PRENTICE HALL
MATHEMATICS

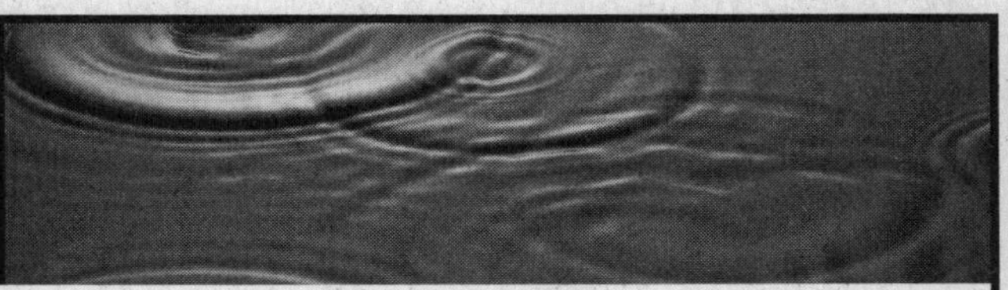

ALGEBRA 2

All-In-One Student Workbook

PEARSON
Prentice Hall

Boston, Massachusetts
Upper Saddle River, New Jersey

PEARSON
Prentice Hall

ISBN 0-13-165724-0

4 5 6 7 8 9 10 10 09 08

Daily Notetaking Guide

Practice, Guided Problem Solving, Vocabulary

Chapter 1 Tools of Algebra

Chapter 2 Functions, Equations, and Graphs

Chapter 3 Linear Systems

Chapter 4 Matrices

Chapter 5 Quadratic Equations and Functions

Chapter 6 Polynomials and Polynomial Functions

Chapter 7 Radical Functions and Rational Exponents

Chapter 8 Exponential and Logarithmic Functions

Chapter 9 Rational Functions

Chapter 10 Quadratic Relations and Conic Sections

Chapter 11 Sequences and Series

Chapter 12 Probability and Statistics

Chapter 13 Periodic Functions and Trigonometry

Chapter 14 Trigonometric Identities and Equations

A Note to the Student:

This section of your workbook contains notetaking pages for each lesson in your student edition. They are structured to help you take effective notes in class. They will also serve as a study guide as you prepare for tests and quizzes.

Name______________________ Class______________________ Date______________

Lesson 1-1

Properties of Real Numbers

Lesson Objectives	**NAEP 2005 Strand:** Number Properties and Operations
1 Graphing and ordering real numbers 2 Identifying and using properties of real numbers	**Topics:** Number Sense; Properties of Number and Operations **Local Standards:** ____________

Vocabulary and Key Concepts

Subsets of Real Numbers

Natural numbers 1, 2, 3, 4, . . .

Natural numbers are ______________________

Whole numbers 0, 1, 2, 3, 4, . . .

Whole numbers are ______________________

Integers . . . −3, −2, −1, 0, 1, 2, 3, 4, . . .

The integers are ______________________

Each negative integer is the [ ], or additive [ ], of a positive integer.

Rational numbers

Rational numbers are ______________________

Each quotient must have a [Common] denominator.

Some rational numbers can be written as ______________________

All other rational numbers can be written as ______________________

Examples $\frac{7}{5}, \frac{-3}{2}, -\frac{4}{5}, 0, 0.3, -1.2, 9$

Irrational numbers

Irrational numbers are ______________________

Their decimal representations neither [ ] nor [ ].

If a positive rational number is not a perfect square such as 25 or $\frac{4}{9}$, then its square root is [ ].

Examples $\sqrt{2}, \sqrt{7}, \sqrt{\frac{2}{3}}, \pi, 1.011011101111011111\ldots$

The opposite or additive inverse of any number a is ______________________

The reciprocal or multiplicative inverse of any nonzero number a is ______________________

The absolute value of a real number is its ______________________

Name______________________ Class______________________ Date ______________

Properties of Real Numbers

Let a, b, and c represent real numbers.

Property	Addition	Multiplication
Real Numbers	$a + b$ is a real number	ab is a real number
Commutative	$a + b = b + a$	$ab = ba$
Associative	$(a + b) + c = a + (b + c)$	$(ab)c = a(bc)$
Identity	$a + 0 = a, \quad 0 + a = a$	$a \cdot 1 = a, \quad 1 \cdot a = a$
Inverse	$a + (-a) = 0$	$a \cdot \frac{1}{a} = 1, \quad a \neq 0$
Distributive	$a(b + c) = ab + ac$	

Examples

1 Graphing Numbers on the Number Line Graph the numbers $-\frac{3}{4}$, $\sqrt{7}$, and 3.6 on a number line.

$-\frac{3}{4}$ is between [−1] and 0. Use a calculator to find that $\sqrt{7} \approx$ [2.6].

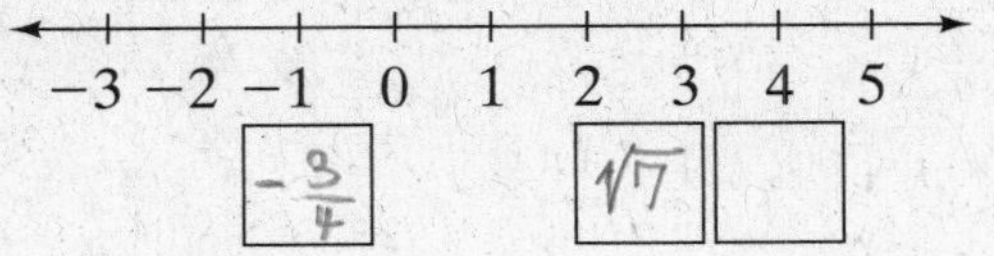

2 Ordering Real Numbers Compare −9 and $-\sqrt{9}$. Use the symbols < and >.

$\sqrt{9} =$ [3], so $-\sqrt{9} =$ [−3].

Since −9 < −3, it follows that −9 < −[ ].

Quick Check

1. Graph the numbers $-\sqrt{2}$, $0.\overline{3}$, and $-2\frac{1}{4}$.

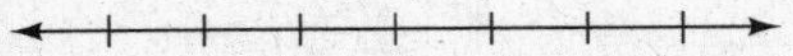

2. Compare $-\sqrt{0.08}$ and $-\sqrt{0.1}$ using the symbols < and >.

Name_______________________________ Class_______________________ Date_____________

Examples

❸ Finding Inverses Find the opposite and the reciprocal of each number.

a. $-3\frac{1}{7}$

Opposite: $-\left(-3\frac{1}{7}\right) =$ [$3\frac{1}{7}$]

Reciprocal: $\dfrac{1}{-3\frac{1}{7}} = \dfrac{1}{-\frac{22}{7}} =$ [$-\frac{7}{22}$]

b. 4

Opposite: [-4]

Reciprocal: [$\frac{1}{4}$]

❹ Identifying Properties of Real Numbers Which property is illustrated?

a. $(-7)(2 \cdot 5) = (-7)(5 \cdot 2)$

b. $3 \cdot (8 + 0) = 3 \cdot 8$

❺ Finding Absolute Value Simplify $\left|4\frac{1}{3}\right|$, $|-9.2|$, and $|3 - 8|$.

$4\frac{1}{3}$ is $4\frac{1}{3}$ units from 0, so $\left|4\frac{1}{3}\right| =$ [$4\frac{1}{3}$].

-9.2 is 9.2 units from 0, so $|-9.2| =$ [9.2].

$|3 - 8| = |$ [-5] $|$ and [-5] is [5] units from 0; $|$ [-5] $| =$ [5], thus $|3 - 8| =$ [5].

Quick Check

3. Find the opposite and reciprocal of each number.

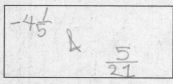

a. $4\frac{1}{5}$

$-4\frac{1}{5}$ & $\frac{5}{21}$

b. -0.002

0.002 & $-\frac{2}{1000} = \frac{1000}{2} = -500$

c. $-\frac{4}{9}$

$\frac{4}{9}$ & $-\frac{9}{4} = -2\frac{1}{4}$

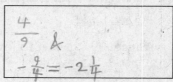

4. Which property is illustrated?

a. $(3 + 0) - 5 = 3 - 5$

b. $-5 + [2 + (-3)] = (-5 + 2) + (-3)$

5. a. Simplify $|-10|$, $|1.5|$, $|0 - 3|$.

10 & 1.5 & 3

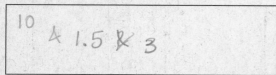

b. For what values of x does $|x| = -x$?

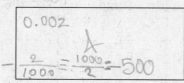

Name________________ Class________________ Date ________

Lesson 1-2

Algebraic Expressions

Lesson Objectives	NAEP 2005 Strand: Algebra
▼1 Evaluating algebraic expressions	**Topic:** Variables, Expressions, and Operations
▼2 Simplifying algebraic expressions	**Local Standards:** ____________

Vocabulary and Key Concepts

Properties for Simplifying Algebraic Expressions

Let a, b, and c represent real numbers.

Definition of [Inverse]
$a - b = a + (-b)$

Definition of [Associative]
$a \div b = \frac{a}{b} = a \cdot \frac{1}{b}, b \neq 0$

Distributive Property for [ ]
$a(b - c) = ab - ac$

Multiplication by 0
[0] $\cdot a = 0$

Multiplication by −1
[−1] $\cdot a = -a$

Opposite of a [ ]
$-(a + b) = -a + (-b)$

Opposite of a [ ]
$-(a - b) = b - a$

Opposite of a [ ]
$-(ab) = -a \cdot b = a \cdot (-b)$

Opposite of an [ ]
$-(-a) = a$

A variable is ____________

An algebraic expression or a variable expression is an expression that contains ____________

To evaluate an expression, ____________

A term is ____________

A coefficient is ____________

Examples

1 Evaluating an Expression with Exponents Evaluate $(k - 18)^2 - 4k$ for $k = 6$.

$(k - 18)^2 - 4k = ([6] - 18)^2 - 4([6])$ — **Substitute [6] for *k*.**

$= ([-6])^2 - 4([6])$ — **Subtract within parentheses.**

$= [36] - 4([6])$ — **Simplify the power.**

$= [36] - [24] = [12]$ — **Multiply and subtract.**

Name____________________ Class____________________ Date______________

❷ **Elections** The expression $-0.08y^2 + 3y$ models the percent increase of voters in a town from 1990 to 2000. In the expression, y represents the number of years since 1990. Find the approximate percent of increase of voters by 1998.

Since $1998 - 1990 = \boxed{8}$, $y = 8$ represents the year 1998.

$-0.08y^2 + 3y = -0.08(\boxed{8})^2 + 3(\boxed{8})$ **Substitute** $\boxed{8}$ **for** y.

$\approx \boxed{29}$

The number of voters had increased by about $\boxed{29}$%.

❸ **Combining Like Terms** Simplify $2h - 3k + 7(2h - 3k)$ by combining like terms.

$2h - 3k + 7(2h - 3k) = 2h - 3k + \boxed{14h} - \boxed{21k}$ $\boxed{}$ **Property**

$= 2h + 14h - 3k - \boxed{21k}$ $\boxed{}$ **Property**

$= \boxed{16h} - \boxed{18k}$ **Simplify.**

Quick Check

1. Evaluate each expression for $c = -3$ and $d = 5$.

a. $c^2 - d^2$

9−25=16

b. $c(3 - d) - c^2$

−9+15−9=
6−9=
−3

c. $-d^2 - 4(d - 2c)$

−25−20+6=−39
or
25−20+6=11

2. a. Assume that the model in Example 2 holds for future years. What percent of the eligible voters will vote in 2012? In 2020?

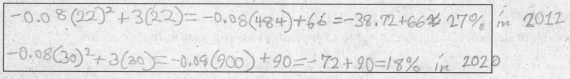

−0.08(22)²+3(22)=−0.08(484)+66=−38.72+66≈27% in 2012
−0.08(30)²+3(30)=−0.08(900)+90=−72+90=18% in 2020

b. **Critical Thinking** Give some reasons that the model may not hold in future years.

3. Simplify by combining like terms.

a. $2x^2 + 5x - 4x^2 + x - x^2$

−3x²+6x

b. $-2(r + s) - (2r + 2s)$

−4r−4s

Example

❹ Finding Perimeter Find the perimeter of this figure. Simplify the answer.

$P = c + \frac{\boxed{c}}{2} + d + (d - c) + d + \frac{\boxed{c}}{2} + c + d$

$= c + \frac{c}{2} + d + d \boxed{-} c + d + \frac{c}{2} + c + d$

$= \frac{c}{2} + \frac{c}{2} + c + \boxed{4d}$

$= \frac{\boxed{2c}}{2} + c + \boxed{4d}$

$= \boxed{c} + c + \boxed{4d}$

$= \boxed{2c} + \boxed{4d}$

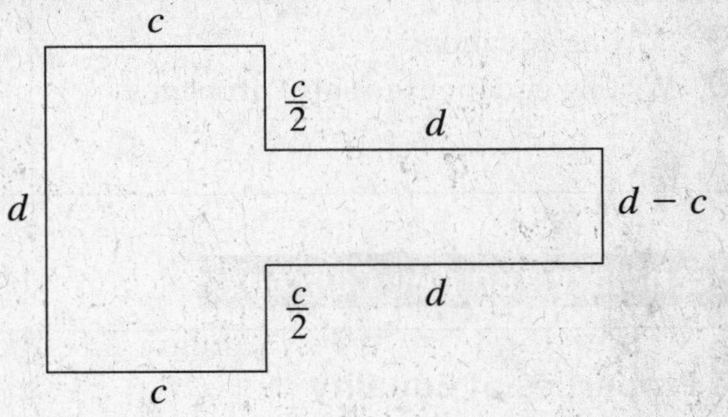

Quick Check

4. Find the perimeter of each figure. Simplify the answer.

a.

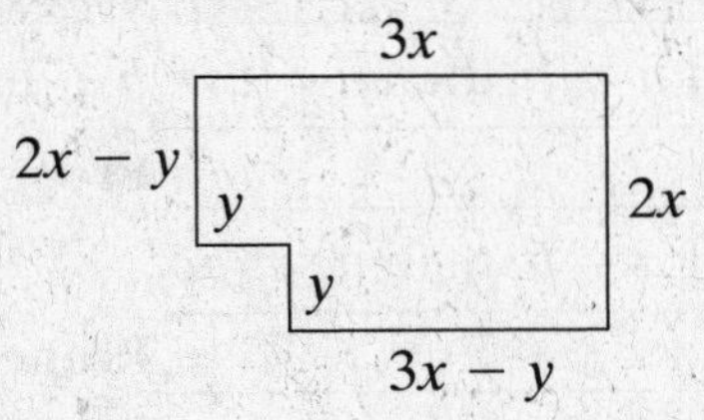

$3x + 2x + (3x - y) + y + y + (2x - y)$

$3x + 2x + 3x - y + y + y + 2x - y$

$3x + 2x + 3x + 2x - y + y + y - y$

$10x$

b.

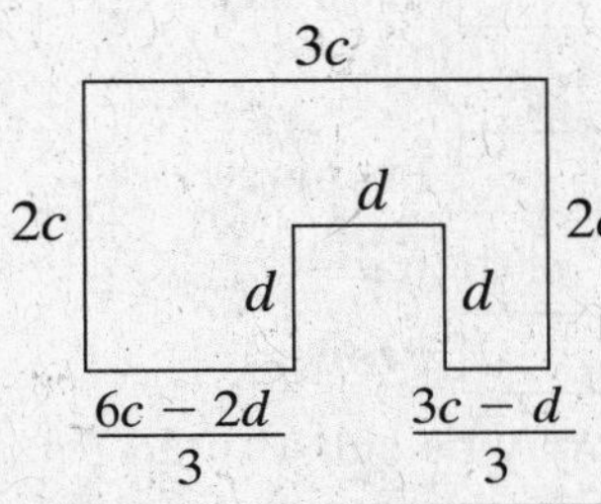

$3c + 2c + \left(\frac{3c-d}{3}\right) + d + d + d + \left(\frac{6c-2d}{3}\right) + 2c$

$3c + 2c + \frac{3c-d}{3} + d + d + d + \frac{6c-2d}{3} + 2c$

$7c + \frac{9c-3d}{3} + 3d$

$\frac{21c}{3} + \frac{9c-3d}{3} + \frac{9d}{3} =$

$\frac{30c-3d}{3} + \frac{9d}{3} = \frac{30c+6d}{3}$

$10c + 2d$

Name__________ Class__________ Date__________

Lesson 1-3

Solving Equations

Lesson Objectives	
1 Solving equations 2 Writing equations to solve problems	**NAEP 2005 Strand:** Algebra **Topics:** Variables, Expressions, and Operations; Equations and Inequalities **Local Standards:** __________

Vocabulary and Key Concepts

Properties of Equality

Let a, b, and c represent real numbers.

________ **Property**
$a = a$

________ **Property**
If $a = b$, then $b = a$.

________ **Property**
If $a = b$ and $b = c$, then $a = c$.

________ **Property**
If $a = b$, then b may be substituted for a in any expression to obtain an equivalent expression.

________ **Property**
If $a = b$, then $a + c = b + c$.

________ **Property**
If $a = b$, then $a - c = b - c$.

________ **Property**
If $a = b$, then $ac = bc$.

________ **Property**
If $a = b$ and $c \neq 0$, then $\frac{a}{c} = \frac{b}{c}$.

A solution of an equation is __________

Example

1 Using the Distributive Property Solve $4(m + 9) = -3(m - 4)$.

$4m +$ [36] $=$ [−3m] $+$ [12] — ________ **Property**

[7m] $+ 36 = 12$ — **Add** ____ **to each side.**

$7m =$ [−24] — **Subtract** ____ **from each side.**

$m =$ [−3.4] — **Divide each side by** ____.

Quick Check

1. Solve each equation. Check your answers.

a. $2(y - 3) + 6 = 70$

2y−6+6=70
2y=70
y=35

b. $6(t - 2) = 2(9 - 2t)$

6t−12=18−4t
10t−12=18
10t=30
t=3

Name______________________ Class______________________ Date ______________

Examples

❷ Solving a Formula for One of Its Variables The formula for the surface area of a rectangular prism ℓ units long, w units wide, and h units high is $A = 2(\ell w + \ell h + wh)$. Solve the formula for w.

$A = 2(\ell w + \ell h + wh)$

$A = \boxed{2}\ell w + \boxed{2}\ell h + \boxed{2}wh$ — ______ **Property**

$A - \boxed{2LH} = 2\ell w + 2wh$ — **Subtract** ______ **from each side.**

$A - 2\ell h = (2\ell + 2h)\boxed{w}$ — ______ **Property**

______ $= w$ — **Divide both sides by** ______ + ______.

❸ Solving an Equation for One of Its Variables Solve $\frac{x}{a} + 8 = b$ for x. Find any restrictions on a and b.

$\frac{x}{a} + 8 = b$

$\boxed{a}\left(\frac{x}{a}\right) + \boxed{a}(8) = ab$ — **Multiply each side by the least common denominator (LCD), *a*.**

$\boxed{X} + \boxed{8a} = ab$ — **Simplify.**

$x = \boxed{-8a + ab}$ — **Subtract** ______ **from each side.**

The denominator cannot be zero, so $a \neq$ ______.

Quick Check

2. The formula for the area of a trapezoid is $A = \frac{1}{2}h(b_1 + b_2)$. Solve it for b_1.

$2A = h(b_1 + b_2)$

$\frac{2A}{h} - b_2 = b_1$

3. Solve each equation for x. Find any restrictions.

a. $ax + bx - 15 = 0$

$ax + bx = 15$

$x(a + b) = 15$

$x = \frac{15}{a+b}$

b. $d = \frac{2x}{a} + b$

$d - b = \frac{2x}{a}$

$ad - ab = 2x$

$\frac{ad - ab}{2} = X$

Name________________________ Class________________________ Date________________

Examples

❹ Using Ratios The sides of a quadrilateral are in the ratio 1 : 2 : 3 : 6. The perimeter is 138 cm. Find the lengths of the sides.

Relate Perimeter equals the sum of the lengths of the four sides.

Define Let [x] = the length of the shortest side.

Then [2x] = the length of the second side.

Then [3x] = the length of the third side.

Then [6x] = the length of the fourth side.

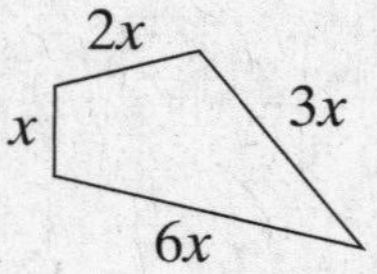

Write $138 =$ [x] $+$ [2x] $+$ [3x] $+ 6x$

$138 =$ [12x] **Combine like terms.**

[11.5] $= x$

$2x = 2($[11.5]$)$ $3x = 3($[11.5]$)$ $6x = 6($[11.5]$)$ **Find the length of each side.**

$=$ [23.0] $=$ [34.5] $=$ [69.0]

The lengths of the sides are [11.5] cm, [23] cm, [34.5] cm, and [69] cm.

❺ Aeronautics A plane takes off and flies east at a speed of 350 mi/h. Thirty-five minutes later, a second plane takes off from the same airport and flies east at a higher altitude at a speed of 400 mi/h. How long does it take the second plane to overtake the first plane?

Relate distance second plane travels = [ ]

Define Let [x] = the time in hours for the second plane.

Then $t + \frac{35}{60} = t + \frac{[x]}{12}$ = the time in hours for the first plane.

Write [ ]$t =$ [ ]$\left(t + \frac{7}{[\ ]}\right)$ **Find the distance each plane travels.**

[ ]$t =$ [ ]$t + \frac{[\ ]}{6}$ **Distributive Property.**

[ ]$t = \frac{[\ ]}{6}$ **Solve for *t*.**

$t =$ [ ] h or 4 h 5 min

Check Is the answer reasonable? In 4 h, the second plane travels [ ] mi. In $4\frac{2}{3}$ h, the first plane travels about [ ] mi. The answer [ ] reasonable.

Name________________________ Class________________________ Date ____________

Quick Check

4. The sides of a triangle are in the ratio 12 : 13 : 15. The perimeter is 120 cm. Find the lengths of the sides of the triangle.

$12x + 13x + 15x = 120$

$40x = 120$

$x = 3$

$40\overline{)120}$ 3

5. A space probe leaves Earth at the rate of 3 km/s. After 100 days, a radio signal is sent to the probe. Radio signals travel at the speed of light, about 3×10^5 km/s. About how long does the signal take to reach the probe?

300,000 km/s

Probe = 25,920,000 km from Earth

86.4 seconds or

About 87 seconds

Name______________________ Class______________________ Date______________

Lesson 1-4

Solving Inequalities

Lesson Objectives	**NAEP 2005 Strand:** Algebra
1 Solving and graphing inequalities	**Topic:** Equations and Inequalities
2 Compound inequalities	**Local Standards:** ____________________

Vocabulary and Key Concepts

Properties of Inequalities

Let a, b, and c represent real numbers.

________ Property	If $a \le b$ and $b \le c$, then $a \le c$.
________ Property	If $a \le b$, then $a + c \le b + c$.
________ Property	If $a \le b$, then $a - c \le b - c$.
________ Property	If $a \le b$ and $c > 0$, then $ac \le bc$.
	If $a \le b$ and $c < 0$, then $ac \ge bc$. ←
________ Property	If $a \le b$ and $c > 0$, then $\frac{a}{c} \le \frac{b}{c}$.
	If $a \le b$ and $c < 0$, then $\frac{a}{c} \ge \frac{b}{c}$. ←

Notice that the inequality is reversed when *c* is negative.

A compound inequality is ____

____

Example

1 Solving and Graphing Inequalities Solve $-2x < 3(x - 5)$. Graph the solution.

$-2x < 3(x - 5)$

$-2x <$ ____ $-$ ____ ________ **Property**

____ $<$ ____ **Subtract** ____ **from both sides.**

x ____ ____ **Divide each side by** ____ **and** ________ **the inequality.**

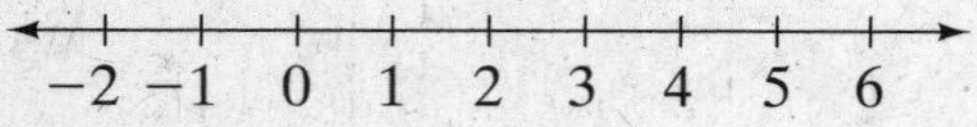

Quick Check

3x − 6 < 27
3x < 33

12 ≥ 6n + 2 + 22
12 ≥ 6n + 24
−12 ≥ 6n
n ≤ −2

1. Solve each inequality. Graph the solution.

a. $3x - 6 < 27$

x < 11

b. $12 \ge 2(3n + 1) + 22$

n ≤ −2

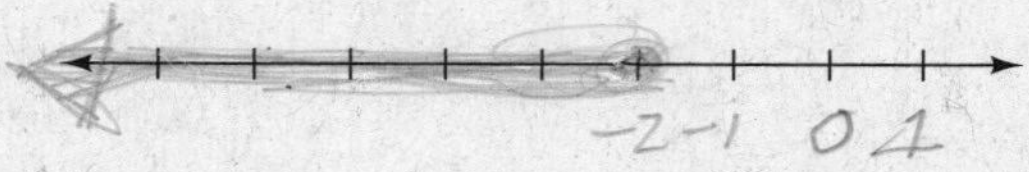

Name______________________ Class______________________ Date ______________

Examples

❷ No Solutions or All Real Numbers as Solutions Solve $7x \geq 7(2 + x)$. Graph the solution.

$7x \geq 7(2 + x)$

$7x \geq$ [14] + [7x] [ ] **Property**

[0] ≥ 14 **Subtract** [ ] **from both sides.**

The last inequality is always false, so $7x \geq 7(2 + x)$ is always [False].

It has [No] solution.

❸ Compound Inequality Containing *And* Graph the solution of $2x - 1 \leq 3x$ and $x > 4x - 9$.

$2x - 1 \leq 3x$ and $x > 4x - 9$

$-1 \leq$ [X] | [9] $> 3x$

[-1] $\leq x$ and [3] $> x$

This compound inequality can be written as -1 [≤] x [<] [3].

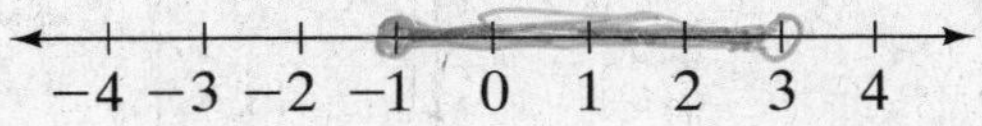

Quick Check

2. Solve each inequality. Graph the solution.

a. $2x < 2(x + 1) + 3$

2x < 2x + 2 + 3
2x < 2x + 5
0 < 5
or x < 1/2 x 7 5/2
No Solution

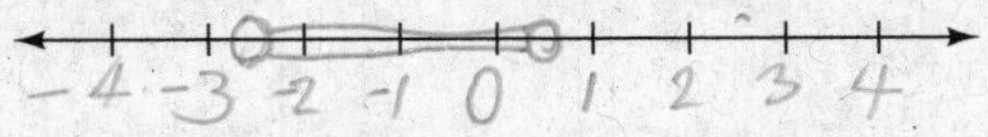

b. $4(x - 3) + 7 \geq 4x + 1$

4x − 12 + 7 ≥ 4x + 1
4x − 5 ≥ 4x + 1
No Solution or
x ≥ 5/4
x ≤ −1/4

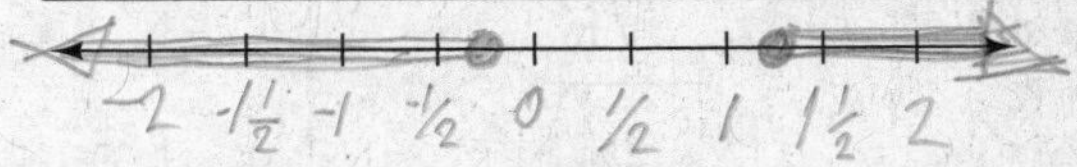

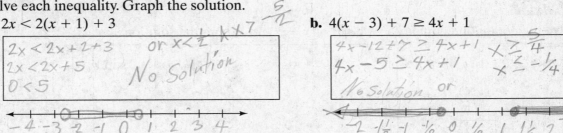

c. Critical Thinking Find values of a such that $2x + a > 2x$ has no solution. Then find values of a such that all real numbers are solutions.

2x + a > 2x
a < −2x
a > 0

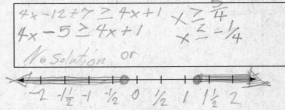

3. Graph the solution of $2x > x + 6$ and $x - 7 < 2$.

x > 6
x < 9

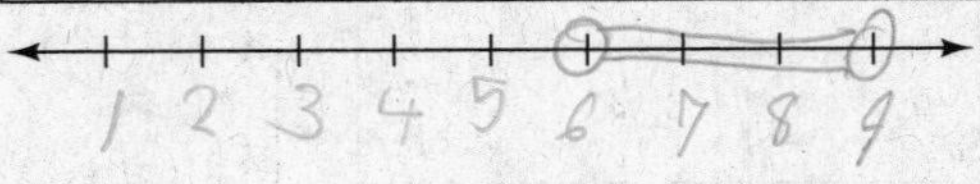

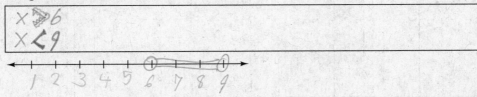

Name________________________ Class________________________ Date________________

Examples

❹ Compound Inequality Containing *Or* Graph the solution of $3x + 9 < -3$ or $-2x + 1 < 5$.

$3x + 9 < -3$ or $-2x + 1 < 5$

$3x <$ [-12] | $-2x <$ [4]

$x <$ [-4] or x [>] [-2]

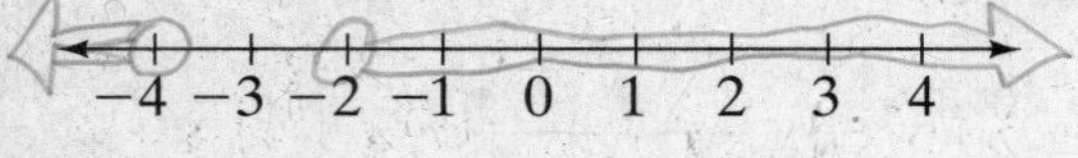

❺ Applying Compound Inequalities A strip of wood is to be 17 cm long with a tolerance of ±0.15 cm. How much should be trimmed from a strip 18 cm long to allow it to meet specifications?

18.00
17.15
00.85

Relate [minimum length] ≤ [final length] ≤ [maximum length]

Define Let [x] = number of centimeters to remove.

Write $17 - 0.15$ ≤ $18 -$ [ ] ≤ $17 + 0.15$

[16.85] $\leq 18 - x \leq 17.15$ **Simplify.**

[-1.15] $\leq -x \leq$ [-0.85] **Subtract** [18].

1.15 [≥] x [≥] 0.85 **Multiply by** [-1].

At least [0.85] cm and no more than [1.15] cm should be trimmed.

Quick Check

4. Solve the compound equality $x - 1 < 3$ or $x + 3 > 8$. Graph the solution.

x<4
x>5

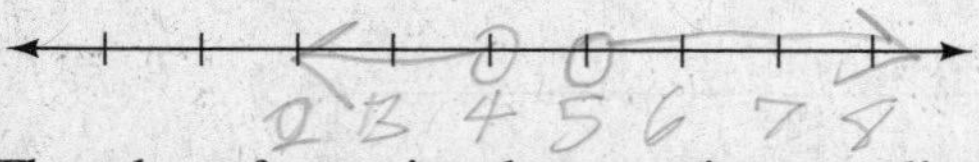

5. The plans for a circular part in a medical instrument require a diameter to be within 0.2 in. of 1.5 in. A machinist finds that the diameter is now 1.73 in. By how much should the diameter be decreased?

1.3 ≤ 1.73 − x ≤ 1.7
−0.43 ≤ −x ≤ −0.03
Most → 0.43 ≥ x ≥ 0.03 ← Least

Name______________________ Class______________________ Date ______________

Lesson 1-5

Absolute Value Equations and Inequalities

Lesson Objectives	**NAEP 2005 Strand:** Number Properties and Operations; Algebra
1 Absolute value equations	**Topics:** Number Sense; Equations and Inequalities
2 Absolute value inequalities	**Local Standards:** ______________

Vocabulary and Key Concepts

Algebraic Definition of Absolute Value

If $x \geq 0$, then $|x| =$ [x]. If $x < 0$, then $|x| =$ [x].

Absolute Value Inequalities

Let k represent a positive real number.

$|x| \geq k$ is equivalent to $x \leq$ [ ] or $x \geq$ [ ].

$|x| \leq k$ is equivalent to $-k \leq$ [ ] $\leq k$.

An extraneous solution is ______________________________

____

The tolerance is ______________________________

____

Examples

1 Solving Multi-Step Absolute Value Equations Solve $4 - 2|x + 9| = -5$.

$4 - 2|x + 9| = -5$

$-2|x + 9| =$ [−9] **Add [ ] to each side.**

$|x + 9| =$ [9/2] **Divide each side by [ ].**

$x + 9 =$ [4.5] or $x + 9 =$ [ ] **Rewrite as two equations.**

$x =$ [−4.5] or $x =$ [ ] **Subtract [ ] from each side of both equations.**

Check

$4 - 2\|x + 9\| = -5$	$4 - 2\|x + 9\| = -5$
$4 - 2\|$ [ ] $+ 9\| \stackrel{?}{=} -5$	$4 - 2\|$ [ ] $+ 9\| \stackrel{?}{=} -5$
$4 - 2\|$ [ ] $\| \stackrel{?}{=} -5$	$4 - 2\|$ [ ] $\| \stackrel{?}{=} -5$
$4 - 2($ [ ] $) \stackrel{?}{=} -5$	$4 - 2($ [ ] $) \stackrel{?}{=} -5$
[ ] $= -5$ ✔	[ ] $= -5$ ✔

2 Checking for Extraneous Solutions Solve $|3x - 4| = -4x - 1$.

$|3x - 4| = -4x - 1$

$3x - 4 = \square - \square$ or $3x - 4 = -(\square - \square)$ **Rewrite as two equations.**

$\square - 4 = \square$ $\quad$ $3x - 4 = \square + \square$ **Solve each equation.**

$7x = \square$ $\quad$ $-x = \square$

$x = \square$ or $x = \square$

Check $\quad |3x - 4| = -4x - 1$ $\qquad\qquad$ $|3x - 4| = -4x - 1$

$\left|3(\square) - 4\right| \stackrel{?}{=} -4(\square) - 1$ $\qquad$ $\left|3(\square) - 4\right| \stackrel{?}{=} -4(\square) - 1$

$\left|-\frac{19}{7}\right| \stackrel{?}{=} \square$ $\qquad$ $|-19| \stackrel{?}{=} \square$

$\frac{19}{7} \neq -\frac{19}{7}$ $\qquad$ $19 = 19$ ✔

$\square$ is an extraneous solution. The only solution is $\square$.

3 Solving Inequalities of the Form $|A| \geq b$ Solve $|2x - 5| > 3$. Graph the solution.

$|2x - 5| > 3$

$2x - 5 < \square$ or $2x - 5 > \square$ **Rewrite as a compound inequality.**

$2x < \square$ $\quad$ $2x > \square$ **Solve for *x*.**

$x < \square$ or $x > \square$

−2 −1 0 1 2 3 4 5 6

$-(2x+3) = 3x+2$ $\qquad$ $2x+3 = 3x+2$

$-2x - 3 = 3x+2$ $\qquad$ $-x = -1$

$-5x = 5$ $\qquad$ $x = 1$

$x = -1$

Quick Check

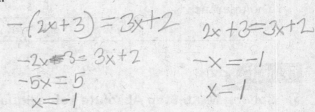

Solve each equation. Check for extraneous solutions.

1. $2|3x - 1| + 5 = 33$

2. $|2x + 3| = 3x + 2$

$-(2(-1)+3) = 3(-1)+2$

$2 - 3 = -3 + 2$

$-1 = -1$

$2(1)+3 = 3(1)+2$

$5 = 5$

3. Solve $|2x - 3| > 7$. Graph the solution.

Name______________________ Class______________________ Date ______________

Examples

❹ Solving Inequalities of the Form $|A| < b$ Solve $-2|x + 1| + 5 \geq -3$. Graph the solution.

$-2\lvert x + 1\rvert + 5 \geq -3$	
$-2\lvert x + 1\rvert \geq \square$	**Isolate the absolute value expression. Subtract $\square$ from each side.**
$\lvert x + 1\rvert \leq \square$	**Divide each side by $\square$ and reverse the inequality.**
$\square \leq x + 1 \leq \square$	**Rewrite as a compound inequality.**
$\square \leq x \leq \square$	**Solve for *x*.**

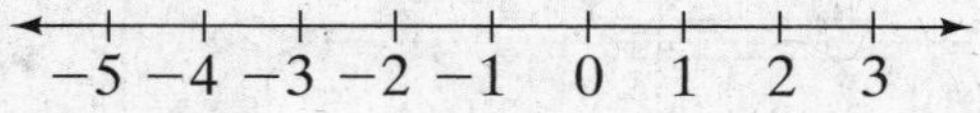

❺ Writing an Absolute Value Inequality The area A in square inches of a square photo is required to satisfy $8.5 \leq A \leq 8.9$. Write this requirement as an absolute value inequality.

$\frac{8.9 - 8.5}{2} = \frac{0.4}{2} = \square$	**Find the tolerance.**
$\frac{8.9 + 8.5}{2} = \frac{\square}{2} = \square$	**Find the average of the maximum and minimum values.**
$-0.2 \leq A - \square \leq \square$	**Write an inequality.**
$\lvert A - \square\rvert \leq \square$	**Rewrite as an absolute value inequality.**

Quick Check

4. Solve $|5z + 3| - 7 < 34$. Graph the solution.

5. The specification for the circumference C in inches of a basketball for junior high school is $27.75 \leq C \leq 28.5$. Write the specification as an absolute value inequality.

Name______________________ Class______________________ Date______________

Lesson 1-6

Probability

Lesson Objectives	**NAEP 2005 Strand:** Data Analysis and Probability
▼1 Experimental probability	**Topic:** Probability
▼2 Theoretical probability	**Local Standards:** ______________________

Vocabulary and Key Concepts

Experimental Probability

experimental probability of event = P(event)

$$= \frac{\text{number of times the } \boxed{} \text{ occurs}}{\text{number of } \boxed{}}$$

Theoretical Probability

If a sample space has n equally likely outcomes and an event A occurs in m of these outcomes, then the theoretical probability of event A is $P(A) = \frac{\boxed{}}{\boxed{}}$.

A simulation is ______________________________

A sample space is ______________________________

Examples

1 Finding Experimental Probability A player hit the bull's-eye on a circular dartboard 8 times out of 50. Find the experimental probability that the player hits the bull's-eye.

$P(\text{bull's-eye}) = \frac{\boxed{8}}{50} = \boxed{0.16}$, or $\boxed{16}$%

2 Finding Theoretical Probability Find the theoretical probability of getting a multiple of 3 when you roll a number cube.

$\boxed{2}$ **outcomes result in a multiple of 3.** → $\frac{2}{\boxed{6}}$ ← $\boxed{6}$ **equally likely outcomes are in the sample space.**

$= \frac{\boxed{1}}{\boxed{3}}$

Name______________________ Class______________________ Date ______________

3 Biology Brown is a dominant eye color for human beings. If a father and mother each carry a gene for brown eyes and a gene for blue eyes, what is the probability of their having a child with blue eyes?

		Gene from Mother	
		B	b
Gene from Father	B	BB	Bb
	b	Bb	bb

Let [B] represent the dominant gene for brown eyes. Let [b] represent the recessive gene for blue eyes.

The sample space {[BB], [Bb], [Bb], [bb]} contains [ ] equally likely outcomes.

The outcome [bb] is the only one for which a child will have blue eyes.

So, P(blue eyes) = [1/4]. The theoretical probability that the child will have blue eyes is [.25], or [25]%.

Quick Check

1. A basketball player has made 32 free throws in 50 tries. What is the experimental probability of her making a free throw?

$\frac{32}{50} = 0.64$

64%

2. Find the theoretical probability of getting a prime number when you roll a number cube.

$\frac{4}{6} = \frac{2}{3}$

3. Use the information from Example 3. What is the probability the parents will have a child with brown eyes?

$\frac{3}{4} = .75 = 75\%$

Name________________________ Class________________________ Date______________

Example

4 Finding Geometric Probability Find the probability that a dart that lands at random on the dartboard hits the outer ring.

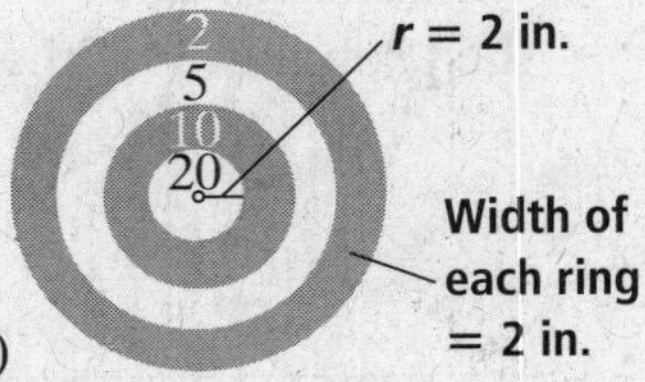

$$P(\text{outer ring}) = \frac{\text{area of outer ring}}{\text{area of circle with radius } 4r}$$

$$= \frac{(\text{area of circle with radius } 4r) - (\text{area of circle with radius } 3r)}{\text{area of circle with radius } 4r}$$

$$= \frac{\pi(\boxed{4r})^2 - \pi(\boxed{3r})^2}{\pi(4r)^2}$$

$$= \frac{\boxed{4}\pi r^2 - \boxed{3}\pi r^2}{\boxed{4}\pi r^2}$$

$$= \frac{\boxed{1}\pi r^2}{\boxed{4}\pi r^2}$$

$$= \boxed{1/4}$$

The theoretical probability of hitting the outer ring is $\boxed{1/4}$, or about $\boxed{25}$%.

Quick Check

4. Use the dartboard from Example 4. Find each probability.

a. P(scoring 20 points)

1/4 25%

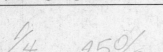

b. P(scoring 5 points)

1/4 25%

Name________________________ Class____________________ Date ____________

Lesson 2-1

Relations and Functions

Lesson Objectives	NAEP 2005 Strand: Algebra
1 Graphing relations	Topic: Algebraic Representations
2 Identifying functions	Local Standards: ____________________

Vocabulary

A relation is ______________________________

The domain of a relation is ______________________________

____

The range of a relation is ______________________________

____

A mapping diagram links ______________________________

____

A function is ______________________________

____

Use the vertical-line test to determine whether ______________________________

____

Function notation $f(x)$ is read as ______________________________

Note that $f(x)$ does *not* mean "f [ ] x."

Examples

1 Finding Domain and Range Write the ordered pairs for the relation. Find the domain and range.

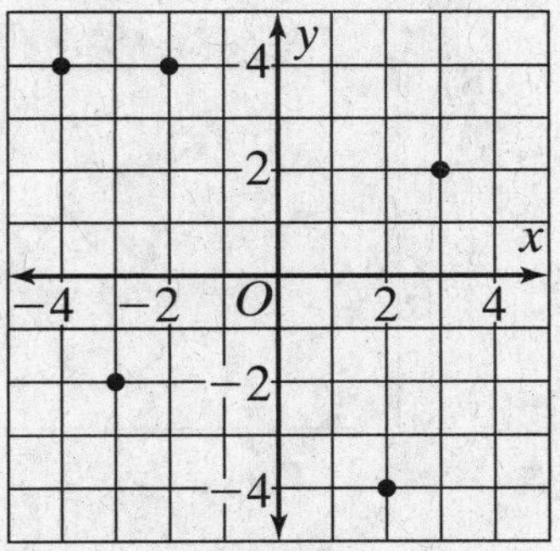

{(−4, 4), [−3, −2], [−2, 4], [2, −4], [3, 2]}

The domain is {−4, [−3], [−2], [2], [3]}.

The range is {[−4], [−2], [2], 4}.

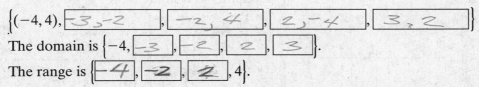

❷ Making a Mapping Diagram Make a mapping diagram for the relation $\{(-1, 7), (1, 3), (1, 7), (-1, 3)\}$.

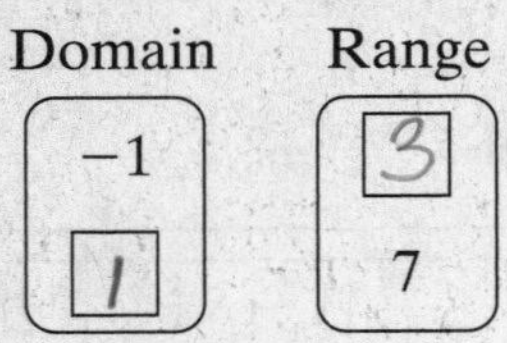

Pair the domain elements with the range elements.

❸ Identifying Functions Determine whether the relation is a function.

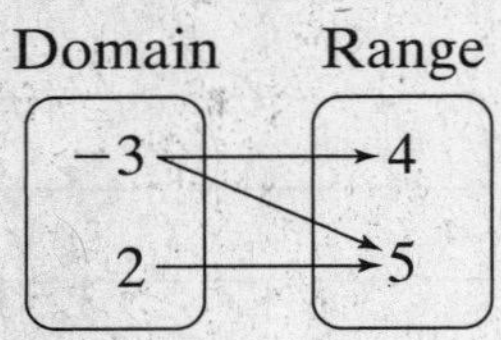

The element −3 of the domain is paired with both 4 **and** 5 **of the range.**

The relation ______ **a function.**

Quick Check

1. Find the domain and range of each relation.

a.

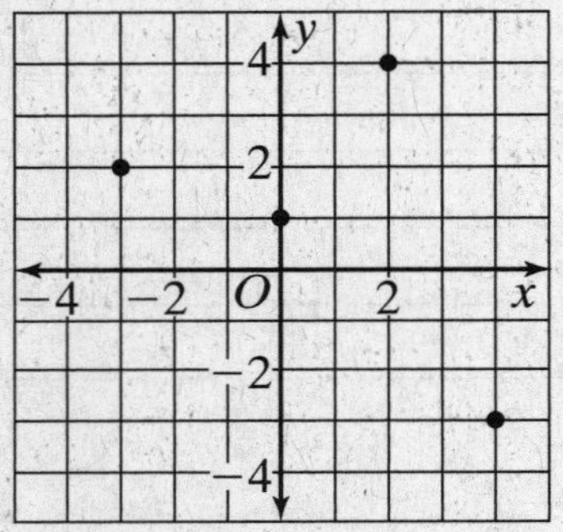

domain: ______

range: ______

b.

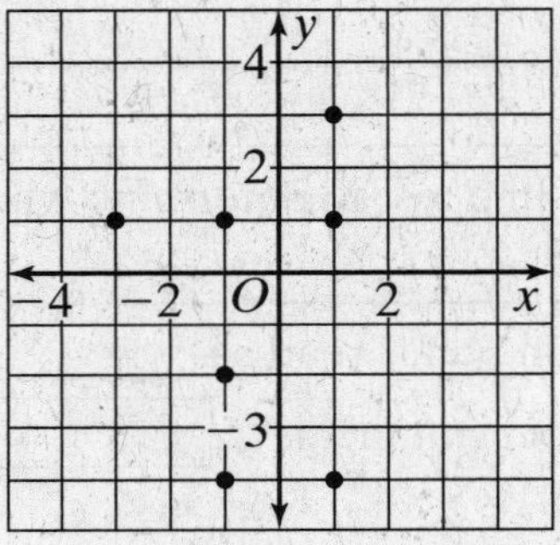

domain: ______

range: ______

2. Make a mapping diagram for each relation.

a. $\{(0, 2), (1, 3), (2, 4)\}$

b. $\{(2, 8), (-1, 5), (0, 8), (-1, 3), (-2, 3)\}$

3. Determine whether each relation is a function.

a.

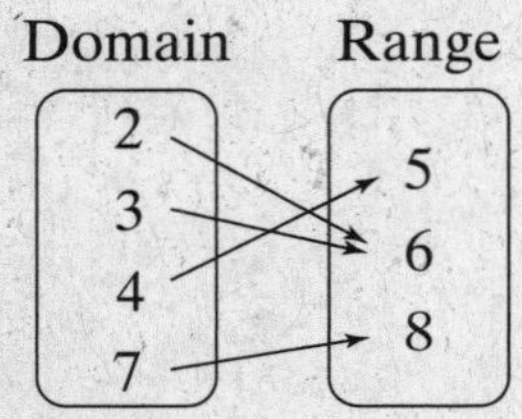

b.

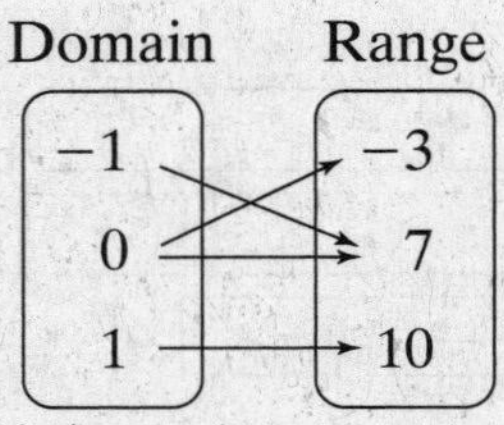

Name_______________ Class_______________ Date_______________

Examples

4 Using the Vertical-Line Test Use the vertical-line test to determine whether the graph represents a function.

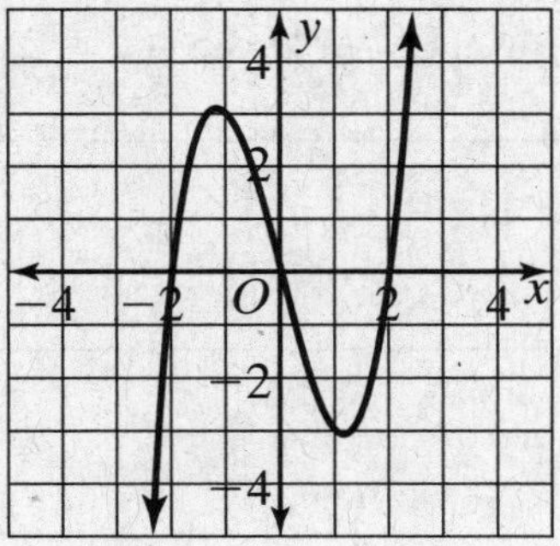

If you move an edge of a ruler from left to [ ] across the graph, keeping the edge [ ] as you do so, you see that the edge of the ruler never intersects the graph in more than one point in any position. Therefore, the graph [ ] represent a function.

5 Evaluating Functions Find $f(2)$ for each function.

a. $f(x) = -x^2 + 1$

$f(2) = -[2]^2 + 1 = [4] + 1 = [5]$

b. $f(x) = |3x|$

$f([2]) = |3 \cdot [2]| = |[6]| = [6]$

c. $f(x) = \dfrac{9}{1 - x}$

$f([2]) = \dfrac{9}{1 - [2]} = \dfrac{9}{[-1]} = [-9]$.

Quick Check

4. Use the vertical-line test to determine whether each graph represents a function.

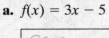

a.

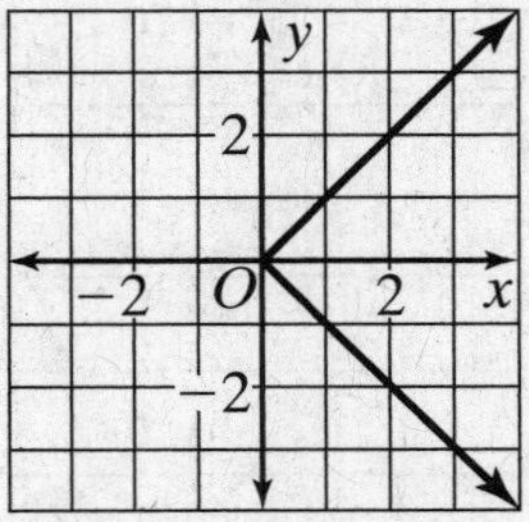

No

b.

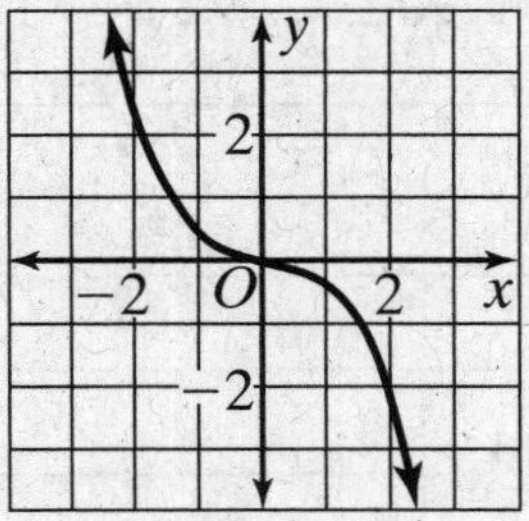

Yes

c.

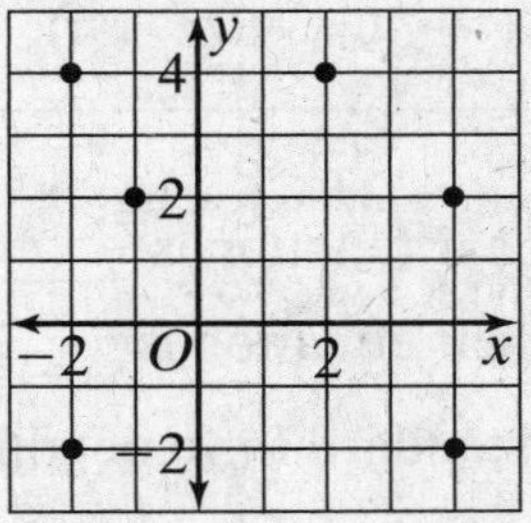

Yes

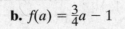

5. Find $f(-3)$, $f(0)$, and $f(5)$ for each function.

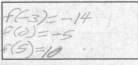

a. $f(x) = 3x - 5$

f(-3) = -14
f(0) = -5
f(5) = 10

b. $f(a) = \frac{3}{4}a - 1$

f(-3) = 5/4 = 1 1/4
f(0) = -1
f(5) = 11/4 = 2 3/4

c. $f(y) = -\frac{1}{5}y + \frac{3}{5}$

f(-3) = 6/5 = 1 1/5
f(0) = 3/5
f(5) = -2/5

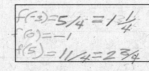

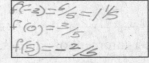

Name______________________ Class______________________ Date______________

Lesson 2-2

Linear Equations

Lesson Objectives	**NAEP 2005 Strand:** Algebra
1 Graphing linear equations 2 Writing equations of lines	**Topics:** Patterns, Relations, and Functions; Algebraic Representations **Local Standards:** ____________

Vocabulary and Key Concepts

Slope Formula

$$\text{slope} = \frac{\boxed{y_2 - y_1}\ \text{change (rise)}}{\boxed{x_2 - x_1}\ \text{change (run)}} = \frac{\boxed{} - \boxed{}}{\boxed{} - \boxed{}},\ \text{where } x_2 - x_1 \neq 0$$

Point-Slope Form

The line through point (x_1, y_1) with ______ m has the equation below.

$$y - y_1 = \boxed{}(x - x_1)$$

Slope-Intercept Form

Slope ↓ y-intercept ↓

$$y = mx + b$$

Equations of a Line

Point-Slope Form	No Form	Slope-intercept Form
$y - 2 = -3(x + 4)$	$3x + y = -10$	$y = -3x - 10$

A linear function is ______________________

A linear equation is ______________________

The standard form of a linear equation is ______________________

____

In a linear equation, the dependent variable is ______________________

____

In a linear equation, the independent variable is ______________________

The y-intercept of a line is ______________________

____

The x-intercept of a line is ______________________

____

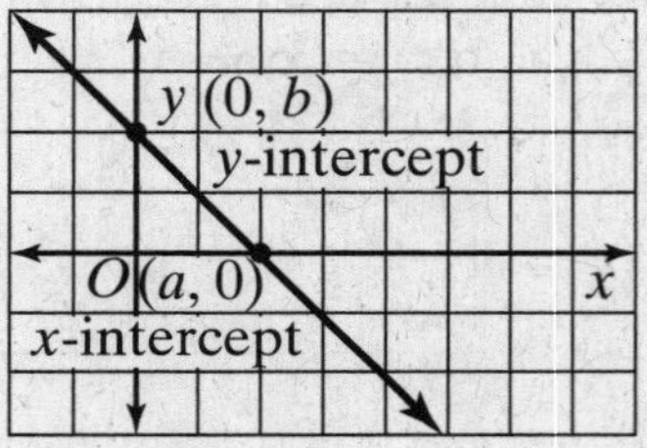

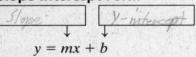

Name______________________ Class______________________ Date ____________

Examples

1 Graphing a Linear Equation The equation $10x + 5y = 40$ models how you can give \$.40 change if you have only dimes and nickels. The variable x is the number of dimes, and y is the number of nickels. Graph the equation. Explain what the x- and y-intercepts represent. Describe the domain and the range.

$10x + 5y = 40$	$10x + 5y = 40$	
$10x + 5(\boxed{0}) = 40$	$10(\boxed{0}) + 5y = 40$	**Set x or y equal to zero to find each intercept.**
$\boxed{10x} = 40$	$\boxed{5y} = 40$	
$x = \boxed{4}$	$y = \boxed{8}$	

Use the intercepts to graph the equation.

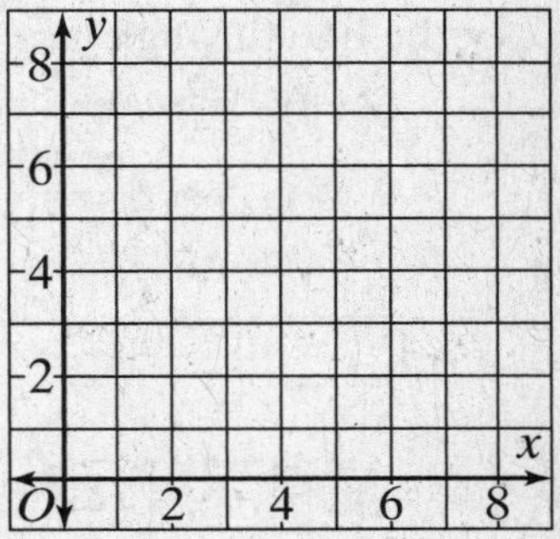

The x-intercept is [4], which means that the change can be given using [4] dimes and 0 nickels. The y-intercept is [8], which means that the change can be given using [0] dimes and [8] nickels.

The number of dimes and the number of nickels must each be a whole number. The possible solutions for this situation are limited to those points on the line segment connecting (0, 8) and (4, 0) whose x- and y-coordinates are whole numbers. Therefore, the domain is {[0, 4]} and the range is {[0, 8]}.

2 Finding Slope Find the slope of the line through the points $(-2, 7)$ and $(8, -6)$.

$\text{Slope} = \dfrac{y_2 - y_1}{x_2 - x_1}$ — **Use the slope formula.**

$= \dfrac{-6 - \boxed{7}}{\boxed{8} - (-2)}$ — **Substitute $(-2, 7)$ for (x_1, y_1) and $(\boxed{8}, \boxed{-6})$ for (x_2, y_2).**

$= \boxed{\dfrac{-13}{10}}$ — **Simplify.**

The slope of the line is $\boxed{\dfrac{-13}{10}}$.

Quick Check

1. Find the slope of the line through each pair of points.

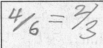

a. $(-2, -2)$ and $(4, 2)$

[$4/6 = 2/3$]

b. $(0, -3)$, and $(7, -9)$

[$-6/7$]

Name____________________ Class____________________ Date____________________

Examples

3 Writing an Equation Given the Slope and a Point Write in standard form an equation of the line with slope 3 through the point $(-1, 5)$.

$y - y_1 = m(x - x_1)$	**Use the point-slope equation.**
$y - \boxed{5} = \boxed{3}[x - (-1)]$	**Substitute $\boxed{3}$ for m, $\boxed{5}$ for y_1, and $\boxed{-1}$ for x_1.**
$y - 5 = 3[(x + \boxed{1})]$	**Simplify.**
$y - 5 = \boxed{3}x + \boxed{3}$	**$\boxed{}$ Property**
$3x - y = \boxed{-8}$	**Write in standard form.**

4 Writing an Equation Given Two Points Write in point-slope form an equation of the line through $(4, -3)$ and $(5, -1)$.

$y - y_1 = m(x - x_1)$ $\frac{2}{1}$	**Write the point-slope equation.**
$y - y_1 = \frac{y_2 - y_1}{x_2 - x_1}(x - x_1)$	**Substitute the $\boxed{}$ formula for m.**
$y - (\boxed{-3}) = \frac{\boxed{-1} - (\boxed{-3})}{5 - \boxed{4}}(x - \boxed{4})$	**Substitute: $x_1 = \boxed{}$, $y_1 = \boxed{}$, $x_2 = \boxed{}$, $y_2 = \boxed{}$.**
$y + \boxed{3} = \boxed{2}(x - \boxed{4})$	**Simplify.**

You can also use $(5, -1)$ for (x_1, y_1) and $(4, -3)$ for (x_2, y_2). This gives the equation $y + 1 = 2(x - 5)$. Both equations define the same line.

Quick Check

$\frac{5}{6} \times \frac{5}{1} = \frac{25}{6}$

2. Write in standard form the equation of each line.

a. slope 2, through $(4, -2)$

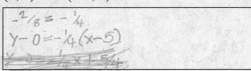

$y - (-2) = 2[(x - 4)]$
$y + 2 = 2x - 8$
$2x - y = 10$

b. slope $\frac{5}{6}$, through $(5, 6)$

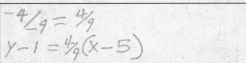

$y - 6 = \frac{5}{6}(x - 5)$
$y - 6 = \frac{5}{6}x - \frac{25}{6}$
$\frac{5}{6}x - y = -\frac{11}{6}$

3. Write in point-slope form the equation of the line through each pair of points.

a. $(5, 0)$ and $(-3, 2)$

$-\frac{2}{8} = -\frac{1}{4}$
$y - 0 = -\frac{1}{4}(x - 5)$
~~$y = -\frac{1}{4}x + \frac{5}{4}$~~

b. $(5, 1)$ and $(-4, -3)$

$\frac{-4}{-9} = \frac{4}{9}$
$y - 1 = \frac{4}{9}(x - 5)$

$\frac{1}{4} \times \frac{5}{1}$

$\frac{5}{4}$

Name________________________ Class________________________ Date ______________

Examples

5 Finding Slope Using Slope-Intercept Form Find the slope of $-7x + 2y = 8$.

$2y = 7x + 8$ — **Add** [7x] **to both sides.**

$y = \frac{7}{[2]}x + 4$ — **Write in the slope-intercept form.**

The slope of the line is [7/2].

6 Writing an Equation of a Perpendicular Line Write an equation of the line through $(5, -3)$ and perpendicular to $y = 4x + 1$. Graph both lines.

$m =$ [$-\frac{1}{4}$] — **Find the negative reciprocal of 4.**

$y = mx + b$ — **Use slope-intercept form.**

$y =$ [$-\frac{1}{4}$] $x + b$ — **Slope is** [$-\frac{1}{4}$].

[−3] $=$ [$-\frac{1}{4}$]([5]) $+ b$ — **Substitute** (5, [ ]) **for (*x*, *y*).**

[−3] $=$ [$-\frac{5}{4}$] $+ b$ — **Simplify.**

[$\frac{7}{4}$] $= b$ — **Solve for *b*.**

$y = -\frac{1}{4}x -$ [$\frac{7}{4}$] — **Write the equation.**

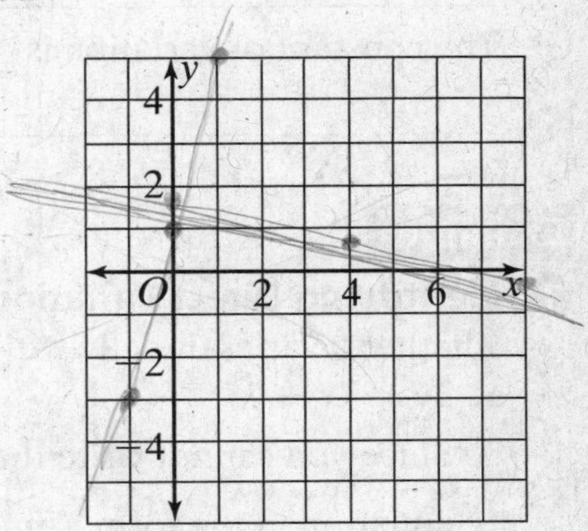

Quick Check

4. Find the slope of each line.

a. $3x + 2y = 1$

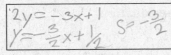

$2y = -3x + 1$
$y = -\frac{3}{2}x + \frac{1}{2}$ $S = -\frac{3}{2}$

b. $\frac{2}{3}x + \frac{1}{2}y = 1$

$\frac{1}{2}y = -\frac{2}{3}x + 1$
$y = -\frac{4}{3}x + 2$ $S = -\frac{4}{3}$

c. $Ax + By = C$

$By = -Ax + C$
$y = -\frac{A}{B}x + \frac{C}{B}$

5. Write an equation for each line. Then graph the line.

a. through $(-1, 3)$ and perpendicular to the line $y = 5x - 3$

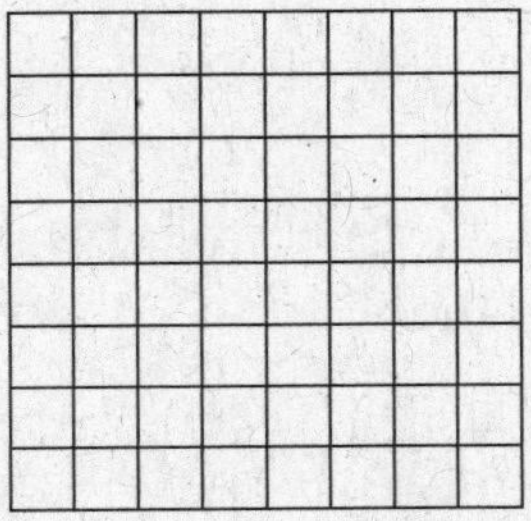

[   ]

b. through $(2, 1)$ and parallel to the line $y = \frac{2}{3}x + \frac{5}{8}$

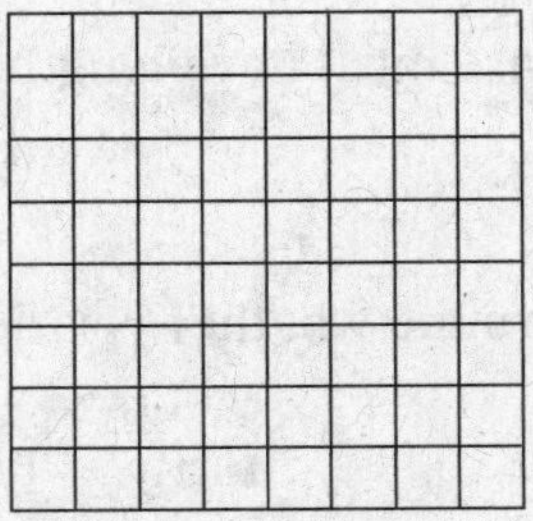

[   ]

Name______________________ Class______________________ Date______________

Lesson 2-3

Direct Variation

Lesson Objective	**NAEP 2005 Strand:** Algebra
1 Writing and interpreting a direct variation	**Topic:** Algebraic Representations
	Local Standards: ____________________

Vocabulary

Direct variation is ______________________________

____

The constant of variation is ______________________________

____

Examples

1 Identifying Direct Variation from an Equation For each function, tell whether y varies directly with x. If so, find the constant of variation.

a. $3y = 7x + 7$

Since you cannot write the equation in the form $y = kx$, y does [Not] vary directly with x.

b. $5x = -2y$

$5x = -2y$ is equivalent to $y =$ [$\frac{5}{2}x$], so y varies directly with x.

The constant of variation is [$-\frac{5}{2}$].

2 Finding Constant Variation The perimeter of a square varies directly as the length of a side of the square. The formula $P = 4s$ relates the perimeter to the length of a side.

a. Find the constant of variation.

The equation $P = 4s$ has the form of a [Constant] variation equation with $k =$ [4].

b. Find how long a side of the square must be for the perimeter to be 64 cm.

$P = 4s$ **Use the direct variation.**

[64] $= 4s$ **Substitute 64 for** [P].

[16] $= s$ **Solve for** s.

The sides of the square must have length [16] cm.

Quick Check

1. For each function, determine whether y varies directly with x. If so, find the constant of variation.

a. $y = \frac{x}{2}$ [Yes $\frac{1}{2}$]

b. $2y - 1 = x$ [No]

c. $\frac{5}{6}x = \frac{1}{3}y$ [yes 5/2]

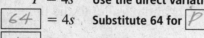

Name_______________ Class_______________ Date_______________

Example

❸ Using a Proportion Suppose y varies directly with x, and $y = 15$ when $x = 27$. Find y when $x = 18$. Let $(x_1, y_1) = (27, 15)$ and let $(x_2, y_2) = (18, y)$.

$\frac{y_1}{x_1} = \frac{y_2}{x_2}$ **Write a proportion.**

$\frac{15}{27} = \frac{y}{18}$ **Substitute.**

$15(18) = 27(y)$ **Write the cross products.**

$y = \frac{270}{27}$ **Solve for *y*.**

$y = 10$ **Simplify.**

$\frac{15}{27} = \frac{y}{18}$

$y = 10$

Quick Check

2. The circumference of a circle varies directly with the diameter of the circle. The formula $C = \pi d$ relates the circumference to the diameter.

   a. What is the constant of variation?

   π

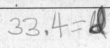

   b. Find the diameter of a circle with circumference 105 cm to the nearest tenth.

   $33.4 = d$

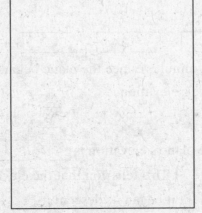

3. Find the missing value for each direct variation.

   a. If $y = 4$ when $x = 3$, find y when $x = 6$.

   b. If $y = 7$ when $x = 2$, find y when $x = 8$.

   c. If $y = 10$ when $x = -3$, find x when $y = 2$.

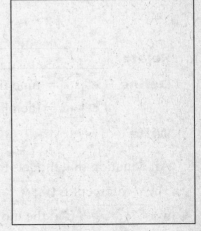

Name______________________ Class______________________ Date______________

Lesson 2-4

Using Linear Models

Lesson Objectives	**NAEP 2005 Strand:** Algebra
1 Modeling real-world data 2 Predicting with linear models	**Topics:** Algebraic Representations; Variables, Expressions, and Operations; Equations and Inequalities **Local Standards:** ____________________

Vocabulary

A scatter plot is ____

____

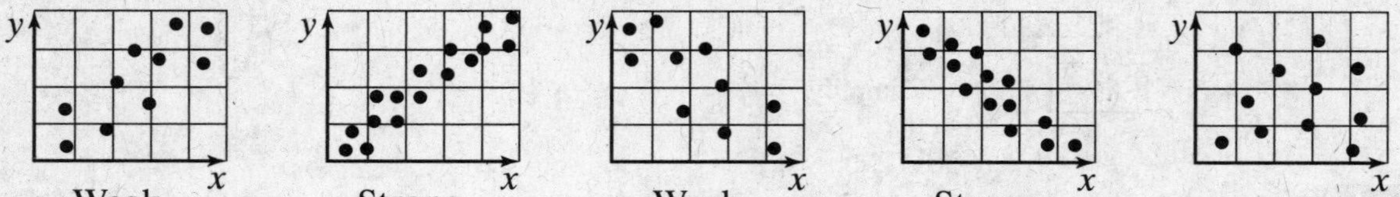

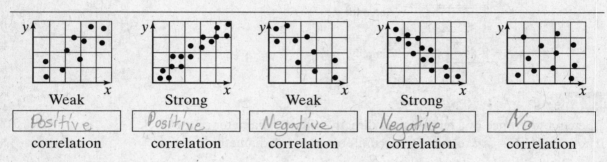

Weak	Strong	Weak	Strong	
Positive correlation	Positive correlation	Negative correlation	Negative correlation	No correlation

A trend line is ____

____

Examples

1 Transportation Suppose an airplane descends at a rate of 300 ft/min from an elevation of 8000 ft.

Write and graph an equation to model the plane's elevation as a function of the time it has been descending. Interpret the intercept at which the graph intersects the vertical axis.

8000 − 300x

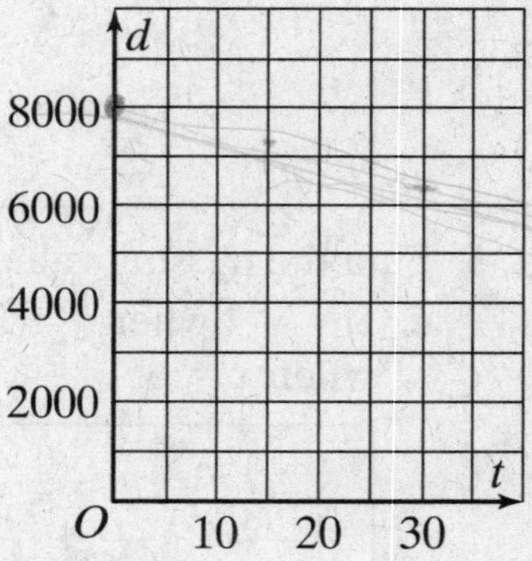

Relate [ ] = [ ] · [ ] + [ ]

Define Let [T] = time (in minutes) since the plane began its descent.

Let [E] = the plane's elevation.

Write [E] = −300 · [T] + [8000]

An equation that models the plane's elevation is [E] = [−300T] + [8,000].

The d-intercept is (0, [8,000]). This tells you that the elevation of the plane was [8000] ft at the moment it began its descent.

Name______________________ Class______________________ Date ______________

❷ Using a Linear Model A spring has a length of 8 cm when a 20-g mass is hanging at the bottom end. Each additional gram stretches the spring another 0.15 cm. Write an equation for the length y of the spring as a function of the mass x of the attached weight.

Step 1 Identify two points as (x_1, y_1) and (x_2, y_2).
Adding another 20 g of mass at the end of the spring will give a total mass of 40 g and a length of $8 + 0.15(20) = 11$ cm. Use the points $(x_1, y_1) = (20, \square)$ and $(x_2, y_2) = (40, \square)$ to find the linear equation.

Step 2 Find the slope of the line.

$$m = \frac{y_2 - y_1}{x_2 - x_1} \qquad \textbf{Use the slope formula.}$$

$$= \frac{11 - \square}{40 - 20} \qquad \textbf{Substitute.}$$

$$m = \frac{\square}{\square}, \text{ or } 0.15 \qquad \textbf{Simplify.}$$

Step 3 Use one of the points and the point-slope form to write an equation for the line.

$$y - y_1 = m(x - x_1) \qquad \textbf{Use point-slope form.}$$

$$y - 8 = \square(x - \square) \qquad \textbf{Substitute.}$$

$$y = \square + \square \qquad \textbf{Solve for } y\textbf{.}$$

An equation of the line that models the length of the spring is $y = \square$.

❸ Determining Whether a Linear Model Is Reasonable An art expert guessed the selling prices of five paintings. Then, she checked the actual prices. The data points (guess, actual) show the results, where each number is in thousands of dollars. Graph the data points. Decide whether a linear model is reasonable. If so, draw a trend line and write its equation.

$\{(12, 11), (7, 8.5), (10, 12), (5, 3.8), (9, 10)\}$

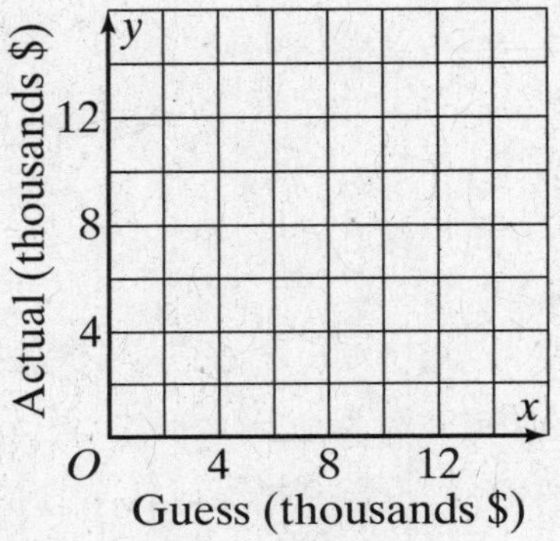

A linear model seems $\square$ since the points fall close to a line.

A possible trend line is the line through (6, 6) and (10.5, 11). Using these two points, the equation in slope-intercept form is $y = \square - \square$.

Name________________________________ Class________________________ Date______________

Quick Check

1. Suppose a balloon begins descending at a rate of 20 ft/min from an elevation of 1350 ft.

   a. Write an equation to model the balloon's elevation as a function of time. What is true about the slope of this line?

   b. Graph the equation. Interpret the h-intercept.

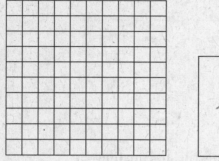

2. A candle is 7 in. tall after burning for 1 h, and 5 in. tall after burning for 2 h. Write a linear equation to model the height of the candle.

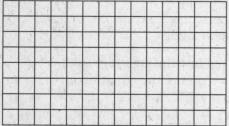

3. Graph the data points. Decide whether a linear model is reasonable. If so, draw a trend line and write its equation.
   $\{(-7.5, 19.75), (-2, 9), (0, 6.5), (1.5, 3), (4, -1.5)\}$

Name________________________________ Class________________________ Date ______________

Lesson 2-5

Absolute Value Functions and Graphs

Lesson Objective	**NAEP 2005 Strand:** Algebra
1 Graphing absolute value functions	**Topic:** Algebraic Representations
	Local Standards: ____________________

Vocabulary

An absolute value function is ____

____

The vertex of a function is ____

____

Examples

1 Graphing an Absolute Value Function Graph $y = |2x - 1|$ by using a table of values. Evaluate the equation for several values of x. Make a table of values.

x	−1.5	−1	−0.5	0	0.5	1	1.5	2	2.5
y	4	3	2	1	0	1	2	3	5

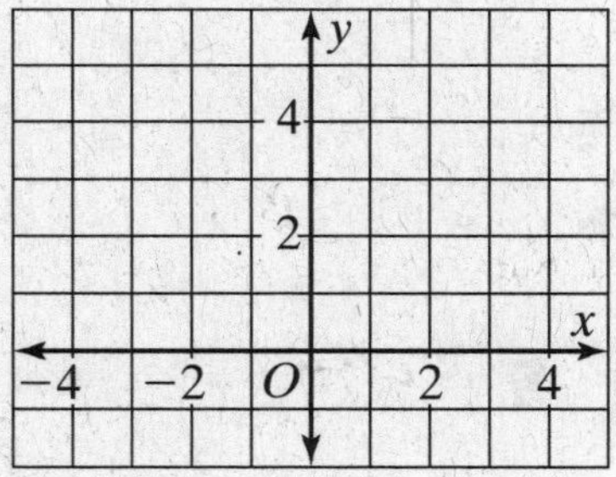

Graph the function.

2 Using a Graphing Calculator Graph $y = |x - 1| - 1$ on a graphing calculator. Use the absolute value key. Graph the equation $Y_1 = \text{abs}(X - 1) - 1$.

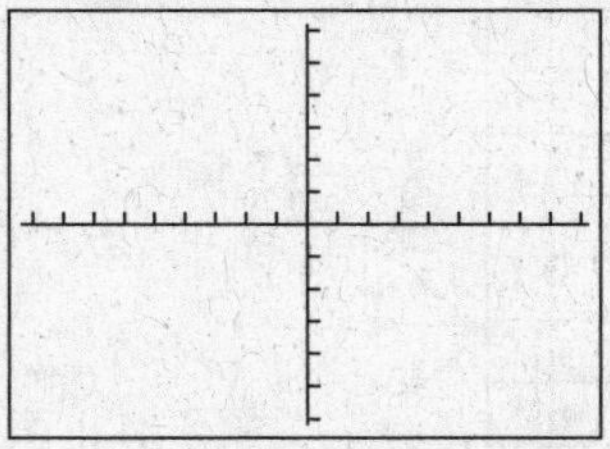

Name______________________________ Class______________________ Date______________

❸ **Writing Two Linear Equations** Use the definition of absolute value to graph $y = |3x + 6| - 2$.

Step 1 Isolate the absolute value.

$$y = |3x + 6| - 2$$
$$y + \boxed{2} = |3x + 6|$$

Step 2 Use the definition of absolute value. Write one equation for $3x + 6 \geq 0$ and a second equation for $3x + 6 < 0$.

when $3x + 6 \geq 0$

$y + 2 = \square + \square$

$y = \square + \square$

when $3x + 6 < 0$

$y + 2 = \square(3x + 6)$

$y = \square - \square$

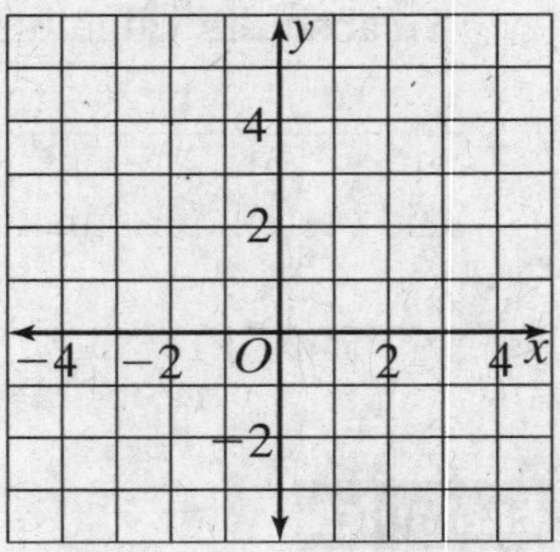

Step 3 Graph each equation for the appropriate domain.

When $3x + 6 \geq 0$, or $x \geq -2$, $y = \square$.

When $3x + 6 < 0$, or $x < -2$, $y = \square$.

❹ **Travel** A train traveling on a straight track at 50 mi/h passes a certain crossing halfway through its journey each day. Sketch a graph of its trip based on its distance and time from the crossing.

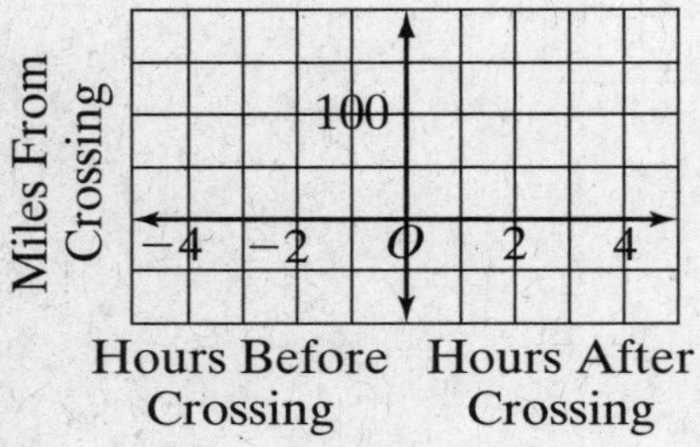

The equation $d = |50t|$ models the train's distance from the crossing.

Quick Check

1. Graph each equation.

a. $y = |2x - 5|$

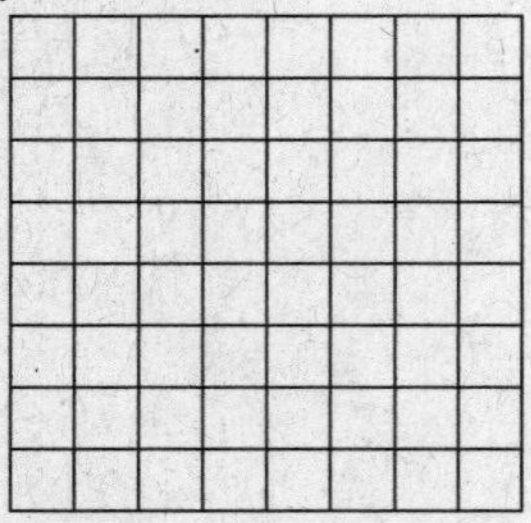

b. $y = -|x + 1| - 2$

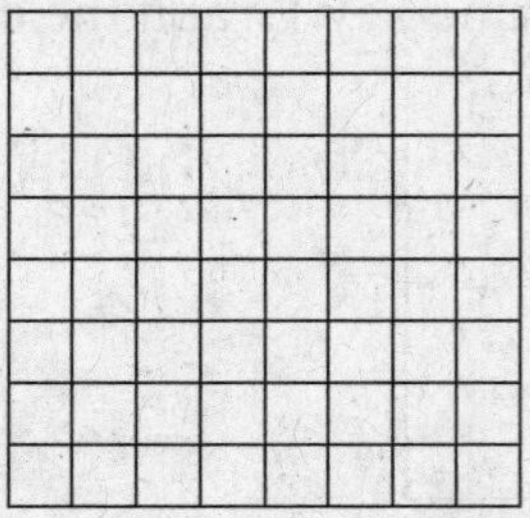

Name______________________________ Class______________________ Date ____________

2. Graph each equation on a graphing calculator. Then sketch the graph.

a. $y = -|-x| + 5$

b. $y = 3 - \left|\frac{x}{2}\right|$

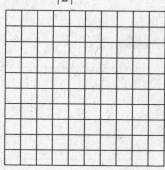

3. Graph each equation by writing two equations.

a. $y = \left|\frac{3}{2}x + 4\right| - 3$

b. $y = 2 - |x + 1|$

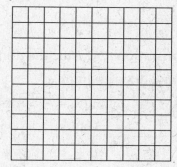

4. a. Use the information from Example 4. Suppose the same train travels at a speed of 25 mi/h. How would the graph of the train's journey change?

b. Sketch a new graph.

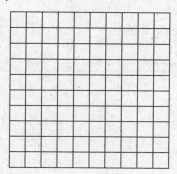

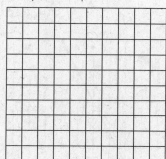

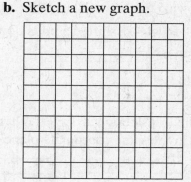

Name______________________ Class______________________ Date______________

Lesson 2-6

Families of Functions

Lesson Objectives	**NAEP 2005 Strand:** Algebra
1 Analyzing translations 2 Analyzing stretches, shrinks, and reflections	**Topic:** Algebraic Representations **Local Standards:** ____________________

Vocabulary

A translation is ____

____

A parent function is ____

____

Examples

1 a. Vertical Translation Describe the translation $y = 2x - 3$ and draw its graph.

The parent is $y = 2x$, and $k = -$[3]. Translate the graph of $y = 2x$ [Right] 3 units.

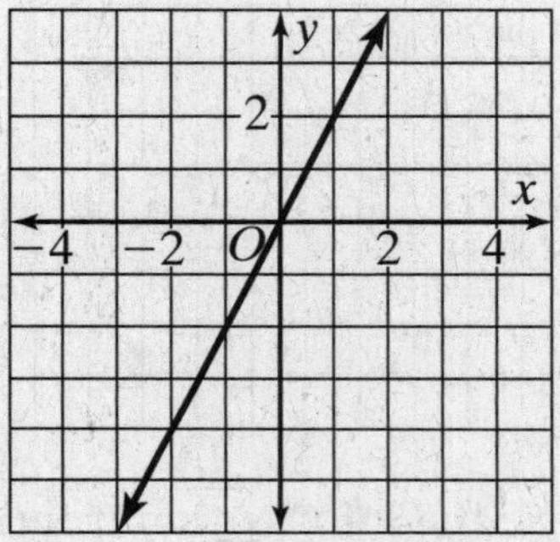

b. Write an equation to translate the graph of $y = |4x|$ down 5 units.

The graph of $y = |4x|$, shifted 5 units down, means $k =$ [−5].

An equation is $y =$ [4x + 5].

Quick Check

1. **a.** Describe the translation $y = |x| + 1$. Then draw the graphs of $y = |x|$ and $y = |x| + 1$ in the same coordinate plane.

[ ]

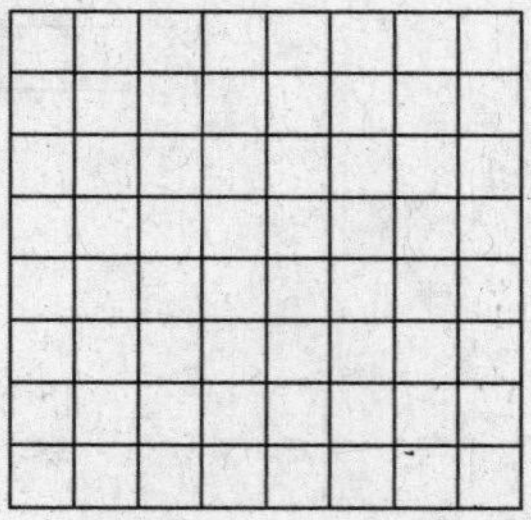

b. Write an equation for the translation of $y = |x|$

i. down $\frac{1}{2}$ unit. **ii.** up 3.5 units.

[ ] [ ]

Name________________________________ Class____________________________ Date ______________

Examples

❷ **a. Horizontal Translations** The dashed graph at the right is a translation of $y = |x|$. Write an equation for the graph.

The parent function is $y =$ ______, and $h =$ ______. Translate the graph of $y = |x|$ right ______ units. The equation of the translated graph is $y =$ ______.

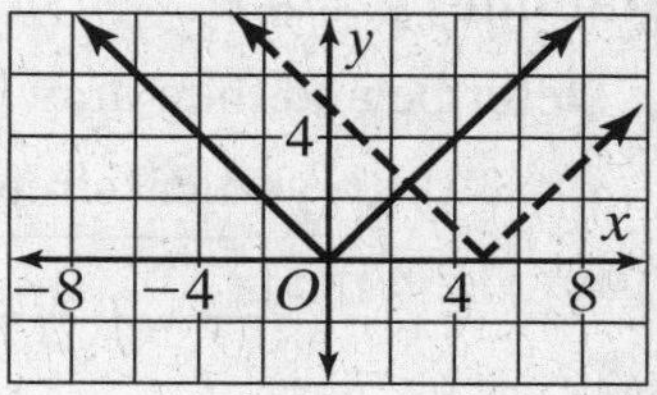

b. Describe the translation $y = -|x + 3|$ and draw its graph.

Translate the graph of $y = -|x|$, 3 units ______.

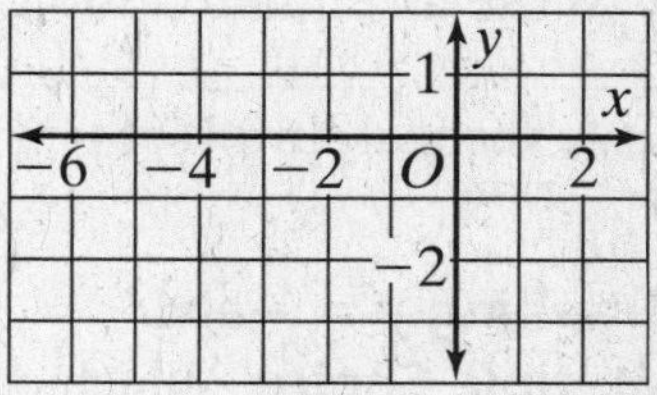

Quick Check

2. a. The graph is a translation of $y = |x|$. Write an equation for the graph.

______

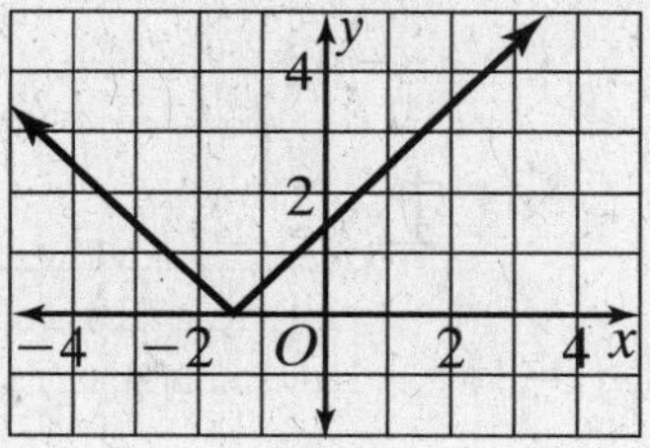

b. Describe the translation $y = |x - 1|$. Then draw the graphs of $y = |x|$ and $y = |x - 1|$ in the same coordinate plane.

______

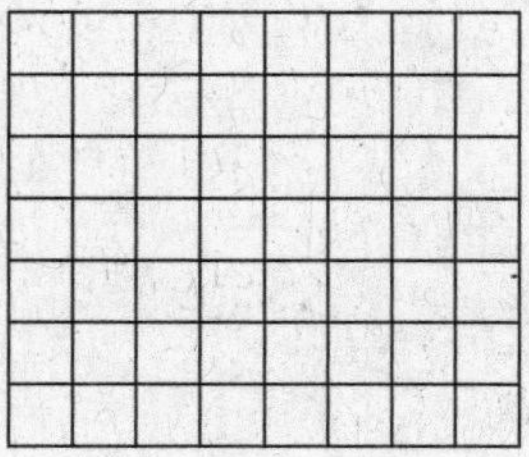

Name______________________________ Class______________________ Date____________

Examples

❸ Graphing $y = a|x|$.

a. Describe and then draw the graph of $y = 3|x|$.

$y = 3|x|$ is a vertical stretch of $y = |x|$ by a factor of ____. Each y-value for $y = 3|x|$ is ________ the corresponding y-value for $y = |x|$.

Note that $(1, 1)$ lies on $y = |x|$, whereas ____ lies on $y = 3|x|$.

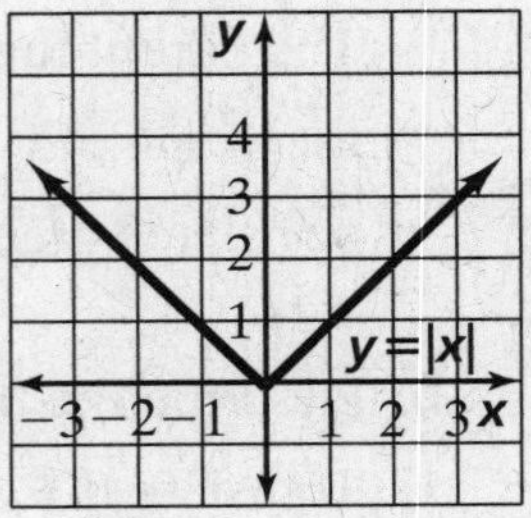

b. Write an equation for a vertical shrink of $y = |x|$ by a factor of $\frac{1}{4}$.

A vertical shrink of $y = |x|$ by a factor of ____ is ________.

❹ Graphing $y = -a|x|$.

Multiple Choice Which equation describes the graph?

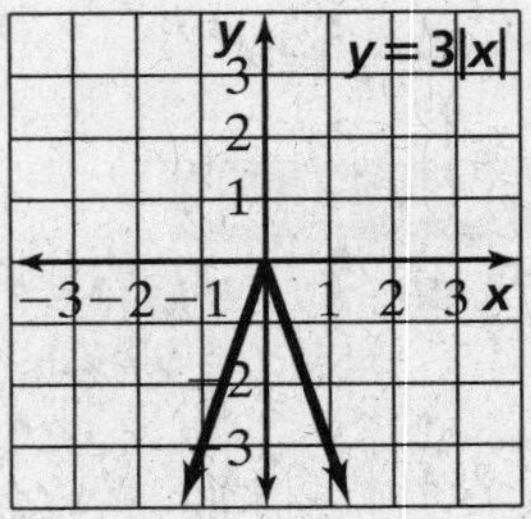

A. $y = 3|x|$

B. $y = -3|x|$

C. $y = \frac{1}{3}|x|$

D. $y = -\frac{1}{3}|x|$

The parent function is $y = |x|$. This is a reflection across the x-axis of $y =$ ____. The answer is ____.

Quick Check

3. a. Describe the stretch or shrink $y = \frac{1}{3}|x|$. Then draw the graphs of $y = |x|$ and $y = \frac{1}{3}|x|$ in the same coordinate plane.

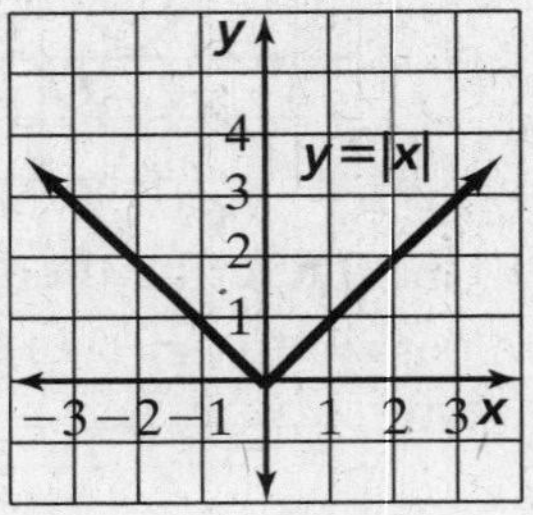

b. Write an equation for the vertical stretch of $y = |x|$ by a factor of 3.

____

4. A function is a vertical stretch of $y = |x|$ by a factor of 5. Write an equation for the reflection of the function across the x axis.

____

Name______________________ Class______________________ Date______________

Lesson 2-7

Two-Variable Inequalities

Lesson Objectives	**NAEP 2005 Strand:** Algebra
1 Graphing linear inequalities	**Topic:** Equations and Inequalities
2 Graphing absolute value inequalities	**Local Standards:** ____________________

Vocabulary

A linear inequality is ____

____

$y > \frac{1}{2}x - 1$

To satisfy the inequality, y-values must be greater than those on the boundary lines.

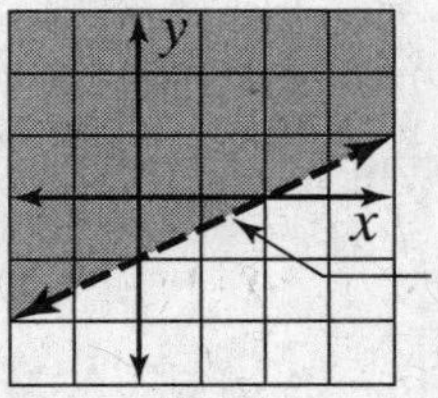

A [ ] boundary line indicates that the line is not part of the solution.

A [ ] boundary line indicates that the line is part of the solution.

$2x + 3y \leq 6$

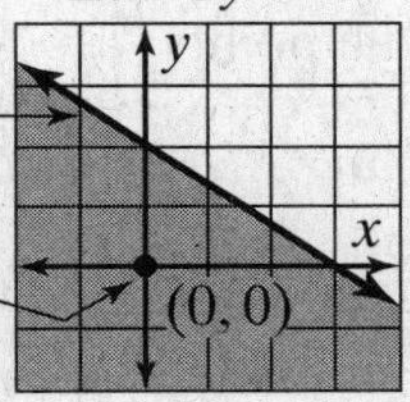

Choose a test point above or below the boundary line.

The test point (0, 0) makes the inequality [ ].

Shade the region [ ] this point.

Examples

1 Graphing a Linear Inequality Graph $y > \frac{3}{2}x + 1$.

Step 1 Graph the boundary line [ ]. Since the inequality is *greater than*, not *greater than or equal to*, use a [ ] boundary line.

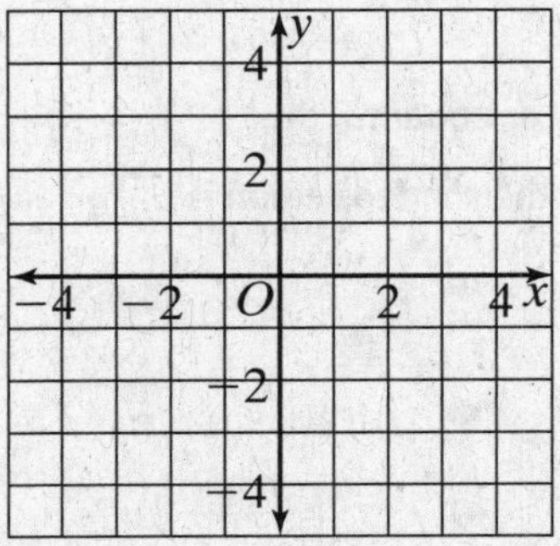

Step 2 Since the inequality is *greater than*, y-values must be [ ] than those on the boundary line. Shade the region [ ] the boundary line.

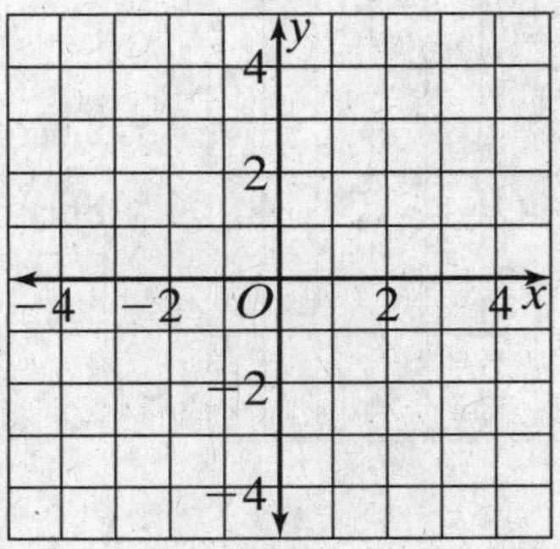

Name____________________ Class____________________ Date____________

❷ Graphing a Linear Inequality A restaurant has only 15 eggs until more are delivered. An order of scrambled eggs requires 2 eggs. An omelet requires 3 eggs. Write an inequality to model all possible combinations of orders of scrambled eggs and omelets the restaurant can fill until more eggs arrive. Graph the inequality.

Relate	number of eggs needed for x orders of scrambled eggs	plus	number of eggs needed for y orders of omelets	is less than or equal to	15

Define Let x = the number of orders for scrambled eggs.

Let y = the number of orders for omelets.

Write 2____ + 3____ ____ ____

Step 1 Find two points on the boundary line.

When $y = 0$, $2x + 3($____$) = 15$ When $x = 0$, $2($____$) + 3y = 15$

____ $= 15$ ____ $= 15$

$x =$ ____ $y =$ ____

Graph the points (____, ____) and (____, ____). Since the inequality is *less than or equal to*, use a ____ boundary line.

Step 2 Since the inequality is *less than*, y-values must be ____ than those on the boundary line. Shade the region ____ the boundary line.

All ordered pairs with whole-number coordinates in the shaded area and on the boundary line represent a combination of x orders of scrambled eggs and y orders of omelets that the restaurant could fill.

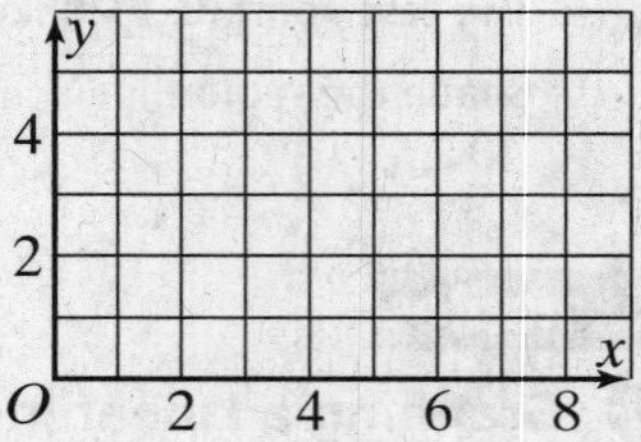

❸ Graphing Absolute Value Inequalities Graph $y \geq |2x| - 3$.

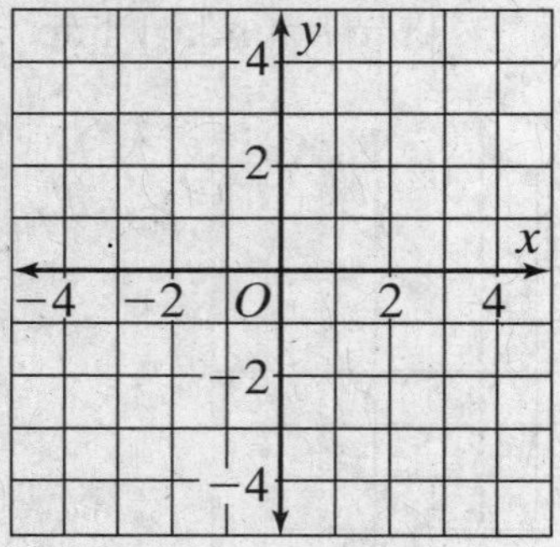

Since the inequality is *greater than* or *equal to*, the boundary is ____ and the shaded region is ____ the boundary.

Name______________________________ Class______________________ Date ____________

❹ **Writing Inequalities** Write an inequality for the graph. The boundary line is given.

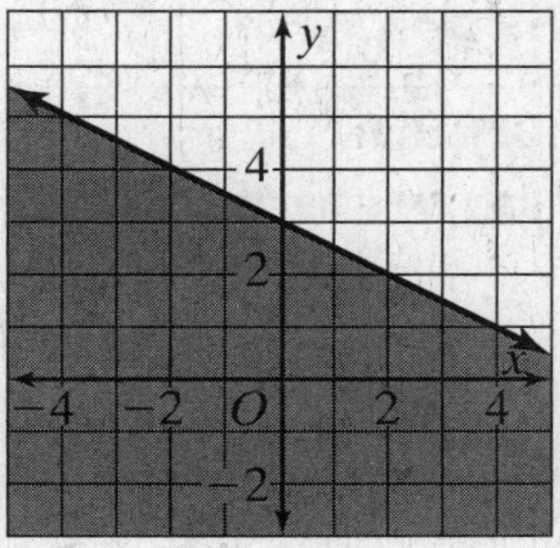

Boundary: $y = -\frac{1}{2}x + 3$

The boundary line is ____________. The shaded region is ____________ the boundary. This is the graph of

$y \;\square\; -\frac{1}{2}x + 3$.

Quick Check

1. Graph each inequality.

a. $4x + 2y \leq 4$

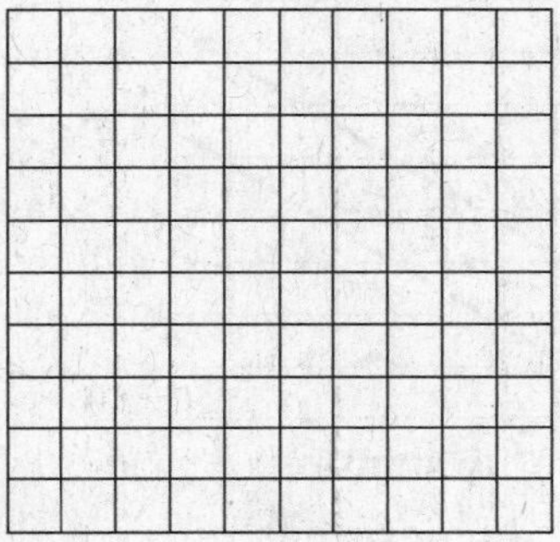

b. $y \geq 3x$

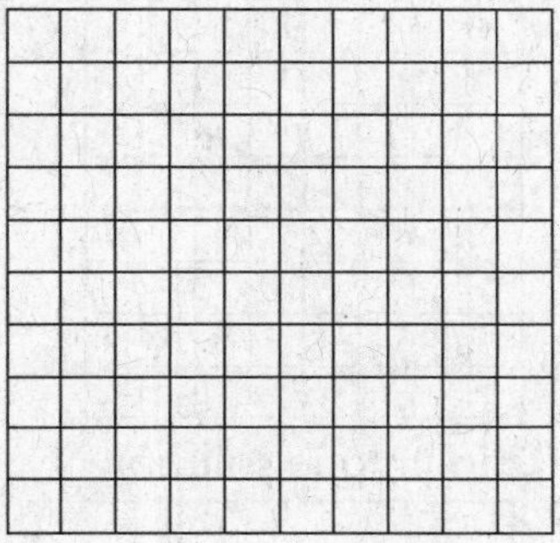

c. $\frac{x}{3} < -y + 2$

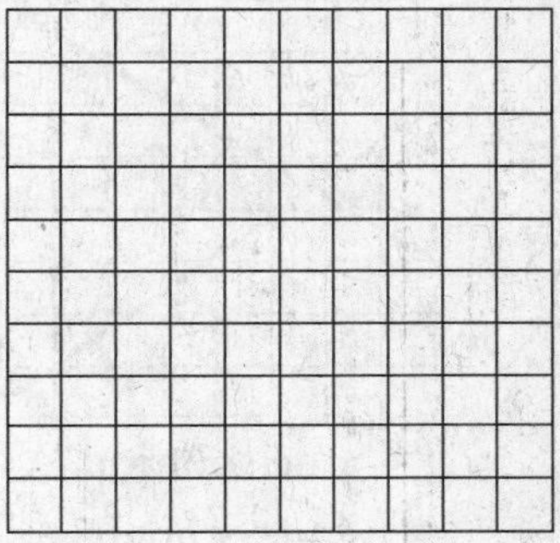

2. Graph each absolute value inequality.

a. $y > -|x + 2| - 3$

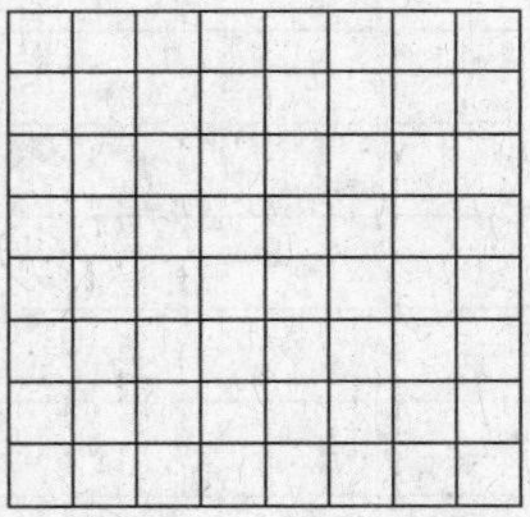

b. $2y + 3 \leq -|x - 5|$

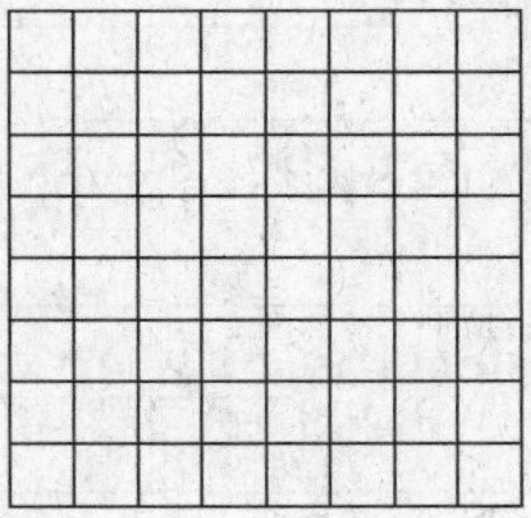

3. Write an inequality for each graph.

a.

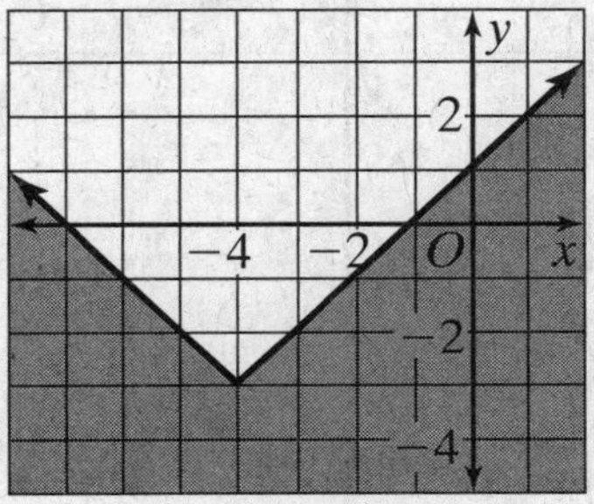

b.

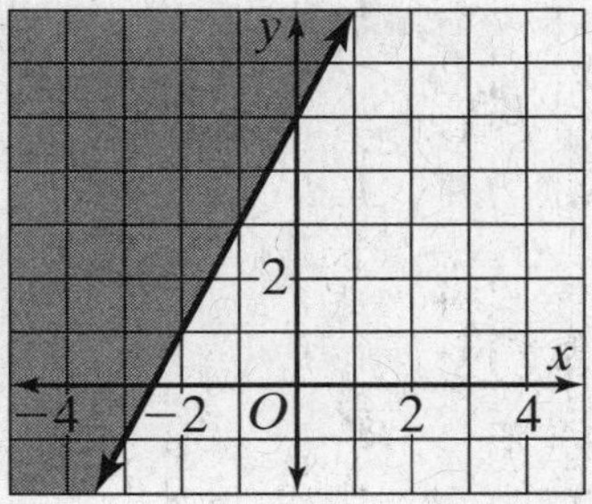

Name________________________ Class________________________ Date____________

Lesson 3-1

Graphing Systems of Equations

Lesson Objective 1 Solving a system by graphing	**NAEP 2005 Strand:** Algebra **Topic:** Equations and Inequalities **Local Standards:** ____________________

Vocabulary and Key Concepts

Graphical Solutions of Linear Systems in Two Variables

________ Lines	Coinciding Lines	________ Lines
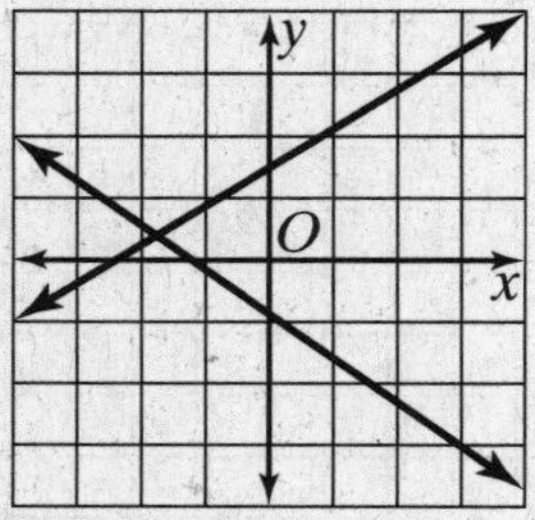	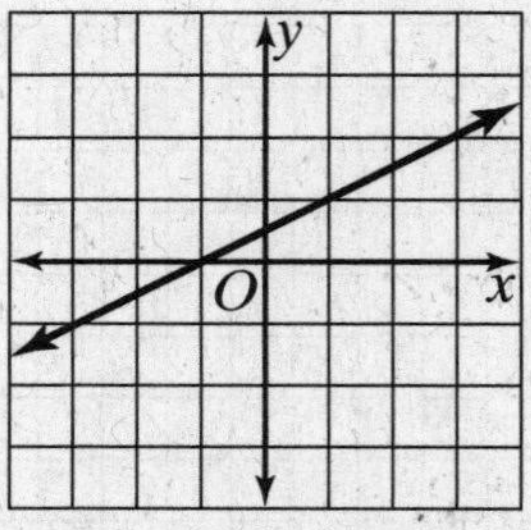	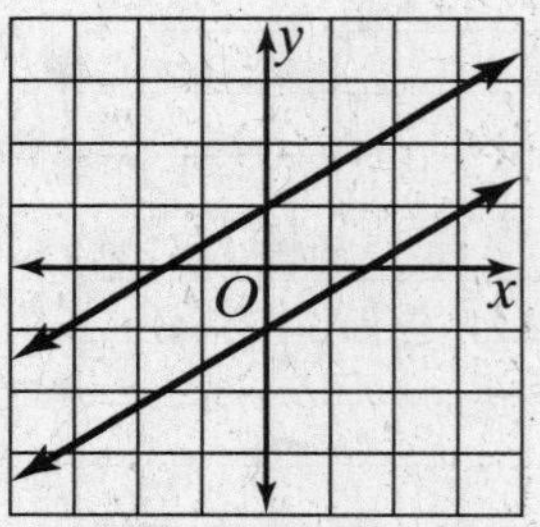
one solution Independent	no unique solution dependent	no solution Inconsistent

A system of equations is ______________________________

____

A system is a linear system if the graph of ______________________________

____

An independent system has ______________________________

____

A dependent system does ______________________________

____

An inconsistent system has ______________________________

Name________________ Class________________ Date ____________

Examples

1 Solving by Graphing Solve the system by graphing the equations and finding the intersection.

$$\begin{cases} x + 3y = 2 \\ 3x + 3y = -6 \end{cases}$$

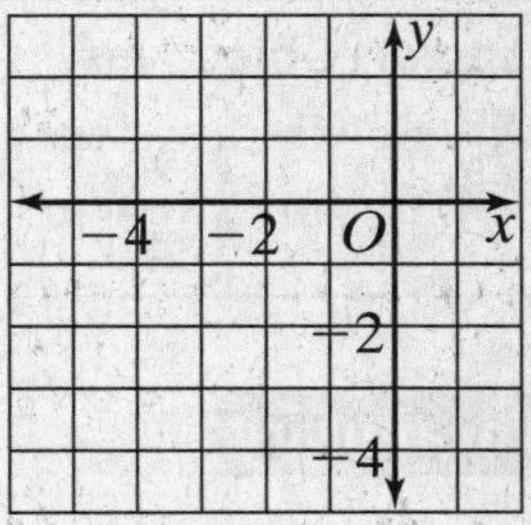

The solution appears to be $(\square, \square)$.

Check Show that (–4, 2) makes both equations true.

$x + 3y = 2$	$3x + 3y = -6$
$(\square) + 3(\square) \stackrel{?}{=} 2$	$3(\square) + 3(\square) \stackrel{?}{=} -6$
$(\square) + \square \stackrel{?}{=} 2$	$\square + \square \stackrel{?}{=} -6$
$\square = 2$	$\square = -6$

2 Classifying Systems Without Graphing Classify the system without graphing.

$$\begin{cases} y = 3x + 2 \\ -6x + 2y = 4 \end{cases}$$

$y = 3x + 2$	$-6x + 2y = 4$	
$y = 3x + 2$	$y = \square + \square$	**Rewrite in slope-intercept form.**
$m = \square, b = \square$	$m = \square, b = \square$	**Find the slope and *y*-intercept.**

Since the slopes are $\square$, the lines could be $\square$ or coinciding. Since the *y*-intercepts are $\square$, the lines $\square$. It is a $\square$ system.

Quick Check

1. Solve $\begin{cases} 2x + y = 5 \\ -x + y = 2 \end{cases}$ by graphing. Check your solution.

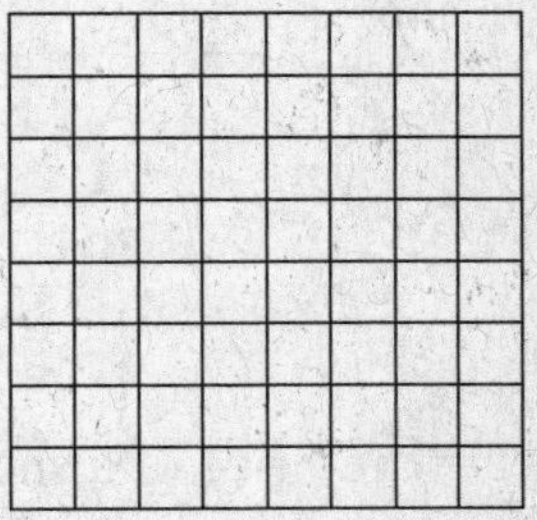

2. Without graphing, classify each system as *independent*, *dependent*, or *inconsistent*.

a. $\begin{cases} 3x + y = 5 \\ 15x + 5y = 2 \end{cases}$

b. $\begin{cases} y = 2x + 3 \\ -4x + 2y = 6 \end{cases}$

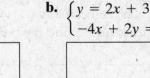

c. $\begin{cases} x - y = 5 \\ y + 3 = 2x \end{cases}$

Name______________________ Class______________________ Date______________

Lesson 3-2

Solving Systems Algebraically

Lesson Objectives	**NAEP 2005 Strand:** Algebra
1 Solving a system by substitution	**Topic:** Equations and Inequalities
2 Solving a system by elimination	**Local Standards:** ______________

Vocabulary

An equivalent system is ____

____

Example

1 Solving by Substitution At Renaldi's Pizza, a soda and two slices of the pizza-of-the-day costs $10.25. A soda and four slices of the pizza-of-the-day costs $18.75. Find the cost of each item.

Relate ☐ · price of a slice of pizza + price of a soda = $10.25
☐ · price of a slice of pizza + price of a soda = $18.75

Define Let p = the price of a slice of pizza.
Let s = the price of a soda.

Write $\begin{cases} \square + \square = 10.25 \\ \square + \square = 18.75 \end{cases}$

$2p + s = 10.25$ **Solve for one of the variables.**

$s = 10.25 - \square$

$4p + (\square - \square) = 18.75$ **Substitute the expression for *s* into the other equation.**

$p = \square$ **Solve for *p*.**

$2(\square) + s = 10.25$ **Substitute the value of *p* into the first equation.**

$s = \square$ **Solve for *s*.**

The price of a slice of pizza is $☐, and the price of a soda is $☐.

Quick Check

1. You can buy CDs at a local store for $15.49 each. You can buy CDs online for $13.99 each plus $6 for shipping. Solve a system of equations to find the number of CDs you can buy for the same amount at each place.

☐

Name______________________ Class______________ Date ___________

Examples

2 Solving by Elimination Use the elimination method to solve the system.

$$\begin{cases} 3x + y = -9 \\ -3x - 2y = 12 \end{cases}$$

$3x + y = -9$

$-3x - 2y = 12$ **Two terms are additive inverses, so ______.**

$-y = \square$ **Solve for *y*.**

$y = \square$

$3x + y = -9$ **Choose one of the original equations.**

$3x + (\square) = -9$ **Substitute for *y*. Solve for *x*.**

$x = \square$

The solution is $(\square, \square)$.

3 Solving an Equivalent System Solve the system by elimination.

$$\begin{cases} 2m + 4n = -4 \\ 3m + 5n = -3 \end{cases}$$

To eliminate the n terms, make them additive inverses by multiplying.

① $2m + 4n = -4$ $\quad \square m + \square n = -20$ **Multiply ① by ☐.**

② $3m + 5n = -3$ $\quad \square m - 20n = \square$ **Multiply ② by ☐.**

$\square m = \square$ **Add.**

$m = \square$ **Solve for *m*.**

$2m + 4n = -4$ **Choose one of the original equations.**

$2(\square) + 4n = -4$ **Substitute for *m*.**

$\square + 4n = -4$

$4n = \square$ **Solve for *n*.**

$n = \square$

The solution is $(\square, \square)$.

Name______________________ Class______________________ Date ______________

❹ Solving a System Without a Unique Solution Solve each system by elimination.

a.

$$\begin{cases} -3x + 5y = 6 \\ 6x - 10y = 0 \end{cases}$$

$$\begin{cases} -\square x + \square y = \square \\ 6x - 10y = 0 \end{cases}$$

$$\square = \square$$

Elimination gives an equation that is always false. The two equations in the system represent parallel lines. The system has ______ solution.

b.

$$\begin{cases} -3x + 5y = 6 \\ 6x - 10y = -12 \end{cases}$$

$$\begin{cases} -\square x + \square y = \square \\ 6x - 10y = -12 \end{cases}$$

$$\square = \square$$

Multiply the first line by $\square$ **to make the *x* terms additive inverses.**

Elimination gives an equation that is always true. The two equations in the system represent the same line. The system has an ______ number of solutions:

$$\left\{(x, y) \mid y = \frac{\square}{\square}x + \frac{\square}{\square}\right\}$$

Quick Check

2. Solve each system by elimination.

a. $\begin{cases} 3x - 2y = 14 \\ 2x + 2y = 6 \end{cases}$

b. $\begin{cases} 4x + 9y = 1 \\ 4x + 6y = -2 \end{cases}$

3. Explain how to solve the system in Example 3 by eliminating the *m* terms.

4. Solve each system by substitution or elimination.

a. $\begin{cases} -3x + 5y = 7 \\ 6x - 10y = -14 \end{cases}$

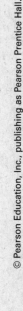

b. $\begin{cases} -2x + 4y = 6 \\ -3x + 6y = 8 \end{cases}$

Name________________________ Class________________________ Date________________

Lesson 3-3

Systems of Inequalities

Lesson Objective	**NAEP 2005 Strand:** Algebra
1 Solving systems of linear inequalities	**Topic:** Equations and Inequalities
	Local Standards: ____________________

Example

1 Solving a System by Using a Table An adventure club has space for 8 boats on a trailer. The 10 members going on the trip can choose either a kayak that holds one person or a canoe that holds 2 people. In how many ways can the boats be filled by the members?

Relate number of kayaks + number of canoes ≤ [8]

1 · number of kayaks + 2 · number of canoes = [10]

Define Let k = number of kayaks

Let c = [number of canoes]

Write $k + c \leq$ [8]

$k +$ [2c] $= 10$

The situation is discrete. The replacement values for k and c must be ______ numbers.

To solve the system $\begin{cases} k + c \leq 8 \\ k + 2c = 10 \end{cases}$

First make a table of values of k and c that solve the inequality.

In the table, look for values of k and c that solve the equation. Circle any that you find.

k	c
0	8, 7, 6, 5, 4, 3, 2, 1, 0
1	7, 6, 5, 4, 3, 2, 1, 0
2	6, 5, 4, 3, 2, 1, 0
3	5, 4, 3, 2, 1, 0
4	4, 3, 2, 1, 0
5	3, 2, 1, 0
6	2, 1, 0
7	1, 0
8	0

There are ☐ possible ways to set up the boats. You can assign all members to ☐ canoes, or ☐ members to 2 kayaks and ☐ members to 4 canoes, or ☐ members to 4 kayaks and ☐ members to 3 canoes, or ☐ members to 6 kayaks and ☐ members to 2 canoes.

Name______________________________ Class______________________ Date ____________

Quick Check

1. Use tables to solve each system. Assume that replacement values for the variables are whole numbers.

a. $\begin{cases} -x + y = 1 \\ x + 2y \leq 20 \end{cases}$

(0, 1), (1, 2), (2, 3), (3, 4), (4, 5), (5, 6), (6, 7)

b. $\begin{cases} x - y \geq 1 \\ 2x + 3y \leq 21 \end{cases}$

(1, 0),
(2, 1,), (2, 0),
(3, 2), (3, 1), (3, 0),
(4, 3), (4, 2), (4, 1), (4, 0),
(5, 3), (5, 2), (5, 1), (5, 0),
(6, 3), (6, 2), (6, 1), (6, 0),
(7, 2), (7, 1), (7, 0)

Examples

❷ Solving a System of Inequalities

Solve the system of inequalities. $\begin{cases} x + y > 3 \\ y > x - 1 \end{cases}$

Graph each inequality. First graph the boundary lines. Then decide which side of each boundary line contains solutions and whether the boundary line is included.

$y > x - 1$

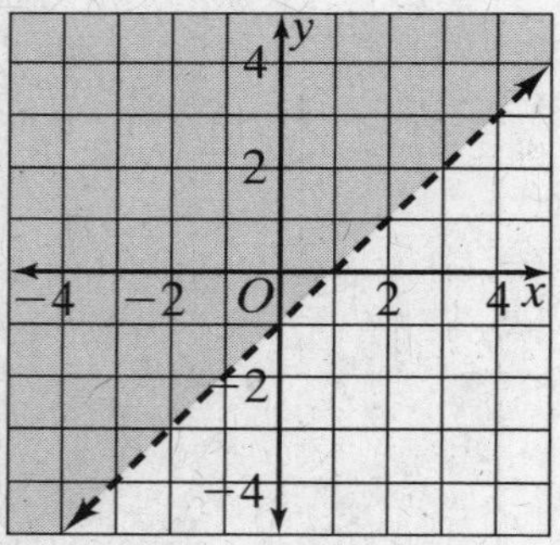

Graph 1

$x + y > 3$

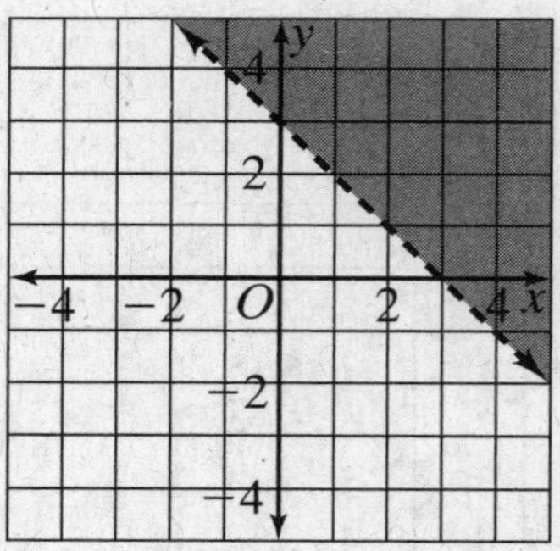

Graph 2

$y > x - 1$
$x + y > 3$

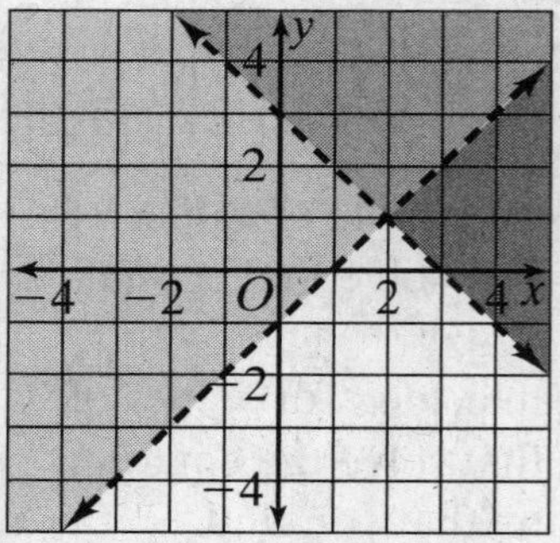

Graph 3

Graph 1 Every point in the shaded region ______ the dashed line is a solution of $y > x - 1$.

Graph 2 Every point in the shaded region ______ the dashed line is a solution of $x + y > 3$.

Graph 3 Every point in the overlapping region where the 2 shaded regions ______ is a solution of the system. For example: (2, 2) is a solution.

Check Check (2, 2) in both inequalities of the system.

$y > x - 1$

☐ > ☐ − 1

2 > ☐ ✓

$x + y > 3$

☐ + ☐ > 3

☐ > 3✓

Name________________________ Class____________________ Date______________

❸ **Solving a Linear Absolute Value System** Solve the system of inequalities.

$$\begin{cases} y \geq 3 \\ y > -|x + 2| + 5 \end{cases}$$

$y \geq 3$

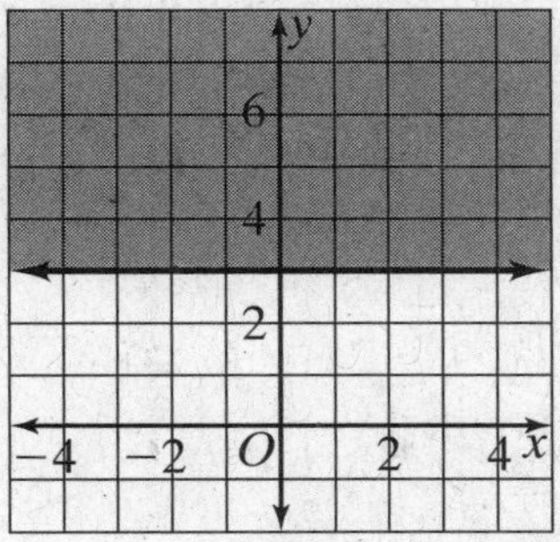

Graph 1

$y > -|x + 2| + 5$

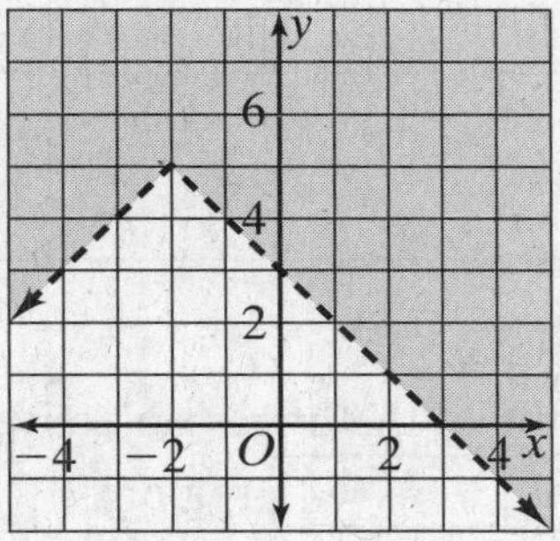

Graph 2

$y \geq 3$
$y > -|x + 2| + 5$

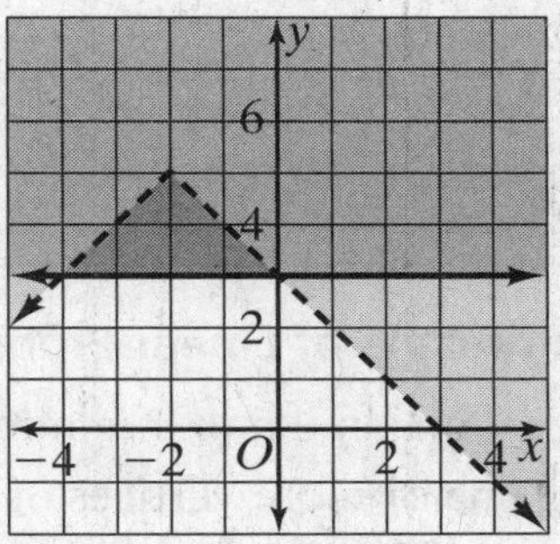

Graph 3

Graph 1 Every point in the shaded region or on the ______ is a solution of $y \geq 3$.

Graph 2 Every point in the shaded region ______ the dashed line is a solution of $y > -|x + 2| + 5$.

Graph 3 Every point in the overlapping region where the 2 shaded regions ______ is a solution of the system. For example: (4, 4) is a solution.

Check Check (4, 4) in both inequalities of the system.

$y \geq 3$

$\square \geq 3$ ✓

$y > -|x + 2| + 5$

$\square > -|\square + 2| + 5$

$\square > \square$ ✓

Quick Check

2. Solve the system of inequalities.

$$\begin{cases} y \leq -2x + 4 \\ x > -3 \end{cases}$$

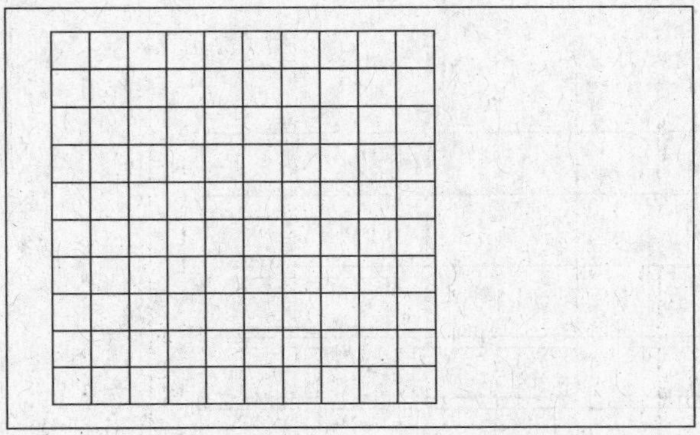

3. Solve the system of inequalities.

$$\begin{cases} y \geq x \\ y \leq |x + 5| - 2 \end{cases}$$

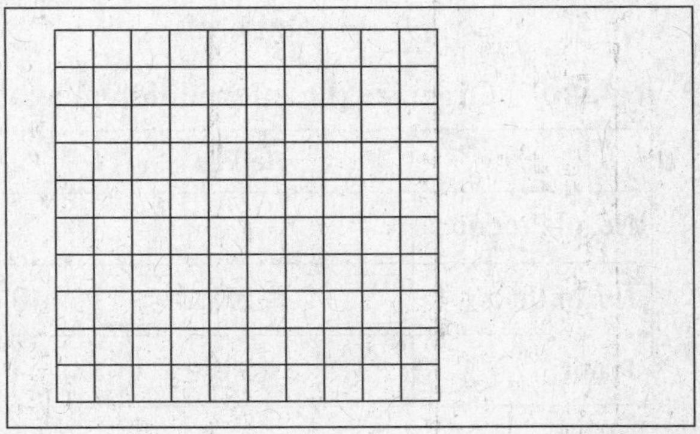

Name_____________________ Class_____________________ Date _____________

Lesson 3-4

Linear Programming

Lesson Objectives	**NAEP 2005 Strand:** Algebra
1 Finding maximum and minimum values 2 Solving problems with linear programming	**Topic:** Equations and Inequalities **Local Standards:** ____________________

Vocabulary and Key Concepts

Vertex Principle of Linear Programming

If there is a maximum or a minimum value of the linear objective function, it occurs at one or more vertices of the ______ region.

Linear programming is a ____________________

____

An objective function is a ____________________

____

Constraints are ____________________

____

The feasible region contains ____________________

____

Example

1 Applying Constraints A furniture manufacturer can make from 30 to 60 tables a day and from 40 to 100 chairs a day. It can make at most 120 units in one day. The profit on a table is $150, and the profit on a chair is $65. How many tables and chairs should they make per day to maximize profit? How much is the maximum profit?

Define Let x = number of tables made in a day.

Let y = number of chairs made in a day.

Let P = total profit.

Relate Organize the information in a table.

	Tables	Chairs	Total
No. of Products	x	y	$x + y$
No. of Units	___ $\leq x \leq$ ___	$40 \leq y \leq 100$	$x + y \leq$ ___
Profit	$150x$	___	___x + ___y

Name____________________ Class____________________ Date____________________

Write Write the constraints. Write the objective function.

$$\begin{cases} x \geq 30 \\ x \leq \square \\ y \geq \square \\ y \leq 100 \\ x + y \leq \square \end{cases} \qquad P = \square x + \square y$$

Step 1
Graph the constraints.

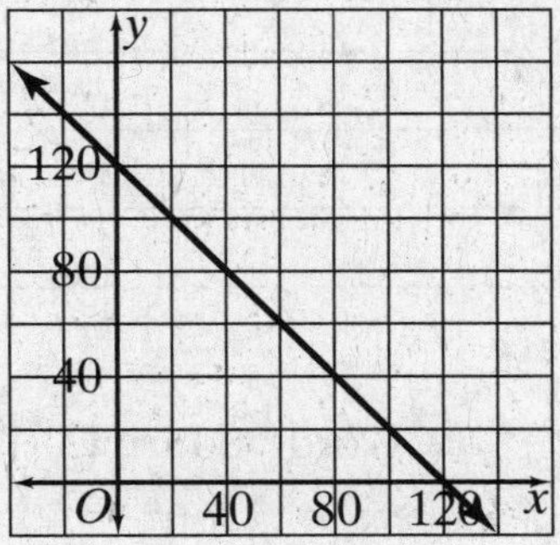

Step 2
Find the coordinates of each vertex.

Vertex

$A(30, 90)$

$B(\square, \square)$

$C(\square, \square)$

$D(30, 40)$

Step 3
Evaluate P at each vertex.

$P = 150x + 65y$

$P = 150(\square) + 65(\square) = \square$

$P = 150(\square) + 65(\square) = \square$

$P = 150(\square) + 65(\square) = \square$

$P = 150(\square) + 65(\square) = \square$

The furniture manufacturer can maximize profit by making ____ tables and ____ chairs. The maximum profit is $____.

Quick Check

1. In Example 1, suppose the profit margin increases so that the profit on a table is $175 and the profit on a chair is $100. How much is the maximum profit?

Name_______________ Class_______________ Date_______________

Lesson 3-5

Graphs in Three Dimensions

Lesson Objectives	**NAEP 2005 Strand:** Algebra
1 Graphing points in three dimensions	**Topic:** Algebraic Representations
2 Graphing equations in three dimensions	**Local Standards:** ____________________

Vocabulary

Coordinate space is ____________________

Ordered triples in the form (x, y, z) represent ____________________

Points in a Plane

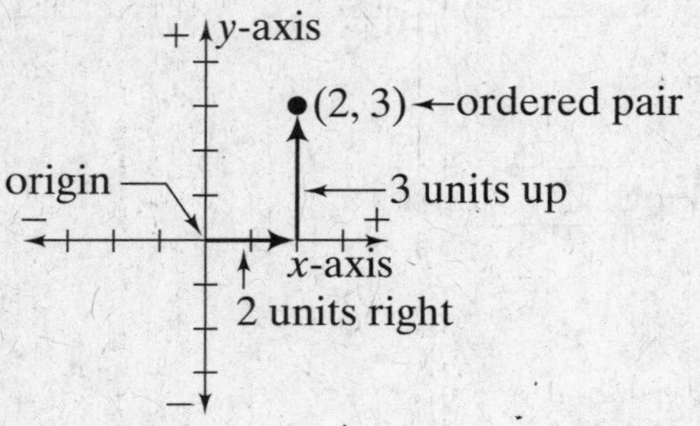

Points in Space

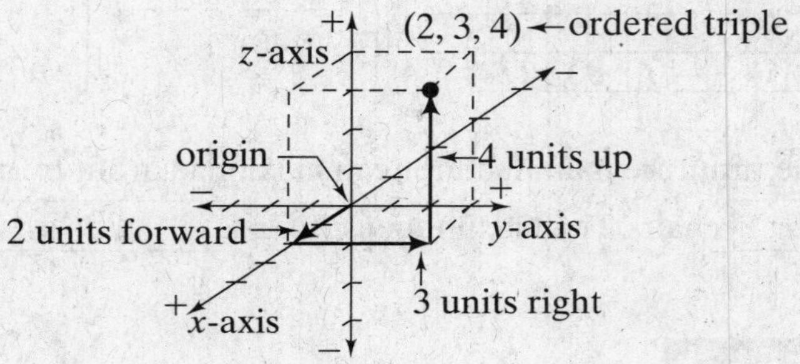

A trace is a ____________________

Examples

1 Graphing in Coordinate Space Graph each point in the coordinate space.

a. $(-3, 3, -4)$

From the origin, move back ☐ units, right ☐ units, and down ☐ units.

b. $(-3, -4, 2)$

From the origin, move back ☐ units, left ☐ units, and up ☐ units.

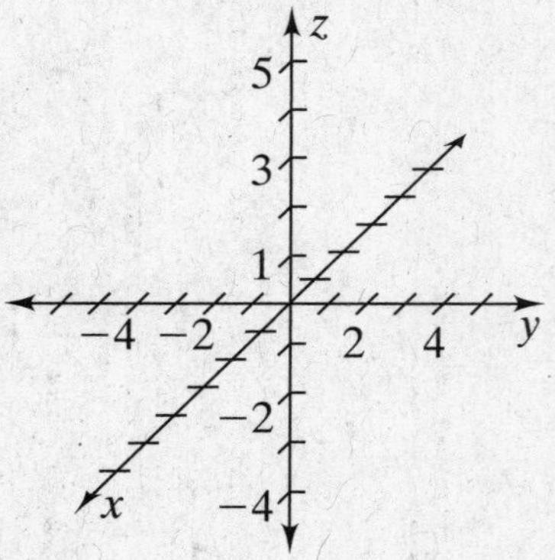

Name______________________ Class______________________ Date ______________

❷ Finding Coordinates for Three-Dimensional Objects In the diagram, the origin is at the center of a cube that has edges 6 units long. The x-, y-, and z-axes are perpendicular to the faces of the cube. Give the coordinates of the corners of the cube.

A(☐, ☐, ☐), B(☐, ☐, ☐),
C(☐, ☐, ☐), D(☐, ☐, ☐),
E(☐, ☐, ☐), F(☐, ☐, ☐),
G(☐, ☐, ☐), H(☐, ☐, ☐)

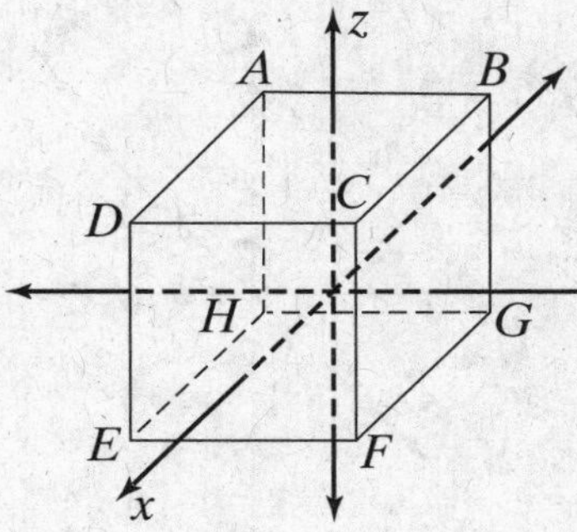

❸ Sketching a Plane Sketch the graph of $-3x - 2y + z = 6$.

Step 1 Find the intercepts.

$-3x - 2y + z = 6$

$-3x - 2(\square) + (\square) = 6$ **To find the x-intercept, substitute 0 for ☐ and ☐.**

$\square x = \square$

$x = \square$ **The x-intercept is ☐.**

$-3(\square) - 2y + (\square) = 6$ **To find the y-intercept, substitute 0 for ☐ and ☐.**

$\square y = \square$

$y = \square$ **The y-intercept is ☐.**

$-3(\square) - 2(\square) + z = 6$ **To find the z-intercept, substitute 0 for ☐ and ☐.**

$z = \square$ **The z-intercept is ☐.**

Step 2 Graph the intercepts.

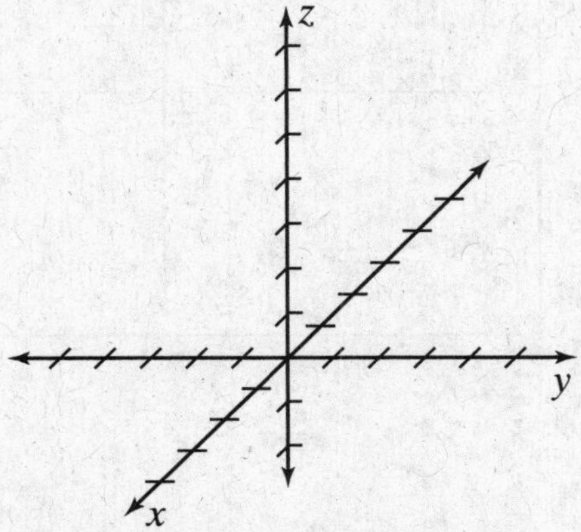

Step 3 Draw the traces. Shade the plane.

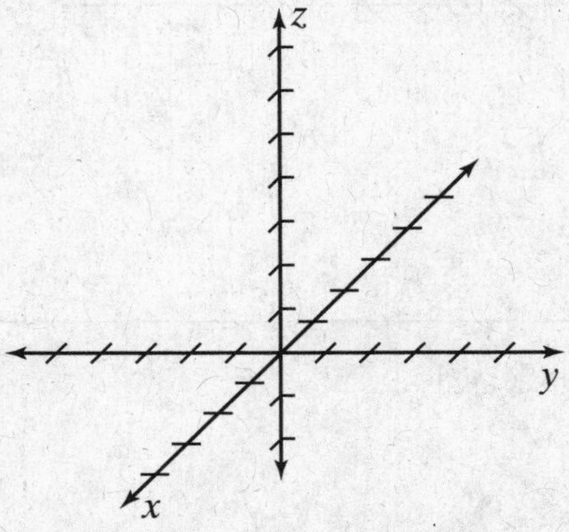

Each point on the plane represents a ☐ to $-3x - 2y + z = 6$.

Name________________________ Class________________ Date____________

Quick Check

1. Graph each point in coordinate space.

a. $(0, -4, -2)$

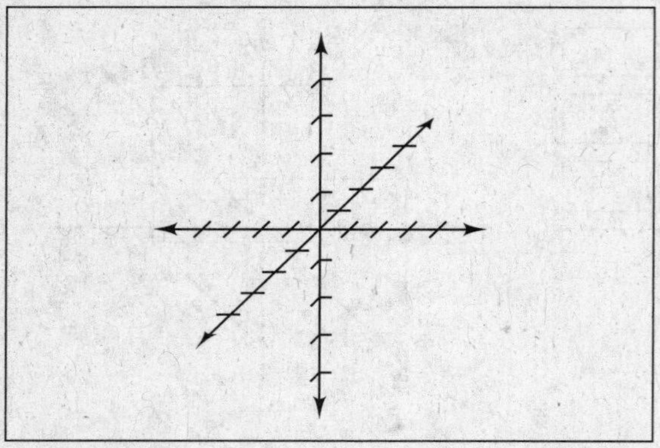

b. $(-1, 1, 3)$

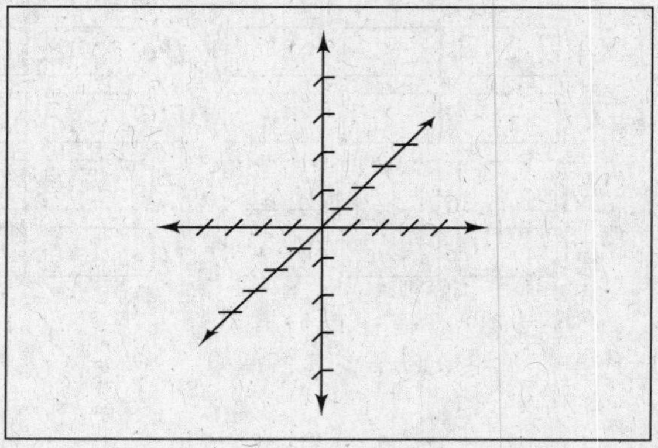

2. Use the diagram in Example 2. The origin is at the center of a cube that has edges 10 units long. The x-, y-, and z-axes are perpendicular to the faces of the cube. Give the coordinates of the corners of the cube.

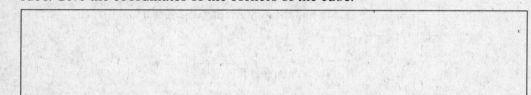

3. Sketch the graph of each equation.

a. $2x - y + 3z = 6$

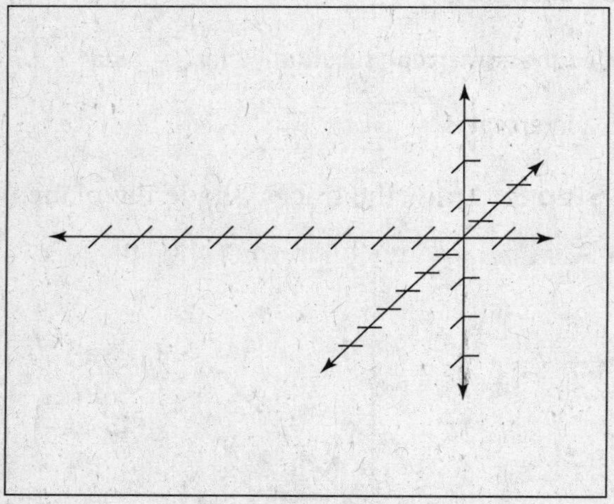

b. $x + 2y - z = -4$

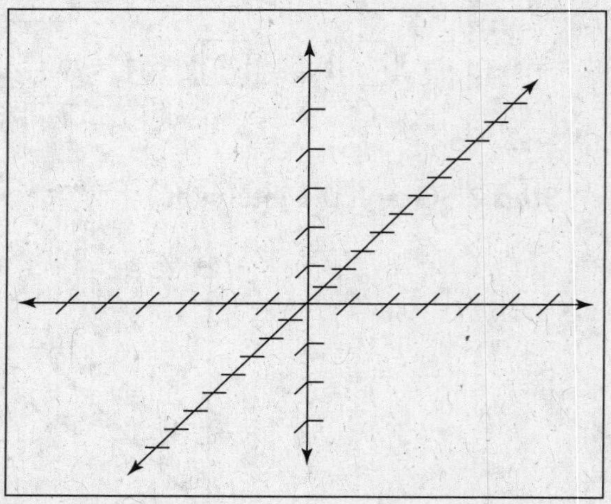

Name________________ Class________________ Date ____________

Lesson 3-6

Systems With Three Variables

Lesson Objectives	NAEP 2005 Strand: Algebra
1 Solving systems in three variables by elimination	**Topic:** Equations and Inequalities
2 Solving systems in three variables by substitution	**Local Standards:** ____________

Examples

1 Solving by Elimination Solve the system by elimination.

$$\begin{cases} -5x + 3y + 2z = 11 & (1)\\ 8x - 5y + 2z = -55 & (2)\\ 4x - 7y - 2z = -29 & (3)\end{cases}$$

Step 1 Pair the equations to eliminate the z-term additive inverses. Then, add.

(2) $8x - 5y + 2z = -55$
(3) $4x - 7y - 2z = -29$
(4) ☐ − ☐ = ☐

(1) $-5x + 3y + 2z = 11$
(3) $4x - 7y - 2z = -29$
(5) ☐ ☐ $4y =$ ☐

Step 2 Write the two new equations as a system. Solve for x and y.

(4) $12x - 12y = -84$
(6) ☐ − ☐ $= -216$ — **Multiply equation (5) by ☐ to make it an additive inverse.**
☐ = ☐ — **Add.**
$y =$ ☐

(4) $12x - 12y = -84$
$12x - 12(☐) = -84$ — **Substitute the value of y.**
$12x =$ ☐
$x =$ ☐

Step 3 Substitute the values for x and y into one of the original equations and solve for z.

(1) $-5x + 3y + 2z = 11$
$-5(☐) + 3(☐) + 2z = 11$
☐ $+ 2z = 11$
$2z =$ ☐
$z =$ ☐

The solution of the system is (☐, ☐, ☐).

Check Show that $(\square, \square, \square)$ makes each equation true.

① $-5x + 3y + 2z = 11$

$-5(\square) + 3(\square) + 2(\square) \stackrel{?}{=} 11$

$\square + \square - \square \stackrel{?}{=} 11$

$\square = 11$ ✔

② $8x - 5y + 2z = -55$

$8(\square) - 5(\square) + 2(\square) \stackrel{?}{=} -55$

$\square\ \square\ 25\ \square\ 14 \stackrel{?}{=} -55$

$\square = -55$ ✔

③ $4x - 7y - 2z = -29$

$4(\square) - 7(\square) - 2(\square) \stackrel{?}{=} -29$

$\square - \square + \square \stackrel{?}{=} -29$

$\square = -29$ ✔

❷ Solving an Equivalent System

Solve the system by elimination.

$$\begin{cases} x + 2y + 5z = 1 & ① \\ -3x + 3y + 7z = 4 & ② \\ -8x + 5y + 12z = 11 & ③ \end{cases}$$

Step 1 Pair the equations to eliminate x.

① $x + 2y + 5z = 1$ → $\boxed{3}x + \boxed{6}y + \boxed{15}z = \boxed{3}$ **Multiply by** $\boxed{3}$.

② $-3x + 3y + 7z = 4$ → $-3x + 3y + 7z = 4$

④ $\boxed{9}y + \boxed{22}z = 7$ **Add.**

① $x + 2y + 5z = 1$ → $\square x + \square y + \square z = \square$ **Multiply by** $\square$.

③ $-8x + 5y + 12z = 11$ → $-8x + 5y + 12z = 11$

⑤ $\square y + \square z = \square$ **Add.**

Step 2 Write the two new equations as a system. Solve for y and z.

④ $9y + 22z = 7$ → $\square y + \square z = \square$ **Multiply by** $\square$.

⑤ $21y + 52z = 19$ → $\square y - \square z = \square$ **Multiply by** $\square$.

$\square z = \square$

$z = \square$

④ $9y + 22z = 7$

$9y + 22(\square) = 7$ **Substitute the value of *z*.**

$9y = \square$

$y = \square$

Name____________________ Class________________ Date __________

Step 3 Substitute the values for y and z into one of the original equations and solve for x.

$$① \; x + 2y + 5z = 1$$
$$x + 2(\square) + 5(\square) = 1$$
$$x = \square$$

The solution of the system is $(\square, \square, \square)$.

❸ Solving by Substitution Solve the system by substitution.
$$\begin{cases} ① & 12x + 7y + 5z = 16 \\ ② & -2x + y - 14z = -9 \\ ③ & -3x - 2y + 9z = -12 \end{cases}$$

Step 1 Choose one equation to solve for one of its variables.

$$③ \; -3x - 2y + 9z = -12$$ **Solve the third equation for *x*.**
$$-3x = \square - \square - 12$$
$$x = \square y + \square z + \square$$

Step 2 Substitute the expression for x into each of the other two equations.

$$① \; 12x + 7y + 5z = 16$$
$$12(\square + \square + \square) + 7y + 5z = 16$$
$$\square y + \square z + \square + 7y + 5z = 16$$
$$\square + \square + \square = 16$$
$$④ \; \square + \square = \square$$

$$② \; -2x + y - 14z = -9$$
$$-2(\square + \square + \square) + y - 14z = -9$$
$$\square y - \square z - \square + y - 14z = -9$$
$$\square - \square - \square = -9$$
$$⑤ \; \square - \square = \square$$

Step 3 Write the two new equations as a system. Solve for y and z.

$$\begin{cases} ④ & -\square + \square z = -32 \\ ⑤ & \frac{7}{3}y - \square z = \square \end{cases}$$

$$\square y + \square z = \square$$ **Multiply by $\frac{7}{3}$.**
$$\frac{7}{3}y - 20z = -1$$
$$\square z = \square$$
$$z = \square$$

$$④ \; -y + 41z = -32$$
$$-y + 41(\square) = -32$$ **Substitute the value of *z*.**
$$-y - \square = -32$$
$$-y = \square$$
$$y = \square$$

Step 4 Substitute the values for y and z into one of the original equations and solve for x.

$$② \; -2x + y - 14z = -9$$

$$-2x + (\square) - 14(\square) = -9$$

$$-2x - \square + \square = -9$$

$$-2x + \square = -9$$

$$\square = \square$$

$$x = \square$$

The solution of the system is $(\square, \square, \square)$.

Quick Check

1. Solve each system by elimination. Check your answers.

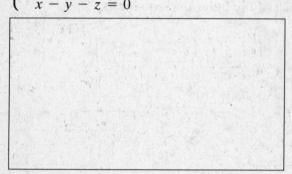

a. $\begin{cases} 2x + y - z = 5 \\ 3x - y + 2z = -1 \\ x - y - z = 0 \end{cases}$

b. $\begin{cases} 2x - y + z = 4 \\ x + 3y - z = 11 \\ 4x + y - z = 14 \end{cases}$

c. Suppose one of the equations in a system contains a variable with a coefficient of zero. When pairing the equations to solve the system, would you use that equation twice? Explain.

2. Solve the system by elimination. Check your answers.

$\begin{cases} x + 4y - 5z = -7 \\ 3x + 2y + 3z = 7 \\ 2x + y + 5z = 8 \end{cases}$

Name______________________________ Class________________________ Date______________

3. Solve each system by substitution. Check your answers.

a. $\begin{cases} x - 3y + z = 6 \\ 2x - 5y - z = -2 \\ -x + y + 2z = 7 \end{cases}$

b. $\begin{cases} 3x + 2y - z = 12 \\ -4x + y - 2z = 4 \\ x - 3y + z = -4 \end{cases}$

Name__________ Class__________ Date__________

Lesson 4-1

Organizing Data into Matrices

Lesson Objectives	
1 Identifying matrices and their elements 2 Organize data into matrices	**NAEP 2005 Strand:** Number Properties and Operations **Topic:** Ratios and Proportional Reasoning **Local Standards:** __________

Vocabulary

A matrix is __________

A matrix element is __________

Examples

1 Dimensions of a Matrix Write the dimensions of each matrix.

a. $\begin{bmatrix} 7 & -4 \\ 12 & 9 \end{bmatrix}$ **The matrix has** [2] **rows and** [2] **columns and is therefore a** [2x2] **matrix.**

b. $\begin{bmatrix} 0 & 6 & 15 \end{bmatrix}$ **The matrix has** [1] **row and** [3] **columns and is therefore a** [1x3] **matrix.**

2 Elements of a Matrix Identify each matrix element.

$$K = \begin{bmatrix} 3 & -1 & -8 & 5 \\ 1 & 8 & 4 & 9 \\ 8 & -4 & 7 & -5 \end{bmatrix}$$

a. k_{32}

$$K = \begin{bmatrix} 3 & -1 & -8 & 5 \\ 1 & 8 & 4 & 9 \\ 8 & -4 & 7 & -5 \end{bmatrix}$$

k_{32} is the element in the [3rd] row and [Second] column.

Element k_{32} is [−4].

b. k_{23}

$$K = \begin{bmatrix} 3 & -1 & -8 & 5 \\ 1 & 8 & 4 & 9 \\ 8 & -4 & 7 & -5 \end{bmatrix}$$

k_{23} is the element in the [2nd] row and [3rd] column.

Element k_{23} is [4].

Quick Check

1. Write the dimensions of each matrix.

a. $\begin{bmatrix} 4 & 5 & 0 \\ -2 & 0.5 & 17 \end{bmatrix}$ [ ]

b. $\begin{bmatrix} 8 & -3 & 15 \end{bmatrix}$ [ ]

c. $\begin{bmatrix} 10 & 0 \\ 1 & -5 \\ -6.2 & 9 \end{bmatrix}$ [ ]

Name____________________________ Class______________________ Date _____________

Example

③ Organizing Data Using a Matrix Three students kept track of the games they won and lost in a chess competition. They showed their results in a chart. Write a 2×3 matrix to show the data.

Let each row represent the number of wins and losses and each column represent a student.

✓ = Win ✗ = Loss

Ed	✓	✗	✓	✓	✗	✓	✓
Jo	✓	✓	✓	✓	✗	✓	✓
Lew	✗	✓	✗	✗	✓	✓	✗

	Ed	Jo	Lew
Wins	5	6	3
Losses	2	1	4

$$\begin{bmatrix} 5 & 6 & 3 \\ 2 & 1 & 4 \end{bmatrix}$$

Quick Check

2. Use the matrix from Example 2 to identify each matrix element.

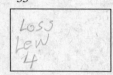

a. k_{33}

Loss
Lew
4

b. k_{11}

Win
Ed
5

c. k_{21}

d. k_{12}

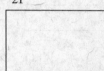

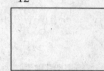

3. **a.** Rewrite the matrix in Example 3 as a 3×2 matrix. Label the rows and columns.

b. How could you modify your matrix to include data from other players?

c. Explain the difference between an $a \times b$ matrix and a $b \times a$ matrix.

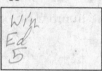

Name_______________ Class_______________ Date _______________

Example

4 Organizing Data and Finding Matrix Elements Refer to the table.

U.S. Passenger Car Imports and Exports (millions)

	1980	1990	1995
Imports	3.116	3.945	4.115
Exports	0.617	0.794	0.989

a. Write a matrix N to represent the information. Use a 2×3 matrix.

Each column represents a different year.

	1980	1990	1995
Imports	3.116	☐	☐
Exports	☐	0.794	☐

$N =$ the matrix above.

Each row represents imports and exports.

b. Which element represents exports for 1995?

Exports are in the ☐ row. The year 1995 is in the ☐ column. Element ☐ represents the number of exports for 1995.

Quick Check

4. a. Write a matrix M to represent the information from the table below.

Passenger Car Imports and Exports (millions)						
	1950	**1955**	**1960**	**1965**	**1970**	**1975**
Imports	1.734	2.002	2.153	2.541	2.976	3.012
Exports	0.289	0.358	0.392	0.464	0.521	0.589

b. Identify element m_{15}. What does this element represent?

Name______________________________ Class______________________ Date______________

Lesson 4-2

Adding and Subtracting Matrices

Lesson Objectives	
1 Adding and subtracting matrices 2 Solving certain matrix equations	**NAEP 2005 Strand:** Algebra; Number Properties and Operations **Topics:** Number Operations; Equations and Inequalities **Local Standards:** ____________

Vocabulary and Key Concepts

Matrix Addition

To add matrices A and B with the same dimensions, add corresponding elements.

$$A = \begin{bmatrix} a & b & c \\ d & e & f \end{bmatrix} \qquad B = \begin{bmatrix} r & s & t \\ u & v & w \end{bmatrix}$$

$$A + B = \begin{bmatrix} a & b & c \\ d & e & f \end{bmatrix} + \begin{bmatrix} r & s & t \\ u & v & w \end{bmatrix} = \begin{bmatrix} a + \boxed{r} & b + s & c + t \\ d + \boxed{u} & \boxed{e} + v & \boxed{f} + w \end{bmatrix}$$

Matrix Addition

If A, B, and C are $m \times n$ matrices, then

$A + B$ is an $m \times n$ matrix.	Closure Property
$A + B = B + A$	______ Property of Addition
$(A + B) + C = A + (B + C)$	______ Property of Addition
There exists a unique $m \times n$ matrix O such that $O + A = A + O = A$.	Additive Identity Property
For each A, there exists a unique opposite, $-A$. $A + (-A) = O$.	______ Property

Matrix Subtraction

If two matrices, A and B, have the same dimensions, then $A - B = A$ ______ $(-B)$.

Matrix addition involves ______________________________

____

A zero matrix is ______________________________

____

A matrix equation is ______________________________

____

Equal matrices are ______________________________

____

Name____________________ Class____________________ Date ____________

Examples

1 Adding Matrices Find each sum.

a. $\begin{bmatrix} 9 & 0 \\ -4 & 6 \end{bmatrix} + \begin{bmatrix} 0 & 0 \\ 0 & 0 \end{bmatrix}$

$= \begin{bmatrix} \square + 0 & \square + 0 \\ -4 + \square & 6 + \square \end{bmatrix}$

$= \begin{bmatrix} \square & 0 \\ -4 & \square \end{bmatrix}$

b. $\begin{bmatrix} 3 & -8 \\ -5 & 1 \end{bmatrix} + \begin{bmatrix} -3 & 8 \\ 5 & -1 \end{bmatrix}$

$= \begin{bmatrix} 3 + \square & \square + 8 \\ -5 + \square & \square + (-1) \end{bmatrix}$

$= \begin{bmatrix} \square & \square \\ \square & \square \end{bmatrix}$

c. $\begin{bmatrix} 198 & 350 \\ 201 & 375 \end{bmatrix} + \begin{bmatrix} 54 & 439 \\ 58 & 386 \end{bmatrix}$

$= \begin{bmatrix} \square + 54 & 350 + \square \\ 201 + \square & \square + 386 \end{bmatrix}$

$= \begin{bmatrix} \square & \square \\ \square & \square \end{bmatrix}$

2 Subtracting Matrices

$A = \begin{bmatrix} 4 & 8 \\ -2 & 0 \end{bmatrix}$ and $B = \begin{bmatrix} 7 & -9 \\ 4 & 5 \end{bmatrix}$. Find $A - B$.

Method 1 Use additive inverses.

$A - B = A + (-B) = \begin{bmatrix} 4 & 8 \\ -2 & 0 \end{bmatrix} + \begin{bmatrix} -7 & 9 \\ -4 & -5 \end{bmatrix}$ **Write the additive inverses of the elements of the second matrix.**

$= \begin{bmatrix} 4 + (\square) & 8 + 9 \\ -2 + (\square) & 0 + \square \end{bmatrix}$ **Add corresponding elements.**

$= \begin{bmatrix} \square & \square \\ -6 & \square \end{bmatrix}$ **Simplify.**

Method 2 Use subtraction.

$A - B = \begin{bmatrix} 4 & 8 \\ -2 & 0 \end{bmatrix} - \begin{bmatrix} 7 & -9 \\ 4 & 5 \end{bmatrix}$

$= \begin{bmatrix} 4 - \square & \square - (-9) \\ \square - 4 & 0 - \square \end{bmatrix}$ **Subtract corresponding elements.**

$= \begin{bmatrix} \square & \square \\ -6 & \square \end{bmatrix}$ **Simplify.**

Name____________________ Class____________________ Date ____________

3 Solving a Matrix Equation Solve $X - \begin{bmatrix} 2 & 5 \\ 3 & -1 \\ 8 & 0 \end{bmatrix} = \begin{bmatrix} 10 & -3 \\ -4 & 9 \\ 6 & -9 \end{bmatrix}$ for the matrix X.

$$X - \begin{bmatrix} 2 & 5 \\ 3 & -1 \\ 8 & 0 \end{bmatrix} = \begin{bmatrix} 10 & -3 \\ -4 & 9 \\ 6 & -9 \end{bmatrix}$$

$$X - \begin{bmatrix} 2 & 5 \\ 3 & -1 \\ 8 & 0 \end{bmatrix} + \begin{bmatrix} 2 & 5 \\ 3 & -1 \\ 8 & 0 \end{bmatrix} = \begin{bmatrix} 10 & -3 \\ -4 & 9 \\ 6 & -9 \end{bmatrix} + \begin{bmatrix} \square & \square \\ \square & \square \\ \square & \square \end{bmatrix}$$

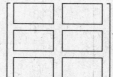

Add $\begin{bmatrix} \square & \square \\ \square & \square \\ \square & \square \end{bmatrix}$ **to each side of the equation.**

$$X = \begin{bmatrix} \square & 2 \\ -1 & \square \\ \square & \square \end{bmatrix}$$

Simplify.

Quick Check

1. Find each sum.

a. $\begin{bmatrix} 1 & -2 & 0 \\ 3 & -5 & 7 \end{bmatrix} + \begin{bmatrix} 3 & 9 & -3 \\ -9 & 6 & 12 \end{bmatrix}$

b. $\begin{bmatrix} -12 & 24 \\ -3 & 5 \\ -1 & 10 \end{bmatrix} + \begin{bmatrix} -3 & 1 \\ 2 & -4 \\ -1 & 5 \end{bmatrix}$

c. $\begin{bmatrix} 14 & 5 \\ 0 & -2 \end{bmatrix} + \begin{bmatrix} -14 & -5 \\ 0 & 2 \end{bmatrix}$

d. $\begin{bmatrix} 0 & 0 & 0 \\ 0 & 0 & 0 \end{bmatrix} + \begin{bmatrix} -1 & 10 & -5 \\ 0 & 2 & -3 \end{bmatrix}$

2. Find each difference.

a. $\begin{bmatrix} 6 & -9 & 7 \\ -2 & 1 & 8 \end{bmatrix} - \begin{bmatrix} -4 & 3 & 0 \\ 6 & 5 & 10 \end{bmatrix}$

b. $\begin{bmatrix} -3 & 5 \\ -1 & 10 \end{bmatrix} - \begin{bmatrix} -3 & 1 \\ 2 & -4 \end{bmatrix}$

Name________________________ Class________________________ Date ______________

Example

❹ Finding Unknown Matrix Elements

Solve $\begin{bmatrix} 2m - n & -3 \\ 8 & -4m + 2n \end{bmatrix} = \begin{bmatrix} 15 & m + n \\ 8 & -30 \end{bmatrix}$ for m and n.

$$\begin{bmatrix} 2m - n & -3 \\ 8 & -4m + 2n \end{bmatrix} = \begin{bmatrix} 15 & m + n \\ 8 & -30 \end{bmatrix}$$

$2m - n = \square$

$\square = m + n$

$-4m + \square = \square$

Since the two matrices are equal, their corresponding elements are equal.

Solve for m and n.

$2m - n = \square$

$m + n = \square$

$3m = \square$ **Add the equations.**

$m = \square$ **Solve for m.**

$\square + n = -3$ **Substitute $\square$ for m.**

$n = \square$ **Solve for n.**

The solutions are $m = \square$ and $n = \square$.

Quick Check

3. Solve $X + \begin{bmatrix} -1 & 0 \\ 2 & 5 \end{bmatrix} = \begin{bmatrix} 10 & 7 \\ -4 & 4 \end{bmatrix}$

4. Solve each for x and y.

a. $\begin{bmatrix} x + 8 & -5 \\ 3 & -y \end{bmatrix} = \begin{bmatrix} 38 & -5 \\ 3 & 4y - 10 \end{bmatrix}$

b. $[3x \quad 4] = [-9 \quad x + y]$

Name____________________ Class____________________ Date____________

Lesson 4-3

Matrix Multiplication

Lesson Objectives	NAEP 2005 Strand: Number Properties and Operations
1 Multiplying a matrix by a scalar	Topic: Number Operations
2 Multiplying two matrices	Local Standards: ____________________

Vocabulary and Key Concepts

Scalar Multiplication

If A, B, and O are $m \times n$ matrices and c and d are scalars, then

cA is an $m \times n$ matrix. ______ Property

$(cd)A = c(dA)$ ______ Property of Multiplication

$c(A + B) = cA + cB$
$(c + d)A = cA + dA$ ______ Property

$1 \cdot A = A$ ______ Property

$0 \cdot A = O$ and $cO = O$ ______ Property of ______

Matrix Multiplication

To find the element c_{ij} of the product matrix AB, multiply each element in the ith ______ of A by the corresponding element in the jth ______ of B, and then add.

Dimensions of a Product Matrix

If matrix A is an $m \times n$ matrix and matrix B is an $n \times p$ matrix, then the product matrix ______ is an ______ $\times$ ______ matrix.

Example **matrix A** $\cdot$ **matrix B**

3 rows $\begin{bmatrix} 1 & 2 \\ 3 & 4 \\ 5 & 6 \end{bmatrix}$ 2 columns

2 rows $\begin{bmatrix} 7 & 8 & 9 & 10 \\ 11 & 12 & 13 & 14 \end{bmatrix}$ 4 columns

equal

dimensions of product matrix

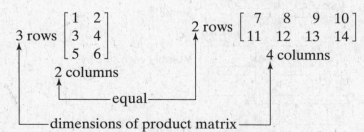

The dimensions of product matrix AB are ______ $\times$ ______.

Name______________________ Class______________ Date ____________

Matrix Multiplication

If A, B, and C are $n \times n$ matrices, then

AB is an $n \times n$ matrix.	________ Property
$(AB)C = A(BC)$	________ Property of Multiplication
$A(B + C) = AB + AC$ $(B + C)A = BA + CA$	________ Property
$OA = AO = O$, where O has the same dimensions as A.	________ Property of ________

A scalar is ____

____

A scalar product is ____

____

Scalar multiplication is ____

____

Examples

1 Solving a Matrix Equation with Scalars Solve the following equation for Y.

$$-3Y + 2\begin{bmatrix} 6 & 9 \\ -12 & 15 \end{bmatrix} = \begin{bmatrix} 27 & -18 \\ 30 & 6 \end{bmatrix}$$

$$-3Y + \begin{bmatrix} \square & \square \\ \square & \square \end{bmatrix} = \begin{bmatrix} 27 & -18 \\ 30 & 6 \end{bmatrix}$$ **Scalar multiplication.**

$$-3Y = \begin{bmatrix} 27 & -18 \\ 30 & 6 \end{bmatrix} - \begin{bmatrix} \square & \square \\ \square & \square \end{bmatrix}$$ **Subtract** $\begin{bmatrix} \square & \square \\ \square & \square \end{bmatrix}$ **from each side.**

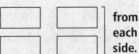

$$-3Y = \begin{bmatrix} \square & \square \\ \square & \square \end{bmatrix}$$ **Simplify.**

$$Y = -\frac{1}{3}\begin{bmatrix} \square & \square \\ \square & \square \end{bmatrix}$$ **Multiply each side by $-\frac{1}{3}$.**

$$= \begin{bmatrix} \square & \square \\ \square & \square \end{bmatrix}$$ **Simplify.**

Name______________________ Class______________________ Date ______________

❷ Multiplying Matrices Find the product of $A = \begin{bmatrix} -2 & 5 \\ 3 & -1 \end{bmatrix}$ and $B = \begin{bmatrix} 4 & -4 \\ 2 & 6 \end{bmatrix}$.

Multiply a_{11} and b_{11}. Then multiply a_{12} and b_{21}. Add the products.

$$\begin{bmatrix} -2 & 5 \\ 3 & -1 \end{bmatrix} \begin{bmatrix} 4 & -4 \\ 2 & 6 \end{bmatrix} = \begin{bmatrix} ? & \blacksquare \\ \blacksquare & \blacksquare \end{bmatrix} \quad (-2)(4) + (5)(\square) = 2$$

The result is the element in the first $\square$ and first column.
Repeat with the rest of the rows and columns.

$$\begin{bmatrix} -2 & 5 \\ 3 & -1 \end{bmatrix} \begin{bmatrix} 4 & -4 \\ 2 & 6 \end{bmatrix} = \begin{bmatrix} 2 & ? \\ \blacksquare & \blacksquare \end{bmatrix} \quad (-2)(\square) + (\square)(6) = \square$$

$$\begin{bmatrix} -2 & 5 \\ 3 & -1 \end{bmatrix} \begin{bmatrix} 4 & -4 \\ 2 & 6 \end{bmatrix} = \begin{bmatrix} 2 & \square \\ ? & \blacksquare \end{bmatrix} \quad (3)(\square) + (\square)(\square) = \square$$

$$\begin{bmatrix} -2 & 5 \\ 3 & -1 \end{bmatrix} \begin{bmatrix} 4 & -4 \\ 2 & 6 \end{bmatrix} = \begin{bmatrix} 2 & \square \\ \square & ? \end{bmatrix} \quad (\square)(\square) + (\square)(\square) = \square$$

The product of $\begin{bmatrix} -2 & 5 \\ 3 & -1 \end{bmatrix}$ and $\begin{bmatrix} 4 & -4 \\ 2 & 6 \end{bmatrix}$ is $\begin{bmatrix} \square & \square \\ \square & \square \end{bmatrix}$.

Quick Check

1. Solve each equation. Check your answers.

a. $2X = \begin{bmatrix} 4 & 12 \\ 1 & -4 \end{bmatrix} + \begin{bmatrix} -2 & 0 \\ 3 & 4 \end{bmatrix}$

b. $-3X + \begin{bmatrix} 7 & 0 & -1 \\ 2 & -3 & 4 \end{bmatrix} = \begin{bmatrix} 10 & 0 & 8 \\ -19 & -18 & 10 \end{bmatrix}$

2. **a.** Find the product of $\begin{bmatrix} -3 & 3 \\ 5 & 0 \end{bmatrix}$ and $\begin{bmatrix} -1 & 0 \\ 3 & -4 \end{bmatrix}$.

b. Critical Thinking Is matrix multiplication commutative? Explain.

Name______________________ Class______________________ Date ______________

Example

❸ Determining Whether a Product Matrix Exists

Use matrices $P = \begin{bmatrix} 3 & -1 & 2 \\ 5 & 9 & 0 \\ 0 & 1 & 8 \end{bmatrix}$ and $Q = \begin{bmatrix} 6 & 5 & 7 & 0 \\ 2 & 0 & 3 & 1 \\ 1 & -1 & 5 & 2 \end{bmatrix}$.

Determine whether products PQ and QP are *defined* or *undefined*.

Find the dimensions of each product matrix.

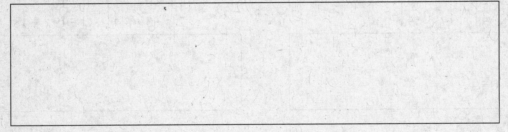

PQ: $(3 \times 3)(3 \times 4) \longrightarrow 3 \times 4$ (the inner 3s are equal; the 3×4 is the product matrix)

QP: $(3 \times 4)(3 \times 3)$ (the 4 and the 3 are *not* equal)

Product PQ is ____ and is a 3×4 matrix.

Product PQ is undefined because the number of ____ of Q is not equal to the number of ____ in P.

Quick Check

3. Let $R = \begin{bmatrix} 4 & -2 \\ 5 & -4 \end{bmatrix}$ and $S = \begin{bmatrix} 8 & 0 & -1 & 0 \\ 2 & -5 & 1 & 8 \end{bmatrix}$.

a. Determine whether products RS and SR are *defined* or *undefined*.

b. Find each defined product.

Name______________________________ Class____________________ Date______________

Lesson 4-4

Geometric Transformations with Matrices

Lesson Objectives	NAEP 2005 Strand: Geometry
1 Representing translations and dilations with matrices 2 Representing reflections and rotations with matrices	**Topic:** Transformation of Shapes and Preservation of Properties **Local Standards:** ____________________

Vocabulary and Key Concepts

Matrices for Reflections in the Coordinate Plane

Reflection in the y-axis $\begin{bmatrix} -1 & 0 \\ 0 & 1 \end{bmatrix}$

Reflection in the x-axis $\begin{bmatrix} 1 & 0 \\ 0 & -1 \end{bmatrix}$

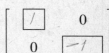

Reflection in the line $y = x$ $\begin{bmatrix} 0 & 1 \\ 1 & 0 \end{bmatrix}$

Reflection in the line $y = -x$ $\begin{bmatrix} 0 & -1 \\ -1 & 0 \end{bmatrix}$

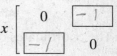

Matrices for Rotations in the Coordinate Plane

Rotation of 90° $\begin{bmatrix} 0 & -1 \\ 1 & 0 \end{bmatrix}$

Rotation of 180° $\begin{bmatrix} -1 & 0 \\ 0 & -1 \end{bmatrix}$

Rotation of 270° $\begin{bmatrix} 0 & 1 \\ -1 & 0 \end{bmatrix}$

Rotation of 360° $\begin{bmatrix} 1 & 0 \\ 0 & 1 \end{bmatrix}$

A transformation is ______________________________

An image is ______________________________

____

A translation is ______________________________

____

A dilation is ______________________________

____

A reflection is ______________________________

____

A rotation is ______________________________

____

The center of rotation is ______________________________

____

Name________________________ Class________________________ Date ____________

Example

1 Translating a Figure Triangle ABC has vertices $A(1, -2)$, $B(3, 1)$ and $C(2, 3)$. Use a matrix to find the vertices of the image translated 3 units left and 1 unit up. Graph ABC and its image $A'B'C'$.

Vertices of the Triangle		Translation Matrix		Vertices of the Image

Subtract 3 from each x-coordinate.

$$\begin{array}{c} \begin{matrix} A & B & C \end{matrix} \\ \begin{bmatrix} 1 & 3 & 2 \\ -2 & 1 & 3 \end{bmatrix} \end{array} + \begin{bmatrix} -3 & -3 & -3 \\ 1 & 1 & 1 \end{bmatrix} = \begin{array}{c} \begin{matrix} A' & B' & C' \end{matrix} \\ \begin{bmatrix} \square & 0 & \square \\ -1 & \square & 4 \end{bmatrix} \end{array}$$

Add 1 to each y-coordinate.

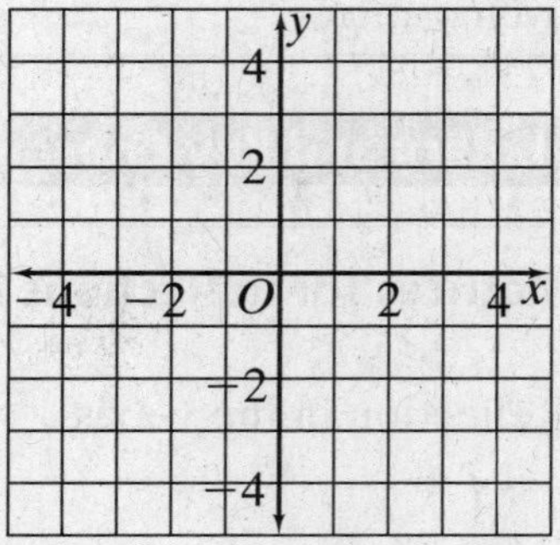

The coordinates of the vertices of the image are $A'(\square, -1)$, $B'(0, \square)$, $C'(\square, 4)$.

Quick Check

1. a. **Critical Thinking** Explain how to translate triangle $A'B'C'$ from Example 1 so that its image is triangle ABC.

b. What matrix would you use to translate the vertices of a triangle 3 units left and 2 units up?

c. Use your answer to part (b) to translate the triangle with vertices $(0, 0)$, $(2, 1)$, and $(1, -2)$. Find the coordinates of the vertices of the image. Graph the preimage and the image.

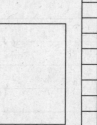

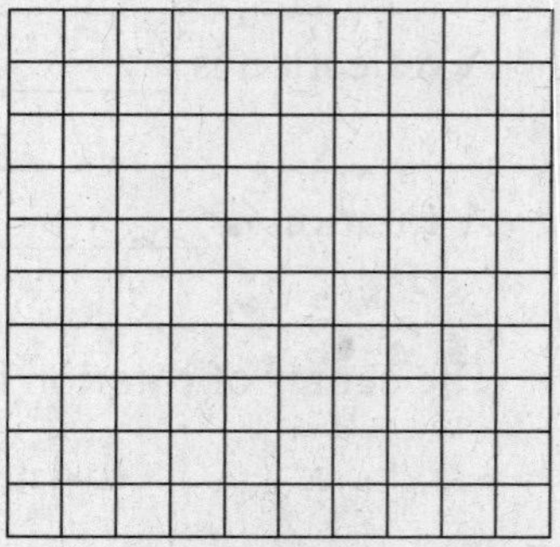

Name________________________ Class____________________ Date ____________

Example

❷ Reflecting a Figure Reflect the triangle with coordinates $A(2, -1)$, $B(3, 0)$, and $C(4, -2)$ in each line. Graph triangle ABC with each reflection.

a. y-axis

$$\begin{bmatrix} \square & 0 \\ 0 & \square \end{bmatrix}\begin{bmatrix} 2 & 3 & 4 \\ -1 & 0 & -2 \end{bmatrix} = \begin{bmatrix} \square & -3 & \square \\ -1 & \square & \square \end{bmatrix}$$

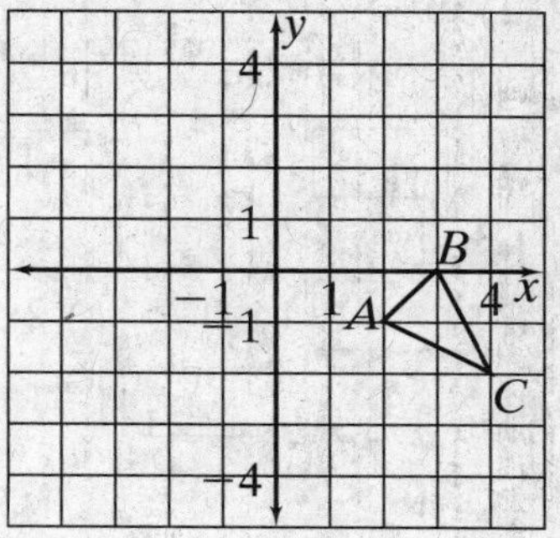

b. $y = x$

$$\begin{bmatrix} 0 & \square \\ \square & 0 \end{bmatrix}\begin{bmatrix} 2 & 3 & 4 \\ -1 & 0 & -2 \end{bmatrix} = \begin{bmatrix} \square & 0 & \square \\ \square & \square & \square \end{bmatrix}$$

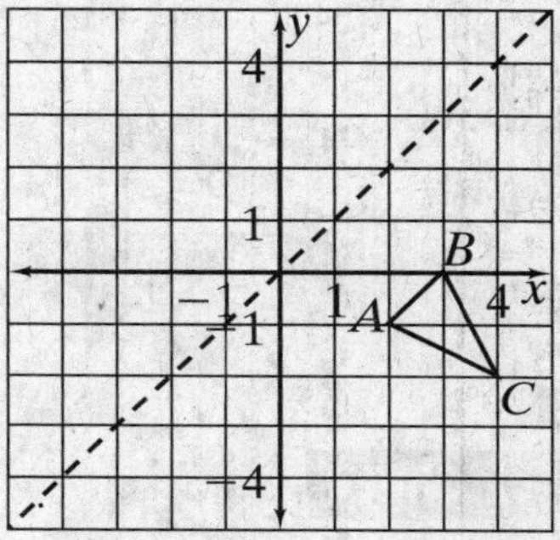

Quick Check

2. Reflect the triangle with coordinates $D(-3, 0)$, $E(-4, 4)$, and $F(1, 1)$ in each line. Graph triangle DEF with each reflection.

a. y-axis

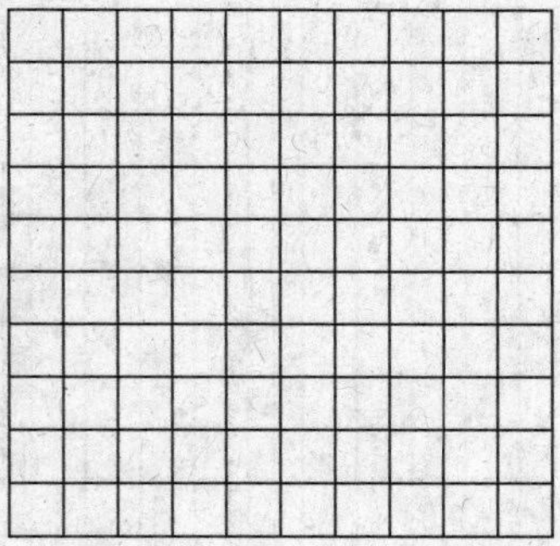

b. $y = x$

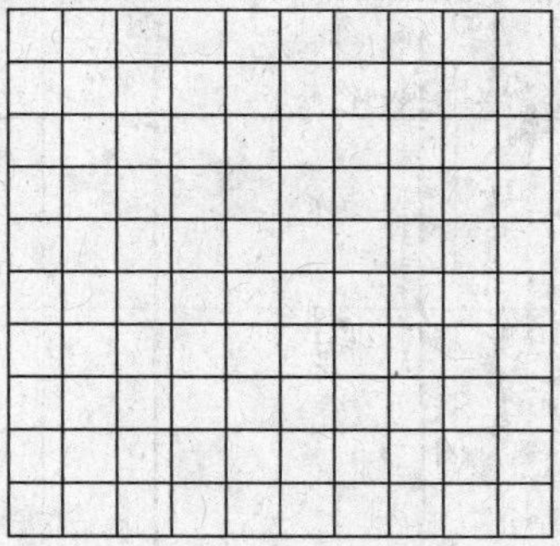

Example

3 Rotating a Figure Rotate the triangle from Example 2 as indicated. Graph the triangle ABC and each image on the same coordinate plane.

a. 90°

$$\begin{bmatrix} 0 & \square \\ \square & 0 \end{bmatrix}\begin{bmatrix} 2 & 3 & 4 \\ -1 & 0 & -2 \end{bmatrix} = \begin{bmatrix} \square & 0 & \square \\ 2 & \square & 4 \end{bmatrix}$$

b. 180°

$$\begin{bmatrix} \square & 0 \\ 0 & \square \end{bmatrix}\begin{bmatrix} 2 & 3 & 4 \\ -1 & 0 & -2 \end{bmatrix} = \begin{bmatrix} -2 & \square & \square \\ 1 & \square & \square \end{bmatrix}$$

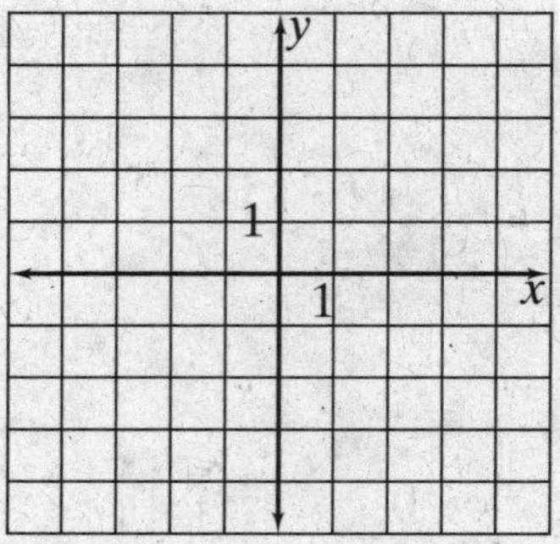

c. 270°

$$\begin{bmatrix} 0 & \square \\ \square & 0 \end{bmatrix}\begin{bmatrix} 2 & 3 & 4 \\ -1 & 0 & -2 \end{bmatrix} = \begin{bmatrix} \square & \square & \square \\ -2 & \square & \square \end{bmatrix}$$

d. 360°

$$\begin{bmatrix} \square & 0 \\ 0 & \square \end{bmatrix}\begin{bmatrix} 2 & 3 & 4 \\ -1 & 0 & -2 \end{bmatrix} = \begin{bmatrix} \square & \square & \square \\ \square & \square & \square \end{bmatrix}$$

Quick Check

3. Rotate the quadrilateral with coordinates $A(1, 1)$, $B(3, 1)$, $C(6, 4)$, and $D(1, 3)$. Then graph $ABCD$ and each image on the same coordinate plane.

a. 90°

b. 180°

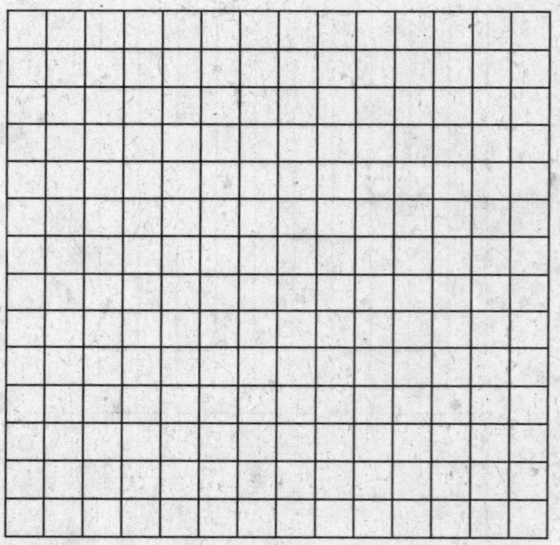

c. 270°

d. 360°

Name_______________ Class_______________ Date_______________

Lesson 4-5

2 x 2 Matrices, Determinants, and Inverses

Lesson Objectives	NAEP 2005 Strand: Number Properties and Operations
1 Evaluating determinants of 2 × 2 matrices and finding inverse matrices 2 Using inverse matrices in solving matrix equations	**Topic:** Number Operations **Local Standards:** ____________________

Vocabulary and Key Concepts

Multiplicative Identity Matrix

For an $n \times n$ square matrix, the **multiplicative identity matrix** is an $n \times n$ square matrix I, or $I_{n \times n}$, with ☐'s along the main diagonal and ☐'s elsewhere.

$I_2 = \begin{bmatrix} 1 & 0 \\ 0 & 1 \end{bmatrix}$, $I_3 = \begin{bmatrix} 1 & 0 & 0 \\ 0 & 1 & 1 \\ 0 & 0 & 1 \end{bmatrix}$, and so forth

Multiplicative Inverse of a Matrix

If A and X are $n \times n$ matrices, and $AX = XA = I$, then X is the multiplicative inverse of ☐, written ☐.

$AA^{-1} = A^{-1}A = I$

Determinant of a 2 x 2 Matrix

The **determinant** of a 2×2 matrix $\begin{bmatrix} a & b \\ c & d \end{bmatrix}$ is ☐.

Write	Read	Evaluate
$A = \begin{bmatrix} a & b \\ c & d \end{bmatrix}$ $\det A = \begin{vmatrix} a & b \\ c & d \end{vmatrix}$	the determinant of A	$\begin{vmatrix} a & b \\ c & d \end{vmatrix} = ad - bc$

Inverse of a 2 x 2 Matrix

Let $A = \begin{bmatrix} a & b \\ c & d \end{bmatrix}$. If $\det A \neq$ ☐, then A has an ☐.

If $\det A \neq 0$, then ☐ $= \frac{1}{\det A}\begin{bmatrix} d & -b \\ -c & a \end{bmatrix} = \frac{1}{\square}\begin{bmatrix} d & -b \\ -c & a \end{bmatrix}$

A square matrix

Name________________________ Class________________________ Date____________

Examples

❶ Verifying Inverses Show that matrices A and B are multiplicative inverses.

$$A = \begin{bmatrix} 3 & -1 \\ 7 & 1 \end{bmatrix} \quad B = \begin{bmatrix} 0.1 & 0.1 \\ -0.7 & 0.3 \end{bmatrix} \quad AB = \begin{bmatrix} 3 & -1 \\ 7 & 1 \end{bmatrix}\begin{bmatrix} 0.1 & 0.1 \\ -0.7 & 0.3 \end{bmatrix}$$

$$= \begin{bmatrix} (3)(\square) + (-1)(\square) & (\square)(0.1) + (\square)(0.3) \\ (\square)(0.1) + (\square)(-0.7) & (7)(\square) + (1)(\square) \end{bmatrix} = \begin{bmatrix} \square & 0 \\ 0 & \square \end{bmatrix}$$

$AB = I$, so B is the ________________ of A.

❷ Evaluating the Determinant of a 2 × 2 Matrix Evaluate each determinant.

a. $\det \begin{bmatrix} 4 & -3 \\ 5 & 6 \end{bmatrix} = \begin{vmatrix} 4 & -3 \\ 5 & 6 \end{vmatrix} = (4)(\square) - (\square)(5) = \square$

b. $\det \begin{bmatrix} a & -b \\ b & a \end{bmatrix} = \begin{vmatrix} a & -b \\ b & a \end{vmatrix} = (a)(\square) - (\square)(b) = a^2 + \square$

❸ Finding an Inverse Matrix Does the matrix have an inverse? If so, find it.

$Y = \begin{bmatrix} 6 & 5 \\ 25 & 20 \end{bmatrix}$ **Find det *Y*.**

$ad - bc = (\square)(\square) - (\square)(\square) = (\square)$ **Simplify.**

Since the determinant $\neq \square$, the inverse of Y ________________.

$Y^{-1} = \frac{1}{\det Y}\begin{bmatrix} \square & \square \\ \square & \square \end{bmatrix}$ **Change signs and positions.**

$= \frac{1}{\square}\begin{bmatrix} \square & \square \\ \square & \square \end{bmatrix} = \begin{bmatrix} \square & \square \\ \square & \square \end{bmatrix}$ **Substitute $\square$ for the determinant and multiply.**

Quick Check

1. Multiply to show that the matrices are multiplicative inverses.

a. $\begin{bmatrix} 2 & 1 \\ 2.5 & 1 \end{bmatrix}$ and $\begin{bmatrix} -2 & 2 \\ 5 & -4 \end{bmatrix}$

b. $\begin{bmatrix} -2 & -5 \\ -3 & -8 \end{bmatrix}$ and $\begin{bmatrix} -8 & 5 \\ 3 & -2 \end{bmatrix}$

Name________________________ Class__________________ Date __________

Example

4 Solving a Matrix Equation Solve $\begin{bmatrix} 9 & 25 \\ 4 & 11 \end{bmatrix} X = \begin{bmatrix} 3 \\ -7 \end{bmatrix}$ for the matrix X.

The matrix equation has the form $AX = \square$. First find $\square$.

$A^{-1} = \dfrac{1}{\square} \begin{bmatrix} d & \square \\ \square & a \end{bmatrix}$ — **Use the definition of inverse.**

$= \dfrac{1}{(\square)(\square) - (\square)(\square)} \begin{bmatrix} 11 & \square \\ \square & 9 \end{bmatrix} = \begin{bmatrix} \square & \square \\ \square & \square \end{bmatrix}$ — **Substitute and simplify.**

Use the equation $X = A^{-1}B$.

$X = \begin{bmatrix} \square & \square \\ \square & \square \end{bmatrix} \begin{bmatrix} 3 \\ -7 \end{bmatrix} = \begin{bmatrix} (\square)(3) + (\square)(-7) \\ (\square)(3) + (\square)(-7) \end{bmatrix} = \begin{bmatrix} \square \\ \square \end{bmatrix}$ — **Substitute, multiply, and simplify.**

Quick Check

2. Evaluate the determinant of each matrix.

a. $\begin{bmatrix} 4 & 2 \\ 4 & 2 \end{bmatrix}$

b. $\begin{bmatrix} 8 & 7 \\ 2 & 3 \end{bmatrix}$

c. $\begin{bmatrix} k & 3 \\ 3 - k & -3 \end{bmatrix}$

3. Determine whether each matrix has an inverse. If an inverse matrix exists, find it.

a. $\begin{bmatrix} 2 & 4 \\ 1 & 3 \end{bmatrix}$

b. $\begin{bmatrix} 0.5 & 2.3 \\ 3 & 7.2 \end{bmatrix}$

4. Solve each matrix equation in the form $AX = B$. Use the equation $X = A^{-1}B$.

a. $\begin{bmatrix} 3 & -4 \\ 4 & -5 \end{bmatrix} X = \begin{bmatrix} 0 & -22 \\ 0 & -28 \end{bmatrix}$

b. $\begin{bmatrix} 7 & 5 \\ 3 & 2 \end{bmatrix} X = \begin{bmatrix} -9 \\ -4 \end{bmatrix}$

Name______________________________ Class____________________ Date______________

Lesson 4-6

3 × 3 Matrices, Determinants, and Inverses

Lesson Objectives	NAEP 2005 Strand: Number Properties and Operations
▼1 Evaluating determinants of 3 × 3 matrices	**Topic:** Number Operations
▼2 Using inverse matrices in solving matrix equations	**Local Standards:** ____________________

Key Concepts

The Determinant of a 3 × 3 Matrix

The determinant of a 3 × 3 matrix $\begin{bmatrix} a_1 & b_1 & c_1 \\ a_2 & b_2 & c_2 \\ a_3 & b_3 & c_3 \end{bmatrix}$ is

$$\begin{vmatrix} a_1 & b_1 & c_1 \\ a_2 & b_2 & c_2 \\ a_3 & b_3 & c_3 \end{vmatrix} = (a_1b_2c_3 + \boxed{a_2b_3c_1} + a_3b_1c_2) - (a_1b_3c_2 + a_2b_1c_3 + \boxed{a_3b_2c_1})$$

Visualize the pattern this way:

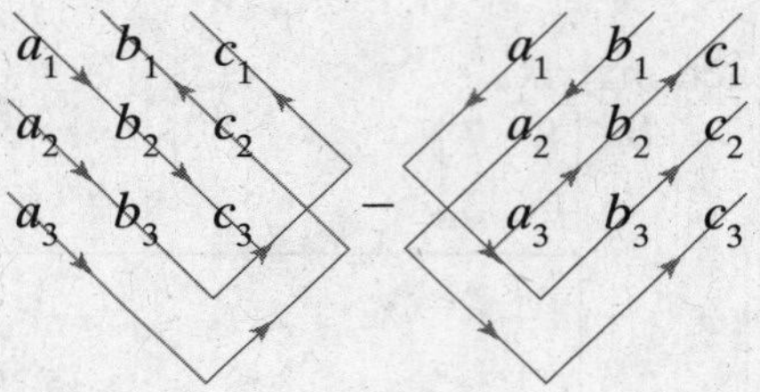

Examples

1 Evaluating the Determinant of a 3 × 3 Matrix Evaluate the determinant of

$X = \begin{bmatrix} 8 & -4 & 3 \\ -2 & 9 & 5 \\ 1 & 6 & 0 \end{bmatrix}$.

$$\begin{vmatrix} 8 & -4 & 3 \\ -2 & 9 & 5 \\ 1 & 6 & 0 \end{vmatrix} = [(8)(\square)(0) + (-2)(\square)(3) + (1)(\square)(5)]$$

$$- [(\square)(6)(\square) + (-2)(\square)(0) + (1)(\square)(3)]$$ **Use the definition.**

$$= [0 + (\square) + (\square)] - [\square + 0 + \square]$$ **Multiply.**

$$= \square - \square = \square$$ **Simplify.**

The determinant of X is $\square$.

Name________________ Class________________ Date ____________

❷ Verifying Inverses Determine whether the matrices are multiplicative inverses.

$$C = \begin{bmatrix} 0.5 & 0 & 0 \\ 0 & 0 & 0.5 \\ 0 & 1 & 1 \end{bmatrix}, D = \begin{bmatrix} 2 & 0 & 0 \\ 0 & 2 & 1 \\ 0 & 2 & 0 \end{bmatrix}$$

$$\begin{bmatrix} 0.5 & 0 & 0 \\ 0 & 0 & 0.5 \\ 0 & 1 & 1 \end{bmatrix} \begin{bmatrix} 2 & 0 & 0 \\ 0 & 2 & 1 \\ 0 & 2 & 0 \end{bmatrix} = \begin{bmatrix} 1 & \square & 0 \\ 0 & \square & 0 \\ 0 & \square & \square \end{bmatrix}$$

Since CD $\square$ I, C and D $\square$ multiplicative inverses.

❸ Solving a Matrix Equation Solve the equation. $\begin{bmatrix} 2 & 0 & 1 \\ 0 & 1 & 4 \\ 1 & 0 & 0 \end{bmatrix} X = \begin{bmatrix} -1 \\ 8 \\ -2 \end{bmatrix}$.

Let $A = \begin{bmatrix} 2 & 0 & 1 \\ 0 & 1 & 4 \\ 1 & 0 & 0 \end{bmatrix}$. Find A^{-1}.

$$X = \begin{bmatrix} 0 & 0 & \square \\ \square & 1 & \square \\ 1 & 0 & \square \end{bmatrix} \begin{bmatrix} -1 \\ 8 \\ -2 \end{bmatrix} = \begin{bmatrix} \square \\ \square \\ \square \end{bmatrix}$$

← **Use the equation $X = A^{-1}C$. Multiply.**

Quick Check

1. Evaluate each determinant.

a. $\begin{vmatrix} -3 & 4 & 0 \\ 2 & -5 & 1 \\ 0 & 2 & 3 \end{vmatrix}$ $\square$

b. $\begin{vmatrix} 1 & -1 & 2 \\ 0 & 4 & 2 \\ 3 & -6 & 10 \end{vmatrix}$ $\square$

2. Verify that C and D from Example 2 are not inverses by showing that $DC \neq I$.

$\square$

3. Solve the equation $\begin{bmatrix} 0 & 0 & 2 \\ 1 & 3 & -2 \\ 1 & -2 & 1 \end{bmatrix} X = \begin{bmatrix} 0 \\ -6 \\ 19 \end{bmatrix}$.

$\square$

Name______________________________ Class____________________ Date ____________

Example

4 Cryptography Use the alphabet table and the encoding matrix.

$$\text{matrix } K = \begin{bmatrix} 0.5 & 0.25 & 0.25 \\ 0.25 & -0.5 & 0.5 \\ 0.5 & 1 & -1 \end{bmatrix}$$

A	26	N	13
B	25	O	12
C	24	P	11
D	23	Q	10
E	22	R	9
F	21	S	8
G	20	T	7
H	19	U	6
I	18	V	5
J	17	W	4
K	16	X	3
L	15	Y	2
M	14	Z	1

a. Find the decoding matrix K^{-1}.

$$K^{-1} = \begin{bmatrix} 0 & \square & 1 \\ 2 & \square & -0.75 \\ \square & -1.5 & \square \end{bmatrix}$$

Use a graphing calculator.

b. Decode $\begin{bmatrix} 11.25 & 16.75 & 24.5 \\ 5.75 & 17 & 5.5 \\ 1.5 & -12 & 15 \end{bmatrix}$. Zero indicates a space holder.

Use the decoding matrix from part (a). Multiply.

$$\begin{bmatrix} 0 & \square & 1 \\ 2 & \square & -0.75 \\ \square & -1.5 & \square \end{bmatrix} \begin{bmatrix} 11.25 & 16.75 & 24.5 \\ 5.75 & 17 & 5.5 \\ 1.5 & -12 & 15 \end{bmatrix} = \begin{bmatrix} \square & 22 & \square \\ 7 & 0 & \square \\ \square & \square & 22 \end{bmatrix}$$

The numbers ____ 22 ____ 7 0 ____ ____ ____ 22 correspond to the letters ____________________.

Quick Check

4. Use the information from Example 4. Decode the matrix at the right, which gives the title of a Pablo Neruda poem.

$$\begin{bmatrix} 13.25 & 8.25 \\ -3.75 & 0.5 \\ 18.5 & 11 \end{bmatrix}$$

Name______________________ Class______________ Date____________

Lesson 4-7

Inverse Matrices and Systems

Lesson Objective	**NAEP 2005 Strand:** Algebra
1 Solving systems of equations using inverse matrices	**Topic:** Equations and Inequalities **Local Standards:** ____________________

Key Concepts

Using a Matrix Equation

You can represent a system of equations with a matrix equation.

System of Equations

$$\begin{cases} x + 2y = 5 \\ 3x + 5y = 14 \end{cases}$$

Matrix Equation

$$\begin{bmatrix} \boxed{1} & \boxed{2} \\ \boxed{3} & \boxed{5} \end{bmatrix} \begin{bmatrix} \boxed{x} \\ \boxed{y} \end{bmatrix} = \begin{bmatrix} \boxed{5} \\ \boxed{14} \end{bmatrix}$$

Each matrix in an equation of the form $AX = B$ has a name.

Coefficient matrix *A* $\begin{bmatrix} \square & \square \\ \square & \square \end{bmatrix}$ **Variable matrix *X*** $\begin{bmatrix} \square \\ \square \end{bmatrix}$ **Constant matrix *B*** $\begin{bmatrix} \square \\ \square \end{bmatrix}$

Examples

1 Solving a System of Two Equations Solve the system $\begin{cases} 2x + 3y = -1 \\ x - y = 12 \end{cases}$.

$$\begin{bmatrix} \boxed{2} & 3 \\ 1 & \boxed{-1} \end{bmatrix} \begin{bmatrix} x \\ y \end{bmatrix} = \begin{bmatrix} \boxed{-1} \\ \boxed{12} \end{bmatrix}$$ **Write the system as a matrix equation.**

$$A^{-1} = \begin{bmatrix} \square & \square \\ \square & \square \end{bmatrix}$$ **Find A^{-1}.**

$$\begin{bmatrix} x \\ y \end{bmatrix} = A^{-1}B = \begin{bmatrix} \square & \square \\ \square & \square \end{bmatrix} \begin{bmatrix} \square \\ \square \end{bmatrix} = \begin{bmatrix} \square \\ \square \end{bmatrix}$$ **Solve for the variable matrix.**

The solution of the system is $(\square, \square)$.

Check $2x + 3y = -1$ $\quad x - y = 12$ **Use the original equations.**

$2(\square) + 3(\square) \stackrel{?}{=} -1$ $\quad (\square) - (\square) \stackrel{?}{=} 12$ **Substitute.**

$\square - \square = -1$ ✓ $\quad \square + \square = 12$ ✓ **Simplify.**

Name______________________ Class______________________ Date ______________

❷ Solving a System of Three Equations Solve the system $\begin{cases} 7x + 3y + 2z = 13 \\ -2x + y - 8z = 26 \\ x - 4y + 10z = -13 \end{cases}$.

Step 1 Write the system as a matrix equation.

$$\begin{bmatrix} \square & 3 & \square \\ -2 & \square & -8 \\ 1 & \square & 10 \end{bmatrix}\begin{bmatrix} x \\ y \\ z \end{bmatrix} = \begin{bmatrix} \square \\ 26 \\ -13 \end{bmatrix}$$

Step 2 Store the coefficient matrix as matrix A and the constant matrix as matrix $\square$.

The solution is $(\square, \square, \square)$.

❸ Unique Solutions Write the coefficient matrix for each system. Use it to determine whether the system has a unique solution.

a. $\begin{cases} 4x - 2y = 7 \\ -6x + 3y = 5 \end{cases}$

$$A = \begin{bmatrix} \square & \square \\ \square & \square \end{bmatrix}; \det A = \begin{vmatrix} \square & \square \\ \square & \square \end{vmatrix} = \square(\square) - (\square)(\square) = \square$$

Since det A = $\square$, the matrix $\square$ an inverse and the system $\square$ a unique solution.

b. $\begin{cases} 12x + 8y = -3 \\ 3x - 7y = 50 \end{cases}$

$$A = \begin{bmatrix} 12 & \square \\ 3 & \square \end{bmatrix}; \det A = \begin{vmatrix} 12 & \square \\ 3 & \square \end{vmatrix} = 12(\square) - \square(3) = \square$$

Since det A $\square$ 0, the matrix $\square$ an inverse and the system $\square$ a unique solution.

Name________________________ Class________________________ Date ____________

Quick Check

1. Solve each system. Check your answers.

a. $\begin{cases} 5a + 3b = 7 \\ 3a + 2b = 5 \end{cases}$

b. $\begin{cases} x + 3y = 22 \\ 3x + 2y = 10 \end{cases}$

2. a. Check the solution from Example 2 in each of the original equations.

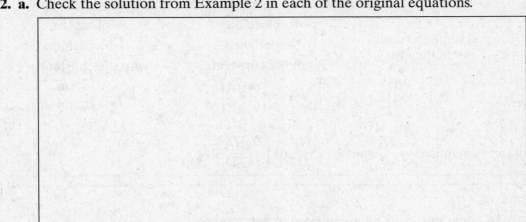

b. Solve the system $\begin{cases} x + y + z = 2 \\ 2x + y = 5 \\ x + 3y - 3z = 14 \end{cases}$. Check your solution.

3. a. Determine whether the system $\begin{cases} 3x + 5y = 1 \\ 2x - y = -8 \end{cases}$ has a unique solution.

b. You can use an inverse matrix to solve a system of equations. What happens when you try to do this with a graphing calculator and the system does not have a unique solution?

Name______________________ Class______________________ Date______________

Lesson 4-8

Augmented Matrices and Systems

Lesson Objectives	**NAEP 2005 Strand:** Algebra
1. Solving a system of equations using Cramer's rule 2. Solving a system of equations using augmented matrices	**Topic:** Equations and Inequalities **Local Standards:** ____________________

Vocabulary and Key Concepts

Cramer's Rule

System	Use the x- and y-coefficients.	Replace the [X]-coefficients with the constants.	Replace the [Y]-coefficients with the constants.
$\begin{cases} ax + by = m \\ cx + dy = n \end{cases}$	$D = \begin{vmatrix} a & b \\ c & d \end{vmatrix}$	$D_x = \begin{vmatrix} m & b \\ n & d \end{vmatrix}$	$D_y = \begin{vmatrix} a & m \\ c & n \end{vmatrix}$

The solution of the system is $x = \frac{D_x}{D}$ and $y = \frac{D_y}{D}$, or $\left(\frac{D_x}{D}, \frac{D_y}{D}\right)$.

Row Operations

To solve a system of equations using an augmented matrix, you can use one or more of the following row operations.

Switch any two [____].

[____] a row by a constant.

[____] one row to another.

Combine one or more of these steps.

An augmented matrix contains ____

____

Examples

1 Using Cramer's Rule Use Cramer's rule to solve the system $\begin{cases} 7x - 4y = 15 \\ 3x + 6y = 8 \end{cases}$.

Evaluate three determinants. Then find x and y.

$$D = \begin{vmatrix} 7 & -4 \\ 3 & 6 \end{vmatrix} = 54 \qquad D_x = \begin{vmatrix} \square & -4 \\ \square & 6 \end{vmatrix} = 122 \qquad D_y = \begin{vmatrix} 7 & \square \\ \square & 8 \end{vmatrix} = \square$$

$$x = \frac{D_x}{D} = \frac{61}{27} \qquad y = \frac{D_y}{D} = \frac{\square}{\square}$$

Name_______________ Class_______________ Date_______________

② Solving a System of Three Equations Find the *y*-coordinate of the solution of the system $\begin{cases} -2x + 8y + 2z = -3 \\ -6x \quad + \quad 2z = 1 \\ -7x - 5y + z = 2 \end{cases}$.

Evaluate two determinants. Then find *y*.

$$D = \begin{vmatrix} -2 & 8 & 2 \\ -6 & \square & 2 \\ -7 & -5 & \square \end{vmatrix} = \square \qquad D_y = \begin{vmatrix} \square & -3 & 2 \\ -6 & \square & 2 \\ -7 & 2 & \square \end{vmatrix} = \square$$

$$y = \frac{D_y}{D} = \frac{\square}{\square} = -\frac{\square}{\square}$$

③ Writing a System from an Augmented Matrix Write a system of equations for the augmented matrix $\left[\begin{array}{cc|c} 9 & -7 & -1 \\ 2 & 5 & -6 \end{array}\right]$.

Augmented Matrix $\left[\begin{array}{cc|c} 9 & -7 & -1 \\ 2 & 5 & -6 \end{array}\right]$

x-coefficients ↕ ↕ *y*-coefficients ↕ ______

System of Equations $\begin{cases} \square - 7y = -1 \\ 2x + \square = -6 \end{cases}$

Quick Check

1. Use Cramer's Rule to solve the system $\begin{cases} 3x + y = 5 \\ 2x + 3y = 8 \end{cases}$.

2. Solve the system in Example 2 for *x* and *z*.

Name________________________ Class________________ Date ____________

Example

④ Using an Augmented Matrix Use an augmented matrix to solve the system

$$\begin{cases} x - 3y = -17 \\ 4x + 2y = 2 \end{cases}$$

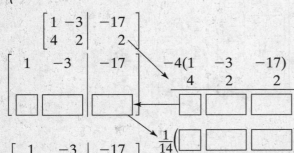

$\left[\begin{array}{cc|c} 1 & -3 & -17 \\ 4 & 2 & 2 \end{array}\right]$ **Write an augmented matrix.**

$-4(1 \quad -3 \quad -17)$
$\;\;\;\;\;4 \quad\; 2 \quad\;\; 2$
$\square \quad \square \quad \square$

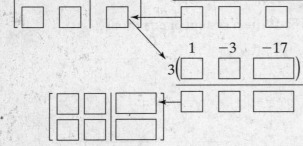

Multiply Row 1 by −4 and add it to Row 2.

$\left[\begin{array}{cc|c} 1 & -3 & -17 \\ \square & \square & \square \end{array}\right]$ **Write the new augmented matrix.**

$\frac{1}{14}(\square \quad \square \quad \square)$
$\square \quad \square \quad \square$

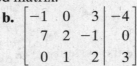

Multiply Row 2 by $\frac{1}{14}$.

$\left[\begin{array}{cc|c} 1 & -3 & -17 \\ \square & \square & \square \end{array}\right]$ **Write the new augmented matrix.**

$1 \quad -3 \quad -17$
$3(\square \quad \square \quad \square)$
$\square \quad \square \quad \square$

Multiply Row 2 by 3 and add it to Row 1.

$\left[\begin{array}{cc|c} \square & \square & \square \\ \square & \square & \square \end{array}\right]$ **Write the final augmented matrix.**

The solution to the system is $(\square, \square)$.

Quick Check

3. Write a system of equations for each augmented matrix.

a. $\left[\begin{array}{cc|c} 5 & 7 & -3 \\ 0 & -8 & 6 \end{array}\right]$

b. $\left[\begin{array}{ccc|c} -1 & 0 & 3 & -4 \\ 7 & 2 & -1 & 0 \\ 0 & 1 & 2 & 3 \end{array}\right]$

4. Solve $\begin{cases} x + y = -10 \\ -x + y = 20 \end{cases}$. Check your solution.

Name______________________ Class______________________ Date______________

Lesson 5-1

Modeling Data With Quadratic Functions

Lesson Objectives	NAEP 2005 Strand: Algebra
1 Identifying quadratic functions and graphs 2 Model data with quadratic functions	**Topics:** Patterns, Relations, and Functions; Algebraic Representations **Local Standards:** ____________________

Vocabulary and Key Concepts

Standard Form of a Quadratic Function

$f(x) = ax^2 + bx + c$

quadratic term — ______ term — constant term

A parabola is ______________________________

The axis of symmetry is ______________________________

____

The vertex of a parabola is ______________________________

____

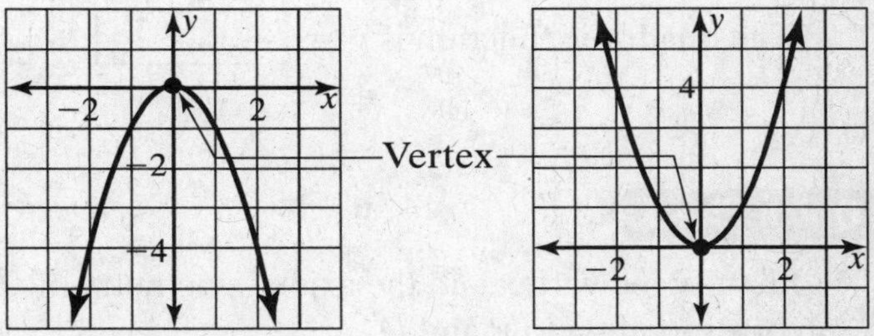

Maximum Value   Minimum Value

Examples

1 Points on a Parabola Below is the graph of $y = x^2 - 6x + 11$. Identify the vertex, axis of symmetry, points P' and Q' corresponding to P and Q, and the range of $f(x)$.

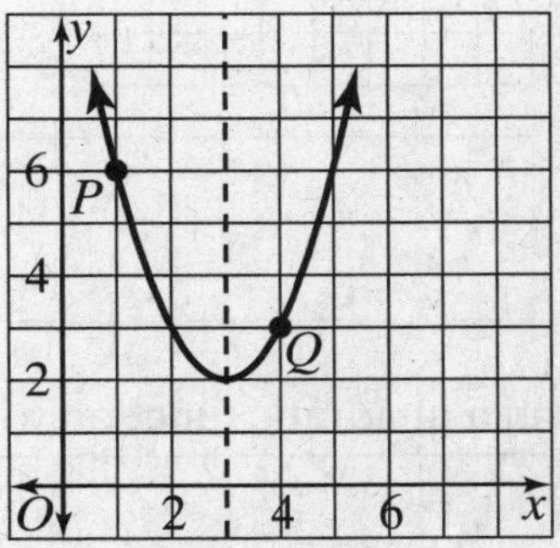

The vertex is (☐, ☐).

The axis of symmetry is $x =$ ☐. $P(1, 6)$ is two units to the left of the axis of symmetry. Corresponding point P' (☐, ☐) is two units to the ☐ of the axis of symmetry.

$Q(4, 3)$ is one unit to the right of the axis of symmetry. Corresponding point Q' (☐, ☐) is one unit to the ☐ of the axis of symmetry.

The range of this function is ☐.

Name________________________ Class________________________ Date ____________

❷ **Finding a Quadratic Model** Find a quadratic function that includes the values in the table.

x	−2	1	5
y	−17	10	−10

Substitute the values of x and y into $y = ax^2 + bx + c$. The result is a system of three linear equations.

$y = ax^2 + bx + c$

$-17 = a(\square)^2 + b(\square) + c = \square a - \square b + c$ **Use (−2, −17).**

$\square = a(\square)^2 + b(\square) + c = \square + \square + \square$ **Use (1, 10).**

$\square = a(\square)^2 + b(\square) + c = \square a + \square b + c$ **Use (5, −10).**

Using one of the methods in Chapter 3, solve the system.

$$\begin{cases} \square a - \square b + c = -17 \\ a + b + c = \square \\ \square a + \square b + c = \square \end{cases}$$

The solution is $a = \square$, $b = \square$, $c = \square$. Substitute these values into standard form.

The quadratic function is $y = \square + \square + \square$.

Quick Check

1. Identify the vertex and the axis of symmetry of each parabola. Identify points corresponding to P and Q.

a.

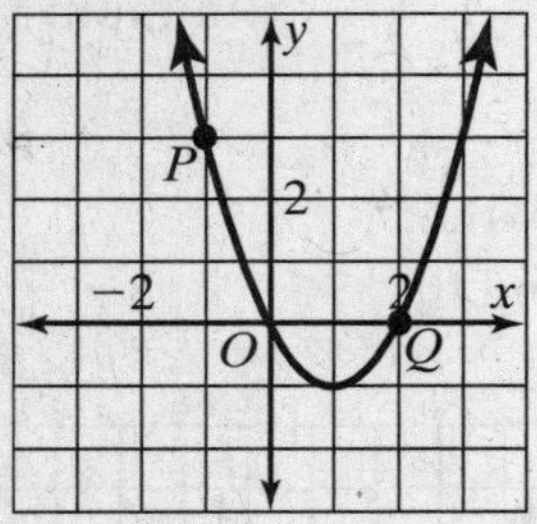

b.

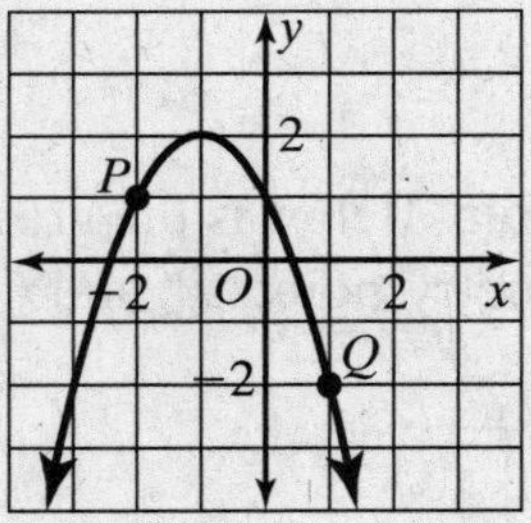

2. Find a quadratic function with a graph that includes (1, 0), (2, −3), and (3, −10).

Name______________________ Class______________________ Date______________

Lesson 5-2

Properties of Parabolas

Lesson Objectives	NAEP 2005 Strand: Algebra
1 Graphing quadratic functions	**Topic:** Algebraic Representations
2 Finding maximum and minimum values of quadratic functions	**Local Standards:** ____________________

Key Concepts

Graph of a Quadratic Function in Standard Form

The graph of $y = ax^2 + bx + c$ is a parabola when $a \neq 0$.

When a $\square$ 0, the parabola opens up. When a $\square$ 0, the parabola opens down.

The axis of symmetry is the line $x = -\frac{b}{2a}$.

The x-coordinate of the vertex is $-\frac{b}{2a}$.

$y = ax^2 + bx + c,\ a\ \square\ 0$

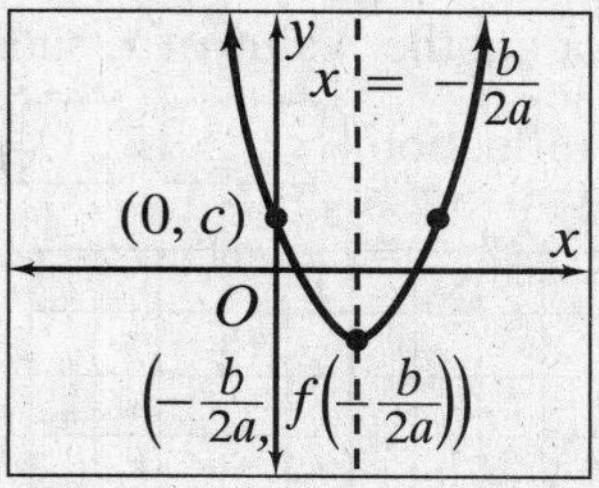

$y = ax^2 + bx + c,\ a\ \square\ 0$

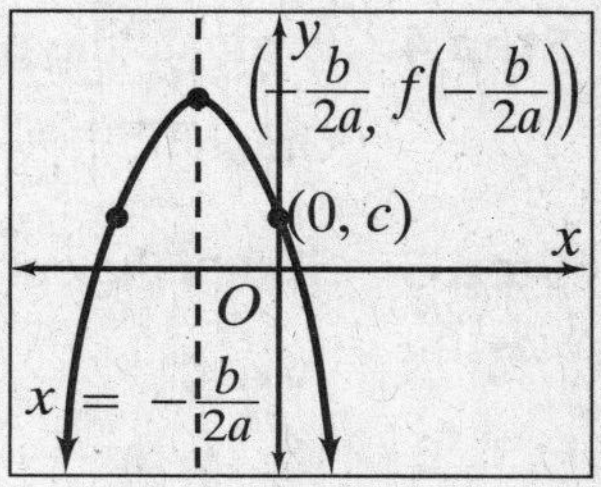

The y-coordinate of the vertex is the value of $\square$ when $x = \square$, or $y = f(-\frac{b}{2a})$.

The $\square$ is $(0, c)$.

Examples

1 Graphing a Function of the Form $y = ax^2 + c$ Graph $y = \frac{1}{3}x^2 + 1$.

Step 1 Graph the vertex, which is the y-intercept $(0, \square)$.

Step 2 Make a table of values to find some points on one side of the axis of symmetry $x = 0$. Graph the points.

x		2	3	4
y	$1\frac{1}{3}$			

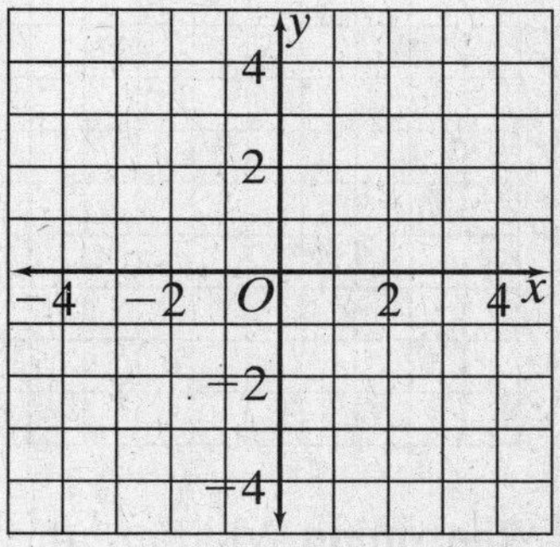

Step 3 Graph corresponding points on the other side of the axis of symmetry.

Step 4 Sketch the curve.

Name____________________ Class____________________ Date____________

❷ Graphing a Function of the Form $y = ax^2 + bx + c$ Graph $y = \frac{1}{2}x^2 + x + 3$.

Label the vertex and the axis of symmetry.

Step 1 Find and graph the axis of symmetry.

$$x = -\frac{b}{2a} = -\frac{\square}{2(\square)} = \square$$

Step 2 Find and graph the vertex. The x-coordinate of the vertex is -1. The y-coordinate is

$y = \square(-1)^2 + (-1) + 3 = \square$. So the vertex is $(\square, \square)$.

Step 3 Find and graph the y-intercept and its reflection. Since $c = 3$, the y-intercept is $(\square, \square)$ and its reflection is $(\square, 3)$.

Step 4 Evaluate the function for another value of x, such as $y = \frac{1}{2}(2)^2 + (2) + 3 = \square$.

Graph $(2, \square)$ and its reflection $(\square, \square)$.

Step 5 Sketch the curve.

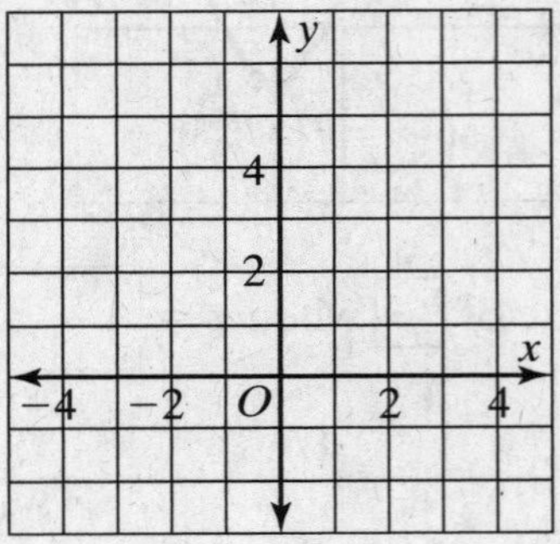

Quick Check

1. a. Graph $y = 2x^2 - 4$.

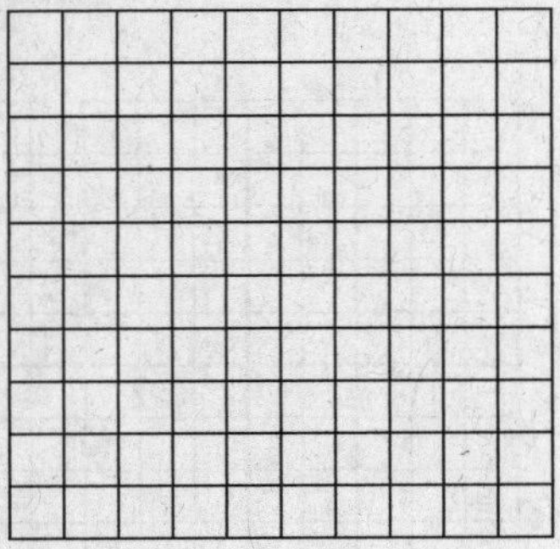

b. Graph $y = -5 + 3x^2$.

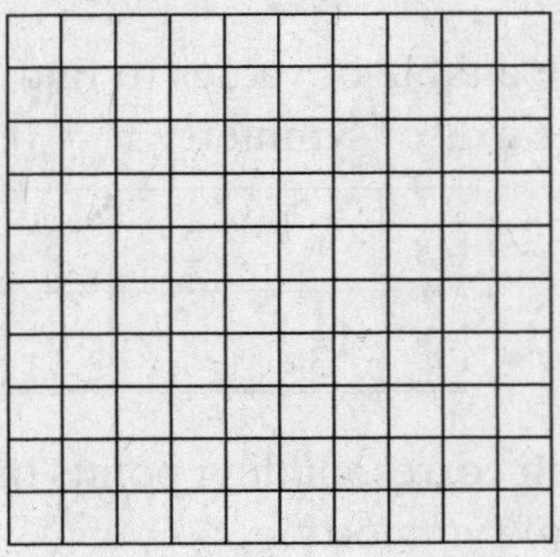

c. **Reasoning** What are the coordinates of the vertex of the graph of a function in the form $y = ax^2$?

Name______________________ Class______________________ Date ______________

Example

3 Finding a Maximum The number of weekend get-away packages a hotel can sell is modeled by $-0.12p + 60$, where p is the price of a get-away package. What price will maximize the revenue? What is the maximum revenue?

Relate [revenue] equals [price] times [number of get-away packages sold]

Define Let [R] = revenue.

Let [p] = price of a get-away package.

Let [$-0.12p + 60$] = number of get-away packages sold.

Write $R \quad = \quad p \quad \cdot \quad (-0.12p + 60)$

$R = -0.12p^2 + 60p$ **Write in standard form.**

Find the maximum value of the function. Since $a < 0$, the graph of the function opens [______] and the vertex represents a maximum value.

$p = -\frac{b}{2a} = -\frac{[\ \ ]}{2([\ \ ])} = [\ \ ]$ **Find *p* at the vertex.**

$R = -0.12([\ \ ])^2 + 60([\ \ ])$ **Evaluate *R* for *p* = 250.**

$= [\ \ ]$ **Simplify.**

A price of \$[______] will maximize revenue. The maximum revenue is \$[______].

Quick Check

2. Graph each function. Label the vertex and the axis of symmetry.

a. $y = -x^2 + 4x + 2$

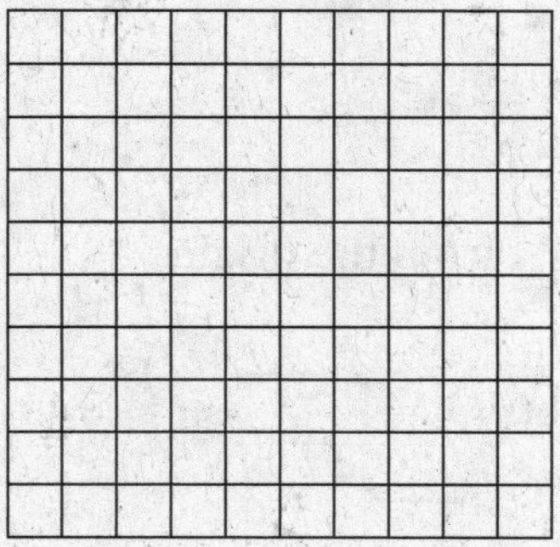

b. $y = -\frac{1}{3}x^2 - 2x - 3$

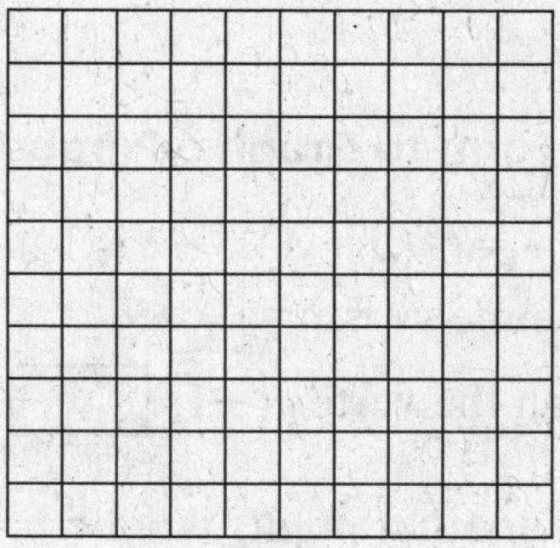

3. The number of dolls a toy company sells can be modeled by $-5p + 100$, where p is the price of a doll. What price will maximize revenue? What is the maximum revenue?

[______________________________]

Name____________________ Class________________ Date____________

Lesson 5-3

Transforming Parabolas

Lesson Objective	**NAEP 2005 Strand:** Geometry
1 Using the vertex form of a quadratic function	**Topic:** Transformation of Shapes and Preservation of Properties
	Local Standards: ________________

Key Concepts

Graph of a Quadratic Function in Vertex Form

The graph of $y = a(x - h)^2 + k$ is the graph of $y = ax^2$ translated h units horizontally and k units vertically.

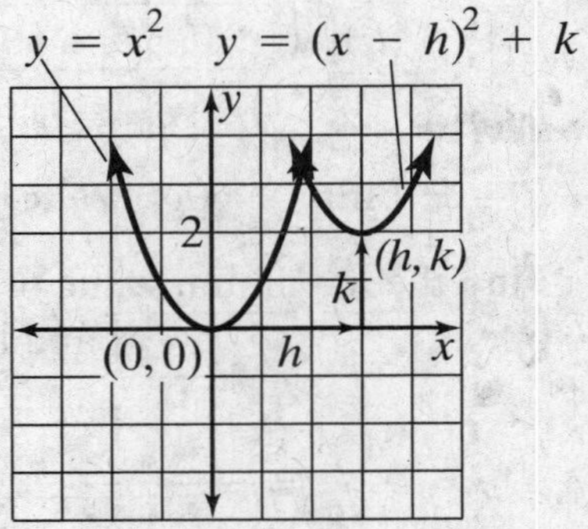

When h is [Positive] the graph shifts right;
when h is [Negative] the graph shifts left.

When k is positive the graph shifts [up];
when k is negative the graph shifts [Down].

The vertex is (h, k), and the axis of symmetry is the line $x = h$.

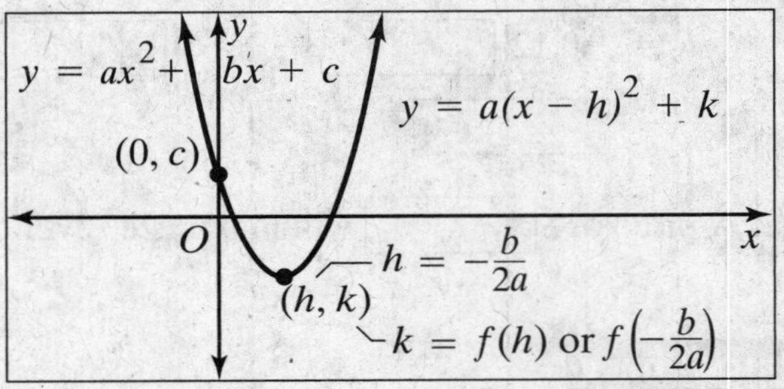

Examples

1 Using Vertex Form to Graph a Parabola Graph $y = \frac{2}{3}(x + 1)^2 - 2$.

The vertex of $y = \frac{2}{3}(x + 1)^2 - 2$ is 1 unit [←] and 2 units [up] from the origin.
The axis of symmetry is $x =$ [ ].

Step 1 Graph the vertex $(-1,$ [ ]$)$. Draw the axis of symmetry $x =$ [ ].

Step 2 Find another point. When $x = 2$, $y = \frac{2}{3}($[ ]$+1)^2 - 2 =$ [ ].
Graph $(2,$ [ ]$)$.

Name____________________ Class____________________ Date__________

Step 3 Graph the point corresponding to $(2, \square)$. It is three units to the left of the axis of symmetry at $(\square, \square)$.

Step 4 Sketch the curve.

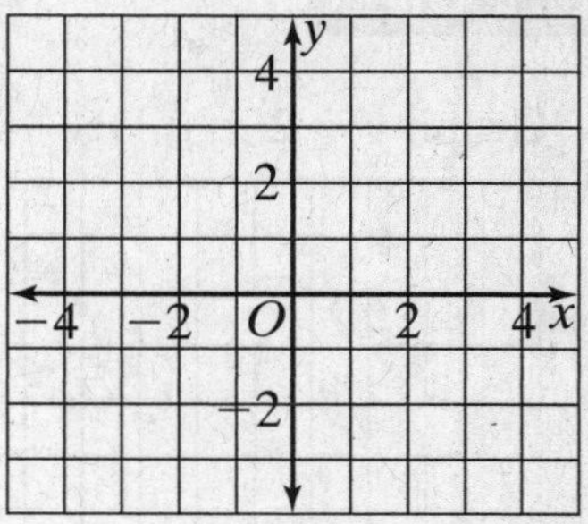

❷ Writing the Equation of a Parabola

Write the equation of the parabola shown.

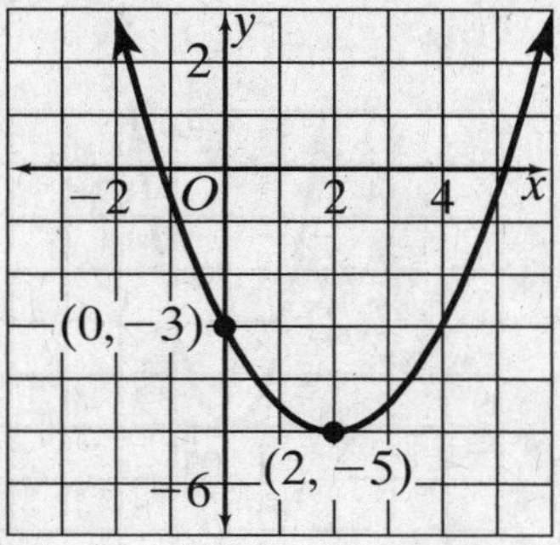

$y = a(x - \square)^2 + \square$ **Use the vertex form.**

$y = a(x - \square)^2 + \square$ **Substitute $h = 2$ and $k = -5$.**

$\square = a(\square - \square)^2 - 5$ **Substitute (0, −3).**

$\square = 4a$ **Simplify.**

$\square = a$ **Solve for a.**

The equation of the parabola is $y = \square(x - \square)^2 - \square$.

❸ Converting to Vertex Form

Write $y = -7x^2 - 70x - 169$ in vertex form.

$x = -\frac{b}{2a}$ **Find the x-coordinate of the vertex.**

$= -\frac{(\square)}{2(\square)}$ **Substitute for a and b.**

$= \square$

$y = -7(\square)^2 - 70(\square) - 169$ **Find the y-coordinate of the vertex.**

$= \square$

The vertex is at (−5, 6).

$y = \square(x - \square)^2 + \square$ **Write in vertex form.**

$= \square(x - (\square))^2 + \square$ **Substitute for a, h and k.**

$= \square$

The vertex form of the function is $y = \square$.

Name____________________ Class________________ Date ____________

Quick Check

1. Graph $y = 2(x + 1)^2 - 4$.

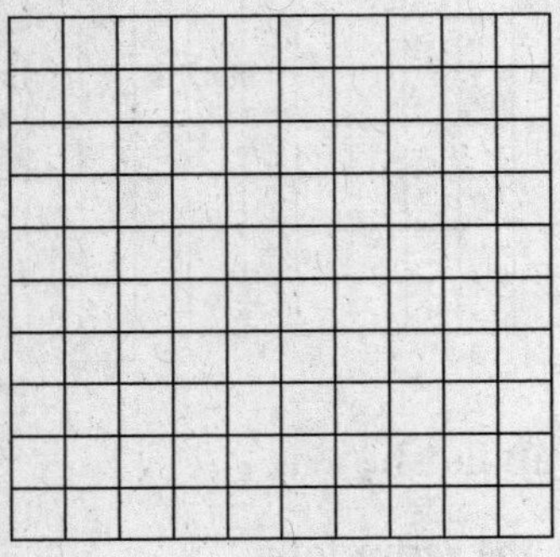

2. Use vertex form to write the equation of the parabola.

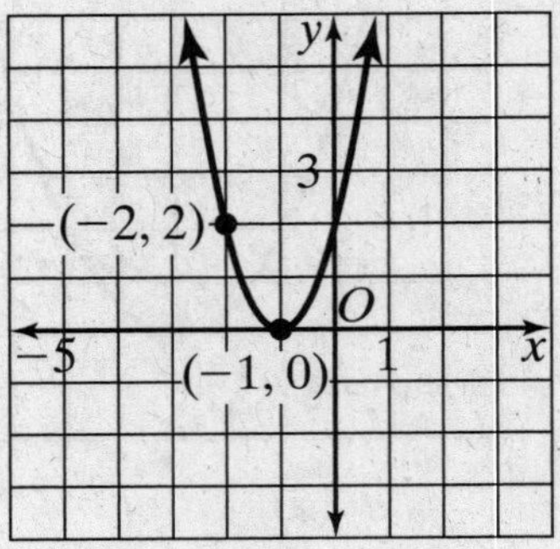

3. Write $y = -3x^2 + 12x + 5$ in vertex form.

Name__________ Class__________ Date__________

Lesson 5-4

Factoring Quadratic Expressions

Lesson Objectives	NAEP 2005 Strand: Algebra
1 Finding common and binomial factors of quadratic expressions	**Topic:** Variables, Expressions, and Operations
2 Factoring special quadratic expressions	**Local Standards:** __________

Vocabulary and Key Concepts

Factoring Perfect Square Trinomials

$a^2 + 2ab + b^2 = (a \square\ b)^2$

$a^2 - 2ab + b^2 = (a \square\ b)^2$

Factoring a Difference of Two Squares

$a^2 - b^2 = (a \square\ b)(a \square\ b)$

Factoring is __________

The greatest common factor (GCF) of an expression is __________

A perfect square trinomial is __________

The difference of two squares is __________

Examples

1 Factoring When $ac > 0$ and $b < 0$ Factor $x^2 - 14x + 33$.

Step 1 Find factors with product ac and sum b.

Since $ac = 33$ and $b = -14$, find negative factors with product 33 and sum -14.

Factors of 33	$\square$, $\square$	$\square$, $\square$
Sum of factors	-34	-14

Name________________________________ Class____________________________ Date ______________

Step 2 Rewrite the term *bx* using the factors you found. Then find common factors and rewrite the expression as a product of two binomials.

$x^2 - 14x + 33$

$x^2 - \square x - \square x + 33$ **Rewrite *bx*.**

$\square(x - 3) - \square(x - 3)$ **Find common factors.**

$(\square - \square)(x - 3)$ **Rewrite as a product of two binomials using the Distributive Property.**

Check $(x - \square)(x - \square) = x^2 - \square - \square + 33$

$= x^2 - \square + 33$ ✔

❷ Factoring When $ac < 0$ Factor $x^2 + 3x - 28$.

Step 1 Find factors with product *ac* and sum *b*.

Since $ac = -28$ and $b = 3$, find factors with product -28 and sum 3.

Factors of −28	1, −28	☐, 28	2, ☐	−2, ☐	4, ☐	−4, ☐
Sum of factors	☐	☐	−☐	12	−3	☐

Step 2 Since $a = 1$, you can write binomials using the factors you found.

$x^2 + 3x - 28$

$(x - \square)(x + \square)$ **Use the factors you found.**

❸ Factoring When $a \neq 1$ and $ac < 0$ Factor $6x^2 + 11x - 35$.

Step 1 Find factors with product *ac* and sum *b*.

Since $ac = -210$ and $b = 11$, find factors with product -210 and sum 11.

Factors of −210	1, −210	☐, 210	2, ☐	−2, ☐	3, ☐
Sum of factors	☐	209	−103	103	−67

Factors of −210	−3, 70	5, ☐	−5, ☐	☐, −21	☐, 21
Sum of factors	☐	−37	☐	☐	☐

Step 2 Rewrite the term *bx* using the factors you found. Then find common factors and rewrite the expression as the product of two binomials.

$6x^2 + 11x - 35$

$6x^2 \square 10x \square 21x \square 35$ **Rewrite *bx*.**

$\square(3x - 5) + \square(3x - 5)$ **Find common factors.**

$(\square + \square)(\square - \square)$ **Rewrite using the Distributive Property.**

Name______________________ Class______________________ Date ______________

Quick Check

1. Factor each expression. Check your answers.

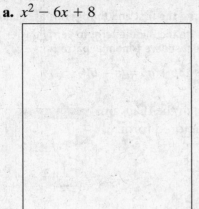

   a. $x^2 - 6x + 8$ b. $x^2 + 6x + 8$ c. $x^2 - 14x - 32$

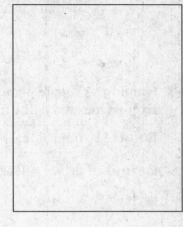

2. Factor each expression.

   a. $2x^2 + 11x + 12$ b. $2x^2 - 7x + 6$ c. $2x^2 + 7x - 9$

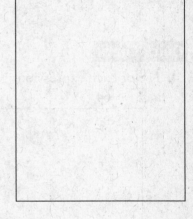

3. Factor each expression.

   a. $4x^2 + 12x + 9$ b. $64x^2 - 16x + 1$ c. $25x^2 + 90x + 81$

Name________________________________ Class________________________ Date ______________

Examples

❹ Factoring a Perfect Square Trinomial Factor $100x^2 + 180x + 81$.

$$100x^2 + 180x + 81 = (\square x)^2 + 180x + (\square)^2$$ **Rewrite the first and third terms as squares.**

$$= (\square x)^2 + 2(10x)(\square) + (\square)^2$$ **Rewrite the middle term to verify the perfect square trinomial pattern.**

$$= (\square + \square)^2$$ $a^2 + 2ab + b^2 = (a + b)^2$

❺ Framing A square photo is enclosed in a square frame, as shown in the diagram. Express the area of the frame (the shaded area) in completely factored form.

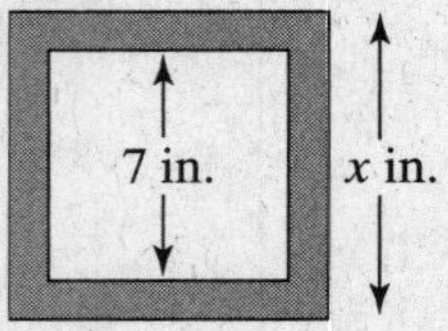

Relate [frame area] = [outer area] − [inner area]

Define Let [x] = length of side of frame.

Write area $= \square^2 - (\square)^2$

$$= (x + \square)(\square - \square)$$

The area of the frame in factored form is $(\square + \square)(\square - \square)$ in.^{2}.

Quick Check

4. Factor each expression.

a. $x^2 - 64$

b. $4a^2 - 49$

c. $9c^2 - 16$

5. In Example 5, write an expression for the area of the frame with the given dimensions.

a. outside length: 10 in.
inside length: x in.

b. outside length: 10 in.
inside length: $x + 2$ in.

Name________________________ Class____________________ Date____________

Lesson 5-5

Quadratic Equations

Lesson Objectives	NAEP 2005 Strand: Algebra
1 Solving quadratic equations by factoring and finding square roots	Topic: Equations and Inequalities
2 Solving quadratic equations by graphing	Local Standards: ____________

Vocabulary and Key Concepts

Zero-Product Property

If $ab = 0$, then $a = 0$ or $b = 0$.

Example If $(x + 3)(x - 7) = 0$, then $(x + 3) = 0$ or $(x - 7) = 0$.

The standard form of a quadratic equation is ______________________

____

A zero of a function is ______________________

____

Examples

1 Solving by Factoring Solve $3x^2 - 20x - 7 = 0$.

$3x^2 - 20x - 7 = 0$	**Write in standard form.**
$3x^2 - \square x + \square - 7 = 0$	**Rewrite *bx* term.**
$3x(\square) + (\square) = 0$	**Find the common factors.**
$(\square)(\square) = 0$	**Factor using the ______ Property.**
$\square = 0$ or $\square = 0$	**Use the ______ Property.**
$x = \square$ or $x = \square$	**Solve for *x*.**

The solutions are $\square$ and $\square$.

Check

$3x^2 - 20x = 7$

$3(\square)^2 - 20(\square) \stackrel{?}{=} 7$

$\frac{\square}{\square} + \frac{\square}{\square} \stackrel{?}{=} 7$

$\square = 7$ ✓

$3x^2 - 20x = 7$

$3(\square)^2 - 20(\square) \stackrel{?}{=} 7$

$\square - \square \stackrel{?}{=} 7$

$\square = 7$ ✓

Name______________________________ Class______________________ Date ____________

❷ **Solving by Finding Square Roots** Solve $6x^2 - 486 = 0$.

$6x^2 - 486 = 0$

$6x^2 = \square$ **Rewrite in the form $ax^2 = c$.**

$\frac{6x^2}{\square} = \frac{486}{\square}$ **Isolate x^2.**

$x^2 = \square$ **Simplify.**

$= \pm\square$ **Take the square root of each side.**

❸ **Solving by Finding Square Roots** The function $y = -16x^2 + 270$ models the height y in feet of a heavy object x seconds after it is dropped from the top of a building that is 270 feet tall. How long does it take the object to hit the ground?

$y = -16x^2 + 270$

$\square = -16x^2 + 270$ **Substitute 0 for *y*.**

$\square = -16x^2$ **Isolate x^2.**

$\square = \square$

$\square \approx x$ **Take the square root of each side.**

The object takes about $\square$ seconds to hit the ground.

Quick Check

1. Solve each equation by factoring. Check your answers.
   a. $x^2 + 7x = 18$
   b. $2x^2 + 4x = 6$
   c. $16x^2 = 8x$

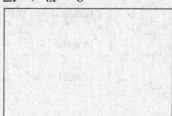

2. Solve each equation by finding square roots.
   a. $4x^2 - 25 = 0$
   b. $3x^2 = 24$
   c. $x^2 - \frac{1}{4} = 0$

Name______________________ Class______________________ Date ______________

Example

4 Solving by Graphing A carpenter wants to cut a piece of plywood in the shape of a right triangle as shown. He wants the hypotenuse of the triangle to be 6 feet long. About how long should the perpendicular sides be?

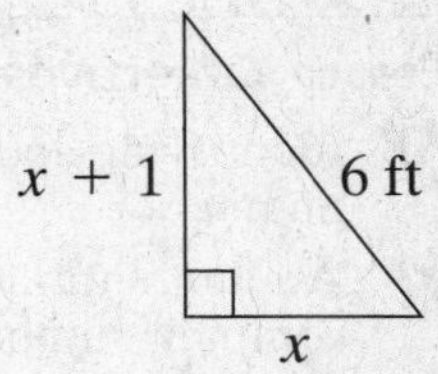

Relate Use the Pythagorean Theorem.

| (hypotenuse)^2 | = | the sum of the squares of the other two sides |

Define Let $\boxed{x}$ = the shorter leg.

Then $\boxed{x + 1}$ = the longer leg.

Write $\square^2 = \square^2 + (\square + \square)^2$

$\square = x^2 + \square + \square + \square$

$0 = \square + \square - \square$

Graph the related function $y = \square$.

Use the **CALC** feature to find the positive solution.

The sides of the triangle are about $\square$ ft and $\square$ ft.

Quick Check

3. a. A smoke jumper is a firefighter who parachutes into areas near forest fires. Smoke jumpers are in free fall from the time they jump out of a plane until they open their parachutes. The function $y = -16t^2 + 1{,}400$ models a jumper's height y in feet at t seconds for a jump from 1,400 ft. Using square roots, find the time during which the jumper is in free fall if the parachute opens at 1,000 ft.

b. Solve the equation in part (a) by factoring. Which method do you prefer—using square roots or factoring? Explain.

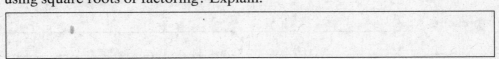

4. Use a graphing calculator to solve each equation. When necessary, round your answers to the nearest hundredth.

a. $x^2 - 2x = 4$ **b.** $x^2 + \frac{1}{2}x - \frac{1}{4} = 0$ **c.** $3x^2 + 5x - 12 = 8$

Name______________________ Class______________________ Date______________

Lesson 5-6

Complex Numbers

Lesson Objectives	NAEP 2005 Strand: Algebra
1. Identifying and graphing complex numbers	Topic: Algebraic Representations
2. Adding, subtracting, and multiplying complex numbers	Local Standards: ____________________

Vocabulary and Key Concepts

Square Root of a Negative Real Number

For any positive real number a, $\sqrt{-a} = i\sqrt{a}$.

Example $\sqrt{-4} = i\sqrt{4} = i \cdot 2 = 2i$

Note that $(\sqrt{-4})^2 = (i\sqrt{4})^2 = i^2(\sqrt{4})^2 = -1 \cdot 4 = -4$ (not 4).

Complex Numbers

A complex number can be written in the form $a + bi$, where a and b are real numbers, including 0.

$a + bi$ — a: Real part; bi: Imaginary part

Complex Numbers

Real Numbers: $-5,\ -\sqrt{3},\ 0,\ \sqrt{5},\ \frac{8}{3},\ 9$

- ________ **Numbers:** $-5,\ 0,\ \frac{8}{3},\ 9$
  - **Integers:** $-5,\ 0,\ 9$
    - **Whole Numbers:** $0,\ 9$
      - **Natural Numbers:** 9
- **Irrational Numbers:** $-\sqrt{3}$, $\sqrt{5}$

________ **Numbers:** $-4i$, $3 + 2i$, $2i\sqrt{2}$

The symbol i represents ____

____

An imaginary number is ____

____

The set of complex numbers is made up of ______________________________

____

Name________________________ Class________________________ Date ____________

A complex number plane can be used to ____________________________________

____

The absolute value of a complex number is ____________________________________

____

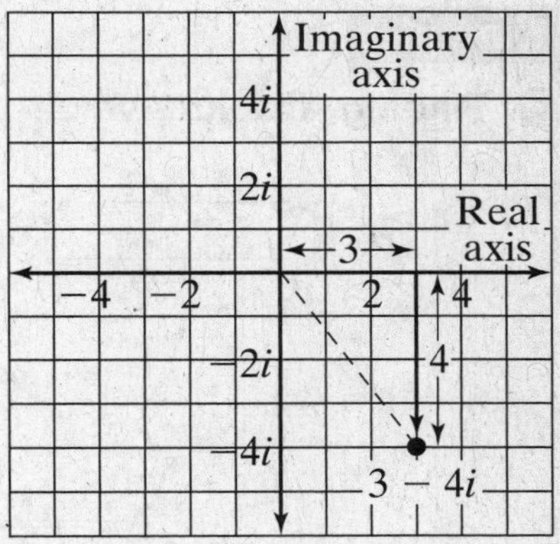

Examples

1 Simplifying Numbers Using *i* Simplify $\sqrt{-54}$ by using the imaginary number i.

$\sqrt{-54} = \sqrt{\square \cdot 54}$

$= \sqrt{\square} \cdot \sqrt{54}$

$= \square \cdot \sqrt{54}$

$= \square \cdot \square\sqrt{\square}$

$= \square$

2 Simplifying Imaginary Numbers Write the complex number $\sqrt{-121} - 7$ in the form $a + bi$.

$\sqrt{-121} - 7 = \square - 7$ **Simplify the radical expression.**

$= \square + \square$ **Write in the form $a + bi$.**

Quick Check

1. Simplify each number by using the imaginary number i.

   a. $\sqrt{-2}$ **b.** $\sqrt{-12}$ **c.** $\sqrt{-36}$

2. Write the complex number $\sqrt{-18} + 7$ in the form $a + bi$.

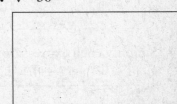

Name________________________ Class________________ Date ____________

Examples

3 Finding Absolute Value Find each absolute value.

a. $|-7i|$

$-7i$ is [ ] units from the origin on the imaginary axis.

So $|-7i| =$ [ ]

b. $|10 + 24i|$

$|10 + 24i| = \sqrt{10^2 + 24^2}$ **Use the Pythagorean Theorem to find distance.**

$= \sqrt{\boxed{} + \boxed{}} = \boxed{}$ **Simplify.**

4 Adding Complex Numbers Simplify the expression $(3 + 6i) - (4 - 8i)$.

$(3 + 6i) - (4 - 8i) = 3 + (-4) + \boxed{} + \boxed{}$ **Use commutative and associative properties.**

$= \boxed{} + \boxed{}$ **Simplify.**

5 Multiplying Complex Numbers

a. Find $(3i)(8i)$.

$(3i)(8i) = \boxed{}\,i^2$ **Multiply the real numbers.**

$= \boxed{}\left(\boxed{}\right) = \boxed{}$ **Substitute −1 for i^2 and multiply.**

b. Find $(3 - 7i)(2 - 4i)$.

$(3 - 7i)(2 - 4i) = 6 - \boxed{} - \boxed{} + 28i^2$ **Multiply the binomials.**

$= 6 - \boxed{} + 28\left(\boxed{}\right)$ **Substitute −1 for i^2.**

$= \boxed{} - \boxed{}$ **Simplify.**

Quick Check

3. Find the absolute value of each complex number.

a. $|6 - 4i|$ **b.** $|-2 + 5i|$ **c.** $|4i|$

4. Simplify each expression.

a. $(8 + 3i) - (2 + 4i)$ **b.** $7 - (3 + 2i)$ **c.** $(4 - 6i) + 3i$

5. Simplify each expression.

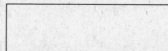

a. $(12i)(7i)$ **b.** $(6 - 5i)(4 - 3i)$ **c.** $(4 - 9i)(4 + 3i)$

Name______________________ Class______________ Date __________

Examples

6 Finding Complex Solutions Solve $9x^2 + 54 = 0$.

$9x^2 + 54 = 0$

$9x^2 = \square$ **Isolate x^2.**

$x^2 = \square$

$x = \pm \square$ **Find the square root of each side.**

7 Output Values Find the first three output values for $f(z) = z^2 - 4i$. Use $z = 0$ as the first input value.

$f(0) = \square^2 - 4i$

$= \square$

$f(-4i) = (-4i)^2 - 4i$ **First output becomes second input. Evaluate for $z = -4i$.**

$= \square - 4i$

$f(\square - \square) = (\square - \square)^2 - 4i$ **Second output becomes third input. Evaluate for $z = \square - \square$.**

$= [(\square)^2 + (-16)(-4i) + (-16)(-4i) + (\square)^2] - 4i$

$= (\square + \square - \square) - 4i$

$= \square + \square$

The first three output values are $\square$, $\square$, and $\square$.

Quick Check

6. Solve for x.

a. $3x^2 + 48 = 0$ **b.** $-5x^2 - 150 = 0$ **c.** $8x^2 + 2 = 0$

7. Find the first three output values for $f(z) = z^2 - 1 + i$. Use $z = 0$ as the first input value.

Name________________ Class________________ Date________________

Lesson 5-7

Completing the Square

Lesson Objectives	
1 Solving equations by completing the square 2 Rewriting functions by completing the square	**NAEP 2005 Strand:** Algebra **Topic:** Equations and Inequalities **Local Standards:** ____________

Vocabulary

Completing the square is a process for ______________________________

____

Examples

1 Solving a Perfect Square Trinomial Equation Solve $x^2 - 12x + 36 = 9$.

$x^2 - 12x + 36 = 9$

$(\square)^2 = 9$ — **Factor the trinomial.**

$\square = \square$ — **Find the square root of each side.**

$x - 6 = \square$ or $x - 6 = -\square$ — **Solve for *x*.**

$x = \square$ or $x = \square$

2 Finding Complex Solutions Solve $x^2 + 6x + 12 = 0$.

$x^2 + 6x + 12 = 0$

$\left(\frac{\square}{2}\right)^2 = \square$ — **Find $\left(\frac{b}{2}\right)^2$.**

$x^2 + 6x = \square$ — **Rewrite so all terms containing *x* are on one side.**

$x^2 + 6x + \square = \square + \square$ — **Complete the square by adding 9 to each side.**

$(\square)^2 = \square$ — **Factor the perfect square trinomial.**

$x + \square = \pm\sqrt{\square}$ — **Find the square root of each side.**

$x = \square \pm \sqrt{\square}$ — **Solve for *x*.**

$= \square \pm \square\sqrt{3}$ — **Simplify.**

Name________________________________ Class________________________ Date ______________

3 Solving When $a \neq 1$ Solve $2x^2 + 7x - 1 = 0$.

$2x^2 + 7x - 1 = 0$

$x^2 + \frac{7}{2}x - \frac{1}{2} = 0$ **Divide each side by 2.**

$x^2 + \frac{7}{2}x = \frac{\square}{\square}$ **Rewrite so all terms containing *x* are on one side.**

$\left(\frac{\frac{7}{2}}{2}\right)^2 = \frac{\square}{\square}$ **Find $\left(\frac{b}{2}\right)^2$.**

$x^2 + \frac{7}{2}x + \frac{\square}{\square} = \frac{1}{2} + \frac{\square}{\square}$ **Complete the square by adding $\frac{49}{16}$ to each side.**

$\left(x + \frac{\square}{4}\right)^2 = \frac{\square}{16}$ **Factor the perfect square trinomial.**

$x + \frac{7}{4} = \pm\frac{\sqrt{57}}{\square}$ **Find the square root of each side.**

$x = \square \pm \square$ **Solve for *x*.**

4 Using Vertex Form The monthly profit P from the sales of rugs woven by a family rug-making business depends on the price r that they charge for a rug. The profit is modeled by $P = -r^2 + 500r - 59{,}500$. Write the function in vertex form. What is the maximum monthly profit, in dollars, determined by this model?

$P = -r^2 + 500r - 59{,}500$

$= -(r^2 - \square) - 59{,}500$ **Factor −1 from the first two terms.**

$= -[r^2 - 500r + (\square)^2] - 59{,}500 + (\square)^2$ **Add and subtract $(-250)^2$ on the right side.**

$= -(r - \square)^2 - 59{,}500 + \square$ **Factor the perfect square trinominal.**

$= -(r - \square)^2 + \square$ **Simplify in vertex form.**

The vertex is $(\square, \square)$. A price of \$$\square$ per rug gives a maximum monthly profit of \$$\square$.

Name________________________ Class________________ Date __________

Quick Check

1. Solve $x^2 - 14x + 49 = 81$.

2. a. Check the solution to Example 2.

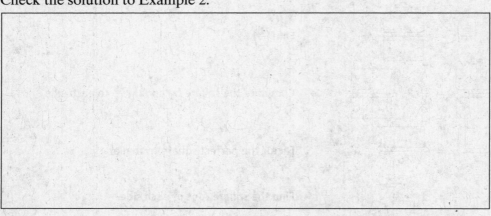

b. Solve $x^2 + 6x = -34$. Check your solution.

c. Solve $x^2 + 4x - 4 = 0$. Check your solution.

3. Solve each quadratic equation by completing the square.

a. $2x^2 + x = 6$

b. $2x^2 = 3x - 4$

4. a. Use the vertex form to find the vertex of $P = -\frac{1}{2}r^2 + 280r - 1{,}200$. Refer to Example 4 if necessary.

b. How do you know the vertex represents a maximum point?

Name____________________ Class____________________ Date____________

Lesson 5-8

The Quadratic Formula

Lesson Objectives	**NAEP 2005 Strand:** Algebra
1 Solving quadratic equations by using the Quadratic Formula	**Topic:** Equations and Inequalities
2 Determining types of solutions by using the discriminant	**Local Standards:** ____________________

Key Concepts

Quadratic Formula

A quadratic equation written in standard form $ax^2 + bx + c = 0$ can be solved with the Quadratic Formula.

$$x = \frac{-b \pm \sqrt{b^2 - 4ac}}{4a}$$

Discriminant of a Quadratic Equation

The discriminant of a quadratic equation in the form $ax^2 + bx + c = 0$ is the value of the expression $b^2 - 4ac$.

$$x = \frac{-b \pm \sqrt{b^2 - 4ac}}{2a} \leftarrow \textbf{discriminant}$$

Methods for Solving Quadratic Equations

Discriminant	Methods
positive square number	• factoring, graphing, Quadratic Formula, or completing the square
positive nonsquare number	• for approximate solutions: graphing, Quadratic Formula, or completing the square • for exact solutions: Quadratic Formula or completing the square
zero	• factoring, graphing, Quadratic Formula, or completing the square
negative	• Quadratic Formula or completing the square

Name____________________ Class________________ Date __________

Examples

1 Using the Quadratic Formula The longer leg of a right triangle is 1 unit longer than the shorter leg. The hypotenuse is 3 units long. What is the length of the shorter leg?

$$x^2 + (\square + \square)^2 = \square$$ **Use the Pythagorean Theorem.**

$$x^2 + \square + \square + \square = \square$$

$$\square + 2x - \square = 0$$ **Write in standard form.**

$$a = \square,\ b = 2,\ c = \square$$ **Find the values of *a*, *b*, and *c*.**

$$x = \frac{-b \pm \sqrt{b^2 - 4ac}}{2a}$$ **Use the Quadratic Formula.**

$$= \frac{\square \pm \sqrt{(\square)^2 - 4(2)(\square)}}{2(\square)}$$ **Substitute for *a*, *b*, and *c*.**

$$= \frac{-\square \pm \sqrt{\square}}{\square}$$ **Simplify.**

The length of the shorter leg is $\frac{\sqrt{17} - 1}{2}$ units.

Check Is the answer reasonable? Since $\frac{-1 - \sqrt{17}}{2}$ is a ________ number, and a length cannot be negative, that answer is ________.
Since $\frac{\sqrt{17} - 1}{2} \approx$ ________, that answer is ________.

2 Using the Discriminant Determine the type and number of solutions of $x^2 + 5x + 10 = 0$.

$$a = \square,\ b = \square,\ c = \square$$ **Find the values of *a*, *b*, and *c*.**

$$b^2 - 4ac = (\square)^2 - 4(\square)(\square)$$ **Evaluate the discriminant.**

$$= 25 - \square = \square$$ **Simplify.**

Since the discriminant is negative, $x^2 + 5x + 10 = 0$ has ________ imaginary solutions.

Name________________________ Class________________________ Date ______________

❸ Evaluating the Discriminant A player throws a ball up and toward a wall that is 17 ft high. The height h in feet of the ball t seconds after it leaves the player's hand is modeled by $h = -16t^2 + 25t + 6$. If the ball makes it to where the wall is, will it go over the wall or hit the wall?

$h = -16t^2 + -5t + 6$

$17 = -16t^2 + 25t + 6$ **Substitute 17 for *h*.**

$0 = -16t^2 + 25t - \square$ **Write the equation in standard form.**

$a = \square,\ b = \square,\ c = \square$ **Find the values of *a*, *b*, and *c*.**

$b^2 - 4ac = (\square)^2 - 4(\square)(\square)$ **Evaluate the discriminant.**

$= \square - \square$ **Simplify.**

$= \square$

Since the discriminant is ______, the equation has no real ______. The ball will hit the wall.

Quick Check

1. Use the Quadratic Formula to solve each equation. Check your solutions.

a. $3x^2 - x = 4$

b. $-2x^2 = 4x + 3$

c. $4x^2 = 8x - 3$

d. $x^2 + 4x = 41$

2. Determine the type and number of solutions of each equation.

a. $x^2 + 6x + 9 = 0$

b. $x^2 + 6x + 10 = 0$

Name______________________________ Class____________________ Date____________

Lesson 6-1

Polynomial Functions

Lesson Objectives	NAEP 2005 Strand: Algebra
1 Classifying polynomials	**Topic:** Algebraic Representations
2 Modeling data using polynomial functions	**Local Standards:** ____________________

Vocabulary and Key Concepts

Polynomial Function

$P(x) = a_nx^n + a_{n-1}x^{n-1} + \ldots + a_1x + a_0$ where n is a nonnegative integer and the coefficients $a_n, \ldots, a_0$ are ________ numbers.

Degree	Name Using Degree	Polynomial Example	Number of Terms	Name Using Number of Terms
0	constant	6	1	monomial
	linear	$x + 6$	2	binomial
2		$3x^2$	1	monomial
3	cubic	$2x^3 - 5x^2 - 2x$		trinomial
4	quartic	$x^4 + 3x^2$	2	
	quintic	$-2x^5 + 3x^2 - x + 4$	4	polynomial of 4 terms

A polynomial is ____

The degree of a term is determined by ____

____

The standard form of a polynomial has ____

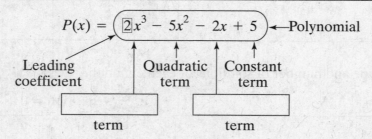

____

$$P(x) = \boxed{2}x^3 - 5x^2 - 2x + 5 \leftarrow \text{Polynomial}$$

Leading coefficient

Quadratic term

Constant term

________ term

________ term

The degree of a polynomial is ____

____

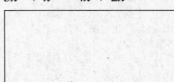

Name____________________ Class____________________ Date____________

Examples

1 Classifying Polynomials Write each polynomial in standard form. Then classify it by degree and by number of terms.

a. $9 + x^3$

$x^3 + \square$

The term with the largest degree is x^3, so the polynomial is degree $\square$. It has two terms. The polynomial is a ____________________.

b. $x^3 - 2x^2 - 3x^4$

$-3x^4 + \square^{\square} - \square^{\square}$

The term with the largest degree is $-3x^4$, so the polynomial is degree $\square$. It has three terms. The polynomial is a ____________________.

2 Comparing Models Using a graphing calculator, determine whether a linear, quadratic, or cubic model best fits the values in the table.

x	*y*
0	2.8
2	5
4	6
6	5.5
8	4

Enter the data. Use the LinReg, QuadReg, and CubicReg options of a graphing calculator to find the best-fitting model for each polynomial classification.

Graph each model and compare.

Cubic model

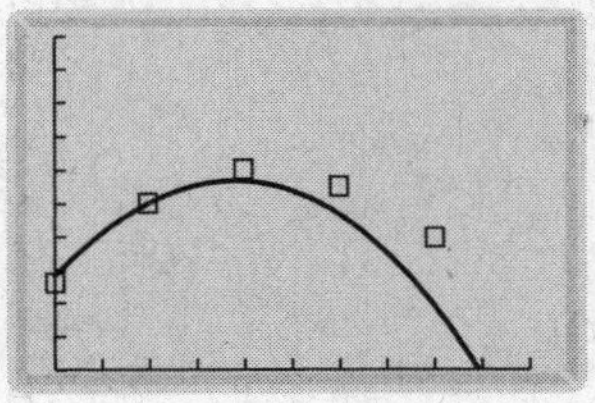

____________________ **model**

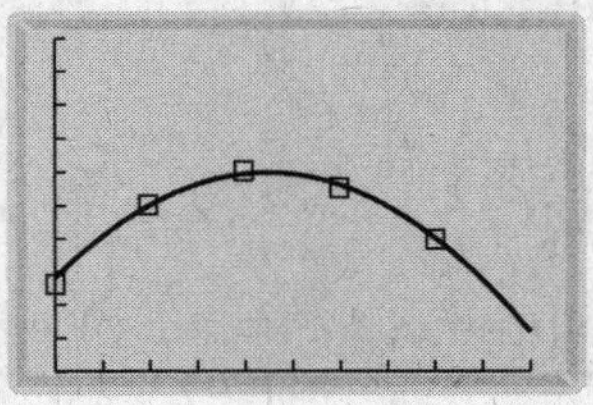

Linear model

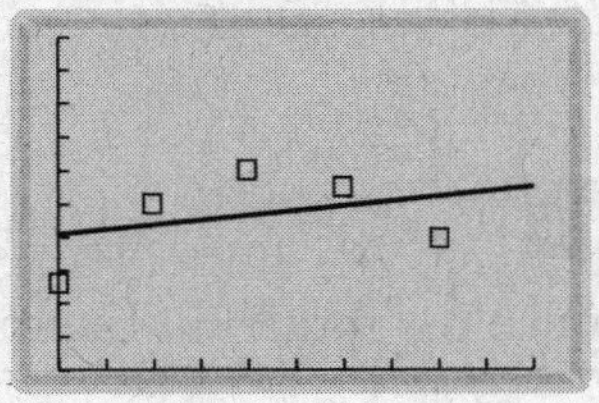

The ____________________ appears to best fit the given values.

Quick Check

1. Write each polynomial in standard form. Then classify it by degree and by number of terms.

a. $4x - 6x + 5$

b. $3x^3 + x^2 - 4x + 2x^3$

c. $6 - 2x^5$

Name________________________ Class________________ Date ____________

Example

3 Using Cubic Functions The table shows data on the number of employees that a small company had from 1975 to 2000. Find a cubic function to model the data. Use it to estimate the number of employees in 1988.

Year	Number of Employees
1975	60
1980	65
1985	70
1990	60
1995	55
2000	64

Enter the data. Let 0 represent 1975. To find a cubic model, use the CubicReg option of a graphing calculator. Graph the model.

CubicReg
y=ax³+bx²+cx+d
a=.0096296296
b=-.3753968254
c=3.541005291
d=58.96031746
R^2=.7827380952

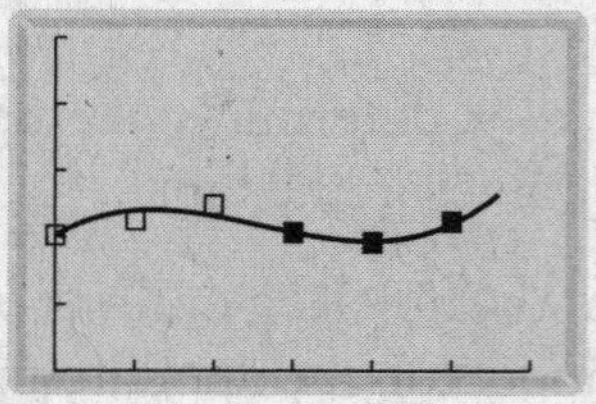

X	Y_1
10	66.46
11	65.305
12	64.035
13	62.708
14	61.38
15	60.111
16	58.958

X=13

The function $f(x) = 0.00963x^3 - 0.3754x^{\square} + 3.541x + 58.96$ is an approximate model for the ______ function.

To estimate the number of employees for 1988, you can use the Table option of a graphing calculator to find that $f(13) \approx 62.71$. According to the model, there were about ______ in 1988.

Quick Check

2. Can you use the model in Example 2 to predict the value of y for $x = 10$?

3. Use the cubic model in Example 3 to estimate the number of employees in 1999.

Name______________________ Class______________________ Date____________

Lesson 6-2

Polynomials and Linear Factors

Lesson Objectives	NAEP 2005 Strand: Algebra
1 Analyzing the factored form of a polynomial	**Topics:** Variables, Expressions, and Operations
2 Writing a polynomial function from its zeros	**Local Standards:** ____________________

Vocabulary and Key Concepts

Factor Theorem

The expression $x - a$ is a linear factor of a polynomial if and only if the value a is a ______ of the related polynomial function.

Equivalent Statements about Polynomials

① -4 is a ______ of $x^2 + 3x - 4 = 0$.

② -4 is an ______ of the graph of $y = x^2 + 3x - 4$.

③ -4 is a ______ of $y = x^2 + 3x - 4$.

④ $x + 4$ is a ______ of $x^2 + 3x - 4$.

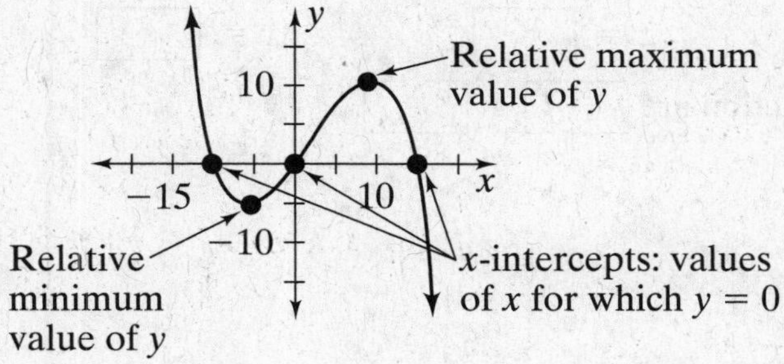

A relative maximum is ____

____

A relative minimum is ____

____

A multiple zero is ____

____

The multiplicity of a zero of a polynomial function is ______________________

____

Name____________________ Class____________________ Date ____________

Examples

1 Writing a Polynomial in Standard Form Write $(x-1)(x+3)(x+4)$ as a polynomial in standard form.

$(x-1)(x+3)(x+4) = (x-1)(x^{\square} + 4x + \square + 12)$	**Multiply $(x+3)$ and $(x+4)$.**
$= (x-1)(x^2 + \square + 12)$	**Simplify.**
$= \square(x^2+7x+12) - \square(x^2+7x+12)$	**Distributive Property**
$= x^{\square} + \square + 12x - \square - 7x \square 12$	**Multiply.**
$= \square + \square + \square - \square$	**Simplify.**

2 Writing a Polynomial in Factored Form Write $3x^3 - 18x^2 + 24x$ in factored form.

$3x^3 - 18x^2 + 24x = \square(x^2 - \square x + 8)$	**Factor out the GCF, $\square$.**
$= \square(x \square 4)(x - \square)$	**Factor $x^2 - 6x + 8$.**

3 Finding Zeros of a Polynomial Function Find the zeros of $y = (x+1)(x-1)(x+3)$. Then graph the function.

$x + 1 = 0$ or $x - 1 = 0$ or $x + 3 = 0$

$x = \square$ $x = \square$ $x = \square$

The zeros of the function are $\square$, 1, $\square$.

Sketch the function.

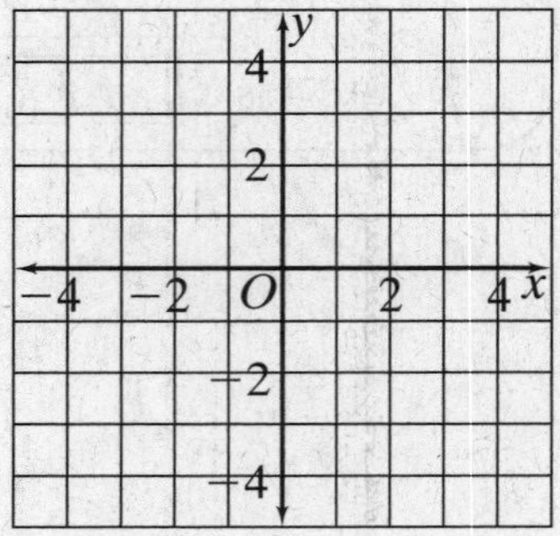

Quick Check

1. Write the expression $(x+1)(x+1)(x+2)$ as a polynomial in standard form.

2. Write $3x^3 - 3x^2 - 36x$ in factored form. Check by multiplication.

Name______________________ Class______________________ Date ______________

Example

④ Writing a Polynomial Function From Its Zeros Write a polynomial in standard form with zeros at 2, −3, and 0.

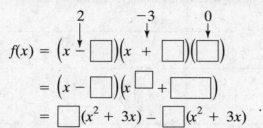

Zeros: 2, −3, 0	**Zeros**
$f(x) = (x - \square)(x + \square)(\square)$	**Write a linear factor for each zero.**
$= (x - \square)(x^{\square} + \square)$	**Multiply (*x* + 3)(*x*).**
$= \square(x^2 + 3x) - \square(x^2 + 3x)$	$\square$ **Property**
$= x^{\square} + \square - 2x^2 - \square$	**Multiply.**
$= \square^{\square} + \square^{\square} - \square$	**Simplify.**

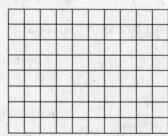

The function $f(x) = \square^{\square} + \square^{\square} - \square$ has zeros at 2, −3, and 0.

Quick Check

3. a. Find the zeros of the function $y = (x - 7)(x - 5)(x - 3)$.

b. Graph the function and label the zeros.

4. a. Write a polynomial function in standard form with zeros at –4, –2, and 1.

b. Write a polynomial function in standard form with zeros at –4, –2, and 0.

c. **Critical Thinking** Explain why the zero at 0 produces more than one possible answer to part (b).

Name________________________________ Class________________________ Date______________

Lesson 6-3

Dividing Polynomials

Lesson Objectives	
1 Dividing polynomials using long division	**NAEP 2005 Strand:** Algebra
2 Dividing polynomials using synthetic division	**Topics:** Variables, Expressions, and Operations
	Local Standards: ____________________

Vocabulary and Key Concepts

Remainder Theorem

If a polynomial $P(x)$ of degree $n \geq 1$ is divided by $(x - a)$, where a is a constant, then the remainder is $P(\square)$.

Synthetic division is ____

____

____

Examples

1 Polynomial Long Division Divide $x^2 + 2x - 30$ by $x - 5$.

$$\begin{array}{r} x \\ x - 5 \overline{) x^2 + 2x - 30} \\ x^{\square} - \square \\ \hline \square - \square \end{array}$$

Divide $\frac{x^2}{x} = \square$.

Multiply: $x(x - 5) = \square - \square$.

Subtract: $(x^2 + 2x) - (x^2 - 5x) = \square$ and bring down -30.

Repeat the process of dividing, multiplying, and subtracting.

$$\begin{array}{r} x + \square \\ x - 5 \overline{) x^2 + 2x - 30} \\ x^2 - 5x \\ \hline 7x - 30 \\ \square - \square \\ \hline \square \end{array}$$

Divide $\frac{7x}{x} = \square$.

Multiply: $7(\square - \square) = \square - 35$.

Subtract: $(7x - 30) - (7x - 35) = \square$.

The quotient is $\square + \square$ with a remainder of $\square$, or simply $\square + \square$, R $\square$.

Name____________________ Class________________ Date __________

❷ **Checking Factors** Determine whether $x + 2$ is a factor of each polynomial.

a. $x^2 + 10x + 16$

$$\begin{array}{r} x + \square \\ x + 2\overline{)x^2 + 10x + 16} \\ x^2 + \square \\ \hline 8x + 16 \\ \square + \square \\ \hline \square \end{array}$$

Since the remainder is $\square$, $x + 2$ $\square$ a factor of $x^2 + 10x + 16$.

b. $x^3 + 7x^2 - 5x - 6$

$$\begin{array}{r} x^{\square} + \square - 15 \\ x + 2\overline{)x^3 + 7x^2 - 5x - 6} \\ x^3 + \square x^2 \\ \hline 5x^2 - \square \\ 5x^2 + \square \\ \hline - \square - 6 \\ -15x - \square \\ \hline \square \end{array}$$

Since the remainder $\square$ 0, $x + 2$ $\square$ a factor of $x^3 + 7x^2 - 5x - 6$.

Quick Check

1. Divide $x^2 - 3x + 1$ by $x - 4$. Check your answer.

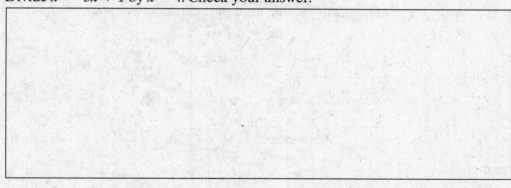

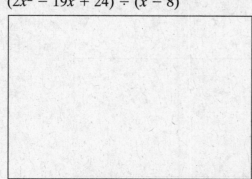

2. Determine whether each divisor is a factor of each dividend.
   a. $(2x^2 - 19x + 24) \div (x - 8)$
   b. $(x^3 - 4x^2 + 3x + 2) \div (x + 2)$

Name______________________ Class______________________ Date ______________

Example

3 Using Synthetic Division Use synthetic division to divide $5x^3 - 6x^2 + 4x - 1$ by $x - 3$.

Step 1 Reverse the sign of the constant term in the divisor. Write the coefficients of the polynomial in standard form.

$x - 3\overline{)5x^3 - 6x^2 + 4x - 1}$

☐ ☐ -6 ☐ -1

Step 2 Bring down the coefficient.

3	5	−6	4	−1
		■	■	■
	☐	■	■	■

Bring down the ☐. This begins the quotient.

Step 3 Multiply the first coefficient by the new divisor. Write the result under the next coefficient. Add.

3	5	−6	4	−1
×		☐	■	■
	5	9	■	■

Multiply 3 by 5. Write the result under −6.

Add −6 and ☐.

Step 4 Repeat the steps of multiplying and adding until the remainder is found.

3	5	−6	4	−1
		15	☐	93
	5	9	☐	☐

☐x^2 + ☐x + ☐ Remainder

The quotient is ☐ + ☐ + ☐, R ☐.

Quick Check

3. Use synthetic division to divide $x^3 + 4x^2 + x - 6$ by $x + 1$.

Name______________________ Class______________ Date__________

Lesson 6-4

Solving Polynomial Equations

Lesson Objectives	NAEP 2005 Strand: Algebra
1 Solving polynomial equations by graphing	Topics: Equations and Inequalities
2 Solving polynomial equations by factoring	Local Standards: ______________

Key Concepts

Sum and Difference of Cubes

$a^3 + b^3 = (a + b)(a^2 \square ab + \square)$ $\qquad$ $a^3 - b^3 = (a \square b)(a^2 \square ab + b^2)$

Examples

1 Solving a Polynomial Equation Solve $8x^3 + 125 = 0$. Find all complex roots.

$8x^3 + 125 = (\square)^3 + (5)^3$ — **Rewrite the expression as the sum of cubes.**

$= (2x + 5)((2x)^2 - \square x + (\square)^2)$ — **Factor.**

$= (2x + 5)(\square - \square + \square)$ — **Simplify.**

Since $2x + 5$ is a factor, $x = -\square$ is a root. Since $4x^2 - \square + \square$ cannot be factored, use the Quadratic Formula to solve the related equation $4x^2 - \square + \square = 0$.

$x = \frac{-b \pm \sqrt{b^2 - 4ac}}{2a}$ — **Quadratic Formula**

$= \frac{-(\square) \pm \sqrt{(-10)^2 - 4(\square)(\square)}}{2(\square)}$ — **Substitute 4 for a, −10 for b, and 25 for c.**

$= \frac{-(\square) \pm \sqrt{-\square}}{\square}$ — **Use order of operations.**

$= \frac{\square \pm 10i\sqrt{\square}}{8}$ — $\sqrt{-1} = i$

$= \frac{\square \pm \square i\sqrt{3}}{\square}$ — **Simplify.**

The solutions are $\square$ and $\square$.

❷ Factoring a Sum or Difference of Cubes Factor $x^3 - 125$.

$x^3 - 125 = (x)^3 - (\square)^3$ **Rewrite the expression as the difference of cubes.**

$= (x - 5)(x^2 + \square + (5)^2)$ **Factor.**

$= (x - 5)(x^2 + \square + \square)$ **Simplify.**

❸ Factoring by Using a Quadratic Pattern Factor $x^4 - 6x^2 - 27$.

Step 1 Since $x^4 - 6x^2 - 27$ has the form of a quadratic expression, you can factor it like one. Make a temporary substitution of variables.

$x^4 - 6x^2 - 27 = (\square)^2 - 6(\square) - 27$ **Rewrite in the form of a quadratic expression.**

$= (\square)^2 - 6(\square) - 27$ **Substitute *a* for x^2.**

$= (a + \square)(a - \square)$ **Factor.**

Step 2 Substitute back to the original variables.

$(a + 3)(a - 9) = (\square + 3)(\square - 9)$ **Substitute x^2 for *a*.**

$= (\square + 3)(x + \square)(x - \square)$ **Factor completely.**

The factored form of $x^4 - 6x^2 - 27$ is $(\square + \square)(\square + \square)(\square - \square)$.

Quick Check

1. Solve each equation.

   a. $x^3 + 8 = 0$

   b. $27x^3 - 1 = 0$

2. Factor $8x^3 - 1$.

Name________________ Class________________ Date ____________

Example

❹ Solving a Higher-Degree Polynomial Equation
Solve $x^4 - 4x^2 - 45 = 0$.

$$x^4 - 4x^2 - 45 = 0$$

Write in the form of a quadratic expression. Think of the expression as $a^2 - 4a - 45$, which factors as $(a - 9)(\square + \square)$.

$$(x^2)^{\square} - \square(x^2) - 45 = 0$$

$$(x^2 \square 9)(\square + \square) = 0$$

$$(x \square 3)(x + \square)(x^2 + 5) = 0$$

$x = \square$ or $x = \square$ or $x^2 = \square$ Use the ________ Theorem.

$x = \square$ or $x = \pm i\sqrt{\square}$ Solve for x, and simplify.

The solutions are ______, ______, ______, and ______.

Quick Check

3. Factor each expression.

a. $x^4 + 7x^2 + 6$

b. $x^4 - 3x^2 - 10$

4. Solve $x^4 + 11x^2 + 18 = 0$.

Name________________________________ Class________________________ Date______________

Lesson 6-5

Theorems About Roots of Polynomial Equations

Lesson Objectives	**NAEP 2005 Strand:** Algebra
1 Solving equations using the Rational Root Theorem	**Topics:** Equations and Inequalities
2 Using the Irrational Root Theorem and the Imaginary Root Theorem	**Local Standards:** ____________________

Vocabulary and Key Concepts

Rational Root Theorem

If $\frac{p}{q}$ is in simplest form and is a rational root of the polynomial equation $a_nx^n + a_{n-1}x^{n-1} + \ldots + a_1x + a_0 = 0$ with integer coefficients, then p must be a [ ] of a_0 and [ ] must be a factor of a_n.

Irrational Root Theorem

Let a and b be rational numbers and let $\sqrt{b}$ be an irrational number. If $a + \sqrt{b}$ is a root of a polynomial equation with rational coefficients, then the conjugate [ ] also is a root.

Imaginary Root Theorem

If the imaginary number $a + bi$ is a root of a polynomial equation with real coefficients, then the conjugate [ ] also is a root.

Conjugates are ____

Complex conjugates are ____

Examples

1. **Finding Irrational Roots** A polynomial equation with rational coefficients has the roots $2 - \sqrt{5}$ and $\sqrt{7}$. Find two additional roots.

By the Irrational Root Theorem, if $2 - \sqrt{5}$ is a root, then its conjugate [ ] is also a root. If $\sqrt{7}$ is a root, then its conjugate [ ] is a root.

Name______________________ Class______________________ Date ______________

❷ Using the Rational Root Theorem Find the roots of $5x^3 - 24x^2 + 41x - 20 = 0$.

Step 1 List the possible rational roots.

The leading coefficient is $\square$. The constant term is $\square$. By the Rational Root Theorem, the only possible roots of the equation have the form $\frac{\text{factor of } -20}{\text{factor of } 5}$.

The factors of -20 are ± 1 and $\square$, ± 2 and $\square$, and ± 4 and $\square$.

The only factors of 5 are ± 1 and ± 5. The only possible rational roots are

$\pm\frac{1}{5}, \pm\frac{2}{5}, \pm\frac{\square}{\square}, \pm 1, \pm 2, \pm 4, \pm 5, \pm 10$, and $\square$.

Step 2 Test each possible rational root until you find a root.

Test $\frac{1}{5}$: $5(\square)^3 - 24(\square)^2 + 41(\square) - 20 = \square \neq 0$

Test $-\frac{1}{5}$: $5\left(-\frac{1}{5}\right)^3 - 24\left(-\frac{1}{5}\right)^2 + 41\left(-\frac{1}{5}\right) - 20 = \square \neq 0$

Test $\frac{4}{5}$: $5(\square)^3 - 24(\square)^2 + 41(\square) - 20 = \square$, so $\square$ $\square$ a root.

Step 3 Use synthetic division with the root you found in Step 2 to find the quotient.

$\frac{4}{5}$	5	−24	41	−20
		$\square$	−16	20
	5	$-\square$	$\square$	0
	↓	↓	↓	↓
	$\square x^2$	$- \square$	$+ \square$	Remainder

Step 4 Find the roots of $5x^2 - 20x + 25 = 0$.

$5(x^2 - \square + \square) = 0$ — **Factor out the GCF, $\square$.**

$x^2 - 4x + 5 = 0$ — **Divide both sides of the equation by $\square$.**

$x = \frac{-b \pm \sqrt{b^2 - 4ac}}{2a}$ — **Quadratic Formula**

$= \frac{-(\square) \pm \sqrt{(-4)^2 - 4(\square)(\square)}}{2(\square)}$ — **Substitute $\square$ for *a*, $\square$ for *b*, and $\square$ for *c*.**

$= \frac{\square \pm \sqrt{-\square}}{2}$ — **Use order of operations.**

$= \frac{4 \pm \square}{2} = \square \pm \square$ — **$\sqrt{-1} = \square$. Simplify.**

The roots of $5x^3 - 24x^2 + 41x - 20 = 0$ are $\frac{\square}{\square}$, $\square + \square$, and $\square - \square$.

Name______________________ Class______________________ Date ______________

③ Finding Imaginary Roots A polynomial equation with real coefficients has the roots $2 + 9i$ and $7i$. Find two additional roots.

By the Imaginary Root Theorem, if $2 + 9i$ is a root, then its ______ conjugate ______ is a root. If $7i$ is a root, then its complex conjugate ______ is a root.

Quick Check

1. a. A polynomial equation with rational coefficients has the roots $2 - \sqrt{7}$ and $\sqrt{5}$. Find two additional roots.

b. Critical Thinking One of the roots of a polynomial equation is $4 + \sqrt{2}$. Can you be certain that $4 - \sqrt{2}$ is a root of the equation? Explain.

2. Find the roots of each equation.

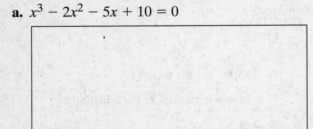

a. $x^3 - 2x^2 - 5x + 10 = 0$

b. $3x^3 + x^2 - x + 1 = 0$

3. a. If a polynomial equation with real coefficients has $3i$ and $-2 + i$ among its roots, then what two other roots must it have?

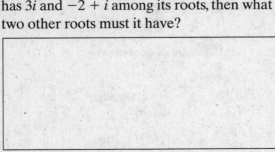

b. Critical Thinking Describe the degree of the equation.

Name______________________________ Class____________________ Date____________

Lesson 6-6

The Fundamental Theorem of Algebra

Lesson Objective	**NAEP 2005 Strand:** Algebra
1 Using the Fundamental Theorem of Algebra in solving polynomial equations with complex roots	**Topics:** Equations and Inequalities **Local Standards:** ____________________

Key Concepts

Fundamental Theorem of Algebra

If $P(x)$ is a polynomial of degree $n \geq 1$ with complex coefficients, then $P(x) = 0$ has at least ______ complex root.

Corollary

Including imaginary roots and multiple roots, an ______ degree polynomial equation has exactly n roots; the related polynomial function has exactly ___ zeros.

Example

1 Using the Fundamental Theorem of Algebra For the equation $x^4 - 3x^3 + 4x + 1 = 0$, find the number of complex roots, the possible number of real roots, and the possible rational roots.

By the corollary to the Fundamental Theorem of Algebra, $x^4 - 3x^3 + 4x + 1 = 0$ has ______ complex roots.

By the Imaginary Root Theorem, the equation has either no imaginary roots, ______ imaginary roots (one conjugate pair), or four imaginary roots (______ conjugate pairs). So the equation has either ______ real roots, ______ real roots, or ______ real roots.

By the Rational Root Theorem, the possible rational roots of the equation are ___ and ___.

Quick Check

1. For the equation $x^4 - 3x^3 + x^2 - x + 3 = 0$, find the number of complex roots, the possible number of real roots, and the possible rational roots.

Name______________________ Class______________________ Date ______________

Example

2 Finding All Zeros of a Polynomial Function Find the number of complex zeros of $f(x) = x^5 + 3x^4 - x - 3$. Find all the zeros.

By the corollary to the Fundamental Theorem of Algebra, there are ☐ complex zeros. You can use synthetic division to find a rational zero.

Step 1 Find a rational root from the possible roots of ±1 and ±3. Use synthetic division to test each possible root until you get a remainder of zero.

−3	1	☐	0	☐	−1	−3
		−3	0	0	0	3
	☐	0	0	0	☐	0

↓ $x^{☐}$ ↓ -1

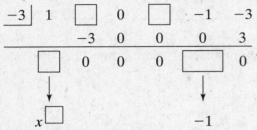

So ☐ is one of the roots.

Step 2 Factor the expression $x^4 - 1$.

$x^4 - 1 = (x^2 - ☐)(x^2 ☐ 1)$

$= (x - 1)(x + 1)(x^{☐} + 1)$ **Factor $x^2 - 1$.**

So ☐ and ☐ are also roots.

Step 3 Solve $x^2 + 1 = 0$.

$x^2 = ☐$

$x = ☐$

So ☐ and ☐ are also roots.

The polynomial function $f(x) = x^5 + 3x^4 - x - 3$ has three real zeros of $x = ☐$, $x = ☐$, and $x = ☐$ and two complex zeros of $x = ☐$ and $x = ☐$.

Quick Check

2. **a.** Find all zeros of $y = x^3 - 2x^2 + 4x - 8$.

b. Explain how you could use a graphing calculator to verify the zeros.

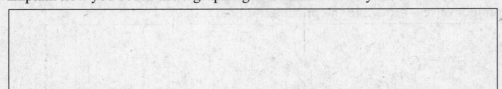

Name______________________ Class______________________ Date______________

Lesson 6-7

Permutations and Combinations

Lesson Objectives	**NAEP 2005 Strand:** Data Analysis and Probability
1 Counting permutations	**Topic:** Probability
2 Counting combinations	**Local Standards:** ____________________

Vocabulary and Key Concepts

***n* Factorial**

For any positive integer n, $n! = n(n-1) \cdot \ldots \cdot 3 \cdot 2 \cdot 1$.

For $n = 0$, $n! = 1$.

Number of Permutations

The number of permutations of n items of a set arranged r items at a time is ${}_n\mathrm{P}_r$.

${}_n\mathrm{P}_r = \frac{n!}{(n-r)!}$ for $0 \le r \le n$

Number of Combinations

The number of combinations of n items of a set chosen r items at a time is ${}_n\mathrm{C}_r$.

${}_n\mathrm{C}_r = \frac{n!}{r!(n-r)!}$ for $0 \le r \le n$

A permutation is ____

____

A combination is ____

____

Examples

1. **Finding Permutations** In how many ways can 6 people line up from left to right for a group photo?

Since everybody will be in the picture, you are using all the items from the original set. You can use the Multiplication Counting Principle or factorial notation.

There are six ways to select the first person in line, five ways to select the next person, and so on. The total number of permutations is

[ ] = 6! = [ ].

The six people can line up in [ ] different orders.

Name____________________ Class____________________ Date ____________

❷ Finding Permutations How many 4-letter codes can be made if no letter can be used twice?

Method 1 Use the Multiplication Counting Principle.

$26 \cdot$ ____ $\cdot\ 24 \cdot$ ____ $=$ ____

Method 2 Use the permutation formula. Since there are ____ letters arranged ____ at a time, $n =$ ____ and $r =$ ____.

$${}_{\square}P_{\square} = \frac{\square}{(26 - 4)!} = \frac{\square}{\square} = \square$$

There are ____ possible arrangements of 4-letter codes with no duplicates.

❸ Finding Combinations A disc jockey wants to select 5 songs from a new CD that contains 12 songs. How many 5-song selections are possible?

Relate 12 songs chosen 5 songs at a time

Define Let n = total number of songs.

Let r = number of songs chosen at a time.

Write ${}_{n}C_{r} = {}_{12}C_{5}$

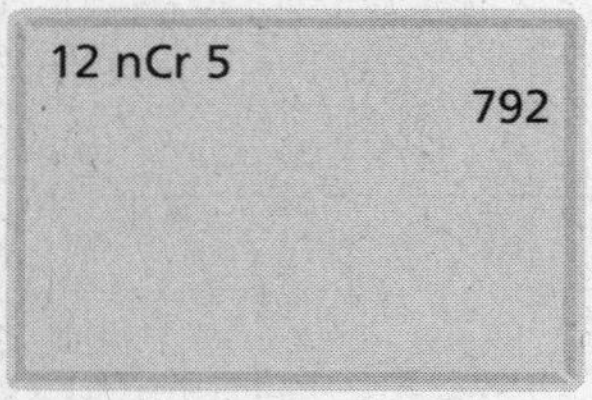

Use the ${}_{n}C_{r}$ feature of your calculator.

The disc jockey can choose five songs in ____ different ways.

Quick Check

1. In how many ways can you arrange six trophies on a shelf?

2. How many 3-letter codes can be made if no letter can be used twice?

Name______________________ Class______________________ Date ______________

Example

4 Finding Combinations A pizza menu allows you to select 4 toppings at no extra charge from a list of 9 possible toppings. In how many ways can you select 4 or fewer toppings?

You may choose

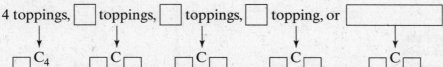

4 toppings, ☐ toppings, ☐ toppings, ☐ topping, or ☐.

$\square C_4$ $\square C \square$ $\square C \square$ $\square C \square$ $\square C \square$

The total number of ways to pick the toppings is

☐ + ☐ + ☐ + ☐ + ☐ = ☐

There are ☐ ways to order your pizza.

Quick Check

3. Evaluate each expression.

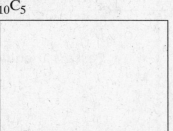

a. ${}_{10}C_5$

b. ${}_{8}C_2$

c. ${}_{25}C_7$

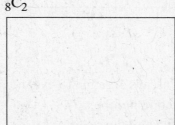

d. Recall Example 3. Of the 12 songs, in how many ways can the disc jockey select seven songs? Twelve songs?

4. Recall Example 4. In how many ways can you select six or fewer toppings?

Name______________________________ Class______________________ Date______________

Lesson 6-8

The Binomial Theorem

Lesson Objectives	NAEP 2005 Strand: Algebra
1 Using Pascal's Triangle	**Topics:** Variables, Expressions, and Operations
2 Using the Binomial Theorem	**Local Standards:** ____________________

Vocabulary and Key Concepts

Binomial Theorem

For every positive integer n, $(a + b)^n =$
$_nC_0a^n + {}_nC_1a^{n-1}b + {}_nC_2a^{n-2}b^2 + \ldots + {}_nC_{n-1}ab^{n-1} + {}_nC_nb^n$

To expand a binomial, ____

____

Pascal's Triangle is ____

____

Example

1 Using Pascal's Triangle Use Pascal's Triangle to expand $(a + b)^5$.

Use the row that has 5 as its second number.

The exponents for a begin with 5 and decrease.

$$1a^5b^0 + 5a^4b^1 + 10a^3b^2 + 10a^2b^3 + 5a^1b^4 + 1a^0b^5$$

The exponents for b begin with 0 and increase.

In its simplest form, the expansion is

☐ + ☐ + ☐ + ☐ + ☐ + ☐.

Pascal's Triangle

1
1 1
1 2 1
1 3 3 1
1 4 6 4 1
1 5 10 10 5 1
1 6 15 20 15 6 1
1 7 21 35 35 21 7 1
1 8 28 56 70 56 28 8 1

Quick Check

1. Use Pascal's Triangle to expand $(a + b)^8$.

Name______________________ Class______________________ Date______________

Example

❷ Using the Binomial Theorem Use the Binomial Theorem to expand $(x - y)^9$.

Write the pattern for raising a binomial to the ninth power.

$(a + b)^9 = \square + \square + \square + \square$
$+ \square + \square + \square + \square$
$+ \square + {}_9C_9b^9$

Substitute x for a and $-y$ for b. Evaluate each combination.

$(x - y)^9 = {}_9C_0x^9 + \square(-y) + {}_9C_2x^7(\square)^{\square} + \square(\square)^{\square}$
$+ \square(\square)^{\square} + \square(\square)^{\square} + \square(\square)^{\square}$
$+ \square(\square)^{\square} + \square(\square)^{\square} + \square(\square)^{\square}$
$= \square^{\square} - 9x^8y + \square - \square + \square$
$- \square + \square - \square + \square - y^9$

The expansion of $(x - y)^9$ is $\square^{\square} - \square + \square - \square$
$+ \square - \square + \square - \square + \square - \square^{\square}$.

Quick Check

2. Use Pascal's Triangle to expand $(x - 2)^4$.

Name________________________ Class________________ Date ____________

Example

3 Probability Dawn Staley makes about 90% of the free throws she attempts. Find the probability that Dawn makes exactly 7 out of 12 consecutive free throws.

Since you want 7 successes (and ☐ failures), use the term p^7q^5. This term has the coefficient $_{\square}C_{\square}$.

Probability (7 out of 12) $= {}_{\square}C_{\square}\, p^{\square} q^{\square}$

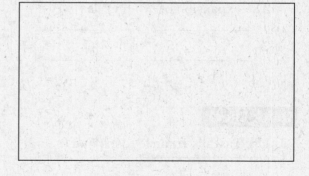

$= \dfrac{\square}{\square \cdot \square} \cdot (\square)^{\square}(0.1)^{\square}$ — **The probability *p* of success = ☐, or ☐.**

$\approx \square$ — **Simplify.**

Dawn Staley has about a ☐% chance of making exactly 7 out of 12 consecutive free throws.

Quick Check

3. Use the Binomial Theorem to expand each binomial.

a. $(v + w)^9$

b. $(c - 2)^5$

4. **a.** Referring to Example 3, find the probability that Dawn Staley will make exactly 9 out of 10 consecutive free-throw attempts.

b. Find the probability that she will make exactly 10 out of 10 attempts.

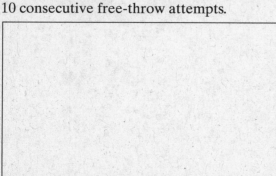

Name________________ Class________________ Date________________

Lesson 7-1

Roots and Radical Expressions

Lesson Objective	**NAEP 2005 Strand:** Number Properties and Operations
1 Simplifying *n*th roots	**Topics:** Number Sense; Properties of Number and Operations
	Local Standards: ________________

Vocabulary and Key Concepts

*n*th Root

For any real numbers a and b, and any positive integer n, if $a^n = b$, then ☐ is an ☐ root of ☐.

*n*th Root of a^n, $a < 0$

For any negative real number a, $\sqrt[n]{a^n} = |\square|$ when n is ☐.

The radicand is ________________

The index indicates ________________

The principal root is ________________

Examples

1 Finding Roots Find each real-number root.

a. $\sqrt[3]{-1000} = \sqrt[3]{(\square)^3}$ **Rewrite −1000 as the third power of a number.**

$= \square$ **Definition of *n*th root: when $n = 3$, there is only ☐ real cube root.**

b. $\sqrt{-81}$

There is ☐ real number whose square is −81.

2 Simplifying Radical Expressions Simplify each radical expression.

a. $\sqrt{9x^{10}} = \sqrt{3^{\square}(x^5)^{\square}} = \sqrt{(3x^5)^{\square}} = \square|\square^{\square}|$

☐ value symbols ensure that the root is positive when x is negative.

b. $\sqrt[3]{a^3b^3} = \sqrt[3]{(\square)^3} = \square$

Absolute value symbols must not be used here. If a or b is negative, then the radicand is ☐ and the root must also be ☐.

Name_______________ Class_______________ Date_______________

3 Applying Cube Roots A cheese manufacturer wants to ship cheese balls that each weigh from 10 to 11 ounces in cartons that will have 3 layers of 3 cheese balls by 4 cheese balls. The weight of a cheese ball is related to its diameter by the formula $w = \frac{d^3}{5}$, where d is the diameter in inches and w is the weight in ounces. What size cartons should be used? Assume whole-inch dimensions.

Find the possible diameters of the cheese balls.

$10 \leq w \leq \square$ **Write an inequality.**

$10 \leq \frac{d^3}{\square} \leq 11$ **Substitute for *w* in terms of *d*.**

$\square \leq d^3 \leq \square$ **Multiply by 5.**

$\sqrt[3]{\square} \leq \sqrt[3]{d^3} \leq \sqrt[3]{\square}$ **Take cube roots. Approximate.**

$\square \leq d \leq \square$ **The diameters range from** ____ **in. to** ____ **in.**

length of a row of 4 of the largest cheese balls = 4 (____ in.) = ____ in.

length of a row of 3 of the largest cheese balls = 3(____ in.) = ____ in.

The manufacturer should order cartons that are ____ in. long by ____ in. wide by ____ in. high to accommodate three dozen of the largest cheese balls.

Quick Check

1. Find each real-number root.

   a. $\sqrt[3]{-27}$

   b. $\sqrt{49}$

2. Simplify each radical expression. Use absolute value symbols when needed.

   a. $\sqrt{4x^2y^4}$

   b. $\sqrt[4]{x^8y^{12}}$

3. The weight of an orange is related to its diameter by the formula $w = \frac{d^3}{4}$, where d is the diameter in inches and w is the weight in ounces. Find the diameter of each orange to the nearest hundredth of an inch.

   a. 3 oz

   b. 5.5 oz

   c. 6.25 oz

Name______________________ Class______________________ Date______________

Lesson 7-2

Multiplying and Dividing Radical Expressions

Lesson Objectives	**NAEP 2005 Strand:** Algebra
1 Multiplying radical expressions	**Topic:** Variables, Expressions, and Operations
2 Dividing radical expressions	**Local Standards:** ____________________

Vocabulary and Key Concepts

Multiplying Radical Expressions

If $\sqrt[n]{a}$ and $\sqrt[n]{b}$ are real numbers, then $\sqrt[n]{a} \cdot \sqrt[n]{b} = \sqrt[n]{\square}$.

Dividing Radical Expressions

If $\sqrt[n]{a}$ and $\sqrt[n]{b}$ are real numbers and $b \neq 0$, then $\dfrac{\sqrt[n]{a}}{\sqrt[n]{b}} = \sqrt[n]{\dfrac{\square}{\square}}$.

To rationalize the denominator of an expression, ______________________________

____

____

Examples

1 Simplifying Radical Expressions Simplify each expression. Assume all variables are positive.

a. $\sqrt{50x^5}$

$\sqrt{50x^5} = \sqrt{\square^2 \cdot 2 \cdot (\square^2)^2 \cdot x}$ **Factor into perfect squares.**

$= \sqrt{\square^2 \cdot (\square^2)^2} \cdot \sqrt{2 \cdot x}$ $\sqrt[n]{a} \cdot \sqrt[n]{b} = \sqrt[n]{\square}$

$= \square$ **Definition of $\square$ root**

b. $\sqrt[3]{54n^8}$

$\sqrt[3]{54n^8} = \sqrt[3]{\square^3 \cdot 2 \cdot (\square^{\square})^3 \cdot n^2}$ **Factor into perfect cubes.**

$= \sqrt[3]{\square^3(\square^{\square})^3} \cdot \sqrt[3]{2n^2}$ $\sqrt[n]{\square} \cdot \sqrt[n]{\square} = \sqrt[n]{ab}$

$= \square$ **Definition of $\square$ root**

❷ **Multiplying Radical Expressions** Multiply and simplify $\sqrt[3]{25xy^8} \cdot \sqrt[3]{5x^4y^3}$. Assume all variables are positive.

$$\sqrt[3]{25xy^8} \cdot \sqrt[3]{5x^4y^3} = \sqrt[3]{\square \cdot \square}$$ **$\sqrt[n]{a} \cdot \sqrt[n]{b} = \sqrt[n]{\square}$**

$$= \sqrt[3]{\square^3 \square^3 \left(\square\square^{\square}\right)^3 \cdot x^2y^2}$$ **Factor into perfect $\square$.**

$$= \sqrt[3]{\square^3 \square^3 \left(\square\square^{\square}\right)^3} \cdot \sqrt[3]{x^2y^2}$$ **$\sqrt[n]{\square} \cdot \sqrt[n]{\square} = \sqrt[n]{ab}$**

$$= \square\square^{\square}\sqrt[3]{\square\square^{\square}\square^{\square}}$$ **Definition of $\square$ root**

❸ **Dividing Radicals** Divide and simplify. Assume all variables are positive.

a. $$\frac{\sqrt[3]{-81}}{\sqrt[3]{3}} = \sqrt[\square]{\left(\frac{-81}{3}\right)} = \sqrt[3]{\square} = \sqrt[3]{\left(\square\right)^3} = \square$$

b. $$\frac{\sqrt[3]{192x^8}}{\sqrt[3]{3x}} = \sqrt[\square]{\left(\frac{192x^8}{3x}\right)} = \sqrt[3]{\square\square^{\square}} = \sqrt[3]{4^{\square}\left(x^{\square}\right)^3} \cdot \square = \square$$

❹ **Rationalizing the Denominator** Rationalize the denominator of $\frac{\sqrt{3}}{\sqrt{5}}$.

Method 1

$$\frac{\sqrt{3}}{\sqrt{5}} = \sqrt{\frac{\square}{\square}} = \sqrt{\frac{3 \cdot \square}{5 \cdot \square}} = \sqrt{\frac{15}{5^{\square}}} = \frac{\square}{\square}$$

Rewrite as a square root of a fraction.
Make the denominator a perfect square.

Method 2

$$\frac{\sqrt{3}}{\sqrt{5}} = \frac{\sqrt{3} \cdot \sqrt{\square}}{\sqrt{5} \cdot \sqrt{\square}} = \frac{\square}{\square}$$

Multiply the numerator and denominator by $\square$ so the denominator becomes a whole number.

❺ **Rationalizing the Denominator** The distance d in meters that an object will fall in t seconds is given by $d = 4.9t^2$. Express t in terms of d and rationalize the denominator.

$$d = 4.9t^2$$

$$t^2 = \frac{d}{\square}$$

$$t = \sqrt{\left(\frac{d}{4.9}\right)} = \sqrt{\left(\frac{d \cdot 10}{\square}\right)} = \frac{\sqrt{\square}}{\square}$$

Name_______________________ Class_______________________ Date _____________

Quick Check

1. Simplify $\sqrt{50x^4}$ and $\sqrt[3]{18x^4}$. Assume that x is positive.

2. Multiply. Simplify if possible. Assume that all variables are positive.

   a. $\sqrt{3} \cdot \sqrt{27}$

   b. $3\sqrt{7x^3} \cdot 2\sqrt{21x^3y^2}$

3. Divide and simplify. Assume that all variables are positive.

   a. $\dfrac{\sqrt{243}}{\sqrt{27}}$

   b. $\dfrac{\sqrt{12x^4}}{\sqrt{3x}}$

4. Rationalize the denominator of each expression. Assume that the variables are positive.

   a. $\sqrt{\dfrac{7}{5}}$

   b. $\dfrac{\sqrt[3]{4}}{\sqrt[3]{6x}}$

5. The formula $a = \frac{d}{t^2}$ relates the acceleration a of a moving object to the distance d it moves in the time t. Solve the formula for t and rationalize the denominator.

Name____________________ Class________________ Date__________

Lesson 7-3

Binomial Radical Expressions

Lesson Objectives	**NAEP 2005 Strand:** Algebra
1 Adding and subtracting radical expressions	**Topic:** Variables, Expressions, and Operations
2 Multiplying and dividing binomial radical expressions	**Local Standards:** ____________

Vocabulary

Like radicals are ____________________________________

____

Examples

1 Adding and Subtracting Radical Expressions Add or subtract if possible.

a. $7\sqrt{xy} + 3\sqrt{xy}$

$7\sqrt{xy} + 3\sqrt{xy} = (\square + \square)\sqrt{xy}$ $\square$ **Property**

$= \square\sqrt{xy}$ **Simplify.**

b. $2\sqrt[3]{x} - 2\sqrt[3]{5}$ **The radicals are not** $\square$ **radicals. They** $\square$ **be combined.**

2 Using Radical Expressions The rectangular window shown at the right is made up of three equilateral triangles and two right triangles. The equilateral triangles have sides 4 feet in length. Find the perimeter of the window to the nearest tenth of a foot.

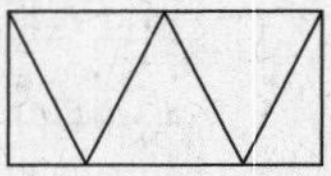

The height of an equilateral triangle with side length 4 ft is $2\sqrt{3}$ ft. So the window's height is $\square$ ft. The length of the window is $\square$ ft. The perimeter is $\square(2\sqrt{3} + 8)$ ft or $\square + \square\sqrt{3}$ ft. To the nearest tenth of a foot, the perimeter is 22.9 ft.

Quick Check

1. Add or subtract if possible.

a. $2\sqrt{7} + 3\sqrt{7}$ **b.** $7\sqrt[4]{5} - 2\sqrt[3]{5}$ **c.** $4\sqrt{xy} + 5\sqrt{xy}$

2. Use the diagram in Example 2. Find the perimeter of the window if the equilateral triangles have sides of length 2.4 feet to the nearest tenth of a foot.

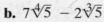

Name____________________ Class____________________ Date ____________

Examples

3 Simplifying Before Adding or Subtracting Simplify $3\sqrt{20} - \sqrt{45} + 4\sqrt{80}$.

$3\sqrt{20} - \sqrt{45} + 4\sqrt{80} = 3\sqrt{\square^2 \cdot 5} - \sqrt{\square^2 \cdot 5} + 4\sqrt{\square^2 \cdot 5}$ **Factor each radicand.**

$= 3 \cdot \square\sqrt{5} - \square\sqrt{5} + 4 \cdot \square\sqrt{5}$ **Simplify each radical.**

$= \square\sqrt{5} - \square\sqrt{5} + \square\sqrt{5}$ **Multiply.**

$= (\square - \square + \square)\sqrt{5}$ **Use the** ______ **Property.**

$= \square$

4 Multiplying Binomial Radical Expressions Multiply $(2 + 4\sqrt{3})(1 - 5\sqrt{3})$.

$(2 + 4\sqrt{3})(1 - 5\sqrt{3}) = 2 \cdot \square - \square \cdot 5\sqrt{3} + \square \cdot 1 - 4\sqrt{3} \cdot \square$ **Use FOIL.**

$= \square + (\square - \square)\sqrt{3} - \square$ **Distributive Property**

$= \square$

Quick Check

3. Simplify $\sqrt{50} + 3\sqrt{32} - 5\sqrt{18}$.

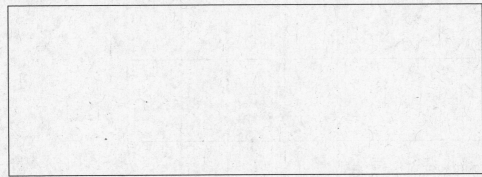

4. Multiply $(\sqrt{2} - \sqrt{3})^2$.

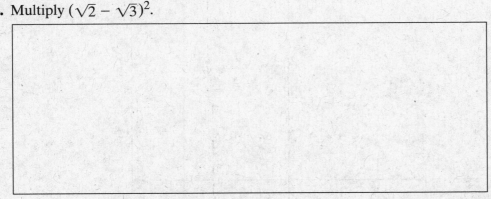

Name______________________ Class______________________ Date ______________

Examples

5 Multiplying Conjugates Multiply $(3 + \sqrt{7})(3 - \sqrt{7})$.

$(3 + \sqrt{7})(3 - \sqrt{7}) = \square^2 - (\square)^2$ **$(a + b)(a - b) = \square^{\square} - \square^{\square}$**

$= \square - \square = \square$

6 Rationalizing Binomial Radical Denominators Rationalize the denominator of $\frac{2 - \sqrt{3}}{4 + \sqrt{3}}$.

$\frac{2 - \sqrt{3}}{4 + \sqrt{3}} = \frac{2 - \sqrt{3}}{4 + \sqrt{3}} \cdot \frac{\square - \sqrt{\square}}{\square - \sqrt{\square}}$ **$\square - \sqrt{\square}$ is the ______________ of $4 + \sqrt{3}$.**

$= \frac{(2 - \sqrt{3})(\square - \sqrt{\square})}{(4 + \sqrt{3})(\square - \sqrt{\square})}$ **Multiply.**

$= \frac{\square - \square\sqrt{3} - \square\sqrt{3} + (\square)^2}{\square^2 - (\square)^2}$ **Simplify.**

$= \frac{\square - \square\sqrt{3}}{\square}$

Quick Check

5. Multiply $(\sqrt{5} + \sqrt{2})(\sqrt{5} - \sqrt{2})$.

6. Rationalize the denominator of $\frac{6 + \sqrt{15}}{4 - \sqrt{15}}$.

Name________________________________ Class________________________ Date______________

Lesson 7-4

Rational Exponents

Lesson Objective	**NAEP 2005 Strand:** Algebra
1 Simplifying expressions with rational exponents	**Topic:** Variables, Expressions, and Operations
	Local Standards: ____________________

Key Concepts

Rational Exponents

If the nth root of a is a real number and m is an integer, then

$a^{\frac{1}{n}} = \sqrt[n]{\square}$ and $a^{\frac{m}{n}} = \sqrt[n]{a^{\square}} = \left(\sqrt[n]{a}\right)^{\square}$ If m is negative, $a \neq 0$.

Properties of Rational Exponents

Let m and n represent rational numbers. Assume that no denominator equals 0.

Property	**Example**
$a^m \cdot a^n = a^{m \square n}$	$8^{\frac{1}{3}} \cdot 8^{\frac{2}{3}} = 8^{\frac{1}{3}+\frac{2}{3}} = 8^1 = 8$
$(a^m)^n = a^{\square}$	$\left(5^{\frac{1}{2}}\right)^4 = 5^{\frac{1}{2} \cdot 4} = 5^2 = 25$
$(ab)^m = a^{\square}b^{\square}$	$(4 \cdot 5)^{\frac{1}{2}} = 4^{\frac{1}{2}} \cdot 5^{\frac{1}{2}} = 2 \cdot 5^{\frac{1}{2}}$
$(a^{-m}) = \frac{1}{a^{\square}}$	$9^{-\frac{1}{2}} = \frac{1}{9^{\frac{1}{2}}} = \frac{1}{3}$
$\frac{a^m}{a^n} = a^{m \square n}$	$\frac{\pi^{\frac{3}{2}}}{\pi^{\frac{1}{2}}} = \pi^{\frac{3}{2} - \frac{1}{2}} = \pi^1 = \pi$
$\left(\frac{a}{b}\right)^m = \frac{a^{\square}}{b^{\square}}$	$\left(\frac{5}{27}\right)^{\frac{1}{3}} = \frac{5^{\frac{1}{3}}}{27^{\frac{1}{3}}} = \frac{5^{\frac{1}{3}}}{3}$

Another way to write a radical expression is ______________________________

Like the radical form, the exponent form ______________________________

A rational exponent may have ______________________________

All of the properties of integer exponents also apply ______________________________

You can simplify a number with a rational exponent ______________________________

____

To write an expression with rational exponents in simplest form, ____________________

____

Name________________________ Class________________________ Date ____________

Examples

1 Simplifying Expressions With Rational Exponents Simplify each expression.

a. $64^{\frac{1}{3}}$

$64^{\frac{1}{3}} = \sqrt[\square]{64}$ **Rewrite as a radical.**

$= \sqrt[3]{4^{\square}}$ **Rewrite 64 as a cube.**

$= \square$ **Definition of □ root.**

b. $7^{\frac{1}{2}} \cdot 7^{\frac{1}{2}}$

$7^{\frac{1}{2}} \cdot 7^{\frac{1}{2}} = \sqrt{\square} \cdot \sqrt{\square}$ **Rewrite as radicals.**

$= \square$ **By definition, $\sqrt{7}$ is the number whose square is □.**

c. $5^{\frac{1}{3}} \cdot 25^{\frac{1}{3}}$

$5^{\frac{1}{3}} \cdot 25^{\frac{1}{3}} = \sqrt[\square]{5} \cdot \sqrt[3]{\square}$ **Rewrite as radicals.**

$= \sqrt[3]{\square \cdot \square}$ **Property for multiplying radical expressions.**

$= \square$ **By definition, $\sqrt[3]{5}$ is the number whose cube is □.**

2 Converting To and From Radical Form

a. Write $x^{\frac{2}{7}}$ and $y^{-0.4}$ in radical form.

$x^{\frac{2}{7}} = \sqrt[\square]{x^2}$ or $(\sqrt[7]{x})^{\square}$

$y^{-0.4} = y^{-\frac{\square}{\square}} = \frac{\square}{\sqrt[\square]{y^2}}$ or $\frac{\square}{(\sqrt[5]{y})^{\square}}$

b. Write the radical expressions $\sqrt[4]{c^3}$ and $(\sqrt[3]{b})^5$ in exponential form.

$\sqrt[4]{c^3} = c^{\frac{\square}{\square}}$ $(\sqrt[3]{b})^5 = b^{\frac{\square}{\square}}$

3 Simplifying Numbers With Rational Exponents Simplify $25^{-2.5}$.

Method 1

$25^{-2.5} = 25^{-\frac{\square}{\square}} = (5^{\square})^{-\frac{5}{2}} = 5^{2\left(-\frac{\square}{\square}\right)}$

$= 5^{-\square} = \frac{1}{5^{\square}} = \frac{\square}{\square}$

Method 2

$25^{-2.5} = 25^{-\frac{\square}{\square}} = \frac{\square}{25^{\frac{5}{2}}} = \frac{1}{(\sqrt{25})^{\square}}$

$= \frac{1}{5^{\square}} = \frac{\square}{\square}$

Name____________________ Class________________ Date__________

4 Writing Expressions in Simplest Form Write $(243a^{-10})^{\frac{2}{5}}$ in simplest form.

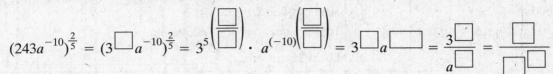

$$(243a^{-10})^{\frac{2}{5}} = (3^{\square}a^{-10})^{\frac{2}{5}} = 3^{5\left(\frac{\square}{\square}\right)} \cdot a^{(-10)\left(\frac{\square}{\square}\right)} = 3^{\square}a^{\square} = \frac{3^{\square}}{a^{\square}} = \frac{\square}{\square^{\square}}$$

Quick Check

1. Simplify each expression.

   a. $16^{\frac{1}{4}}$

   b. $2^{\frac{1}{2}} \cdot 2^{\frac{1}{2}}$

   c. $2^{\frac{1}{2}} \cdot 8^{\frac{1}{2}}$

2. a. Write the expressions $y^{-\frac{3}{8}}$ and $z^{0.4}$ in radical form.

   b. Write the expressions $\sqrt[3]{x^2}$ and $(\sqrt{y})^3$ in exponential form.

   c. **Critical Thinking** Refer to the definition of rational exponents. Explain the need for the following restriction: If m is negative, $a \neq 0$.

3. Simplify each number.

   a. $25^{-\frac{3}{2}}$

   b. $32^{\frac{3}{5}}$

   c. $(-32)^{\frac{4}{5}}$

4. Write $(8x^{15})^{-\frac{1}{3}}$ in simplest form.

Name______________________ Class______________________ Date______________

Lesson 7-5

Solving Square Root and Other Radical Equations

Lesson Objective	NAEP 2005 Strand: Algebra
1 Solving square root and other radical equations	Topic: Equations and Inequalities
	Local Standards: ____________________

Vocabulary

A radical equation is ____

____

Examples

1 Solving Square Root Equations Solve $-10 + \sqrt{2x + 1} = -5$.

$-10 + \sqrt{2x + 1} = -5$

$\sqrt{2x + 1} = \square$ **Isolate the radical.**

$(\sqrt{2x + 1})^{\square} = 5^{\square}$ **Square both sides.**

$2x + 1 = \square$

$2x = \square$

$x = \square$

Check

$-10 + \sqrt{2x + 1} = -5$

$-10 + \sqrt{2(\square) + 1} \stackrel{?}{=} -5$

$-10 + \sqrt{\square} \stackrel{?}{=} -5$

$-10 + \square \stackrel{?}{=} -5$

$-5 \; \square \; -5$ ✓

2 Multiple Choice An artist wants to make a plastic sphere for a sculpture. The plastic weighs 0.8 ounce per cubic inch. The maximum weight in pounds of the sphere and the radius are related by the equation $r = \sqrt[3]{\frac{3w}{3.2\pi}}$. What is the approximate maximum weight for a sphere with a radius of 3 inches?

A. 0.3 lb **B.** 90.5 lb **C.** 30.2 lb **D.** 6.0 lb

$r = \sqrt[3]{\frac{3w}{3.2\pi}}$

$\square = \sqrt[3]{\frac{3w}{3.2\pi}}$ **Substitute** $\square$ **for *r*.**

$27 = \frac{3w}{3.2\pi}$ $\square$ **both sides.**

$\square = w$ **Multiply both sides by** $\square$.

$\square = w$ **Simplify. Round to one decimal place.**

A sphere with a radius of 3 inches has a maximum weight of $\square$.
The correct choice is $\square$.

Name________________________________ Class_________________________ Date ______________

❸ Checking for Extraneous Solutions Solve $\sqrt{x+2} - 3 = 2x$. Check for extraneous solutions.

$\sqrt{x+2} = 2x + \square$ — **Isolate the radical.**

$(\sqrt{x+2})^{\square} = (2x+3)^{\square}$ — **Square both sides.**

$x + 2 = \square x^2 + \square x + \square$ — **Simplify.**

$0 = 4x^2 + \square + \square$ — **Combine like terms.**

$0 = (x+1)(\square + 7)$ — **Factor.**

$x + 1 = 0$ or $\square + \square = 0$ — $\square$ **Property**

$x = \square$ or $x = \square$

Check $\sqrt{\square + 2} - 3 \stackrel{?}{=} 2(\square)$

$\sqrt{\square} - 3 \stackrel{?}{=} -\square$

$-2 \ \square \ -2$ ✓

$\sqrt{(\square) + 2} - 3 \stackrel{?}{=} 2(\square)$

$\sqrt{\frac{\square}{\square}} - 3 \stackrel{?}{=} -\frac{\square}{\square}$

$-\frac{\square}{\square} \ \square \ -\frac{7}{2}$

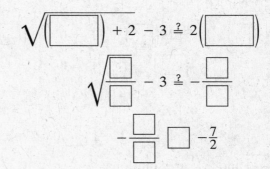

The only solution is $\square$.

Quick Check

1. Solve $\sqrt{5x+1} - 6 = 0$.

2. Using the information in Example 2, find the maximum weight the sphere can have if the radius of the sculpture is to be 2 in.

Name________________ Class________________ Date ________

Example

❹ Solving Equations With Two Rational Exponents

Solve $(x+1)^{\frac{2}{3}} - (9x+1)^{\frac{1}{3}} = 0$. Check for extraneous solutions.

$$(x+1)^{\frac{2}{3}} = (9x+1)^{\frac{1}{3}}$$

$$\left((x+1)^{\frac{2}{3}}\right)^{\square} = \left((9x+1)^{\frac{1}{3}}\right)^{\square}$$

$$(x+1)^{\square} = 9x+1$$

$$x^2 + \square x + \square = 9x+1$$

$$x^2 - \square = 0$$

$$x(\square) = 0$$

$$x = \square \text{ or } x = \square$$

Check

$$(\square + 1)^{\frac{2}{3}} - (9(\square) + 1)^{\frac{1}{3}} \stackrel{?}{=} 0 \qquad (\square + 1)^{\frac{2}{3}} - (9(\square) + 1)^{\frac{1}{3}} \stackrel{?}{=} 0$$

$$(\square)^{\frac{2}{3}} - (\square)^{\frac{1}{3}} \stackrel{?}{=} 0 \qquad (\square)^{\frac{2}{3}} - (\square)^{\frac{1}{3}} \stackrel{?}{=} 0$$

$$(1)^{\frac{2}{3}} - (1)^{\frac{1}{3}} \stackrel{?}{=} 0 \qquad (8)^{\frac{2}{3}} - (8^{\square})^{\frac{1}{3}} \stackrel{?}{=} 0$$

$$1 - 1 \square 0 \checkmark \qquad 8^{\frac{2}{3}} - 8^{\square} = 0 \checkmark$$

Both $\square$ and $\square$ are solutions.

Quick Check

3. Solve $\sqrt{5x-1} + 3 = x$. Check for extraneous solutions.

4. Solve $\sqrt{3x+2} - \sqrt{2x+7} = 0$. Check for extraneous solutions.

Name______________________ Class______________________ Date______________

Lesson 7-6

Function Operations

Lesson Objectives	NAEP 2005 Strand: Algebra
1 Adding, subtracting, multiplying, and dividing functions **2** Finding the composite of two functions	**Topics:** Variables, Expressions, and Operations; Patterns, Relations, and Functions **Local Standards:** ____________________

Key Concepts

Function Operations

Addition $(f + g)(x) = f(x) \square g(x)$

Multiplication $(f \cdot g)(x) = f(x) \square g(x)$

Subtraction $(f - g)(x) = f(x) \square g(x)$

Division $\left(\frac{f}{g}\right)(x) = \frac{\square(x)}{\square(x)}, g(x) \neq 0$

Composition of Functions

The composition of function g with function f is written as $g \circ f$ and is defined as $(g \circ f)(x) = g(f(x))$, where the domain of $g \circ f$ consists of the values a in the domain such that $f(a)$ is in the domain of g.

$(g \circ f)(x) = g(f(x))$ ① Evaluate the ____________ function $f(x)$ first.

② Then use your answer as the ____________ of the outer function $g(x)$.

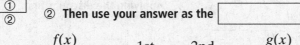

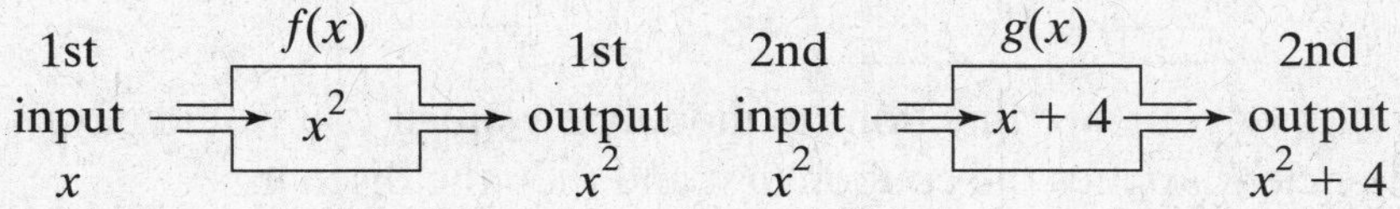

Examples

1 Adding and Subtracting Functions Let $f(x) = -2x + 6$ and $g(x) = 5x - 7$. Find $f + g$ and $f - g$ and their domains.

$(f + g)(x) = f(x) \square g(x) = (-2x + 6) \square (5x - 7) = \square - \square$

$(f - g)(x) = f(x) \square g(x) = (-2x + 6) \square (5x - 7) = \square + \square$

The domains of $f + g$ and $f - g$ are the set of ____________ numbers.

Name______________________________ Class______________________ Date ______________

❷ Multiplying and Dividing Functions Let $f(x) = x^2 + 1$ and $g(x) = x^4 - 1$. Find $f \cdot g$ and $\frac{f}{g}$ and their domains.

$(f \cdot g)(x) = f(x)\square g(x) = (x^2 + 1)(x^4 - 1) = \square + \square - \square - \square$

$\left(\frac{f}{g}\right)(x) = \frac{\square(x)}{\square(x)} = \frac{x^2+1}{x^4-1} = \frac{x^2+1}{(x^2\square 1)(x^2\square 1)} = \frac{\square}{\square}$

The domains of f and g are the set of real numbers, so the domain of $f \cdot g$ is also the set of $\square$ numbers. The domain of $\frac{f}{g}$ does not include 1 and -1 because $g(1)$ and $g(-1) = \square$.

❸ Using Composite Functions A store offers a 20% discount on all items. You have a coupon worth \$3.

a. Use functions to model discounting an item by 20% and to model applying the coupon.

Let $\boxed{x}$ = the original price.

$f(x) = x - 0.2x = \square$ **Cost with 20% discount.**

$g(x) = x - 3$ **Cost with a coupon for \$3.**

b. Use a composition of your two functions to model how much you would pay for an item if the clerk applies the discount first and then the coupon.

$(g \circ \square)(x) = g(f(x))$ **Applying the discount first.**

$= g(\square) = \square - 3$

c. Use a composition of your two functions to model how much you would pay for an item if the clerk applies the coupon first and then the discount.

$(\square \circ g)(x) = f(g(x))$ **Applying the coupon first.**

$= f(x - \square) = \square(x - \square) = 0.8x - \square$

d. How much more is any item if the clerk applies the coupon first?

$(f \circ g)(x) - (g \circ f)(x) = (\square x - \square) - (\square x - 3) = \square$

Any item would cost \$$\square$ more.

Name______________________ Class______________________ Date ______________

Quick Check

1. Let $f(x) = 5x^2 - 4x$ and $g(x) = 5x + 1$. Find $f + g$ and $f - g$ and their domains.

2. Let $f(x) = 6x^2 + 7x - 5$ and $g(x) = 2x - 1$. Find $f \cdot g$ and $\frac{f}{g}$ and their domains.

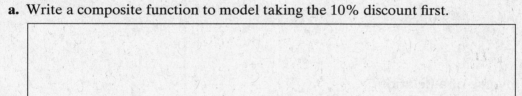

3. A store is offering a 10% discount on all items. In addition, employees get a 25% discount.

   a. Write a composite function to model taking the 10% discount first.

   b. Write a composite function to model taking the 25% discount first.

   c. Suppose you are an employee buying an item from the store. Which discount would you prefer to take first?

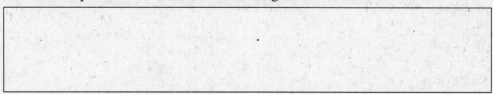

Name________________________________ Class____________________ Date______________

Lesson 7-7

Inverse Relations and Functions

Lesson Objective	**NAEP 2005 Strand:** Algebra
1 Finding the inverse of a relation or a function	**Topic:** Patterns, Relations, and Functions
	Local Standards: ____________________

Vocabulary and Key Concepts

Composition of Inverse Functions

If f and f^{-1} are inverse functions, then $(f^{-1} \circ f)(x) = \square$ and $(f \circ f^{-1})(x) = \square$.

If a relation maps element a of its domain to element b of its range, the inverse relation ____________

____

____

Relation r

Domain Range

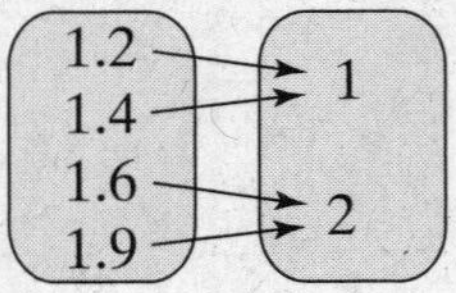

Inverse of r

Domain Range

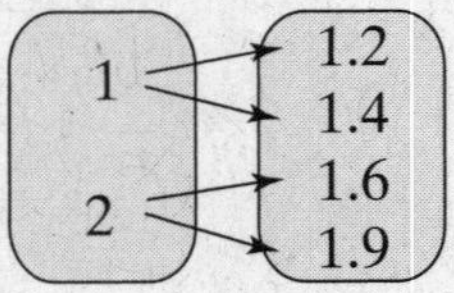

Domain of f Range of f

Range of f^{-1} Domain of f^{-1}

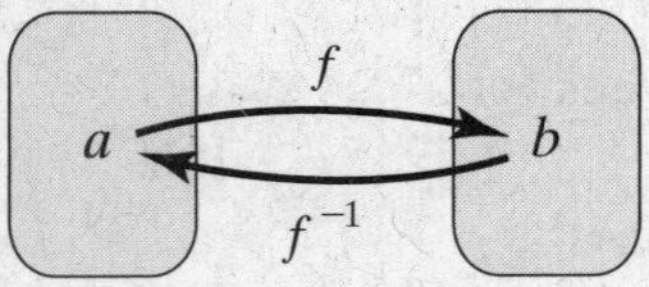

The inverse of function f is denoted by ____________.

If a function f pairs a with b, then f^{-1} must ____________

____

Examples

1 Finding the Inverse of a Relation

a. Find the inverse of relation m.

Relation m

x	−1	0	1	2
y	−2	−1	−1	−2

Inverse of Relation m

x		−1		−2
y	−1		1	

Interchange the x and y columns.

b. Graph m and its inverse on the same graph. Reverse the ordered pairs of relation m to graph the inverse of m.

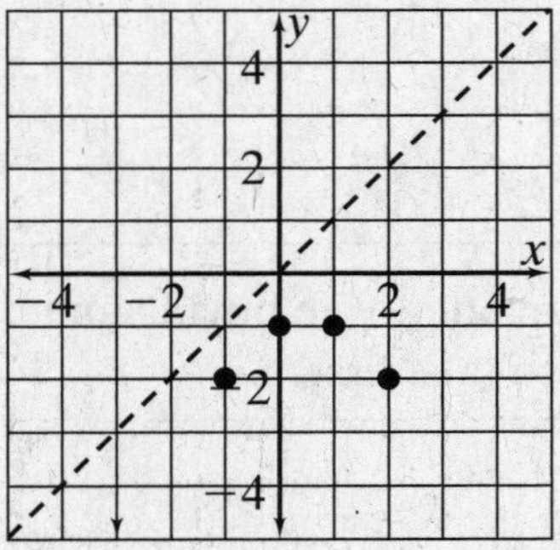

Name______________________ Class______________________ Date ______________

❷ Interchanging *x* and *y* Find the inverse of $y = x^2 - 2$.

$x = y^2 - 2$ **Interchange *x* and *y*.**

$x + \square = y^2$ **Add $\square$ to each side.**

$\pm\sqrt{x + \square} = \square$ **Find the square root of each side.**

❸ Finding an Inverse Function Consider the function $f(x) = \sqrt{2x + 2}$.

a. Find the domain and range of f.

Since the radicand cannot be negative, the domain is the set of numbers greater than or equal to $\square$. Since the principal square root is nonnegative, the range is the set of $\square$ numbers.

b. Find f^{-1}.

$\square = \sqrt{2x + 2}$ **Rewrite the equation using *y*.**

$\square = \sqrt{2\square + 2}$ **Interchange *x* and *y*.**

$\square^{\square} = 2\square + 2$ **Square both sides.**

$y = \dfrac{\square}{\square}$ **Solve for *y*.**

So, $f^{-1}(x) = \dfrac{\square}{\square}$.

c. Find the domain and range of f^{-1}.

The domain of f^{-1} equals the $\square$ of f, which is the set of $\square$ numbers.

Since $x^2 \geq 0$, $\dfrac{x^2 - 2}{2} \geq -1$. The range of f^{-1} is the set of numbers greater than or equal to $\square$.

The range of f^{-1} is the same as the $\square$ of f.

d. Is f^{-1} a function? Explain.

For each x in the domain of f^{-1}, there is only $\square$ value of $f^{-1}(x)$.

So f^{-1} $\square$ a function.

Quick Check

1. a. Describe how the line $y = x$ is related to the graphs of m and its inverse in Example 1.

$\square$

b. Is relation m a function? Is the inverse of m a function?

$\square$

Name________________ Class________________ Date ________________

Example

4 Composition of Inverse Functions For the function $f(x) = \frac{1}{2}x + 5$, find $(f^{-1} \circ f)(652)$ and $(f \circ f^{-1})(-\sqrt{86})$.

Since f is a linear function with nonzero slope, f^{-1} is also a linear function. Therefore f^{-1} is a function. So $(f^{-1} \circ f)(652) =$ ☐ and $(f \circ f^{-1})(-\sqrt{86}) =$ ☐.

Quick Check

2. a. Does $y = x^2 + 3$ define a function? Is its inverse a function? Explain.

b. Find the inverse of $y = 10 - 3x$. Is the inverse a function? Explain.

3. Let $f(x) = 10 - 3x$. Find each of the following.

a. the domain and range of f

b. f^{-1}

c. the domain and range of f^{-1}

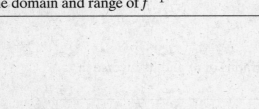

d. $f^{-1}(f(3))$

4. For $f(x) = 5x + 11$, find $(f^{-1} \circ f)(777)$ and $(f \circ f^{-1})(-5802)$.

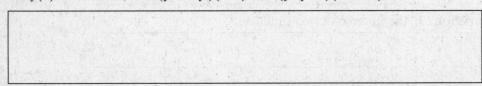

Name________________ Class________________ Date________________

Lesson 7-8

Graphing Square Root and Other Radical Functions

Lesson Objective	NAEP 2005 Strand: Algebra
1 Graphing square root and other radical functions	Topic: Algebraic representation
	Local Standards: ____________

Vocabulary

A radical function is ______________________________

Examples

1 Translating Square Root Functions Vertically Graph $y = \sqrt{x} + 5$ and $y = \sqrt{x} - 7$.

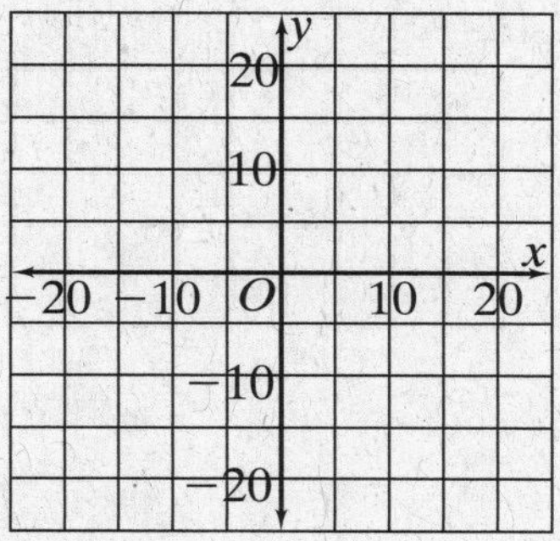

The graph of $y = \sqrt{x} + 5$ is the graph of $y =$ ☐ shifted ☐ ☐ units.

The graph $y = \sqrt{x} - 7$ is the graph of $y =$ ☐ shifted ☐ ☐ units.

The domains of both functions are the set of ☐ numbers, but their ☐ differ.

2 Translating Square Root Functions Horizontally Graph $y = \sqrt{x + 7}$ and $y = \sqrt{x - 5}$.

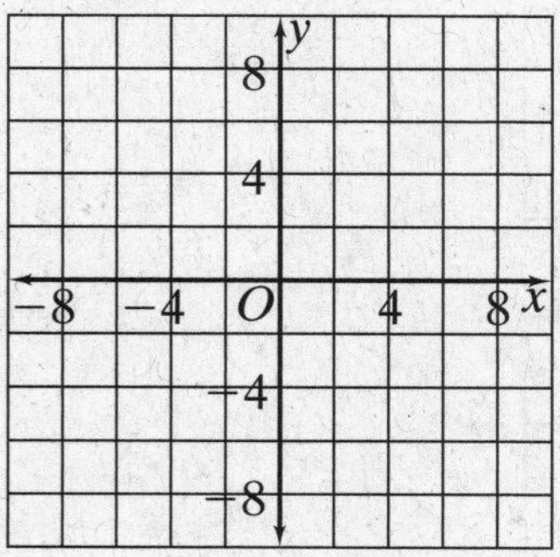

The graph of $y = \sqrt{x + 7}$ is the graph of $y =$ ☐ shifted ☐ ☐ units.

The graph $y = \sqrt{x - 5}$ is the graph of $y =$ ☐ shifted ☐ ☐ units.

The ranges of both functions are the set of ☐ numbers, but their ☐ differ.

Name________________________ Class________________________ Date ______________

❸ Graphing Square Root Functions Graph $y = -3\sqrt{x - 2} + 4$.

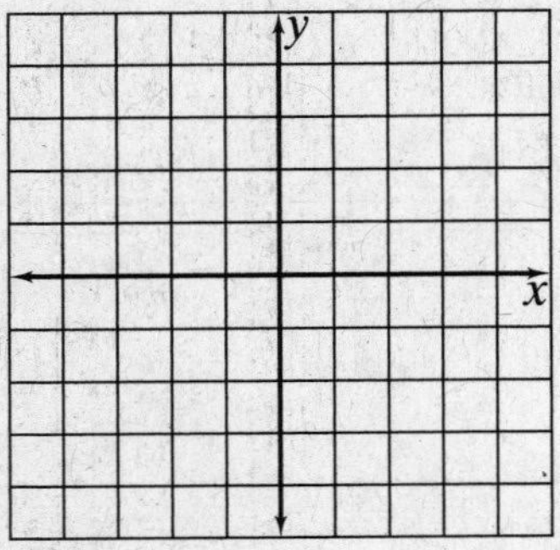

The graph of $y = -3\sqrt{x}$ is a stretch of $y = \sqrt{x}$ by a factor of ______ and a reflection across the ______. Then translate right ______ and up ______.

❹ Graphing Cube Root Functions Graph $y = 2\sqrt[3]{x + 2} - 2$.

The graph of $y = 2\sqrt[3]{x + 2} - 2$ is the graph of $y =$ ______ translated 2 units ______ and 2 units ______.

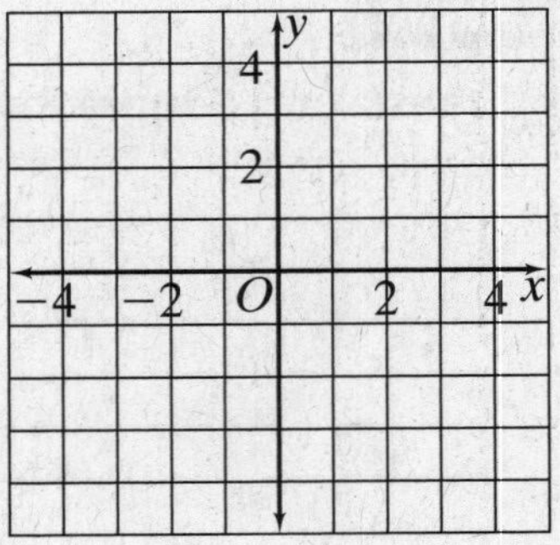

Quick Check

1. Graph $y = \sqrt{x} - 3$ and $y = \sqrt{x} + 3$.

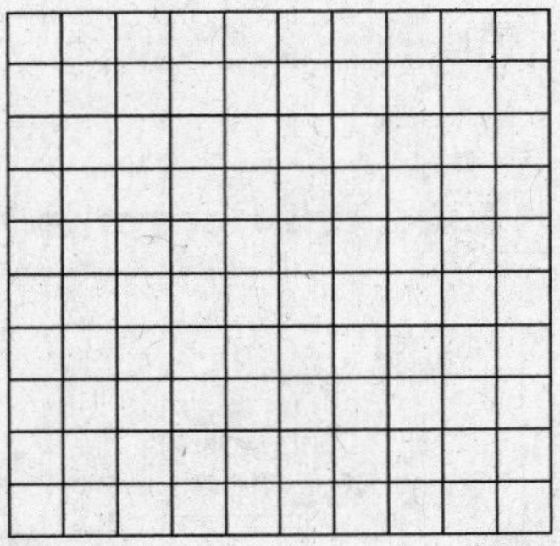

2. Graph $y = \sqrt{x - 1}$ and $y = \sqrt{x + 4}$.

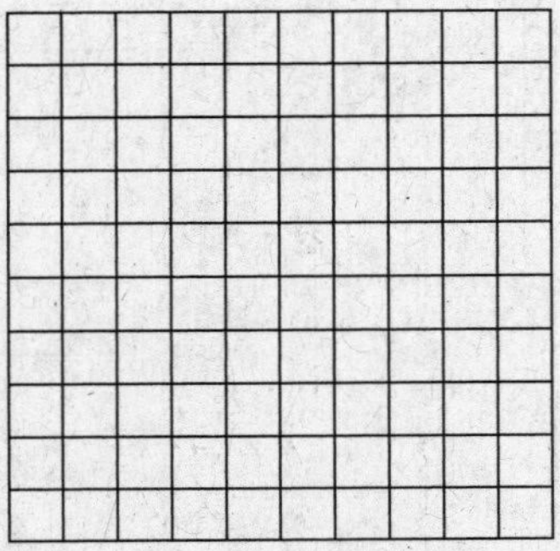

Name______________________ Class______________________ Date ______________

Quick Check

3. Graph $y = \frac{1}{4}\sqrt{x - 2} - 4$.

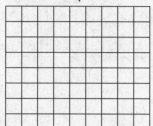

4. Graph $y = 3 - \sqrt[3]{x + 1}$.

Examples

5 Solving Square Root Equations by Graphing

You can model the speed s, in miles per hour, a car is traveling when it begins to skid by $s = \sqrt{30fnd}$, where f is the drag factor, n is the breaking efficiency, and d is the length of the skid mark in feet. What is the length of the skid mark of a car that travels 30 miles per hour on a road with a drag factor of 0.75 and a breaking efficiency of 1?

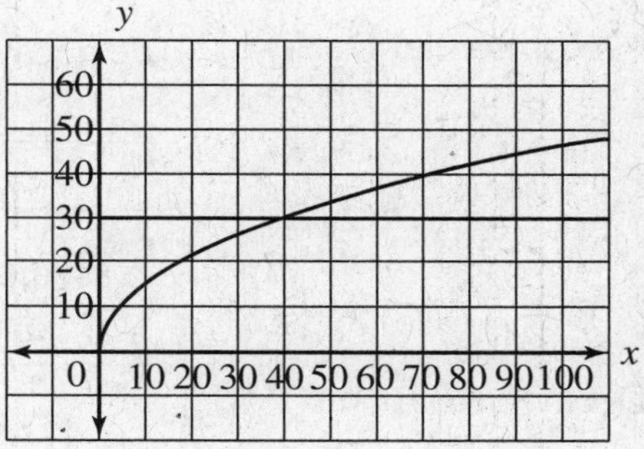

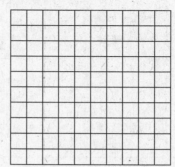

Graph $Y_1 =$ ______ and $Y_2 =$ ______.

Adjust the window to find where the graphs intersect.
Use the Intersect feature to find the x-coordinate of the intersection.

The length of the skid mark is ______ feet.

6 Transforming Radical Equations

Rewrite $y = \sqrt{9x + 18}$ to make it easy to graph using a translation. Describe the graph.

$y = \sqrt{9x + 18} = \sqrt{9(x + \square)} = \square\sqrt{x + \square}$

The graph of $y = \sqrt{9x + 18}$ is the graph of $y =$ ______ translated 2 units ______.

Quick Check

5. Refer to Example 5. What is the length of the skid mark of a car that travels 45 miles per hour?

Name________________________ Class________________________ Date____________

Lesson 8-1

Exploring Exponential Models

Lesson Objectives	NAEP 2005 Strand: Algebra
1 Modeling exponential growth	**Topic:** Algebraic Representation
2 Modeling exponential decay.	**Local Standards:** ____________________

Vocabulary

An exponential function is ____

____

The growth factor is ____________________________

____

____

Exponential Growth

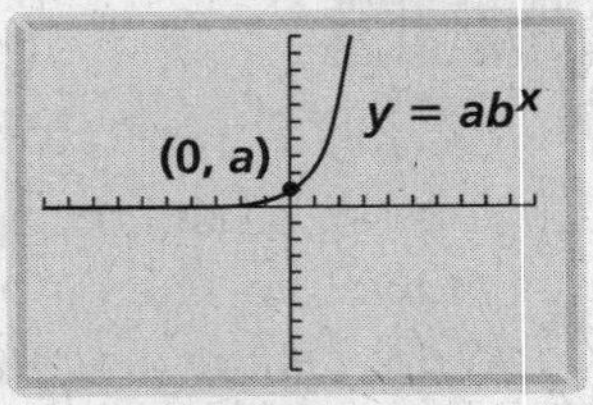

Growth factor $b > 1$

Exponential Decay

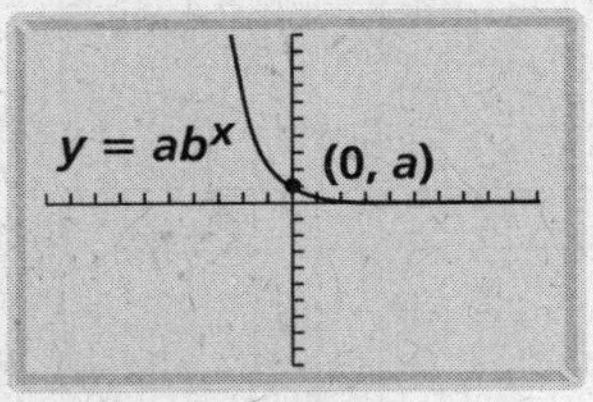

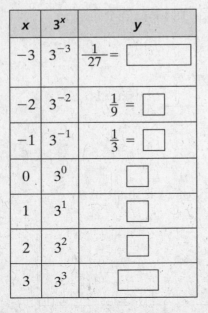

Decay factor $0 < b < 1$

The decay factor is ____________________

____

____

An asymptote is ____________________________

____

Examples

1 Graphing Exponential Growth Graph $y = 3^x$.

Step 1 Make a table of values.

x	3^x	y
-3	3^{-3}	$\frac{1}{27} =$ ☐
-2	3^{-2}	$\frac{1}{9} =$ ☐
-1	3^{-1}	$\frac{1}{3} =$ ☐
0	3^0	☐
1	3^1	☐
2	3^2	☐
3	3^3	☐

Step 2 Graph the coordinates.
Connect the points with a smooth curve.

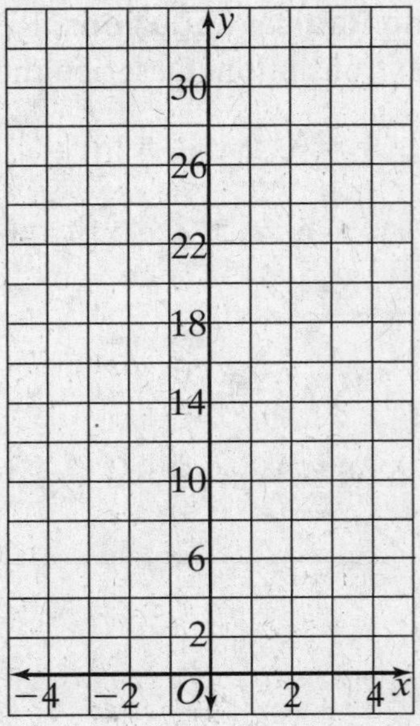

Name______________________ Class______________________ Date ______________

❷ **Writing an Exponential Function** Write an exponential function $y = ab^x$ for a graph that includes (1, 6) and (0, 2).

$y = ab^x$ — **Use the general term.**

$\square = ab^{\square}$ — **Substitute for *x* and *y* using (1, 6).**

$\frac{\square}{b} = a$ — **Solve for *a*.**

$\square = \frac{\square}{b} b^{\square}$ — **Substitute for *x* and *y* using (0, 2) and for *a* using $\frac{\square}{b}$.**

$\square = \frac{\square}{b} \cdot \square$ — **Any nonzero number to the zero power equals $\square$.**

$b = \square$ — **Solve for *b*.**

$a = \frac{6}{b} = \frac{6}{\square} = \square$ — **Use your equation for *a*, substitute 3 for *b*, and simplify.**

$y = \square \cdot \square^x$ — **Substitute $\square$ for *a* and $\square$ for *b* in $y = ab^x$.**

The exponential function for a graph that includes (1, 6) an (0, 2) is

$y = \square$.

Quick Check

1. Graph the function $y = 4(2)^x$.

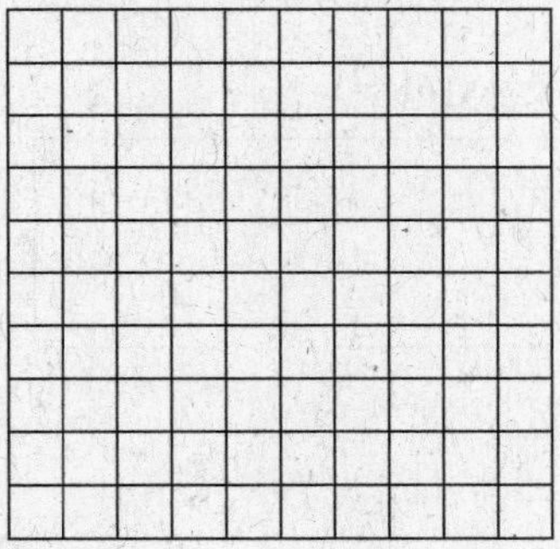

2. Write an exponential function $y = ab^x$ for a graph that includes (2, 4) and (3, 16).

Name______________________________ Class______________________ Date ____________

Example

3 Graphing Exponential Decay Graph $y = 36(0.5)^x$. Identify the horizontal asymptote.

Step 1 Make a table of values.

x	y
−3	
−2	
−1	
0	
1	
2	
3	

Step 2 Graph the coordinates. Connect the points with a smooth curve.

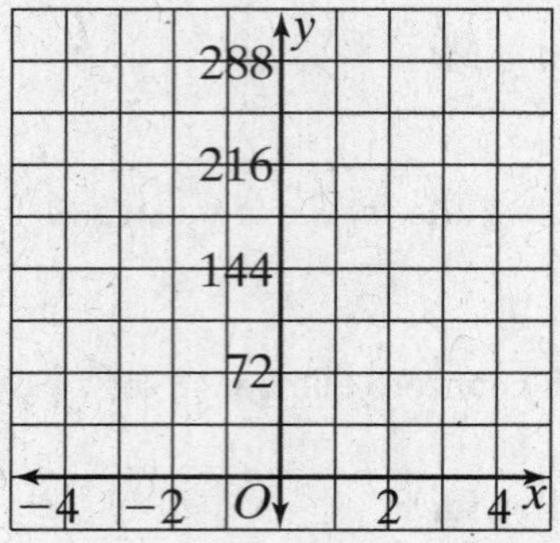

As x increases, y approaches ☐.

The horizontal asymptote is the ☐-axis, $y =$ ☐.

Quick Check

3. Without graphing, determine whether each function represents exponential growth or exponential decay.

a. $y = 100(0.12)^x$

b. $y = 0.2(5)^x$

c. $y = 16\left(\frac{1}{2}\right)^x$

Graph each decay function. Identify the horizontal asymptote.

d. $y = 24\left(\frac{1}{3}\right)^x$

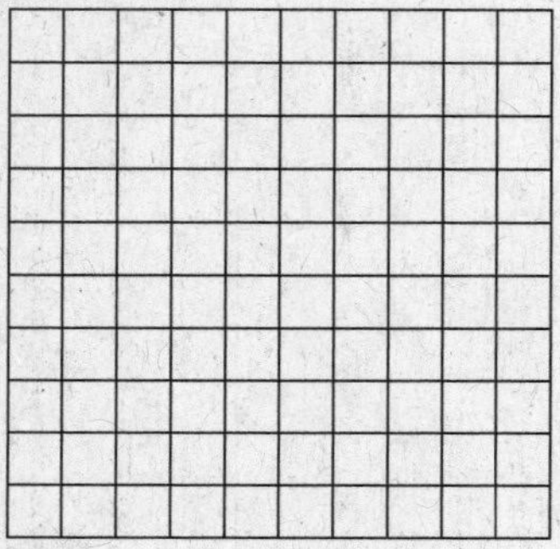

e. $y = 100(0.1)^x$

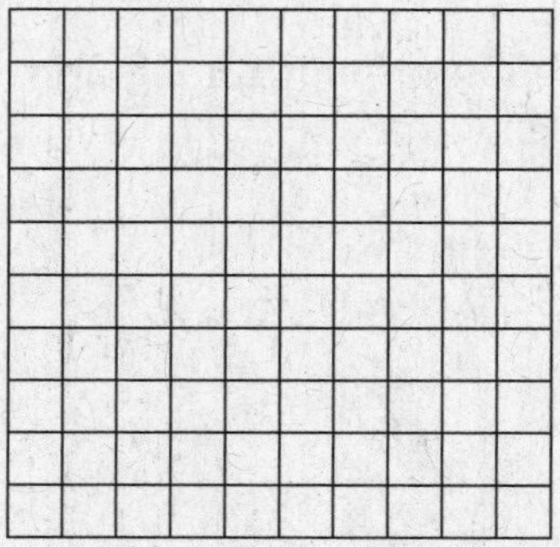

Name______________________ Class______________________ Date______________

Lesson 8-2

Properties of Exponential Functions

Lesson Objectives	**NAEP 2005 Strand:** Algebra
1 Identifying the role of constants in $y = ab^{cx}$	**Topic:** Patterns, Relations, and Functions
2 Using e as a base	**Local Standards:** ______________

Key Concepts

Continuously Compounded Interest Formula

amount in account → A

annual rate of interest → r

$$A = Pe^{rt}$$

t ← ______________________

P ← ______________

Example

1 Translating $y = ab^x$ Graph $y = 6\left(\frac{1}{2}\right)^x$ and $y = 6\left(\frac{1}{2}\right)^{x-3} - 2$.

Step 1 Graph $y = 6\left(\frac{1}{2}\right)^x$. The horizontal asymptote is $y =$ ____.

Step 2 For $y = 6\left(\frac{1}{2}\right)^{x-3} - 2$, $h = 3$ and $k = -2$. So shift the graph of the parent function ____ units right and 2 units __________. The horizontal asymptote is $y =$ ______.

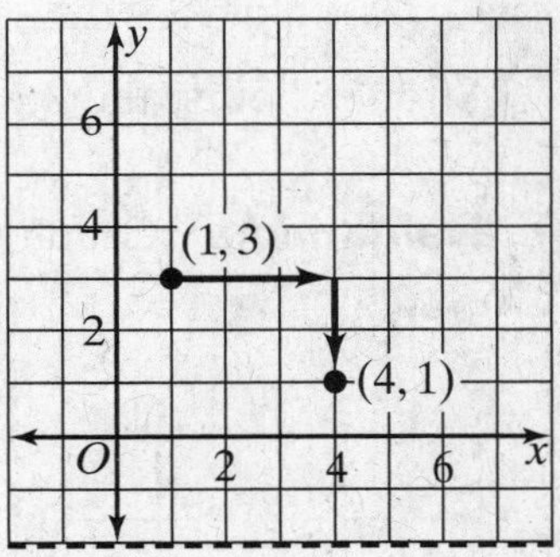

Quick Check

1. Graph each function as a translation of $y = 9(3)^x$.

a. $y = 9(3)^{x+1}$

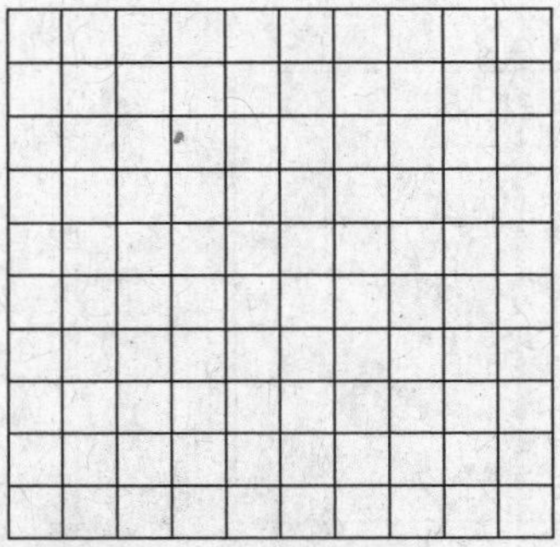

b. $y = 9(3)^x - 4$

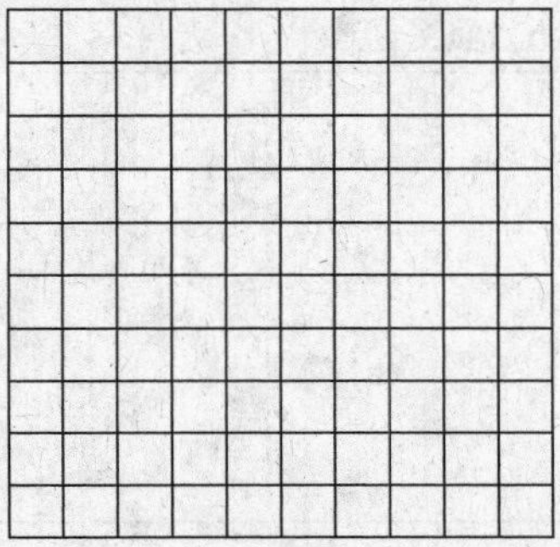

c. $y = 9(3)^{x-3} - 1$

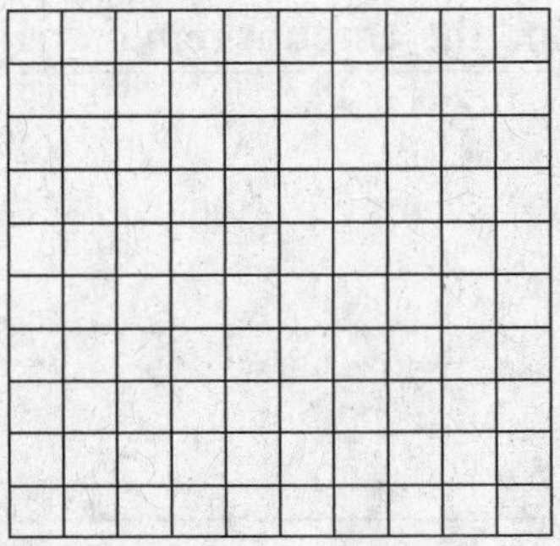

Name____________________________ Class____________________ Date ____________

Examples

2 Medicine Technetium-99*m* has a half-life of 6 hours. Find the amount of technetium-99*m* that remains from a 50-mg supply after 25 hours.

Relate The amount of technetium-99*m* is an exponential function of the number of half-lives. The initial amount is 50 mg. The decay factor is $\frac{1}{2}$. One half-life equals $\square$.

Define Let $\boxed{y}$ = the amount of technetium-99*m*. Let x = the number of hours elapsed. Then $\square$ = the number of half-lives.

Write $\boxed{y} = 50\left(\frac{1}{2}\right)^{\square}$

$y = 50\left(\frac{1}{2}\right)^{\square \cdot \square}$ **Substitute** $\square$ **for *x*.**

$= 50\left(\frac{1}{2}\right)^{\square}$ **Simplify.**

$\approx \square$

After 25 hours, about $\square$ mg of technetium-99*m* remain.

3 Evaluating e^x Graph $y = e^x$. Evaluate e^3 to four decimal places.

Step 1

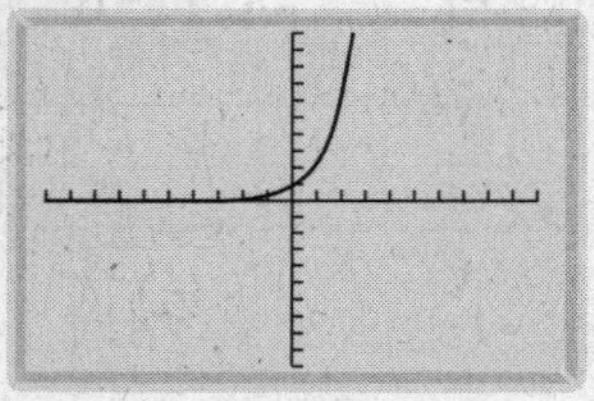

Step 2

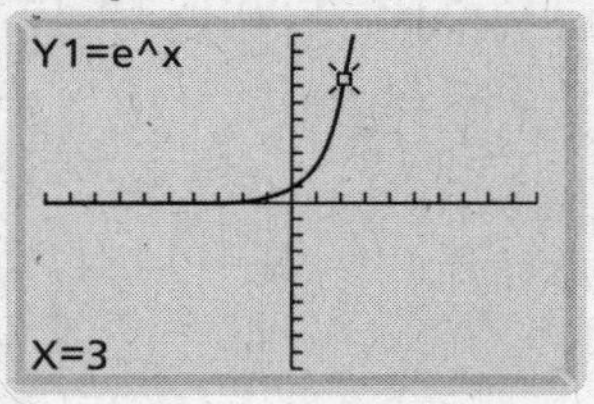

The value of e^3 is about $\square$.

Quick Check

2. Arsenic-74 is used to locate brain tumors. It has a half-life of 17.5 days. Write an exponential decay function for a 90-mg sample. Use the function to find the amount remaining after 6 days.

Name______________________ Class______________________ Date______________

Example

4 Investments Suppose you invest $100 at an annual interest rate of 4.8% compounded continuously. How much will you have in the account after 3 years?

$A = Pe^{rt}$

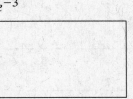

$= 100 \cdot e^{\square \square}$ **Substitute 100 for *P*, ☐ for *r* and ☐ for *t*.**

$= 100 \cdot e^{\square}$ **Simplify.**

$\approx 100 \cdot (\square)$ **Evaluate $e^{\square}$.**

$\approx \square$ **Simplify.**

You will have $☐ in the account after three years.

Quick Check

3. Use the graph of $y = e^x$ to evaluate each expression to four decimal places.

a. e^4 **b.** e^{-3} **c.** $e^{\frac{1}{2}}$

4. Suppose you invest $1300 at an annual interest rate of 4.3% compounded continuously. Find the amount you will have in the account after three years.

Name____________________ Class____________________ Date________________

Lesson 8-3

Logarithmic Functions as Inverses

Lesson Objectives	NAEP 2005 Strand: Algebra
1 Writing and evaluating logarithmic expressions 2 Graphing logarithmic functions	**Topics:** Algebraic Representations; Algebraic Variables, Expressions, and Operations **Local Standards:** ________________

Vocabulary and Key Concepts

Logarithm

The logarithm to the base b of a positive number y is defined as follows:

If $y = b^x$, then $\log_b \square = \square$.

Translations of Logarithmic Functions

Characteristic	$y = \log_b x$	$y = \log_b (x - h) + k$
Asymptote	$x = \square$	$x - h = \square$, or $x = \square$
Domain	$x > \square$	$x > \square$
Range		

A common logarithm is ____________________________

A logarithmic function is ____________________________

Examples

1. **Writing in Logarithmic Form** Write $32 = 2^5$ in logarithmic form.

If $y = b^x$, then $\log_b \square = \square$. **Write the definition.**

If $32 = 2^5$, then $\log_2 \square = \square$. **Substitute.**

The logarithmic form of $32 = 2^5$ is $\log_2 \square = \square$.

Name______________________ Class______________________ Date______________

❷ Seismology Compare the amount of energy released in an earthquake that registers 6 on the Richter scale with one that registers 3.

The Richter Scale

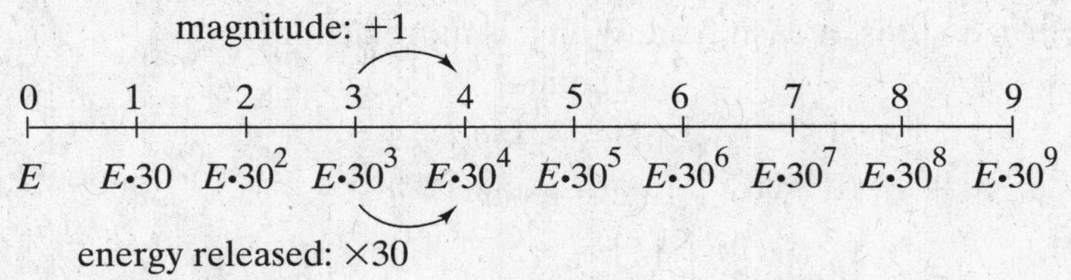

$\frac{E \cdot 30^6}{E \cdot 30^3} = \frac{30^6}{30^3}$ **Write a ratio and simplify.**

$= 30^{\square - \square} = 30^{\square}$ $\square$ **Property of Exponents.**

$= \square$ **Use a calculator.**

The first earthquake released about $\square$ times as much energy as the second.

❸ Evaluating Logarithms Evaluate $\log_3 81$.

$\log_3 81 = x$ **Write in logarithmic form.**

$81 = 3^x$ **Convert to exponential form.**

$3^{\square} = 3^x$ **Write each side using base 3.**

$\square = x$ **Set the exponents equal to each other.**

Quick Check

1. Write each equation in logarithmic form.

a. $729 = 3^6$ **b.** $\left(\frac{1}{2}\right)^3 = \frac{1}{8}$ **c.** $10^0 = 1$

2. In 1997, an earthquake in Alabama registered 4.9 on the Richter scale. In 1999, one in California registered 7.0. Compare the energy released in the two quakes.

3. Evaluate each logarithm.

a. $\log_{64} \frac{1}{32}$ **b.** $\log_9 27$ **c.** $\log_{10} 100$

Name______________________________ Class____________________ Date ____________

Examples

4 Chemistry The pH of an apple is about 3.3 and that of a banana is about 5.2. The pH of a substance equals $-\log[H^+]$, where $[H^+]$ is the concentration of hydrogen ions. Find the concentration of hydrogen ions in each fruit. Which is more acidic?

Apple

$$\text{pH} = -\log[H^+]$$
$$3.3 = -\log[H^+]$$
$$\log[H^+] = -3.3$$
$$[H^+] = 10^{-3.3}$$
$$\approx \square$$

Banana

$$\text{pH} = -\log[H^+]$$
$$5.2 = -\log[H^+]$$
$$\log[H^+] = -5.2$$
$$[H^+] = 10^{-5.2}$$
$$\approx \square$$

The apple has a higher concentration of hydrogen ions, so it is ☐ acidic.

5 Translating $y = \log_b x$ Graph $y = \log_5 (x - 1) + 2$.

Step 1 Make a table of values for the parent function.

x	$y = \log_5 x$
$\frac{1}{125}$	-3
$\frac{1}{25}$	☐
$\frac{1}{5}$	-1
1	☐
5	1

Step 2 Graph the function by shifting the points from the table to the right ☐ unit and up ☐ units.

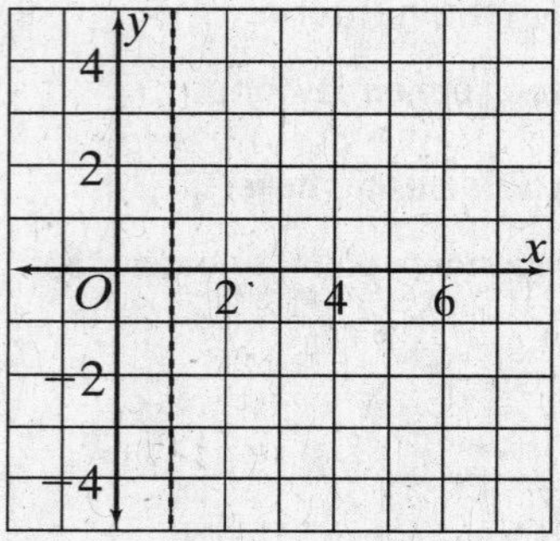

Quick Check

4. Refer to Example 4. Find the concentration of hydrogen ions in seawater of pH 8.5.

☐

5. a. Graph $y = \log_3 x$.

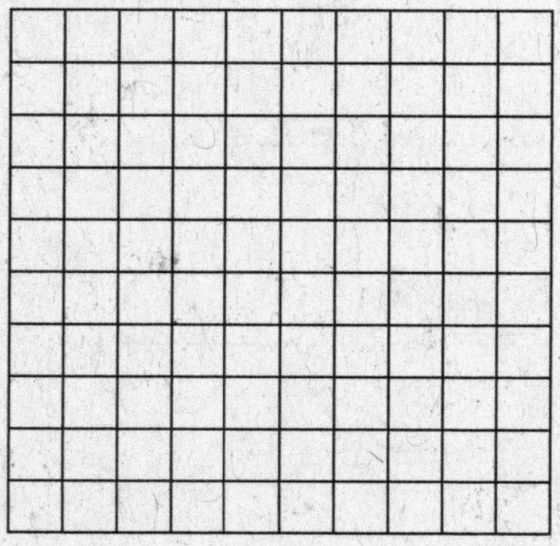

b. Graph $y = \log_3 (x + 3)$.

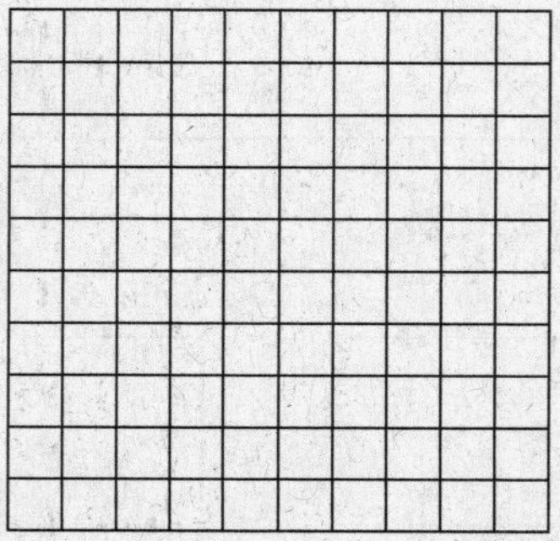

Name______________________________ Class____________________ Date______________

Lesson 8-4

Properties of Logarithms

Lesson Objective	**NAEP 2005 Strand:** Algebra
1 Using the properties of logarithms	**Topic:** Algebraic Representations
	Local Standards: ____________________

Key Concepts

Properties of Logarithms

For any positive numbers, M, N, and b, $b \neq 1$,

$\log_b MN = \log_b M + \log_b N$ ☐ Property

$\log_b \frac{M}{N} = \log_b M - \log_b N$ ☐ Property

$\log_b M^x = x \log_b M$ ☐ Property

Examples

1 Identifying the Properties of Logarithms State the property or properties used to rewrite each expression.

a. $\log 6 = \log 2 + \log 3$

☐ Property: $\log 6 = \log (2 \cdot 3) = \log 2 + \log 3$

b. $\log_b \frac{x^2}{y} = 2 \log_b x - \log_b y$

☐ Property: $\log_b \frac{x^2}{y} = \log_b x^2 - \log_b y$

☐ Property: $\log_b x^2 - \log_b y = 2 \log_b x - \log_b y$

2 Simplifying Logarithms Write each expression as a single logarithm.

a. $\log_4 64 - \log_4 16$

$\log_4 64 - \log_4 16 = \log_4 \frac{\square}{\square}$ **Quotient Property**

$= \log_4 \square$, or $\square$ **Simplify.**

b. $6 \log_5 x + \log_5 y$

$6 \log_5 x + \log_5 y = \log_5 x^{\square} + \log_5 y$ **Power Property**

$= \log_5 (\square\square)$ **Product Property**

Name_______________ Class_______________ Date _______________

3 Expanding Logarithms Expand each logarithm.

a. $\log_7 \left(\frac{t}{u}\right)$

$\log_7 \left(\frac{t}{u}\right) = \log_7 \square - \log_7 \square$ ______ **Property**

b. $\log (4p^3)$

$\log (4p^3) = \log \square + \log p^3$ ______ **Property**

$= \log \square + \square \log p$ ______ **Property**

Quick Check

1. State the property or properties used to rewrite each expression.

a. $\log_5 2 + \log_5 6 = \log_5 12$

b. $3 \log_b 4 - 3 \log_b 2 = \log_b 8$

2. a. Write $3 \log 2 + \log 4 - \log 16$ as a single logarithm.

b. Critical Thinking Can you write $3 \log_2 9 - \log_6 9$ as a single logarithm? Explain.

3. Expand each logarithm.

a. $\log_2 7b$

b. $\log \left(\frac{y}{3}\right)^2$

c. $\log_7 a^3b^4$

Name_______________ Class_______________ Date_______________

Lesson 8-5

Exponential and Logarithmic Equations

Lesson Objectives	NAEP 2005 Strand: Algebra
1 Solving exponential equations	Topic: Algebraic Representation
2 Solving logarithmic equations	Local Standards: ____________

Vocabulary and Key Concepts

Change of Base Formula

For any positive numbers M, b, and c, with $b \neq 1$ and $c \neq 1$, $\log_b M = \dfrac{\log_c \square}{\log_c \square}$.

An exponential equation is _______________

____

A logarithmic equation is _______________

Example

1 Solving an Exponential Equation Solve $5^{2x} = 16$.

$\log 5^{2x} = \log 16$ — **Take the ______ logarithm of each side.**

$\square \log \square = \log 16$ — **Use the ______ property of logarithms.**

$x = \dfrac{\log 16}{\square}$ — **Divide each side by ______.**

$\approx \square$ — **Use a calculator.**

Check $5^{2x} \stackrel{?}{=} 16$

$5^{2(\square)} \approx 16$

Quick Check

1. Solve each equation. Round to the nearest ten-thousandth. Check your answers.

a. $3^x = 4$ **b.** $6^{2x} = 21$ **c.** $3^{x+4} = 101$

Name_______________________________ Class_________________________ Date _______________

Examples

X	Y_1
1.4850	−.8920
1.4860	−.508
1.4870	
1.4880	
1.4890	
1.4900	1.0405
1.4910	1.4307

2 **Solving an Exponential Equation by Tables** Solve $5^{2x} = 120$ to the nearest hundredth.

Enter $y_1 =$ ______ $- 120$.

Use tabular zoom-in to find the sign change, as shown at the right.

The solution is $x \approx$ ______.

3 **Zoology** The population of trout in a certain stretch of the Platte River for five consecutive years is shown in the table, where 0 represents the year 1997. If the decay rate remains constant, in the beginning of which year might at most 100 trout remain in this stretch of river?

Time t	0	1	2	3	4
Pop. $P(t)$	5,000	4,000	3,201	2,561	2,049

Step 1 Enter the data into your calculator.

Step 2 Use the ExpReg feature to find the exponential function that fits the data.

ExpReg
y=a*b^x
a= ______
b= ______

Step 3 Graph the function and the line $y = 100$.

Step 4 Find the point of intersection.

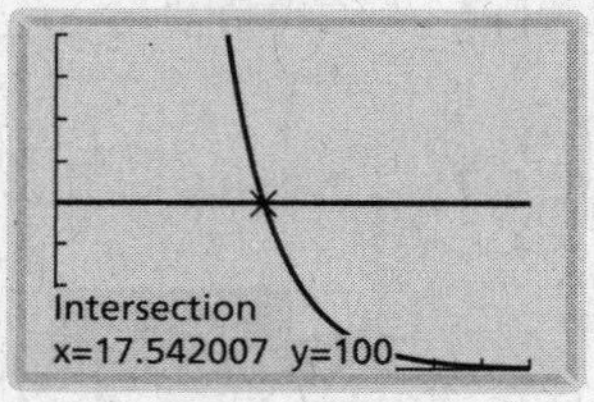

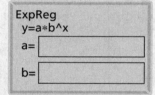

The solution is $x \approx$ ______, so there may be only 100 trout remaining in the beginning of the year ______.

Quick Check

2. Solve $11^{6x} = 786$ using tables.

Name________________________ Class________________________ Date ______________

Example

4 Using Logarithmic Properties to Solve an Equation Solve $3 \log x - \log 2 = 5$.

$\log\left(\frac{x^3}{\square}\right) = 5$ **Write as a single logarithm.**

$\frac{x^3}{\square} = \square$ **Write in exponential form.**

$x^3 = 2(\square)$ **Multiply each side by 2.**

$x = 10\sqrt[3]{\square}$, or about $\square$.

The solution is $10\sqrt[3]{\square}$, or about $\square$.

Quick Check

3. a. Use a graphing calculator to solve $11^{6x} = 786$.

b. The population of peninsular bighorn sheep in Mexico was approximately 6200 in 1971. By 1999, about 2300 remained. Determine the year by which only 200 peninsular bighorn sheep might remain in Mexico.

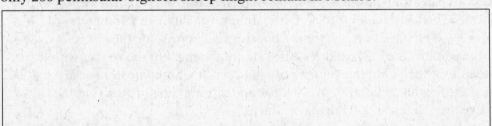

4. a. Solve $\log(7 - 2x) = -1$.

b. Solve $\log 6 - \log 3x = -2$.

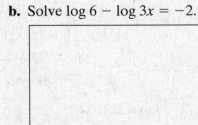

Name________________________ Class____________________ Date____________

Lesson 8-6

Natural Logarithms

Lesson Objectives	**NAEP 2005 Strand:** Algebra
1 Evaluating natural logarithmic expressions	**Topic:** Variables, Expressions, and Operations
2 Solving equations using natural logarithms	**Local Standards:** ____________________

Key Concepts

Natural Logarithmic Function

If $y = e^x$, then $\log_{\square} \square = x$, which is commonly written as $\ln y = x$.

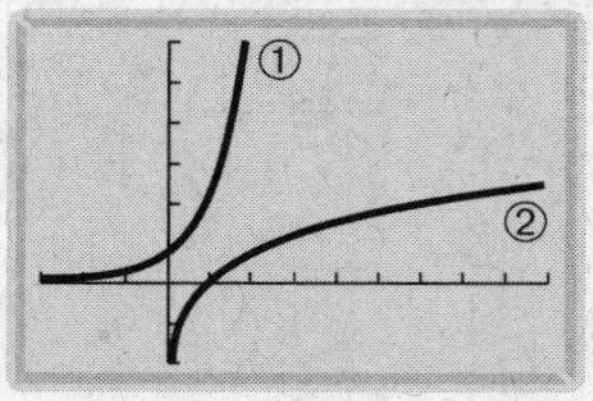

① $y = e^x$

② $y = \ln x$

Examples

1 Simplifying Natural Logarithms Write $2 \ln 12 - \ln 9$ as a single natural logarithm.

$2 \ln 12 - \ln 9 = \ln 12^{\square} - \ln \square$ **Power Property**

$= \ln \frac{12^{\square}}{\square}$ **Quotient Property**

$= \ln \square$ **Simplify.**

2 Space A spacecraft can attain a stable orbit 300 km above Earth if it reaches a velocity of 7.7 km/s. The formula for a rocket's maximum velocity v in kilometers per second is $v = -0.0098t + c \ln R$, where the booster rocket fires for t seconds, the velocity of the exhaust is c km/s, and R is the ratio of the mass of the rocket with fuel to its mass without fuel. Find the velocity of a spacecraft whose booster rocket has a mass ratio 22, an exhaust velocity of 2.3 km/s, and a firing time of 50 s. Can the spacecraft achieve a stable orbit 300 km above Earth?

Let $R = 22$, $c = 2.3$, and $t = 50$. **Find v.**

$v = -0.0098t + c \ln R$ **Use the formula.**

$= -0.0098(\square) + \square \ln \square$ **Substitute.**

$\approx -\square + \square(\square)$ **Use a calculator.**

$\approx \square$ **Simplify.**

The velocity is about $\square$ km/s. This is $\square$ than the 7.7 km/s needed for a stable orbit. The spacecraft $\square$ achieve a stable orbit 300 km above the Earth.

Name________________________ Class________________________ Date ____________

❸ Solving a Natural Logarithmic Equation Solve $\ln(2x - 4)^3 = 6$.

$\ln(2x - 4)^3 = 6$

$\square \ln(2x - 4) = 6$ **Power Property**

$\ln(2x - 4) = 2$ **Divide each side by $\square$.**

$2x - 4 = e^{\square}$ **Rewrite in exponential form.**

$x = \dfrac{\square + 4}{\square}$ **Solve for *x*.**

$x \approx \square$ **Use a calculator.**

Check $\ln\left(2 \cdot \square - 4\right)^3 \stackrel{?}{=} 6$

$\ln \square \stackrel{?}{=} 6$

$\square \approx 6$ ✓

Quick Check

1. Write each expression as a single natural logarithm.

a. $5 \ln 2 - \ln 4$ **b.** $3 \ln x + \ln y$ **c.** $\frac{1}{4} \ln 3 + \frac{1}{4} \ln x$

2. A booster rocket for a spacecraft has a mass ratio of about 15, an exhaust velocity of 2.1 km/s, and a firing time of 30 s. Find the velocity of the spacecraft. Can the spacecraft achieve a stable orbit 300 km above Earth?

3. Solve each equation. Check your answers.

a. $\ln x = 0.1$ **b.** $\ln(3x - 9) = 21$ **c.** $\ln\left(\frac{x + 2}{3}\right) = 12$

Name____________________ Class____________________ Date ____________

Examples

④ Solving an Exponential Equation Use natural logarithms to solve $4e^{3x} + 1.2 = 14$.

$4e^{3x} = \square$ **Subtract 1.2 from each side.**

$e^{3x} = \square$ **Divide each side by 4.**

$\ln e^{3x} = \ln \square$ **Take the natural logarithm of each side.**

$\square x = \ln \square$ **Simplify.**

$x = \dfrac{\ln \square}{\square}$ **Solve for *x*.**

$x \approx \square$

⑤ Investing An initial investment of \$200 is now valued at \$254.25. The interest rate is 6%, compounded continuously. How long has the money been invested?

$A = Pe^{rt}$ **Continuously compounded interest formula.**

$\square = \square e^{0.06t}$ **Substitute $\square$ for *A*, $\square$ for *P*, and 0.06 for *r*.**

$\square = e^{0.06t}$ **Divide each side by $\square$.**

$\ln \square = \ln e^{0.06t}$ **Take the natural logarithm of each side.**

$\ln \square = \square t$ **Simplify.**

$\dfrac{\ln \square}{\square} = t$ **Solve for *t*.**

$\square \approx t$ **Use a calculator.**

The money has been invested for $\square$ years.

Quick Check

4. Use natural logarithms to solve each equation.

   a. $e^{x+1} = 30$

   b. $e^{\frac{2x}{5}} + 7.2 = 9.1$

5. An initial investment of \$200 is worth \$315.24 after seven years of continuous compounding. Find the interest rate.

Name______________________________ Class____________________ Date____________

Lesson 9-1

Inverse Variation

Lesson Objectives	**NAEP 2005 Strand:** Algebra
1 Using inverse variation 2 Using joint and other variations	**Topic:** Patterns, Relations, and Functions **Local Standards:** ____________________

Vocabulary

An inverse variation is ____

____

A combined variation combines ____

____

Examples of Combined Variations

Combined Variation	Equation Form
y varies ☐ with the square of x.	$y = kx^2$
y varies ☐ with the cube of x.	$y = \frac{k}{x^3}$
z varies ☐ with x and y.	$z = kxy$
z varies ☐ with x and y and ☐ with w.	$z = \frac{kxy}{w}$
z varies ☐ with x and ☐ with the product of w and y.	$z = \frac{kx}{wy}$

Examples

1 Modeling Inverse Variation Suppose that x and y vary inversely, and $x = 7$ when $y = 4$. Write the function that models the inverse variation.

$y = \frac{k}{x}$ **x and y vary inversely.**

$\square = \frac{k}{\square}$ **Substitute the given values of x and y.**

$\square = k$ **Find k.**

$y = \frac{\square}{x}$ **Use the value of k to write the function.**

Name________________________ Class________________ Date________________

❷ **Identifying Direct and Inverse Variations** Is the relationship between the variables in each table a direct variation, an inverse variation, or neither? Write functions to model the direct and inverse variations.

a.

x	2	4	14
y	0.7	0.35	0.1

As x increases, y ______. The product of each pair of x- and y-values is ______. y varies ______ with x and the constant of variation is ______.

So $xy =$ ______ and the function is $y = \frac{\square}{x}$.

b.

x	−2	−1.3	7
y	6	5	−4

As x increases, y ______, but this is not an inverse variation. Not all the products of x and y are the ______ $(-2 \cdot 6 \neq -1.3 \cdot 5)$. This is neither a ______ variation nor an inverse variation.

c.

x	−2	4	6
y	5	−10	−15

As x increases, y ______. Since each y-value is −2.5 times the corresponding x-value, y varies ______ with x and the constant of variation is ______, and the function is $y =$ ______.

❸ **Finding a Formula** The area of an equilateral triangle varies directly as the square of the radius r of its circumscribed circle. The area of an equilateral triangle for which $r = 2$ is $3\sqrt{3}$. Find the formula for the area A of an equilateral triangle in terms of r.

$A = kr^2$ — **A varies ______ as the square of r.**

$\square = k(\square)^2$ — **Substitute the values for A and r.**

$\frac{\square}{\square} = k$ — **Solve for k.**

$A = \frac{\square}{\square}r^2$ — **Substitute the value for k.**

Name______________________________ Class______________________ Date ____________

Quick Check

1. Suppose that x and y vary inversely, and $x = 0.3$ when $y = 1.4$. Write the function that models the inverse variation.

2. Is the relationship between the values in each table a direct variation, an inverse variation, or neither? Write functions to model the direct and inverse variations.

a.

x	0.8	0.6	0.4
y	0.9	1.2	1.8

b.

x	2	4	6
y	3.2	1.6	1.1

c.

x	1.2	1.4	1.6
y	18	21	24

3. The volume of a square pyramid with congruent edges varies directly as the cube of the length of an edge. The volume of a square pyramid with edge length 4 is $\frac{32\sqrt{2}}{3}$. Find the formula for the volume V of a square pyramid with congruent edges of length e.

Name________________________ Class________________ Date____________

Lesson 9-2

Graphing Rational Functions

Lesson Objectives	
1 Graphing reciprocal functions **2** Graphing translations of reciprocal functions	**NAEP 2005 Strand:** Algebra **Topic:** Patterns, Relations, and Functions; Algebraic Representations **Local Standards:** ____________________

Vocabulary and Key Concepts

The Reciprocal Function Family

Parent function: $y = \frac{1}{x}$

Stretch ($|a| > 1$)
Shrink ($0 < |a| < 1$)
Reflection ($a < 0$) in x-axis
} $y = \square$

Translation (horizontal by h; vertical by k) with vertical asymptote $x = \square$, horizontal asymptote $y = \square$: $y = \frac{1}{x - \square} + \square$

Combined: $y = \frac{\square}{x - \square} + \square$

A branch is ____

Examples

1 **Graphing an Inverse Variation** Sketch a graph of $y = \frac{0.5}{x}$. Make a table of values that include positive and negative values of x. Notice that x cannot be 0.

x	-10		-2	$-\frac{1}{2}$	$-\frac{1}{4}$		$\frac{1}{10}$		$\frac{1}{2}$	2	5	
y	-0.05	-0.1		-1		-5	5	2		0.25	0.1	

Graph the points and connect them with a smooth curve. The graph has two parts. Each part is called a branch.

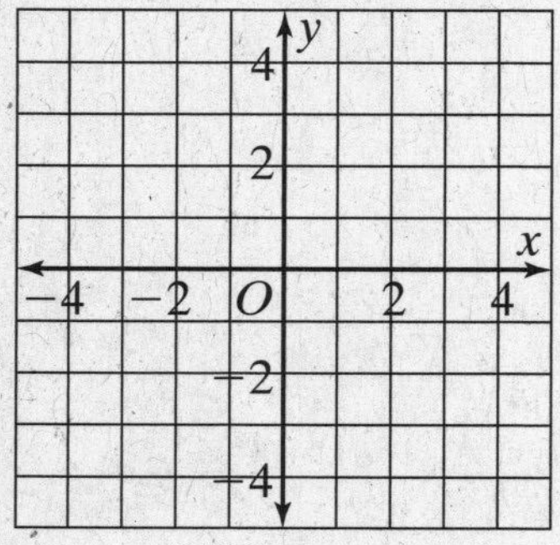

The x-axis is the $\square$ asymptote. The y-axis is the $\square$ asymptote.

Name________________________________ Class________________________ Date ______________

❷ **Sound** The frequency f in hertz of a sound wave varies inversely with its wavelength w. The function $f = \frac{343}{w}$ models the relationship between f and w for a wave with a velocity of 343 m/s. Find the wavelength of a sound wave with a frequency of 440 Hz. Graph the functions $f = \frac{343}{w}$ and $f = 440$. Use the Intersection feature of a graphing calculator.

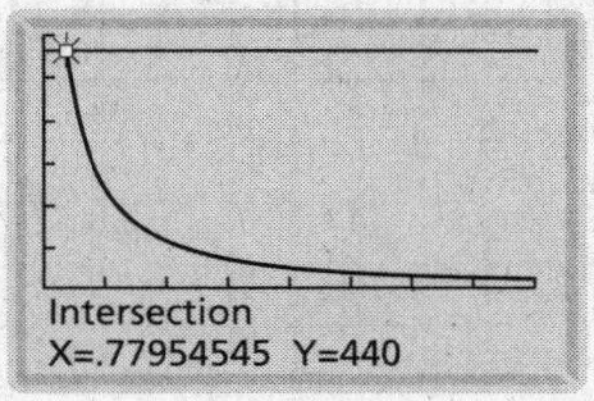

Xmin=0 Ymin=0
Xmax=40 Ymax=500
Xscl=5 Yscl=50

The wavelength is about ☐ m.

Quick Check

1. Sketch a graph of $y = \frac{16}{x}$.

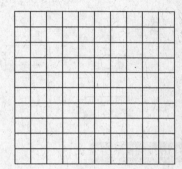

2. The pitch y produced by a panpipe varies inversely with the length x of the pipe. The function $y = \frac{564}{x}$ models the inverse variation where x is the length in feet.

a. Pitches of 247 Hz, 311 Hz, and 370 Hz form a musical chord. Find the length of pipe that will produce each pitch.

b. Writing The asymptotes of $y = \frac{564}{x}$ are $x = 0$ and $y = 0$. Explain why this makes sense in terms of the panpipe.

Name______________________________ Class________________________ Date ____________

Examples

3 Graphing a Translation Sketch the graph of $y = \frac{1}{x+2} + 2$.

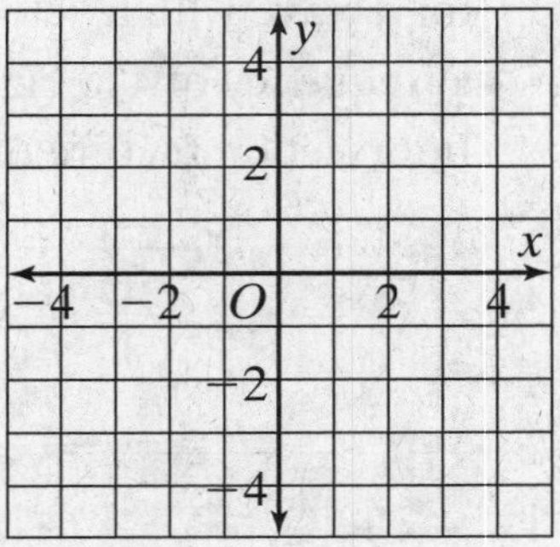

Step 1 Draw the asymptotes.

For $y = \frac{1}{x+2} + 2$, $b = \square$ and $c = \square$. The vertical asymptote is $x = \square$. The horizontal asymptote is $y = \square$.

Step 2 Translate $y = \frac{1}{x}$.

The graph $y = \frac{1}{x}$ includes $(1, 1)$ and $(-1, -1)$. Translate these points $\square$ units to the left and $\square$ units up to $(\square, \square)$ and $(\square, \square)$. Draw the branches through these points.

4 Writing the Equation of a Translation Write an equation for the translation of $y = -\frac{7}{x}$ that has asymptotes at $x = 8$ and $y = -4$.

$y = \frac{-7}{x - b} + c$ **Use the general form of a translation.**

$= \frac{-7}{x - \square} + (\square)$ **Substitute 8 for *b* and $\square$ for *c*.**

$= \frac{-7}{x - \square} - \square$ **Simplify.**

Quick Check

3. Find the asymptotes and sketch the graph of $y = -\frac{1}{x+7} - 3$.

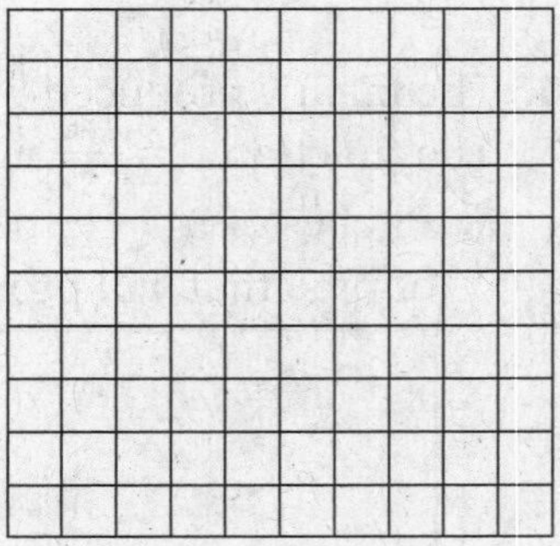

4. a. Write an equation for the translation of $y = -\frac{1}{x}$ that is 4 units left and 5 units up.

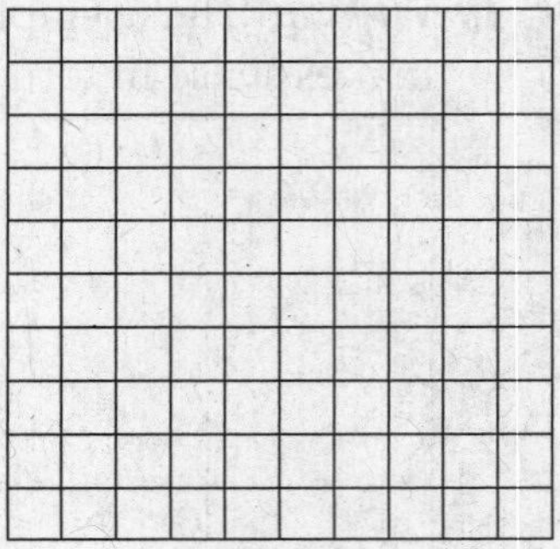

b. Check your work by graphing your solution to part (a).

Name__________ Class__________ Date__________

Lesson 9-3

Rational Functions and Their Graphs

Lesson Objectives	NAEP 2005 Strand: Algebra
1 Identifying properties of rational functions	Topic: Algebraic Representations
2 Graphing rational functions	Local Standards: __________

Key Concepts

Rational Function

A **rational function** $f(x)$ is a function that can be written as $f(x) = \frac{P(x)}{Q(x)}$, where ☐ and ☐ are polynomial functions. The domain of $f(x)$ is all real numbers except those for which $Q(x) =$ ☐.

Vertical Asymptotes

The rational function $f(x) = \frac{P(x)}{Q(x)}$ has a point of discontinuity for each real ☐ of $Q(x)$.

If $P(x)$ and $Q(x)$ have no common real zeros, then the graph of $f(x)$ has a ☐ asymptote at each real zero of $Q(x)$.

If $P(x)$ and $Q(x)$ have a common real zero a, then there is a ☐ in the graph or a vertical asymptote at $x =$ ☐.

Horizontal Asymptotes

- The graph of a rational function has at most ☐ horizontal asymptote.
- The graph of a rational function has a ☐ asymptote at $y = 0$ if the degree of the ☐ is ☐ than the degree of the ☐.
- If the ☐ of the numerator and the denominator are equal, then the graph has a ☐ asymptote at $y =$ ☐, where a is the coefficient of the term of highest ☐ in the numerator and b is the coefficient of the term of highest degree in the ☐.
- If the degree of the ☐ is greater than the degree of the ☐, then the graph has ☐ horizontal asymptote.

Name_________________________ Class_________________________ Date _______________

Example

1 Finding Points of Discontinuity For each rational function, find any points of discontinuity.

a. $y = \frac{3}{x^2 - x - 12}$

The function is undefined at values of x for which $x^2 - x - 12 = 0$.

$x^2 - x - 12 = \square$ **Set the denominator equal to** $\square$.

$(x \square 4)(x + \square) = 0$ **Solve by factoring or using the Quadratic Formula.**

$x - 4 = \square$ or $x + 3 = \square$ $\square$ **Property.**

$x = \square$ or $x = \square$ **Solve for *x*.**

There are points of discontinuity at $x = \square$ and $x = \square$.

b. $y = \frac{2x}{3x^2 + 4}$

The function is undefined at values of $3x^2 + 4 = 0$.

$3x^2 + 4 = \square$ **Set the denominator equal to zero.**

$x^2 = -\frac{\square}{\square}$ **Solve for *x*.**

$x = \pm\sqrt{\frac{\square}{3}} = \frac{\pm\square}{\sqrt{\square}} = \frac{\pm 2i\sqrt{3}}{3}$

Since $\frac{\pm 2i\sqrt{3}}{3}$ $\square$ a real number, there is $\square$ real value for x for which the function $y = \frac{2x}{3x^2 + 4}$ is undefined. There is $\square$ point of discontinuity.

Quick Check

1. For each rational function, find any points of discontinuity.

a. $y = \frac{1}{x^2 - 16}$ **b.** $y = \frac{x^2 - 1}{x^2 + 3}$ **c.** $y = \frac{x + 1}{x^2 + 2x - 8}$

Name______________________________ Class______________________ Date ______________

Example

2 Finding Vertical Asymptotes Describe the vertical asymptotes and holes for the graph of each rational function.

a. $y = \frac{x - 7}{(x + 1)(x + 5)}$

Since -1 and -5 are the zeros of the [ ] and neither is a zero of the numerator, $x = -1$ and $x = -5$ are [ ] asymptotes.

b. $y = \frac{(x + 3)x}{x + 3}$

-3 is a zero of [ ] the numerator and the denominator. The graph of this function is the same as the graph $y = x$, except it has a hole at $x =$ [ ].

Quick Check

2. Describe the vertical asymptotes and holes for the graph of each rational function.

a. $y = \frac{x - 2}{(x - 1)(x + 3)}$

[ ]

b. $y = \frac{x - 2}{(x - 2)(x + 3)}$

[ ]

c. $y = \frac{x^2 - 1}{x + 1}$

[ ]

Name________________________ Class________________________ Date ____________

Examples

❸ Finding Horizontal Asymptotes Find the horizontal asymptote of $y = \frac{-4x + 3}{2x + 1}$.

Divide the numerator by the denominator as shown at the right.

$$\begin{array}{r} -2 \\ 2x + 1 \overline{\big)\; -4x + 3} \\ -(-4x - \square) \\ \hline 5 \end{array}$$

The function $y = \frac{-4x + 3}{2x + 1}$ can be written as $y = \frac{\square}{2x + 1} - \square$.

Its graph is a translation of $y = \frac{5}{2x + 1}$.

The horizontal asymptote is $y = \square$.

❹ Sketching Graphs of Rational Functions Sketch the graph $y = \frac{x + 1}{(x - 3)(x + 2)}$.

The degree of the denominator is greater than the degree of the numerator, so the x-axis is the ______________. When $x > 3$, y is positive. So as x increases, the graph approaches the y-axis from above. When $x < -2$, y is __________. So as x decreases, the graph approaches the y-axis from __________.

Since ____ is the zero of the numerator, the x-intercept is at ____. Since ____ and ____ are the zeros of the denominator, the vertical asymptotes are at $x = \square$ and $x = \square$.
Calculate the values of y for values of x near the asymptotes.
Plot those points and sketch the graph.

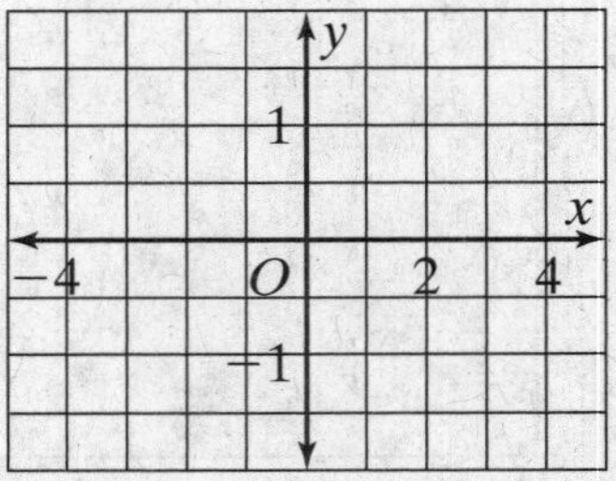

Quick Check

3. Find the horizontal asymptote of the graph of each rational function.

a. $y = \frac{-2x + 6}{x - 1}$

b. $y = \frac{2x^2 + 5}{x^2 + 1}$

4. Sketch the graph of $y = \frac{x + 3}{(x - 1)(x - 5)}$.

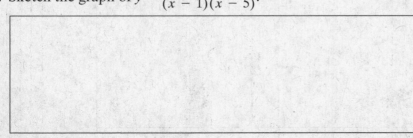

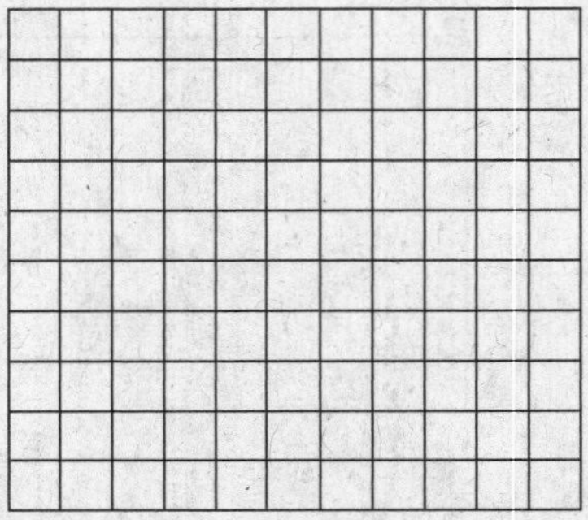

Name________________ Class________________ Date________________

Lesson 9-4

Rational Expressions

Lesson Objectives	NAEP 2005 Strand: Algebra
1 Simplifying rational expressions	**Topic:** Variables, Expressions, and Operations
2 Multiplying and dividing rational expressions	**Local Standards:** ________________

Vocabulary

A rational expression is in its simplest form when ________________________________

____

Example

1 Multiplying Rational Expressions Multiply $\frac{3x^2 + 5x - 2}{x - 5}$ and $\frac{x^2 - 25}{3x^2 - 7x + 2}$. State any restrictions on the variable.

$$\frac{3x^2 + 5x - 2}{x - 5} \cdot \frac{x^2 - 25}{3x^2 - 7x + 2} = \frac{(3x - \square)(x + \square)}{x - 5} \cdot \frac{(x + \square)(x - \square)}{(3x - \square)(x - \square)}$$ **Factor.**

$$= \frac{\cancel{(3x - 1)}^{\square}(x + \square)}{\cancel{x - 5}_{\square}} \cdot \frac{(x + \square)\cancel{(x - 5)}^{\square}}{\cancel{(3x - 1)}_{\square}(x - \square)}$$ **Divide out common factors.**

$$= \frac{(x + \square)(x + \square)}{x - \square} = \frac{x^2 + \square x + \square}{x - \square}$$

The product is $\frac{x^2 + \square x + \square}{x - \square}$ for $x \neq \square, \square,$ or $\square$.

Quick Check

1. Multiply $\frac{a^2 - 4}{a^2 - 1}$ and $\frac{a + 1}{a^2 + 2a}$. State any restrictions on the variable.

Name________________________ Class________________________ Date ____________

Example

2 Dividing Rational Expressions Divide $\frac{3-y}{(2x-1)(x+5)}$ by $\frac{6(y-3)}{(2x-1)(x-7)}$. State any restrictions on the variables.

$$\frac{3-y}{(2x-1)(x+5)} \div \frac{6(y-3)}{(2x-1)(x-7)} = \frac{3-y}{(2x-1)(x+5)} \;\square\; \frac{(2x-1)(x-7)}{6(y-3)}$$ **Multiply by the reciprocal.**

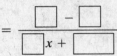

$$= \frac{\overset{\square}{\cancel{3-y}}}{\underset{\square}{\cancel{(2x-1)}(x+5)}} \cdot \frac{\overset{\square}{\cancel{(2x-1)}(x-7)}}{\underset{\square}{6\cancel{(y-3)}}}$$ **Divide out common factors.**

$$= \frac{\square}{(x+\square)} \cdot \frac{(x-\square)}{\square}$$ **Rewrite the expression.**

$$= \frac{\square - \square}{\square x + \square}$$ **Multiply.**

The quotient is $\frac{\square - \square}{\square x + \square}$ for $x \neq \square$, $\square$, or $\square$, and $y \neq \square$.

Quick Check

2. Divide $\frac{a^2 + 2a - 15}{a^2 - 16}$ by $\frac{a+1}{3a-12}$. State any restrictions on the variable.

Name______________________________ Class____________________ Date______________

Lesson 9-5

Adding and Subtracting Rational Expressions

Lesson Objectives	NAEP 2005 Strand: Algebra
1 Adding and subtracting rational expressions	**Topic:** Variables, Expressions, and Operations
2 Simplifying complex fractions	**Local Standards:** ____________________

Vocabulary

A complex fraction is ____

____

Example

1 Finding Least Common Multiples Find the least common multiple of $2x^2 - 8x + 8$ and $15x^2 - 60$.

Step 1 Find the prime factors of each expression.

$2x^2 - 8x + 8 = (\square)(x^2 - 4x + 4) = (\square)(x - \square)(x - \square)$

$15x^2 - 60 = (\square)(x^2 - 4) = (\square)(\square)(x - \square)(x + \square)$

Step 2 Write each prime factor the greatest number of times it appears in either expression. Simplify where possible.

$(\square)(\square)(\square)(x - \square)(x - \square)(x + \square) = \square(x - \square)^2(x + \square)$

The least common multiple is $30(x + 2)(x - 2)^2$.

Quick Check

1. Find the least common multiple of each pair of expressions.

a. $3x^2 - 9x - 30$ and $6x + 30$.

b. $5x^2 + 15x + 10$ and $2x^2 - 8$.

Name________________________ Class________________________ Date ________________

Examples

❷ Adding Rational Expressions Simplify $\frac{1}{3x^2 + 21x + 30} + \frac{4x}{3x + 15}$.

$$\frac{1}{3x^2 + 21x + 30} + \frac{4x}{3x + 15}$$

$$= \frac{1}{\square(x + \square)(x + \square)} + \frac{4x}{\square(x + \square)}$$ **Factor the denominators.**

$$= \frac{1}{\square(x + \square)(x + \square)} + \frac{4x}{\square(x + \square)} \cdot \frac{x + \square}{x + \square}$$ **identity for multiplication**

$$= \frac{1}{\square(x + \square)(x + \square)} + \frac{4x(x + 2)}{\square(x + \square)(x + \square)}$$ **Multiply.**

$$= \frac{1 + 4x(x + 2)}{\square(x + \square)(x + \square)} = \frac{\square x^2 + \square x + \square}{\square(x + \square)(x + \square)}$$ **Simplify the numerator.**

❸ Subtracting Rational Expressions Simplify $\frac{2x}{x^2 - 2x - 3} - \frac{3}{4x + 4}$.

$$\frac{2x}{x^2 - 2x - 3} - \frac{3}{4x + 4}$$

$$= \frac{2x}{(x - \square)(x + \square)} - \frac{3}{4(x + \square)}$$ **Factor the denominators.**

$$= \frac{2x}{(x - 3)(x + 1)} \cdot \frac{\square}{\square} - \frac{3}{4(x + 1)} \cdot \frac{x - \square}{x - \square}$$ **identity for multiplication**

$$= \frac{\square(2x) - (3)(x - \square)}{\square(x + 1)(x - \square)} = \frac{\square x + \square}{\square(x + 1)(x - \square)}$$ **Simplify.**

Quick Check

2. Simplify $\frac{1}{x^2 - 4x - 12} + \frac{3x}{4x + 8}$.

Name________________________ Class________________________ Date ______________

Example

④ Simplifying Complex Fractions Simplify $\dfrac{\frac{1}{x}+\frac{1}{y}}{\frac{2}{y}-\frac{1}{x}}$.

First find the LCD of all the rational expressions.

$$\frac{\frac{1}{x}+\frac{1}{y}}{\frac{2}{y}-\frac{1}{x}} = \frac{\left(\frac{1}{x}+\frac{1}{y}\right)\cdot \square}{\left(\frac{2}{y}-\frac{1}{x}\right)\cdot \square}$$

The LCD is ☐**. Multiply the numerator and denominator by** ☐**.**

$$= \frac{\frac{1\cdot\square}{x}+\frac{1\cdot\square}{y}}{\frac{2\cdot\square}{y}-\frac{1\cdot\square}{x}} = \frac{\square+\square}{2\square-\square}$$

Use the Distributive Property and simplify.

Quick Check

3. Simplify each expression.

a. $\dfrac{-2}{3x^2+36x+105}-\dfrac{3x}{6x+30}$

b. $\dfrac{x}{3x^2-9x+6}-\dfrac{2x+1}{3x^2+3x-6}$

4. Simplify each complex fraction.

a. $\dfrac{\frac{1}{x}}{y}$

b. $\dfrac{3}{1-\frac{1}{2y}}$

c. $\dfrac{\frac{x-2}{x}-\frac{2}{x+1}}{\frac{3}{x-1}-\frac{1}{x+1}}$

Name________________ Class________________ Date________________

Lesson 9-6

Solving Rational Equations

Lesson Objectives	NAEP 2005 Strand: Algebra
1 Solving rational equations	**Topic:** Variables, Expressions, and Operations
2 Using rational equations	**Local Standards:** ________________

Example

1 Solving Rational Equations Solve $\frac{1}{x-3} = \frac{6x}{x^2-9}$. Check each solution.

$x^2 - \square = \square(\square - \square)$ **Write the cross products.**

$x^2 - \square = \square x^2 - \square x$ ________ **Property**

$\square x^2 + \square x - \square = 0$ **Write in standard form.**

$\square x^2 - \square x + \square = 0$ **Multiply each side by** ____.

$(\square - \square)(\square - \square) = 0$ **Factor.**

$x = \frac{\square}{\square}$ or $x = \square$ ________ **Property**

Check When $x = \square$, both denominators in the original equation are ____.

The original equation is undefined at $x = \square$. So $x = \square$ ____ a solution.

When ____ is substituted for x in the original equation, both sides equal ____.

Quick Check

1. Solve each equation. Check each solution.

a. $\frac{-4}{5(x+2)} = \frac{3}{x+2}$

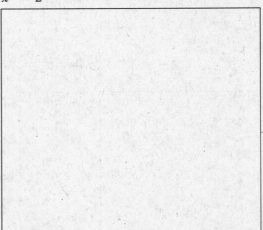

b. $\frac{-2}{x^2-2} = \frac{2}{x-4}$

Name______________________ Class______________ Date ____________

Example

❷ Solving Rational Equations Josefina can row 4 miles upstream in a river in the same time it takes her to row 6 miles downstream. Her rate of rowing in still water is 2 miles per hour. Find the speed of the river current.

Relate speed with the current = speed in still water + speed of the current
speed against the current = speed in still water − speed of the current
time to row 4 miles upstream = time to row 6 miles downstream

Define

	Distance (mi)	Rate (mi/h)	Time (h)
With Current	6	$2 + r$	$\frac{6}{(2+r)}$
Against Current	4	$2 - r$	$\frac{6}{(2-r)}$

Write

$$\frac{6}{2+r} = \frac{4}{2-r}$$

$$(\square)(\square)\left(\frac{6}{2+r}\right) = (\square)(\square)\left(\frac{4}{2-r}\right)$$ **Multiply by the LCD** $(\square)(\square)$.

$$(\square)(6) = (\square)(4)$$ **Simplify.**

$$\square - \square r = \square + \square r$$ **Distributive Property**

$$\square = \square r$$ **Solve for *r*.**

$$\square = r$$ **Simplify.**

The speed of the river current is $\square$ mi/h.

Quick Check

2. Rosa can jog 5 mi downhill in the same time it takes her to jog 3 mi uphill. She jogs downhill 4 mi/h faster than she jogs uphill. Find her jogging rate each way.

Name______________________ Class______________________ Date______________

Lesson 9-7

Probability of Multiple Events

Lesson Objectives	**NAEP 2005 Strand:** Data Analysis and Probability
1 Finding the probabilities of events *A* and *B*	**Topic:** Probability
2 Finding the probabilities of events *A* or *B*	**Local Standards:** ____________________

Vocabulary and Key Concepts

Probability of *A* and *B*

If *A* and *B* are independent events, then $P(A \text{ and } B) = P(A) \cdot P(B)$.

Example: If $P(A) = \frac{1}{2}$ and $P(B) = \frac{1}{3}$, then $P(A \text{ and } B) = \frac{1}{2} \cdot \frac{1}{3} = \frac{1}{6}$.

Probability of *A* or *B*

If *A* and *B* are mutually exclusive events, then $P(A \text{ or } B) = P(A) + P(B)$.

If *A* and *B* are not mutually exclusive events, then
$P(A \text{ or } B) = P(A) + P(B) - P(A \text{ and } B)$.

Dependent events are two events where ______________________________

____

Independent evens are two events where ______________________________

____

Mutually exclusive events are two events that ______________________________

____

Examples

1 Mutually Exclusive Events Are the events mutually exclusive? Explain.

a. rolling an even number or a prime number on a number cube

By rolling a 2, you can roll an [ ] number and a [ ] number at the same time. So the events [ ] mutually exclusive.

b. rolling a prime number or a multiple of 6 on a number cube

Since 6 is [ ] multiple of 6 you can roll at a time and it is not a [ ], the events [ ] mutually exclusive.

❷ Probability and Mutually Exclusive Events At a restaurant, customers get to choose one of four vegetables with any main course. About 33% of the customers choose green beans, and about 28% choose spinach. What is the probability that a customer will choose beans or spinach?

Since a customer [ ] choose both beans and spinach,

the events [ ].

$P(\text{beans or spinach}) = P(\text{beans})$ [ ] $P(\text{spinach})$ **Use the *P*(*A* or *B*) formula for mutually exclusive events.**

= [ ] [ ] [ ]

= [ ]

The probability that a customer will choose beans or spinach is about [ ] or about [ ]%.

❸ Probability A box contains 20 red marbles and 30 blue marbles. A second box contains 10 white marbles and 47 black marbles. If you choose one marble from each box without looking, what is the probability that you get a blue marble and a black marble?

Relate [Probability of both events] is [Probability of first event] times [Probability of second event]

Define [Event A] = first marble is blue. Then [$P(A)$] = [ ].

[Event B] = second marble is black. Then [$P(A)$] = [ ].

Write [$P(A \text{ and } B)$] = [ ] · [ ]

$P(A \text{ and } B) =$ [ ] · [ ] = [ ] = [ ] **Multiply and simplify.**

The probability that a blue and a black marble will be drawn is [ ], or about [ ]%.

Quick Check

1. Are the events of rolling an even number and rolling a number less than 2 on a 1–6 number cube mutually exclusive? Explain.

[ ]

2. About 53% of U.S. college students are under 25 years old. About 21% of U.S. college students are over 34 years old. A U.S. college student is chosen at random. Find the probability that the chosen student falls in each age range.

a. 25–34 [ ]

b. 34 or under [ ]

Name______________________ Class______________________ Date ____________

Example

4 Probabilities of Events A spinner has twenty equal-sized sections numbered from 1 to 20. If you spin the spinner, what is the probability that the number you spin will be a multiple of 2 or a multiple of 3?

$P(\text{multiple of 2 or 3}) = P(\text{multiple of 2})$ $\square$

$P(\text{multiple of 3})$ $\square$ $P(\text{multiple of 2}$ $\square$ $3)$

$= \frac{\square}{20} \;\square\; \frac{\square}{20} \;\square\; \frac{\square}{20} = \frac{\square}{20}$

The probability of spinning a multiple of 2 or 3 is $\square$.

Quick Check

3. Suppose your favorite radio station is running a promotional campaign. Every hour, 5 callers chosen at random get to select two songs each. You call the station once after 7:00 A.M. and again after 3:00 P.M. Use the table to answer each question.

Radio Station Statistics

Hour	Calls Received That Hour
7:00 A.M.	125
3:00 P.M.	200

a. What is the probability of being one of the five callers after 7 A.M.? After 3 P.M.?

b. Find the probability of being one of the five callers both times you call.

4. A fruit bowl contains 3 red apples, 2 green apples, 2 oranges, 1 lime, and 1 lemon. Suppose you reach into the fruit bowl and select a piece of fruit at random. What is the probability that the piece of fruit is green or citrus?

Name______________________ Class______________________ Date______________

Lesson 10-1

Exploring Conic Sections

Lesson Objectives	NAEP 2005 Strand: Geometry
1 Graphing conic sections	Topic: Position and Direction
2 Identifying conic sections	Local Standards: ____________

Vocabulary

A conic section is ____

____

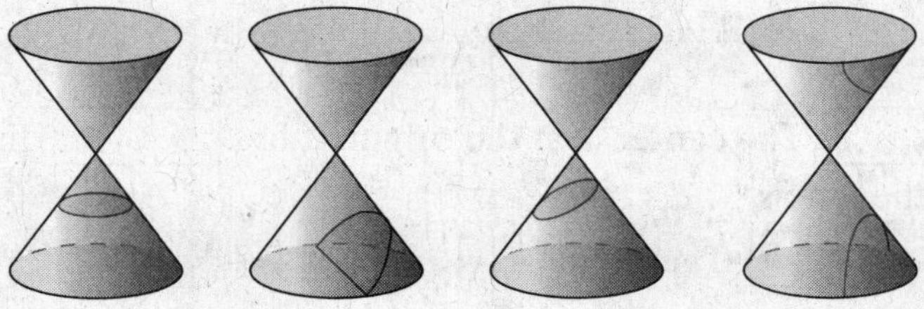

Examples

1 Graphing a Circle Graph the equation $x^2 + y^2 = 16$. Describe the graph and its lines of symmetry. Then find the domain and range.

Make a table of values.

x	y
−4	☐
−3	$\pm\sqrt{7} \approx \pm$ ☐
−2	$\pm 2\sqrt{3} \approx \pm$ ☐
−1	$\pm\sqrt{15} \approx \pm$ ☐
0	$\pm$ ☐
1	$\pm\sqrt{15} \approx \pm$ ☐
2	$\pm 2\sqrt{3} \approx \pm$ ☐
3	$\pm\sqrt{7} \approx \pm$ ☐
4	☐

Plot the points and connect them with a smooth curve.

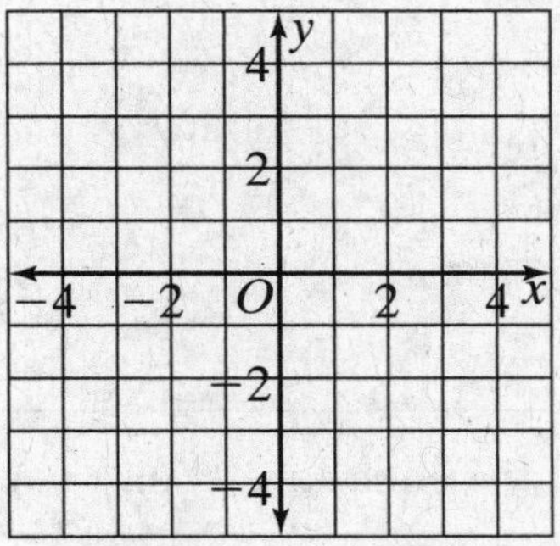

The graph is a circle with radius ☐.

Its center is at the origin. Every line through the center is a line of symmetry.

Recall from Chapter 2 that you can use set notation to describe a domain or a range. The domain is $\{x \mid -☐ \leq x \leq ☐\}$. The range is $\{y \mid -☐ \leq y \leq ☐\}$.

❷ Graphing an Ellipse Graph the equation $9x^2 + 4y^2 = 36$. Describe the graph and the lines of symmetry. Then find the domain and range.

Make a table of values.

x	____
−2	0
−1	± ____
0	± ____
____	±2.6
____	0

Plot the points and connect them with a smooth curve.

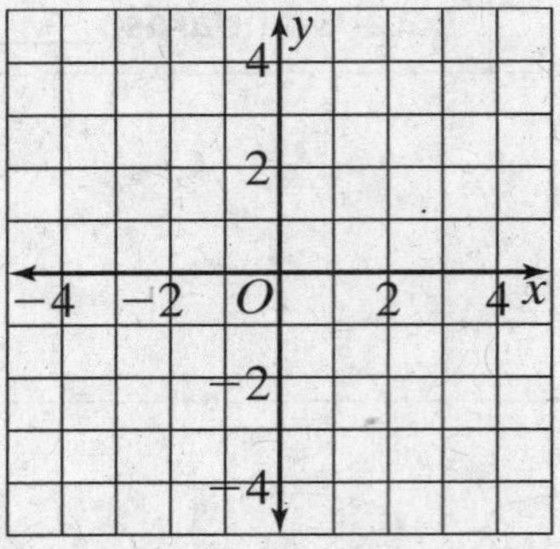

The graph is an ____________. The center is at the origin. It has ________ lines of symmetry, the x-axis and the y-axis.

The domain is $\{x \mid -\underline{\quad} \le x \le \underline{\quad}\}$. The range is $\{y \mid -\underline{\quad} \le y \le \underline{\quad}\}$.

Quick Check

1. a. Graph the functions $y = \sqrt{25 - x^2}$ and $y = -\sqrt{25 - x^2}$ on the same grid. Compare this graph to the one in Example 1.

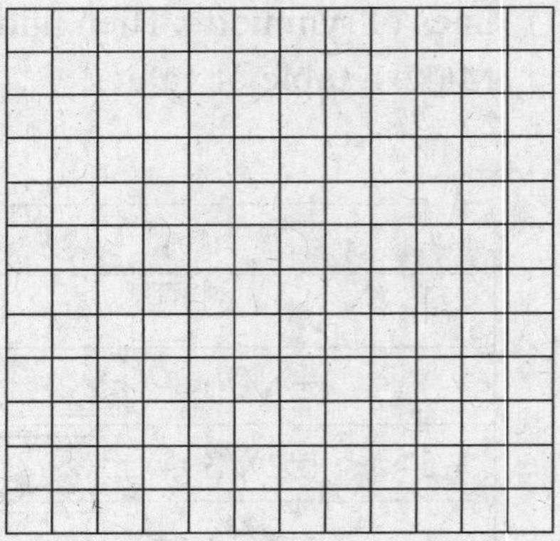

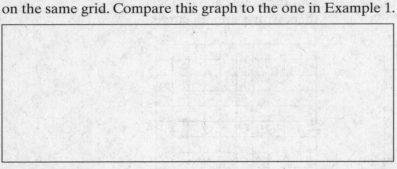

b. Explain how you can get the equations in part (a) from $x^2 + y^2 = 25$.

c. **Critical Thinking** Why is there no point on the graph of Example 1 with an x-coordinate of 6?

Name__________________________ Class__________________________ Date __________________

Example

③ Graphing a Hyperbola Graph the equation $x^2 - y^2 = 4$. Describe the graph and its lines of symmetry. Then find the domain and range.

Make a table of values.

x	☐
−5	± ☐
−4	± ☐
−3	± ☐
−2	0
−1	–
0	–
1	–
2	☐
3	± ☐
4	± ☐
5	± ☐

Plot the points and connect them with smooth curves.

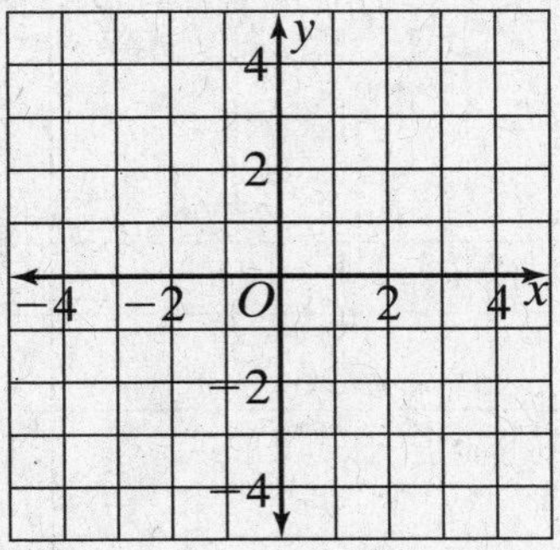

The graph is a ______ that consists of ______ branches. Its center is at the origin. It has ______ lines of symmetry, the x-axis and the y-axis.

The domain is $\{x \mid x$ ☐ -2 or x ☐ $2\}$.

The range is ______ numbers.

Quick Check

2. Graph the equation $2x^2 + y^2 = 18$. Describe the graph and give the coordinates of the center and the x- and y-intercepts.

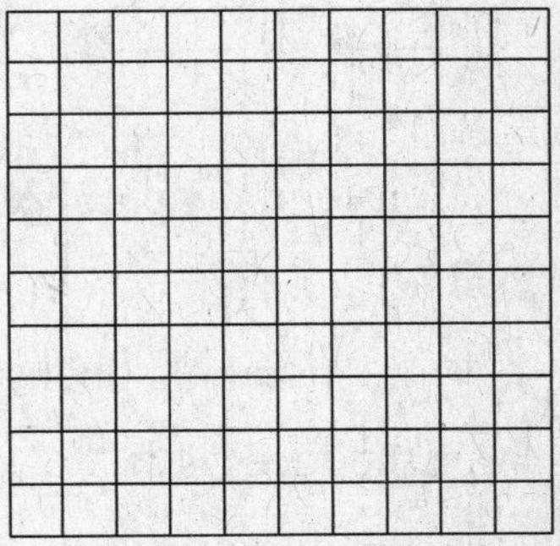

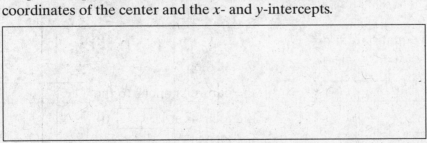

3. **a.** Does the graph in Example 3 represent a function? Explain.

   b. In the table in Example 3, why is the y-value undefined when $x = -1, 0$, or 1?

Name______________________ Class______________________ Date______________

Lesson 10-2

Parabolas

Lesson Objectives	**NAEP 2005 Strand:** Geometry
1 Writing the equation of a parabola	**Topic:** Position and Direction
2 Graphing parabolas	**Local Standards:** ____________

Vocabulary

The focus of a parabola is ____

____

The directrix of a parabola is ____

____

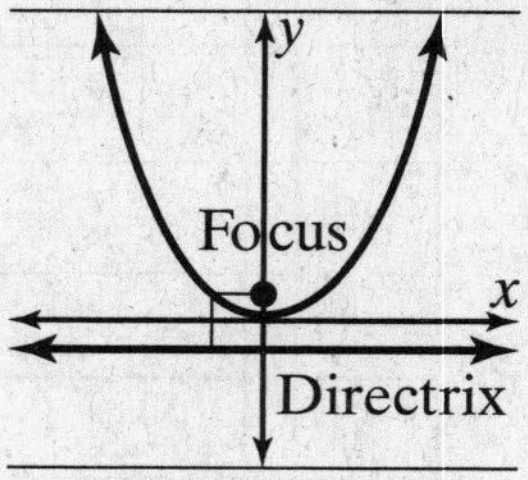

Consider any parabola with equation $y = ax^2$ and vertex at the origin.

If $a > 0$, then
- the parabola opens ______
- the focus is at $(0, \square)$
- the directrix is $y = \square$

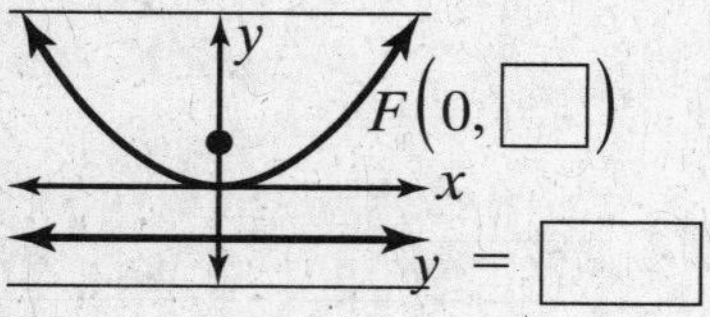

If $a < 0$, then
- the parabola opens ______
- the focus is at $(0, \square)$
- the directrix is at $y = \square$

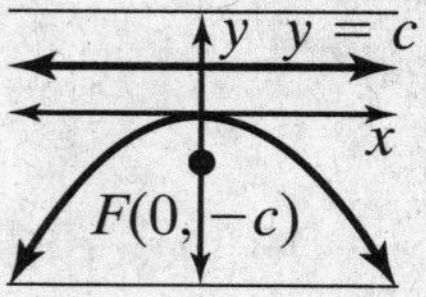

Consider any parabola with equation $x = ay^2$.

If $a > 0$, then
- the parabola opens to the ______
- the focus is at $(\square, 0)$
- the directrix is at $x = \square$

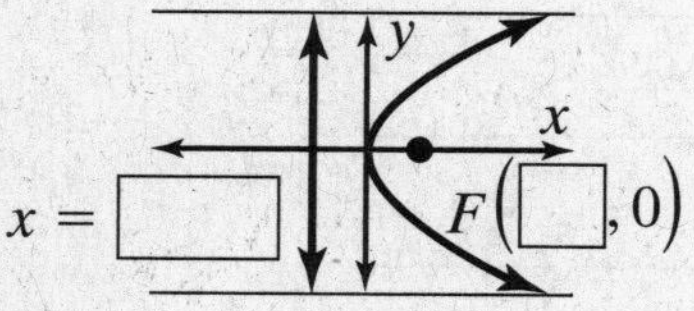

If $a < 0$, then
- the parabola opens to the ______
- the focus is at $(\square, 0)$
- the directrix is at $x = \square$

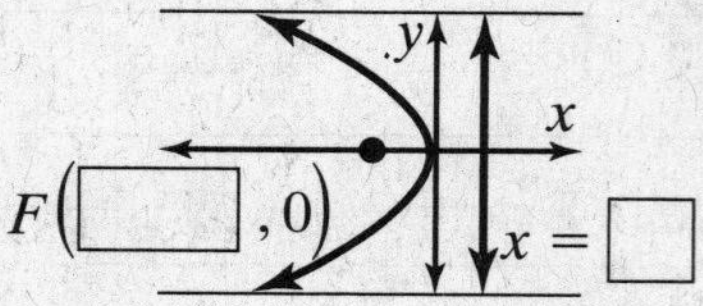

Name______________________ Class______________________ Date ______________

Examples

1 Using the Definition of a Parabola Write an equation for a graph that is the set of all points in the plane that are equidistant from point $F(0, 1)$ and the line $y = -1$.

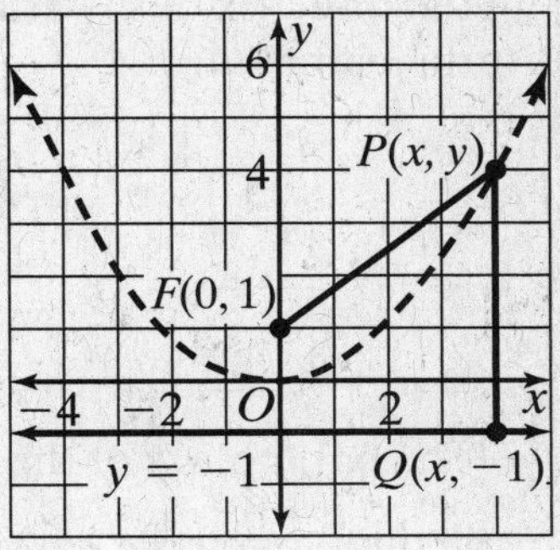

You need to find all points $P(x, y)$ such that FP and the distance from P to the given line are equal.

$$FP = PQ$$

$$\sqrt{(x - \square)^2 + (y - \square)^2} = \sqrt{(x - \square)^2 + (y - (\square))^2}$$

$$x^2 + (y - \square)^2 = \square^2 + (y + \square)^2$$

$$x^2 + y^2 - \square + \square = y^2 + \square + 1$$

$$x^2 = \square y$$

$$y = \square x^2$$

An equation for a graph that is the set of all points in the plane that are equidistant from the point $F(0, 1)$ and the line $y = -1$ is $y = \square x^2$.

2 Writing the Equation of a Parabola Write an equation for a parabola with a vertex at the origin and a focus at $(0, -7)$.

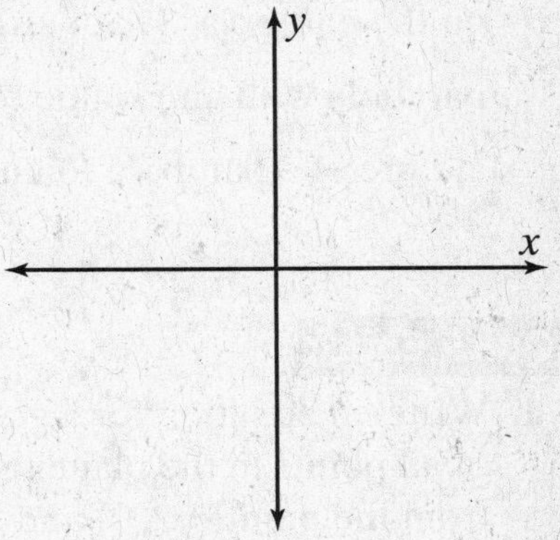

Step 1 Determine the orientation of the parabola. Make a sketch. Since the focus is located below the vertex, the parabola must open ______________.
Use $y = ax^2$.

Step 2 Find a.

$$|a| = \frac{1}{4c}$$

$$= \frac{1}{4(\square)}$$ **Since the focus is a distance of $\square$ units from the vertex, c = $\square$.**

$$= \frac{1}{\square}$$

Since the parabola opens ______________, a is negative. So $a = -\frac{1}{\square}$.

An equation for the parabola is $y = -\frac{1}{\square}x^2$.

Name________________________ Class________________________ Date ________________

❸ Graphing the Equation of a Parabola Identify the vertex, the focus, and the directrix of the graph of the equation $x^2 + 4x + 8y - 4 = 0$. Then graph the parabola.

$8y = -x^2 \square 4x \square 4$ — **Solve for *y*, since *y* is in only one term.**

$8y = -(x^2 + 4x + \square) + 4 + \square$ — **Complete the square in *x*.**

$y = -\square(x + \square)^2 + 1$ — **Vertex form**

The parabola is of the form $y = a(x - h)^2 + k$, so the vertex is at $(\square, \square)$ and the parabola has a vertical axis of symmetry. Since $a < 0$, the parabola opens $\square$.

$|a| = \frac{1}{4c}$

$|\square| = \frac{1}{4c}$ — **Substitute** $\square$ **for *a*.**

$4c = \square$ — **Solve for *c*.**

$c = \square$

The vertex is at $(\square, \square)$ and the focus is at $(\square, \square)$. The equation of the directrix is $y = \square$. Locate one or more points on the parabola. Select a value for x such as -6. The point on the parabola with an x-value of -6 is $(-6, \square)$. Use the symmetric nature of a parabola to find the corresponding point $(\square, \square)$.

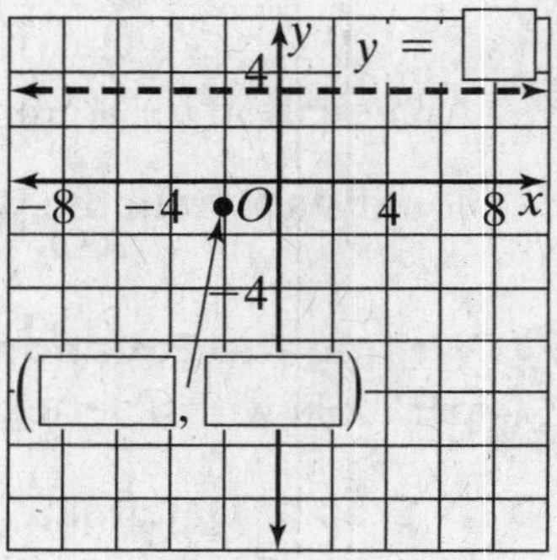

Quick Check

1. Write an equation for a graph that is the set of all points in the plane that are equidistant from the point $F(2, 0)$ and the line $x = -2$.

2. Write an equation of a parabola with a vertex at the origin and a focus at $\left(\frac{1}{2}, 0\right)$.

3. Identify the vertex, the focus, and the directrix of the graph of $x^2 + 6x + 3y + 12 = 0$. Then graph the equation.

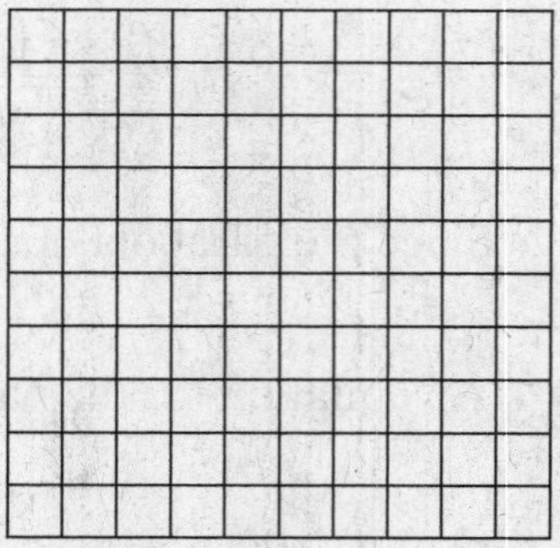

Name________________ Class________________ Date________________

Lesson 10-3

Circles

Lesson Objectives	**NAEP 2005 Strand:** Geometry
1 Writing and graphing the equation of a circle	**Topic:** Position and Direction
2 Finding the center and radius of a circle and using it to graph the circle	**Local Standards:** ____________________

Vocabulary and Key Concepts

Standard Form of an Equation of a Circle

The standard form of an equation of a circle with center (h, k) and radius r is $(x - h)^2 + (y - k)^2 = r^2$.

A circle is ______________________________

____

The center of a circle is ______________________________

____

____

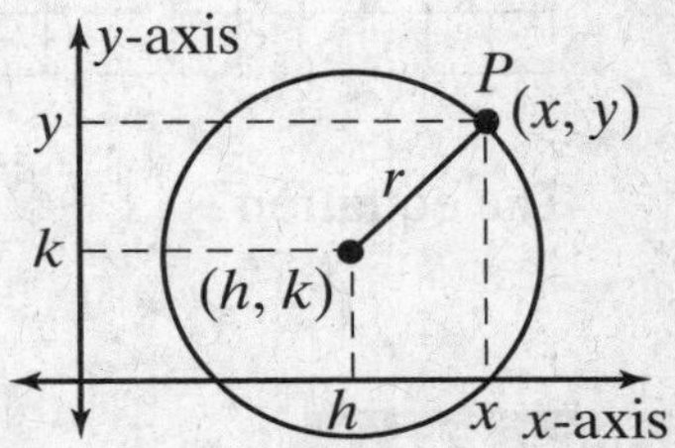

The radius r of a circle is ______________________________

____

____

Examples

1 Writing the Equation of a Circle Write the equation of a circle with center (3, −2) and radius 3.

$(x - h)^2 + (y - k)^2 = r^2$ **Use the standard form of the equation of a circle.**

$\left(x - \square\right)^2 + \left(y - \left(\square\right)\right)^2 = \square^2$ **Substitute $\square$ for *h*, $\square$ for *k*, and $\square$ for *r*.**

$\left(x - \square\right)^2 + \left(y + \square\right)^2 = \square$ **Simplify.**

Check Solve the equation for y and enter both functions into your graphing calculator.

$\left(x - \square\right)^2 + \left(y + \square\right)^2 = \square$

$\left(y + \square\right)^2 = \square - \left(x - \square\right)^2$

$y + \square = \pm\sqrt{\square - \left(x - \square\right)^2}$

$y = \square \pm \sqrt{\square - \left(x - \square\right)^2}$

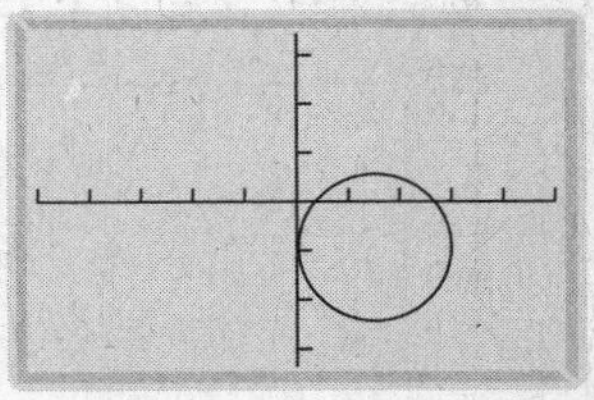

Xmin=−10 Ymin=−7
Xmax=10 Ymax=7
Xscl=2 Yscl=2

❷ Using Translations to Write an Equation Write an equation for the translation of $x^2 + y^2 = 16$ two units right and one unit down. Then graph the translation.

$(x - h)^2 + (y - k)^2 = r^2$ **Use the standard form of the equation of a circle.**

$(x - \square)^2 + (y - (\square))^2 = \square$ **Substitute $\square$ for h, $\square$ for k, and $\square$ for r^2.**

$(x - \square)^2 + (y + \square)^2 = \square$ **Simplify.**

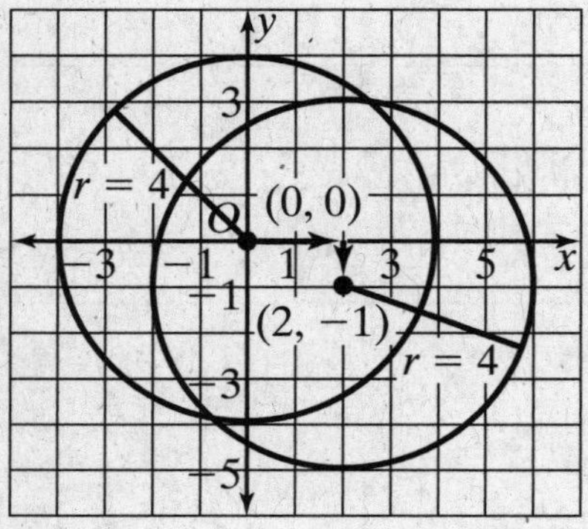

The equation is $(x - \square)^2 + (y + \square)^2 = \square$.

Quick Check

1. Write an equation for a circle with center at (5, −2) and radius 8. Check your answer.

2. Write an equation for each translation.

   a. $x^2 + y^2 = 1$; left 5 and down 3

   b. $x^2 + y^2 = 9$; right 2 and up 3

Name________________ Class________________ Date________________

Examples

3 Finding the Center and Radius Find the center and radius of the circle with equation $(x + 4)^2 + (y - 2)^2 = 36$.

$(x - h)^2 + (y - k)^2 = r^2$ **Use the standard form.**

$(x + 4)^2 + (y - 2)^2 = 36$ **Write the equation.**

$\left(x - (\square)\right)^2 + (y - 2)^2 = \square^2$ **Rewrite the equation in standard form.**

$h = \square$ $k = \square$ $r = \square$ **Find *h*, *k*, and *r*.**

The center of the circle is $(\square, \square)$. The radius is $\square$.

4 Graphing a Circle Using Center and Radius Graph $(x - 3)^2 + (y + 1)^2 = 4$.

$(x - h)^2 + (y - k)^2 = r^2$ **Find the center and radius of the circle.**

$(x - 3)^2 + (y - (-1))^2 = 4$

$h = \square$ $k = \square$ $r^2 = \square$, or $r = \square$

Draw the center $(\square, \square)$ and radius $\square$.

Draw a smooth curve.

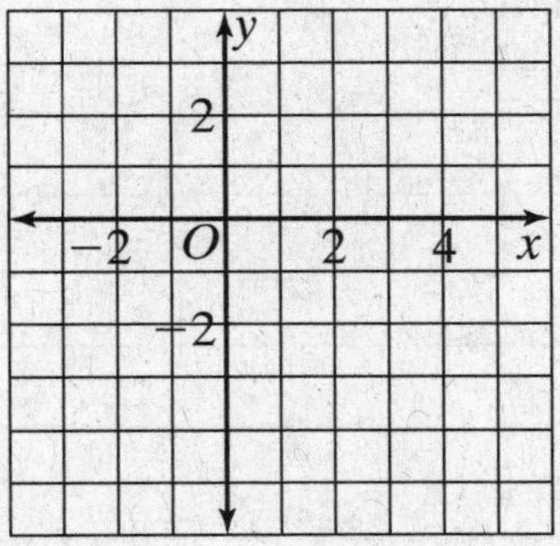

Quick Check

3. Find the center and radius of the circle with equation $(x + 8)^2 + (y + 3)^2 = 121$.

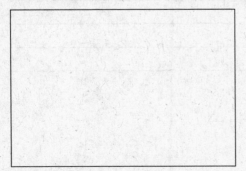

4. Graph $(x - 4)^2 + (y + 2)^2 = 49$.

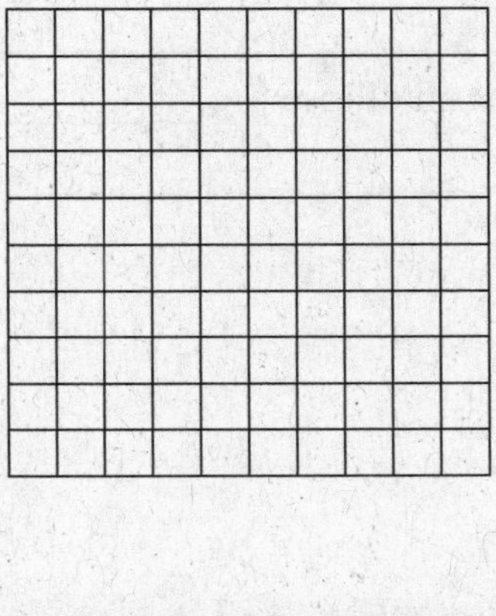

Name________________________ Class____________________ Date____________

Lesson 10-4

Ellipses

Lesson Objectives	**NAEP 2005 Strand:** Geometry
1. Writing the equation of an ellipse	**Topic:** Position and Direction
2. Finding the foci of an ellipse and graphing an ellipse	**Local Standards:** ____________

Vocabulary and Key Concepts

Ellipse

An **ellipse** is a set of points P in a plane such that the sum of the distances from P to two fixed points F_1 and F_2 is a given constant k.

$PF_1 + PF_2 = \square$, where $k > \square$

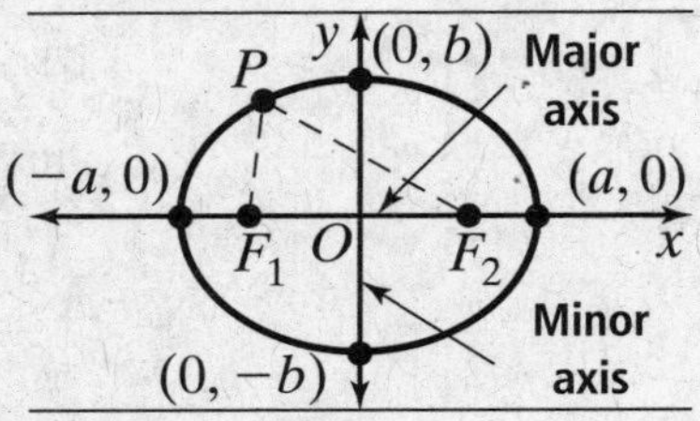

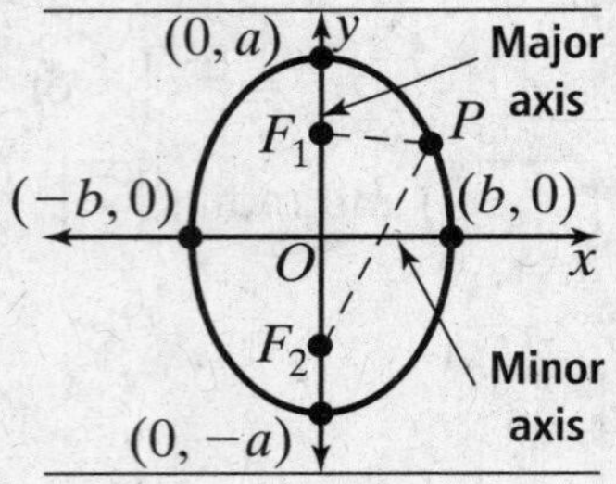

The focus of an ellipse is ____

____

The major axis of an ellipse is ____

____

The vertices of an ellipse are ____

____

The minor axis of an ellipse is ____

____

The co-vertices of an ellipse are ____

____

Name______________________ Class______________________ Date ______________

Examples

1 Writing the Equation of an Ellipse Write an equation in standard form of an ellipse that has a vertex at $(0, -4)$, a co-vertex at $(3, 0)$, and a center at the origin.

Since $(0, -4)$ is a vertex of the ellipse, the other vertex is at $(0, \square)$, and the major axis is $\square$. Since $(3, 0)$ is a co-vertex, the other co-vertex is at $(\square, 0)$, and the minor axis is $\square$. So, $a = \square$, $b = \square$, $a^2 = \square$, and $b^2 = \square$.

$$\frac{x^2}{b^2} + \frac{y^2}{a^2} = 1$$ **Standard form for an equation of an ellipse with a vertical major axis.**

$$\frac{x^2}{\square} + \frac{y^2}{\square} = 1$$ **Substitute $\square$ for b^2 and $\square$ for a^2.**

An equation of the ellipse is $\frac{x^2}{\square} + \frac{y^2}{\square} = 1$.

2 Finding the Foci of an Ellipse Find the foci of the ellipse with the equation $9x^2 + y^2 = 36$. Graph the ellipse.

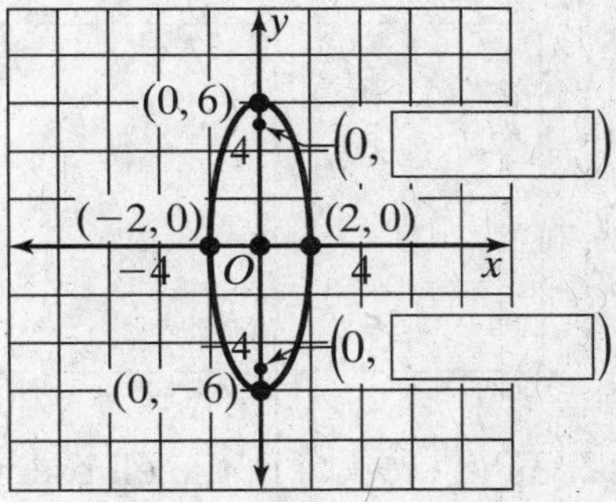

$$9x^2 + y^2 = 36$$

$$\frac{x^2}{\square} + \frac{y^2}{\square} = 1$$ **Write in standard form.**

Since $36 > 4$ and $\square$ is with y^2, the major axis is $\square$, $a^2 = \square$, and $b^2 = \square$.

$c^2 = a^2 - b^2$ **Find c.**

$= \square - \square$ **Substitute $\square$ for a^2 and $\square$ for b^2.**

$= \square$

$c = \pm\sqrt{\square} = \pm\square$

The major axis is $\square$, so the coordinates of the foci are $(0, \pm c)$. The foci are $(0, \square)$ and $(0, \square)$.

The vertices are $(0, \pm 6)$. The co-vertices are $(\pm 2, 0)$.

Name______________________ Class______________________ Date ______________

3 Using the Foci of an Ellipse Write an equation of the ellipse with foci at $(0, \pm 4)$ and co-vertices at $(\pm 2, 0)$.

Since the foci have coordinates $(0, \pm 4)$, the major axis is $\square$.

Since $c = \square$ and $b = \square$, $c^2 = \square$, and $b^2 = \square$.

$c^2 = a^2 - b^2$ **Use the equation to find a^2.**

$\square = a^2 - \square$ **Substitute $\square$ for c^2 and $\square$ for b^2.**

$a^2 = \square$ **Simplify.**

$\frac{x^2}{\square} + \frac{y^2}{\square} = 1$ **Substitute $\square$ for a^2 and $\square$ for b^2.**

An equation of the ellipse is $\frac{x^2}{\square} + \frac{y^2}{\square} = 1$.

Quick Check

1. Write an equation in standard form for an ellipse that has a vertex at $(0, -6)$, a co-vertex at $(3, 0)$, and a center at the origin.

2. Find the foci of the ellipse with the equation $x^2 + 9y^2 = 9$. Graph the ellipse.

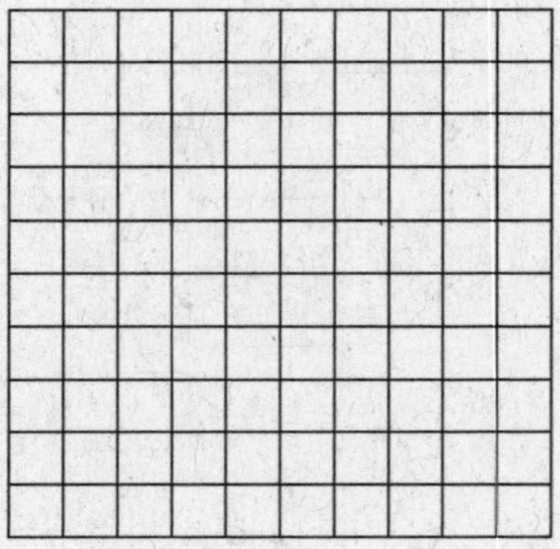

3. Write an equation of the ellipse with foci at $(0, \pm\sqrt{17})$ and co-vertices at $(\pm 8, 0)$.

Name________________________ Class________________________ Date____________

Lesson 10-5

Hyperbolas

Lesson Objectives	**NAEP 2005 Strand:** Geometry
1 Graphing hyperbolas	**Topic:** Position and Direction
2 Finding and using the foci of a hyperbola	**Local Standards:** ____________________

Vocabulary and Key Concepts

Hyperbola

A **hyperbola** is a set of points P in a plane such that the absolute values of difference between the distances from P to two fixed points F_1 and F_2 is a given constant k.

$|PF_1 - PF_2| = \square$, where $k < \square$

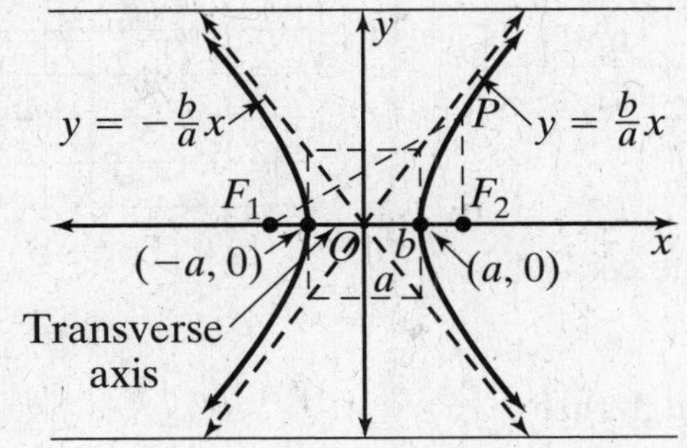

$$\frac{x^2}{a^2} - \frac{y^2}{b^2} = 1$$

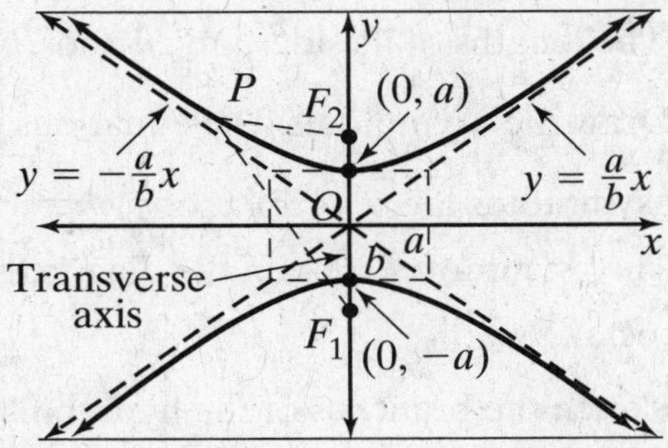

$$\frac{y^2}{a^2} - \frac{x^2}{b^2} = 1$$

The focus of a hyperbola is ______________________________________

____

The transverse axis of a hyperbola is ______________________________

____

The vertices of a hyperbola are ___________________________________

Name____________________ Class________________ Date ____________

Examples

1 Graphing a Hyperbola Graph $4x^2 - 16y^2 = 64$.

$\frac{x^2}{\square} - \frac{y^2}{\square} = 1$ **Rewrite the equation in standard form.**

The equation is of the form $\frac{x^2}{a^2} - \frac{y^2}{b^2} = 1$, so the transverse axis is $\square$.

Since $a^2 = \square$ and $b^2 = \square$, $a = \square$ and $b = \square$.

Step 1 Graph the vertices. Since the transverse axis is $\square$, the vertices lie on the $\square$-axis. The coordinates are $(\pm a, 0)$, or $(\pm\square, 0)$.

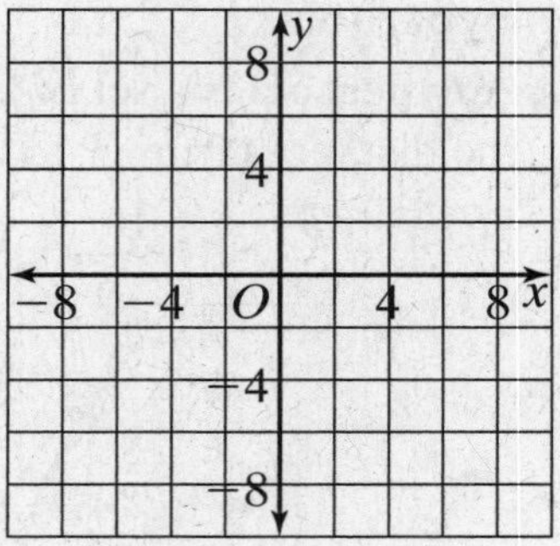

Step 2 Use the values a and b to draw the central rectangle. The lengths of its sides are $2a$ and $2b$, or $\square$ and $\square$.

Step 3 Draw the asymptotes. The equations of the asymptotes are $y = \pm\frac{b}{a}x$, or $y = \pm\square x$. The asymptotes contain the diagonals of the central rectangle.

Step 4 Sketch the branches of the hyperbola through the vertices so they approach the asymptotes.

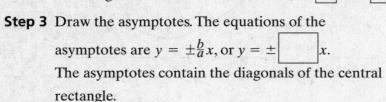

2 Finding the Foci of a Hyperbola Find the foci of the graph $\frac{y^2}{4} - \frac{x^2}{9} = 1$.

Draw the graph.

The equation is in the form $\frac{y^2}{a^2} - \frac{x^2}{b^2} = 1$, so the transverse axis is $\square$;

$a^2 = \square$ and $b^2 = \square$.

$c^2 = a^2 + b^2$ **Use the Pythagorean Theorem.**

$= \square + \square$ **Substitute $\square$ for a^2 and $\square$ for b^2.**

$c = \sqrt{\square} \approx \square$ **Find the square root of each side of the equation.**

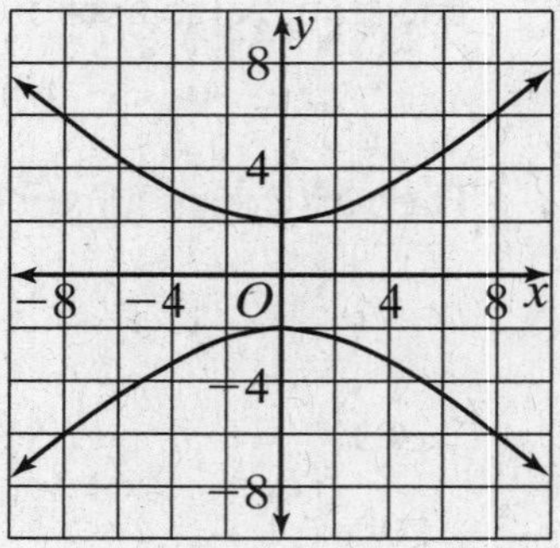

The foci $(0, \pm c)$ are approximately $(0, \square)$ and $(0, \square)$.

The vertices $(0, \pm a)$ are $(0, \square)$ and $(0, \square)$.

The asymptotes are the lines $y = \pm\frac{a}{b}x$, or $y = \pm\square x$.

Name______________________ Class______________________ Date ______________

3 **Space** As a spacecraft approaches a planet, the gravitational pull of the planet changes the spacecraft's path to a hyperbola that diverges from its asymptote. Find an equation that models the path of a spacecraft around a planet if $a = 300{,}765$ km and $c = 424{,}650$ km.

Assume that the center of the hyperbola is at the origin and that the transverse axis is horizontal. The equation will be in the form $\frac{x^2}{a^2} - \frac{y^2}{b^2} = 1$.

$c^2 = a^2 + b^2$ **Use the Pythagorean Theorem.**

$(\square)^2 = (\square)^2 + b^2$ **Substitute.**

$b^2 = (\square)^2 - (\square)^2$ **Solve for b^2.**

$\approx \square$

$\frac{x^2}{\square} - \frac{y^2}{\square} = 1$ **Substitute for a^2 and b^2.**

The path of the spacecraft around the planet can be modeled by

$\frac{x^2}{\square} - \frac{y^2}{\square} = 1$.

Quick Check

1. Graph the hyperbola with equation $\frac{y^2}{16} - \frac{x^2}{9} = 1$.

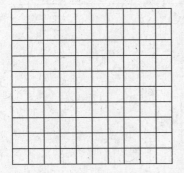

2. Find the foci of $\frac{x^2}{25} - \frac{y^2}{9} = 1$.

   Draw the graph.

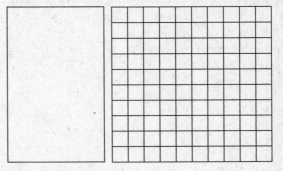

3. Refer to the information in Example 3. Find an equation that models the path of *Voyager 2* around Jupiter, given that $a = 2{,}184{,}140$ km and $c = 2{,}904{,}906.2$ km.

Name______________________ Class______________________ Date______________

Lesson 10-6

Translating Conic Sections

Lesson Objectives	**NAEP 2005 Strand:** Geometry
1 Writing the equation of a translated conic section	**Topic:** Position and Direction
2 Identifying the equation of a translated conic section	**Local Standards:** ____________________

Key Concepts

Equations of Conic Sections

Conic Section		Standard Form of Equation
______	Vertex (0, 0) $y = ax^2$ $x = ay^2$	Vertex (h, k) $y - \square = a(x - \square)^2$ or $y = a(x - \square)^2 + \square$ $x - \square = a(y - \square)^2$ or $x = a(y - \square)^2 + \square$
______	Center (0, 0) $x^2 + y^2 = r^2$	Center (h, k) $(\square - h)^2 + (\square - k)^2 = r^2$
______	Center (0, 0) $\frac{x^2}{\square} + \frac{y^2}{\square} = 1$ $\frac{x^2}{b^2} + \frac{y^2}{a^2} = 1$	Center (h, k) $\frac{(\square - h)^2}{a^2} + \frac{(\square - k)^2}{b^2} = 1$ $\frac{(x - \square)^2}{b^2} + \frac{(y - \square)^2}{a^2} = 1$
______	Center (0, 0) $\frac{x^2}{\square} - \frac{y^2}{\square} = 1$ $\frac{y^2}{a^2} - \frac{x^2}{b^2} = 1$	Center (h, k) $\frac{(\square - h)^2}{a^2} - \frac{(\square - k)^2}{b^2} = 1$ $\frac{(x - \square)^2}{b^2} - \frac{(y - \square)^2}{a^2} = 1$

Name______________________ Class______________________ Date ____________

Examples

1 Writing the Equation of a Translated Ellipse Write an equation of an ellipse with center $(-2, 4)$, a vertical major axis of length 10, and minor axis of length 8.

The length of the $\square$ axis is $2a$. So $2a = \square$ and $a = \square$.

The length of the $\square$ axis is $2b$. So $2b = \square$ and $b = \square$.

Since the center is $(-2, 4)$, $h = \square$ and $k = \square$.

The major axis is vertical, so the equation has the form $\dfrac{(x-h)^2}{b^2} + \dfrac{(y-k)^2}{a^2} = 1$.

$$\frac{(x - (\square))^2}{\square^2} + \frac{(y - \square)^2}{\square^2} = 1$$ **Substitute** $\square$ **for** h, $\square$ **for** k, $\square$ **for** a, **and** $\square$ **for** b.

The equation of the ellipse is $\dfrac{(x + \square)^2}{\square} + \dfrac{(y - \square)^2}{\square} = 1$.

2 Writing the Equation of a Translated Hyperbola Write an equation of a hyperbola with vertices $(-1, 2)$ and $(3, 2)$, and foci $(-3, 2)$ and $(5, 2)$.

The center is the midpoint of the line joining the vertices. Its coordinates are $(\square, \square)$. The distance between the vertices is $2a$, and the distance between the foci is $2c$.

$2a = \square$, so $a = \square$; $2c = \square$, so $c = \square$.

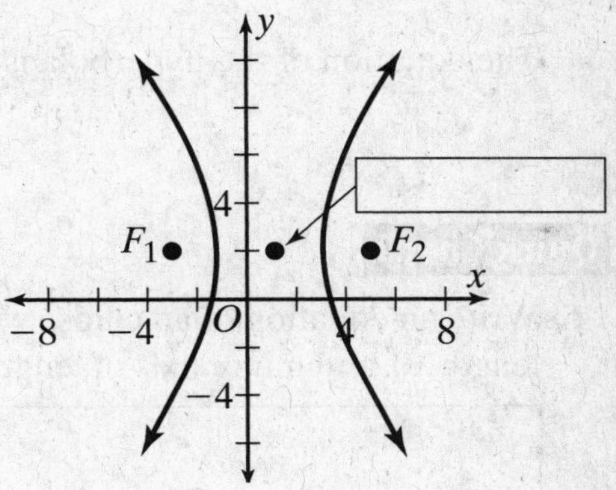

Find b^2 using the Pythagorean Theorem.

$$c^2 = a^2 + b^2$$

$$\square = \square + b^2$$

$$b^2 = \square$$

The transverse axis is $\square$, so the equation has the form $\dfrac{(x-h)^2}{a^2} - \dfrac{(y-k)^2}{b^2} = 1$.

The equation of the hyperbola is $\dfrac{(x - \square)^2}{\square} - \dfrac{(y - \square)^2}{\square} = 1$.

Name________________________ Class________________ Date ____________

❸ Navigation Some ships navigate using "long range navigation" (or LORAN). Navigators use a system of radio transmitters to pinpoint their locations using hyperbolas. Find the equation of the hyperbola if the transmitters are 80 miles apart located at (0, 0) and (80, 0), and all points on the hyperbola are 30 miles closer to one transmitter than the other.

Find c. Since $2c = 80$, $c = 40$. The center of the hyperbola is $(\square, \square)$.

Find a by calculating the difference in the distances from the vertex at $(a + 40, 0)$ to the two foci.

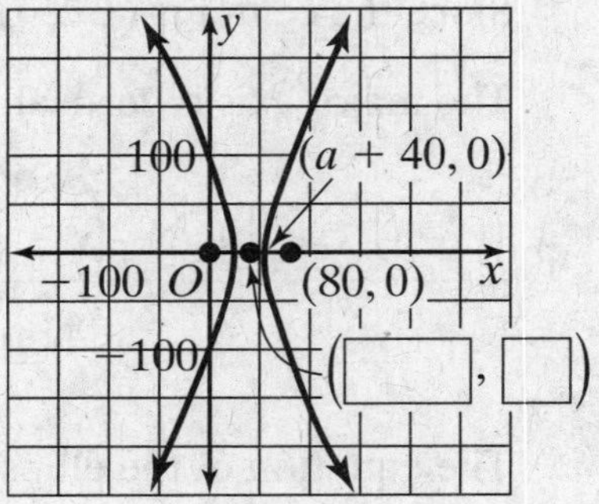

$30 = (a + 40) - (80 - (a + 40))$

$= \square a$

$\square = a$

Find b^2.

$c^2 = a^2 + b^2$

$(\square)^2 = (\square)^2 + b^2$

$\square = \square + b^2$

$b^2 = \square$

The equation of the hyperbola is $\dfrac{(x - \square)^2}{\square} - \dfrac{y^2}{\square} = 1$.

Quick Check

1. Write an equation of an ellipse with center (1, −4), horizontal major axis of length 10, and minor axis of length 4. Check your answer.

2. Write an equation of a hyperbola with vertices (2, −1) and (2, 7), and foci (2, 10) and (2, −4).

3. Using the information from Example 3, find the equation of the hyperbola with all points 56 miles closer to one transmitter than the other.

Name____________________ Class____________________ Date ____________

Example

4 Identifying a Translated Conic Section Identify the conic section with equation $9x^2 - 4y^2 + 18x = 27$. If it is a parabola, give the vertex. If it is a circle, give the center and the radius. If it is an ellipse or a hyperbola, give the center and foci. Sketch the graph.

Complete the square for the x- and y-terms to write the equation in standard form.

$9x^2 + 18x - 4y^2 = 27$	**Group the x- and y-terms.**
$9(x^2 + 2x + \blacksquare) - 4y^2 = 27$	**Complete the square.**
$9\left(x^2 + 2x + \square\right) - 4y^2 = 27 + 9\left(\square^2\right)$	**Add (9)$\left(\square^2\right)$ to each side.**
$9\left(x + \square\right)^2 - 4y^2 = \square$	**Write the trinomial as a binomial squared.**
$\dfrac{9\left(x + \square\right)^2}{\square} - \dfrac{4y^2}{\square} = 1$	**Divide each side by $\square$.**
$\dfrac{\left(x + \square\right)^2}{\square} - \dfrac{y^2}{\square} = 1$	**Simplify.**

The equation represents a hyperbola. The center is $\left(\square, 0\right)$.

The transverse axis is $\square$.

Since $a^2 = \square$, $a = \square$; $b^2 = \square$, so $b = \square$.

$c^2 = a^2 + b^2$

$= \square + \square = \square$

$c = \square$

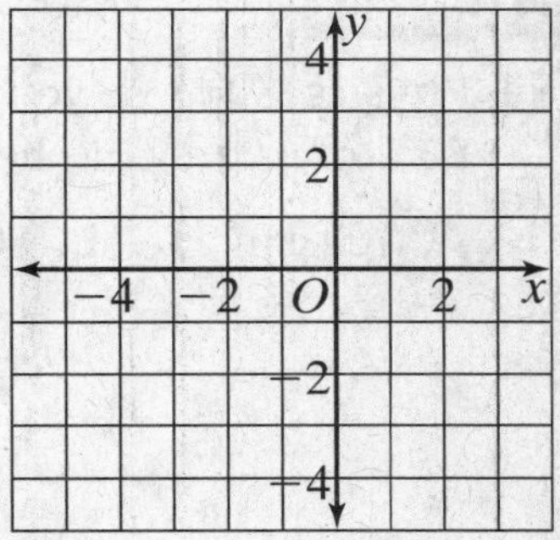

The distance from the center of the hyperbola to the foci is $\square$.

Since the hyperbola is centered at $\left(\square, 0\right)$, and the transverse axis is $\square$, the foci are located $\square$ to the left and right of the center. The foci are at $\left(-1 + \square, 0\right)$ and $\left(-1 - \square, 0\right)$.

Quick Check

4. Identify the conic section represented by $x^2 + y^2 - 12x + 4y = 8$. Sketch the graph.

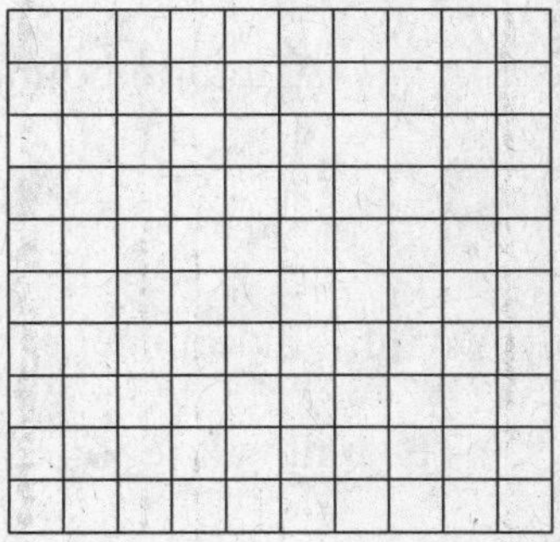

Name______________________ Class______________________ Date______________

Lesson 11-1

Mathematical Patterns

Lesson Objectives	NAEP 2005 Strand: Algebra
1 Identifying mathematical patterns	**Topic:** Patterns, Relations, and Functions
2 Using a formula for finding the *n*th term in a sequence	**Local Standards:** ______________________

Vocabulary

A sequence is ______________________________

A term in a sequence is ______________________________

____

A recursive formula ______________________________

____

An explicit formula ______________________________

____

Examples

1 **Physics** Suppose you drop a ball from a height of 100 cm. It bounces back to 80% of its previous height. About how high will it go after its fifth bounce?

A. 100 cm **B.** 80 cm **C.** 32.8 cm **D.** 26.2 cm

Original height of ball: 100 cm →

After first bounce: 80% of 100 = 0.80(100) = 80 →

After 2nd bounce: 0.80(80) = ____ →

After 3rd bounce: 0.80(____) = ____ →

After 4th bounce: 0.80(____) = ____ →

After 5th bounce: 0.80(____) = ____ →

The ball will rebound about 32.8 cm after the fifth bounce.

The correct choice is C.

Name______________________ Class______________________ Date______________

❷ Using a Recursive Formula

a. Describe the pattern that allows you to find the next term in the sequence 2, 6, 18, 54, 162, ... Write a recursive formula for the sequence.

Multiply a term by 3 to find the next term. A recursive formula is

$a_n = \square\,\square \cdot \square$, where $a_1 = \square$.

b. Find the sixth and seventh terms in the sequence.

Since $a_5 = 162$, $a_6 = 162 \cdot 3 = \square$, and $a_7 = \square \cdot 3 = \square$.

c. Find the value of a_{10} in the sequence.

The term a_{10} is the tenth term. $a_{10} = a_9 \cdot 3 = (a_8 \cdot 3) \cdot 3 = ((a_7 \cdot 3) \cdot 3) \cdot 3 =$ $((\square \cdot 3) \cdot 3) \cdot 3 = \square$.

Quick Check

1. Use the information from Example 1.

a. About how high will the ball rebound after the eighth bounce?

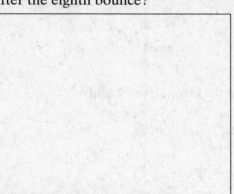

b. After what bounce will the rebound height be less than 11 cm?

2. Use the sequence from Example 2. Find terms a_{11} and a_{13} in the sequence.

Name________________________ Class________________________ Date ____________

Example

3 Geometry The spreadsheet shows the perimeters of regular pentagons with sides from 1 to 4 units long. The numbers in each row form a sequence.

	A	B	C	D	E	F
1		a_1	a_2	a_3	a_4	...
2	Length of a Side	1	2	3	4	...
3	Perimeter	5	10	15	20	...

a. For each sequence, find the next term (a_5) and the twentieth term (a_{20}).

In the sequence in row 2, each term is the same as its subscript. Therefore, $a_5 = \square$ and $a_{20} = \square$.

In the sequence in row 3, each term is $\square$ times its subscript. Therefore, $a_5 = 5(\square) = \square$ and $a_{20} = 5(\square) = \square$.

b. Write an explicit formula for each sequence.

The explicit formula for the sequence in row 2 is $\square_{\square} = \square$. The explicit formula for the sequence in row 3 is $\square_{\square} = \square$.

Quick Check

3. The spreadsheet shows the perimeters of squares with sides from 2 to 12 units long.

	A	B	C	D	E	F	G	H
1		a_1	a_2	a_3	a_4	a_5	a_6	...
2	Length of a Side	2	4	6	8	10	12	...
3	Perimeter	8	16	24	32	40	48	...

a. Write the first six terms in the sequence showing the areas of the squares. Then find a_{20}.

b. Write an explicit formula for the sequence from part (a).

Name________________ Class________________ Date________________

Lesson 11-2

Arithmetic Sequences

Lesson Objective	
1 Identifying and generating arithmetic sequences	**NAEP 2005 Strand:** Algebra **Topic:** Patterns, Relations, and Functions **Local Standards:** ____________________

Vocabulary and Key Concepts

Arithmetic Sequence Formulas

[________] **Formula**

a_1 = a given value, $a_n = a_{n-1} + d$

[________] **Formula**

$a_n = a_1 + (n - 1)d$

In these formulas, a_n is the nth term, a_1 is the first term, n is the number of the term, and d is the common difference.

In an arithmetic sequence, ____

____

A common difference is ____

____

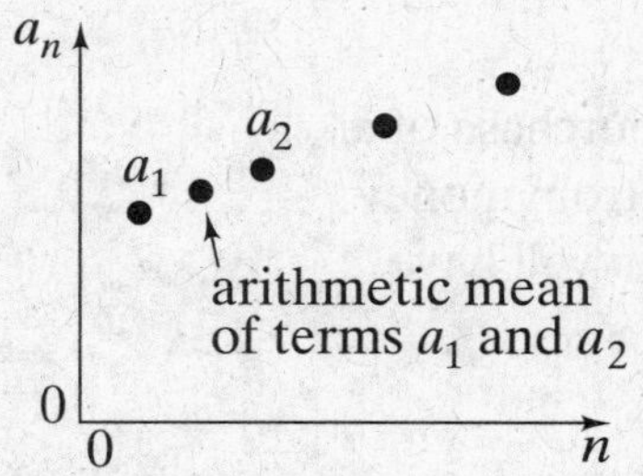

The arithmetic mean of any two numbers is ______________________________

____

Name____________________________ Class____________________ Date ____________

Examples

1 Identifying an Arithmetic Sequence Is the given sequence arithmetic?

a. 7, 10, 13, 16, …

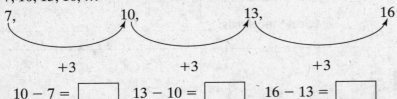

7, 10, 13, 16

+3 +3 +3

10 − 7 = ____ 13 − 10 = ____ 16 − 13 = ____

The common difference is ____. This ____ an arithmetic sequence.

b. the sequence of dots in the triangles shown below

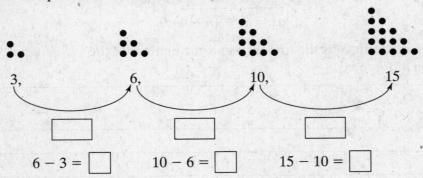

3, 6, 10, 15

____ ____ ____

6 − 3 = ____ 10 − 6 = ____ 15 − 10 = ____

There is no common difference. This ____ an arithmetic sequence.

2 Saving Money Suppose you have already saved \$75 toward the purchase of a new CD player and speakers. You plan to save at least \$12 a week from money you earn at a part-time job. In all, what is the minimum amount you will have saved after 26 weeks?

Find the 27th term of the sequence 75, 87, 99, … .

$a_n = a_1 + (n - 1)d$	**Use the explicit formula.**
a_{27} = ____ + (____ − ____)(____)	**Substitute a_1 = ____, n = ____, and d = ____.**
= 75 + (____)(____)	**Subtract within parentheses.**
= 75 + ____	**Multiply.**
= ____	**Simplify.**

After 26 weeks, you will have saved a minimum of \$____.

Name________________________ Class________________ Date __________

3 **Using the Arithmetic Mean** Find the missing term of the arithmetic sequence 50, ▢, 92.

arithmetic mean $= \dfrac{\square + \square}{\square}$ **Write the average.**

$= \dfrac{\square}{\square}$ **Simplify the numerator.**

$= \square$ **Divide.**

The missing term is ▢.

Quick Check

1. Is the given sequence arithmetic? If so, identify the common difference.
   a. 2, 5, 7, 12, . . .
   b. 48, 45, 42, 39, . . .

2. **a.** Refer to the formula in Example 2. Why was it necessary to find the value of the 27th term, not the 26th term?
   b. Use the explicit formula to find the 25th term in the sequence 5, 11, 17, 23, 29, . . .

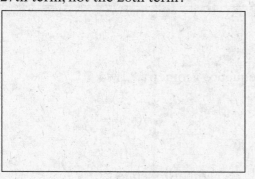

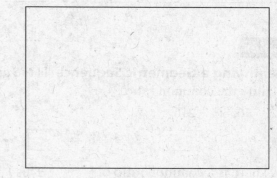

3. **a.** Find the missing term of the arithmetic sequence 24, ▢, 57.
   b. Write an expression that shows the arithmetic mean of a_6 and a_7.

Name________________________ Class____________________ Date______________

Lesson 11-3

Geometric Sequences

Lesson Objective	**NAEP 2005 Strand:** Algebra
1 Identifying and generating geometric sequences	**Topic:** Patterns, Relations, and Functions
	Local Standards: ____________________

Vocabulary and Key Concepts

Geometric Sequence Formulas

______ **Formula**

a_1 = a given value, $a_n = a_{n-1} \cdot r$

______ **Formula**

$a_n = a_1 \cdot r^{n-1}$

In these formulas, a_n is the nth term, a_1 is the first term, n is the number of the term, and r is the common ratio.

In a geometric sequence, ____

____

The common ratio is ____

____

The geometric mean of any two positive numbers can be found by ______________

____

Examples

1 Identifying a Geometric Sequence Is the given sequence geometric? If so, identify the common ratio.

a. 1, −6, 36, −216, …

$-6 \div 1 =$ ☐ $\quad 36 \div -6 =$ ☐ $\quad -216 \div 36 =$ ☐

There is a common ratio of ☐. This ☐ a geometric sequence.

b. 2, 4, 6, 8, …

$4 \div 2 =$ ☐ $\quad 6 \div 4 = \frac{☐}{☐}$ $\quad 8 \div 6 = \frac{☐}{☐}$

There is no common ratio. This ☐ a geometric sequence.

Name____________________ Class____________________ Date____________

2 **Design** Suppose you have equipment that can enlarge a photo to 120% of its original size. A photo has a length of 10 cm. Find the length of the photo after 5 enlargements of 120%.

$a_n = a_1 \cdot r^{n-1}$ — **Use the explicit formula.**

$a_6 = \square \cdot \square^{\square - \square}$ — **Substitue a_1 = $\square$, n = $\square$, and r = $\square$.**

$= \square \cdot \square^{\square}$ — **Simplify the exponent.**

$\approx \square$ — **Use a calculator.**

After five enlargements of 120%, the photo has a length of about $\square$ cm.

3 **Real Estate** A family purchased a home for $150,000. Two years later the home was valued at $188,160. If the value of the home is increasing geometrically, how much was the home worth after one year?

geometric mean $= \sqrt{\square \cdot \square}$ — **Use the definition.**

$= \sqrt{\square}$ — **Multiply.**

$= \square$ — **Take the square root.**

Quick Check

1. Determine whether each sequence is arithmetic, geometric, or neither. Explain.
   a. 6, −24, 96, −384, . . .
   b. 8, 20, 32, 44, . . .

2. Find the 19th term in each sequence.
   a. 11, 33, 99, 297, . . .
   b. 20, 17, 14, 11, 8, . . .

3. Find the missing term of each geometric sequence.
   a. 20, ▢, 80 . . .
   b. 3, ▢, 18.75 . . .
   c. 28, ▢, 5103 . . .

Name________________________ Class____________________ Date______________

Lesson 11-4

Arithmetic Series

Lesson Objectives	NAEP 2005 Strand: Algebra
1 Writing and evaluating arithmetic series	**Topic:** Patterns, Relations, and Functions
2 Using summation notation	**Local Standards:** ____________________

Vocabulary and Key Concepts

Sum of a Finite Arithmetic Series

The sum of S_n of a finite arithmetic series $a_1 + a_2 + a_3 + \ldots + a_n$ is

$$S_n = \frac{n}{2}(a_1 + a_n)$$

where a_1 is the first term, a_n is the nth term, and n is the __________.

A series is ____

____

Finite sequence	**Finite series**	**Infinite sequence**	**Infinite series**
6, 9, 12, 15, 18	6 + 9 + 12 + 15 + 18	3, 7, 11, 15, . . .	3 + 7 + 11 + 15 + . . .

An arithmetic series is ____

____

upper limit, greatest value of n → 3

explicit formula for the sequence → $(5n + 1)$

$$\sum_{n=1}^{3} (5n + 1)$$

lower limit, least value of n → $n = 1$

The limits are ____

____

Name______________________ Class______________________ Date ______________

Examples

❶ Writing and Evaluating a Series Use the finite sequence 5, 9, 13, 17, 21, 25, 29. Write the related series. Evaluate the series.

Related series → $5 + 9 + 13 + 17 + 21 + 25 + 29 = \square$ ← Add to evaluate.

The sum of the terms of the sequence is $\square$.

❷ Finding the Sum of a Series A staircase uses same-size cement blocks arranged 4 across, as shown. Find the total number of blocks in the staircase.

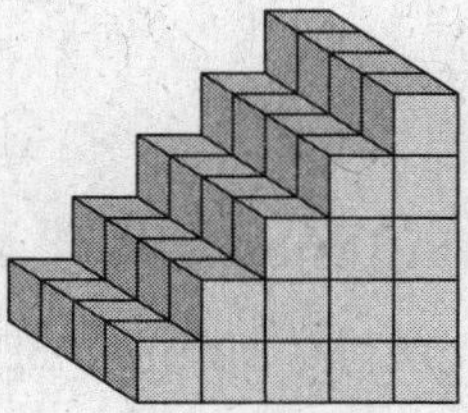

Relate $\boxed{\text{sum of the series}} = \dfrac{\boxed{\text{number of terms}}}{2} \times \left(\boxed{\text{the first term}} + \boxed{\text{the last term}}\right)$

Define Let $\boxed{S_n}$ = total number of blocks, and let $\boxed{n}$ = the number of stairs.

Then $\boxed{a_1}$ = the number of blocks in the first stair,

and $\boxed{a_n}$ = the number of blocks in the last stair.

Write $\boxed{S_n} = \dfrac{\boxed{n}}{\square} \times \left(\boxed{a_1} + \boxed{a_n}\right)$ **Use the formula.**

$= \dfrac{\square}{\square}\left(\square + \square\right)$ **Substitute $n = \square$, $a_1 = \square$, $a_n = \square$.**

$= \square\left(\square\right) = \square$ **Simplify.**

There are $\square$ blocks in the stairs.

Quick Check

1. Write the related series for each finite sequence. Then evaluate the series.

a. 0.3, 0.6, 0.9, 1.2, 1.5, 1.8, 2.1, 2.4, 2.7, 3.0

b. 100, 125, 150, 175, 200, 225

2. Suppose the pattern from Example 2 extends to 10 stairs.

a. Find the 10th term of the sequence.

b. Find the value of the series to the 10th term.

Name______________________ Class______________________ Date ____________

Examples

3 Writing a Series in Summation Notation Use the summation notation to write the series 8 + 16 + 24 + . . . for 50 terms.

$\square \cdot 1 = 8, \square \cdot 2 = 16, \square \cdot 3 = 24, \ldots$ **The explicit formula for the sequence is** $\square$ ***n*.**

$8 + 16 + 24 + \ldots + 400 = \sum_{n=\square}^{\square} \square n$ **The lower limit is** $\square$ **and the upper limit is** $\square$**.**

4 Finding the Sum of a Series Use the series $\sum_{n=1}^{4}(-2n + 3)$.

a. Find the number of terms in the series.

Since the values of n are $\square$, there are $\square$ terms in the series.

b. Evaluate the series.

$\sum_{n=1}^{4}(-2n + 3) = (-2(\square) + 3) + (-2(\square) + 3) + (-2(\square) + 3) + (-2(\square) + 3)$ **Substitute.**

$= \square + (\square) + (\square) + (\square) = \square$ **Simplify within parentheses. Add.**

The sum of the series is $\square$.

Quick Check

3. Use summation notation to write each series for the specified number of terms.

a. $1 + 2 + 3 + \ldots; n = 6$

b. $3 + 8 + 13 + 18 + \ldots; n = 9$

4. For each sum, find the number of terms, the first term, and the last term. Then evaluate the series.

a. $\sum_{n=1}^{10}(n - 3)$

b. $\sum_{n=1}^{4}\left(\frac{1}{2}n + 1\right)$

c. $\sum_{n=2}^{5}n^2$

Name______________________ Class______________________ Date______________

Lesson 11-5

Geometric Series

Lesson Objectives	**NAEP 2005 Strand:** Algebra
1 Evaluating a finite geometric series	**Topic:** Patterns, Relations, and Functions
2 Evaluating an infinite geometric series	**Local Standards:** ____________________

Vocabulary and Key Concepts

Sum of a Finite Geometric Series

The sum S_n of a finite geometric series $a_1 + a_2 + a_3 + \ldots + a_n, r \neq 1$, is

$$S_n = \frac{a_1(1 - r^n)}{1 - r}$$

where a_1 is the first term, a_n is the nth term, and n is the ______.

Sum of an Infinite Geometric Series

An infinite geometric series with $|r| < 1$ converges to the sum

$$S_n = \frac{a_1}{1 - r}$$

where a_1 is the first term, and r is the ______.

An infinite geometric series diverges when $|r| \geq 1$.

A geometric series is ____

____

Examples

1 Determining Divergence and Convergence Decide whether each infinite geometric series diverges or converges. State whether the series has a sum.

a. $\sum_{n=1}^{\infty} \left(\frac{2}{3}\right)^n$

$a_1 = \left(\frac{2}{3}\right)^{\square} = \frac{2}{3}, a_2 = \left(\frac{2}{3}\right)^{\square} = \frac{4}{9}$

$r = \frac{4}{9} \div \frac{2}{3} = \frac{\square}{\square}$

Since $|r|$ ☐ 1, the series ______,
and the series ______ a sum.

b. $2 + 6 + 18 + \ldots$

$a_1 = 2, a_2 = 6$

$r = 6 \div 2 = \square$

Since $|r|$ ☐ 1, the series ______,
and the series ______ a sum.

Name_______________________ Class_______________________ Date_____________

❷ **Physics** The weight at the end of a pendulum swings through an arc of 30 inches on its first swing. After that, each successive swing is 85% of the length of the previous swing. What is the total distance the weight will swing by the time it comes to rest?

A. 230 in. **B.** 200 in. **C.** 35.3 in. **D.** 25.5 in.

The largest arc the pendulum swings through is on the first swing of 30 in., so $a_1 = 30$.

$S_n = \frac{a_1}{1 - r} = \frac{30}{1 - \square} = \square$ **Use the formula and substitute.**

The total distance that the pendulum swings through is $\square$ in.

The correct choice is B.

❸ **Financial Planning** The Floyd family starts saving for a vacation that is one year away. They start with $125. Each month they save 8% more than the previous month. How much money will they have saved 12 months later?

Relate $\boxed{S_n} = \frac{\boxed{a_1}\left(1 - \boxed{r}^{n}\right)}{1 - \boxed{r}}$ **Write the formula for the sum of a geometric series.**

Define $\boxed{S_n}$ = total amount saved

$\boxed{a_1} = \square$ **Initial amount.**

$\boxed{r} = 1.08$ **Common ratio.**

$\boxed{n} = \square$ **Number of months.**

Write $\boxed{S_{12}} = \frac{\square\left(1 - \square^{\square}\right)}{1 - \square}$ **Substitute.**

$\approx \square$ **Use a calculator.**

The amount of money the Floyds will have saved will be $\square$.

Quick Check

1. Determine whether each series has a sum.

a. $1 + \frac{1}{5} + \frac{1}{25} + \dots$

b. $4 + 8 + 16 + \dots$

2. Evaluate each infinite geometric series.

a. $1 + \frac{1}{2} + \frac{1}{4} + \frac{1}{8} + \ldots$

b. $3 - \frac{3}{2} + \frac{3}{4} - \frac{3}{8} + \ldots$

3. a. Explain how the common ratio 1.08 was found in Example 3.

b. Suppose each month the Floyds deposit 15% more than the previous month instead of 8% more. Describe how this changes the problem.

c. At the 15% rate, how much money will the Floyds have saved after 12 months?

4. Identify a_1, r, and n for each series. Then evaluate each series.

a. $-45 + 135 - 405 + 1215 - 3645$

b. $\frac{1}{3} + \frac{1}{9} + \frac{1}{27} + \frac{1}{81}$

Name________________________________ Class____________________ Date______________

Lesson 11-6

Area Under a Curve

Lesson Objective	
▼1 Finding area under a curve	**Local Standards:** ____________________

Vocabulary

When approximating the area under a curve, inscribed rectangles are ______

____

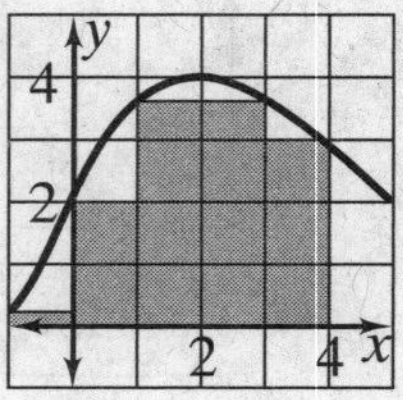

When approximating the area under a curve, circumscribed rectangles ______

____

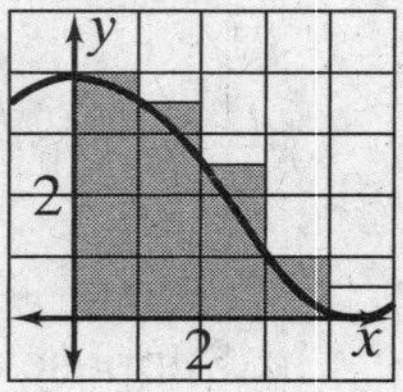

Examples

1 Data Analysis The curve at the right approximates the speed of a car during a 12-minute drive.

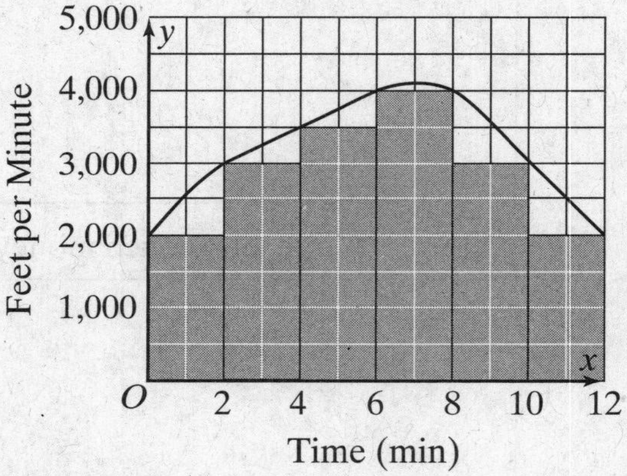

a. What does the area under the curve represent?

Area = $\frac{\text{feet}}{\cancel{\text{minutes}}} \cdot \cancel{\text{minutes}}$ **Use dimensional analysis.**

= feet **Simplify.**

The area under the curve approximates the [________________].

b. The inscribed rectangles are each 2 units wide. Use them to estimate the area under the curve.

Width of each rectangle ↓ **Total area** ↓

2([ ]) + 2([ ]) + 2([ ]) + 2([ ]) + 2([ ]) + 2([ ]) = [ ]

↑ **Value of the curve at the upper edge of each rectangle.**

The indicated area is [ ] units^2.

Name______________________________ Class______________________ Date ____________

❷ Using a Sum to Estimate Area Under a Curve Estimate the area under the curve $f(x) = -0.5x^2 + 6$ for the domain $0 \le x \le 2$ by evaluating the sum A.

$$A = \sum_{n=1}^{4} (0.5)f(a_n), \text{ where } a_1 = 0.5, a_2 = 1, a_3 = 1.5, a_4 = 2.$$

4 ← number of rectangles

width of each rectangle (0.5); function value at a_n ($f(a_n)$)

The expression $f(a_n)$ gives the height of the nth rectangle.

$A = 0.5f(0.5) + 0.5f(1) + 0.5f(1.5) + 0.5f(2)$ — **Add the areas of the rectangles.**

$= 0.5(\_\_\_\_\_\_\_\_)$ — **total area = width of each rectangle · sum of the heights.**

$= 0.5(\_\_\_\_) = \_\_\_\_$

The indicated area is about ______ units^2.

Quick Check

1. The graph at the right shows the curve from Example 1, but it shows circumscribed rectangles rather than inscribed rectangles.

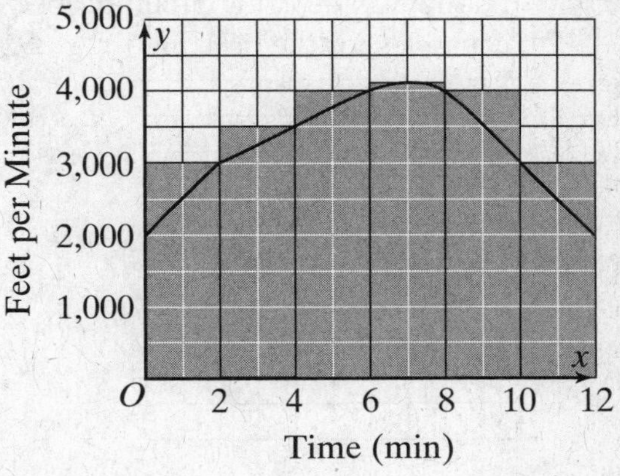

a. Estimate the area under the curve using circumscribed rectangles. How does your answer differ from the answer to Example 1?

b. Find the mean of the answer using inscribed rectangles and the answer using circumscribed rectangles. Of the three answers, which is the most accurate? Explain.

Name______________________ Class______________________ Date ______________

Example

❸ Using a Graphing Calculator Use a graphing calculator to graph $f(x) = -x^2 + 4x + 5$. Find the area under the curve for the domain $1 \le x \le 4$.

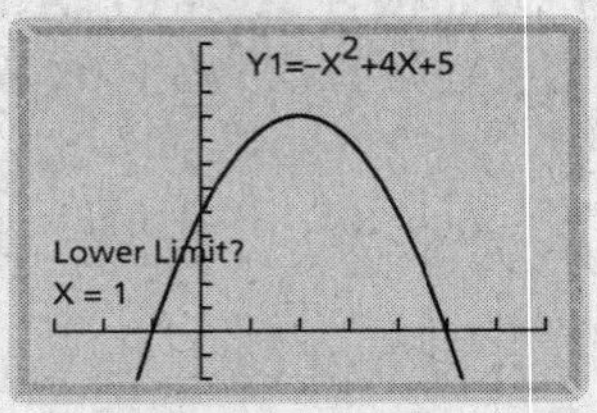

Xmin=–3 Ymin=–2
Xmax=7 Ymax=12
Xscl=1 Yscl=1

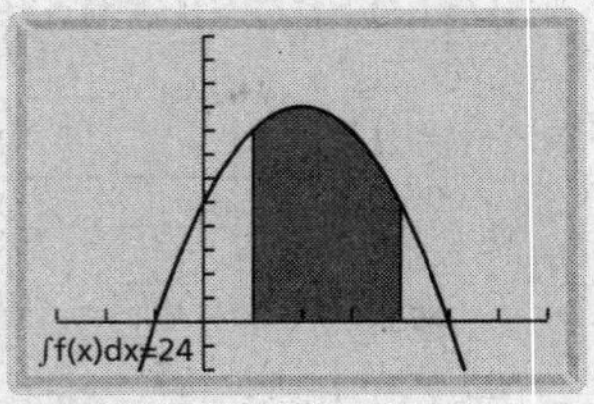

Step 1 Input the equation. Adjust the window values.

Step 2 Access the $\int f(x)dx$ feature from the CALC menu.

Step 3 Use the lower limit of $x =$ ☐.

Step 4 Use the upper limit of $x =$ ☐.

The area under the curve between $x =$ ☐ and $x =$ ☐ is ☐ units^2.

Quick Check

2. a. Sketch a graph using the equation from Example 2 and draw circumscribed rectangles for the domain $0 \le x \le 2$.

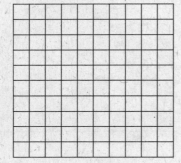

b. To find the area using these rectangles, you should evaluate the function at the left side of each rectangle. Explain why.

c. Use the circumscribed rectangles to write and evaluate a sum that approximates the area under the curve for the domain $0 \le x \le 2$. Compare your answer to the answer in Example 2.

3. Use the equation from Example 3 and a graphing calculator. Find the area under the curve for each domain.

a. $0 \le x \le 1$ **b.** $-1 \le x \le 1$ **c.** $-1.5 \le x \le 0$

Name________________________ Class____________________ Date______________

Lesson 12-1

Probability Distributions

Lesson Objectives	
1 Making a probability distribution **2** Using a probability distribution in conducting a simulation	**NAEP 2005 Strand:** Data Analysis and Probability **Topic:** Probability **Local Standards:** ____________________

Vocabulary

A frequency table is ____

____

Cumulative probability is ____

____

A probability distribution is ____

____

Example

1 Finding Probability Use the frequency table. Find the probability that a student is involved in at least one extra-curricular activity.

More than one activity	144
One activity	360
No activities	216
Total Students	**720**

$P(\text{more than one activity}) = \dfrac{\square}{720}$

$P(\text{one activity}) = \dfrac{\square}{720}$

Find the experimental probability for each event in the table that represents at least one extra-curricular activity.

$\dfrac{\square}{720} + \dfrac{\square}{720} = \dfrac{\square}{720} = \square$

Add to find the cumulative probability.

Quick Check

1. Use the information in Example 1. Find the probability that a student is involved in one activity or no activities.

Name________________________________ Class________________________ Date ______________

Example

❷ Probability Distributions Suppose you spin two spinners. Each spinner has 4 possible outcomes: 1, 2, 3, and 4. Show the probability distribution for the sum of the numbers.

Method 1 Make a frequency table. Extend the table to include probabilities.

Spinning Two Spinners

Sum	2	3	4	5	6	7	8
Frequency							
Probability	$\frac{\square}{16}$	$\frac{\square}{16}$	$\frac{\square}{16}$	$\frac{\square}{16}$	$\frac{\square}{16}$	$\frac{\square}{16}$	$\frac{\square}{16}$

There are 16 possible outcomes.

Divide to find the probability.

Method 2 Graph.

Spinning Two Spinners

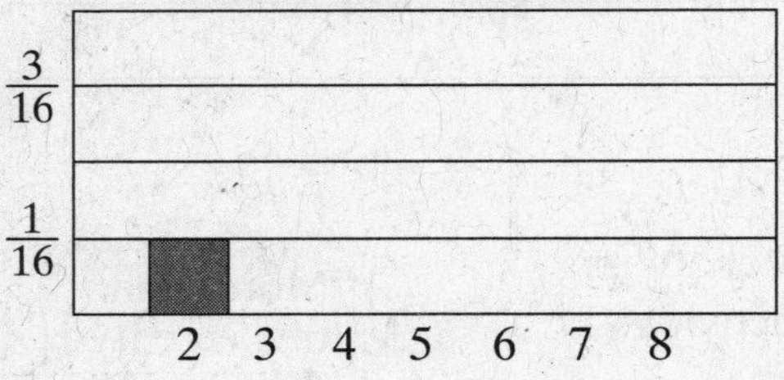

Quick Check

2. Use a table or a graph to show the probability distribution for the roll of one number cube labeled with numbers 1–6.

Name________________________________ Class________________________ Date ______________

Example

❸ Genetics Use the information in the chart. Graph the probability distribution for each sample space.

Inherited Gene Pairs From
One Recessive and One Hybrid Pea Plant

		Parent Plant	
		r	r
Parent Plant	R	Rr	Rr
	r	rr	rr

RR = dominant gene pair (red flower)
Rr = hybrid gene pair (pink flower)
rr = recessive gene pair (white flower)

Genotype Distribution
$\{RR, Rr, rr\}$

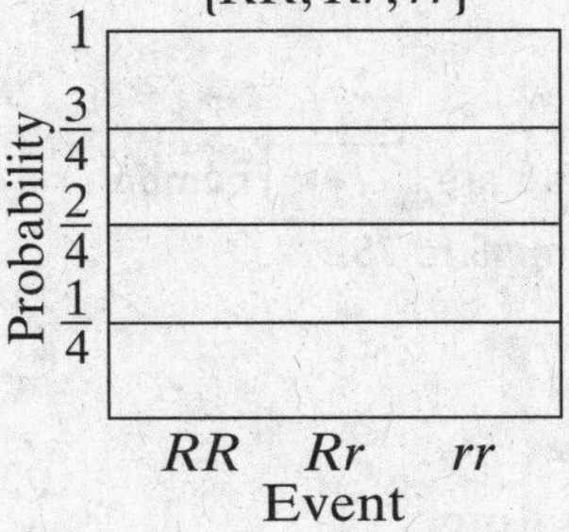

Plant Color Distribution
{red, pink, white}

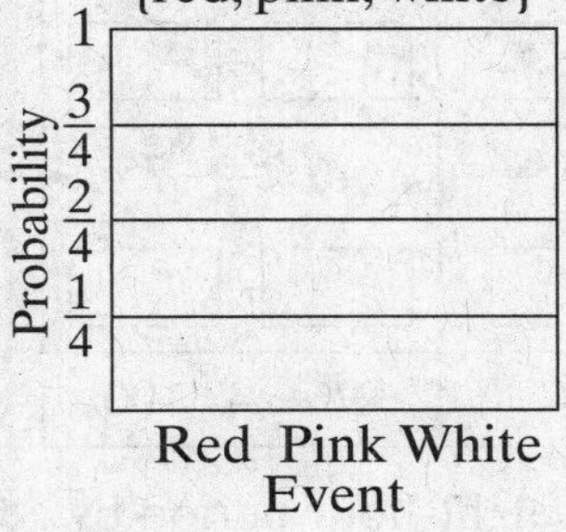

Quick Check

3. Make a probability distribution table for each sample space in Example 3.

Name______________________ Class______________________ Date______________

Example

4 Market Research The probability of an information desk at a library receiving C calls each hour varies according to the following distribution.

C	0	1	2	3	4	5
$P(C)$	0.05	0.15	0.25	0.3	0.2	0.05

Use random numbers to predict the number of calls received during an eight-hour shift.

Step 1 Set up a random-number simulation. Assign numbers from 1 to 100 based on the probability of each event. Use cumulative probabilities.

Outcome	Probability	Cumulative Probability	Assigned Numbers
0	0.05	0.05	01 – 05
1	0.15	0.20	☐ – ☐
2	0.25	☐	☐ – ☐
3	0.30	0.75	46 – 75
4	0.20	☐	☐ – ☐
5	0.05	1.00	96 – 100

Since $P(0) = 0.05$, assign ☐ numbers to this outcome.

There are ☐ numbers from 46 to 75.

Step 2 Conduct the simulation. Model an eight-hour period by generating eight random numbers from 1 to 100.

Hour →	1st	2nd	3rd	4th	5th	6th	7th	8th
Random numbers →	95	91	15	52	41	74	5	34
Number of calls →	4	4	☐	3	☐	☐	0	☐

Step 3 Interpret the simulation. A total of ☐ calls came in over an eight-hour period.

Quick Check

4. Use the information in Example 4. Conduct a simulation to predict the number of calls received during a 16-hour period.

Name______________________ Class______________________ Date______________

Lesson 12-2

Conditional Probability

Lesson Objectives	**NAEP 2005 Strand:** Data Analysis and Probability
1 Finding conditional probabilities	**Topic:** Probability
2 Using formulas and tree diagrams	**Local Standards:** ____________

Vocabulary and Key Concepts

Conditional Probability Formula

For any two events A and B from a sample space with $P(A) \neq 0$,

$$P(B \mid A) = \frac{P(A \; \boxed{} \; B)}{P(A)}.$$

A conditional probability contains ______________________________

____

Example

1 **Recycling** Using the data in the table, find the probability that a sample of non-recycled waste was plastic.

A 1% **B** 15% **C** 24% **D** 56%

Material	Recycled	Not Recycled
Paper	36.7	45.1
Metal	6.3	11.9
Glass	2.4	10.1
Plastic	1.4	24.0
Other	21.1	70.1

The given condition limits the sample space to non-recycled waste. A favorable outcome is non-recycled ☐.

$$P(\text{plastic} \mid \text{non-recycled}) = \frac{24.0}{\boxed{} + \boxed{} + \boxed{} + 24.0 + \boxed{}}$$

$$= \frac{24.0}{\boxed{}} \approx \boxed{}$$

The probability that the non-recycled waste was plastic is about ☐%.
The correct choice is B.

Quick Check

1. Refer to the table in Example 1. Find the probability that a sample of recycled waste was plastic.

Name__________________________ Class__________________ Date __________

Examples

❷ **Market Research** Researchers asked people who exercise regularly whether they jog or walk. Fifty-eight percent of the respondents were male. Twenty percent of all respondents were males who said they jog. Find the probability that a male respondent jogs.

Relate $P(\_\_\_\_) = 58\%$

$P(\_\_\_\_ \text{ and } \boxed{\text{jogs}}) = \_\_\_\_\%$

Define Let $\boxed{A}$ = male.

Let $\boxed{B}$ = jogs.

Write $P(\boxed{B} \mid \boxed{A}) = \dfrac{P(\boxed{A}\ \_\_\_\_\ \boxed{B})}{P(\boxed{A})}$

$= \dfrac{\_\_\_\_}{\_\_\_\_} \approx \_\_\_\_$ **Substitute ____ for $P(A \text{ and } B)$ and ____ for $P(A)$ and simplify.**

The probability that a male respondent jogs is about ____%.

❸ **Using a Tree Diagram** The diagram shows the probability that a day will begin clear or cloudy, and then the probability of rain on days that begin clear and cloudy. Find the probability that a day will start out clear, and then rain. The path containing *clear* and *rain* represents days that start out clear and then rain.

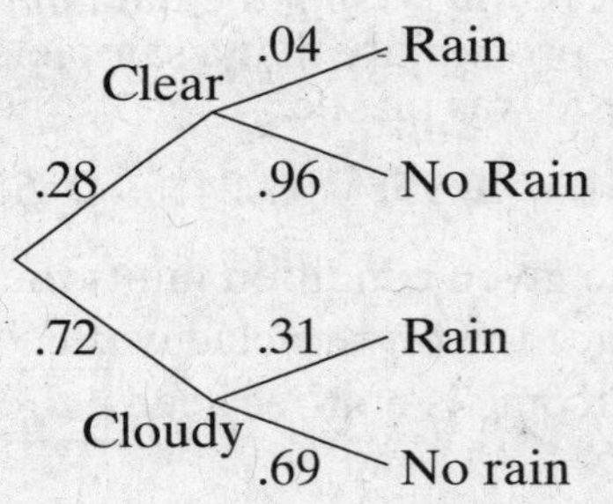

$P(\text{clear and rain}) = P(\text{rain} \mid \text{clear}) \cdot P(\_\_\_\_)$

$= \_\_\_\_ \cdot \_\_\_\_ = \_\_\_\_$

The probability that a day will start out clear and then rain is about ____%.

Quick Check

2. Eighty percent of an airline's flights depart on schedule. Seventy-two percent of its flights depart and arrive on schedule. Find the probability that a flight that departs on time also arrives on time.

3. Use the tree diagram in Example 3. Find $P(\text{cloudy and no rain})$.

Name______________________ Class______________________ Date______________

Lesson 12-3

Analyzing Data

Lesson Objectives	NAEP 2005 Strand: Data Analysis and Probability
1 Calculating measures of central tendency **2** Draw and interpret box-and-whisker plots	**Topic:** Data Representation (Histograms, line graphs, scatter plots, box plots, circle graphs, stem-and-leaf plots, frequency distributions, and tables.) **Local Standards:** ____________________

Vocabulary and Key Concepts

Measures of Central Tendency

Measure	Definition	Example, using {1, 2, 2, 3, 5, 5}
______	$\frac{\text{sum of the data values}}{\text{number of data values}}$	$\frac{1+2+2+3+5+5}{6} = \frac{18}{6} = 3$
______	middle value *or* mean of the two middle values	$\frac{2+3}{2} = 2.5$
______	most frequently occurring value	2 and 5

Measures of central tendency are ____

____

A bimodal data set has ____

Quartiles are ____________________

____

____

____

Median of lower part (Q_1) = 60.5 **Median of upper part (Q_3) = 83**

56 58 58 ↓ 63 65 71 ↑ 74 78 82 ↓ 84 85 86

Median of data set (Q_2) = 72.5

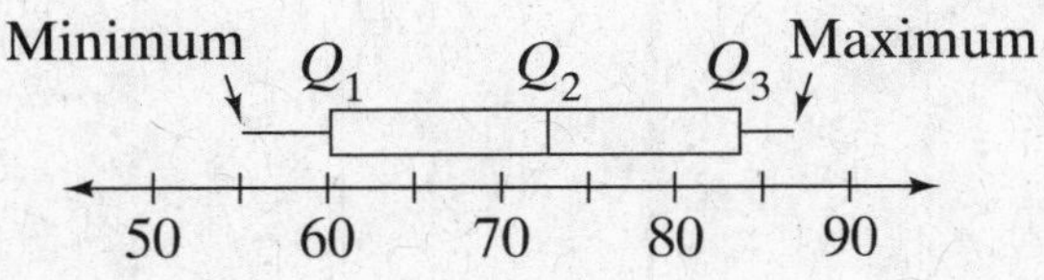

A box-and-whisker plot is ______________________

____

____

____

____

A percentile is ____

____

An outlier is ____

____

Name____________________ Class____________________ Date ______________

Examples

1 Finding Measures of Central Tendency Find the mean, median, and mode for these values: 78, 87, 84, 75, 80, 98, 78, 95, 72.

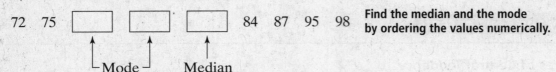

$$\bar{x} = \frac{(78 + 87 + 84 + 75 + 80 + 98 + 78 + 95 + 72)}{\square} = \frac{\square}{\square} = \square$$

Use the $\bar{x}$ symbol to designate the mean.

72 75 ☐ ☐ ☐ 84 87 95 98

(Mode: the first two boxes; Median: the third box)

Find the median and the mode by ordering the values numerically.

The mean is ☐, the median is ☐, and the mode is ☐.

2 Using Percentiles Find the 30th and 60th percentiles for the values below.

54 98 45 87 98 64 21 61 71 82 93 65 62 98 87 24 65 97 31 47

Step 1 Order the values.

☐ 24 31 45 47 54 61 62 64 65 65 71 82 87 87 93 97 98 98 98

Step 2 Find the number of values that fall below the 30th percentile and the number that fall below the 60th percentile.

Of the 20, 30% should fall below the 30th percentile and 60% should fall below the 60th percentile.

$20 \times 30\% = 20 \times 0.30 = \square$

Since ☐ is greater than 6 values, ☐ is at the 30th percentile.

$20 \times 60\% = 20 \times 0.60 = \square$

Since ☐ is greater than 12 values, ☐ is at the 60th percentile.

Quick Check

1. Find the mean, median, and mode for these values: 2.4, 4.3, 3.7, 3.9, 2.8, 5.4, 2.8.

2. Find the value at each percentile for the data in Example 2.
   a. 0th percentile
   b. 45th percentile
   c. 55th percentile

Name________________________ Class________________ Date ____________

Example

❸ Making a Box-and-Whisker Plot Make a box-and-whisker plot for these values: 91, 95, 88, 85, 90, 97, 94, 100, 81.

Step 1 Find the quartile values, the minimum value, and the maximum value.

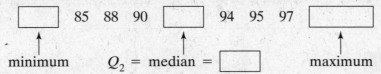

☐ 85 88 90 ☐ 94 95 97 ☐

↑ minimum ↑ Q_2 = median = ☐ ↑ maximum

The median is a value of the data set. Remove it to calculate Q_1 and Q_3.

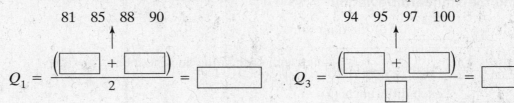

81 85 88 90 94 95 97 100

$$Q_1 = \frac{(\square + \square)}{2} = \square \qquad Q_3 = \frac{(\square + \square)}{\square} = \square$$

Step 2 Draw a number line for the base of your box-and-whisker plot. Above it, plot the three quartiles, the minimum value, and the maximum value.

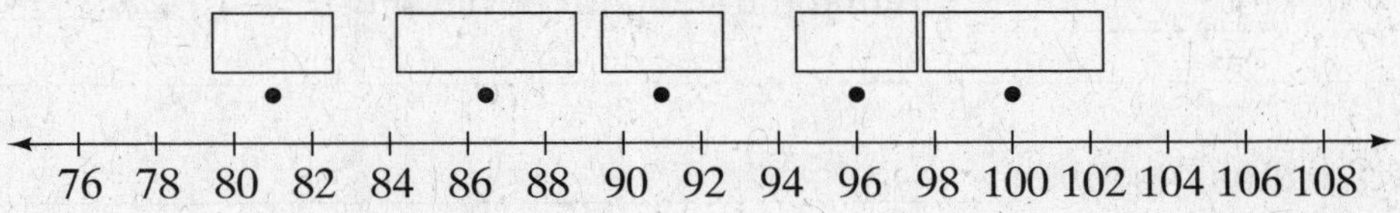

Step 3 Finish your box-and-whisker plot by drawing a box through Q_1 and Q_3, a vertical line through the median, and line segments from the box outward to the minimum and maximum values.

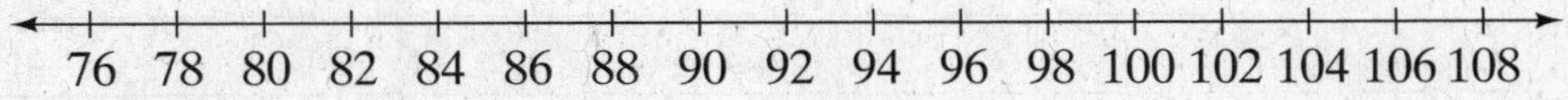

Quick Check

3. Make a box-and-whisker plot for these values: 34, 36, 47, 45, 28, 31, 29, 40.

Name______________________________ Class____________________ Date______________

Lesson 12-4

Standard Deviation

Lesson Objectives	NAEP 2005 Strand: Data Analysis and Probability
1 Finding the standard deviation of a set of values	Topic: Characteristics of Data Sets
2 Using standard deviation in real-world situations	Local Standards: ____________________

Vocabulary and Key Concepts

Finding the Standard Deviation

Find the ______ of the data set: $\bar{x}$.

Find the ______ between each value and the mean: $x - \bar{x}$.

______ each difference: $(x - \bar{x})^2$.

Find the ______ (mean) of these squares: $\frac{\sum(x - \bar{x})^2}{n}$.

Take the ______ to find the standard deviation: $\sigma = \sqrt{\frac{\sum(x - \bar{x})^2}{n}}$.

Measures of variation describe ____________________

____

The range of a set of data is ____________________

____

The interquartile range is ____________________

____

Standard deviation is ____________________

____

The z-score is ____________________

____

Name________________ Class________________ Date ________

Examples

1 Finding the Mean and Standard Deviation Find the mean and the standard deviation for the values 78.2, 90.5, 98.1, 93.7, 94.5.

$$\bar{x} = \frac{(78.2 + 90.5 + 98.1 + 93.7 + 94.5)}{5} = \square$$

Find the mean.

Organize the next steps in a table.

x	$\bar{x}$	$x - \bar{x}$	$(x - \bar{x})^2$
78.2	91	−12.8	163.84
90.5	91	−0.5	
98.1	91		
93.7	91		
94.5	91		

$$\sigma = \sqrt{\frac{\sum(x - \bar{x})^2}{n}}$$

$$= \sqrt{\frac{\square}{5}} \approx \square$$

Find the standard deviation.

2 Applying Standard Deviation The number of points that Darden scored in each of 11 basketball games is listed below. Within how many standard deviations of the mean do all of the values fall? What can Darden's coach do with this information?

8, 12, 13, 10, 7, 5, 10, 9, 13, 11, 8

Step 1 Draw a number line. Plot the data values and the mean.

Step 2 Mark off intervals of 2.4 on either side of the mean.

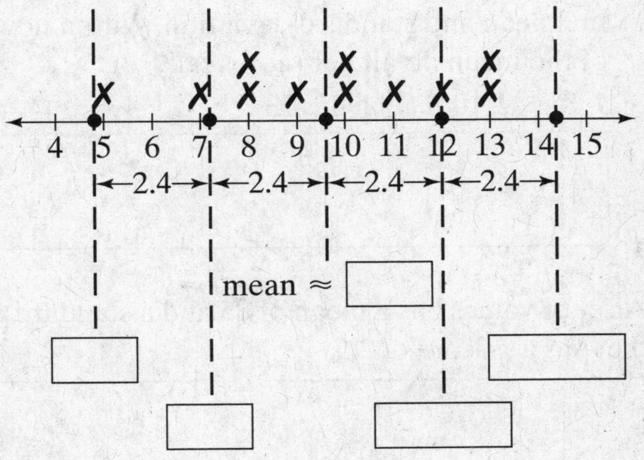

All the values fall within ☐ standard deviations of the mean. The coach can expect that it will be very likely that Darden's score in the next game will be within ☐ points of his mean score of ☐ points.

Name________________________ Class________________________ Date ____________

3 Finding the *z*-score A set of values has a mean of 22 and a standard deviation of 5. Find the *z*-score for a value of 30.

$$z\text{-score} = \frac{\text{value} - \square}{\text{standard deviation}}$$

$$= \frac{30 - \square}{5} \quad \textbf{Substitute.}$$

$$= \frac{\square}{\square} \quad \textbf{Simplify.}$$

$$= \square$$

Quick Check

1. Find the mean and standard deviation for these values: 50, 60, 70, 80, 80, 90, 100, 110.

2. a. Refer to Example 2. Within how many standard deviations of Darden's mean would a score of 7 fall?

b. Melanie played in 9 basketball games. Her scores are shown below. Find the mean and standard deviation. Within how many standard deviations of the mean do all her scores fall?

7 8 9 9 10 11 11 12 13

3. A set of values has a mean of 85 and a standard deviation of 6. Find the value that has a *z*-score of 2.5.

Name__________________ Class__________________ Date______________

Lesson 12-5

Working with Samples

Lesson Objectives	
1 Finding sample proportions 2 Finding the margin of error	**NAEP 2005 Strand:** Data Analysis and Probability **Topic:** Characteristics of Data Sets **Local Standards:** ____________

Vocabulary and Key Concepts

Margin of Error Formula

When a random sample of size n is taken from a large population, the sample proportion has a margin of error of approximately $\pm \frac{1}{\sqrt{n}}$.

A sample represents ________________________

The sample proportion is ________________________

____

In a random sample, ________________________

____

The margin of error is ________________________

____

Examples

1 Finding the Sample Proportion In a sample of 500 teenagers, 328 had never attended a popular music concert. Find the sample proportion for those who have never attended a popular music concert. Write the answer as a percent.

sample proportion $= \frac{\square}{\square}$ **Write the formula.**

$= \frac{328}{500}$ **Substitute 328 for x and 500 for n.**

$= \square$ **Simplify.**

The sample proportion of teenagers who have never attended a popular music concert is about $\square$.

Name________________________ Class________________________ Date ______________

❷ **Sampling Methods** The student council dance committee is trying to decide whether to have a band or a DJ for the fall dance. They decided that each of the four committee members should survey the students in their homeroom classes. Identify any bias in this sampling method.

This is a "convenience" sample that is convenient for the committee members. Four homerooms may not accurately reflect the opinions of the entire school, because four homerooms is probably too ______ of a percentage of all the school's homerooms.

This sampling method ______ a bias and ______ random.

Quick Check

1. In a poll of 1,085 voters, 564 favor Candidate A. Find the sample proportion for those who favor Candidate A.

2. a. Suppose the 500 teenagers in Example 1 all live in a rural area where there are no major concert venues. Is there a bias in this sample? Explain.

   b. The only way to know a true population proportion is to poll every person in the population. Such a poll is no longer a sample, but a census. Describe a situation in which a sample is unsatisfactory and a census is required.

Example

3 **Career Plans** A survey of 528 high school seniors found that 65% already had career plans after high school.

Find the margin of error for the sample.

margin of error $= \pm \frac{1}{\sqrt{\square}}$ **Use the formula.**

$= \pm \frac{1}{\sqrt{\square}}$ **Substitute.**

$\approx \pm \square$ **Use a calculator.**

The margin of error is about $\pm \square$%.

Use the margin of error to find an interval that is likely to contain the true population proportion.

The margin of error forms an interval with the sample proportion at its midpoint.

Sample Proportion

|← − ☐% —— + ☐% →|

☐% 65% ☐%

The proportion of seniors who already have career plans is likely to be from ☐% to ☐%.

Quick Check

3. In a poll of 123 students, 87 have never ridden a ferry. Find the sample proportion, the margin of error, and the interval likely to contain the true population proportion.

Name______________________ Class______________________ Date______________

Lesson 12-6

Binomial Distributions

Lesson Objectives	**NAEP 2005 Strand:** Data Analysis and Probability
1 Finding binomial probabilities	**Topic:** Probability
2 Using binomial distributions	**Local Standards:** ____________________

Vocabulary and Key Concepts

Binomial Probability

Suppose you have repeated independent trials, each with a probability of success p and a probability of failure q (with $p + q = 1$). Then the probability of x successes in n trials is the following product: $\square$.

A binomial experiment involves ______________________________________

____

Examples

1 Merchandising A fast-food restaurant is attaching prize cards to every one of its soft-drink cups. The restaurant awards free drinks as prizes on three out of four cards. Suppose you have three cards. Find the probability that exactly one of these cards will reveal a prize.

Each card represents a trial with a probability of success of $\frac{3}{4}$. The probability of failure is $\frac{1}{4}$. The tree diagram shows the probabilities along each path.

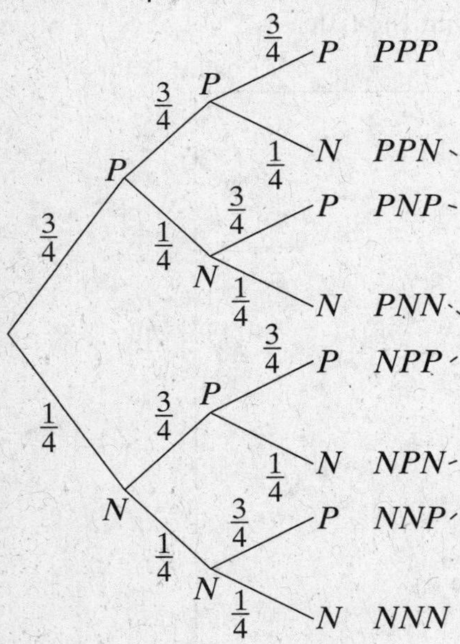

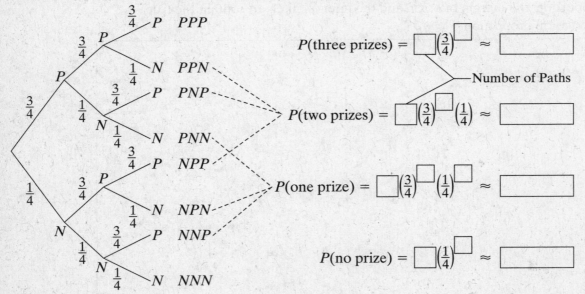

$P(\text{three prizes}) = \square\left(\frac{3}{4}\right)^{\square} \approx \square$

Number of Paths

$P(\text{two prizes}) = \square\left(\frac{3}{4}\right)^{\square}\left(\frac{1}{4}\right) \approx \square$

$P(\text{one prize}) = \square\left(\frac{3}{4}\right)^{\square}\left(\frac{1}{4}\right)^{\square} \approx \square$

$P(\text{no prize}) = \square\left(\frac{1}{4}\right)^{\square} \approx \square$

The probability that exactly one card will reveal a free drink is about $\square$%.

Name________________________ Class________________________ Date ________________

2 Probability Alicia walks to school with her friend Juana. Juana is on time 80% of the time. What is the probability that Juana will be on time five days in a row?

Relate This is a binomial experiment.

- There are five days.
- Each day she'll be on time or late.
- The probability that she'll be on time is 0.8 for each day.

Define Let $\boxed{n} = 5$.

Let $\boxed{p} = 0.8$.

Let $\boxed{q} = 0.2$.

Let $\boxed{x} = 5$.

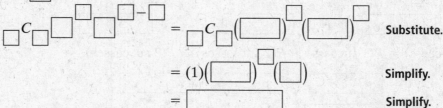

Write $_{\square}C_{\square}\,\square^{\square}\,\square^{\square - \square} = {}_{\square}C_{\square}(\square)^{\square}(\square)^{\square}$ **Substitute.**

$= (1)(\square)^{\square}(\square)$ **Simplify.**

$= \square$ **Simplify.**

The probability that she will be on time five days in a row is about $\square$%.

Quick Check

1. Verify your work for Example 1 by adding the probabilities for three, two, and no prizes to the probability for one prize. What answer should you get?

2. Find the probability of x successes in n trials for the given probability of success p on each trial.

   a. $x = 2, n = 5, p = 0.25$

   b. $x = 8, n = 10, p = 0.7$

Name________________________ Class________________________ Date________________

Example

3 Weather When it rains, there is a 70% chance that soccer practice will be canceled. If it rains for the next three days, what is the probability that practice will be canceled on at least one of the days?

Use the expansion for $(p + q)^n$, with $n = 3, p = 0.7$, and $q = 0.3$.

3 successes	2 successes	1 success	0 successes
↓	↓	↓	↓

$$(p + q)^3 = \square p^{\square} + \square p^{\square} q + \square p q^{\square} + \square q^{\square}$$

$$= \square(0.7)^3 + \square(0.7)^{\square}(0.3) + \square(0.7)(0.3)^{\square} + \square(0.3)^{\square}$$

$$= \square + \square + \square + 0.027$$

$P(\text{at least 1 success}) = P(\text{1 success}) + P(\text{2 successes}) + P(\text{3 successes})$

$$= \square + \square + \square$$

$$= \square$$

The probability that at least one practice will be canceled if it rains for the next three days is about $\square$%.

Quick Check

3. One survey found that 80% of respondents eat corn on the cob in circles rather than from side to side. Assume that this sample accurately represents the population. What is the probability that, out of five people you know, at least two of them eat corn on the cob in circles?

Name______________________ Class______________ Date______________

Lesson 12-7

Normal Distributions

Lesson Objectives	NAEP 2005 Strand: Data Analysis and Probability
1 Using a normal distribution	Topic: Probability
2 Using the standard normal curve	Local Standards: ____________

Vocabulary

Normal distribution shows ______________________________

____

The standard normal curve is ______________________________

____

The Standard Normal Curve

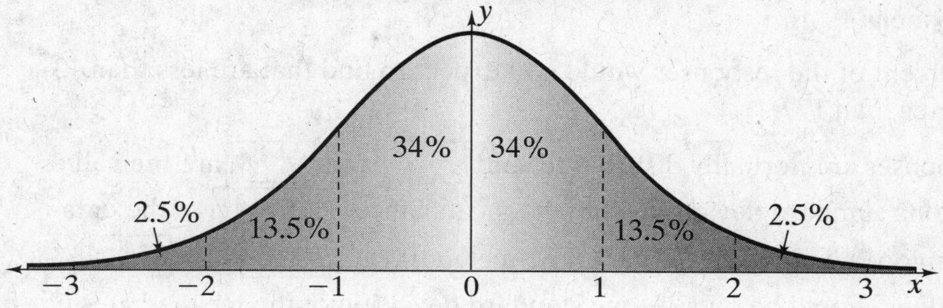

Examples

1 Using a Normal Distribution A survey of the employees of XYZ Corporation found that the mean of the morning commute times to work was 18 minutes. The standard deviation was 4 minutes. Sketch a normal curve showing the commute times at one, two, and three standard deviations from the mean.

Distribution for Commute Times for XYZ Employees

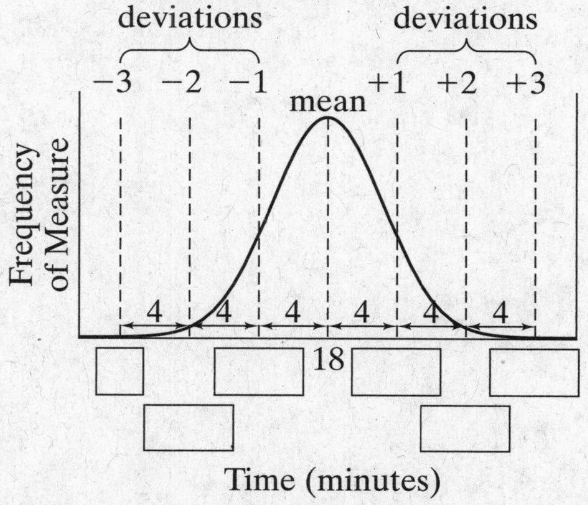

Name______________________ Class______________ Date ___________

❷ Using the Standard Normal Curve In a survey, the responses to the question, "How much time do you spend in the shower every day?" were normally distributed. The mean was 15 minutes; the standard deviation was 2 minutes.

a. What values are one standard deviation from the mean?

Values that are one standard deviation from the mean have z-scores of ☐ and ☐.

$$z\text{-score} = \frac{\text{value} - \text{mean}}{\text{standard deviation}}$$

$$\square = \frac{v - \square}{\square} \qquad \square = \frac{u - \square}{\square}$$

$$v = \square \qquad u = \square$$

The values ☐ minutes and ☐ minutes are one standard deviation from the mean.

b. What percent of the responses would you expect to find that are less than 13 and greater than 17?

The responses are normally distributed, and ☐ and ☐ are the values that are one standard deviation from the mean. Since ☐ of the data are within one standard deviation of the mean, 100% – ☐% = ☐% of the values should be outside one standard deviation of the mean, that is, less than ☐ and greater than ☐.

Quick Check

1. Suppose the mean in Example 1 is 15 minutes and the standard deviation is 3 minutes. Sketch a normal curve showing the commute times at one, two, and three standard deviations from the mean.

Name______________________ Class______________________ Date ______________

Example

3 Using Distribution The professor of a class has found that students who score between one and two standard deviations below the mean need to attend study sessions in order to pass the class. If 92 students are in the class, and the graph below shows their distribution, how many students need to attend study sessions?

Distribution of Final Exam Scores

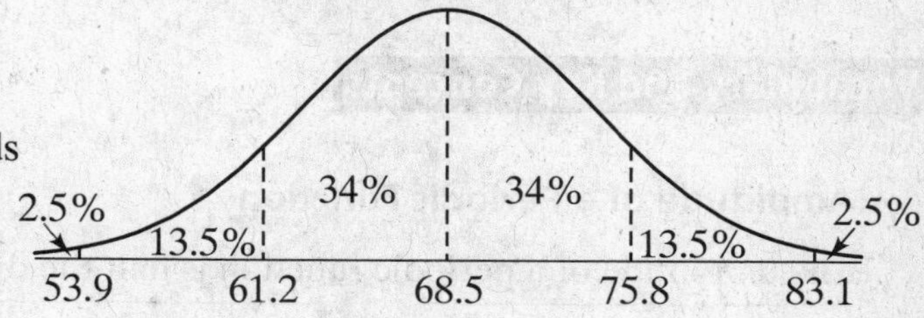

Use the normal curve. About ☐ % of the students receive grades from one to two standard deviations below the mean.

Find the number of students that corresponds to ☐ %.

☐(☐) = ☐

About ☐ or ☐ students need to attend study sessions.

Quick Check

2. a. Suppose there were 100 responses to the survey question from Example 2. How many responses would you expect to be values less than 13 minutes or greater than 17 minutes?

b. Of 100 responses, how many would you expect to be values between 17 minutes and 19 minutes?

3. a. Suppose there are 140 students in the class in Example 3. About how many would receive grades from 69 to 75?

b. How do you know that in a class of 140 students, about 22 students receive grades of 76 or higher?

Name______________________ Class______________________ Date______________

Lesson 13-1

Exploring Periodic Data

Lesson Objectives

1. Identifying cycles and periods of periodic functions
2. Finding the amplitude of periodic functions

Vocabulary and Key Concepts

Amplitude of a Periodic Function

The amplitude of a periodic function is half the difference between the

[ ] and [ ] values of the function.

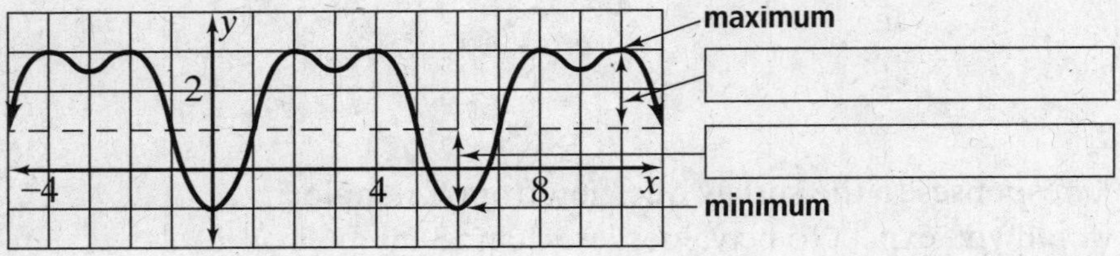

A periodic function repeats a pattern of ______________________

A cycle is ______________________

The period of a function is ______________________

Examples

1 **Identifying Cycles and Periods** Analyze this periodic function. Identify one cycle in two different ways. Then determine the period of the function.

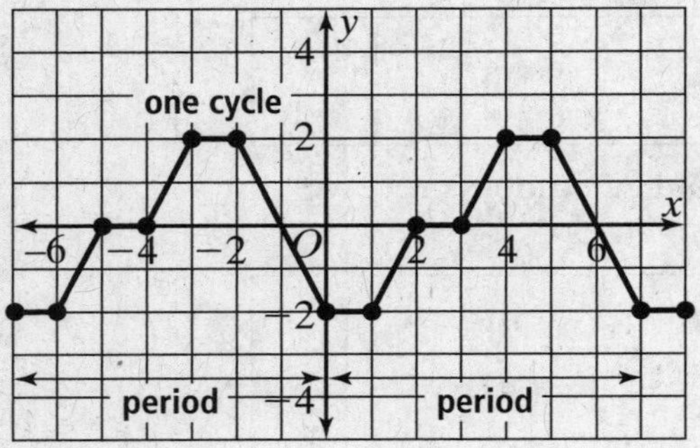

Begin at any point on the graph. Trace one complete pattern.

The beginning and ending [ ]-values of each cycle determine the [ ] of the function.

Each cycle is [ ] units long. The period of the function is [ ].

Name______________________ Class______________________ Date ______________

❷ Identifying Periodic Functions

Identifying Periodic Functions Determine whether the function *is* or *is not* periodic. If it is, find the period.

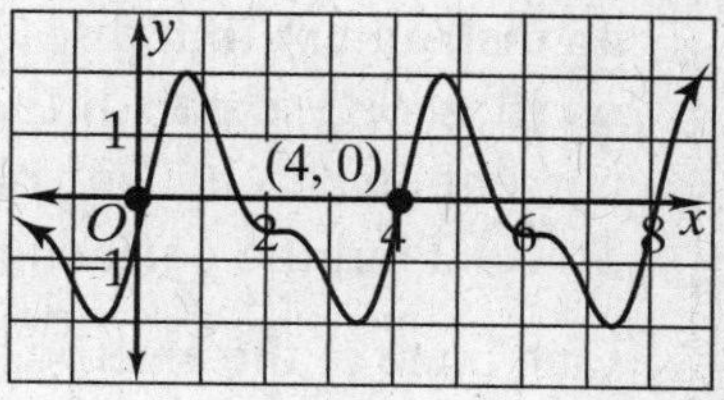

The pattern of ______ in one section ______ exactly in other sections.

The function ______ periodic.

Find points at the beginning and end of one cycle. Subtract the ______ of the points: ☐ − ☐ = ☐.

The pattern of the graph repeats every ☐ units, so the period is ☐.

❸ Finding the Amplitude of a Periodic Function

Finding the Amplitude of a Periodic Function Find the amplitude of the function in Example 2.

amplitude = $\frac{☐}{☐}$(______ value − ______ value) **Use definition of amplitude.**

= $\frac{☐}{☐}$[☐ − (☐)] **Substitute.**

= $\frac{☐}{☐}$(☐) = ☐ **Simplify.**

The amplitude of the function is ☐.

Quick Check

1. For the function below, identify one cycle in two different ways. Then determine the period of the function.

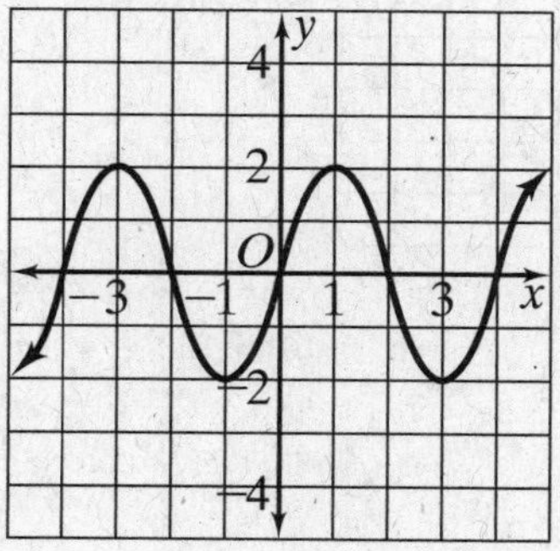

____

2. Determine whether the function is or is not periodic. If it is, find the period.

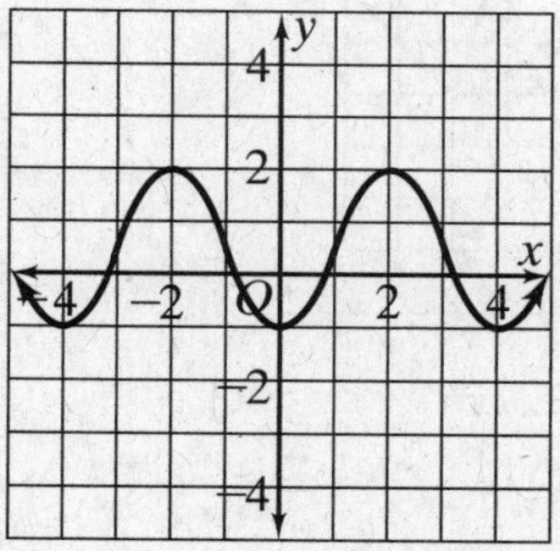

____

Name____________________ Class____________________ Date ____________________

Example

4 Finding the Amplitude and the Period An oscilloscope is an instrument that displays electrical waves on a screen. The oscilloscope screen at the right shows the graph of the alternating current electricity (in volts) supplied to homes in the United States. Find the period and amplitude.

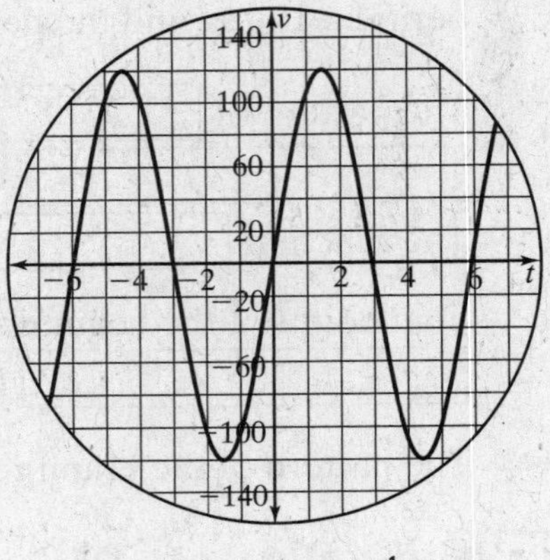

1 unit on the t-axis = $\frac{1}{360}$ s

One cycle of the electric current occurs from 0 s to $\frac{1}{60}$ s.

The maximum value of the function is ☐, and the minimum value is ☐.

period = $\frac{☐}{☐}$ − ☐ **Use the definitions.** amplitude = $\frac{☐}{☐}$[☐ − (☐)]

= $\frac{☐}{☐}$ **Simplify.** = $\frac{☐}{☐}$(☐) = ☐

The period of the electric current is ☐ s. The amplitude is ☐ volts.

Quick Check

3. Find the amplitude of the function.

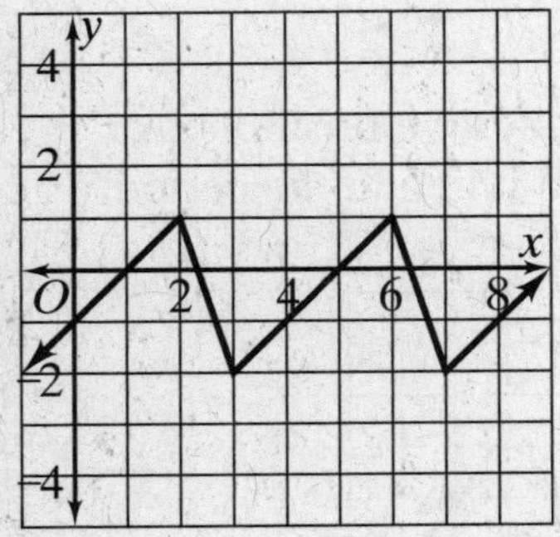

☐

4. Sketch the graph of a sound wave with a period of 0.004 s and an amplitude of 2.

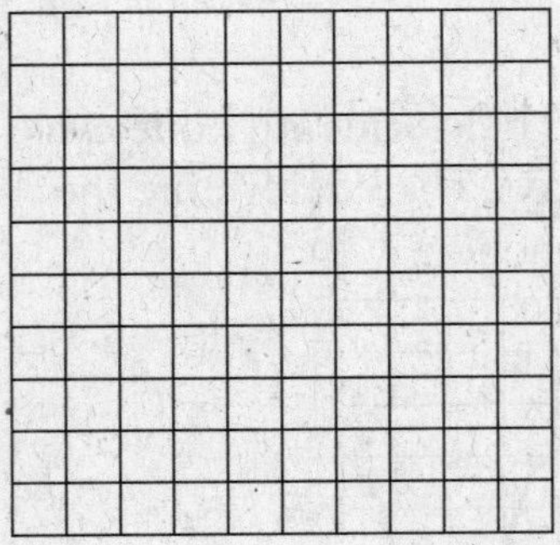

Lesson 13-2

Angles and the Unit Circle

Lesson Objectives	
1 Working with angles in standard position 2 Finding coordinates of points on the unit circle	**Local Standards:** ____________

Vocabulary and Key Concepts

Cosine and Sine of an Angle

Suppose an angle in standard position has measure θ.

The cosine of θ ($\cos\theta$) is the ☐-coordinate of the point at which the terminal side of the angle intersects the unit circle. The sine of θ ($\sin\theta$) is the ☐-coordinate.

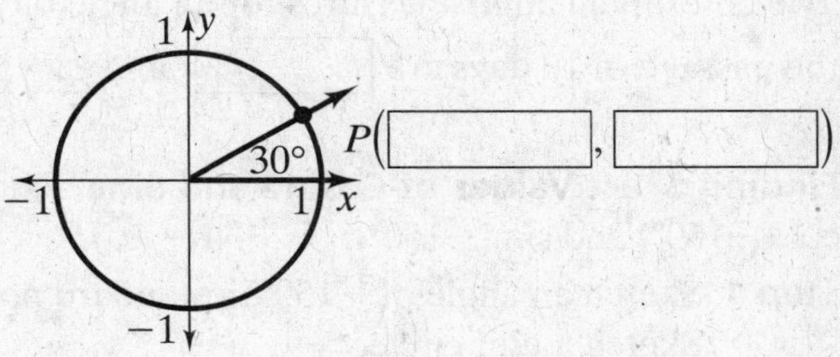

An angle is in standard position when ______________________________

The initial side of the angle is ______________________________

The terminal side of the angle is ______________________________

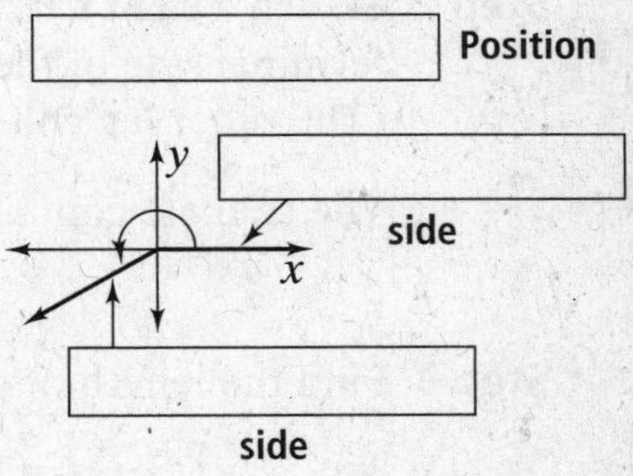

Two angles in standard position are coterminal angles if ______________________________

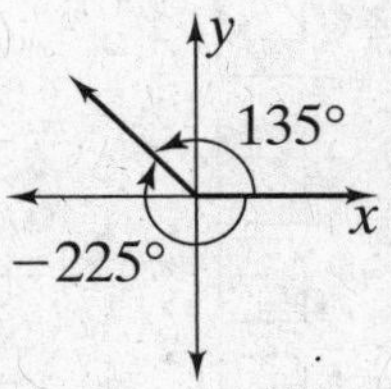

Angles that have measures 135° and −225° are ____________.

The unit circle is a circle that ______________________________

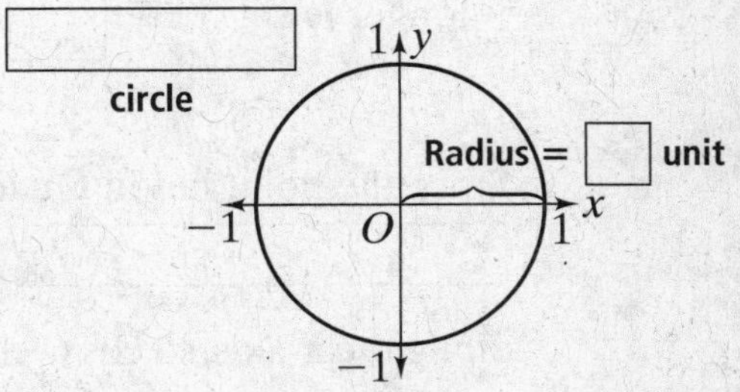

Name______________________________ Class______________________ Date ______________

Examples

1 History The Aztec calendar stone has 20 divisions for the 20 days in each month of the Aztec year. An angle on the Aztec calendar shows the passage of 16 days. Find the measures of the two coterminal angles that coincide with the angle.

The terminal side of the angle is [ ] of a full rotation from the initial side.

[ ] · [ ]° = [ ]°

To find a coterminal angle, subtract one full rotation.

[ ]° − [ ]° = [ ]°

Two coterminal angle measures for an angle on the Aztec calendar that shows the passage of 16 days are [ ]° and [ ]°.

2 Finding Exact Values of Cosine and Sine Find the exact values of cos (−150°) and sin (−150°).

Step 1 Sketch an angle of −150° in standard position. Sketch a unit circle.

x-coordinate = cos (−150°)

y-coordinate = sin (−150°)

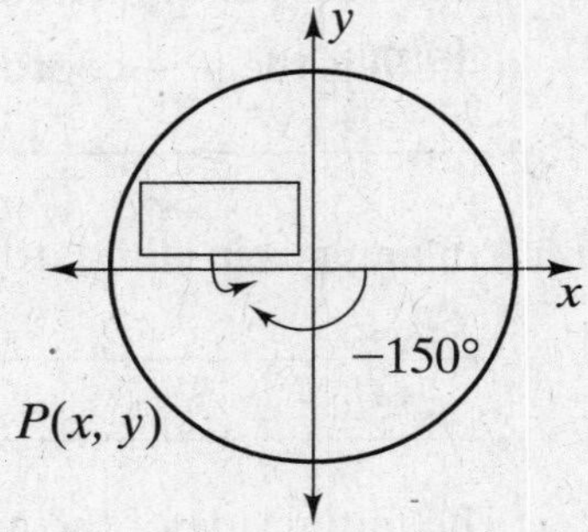

Step 2 Sketch a right triangle. Place the hypotenuse on the terminal side of the angle. Place one leg on the x-axis. (The other leg will be parallel to the y-axis.)

The triangle contains angles of [ ]°, [ ]°, and [ ]°.

Step 3 Find the length of each side of the triangle.

hypotenuse = [ ] — **The hypotenuse is a [ ] of the unit circle.**

shorter leg = [ ]/[ ] — **The shorter leg is [ ] the hypotenuse.**

longer leg = [ ]/[ ] [ ] = [ ]/[ ] — **The longer leg is [ ] times the shorter leg.**

Since the point lies in Quadrant [ ], both coordinates are [ ]. The [ ] leg lies along the x-axis, so cos (−150°) = [ ], and sin (−150°) = [ ].

Name________________________________ Class__________________________ Date ______________

Quick Check

1. a. Find an angle coterminal with 198° by adding one full rotation.

b. Reasoning Are angles with measures of 40° and 680° coterminal? Explain.

c. Make a Conjecture Generalize how the measures of two coterminal angles are related.

2. a. Find the decimal values of $-\frac{1}{2}$ and $-\frac{\sqrt{3}}{2}$. Then use a calculator to find cos (−120°) and sin (−120°). How do these values compare to each other? How do they compare to the exact values found in Example 2?

b. Find the exact values of cos 135° and sin 135°. Use properties of a 45°-45°-90° triangle. Use a calculator to find the decimal equivalents.

c. Find the exact values of cos 150° and sin 150°.

Name______________________ Class______________________ Date______________

Lesson 13-3

Radian Measure

Lesson Objectives	
1 Using radian measure for angles	
2 Finding the length of an arc of a circle	**Local Standards:** ____________

Vocabulary and Key Concepts

Converting Between Radians and Degrees

To convert degrees to radians, multiply by $\frac{\pi \text{ radians}}{180^\circ}$.

To convert radians to degrees, multiply by $\frac{180^\circ}{\pi \text{ radians}}$.

Length of an Intercepted Arc

For a circle of radius r and a central angle of measure θ (in radians), the length s of the intercepted arc is $s =$ ______.

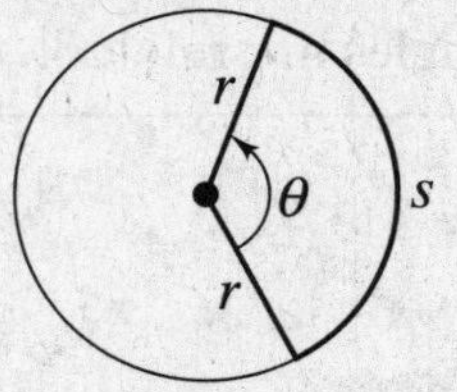

A central angle of a circle is ________________________________

____

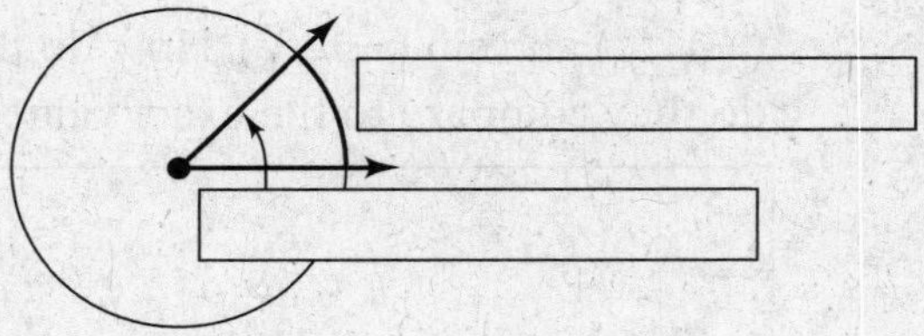

An intercepted arc of a circle is ________________________________

____

____

____

____

A radian is ________________________________

____

____

____

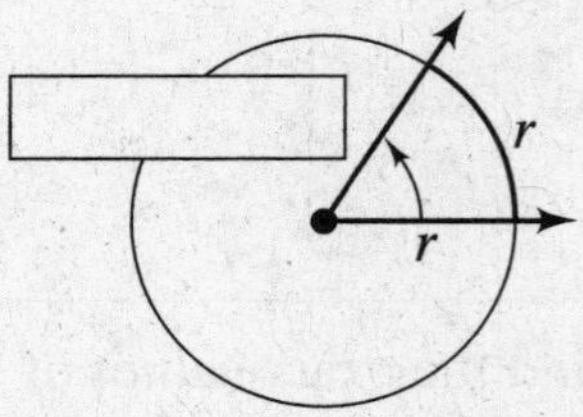

Name______________________ Class______________________ Date ____________

Example

❶ Using a Proportion

a. Find the radian measure of an angle of 45°.

$$\frac{\square^\circ}{\square^\circ} = \frac{r \text{ radians}}{\pi \text{ radians}}$$ **Write a proportion.**

$$\square \cdot \pi = \square \cdot r$$ **Write the cross-products.**

$$r = \frac{\square \cdot \square}{\square}$$ **Divide each side by** $\square$.

$$= \frac{\square}{\square} \approx \square$$ **Simplify.**

An angle of 45° measures about $\square$ radians.

b. Find the degree measure of $\frac{13\pi}{6}$ radians.

$$\frac{\frac{\square}{\square}}{\pi \text{ radians}} = \frac{d^\circ}{180}$$ **Write a proportion.**

$$\frac{\square}{\square} \cdot 180 = \pi \cdot d$$ **Write the cross-products.**

$$d = \frac{\square \not{\pi} \cdot \not{180}\,\square}{\square \not{6} \cdot \not{\pi}}$$ **Divide each side by** $\square$.

$$= \square$$ **Simplify.**

An angle of $\frac{13\pi}{6}$ radians measures $\square$ degrees.

Quick Check

1. Use a proportion for each conversion.

a. 85° to radians

b. 2.5 radians to degrees

Name________________ Class________________ Date ________________

Examples

2 Finding Cosine and Sine of Radian Measures Find the exact values of cos ($\frac{\pi}{3}$ radians) and sin ($\frac{\pi}{3}$ radians).

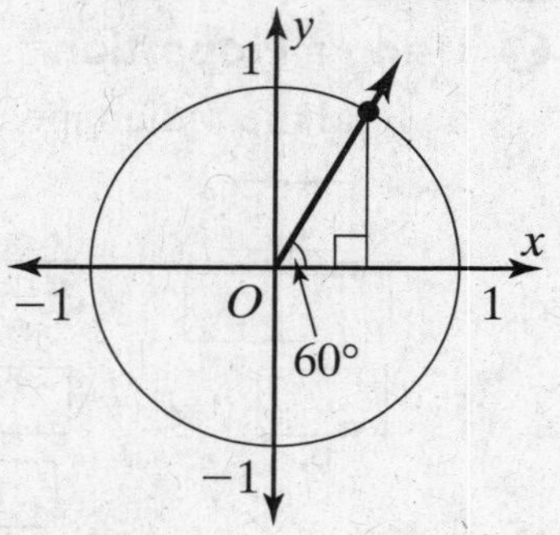

$\frac{\pi}{3}$radians $\cdot \frac{\square°}{\square} = \square°$ **Convert radians to degrees.**

Draw the angle. Complete a 30°-60°-90° triangle.

The hypotenuse has length ☐.

The shorter leg is ☐ the length of the hypotenuse, and the longer leg is ☐ times the length of the shorter leg.

Thus, cos ($\frac{\pi}{3}$ radians) = ☐ and sin ($\frac{\pi}{3}$ radians) = ☐.

3 Finding the Length of an Arc Use the circle at the right. Find length *s* to the nearest tenth.

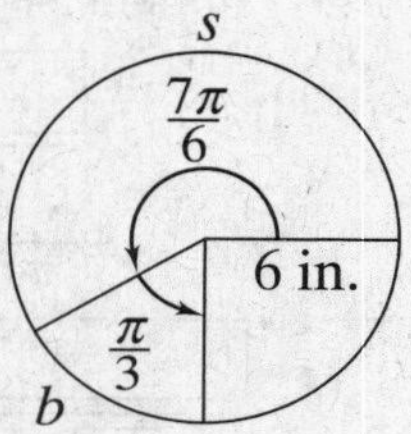

$s = r\theta$ **Use the formula.**

$= \square \cdot \frac{\square}{\square}$ **Substitute ☐ for *r* and $\frac{\square}{\square}$ for θ.**

$= \square$ **Simplify.**

$\approx \square$ **Use a calculator.**

The arc has length ☐ in.

Quick Check

2. a. Use a calculator to find cos ($\frac{\pi}{3}$ radians) and sin ($\frac{\pi}{3}$ radians). How do these values compare to the values found in Example 2?

☐

b. Explain how to use mental math to convert $\frac{\pi}{3}$ radians to degrees.

☐

3. Find length *b* in Example 3. Round your answer to the nearest tenth of an inch.

☐

Name______________________ Class______________________ Date______________

Lesson 13-4

The Sine Function

Lesson Objectives	**NAEP 2005 Strand:** Measurement
1 Identifying the properties of the sine function	**Topic:** Measuring Physical Attributes
2 Graphing sine curves	**Local Standards:** ____________________

Vocabulary and Key Concepts

Properties of Sine Functions

Suppose $y = a \sin b\theta$, with $a \neq 0$, $b > 0$, and θ in radians.

[ ] is the amplitude of the function.

[ ] is the number of cycles in the interval from 0 to 2π.

[ ] is the period of the function.

The sine function, $y = \sin \theta$, ____
____
____

A sine curve is ____

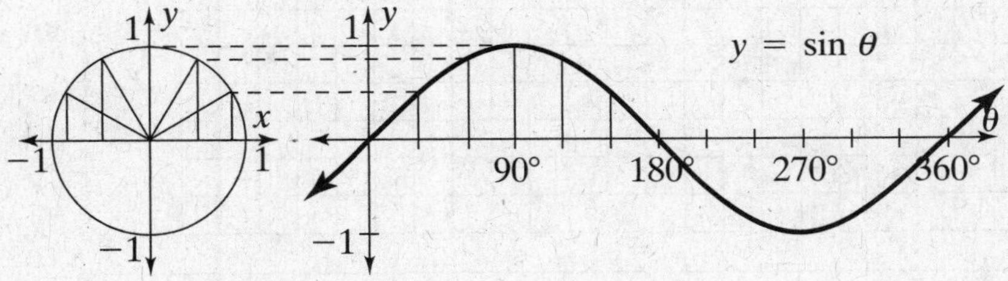

Examples

1 Interpreting the Sine Function in Degrees Use the graph of the sine function above.

a. What is the value of $y = \sin \theta$ for $\theta = 180°$?

The value of the function at $\theta = 180°$ is [ ].

b. For what other value(s) of θ from 0° to 360° does the graph of $y = \sin \theta$ have the same value as for $\theta = 180°$?

When $y = 0$, $\theta =$ [ ]° and [ ]°.

Name______________________ Class______________________ Date______________

2 Estimating Sine Values in Radians Estimate each value from the graph. Check your estimate with a calculator.

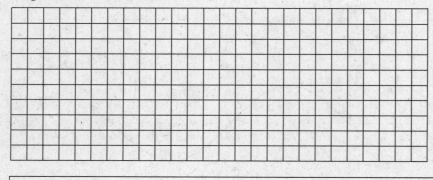

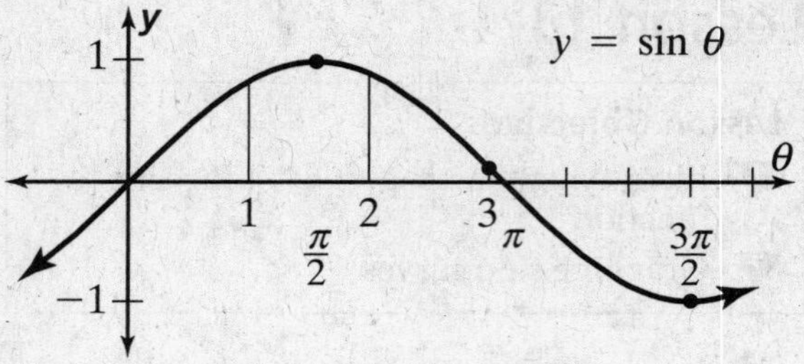

a. sin 3

The sine function reaches its median value of ☐ at $\pi \approx$ ☐. The value of the function at 3 is slightly more than ☐, or about ☐.

sin 3 = ☐ **Use a calculator in radian mode to check your estimate.**

b. $\sin \frac{\pi}{2}$

The sine function reaches its maximum value of ☐ at ☐, so $\sin \frac{\pi}{2} =$ ☐.

$\sin \frac{\pi}{2} =$ ☐ **Use a calculator in radian mode to check your estimate.**

Quick Check

1. a. Extend the graph of $y = \sin \theta$ in the definition above to include angle measures from 360° to 720°. Will the graph reach the maximum value of 1 again, and if so, where?

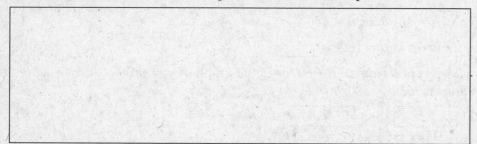

b. Reasoning Is the sine function a periodic function? Explain.

Name______________________ Class______________ Date __________

Example

3 Finding the Equation of a Sine Curve Find the period of the solid sine curve. Then write an equation for the curve.

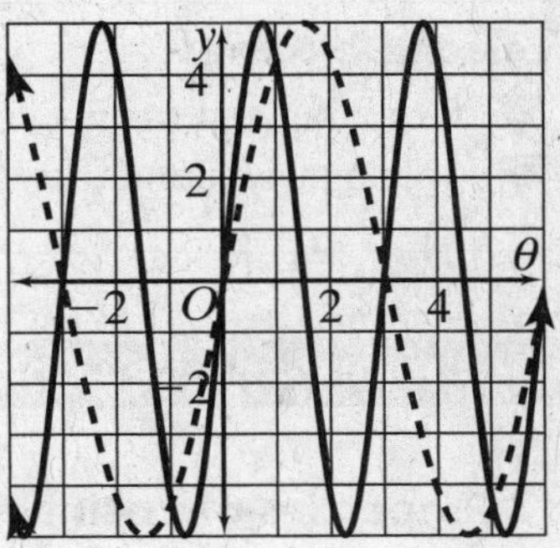

According to the graph, one cycle takes ☐ units to complete, so the period is ☐.

To write the equation, first find b.

period $= \dfrac{\square}{b}$ **Use the relationship between the period and** b**.**

$\square = \dfrac{\square}{b}$ **Substitute.**

$b = \dfrac{\square}{\square}$ **Multiply each side by** $\dfrac{b}{\square}$**.**

$\approx \square$ **Simplify.**

Now find a: the minimum is ☐ and the maximum is ☐, so the amplitude is $a =$ ☐.

Use the form $y = a \sin b\theta$. An equation for the graph is ☐.

Quick Check

2. Use the graphs of $y = \sin \theta$ from the definition and from Example 2.

a. Find the amplitude of the sine function.

b. Express the period of the sine function in degrees and in radians.

c. What are the domain and range of the sine function?

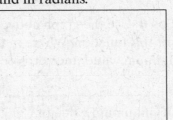

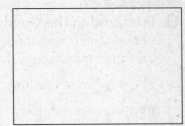

3. Write an equation for the dotted sine curve in Example 3.

Name_______________ Class_______________ Date_______________

Lesson 13-5

The Cosine Function

Lesson Objectives	NAEP 2005 Strand: Measurement
1 Graphing and writing cosine functions	**Topic:** Measuring Physical Attributes
2 Solving trigonometric equations	**Local Standards:** ____________

Vocabulary and Key Concepts

Properties of Cosine Functions

Suppose $y = a \cos b\theta$, with $a \neq 0, b > 0$, and θ in radians.

☐ is the amplitude of the function.

☐ is the number of cycles in the interval from 0 to 2π.

☐ is the period of the function.

The cosine function, $y = \cos\theta$, ______________________________

____

____

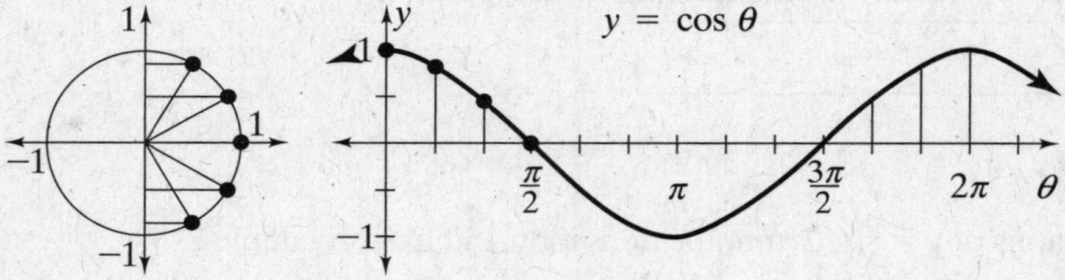

Examples

1 Interpreting the Graph of Cos θ Use the graph above. Find the domain, period, range, and amplitude of this function. Where in the cycle from 0 to 2π do the maximum value, minimum value, and zeros occur?

The domain of this function is ☐. The function goes from its maximum value of ☐ to its minimum value of ☐ and back again in an interval from 0 to ☐. The period is ☐. The range is ☐. The amplitude is ☐(maximum − minimum) = ☐(☐ − (☐)) = ☐(☐) = ☐.

The maximum value occurs at ☐ and ☐. The minimum value occurs at ☐. The zeros occur at ☐ and ☐.

Name______________________ Class______________________ Date ____________

❷ Sketching the Graph of a Cosine Function Sketch the graph of $y = -2 \cos \pi\theta$ in the interval from 0 to 4.

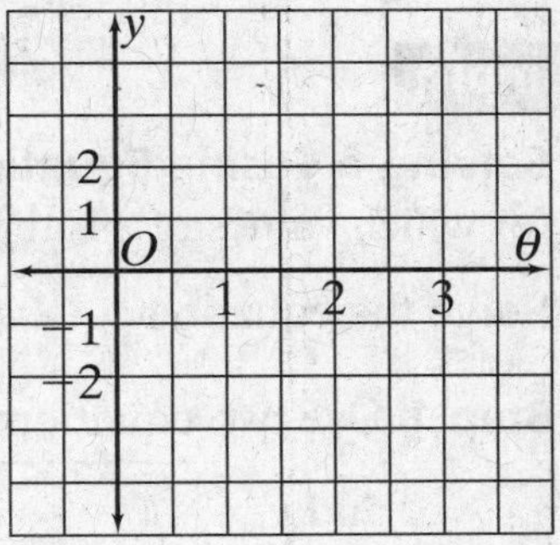

$|a| = \square$, so the amplitude is $\square$.

$b = \square$, so the graph has $\square$ full cycles from 0 to 4.

$\frac{2\pi}{b} = \square$, so the period is $\square$.

Divide the period into fourths. Plot five points for the first cycle. Use $\square$ for the maximum and $\square$ for the minimum. Repeat the pattern for the second cycle. Sketch the curve.

Quick Check

1. Use the graphs at the right. How are the graphs of the sine and cosine functions alike? How are they different?

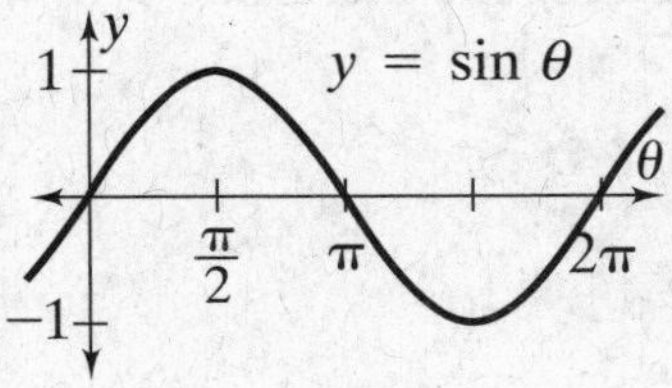

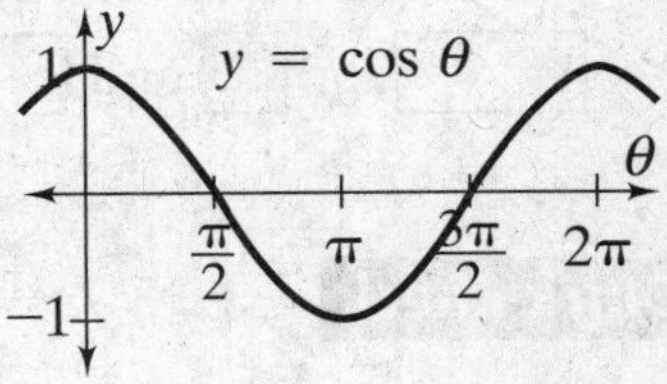

$\square$

2. **a.** Graph the equations $y = \cos x$ and $y = -\cos x$ on the same coordinate plane. Compare the graphs.

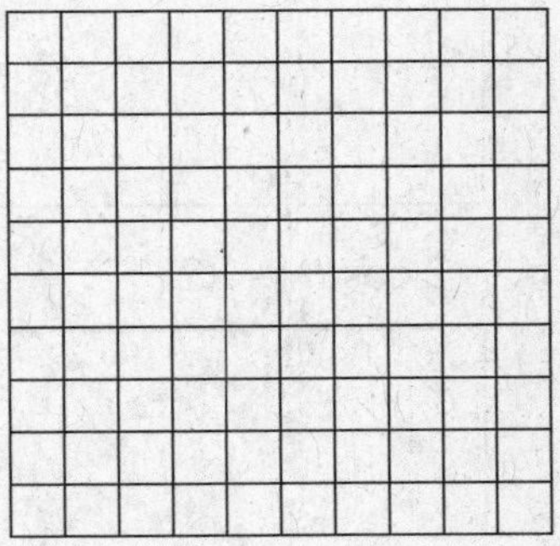

$\square$

b. Critical Thinking Write the five-point pattern to graph $y = a \cos b\theta$ when $a < 0$.

$\square$

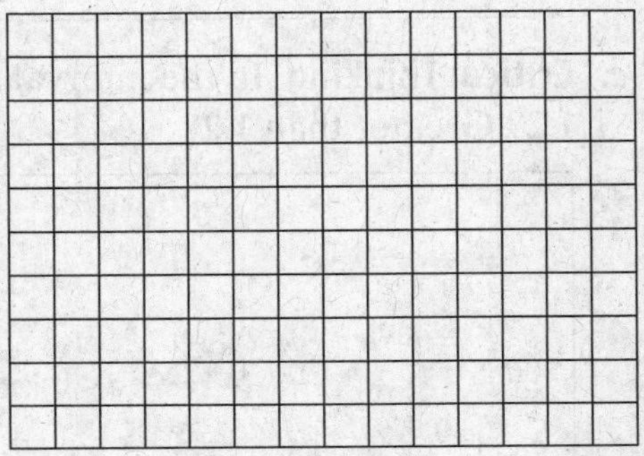

c. Sketch the cosine curve $y = -\frac{1}{2}\cos \pi\theta$ in the interval from 0 to 2π.

Name____________________ Class____________________ Date ____________

Example

3 Solving a Cosine Equation In the function $y = -2 \cos \frac{2x}{3}$, for which values of x is the function equal to 1?

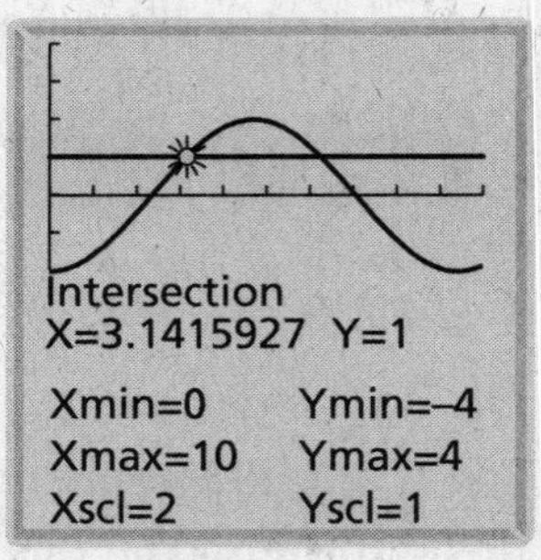

Solve the equation ☐ $= -2 \cos \frac{2x}{3}$ for the interval 0 to 10.

Step 1 Use two equations. Graph the equations $y =$ ☐ and $y =$ ☐ on the same screen.

Step 2 Use the ☐ feature to find the points at which the two graphs intersect.

The graph shows two solutions in the interval. They are $x \approx$ ☐ and ☐.

The solutions to the equation for the interval $0 \le x \le 10$ are about ☐ and ☐, or ☐ and ☐.

Quick Check

3. Find all solutions in the interval from 0 to 2π.

a. $3 \cos 2t = -2$

b. $-2 \cos \theta = 1.2$

c. Critical Thinking In the interval from 0 to 2π, when is $-2 \cos \theta$ less than 1.2? Greater than 1.2?

Name________________________ Class____________________ Date____________

Lesson 13-6

The Tangent Function

Lesson Objective	**NAEP 2005 Strand:** Measurement
1 Graphing the tangent function	**Topic:** Measuring Physical Attributes
	Local Standards: ____________________

Vocabulary and Key Concepts

Properties of Tangent Functions

Suppose $y = a \tan b\theta$, with $b > 0$ and θ in radians.

____ is the period of the function.

One cycle occurs in the interval from $-\frac{\pi}{2b}$ to ____.

There are ____________ asymptotes at each end of the cycle.

The tangent of θ is ____

____

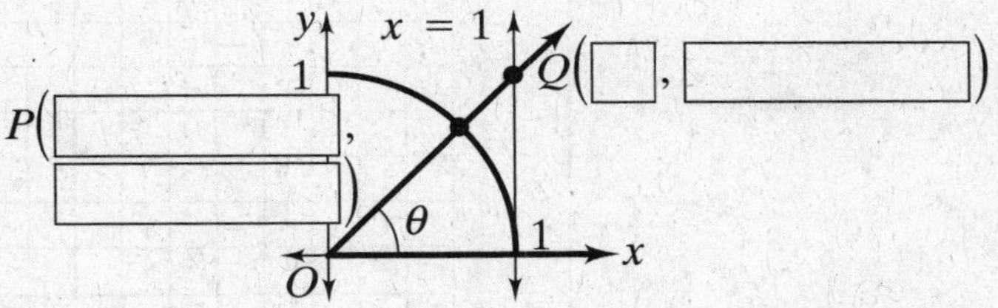

The line containing the terminal side of θ intersects the line $x = 1$ at Q.

The tangent function, $y = \tan \theta$, has a period of ____, and the asymptote that occurs at $\theta =$ ____ repeats every ____ units.

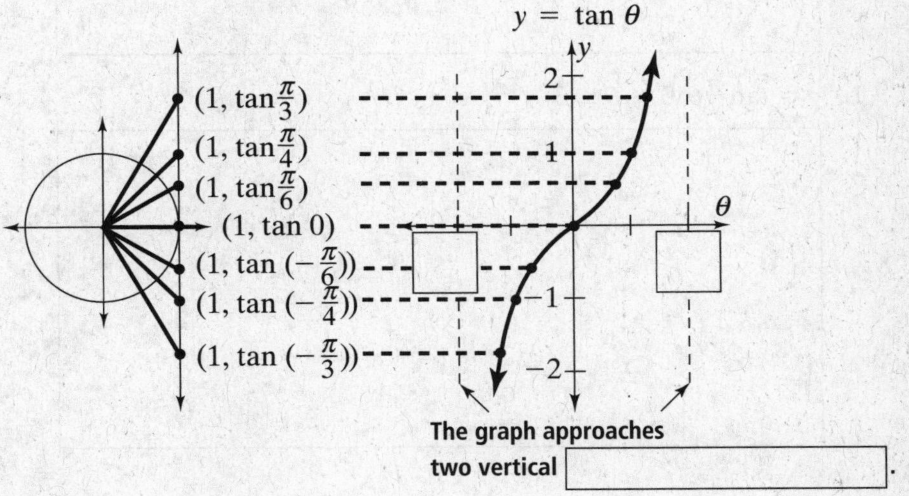

Name______________________ Class______________________ Date ______________

Example

❶ Graphing a Tangent Function Sketch two cycles of the graph of $y = \tan\frac{\theta}{2}$.

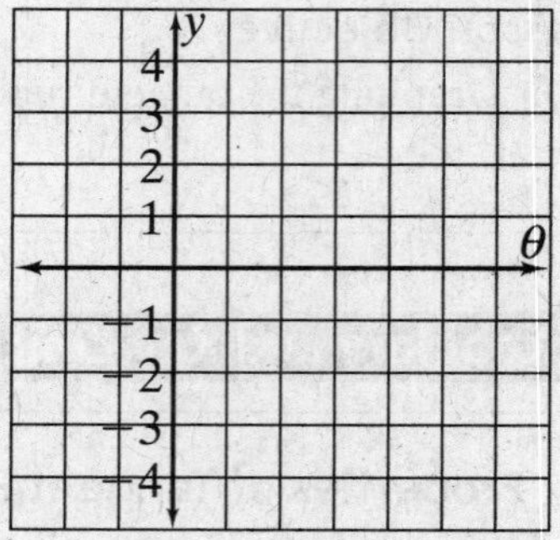

$\text{period} = \frac{\square}{\square}$ **Use the formula for the period.**

$= \frac{\square}{\square} = \square$ **Substitute** ____ **for *b* and simplify.**

One cycle occurs in the interval ____ to ____. Asymptotes occur every 2π units, at $\theta =$ ____, ____, and ____. Sketch the asymptotes. Plot three points in each cycle. Sketch the curve.

Quick Check

1. Sketch the graph of each tangent curve.

a. $y = \tan 3\theta, 0 \leq \theta \leq \pi$

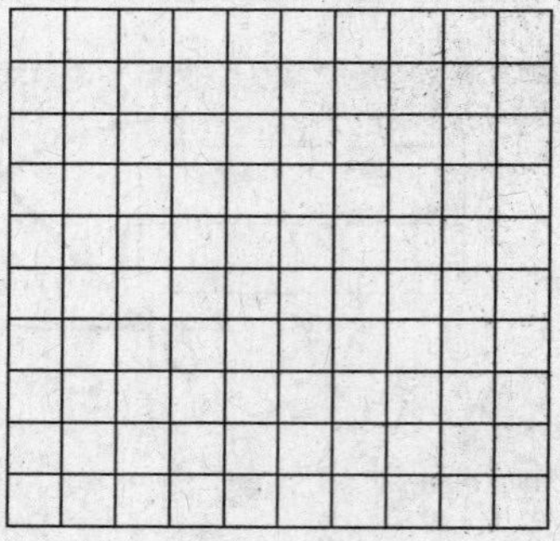

b. $y = \tan\frac{\pi}{2}\theta, 0 \leq \theta \leq 3$

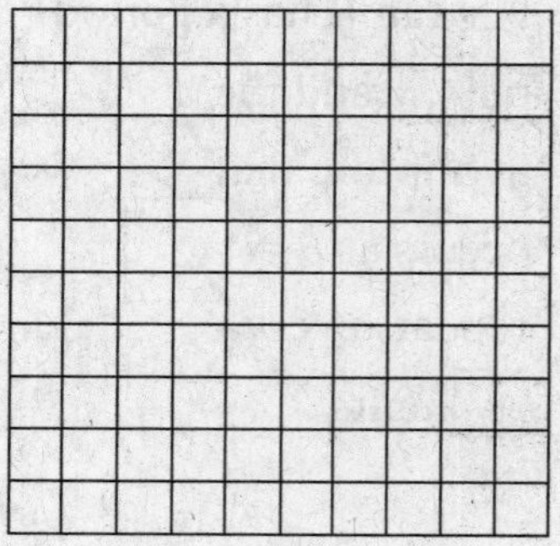

Name______________________ Class______________________ Date ______________

Example

❷ Design An architect is designing a front facade of a building to include a triangle like the one at the right. What is the height of the triangle when $\theta = 18°$? What is the height when $\theta = 20°$?

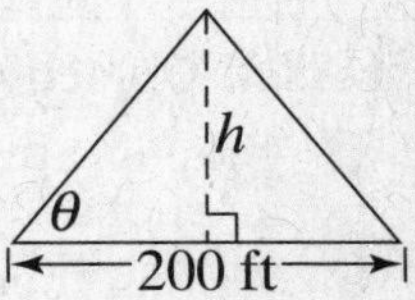

Step 1 Use a graphing calculator to sketch the graph of $y = \square \tan \theta$.

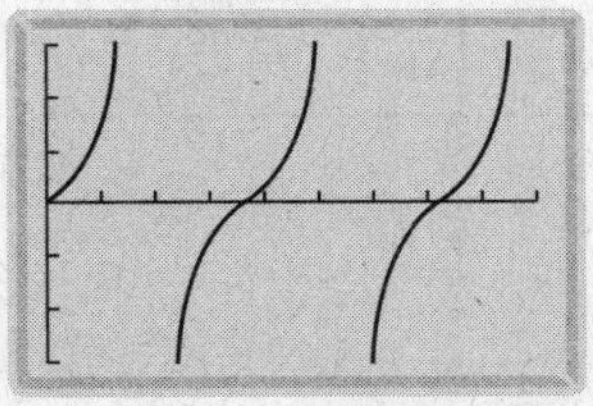

Xmin=0 Ymin=–300
Xmax=470 Ymax=300
Xscl=50 Yscl=90

Step 2 Use the TABLE feature.

X	Y1	
16	28.675	
17	30.573	
18	32.492	
19	34.433	
20	36.397	
21	38.386	
22	40.403	

X=16

When $\theta = 18°$, the height of the triangle is about $\square$ ft.

When $\theta = 20°$, the height of the triangle is about $\square$ ft.

Quick Check

2. a. What is the height of the triangle in Example 2 when $\theta = 25°$?

b. Reasoning The architect wants the triangle to be at least one story tall. The average height of a story is 14 ft. What must the measure of θ be for the height of the triangle to be at least 14 ft?

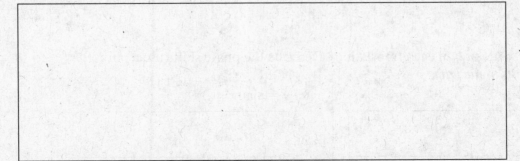

Name______________________ Class______________________ Date______________

Lesson 13-7

Translating Sine and Cosine Functions

Lesson Objectives	**NAEP 2005 Strand:** Measurement, Geometry
1 Graphing translations of trigonometric functions	**Topics:** Measuring Physical Attributes; Transformation of Shapes and Preservation of Properties
2 Writing equations of translations	**Local Standards:** ____________________

Vocabulary and Key Concepts

Translations of Sine and Cosine Functions

Parent Function	**Transformed Function**
$y = a \sin bx$	$y = a \sin b(x - h) + k$
$y = a \cos bx$	$y = a \cos b(x - h) + k$

☐ = amplitude (vertical stretch or shrink)

☐ = period (when x is in radians and $b > 0$)

☐ = phase shift, or horizontal shift

☐ = vertical shift

A phase shift is ____

Example

1 Identifying Phase Shifts What is the value of h in each translation? Describe each phase shift.

a. $g(x) = f(x + 3)$

$h =$ ☐; the phase shift is ☐ units to the ☐.

b. $y = \cos(x - 2)$

$h =$ ☐; the phase shift is ☐ units to the ☐.

Quick Check

1. What is the value of h in each translation? Describe the phase shift (use a phrase such as *3 units to the left*).

a. $g(t) = f(t - 5)$

b. $y = \sin(x + 3)$

Name__________________ Class__________________ Date__________________

Examples

❷ Graphing a Translation of $y = \sin 3x$ Sketch the graph of $y = \sin 3\left(x - \frac{\pi}{2}\right) - \frac{1}{2}$ in the interval $0 \le x \le 2\pi$.

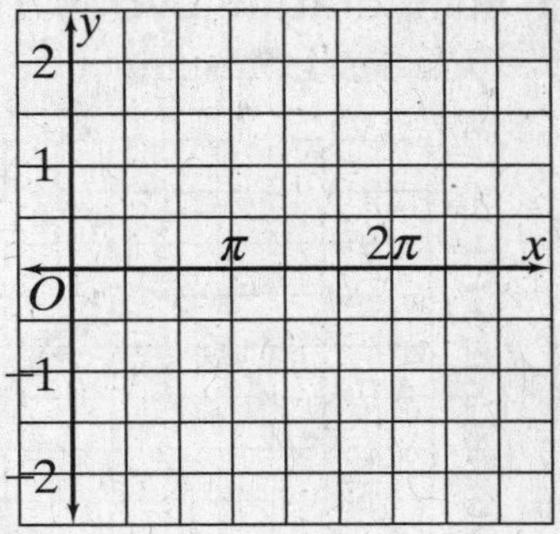

Since $a =$ ☐ and $b =$ ☐, the graph is a translation of $y = \sin 3x$.

Step 1 Sketch one cycle of $y = \sin 3x$. Use five points in the pattern zero-max-zero-min-zero.

Step 2 Since $h =$ ☐ and $k =$ ☐, translate the graph ☐ units to the ☐ and ☐ unit ☐. Extend the period pattern from 0 to 2π. Sketch the graph.

❸ Writing a Translation Write an equation for each translation.

a. $y = \cos x$, π units up

A shift up means ☐ $= \pi$.

An equation is ☐.

b. $y = -\sin x$, 3 units to the right

A shift to the right means ☐ $= 3$.

An equation is ☐.

Quick Check

2. Sketch each graph in the interval from 0 to 2π.

a. $y = -3 \sin 2\left(x - \frac{\pi}{3}\right) - \frac{3}{2}$

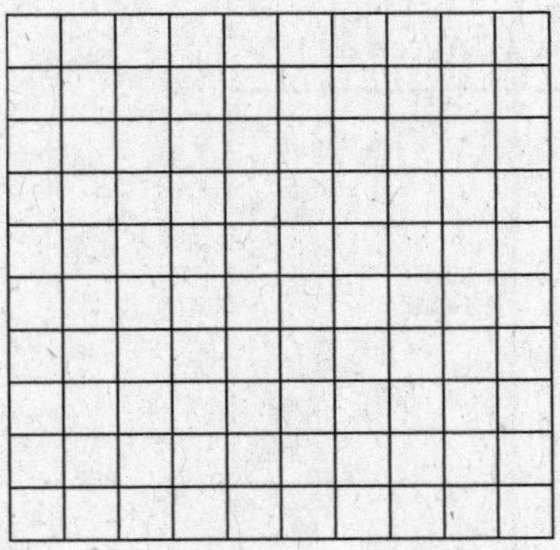

b. $y = 2 \cos \frac{\pi}{2}(x + 1) - 3$

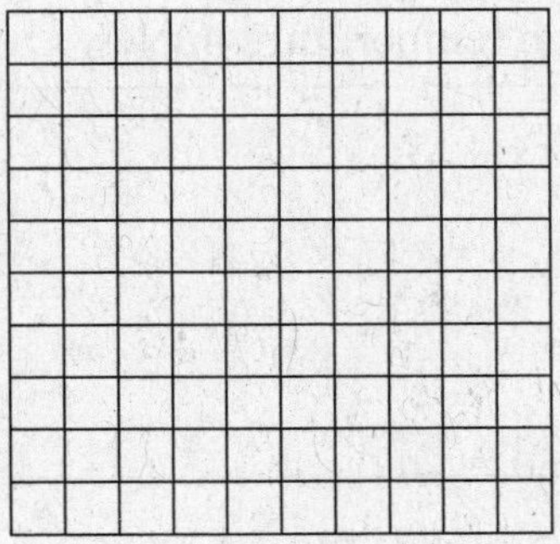

3. Write an equation for each translation.

a. $y = \cos x$, $\frac{\pi}{2}$ units up

☐

b. $y = 2 \sin x$, $\frac{\pi}{4}$ units to the right

☐

Name________________________ Class________________________ Date ____________

Example

4 **Temperature Cycles** The graph below shows typical high temperatures in New Orleans, Louisiana. Use it to draw some conclusions about the weather there.

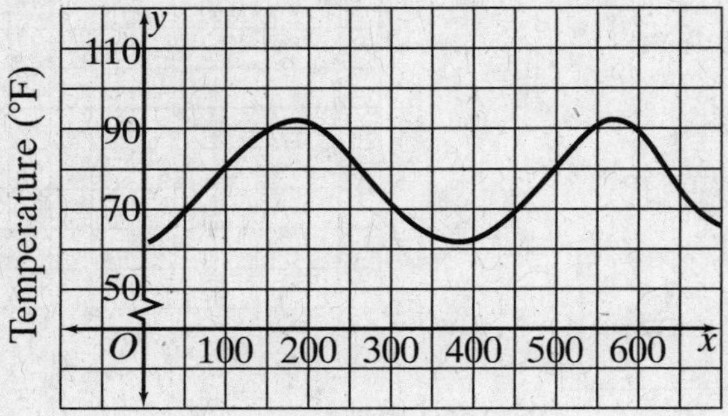

One can draw the conclusion that the temperature for New Orleans is ____________________

____

More exactly, the temperature varies approximately [ ] degrees.

One can also determine that the hottest temperature for the city never gets above [ ] degrees. Nor does the coldest temperature ever get lower than [ ] degrees.

Quick Check

4. Use the graph from Example 4.

a. Estimate the high temperature in New Orleans on September 1 (day 244).

b. An equation that models the data is $y = 14.5 \cos \frac{2\pi}{365}(x - 197) + 76.5$. Graph this model on your calculator. Use it to estimate the first day of the year that the high temperature is likely to reach 75°F.

Name____________________ Class____________________ Date____________

Lesson 13-8

Reciprocal Trigonometric Functions

Lesson Objectives	
1 Evaluating reciprocal trigonometric functions 2 Graphing reciprocal trigonometric functions	**Local Standards:** ____________________

Key Concepts

Cosecant, Secant, and Cotangent Functions

The cosecant (______), secant (______), and cotangent (______) functions are defined as reciprocals.

Their domains include ____

____

$\csc \theta = \dfrac{1}{\square}$ $\quad \sec \theta = \dfrac{1}{\square}$ $\quad \cot \theta = \dfrac{1}{\square}$

Example

1 Using Reciprocals

a. Find csc 45°. Use a calculator in ______________ mode.

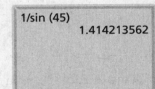

1/sin (45)
1.414213562

b. Suppose $\cos \theta = \frac{4}{5}$. Find $\sec \theta$.

$\sec \theta = \dfrac{1}{\square}$ **Use the definition.**

$= \dfrac{1}{\square}$ **Substitute.**

$= \dfrac{\square}{\square}$ **Simplify.**

Quick Check

1. a. Suppose $\sin \theta = \frac{15}{8}$. Find $\csc \theta$.

b. Find cot 55° to the nearest hundredth.

Name________________________ Class________________________ Date ____________

Examples

② Finding Exact Values Find the exact value of csc 45°.

Use the unit circle to find the exact value of ____________. Then write the reciprocal.

The *y*-coordinate of point *P* is ____.

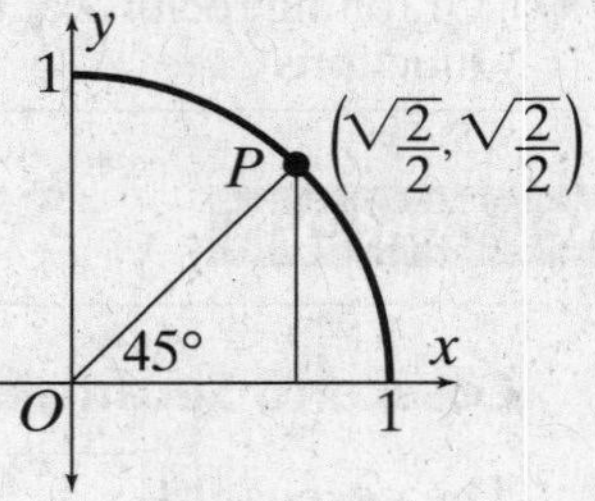

csc 45° $= \frac{1}{\square}$ **Use the definition.**

$= \frac{1}{\square}$ **Substitute.**

$= \frac{\square}{\square}$ **Simplify.**

$= \square$ **Rationalize the denominator.**

③ Sketching a Graph Graph $y = \cos x$ and $y = \sec x$ in the interval from 0 to 2π.

Step 1 Make a table of values.

x	0	$\frac{\pi}{6}$	$\frac{\pi}{3}$	$\frac{\pi}{2}$	$\frac{2\pi}{3}$	$\frac{5\pi}{6}$	π	$\frac{7\pi}{6}$	$\frac{4\pi}{3}$	$\frac{3\pi}{2}$	$\frac{5\pi}{3}$	$\frac{11\pi}{6}$	2π
cos *x*													
sec *x*													

Step 2 Plot the points and sketch the graphs.

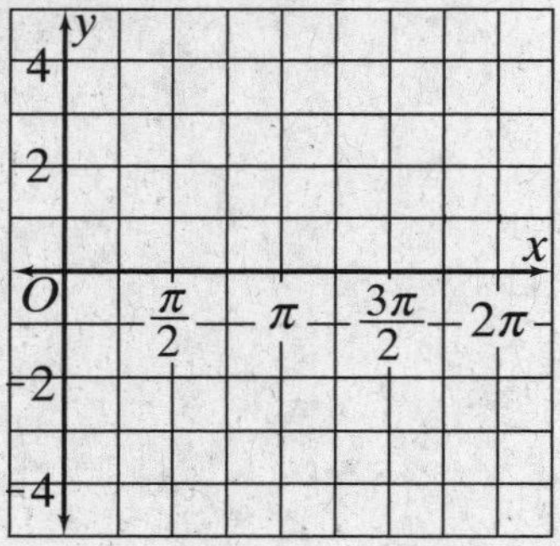

Name________________________ Class________________________ Date____________

❹ Indirect Measurement A handler of a parade balloon holds a line of length y. The length is modeled by the function $y = d \sec \theta$, where d is the distance from the handler of the balloon to the point on the ground just below the balloon, and θ is the angle formed by the line and the ground. Use the graph of the function $y = 6 \sec \theta$ to find the length of string needed to form an angle of 55°.

$$y = 6 \sec \theta = 6\left(\frac{1}{\boxed{}}\right) = \frac{6}{\boxed{}}$$ **Use the definition of secant. Simplify.**

Graph the function. Use the Value feature. To form an angle of 55°, the string must be about ______ ft long.

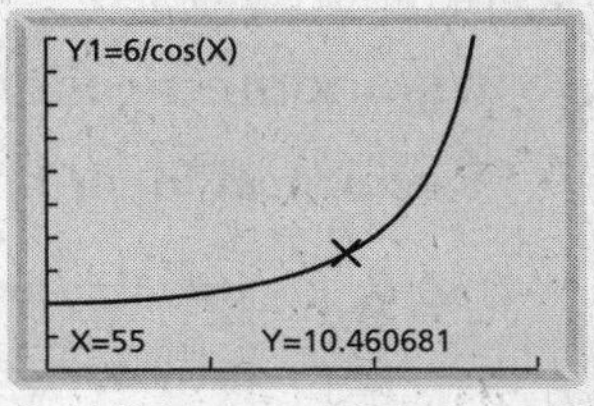

Quick Check

2. Find each exact value.

a. sec 60° **b.** cot 45° **c.** csc 30°

3. Graph $y = \tan x$ and $y = \cot x$ in the interval from 0 to 2π.

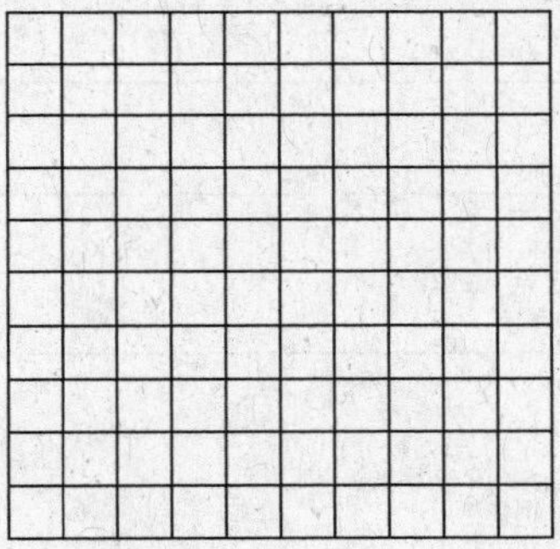

4. Use the model equation in Example 4 to find how long the line must be to form an angle of 30°, 45°, or 85°.

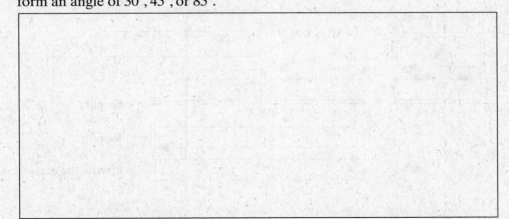

Name______________________ Class______________ Date__________

Lesson 14-1

Trigonometric Identities

Lesson Objective	
1 Verifying trigonometric identities	**NAEP 2005 Strand:** Algebra **Topic:** Variables, Expressions, and Operations **Local Standards:** ____________

Vocabulary and Key Concepts

Trigonometric Identities

Reciprocal identities

$\csc\theta = \dfrac{1}{\square}$ $\sec\theta = \dfrac{1}{\square}$ $\cot\theta = \dfrac{1}{\square}$

Tangent and cotangent identities

$\tan\theta = \dfrac{\square}{\square}$ $\cot\theta = \dfrac{\square}{\square}$

Pythagorean identities

$\cos^2\theta + \sin^2\theta = \square$ $1 + \tan^2\theta = \square$ $1 + \cot^2\theta = \square$

A trigonometric identity is ______________________________

____

____

Examples

1 Verifying Identities Verify the identity $\frac{\sin\theta}{\tan\theta} + \frac{\cos\theta}{\cot\theta} = \sin\theta + \cos\theta$.

$\dfrac{\sin\theta}{(\square)} + \dfrac{\cos\theta}{(\square)} = \sin\theta + \cos\theta$ $\square$ **and** $\square$ **identities**

$\dfrac{\square \cdot \square}{\sin\theta} + \dfrac{\square \cdot \square}{\cos\theta} =$ **Simplify.**

$\square + \square =$ **Simplify.**

$\square + \square$ **Rewrite the expression.**

Name____________________ Class____________________ Date ____________

❷ Simplifying Expressions Simplify the trigonometric expression $(1 + \cot^2 \theta)(\sec^2 \theta - 1)$.

$(1 + \cot^2 \theta)(\sec^2 \theta - 1) =$ ______ · ______ ______ **identities**

$= \frac{1}{\_\_\_\_\_\_} \cdot \frac{\_\_\_\_\_\_}{\_\_\_\_\_\_}$ ______ **and** ______ **identities**

$= \frac{1}{\_\_\_\_\_\_}$ **Simplify.**

$=$ ______ ______ **identity**

Quick Check

1. Verify the identity $\sec^2 \theta - \sec^2 \theta \cos^2 \theta = \tan^2 \theta$.

2. Simplify the trigonometric expression $\sec\theta \cot\theta$.

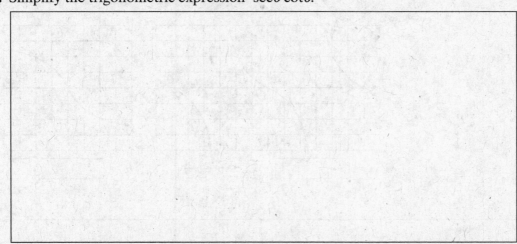

Name________________ Class________________ Date____________

Lesson 14-2

Solving Trigonometric Equations Using Inverses

Lesson Objectives

1. Evaluating inverses of trigonometric functions
2. Solving trigonometric equations

NAEP 2005 Strand: Algebra

Topic: Equations and Inequalities

Local Standards: ________________

Vocabulary and Key Concepts

The ________ of the ________ function can be restricted to $0 \le \theta \le \pi$ so that its inverse is a function. The inverse function is written ________ and is read as "θ is the angle whose ________ is x."

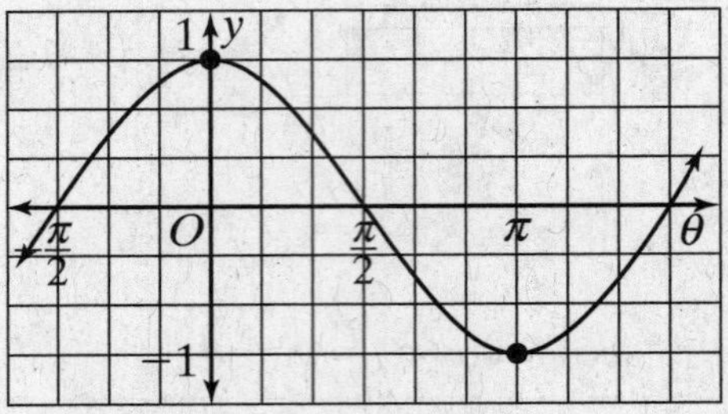

$y =$ ________ $, 0 \le \theta \le \pi$

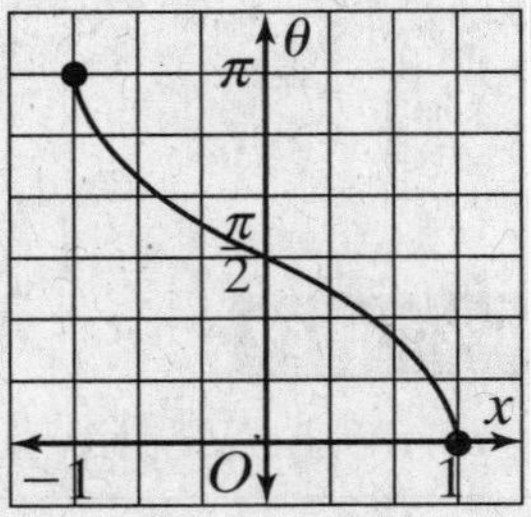

$\theta =$ ________

Similarly, the ________ of $y =$ ________ and $y =$ ________ are restricted to $-\frac{\pi}{2} \le \theta \le \frac{\pi}{2}$ to obtain the inverse functions $\theta =$ ________ and $\theta =$ ________.

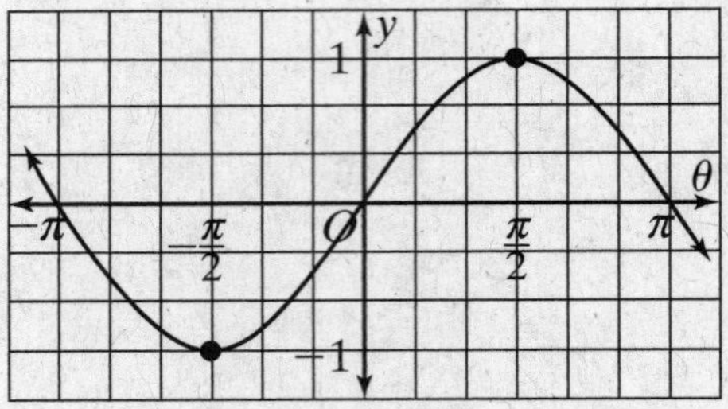

$y =$ ________ $, -\frac{\pi}{2} \le \theta \le \frac{\pi}{2}$

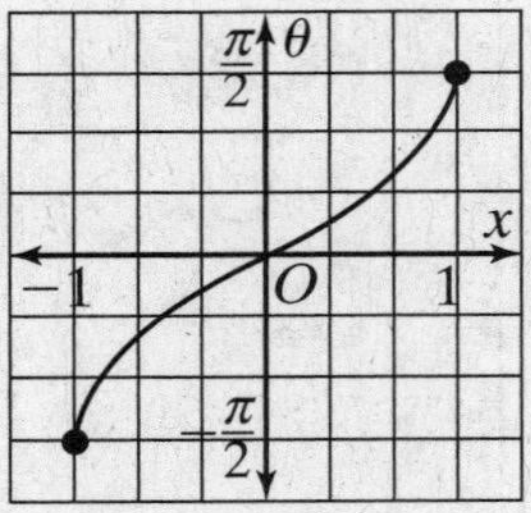

$\theta =$ ________

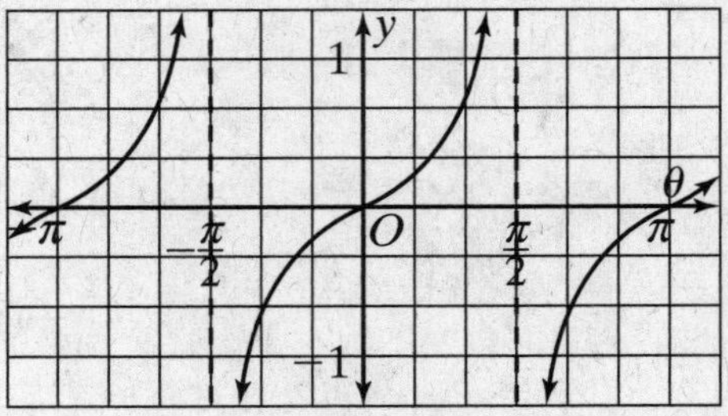

$y =$ ________ $, -\frac{\pi}{2} \le \theta \le \frac{\pi}{2}$

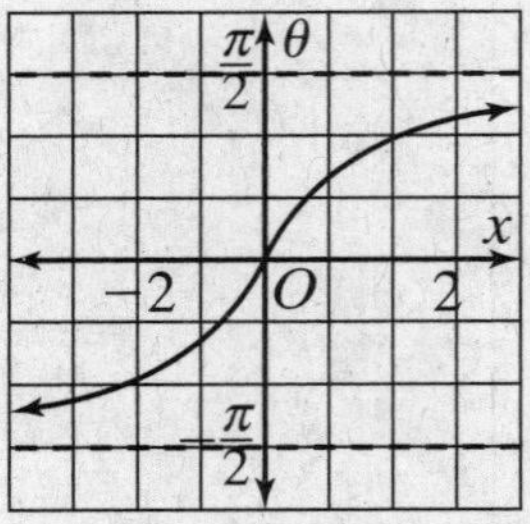

$\theta =$ ________

Name________________________ Class________________________ Date ______________

The cosine function $y = \cos\theta$ is periodic, so a [ ] line, such as the x-axis, can intersect the graph of $y = \cos\theta$ in [ ] many points. Therefore a [ ] line can intersect the graph of the inverse of $y = \cos\theta$ in infinitely many points. The inverse of $y = \cos\theta$ is a relation that [ ] a function.

You can use a graph of an [ ] function to find the measures of angles that have a given value of the function.

Examples

1 Using a Unit Circle Find the degree measures of the angles whose cosine is $\frac{\sqrt{2}}{2}$.

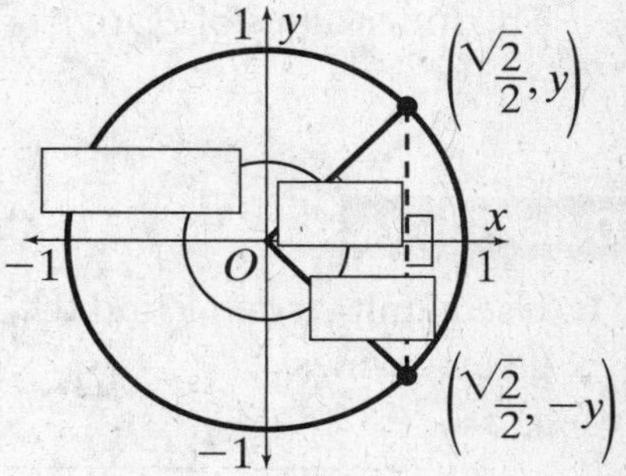

A. $45° + n \cdot 360°$ and $135° + n \cdot 360°$

B. $60° + n \cdot 360°$ and $300° + n \cdot 360°$

C. $60° + n \cdot 360°$ and $300° + n \cdot 360°$

D. $45° + n \cdot 360°$ and $315° + n \cdot 360°$

Find the points on the circle that have [ ]-coordinates of $\frac{\sqrt{2}}{2}$. These points and the origin form [ ] triangles. [ ] and [ ] are the measures of two angles whose cosine is $\frac{\sqrt{2}}{2}$. All their [ ] angles also have a cosine of $\frac{\sqrt{2}}{2}$. The measures of all the angles whose cosine is $\frac{\sqrt{2}}{2}$ can be written [ ] $+ n \cdot 360°$ and [ ] $+ n \cdot 360°$.

The correct choice is [ ].

2 Using a Calculator to Find the Inverse of a Tangent Use a calculator and an inverse function to find the radian measures of all angles whose tangent is 1.34.

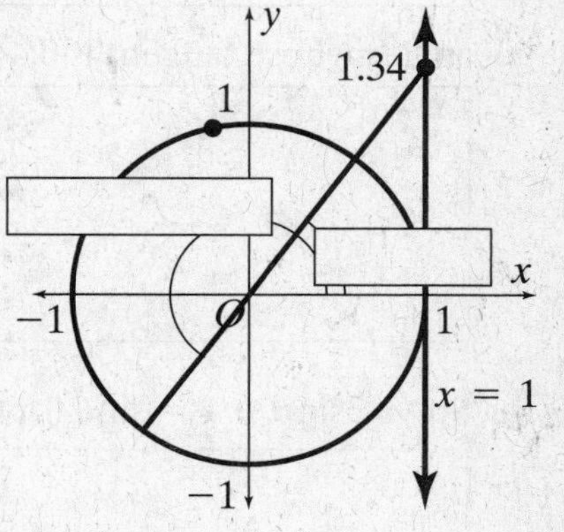

$\tan^{-1} 1.34 \approx$ [ ] **Use a calculator.**

The tangent function is also positive in Quadrant [ ], as shown in the figure at the right. So [ ] + [ ] is another solution.

The radian measures of all angles whose tangent is 1.34 can be written as [ ] + [ ][ ].

Name________________________ Class________________ Date ____________

3 Solving Trigonmic Equations by Factoring Solve $2 \sin \theta \cos \theta - \cos \theta = 0$ for $0 \le \theta < 2\pi$.

$2 \sin \theta \cos \theta - \cos \theta = 0$

$\cos \theta (\square - \square) = 0$ **Factor.**

$\square = 0$ or $\square = 0$ **Use the** ____ **Property.**

$\cos \theta = \square$ $\sin \theta = \square$ **Solve for sin θ.**

$\theta = \square$ and $\square$ $\theta = \square$ and $\square$ **Use the unit circle.**

The four values of θ are $\square$, $\square$, $\square$, and $\square$.

Quick Check

1. Use a unit circle to find the measures in degrees of all the angles with the given cosines.

a. $-\frac{1}{2}$ **b.** $-\frac{\sqrt{3}}{2}$ **c.** $-\frac{\sqrt{2}}{2}$

2. Find the radian measures of the angles.

a. angles whose sine is 0.44

b. angles whose sine is -0.73

c. angles whose tangent is 0.44

d. angles whose tangent is -0.73

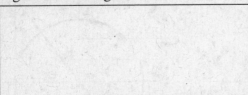

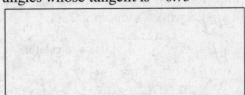

3. **a.** Solve $3\sin\theta + 1 = \sin\theta$ for $0 \le \theta < 2\pi$.

b. Solve $\sin\theta \cos\theta - \cos\theta = 0$ for $0 \le \theta < 2\pi$.

Name______________________________ Class______________________ Date______________

Lesson 14-3

Right Triangles and Trigonometric Ratios

Lesson Objectives	NAEP 2005 Strand: Measurement
1 Finding lengths of sides in a right triangle	**Topic:** Measuring Physical Attributes
2 Finding measures of angles in a right triangle	**Local Standards:** ____________________

Vocabulary

A trigonometric ratio for a right triangle is ______________________________________
____
____

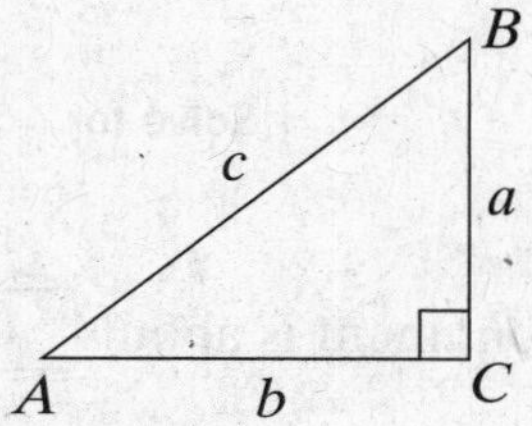

$$\sin A = \frac{\text{length of leg } \underline{\hspace{3cm}} \ \angle A}{\text{length of } \underline{\hspace{3cm}}} = \frac{\square}{\square}$$

$$\cos A = \frac{\text{length of leg } \underline{\hspace{3cm}} \text{ to } \angle A}{\text{length of } \underline{\hspace{3cm}}} = \frac{\square}{\square}$$

$$\tan A = \frac{\text{length of leg } \underline{\hspace{3cm}} \ \angle A}{\text{length of leg } \underline{\hspace{3cm}} \text{ to } \angle A} = \frac{\square}{\square}$$

$$\csc A = \frac{1}{\underline{\hspace{2cm}}} = \frac{\text{length of } \underline{\hspace{3cm}}}{\text{length of leg } \underline{\hspace{3cm}} \ \angle A} = \frac{\square}{\square}$$

$$\sec A = \frac{1}{\underline{\hspace{2cm}}} = \frac{\text{length of } \underline{\hspace{3cm}}}{\text{length of leg } \underline{\hspace{3cm}} \text{ to } \angle A} = \frac{\square}{\square}$$

$$\cot A = \frac{1}{\underline{\hspace{2cm}}} = \frac{\text{length of leg } \underline{\hspace{3cm}} \text{ to } \angle A}{\text{length of leg } \underline{\hspace{3cm}} \ \angle A} = \frac{\square}{\square}$$

Name________________________ Class________________________ Date ____________

Examples

1 Travel A tourist visiting Washington, D.C., is seated on the grass at point A and looks up at the top of the Washington Monument. The angle of her line of sight with the ground is 27°. Find her approximate distance AC from the base of the monument.

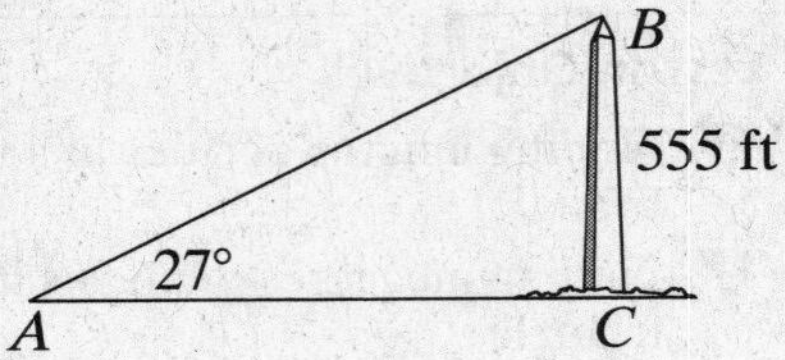

$\tan 27° = \dfrac{\boxed{}\text{ of the monument}}{\boxed{}\text{ from monument}}$ **Definition of tangent**

$\tan 27° = \dfrac{\boxed{}}{AC}$ **Substitute.**

$\boxed{} = \dfrac{\boxed{}}{AC}$ **Use a calculator in ____ mode.**

$AC = \dfrac{\boxed{}}{\boxed{}} \approx \boxed{}$ **Solve for *AC* and simplify.**

The distance between the visitor and the monument is about ____ feet.

2 Indirect Measure A man 6 feet tall is standing 50 feet from a tree. When he looks at the top of the tree, the angle of elevation is 42°. Find the height of the tree to the nearest foot.

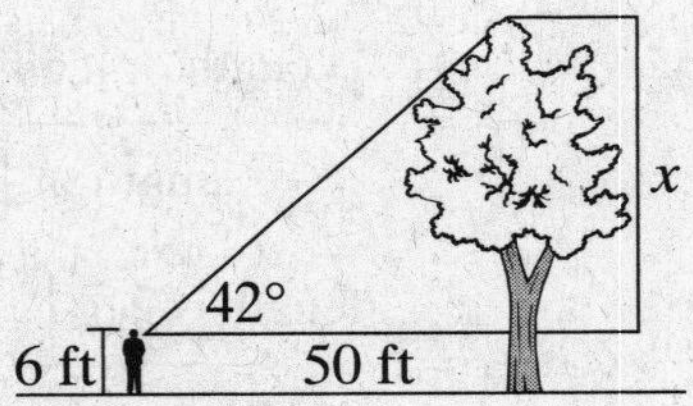

In the right triangle, the length of the leg adjacent to the 42° angle is ____ ft. You need to find the length of the leg opposite the 42° angle. Use the ____ ratio.

$\boxed{}\ 42° = \dfrac{x}{\boxed{}}$ **Definition of tangent**

$x = \boxed{}\ \boxed{}$ **Solve for *x*.**

$\approx \boxed{}$ **Use a calculator in ____ mode.**

The height of the tree is approximately ____ + ____ = ____ ft.

Quick Check

1. Find the distance from the visitor in Example 1 to the top of the monument.

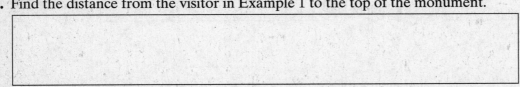

Name________________________ Class________________________ Date ____________

Example

3 Using Trigonometric Ratios to Find an Acute Angle Measure In $\triangle KMN$, $\angle N$ is a right angle, $m = 7$, and $n = 25$. Find $m\angle K$ to the nearest tenth of a degree.

Step 1 Draw a diagram.

Step 2 Use a ______ ratio.

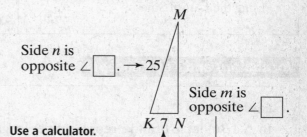

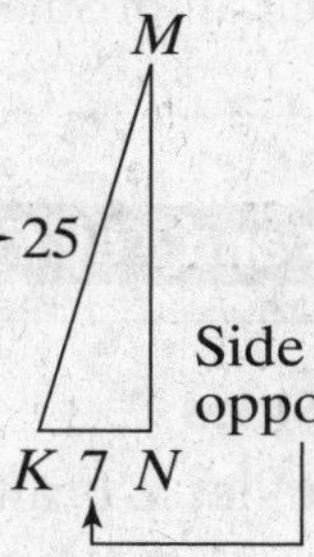

$\cos K = \frac{\square}{\square} = \square$

$m\angle K = \cos^{-1}\square \approx \square$ **Use a calculator.**

Since $\angle K$ is ______, the other solutions of $\cos^{-1}\square$ do not apply. To the nearest tenth of a degree, $m\angle K$ is ______.

Quick Check

2. In $\triangle DEF$, $\angle D$ is a right angle and $\tan E = \frac{3}{4}$. Draw a diagram and find $\sin E$ and $\sec F$ in fraction and in decimal form.

3. Use a trigonometric ratio to find the measure in degrees of $\angle A$ in each triangle.

a.

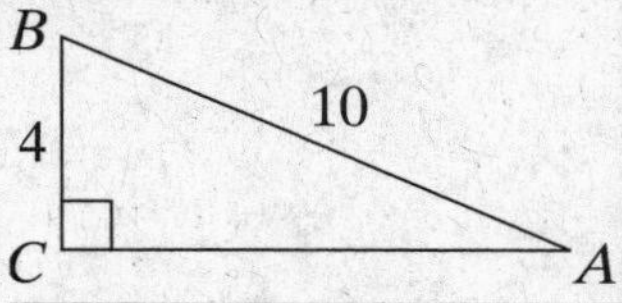

b.

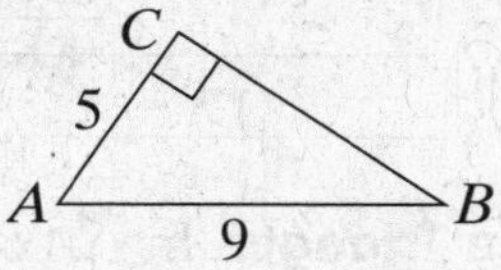

c. In $\triangle DEF$, $\angle F$ is a right angle, $d = 7$, and $f = 10$. Draw a diagram and find the remaining side length and angle measures in degrees. Round to the nearest tenth.

Name________________________ Class________________ Date____________

Lesson 14-4

Area and the Law of Sines

Lesson Objective	**NAEP 2005 Strand:** Algebra
1 Finding the area of any triangle and using the Law of Sines	**Topic:** Equations and Inequalities **Local Standards:** ____________________

Vocabulary and Key Concepts

Law of Sines

In $\triangle ABC$, let a, b, and c represent the lengths of the sides opposite $\angle A$, $\angle B$, and $\angle C$, respectively.

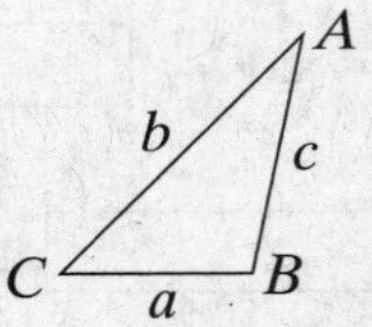

Then $\dfrac{\sin A}{\square} = \dfrac{\sin B}{\square} = \dfrac{\sin C}{\square}$.

The Law of Sines is ____

____

Examples

1 Finding the Area of a Triangle Find the area of the triangle shown at the right.

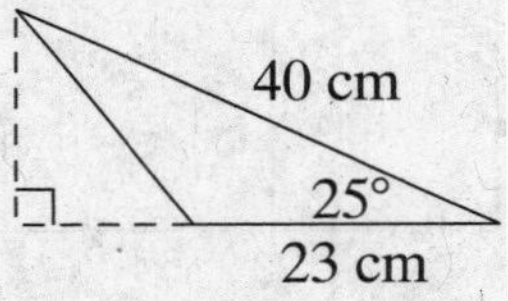

The area $K = \frac{1}{2}bh$.

$b = \square$, and since $\sin 25° = \dfrac{h}{\square}$, $h = \square\ \square°$.

So $K = \frac{1}{2}(\square)(\square) \approx \square$ cm^2.

2 Finding a Side of a Triangle In $\triangle ABC$, $m\angle A = 33°$, $m\angle C = 64°$, and $BC = 8$ cm. Find AC.

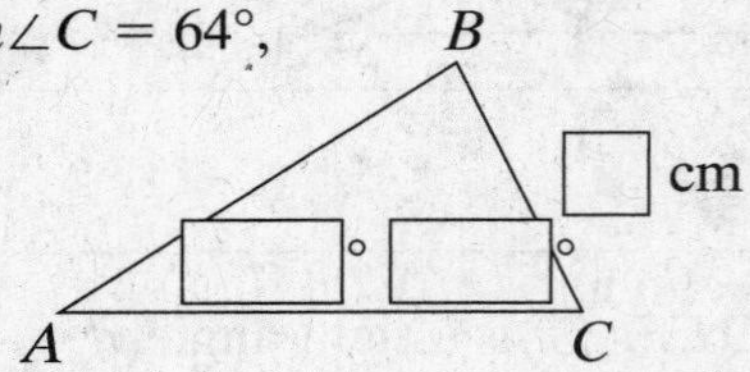

Step 1 Draw and label a diagram.

Step 2 Find the measure of the angle opposite $\overline{AC}$.

$m\angle B = 180° - 33° - 64° = 83°$

Step 3 Find AC.

$\dfrac{\sin 83°}{\square} = \dfrac{\sin 33°}{\square}$ **Law of Sines.**

$AC = \dfrac{\square \sin \square°}{\sin \square°}$ **Solve for AC.**

$AC \approx \square$ cm **Use a calculator.**

Name______________________ Class______________________ Date ____________

❸ Finding an Angle of a Triangle In $\triangle PQR, p = 7$ in., $q = 10$ in., and $m\angle Q = 98°$. Find $m\angle R$.

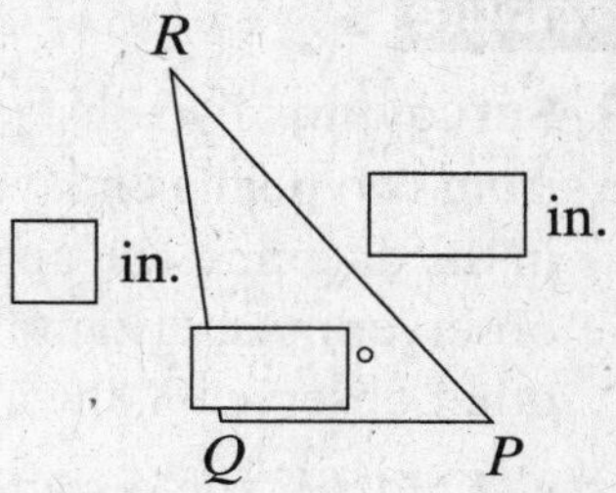

Step 1 Label the diagram.

Step 2 Find the measure of the angle opposite $\square$.

$$\frac{\sin P}{\square} = \frac{\sin 98°}{\square}$$ **Law of Sines.**

$$\sin P = \frac{\square \sin 98°}{\square}$$ **Solve for sin *P*.**

$$m\angle P = \square\left(\frac{\square \sin 98°}{\square}\right)$$ **Solve for *m*∠*P*.**

$$m\angle P \approx \square$$

Step 3 Find the measure of $\angle R$.

$$m\angle R \approx 180° - \square - \square$$
$$= \square$$

Quick Check

1. A triangle has sides of lengths 12 in. and 15 in., and the measure of the angle between them is 24°. Find the area of the triangle.

2. In $\triangle KLM, m\angle K = 120°, m\angle M = 50°$, and $ML = 35$ yd. Find KL.

3. In $\triangle PQR, m\angle R = 97.5°, r = 80$, and $p = 75$. Find $m\angle P$.

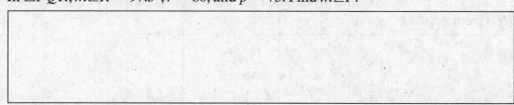

Name______________________ Class______________________ Date ______________

Example

4 **Surveying** Two observers view the same mountain peak from two points on level ground and 2 miles apart, as shown in the diagram. The angle of elevation of the peak for the observer most distant from the mountain, T, is 31°. For the other observer, S, the angle of elevation of the peak is 58°.

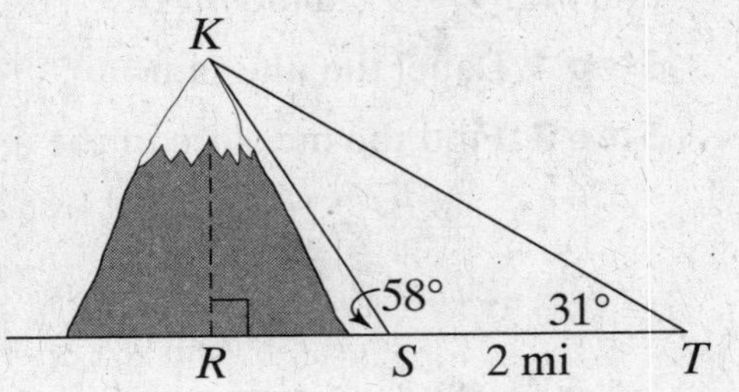

a. Find TK, the distance from T to the summit.

First find $m\angle KST$ and $m\angle SKT$.

$m\angle KST = 180° - \square = \square$

$m\angle SKT = 180° - \square - \square = \square$

Use the Law of Sines in $\triangle SKT$. Write a proportion that includes the side you know, $\square$, and the side you want to know $\square$.

$$\frac{\sin S}{\square} = \frac{\sin K}{\square}$$ **Law of Sines**

$$\frac{\sin \square°}{KT} = \frac{\sin \square°}{\square}$$ **Substitute.**

$$KT = \frac{\square \sin \square°}{\sin \square°} \approx \square$$ **Solve for *KT*. Use a calculator.**

The distance from T to the summit is about $\square$ mi.

b. Find RK, the height of the mountain.

In right $\triangle KRT$, you know KT and $m\angle T$. Use the $\square$ ratio.

$$\sin \square° = \frac{RK}{\square}$$ **Definition of Sine**

$$RK = \square \sin \square° \approx \square$$ **Solve for *RK*. Use a calculator.**

The summit is about $\square$ mi high.

Quick Check

4. In $\triangle MNP$, $m\angle M = 35°$, $m\angle N = 120°$, and $MN = 48$. Find the length of the altitude of $\triangle MNP$ from vertex P.

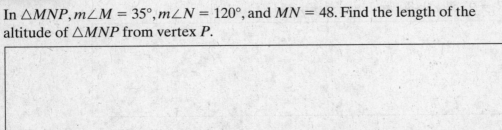

Name____________________ Class____________________ Date____________________

Lesson 14-5

The Law of Cosines

Lesson Objective	NAEP 2005 Strand: Algebra
1 Using the Law of Cosines in finding the measures of sides and angles of a triangle	**Topic:** Equations and Inequalities
	Local Standards: ____________________

Key Concepts

Law of Cosines

In $\triangle ABC$, let a, b, and c represent the lengths of the sides opposite $\angle A$, $\angle B$, and $\angle C$, respectively.

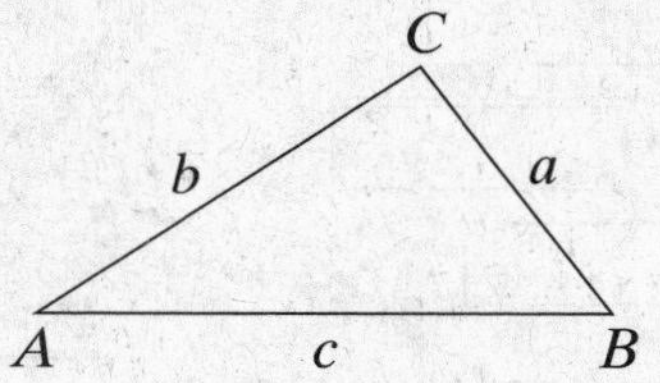

$a^2 = \square^2 + \square^2 - 2\square \cos \square$

$b^2 = \square^2 + \square^2 - 2\square \cos \square$

$c^2 = \square^2 + \square^2 - 2\square \cos \square$

Example

1 Astronomy Suppose two stars are 9.5 and 4.6 light years from Earth. When an astronomer observes the stars with the Earth as a vertex, the angle between the stars is about 43°. What is the approximate distance between the stars?

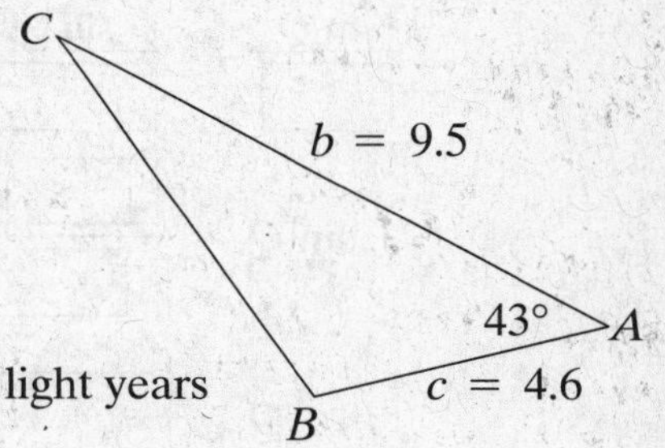

A. 6.9 light years **B.** 47.5 light years **C.** 10.1 light years **D.** 9.5 light years

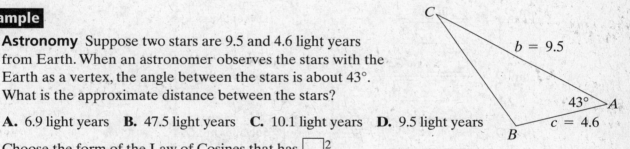

Choose the form of the Law of Cosines that has $\square^2$.

$a^2 = \square^2 + \square^2 - 2\square \cos \square$

$a^2 = (\square)^2 + (\square)^2 - 2(\square)(\square) \cos \square°$ **Substitute.**

$\approx \square$ **Use a calculator.**

$a \approx \square$

The distance between the two stars is about $\square$ light years.

The correct choice is $\square$.

Quick Check

1. The lengths of two sides of a triangle are 8 and 10, and the measure of the angle between them is 40°. Find the length of the third side.

$\square$

Name______________________ Class______________________ Date ______________

Example

2 Finding an Angle Measure In $\triangle PQR$, $r = 10$, $q = 12$, and $m\angle P = 32°$. Find $m\angle Q$.

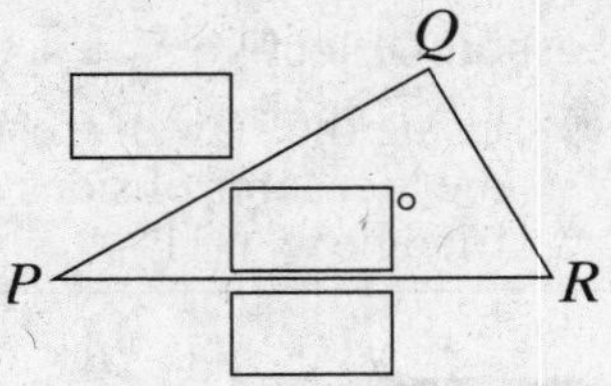

Step 1 Label the diagram.

Step 2 Since you cannot find $m\angle Q$ directly, use the Law of ______ to find p.

$$p^2 = q^2 + r^2 - 2qr\cos 32°$$

$p^2 = \square^2 + \square^2 - 2(\square)(\square)\cos 32°$ **Substitute.**

$p^2 \approx \square$ **Simplify.**

$p \approx \sqrt{\square}$ **Solve for *p*.**

$p \approx \square$ **Find the principal square root.**

Step 3 Now you can use the Law of ______ or the Law of ______ to find $m\angle Q$.

$\dfrac{\sin Q}{\square} = \dfrac{\sin 32°}{\square}$ **Law of Sines.**

$\sin Q = \dfrac{\square \sin 32°}{\square}$ **Solve for sin *Q*.**

$m\angle Q = \square\left(\dfrac{\square \sin 32°}{\square}\right)$ **Solve for $m\angle Q$.**

$m\angle Q \approx \square$ **Use a calculator.**

Quick Check

2. In $\triangle RST$, $s = 41$, $t = 53$, and $m\angle R = 126°$. Find $m\angle T$.

Name_______________ Class_______________ Date_______________

Lesson 14-6

Angle Identities

Lesson Objectives	NAEP 2005 Strand: Algebra
1 Verifying and using angle identities	Topic: Variables, Expressions, and Operations
2 Verifying and using sum and difference identities	Local Standards: ____________

Key Concepts

Angle Identities

Negative Angle Identities

$\sin(-\theta) = \square$ $\quad \cos(-\theta) = \square$ $\quad \tan(-\theta) = \square$

Cofunction Identities

$\sin\left(\frac{\pi}{2} - \theta\right) = \square$ $\quad \cos\left(\frac{\pi}{2} - \theta\right) = \square$ $\quad \tan\left(\frac{\pi}{2} - \theta\right) = \square$

Angle Difference Identities

$\sin(A - B) = \sin\square\cos\square - \cos\square\sin\square$

$\cos(A - B) = \cos\square\cos\square + \sin\square\sin\square$

$\tan(A - B) = \dfrac{\tan\square - \tan\square}{1 + \tan\square\tan\square}$

Angle Sum Identities

$\sin(A + B) = \sin\square\cos\square + \cos\square\sin\square$

$\cos(A + B) = \cos\square\cos\square - \sin\square\sin\square$

$\tan(A + B) = \dfrac{\tan\square + \tan\square}{1 - \tan\square\tan\square}$

Examples

1 Verifying Angle Identities Use the fact that $\pi - \theta = \left(\frac{\pi}{2} - \left(\theta - \frac{\pi}{2}\right)\right)$ to verify the identity $\sin(\pi - \theta) = \sin\theta$.

$\sin(\pi - \theta) = \sin\left(\frac{\pi}{2} - \left(\theta - \frac{\pi}{2}\right)\right)$ **Take the sine of each side.**

$= \square\left(\theta - \frac{\pi}{2}\right)$ **Cofunction identity**

$= \cos\left(\square - \square\right)$ **Negative angle identity**

$= \square\,\theta$ **Cofunction identity**

Name______________________ Class______________________ Date ____________

2 Solving Trigonometric Equations Solve $\cos\left(\frac{\pi}{2} - \theta\right) = \sin\left(\frac{\pi}{2} - \theta\right)$ for $0 \leq \theta < 2\pi$.

$\dfrac{\cos\left(\frac{\pi}{2} - \theta\right)}{\sin\left(\frac{\pi}{2} - \theta\right)} = 1$ **Divide by $\sin\left(\frac{\pi}{2} - \theta\right)$.**

$\dfrac{\boxed{}\,\theta}{\boxed{}\,\theta} = 1$ **Cofunction identities**

$\boxed{}\,\theta = 1$ **Tangent identity**

$\theta = \boxed{} = \dfrac{\boxed{}}{\boxed{}}$ **Solve for θ.**

Another solution is $\boxed{} + \pi = \boxed{}$.

3 Cofunction Identities in a Right Triangle Find a cofunction identity for $\tan(90° - A)$, where A is an acute angle of a right triangle.

In a right triangle, the ______ angles are complementary (the sum of their measures is ______). So $A + B =$ ______ and $B =$ ______ $- A$, where A and B are the measures of the acute angles.

$\tan(90° - A) = \dfrac{\boxed{}\,(90° - A)}{\boxed{}\,(90° - A)}$ **Tangent identity**

$= \dfrac{\boxed{}\,A}{\boxed{}\,A}$ **Cofunction identities**

$= \boxed{}\,A$ **Cotangent identity**

Quick Check

1. Verify the identity $\cos\left(\theta - \frac{\pi}{2}\right) = \sin\theta$.

2. Solve $\sin\left(\frac{\pi}{2} - \theta\right) = \sec\theta$ for $0 \leq \theta < 2\pi$.

3. Derive a cofunction identity for $\sec(90° - A)$.

4 Using Angle Difference Identities Find the exact value of cos 165°.
You know exact values for 180°, 60°, and 45°, and that $165° = 180° - (60° - 45°)$.

$\cos(A - B) = \square A \square B + \square A \square B$ **Cosine Angle Difference Identity**

$\cos(180° - (60° - 45°))$ **Substitute** $\square$° **for** ***A*** **and** $\square$ **for** ***B*****.**

$= \cos \square° \cos(\square) + \sin \square° \sin(\square)$

$= (\square)\cos(\square) + (\square)\sin(\square)$ **Use the exact values for cos 180° and sin 180°.**

$= (\square)\cos(\square)$ **Simplify.**

$= (\square)(\cos \square° \cos \square° + \sin \square° \sin \square°)$ **Substitute** $\square$° **for** ***A*** **and** $\square$° **for** ***B*****.**

$= (\square)\left[\left(\frac{\square}{\square}\right)\left(\frac{\square}{\square}\right) + \left(\frac{\square}{\square}\right)\left(\frac{\square}{\square}\right)\right]$ **Replace with exact values.**

$= -\left(\frac{\square}{\square} + \frac{\square}{\square}\right) = -\left(\frac{\square + \square}{\square}\right)$ **Simplify.**

Since the cosine is $\square$ in Quadrant II, cos 165° = $\square$.

5 Using Angle Sum Identities Find the exact value of sin 195°.
Use the fact that $195° = 135° + 60°$.

$\sin(A + B) = \square A \square B + \square A \square B$ **Sine Angle Sum Identity**

$\sin(135° + 60°) = \sin \square° \cos \square° + \cos \square° \sin \square°$ **Substitute** $\square$° **for** ***A*** **and** $\square$° **for** ***B*****.**

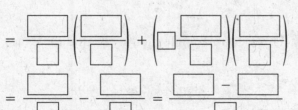

$= \frac{\square}{\square}\left(\frac{\square}{\square}\right) + \left(\square\frac{\square}{\square}\right)\left(\frac{\square}{\square}\right)$ **Replace with exact values.**

$= \frac{\square}{\square} - \frac{\square}{\square} = \frac{\square - \square}{\square}$ **Simplify.**

Quick Check

4. Find the exact value of sin 15°.

5. Find the exact value of tan 105°.

Name______________________ Class______________________ Date______________

Lesson 14-7

Double-Angle and Half-Angle Identities

Lesson Objectives	NAEP 2005 Strand: Algebra
1 Verifying and using double angle identities	Topic: Variables, Expressions, and Operations
2 Verifying and using half-angle identities	Local Standards: ____________________

Key Concepts

Double-Angle Identities

$\cos 2\theta = \underline{\qquad}^2\,\theta - \underline{\qquad}^2\,\theta$ $\sin 2\theta = 2\,\underline{\qquad}\,\theta\,\underline{\qquad}\,\theta$

$\cos 2\theta = 2\,\underline{\qquad}^2\,\theta - \underline{\quad}$

$\tan 2\theta = \dfrac{2\,\underline{\qquad}\,\theta}{1 - \underline{\qquad}^2\,\theta}$

$\cos 2\theta = \underline{\quad} - 2\,\underline{\qquad}^2\,\theta$

Half-Angle Identities

$\sin \frac{A}{2} = \pm\sqrt{\dfrac{1 - \underline{\qquad}\,A}{2}}$

$\tan \frac{A}{2} = \pm\sqrt{\dfrac{1 - \underline{\qquad}\,A}{1 + \underline{\qquad}\,A}}$

$\cos \frac{A}{2} = \pm\sqrt{\dfrac{1 + \underline{\qquad}\,A}{2}}$

Examples

1 Using a Double-Angle Identity Use a double-angle identity to find the exact value of sin 600°.

$\sin 600° = \sin(2 \cdot 300°)$ **Rewrite 600 as (2 · 300).**

$= 2\,\underline{\qquad}\,300°\,\underline{\qquad}\,300°$ **Use a sine ________-angle identity.**

$= 2(\underline{\qquad})(\underline{\qquad}) = \underline{\qquad}$ **Replace with exact values. Simplify.**

Name_______________ Class_______________ Date_______________

2 Verifying an Identity Verify the identity $\frac{\sin 2\theta}{(1 - \sin^2 \theta)} = 2 \tan \theta$.

$\frac{\sin 2\theta}{(1 - \sin^2 \theta)} = \frac{2 \square \theta \cdot \square \theta}{\square \theta}$ ____________-angle and ____________ identities

$= \frac{2 \square \theta}{\square \theta}$ **Simplify.**

$= 2 \square \theta$ ____________ **Identity**

3 Using Half-Angle Identities Use the half-angle identities to find the exact value of sin 75°.

$\sin 75° = \sin \frac{150°}{2}$ **Rewrite 75° as $\left(\frac{150°}{2}\right)$.**

$= \sqrt{\frac{(\square - \square\ 150°)}{2}}$ **Use the ____________ square root, since sin 75° is positive.**

$= \sqrt{\frac{1 - (\square)}{2}}$ **Substitute the exact value for ____________ 150°.**

$= \sqrt{\frac{\square + \square}{4}}$ **Simplify.**

$= \frac{\sqrt{\square + \square}}{\square}$ **Simplify.**

Quick Check

1. Use a double-angle identity to find the exact value of sin 120°.

2. Verify the identity $2 \cos 2\theta = 4 \cos^2 \theta - 2$.

Name____________________ Class____________________ Date ____________

Example

4 Using Half-Angle Identities Given $\cos\theta = -\frac{12}{13}$ and $90^\circ < \theta < 180^\circ$, find $\sin\frac{\theta}{2}$.

Since $90^\circ < \theta < 180^\circ$, $\square < \frac{\theta}{2} < \square$ and $\frac{\theta}{2}$ is in Quadrant $\square$.

$$\sin\frac{\theta}{2} = \pm\sqrt{\frac{\square - \square\,\theta}{2}}$$ **$\square$-angle identity**

$$= \sqrt{\frac{1 - \left(\square\right)}{2}}$$ **Substitute. Choose the $\square$ square root since $\frac{\theta}{2}$ is in Quadrant $\square$.**

$$= \sqrt{\frac{25}{26}}$$ **Simplify.**

$$= \frac{\square\sqrt{26}}{26}$$ **Rationalize the denominator.**

Quick Check

3. Use the half-angle identities to find the exact value of each expression.

a. $\sin 150^\circ$

b. $\tan 150^\circ$

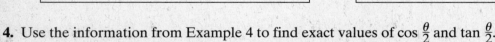

4. Use the information from Example 4 to find exact values of $\cos\frac{\theta}{2}$ and $\tan\frac{\theta}{2}$.

A Note to the Student:

This section of your workbook contains a series of pages that support your mathematics understandings for each chapter and lesson presented in your student edition.

- Practice pages provide additional practice for every lesson.
- Guided Problem Solving pages lead you through a step-by-step solution to an application problem in each lesson.
- Vocabulary pages contain a variety of activities to increase your reading and math understanding, ranging from graphic organizers to vocabulary review puzzles.

Name ____________ Class ____________ Date ____________

Practice 1-1

Properties of Real Numbers

Simplify.

1. $-|4.2|$
2. $|12 - 16|$
3. $\left|-\frac{7}{6}\right|$
4. $|3| - |-2|$
5. $\left|\frac{2}{3}\right|$
6. $0.3|-6|$
7. $|14 - 8|$
8. $|-0.01|$

Replace each \$ with the symbol <, >, or = to make the sentence true.

9. $-\sqrt{6}$ \$ $\sqrt{10}$
10. $\frac{3}{2}$ \$ 1.5
11. 0.06 \$ 0.6
12. 4 \$ $|-4|$
13. -0.4 \$ 0
14. $-|-7|$ \$ $|-7|$
15. 0.9 \$ $\frac{2}{3}$
16. $\sqrt{2}$ \$ $\sqrt{5}$

Name all the sets of numbers to which each number belongs.

17. -5
18. 0
19. $\sqrt{5}$
20. $2.\overline{7}$
21. 9
22. $\frac{10}{7}$
23. 1.2345267831 . . .
24. $-\frac{4}{2}$

Name the property of real numbers illustrated by each equation.

25. $\pi + 3 = 3 + \pi$
26. $\sqrt{2} + 0 = \sqrt{2}$
27. $(2 + x) + 3 = 2 + (x + 3)$
28. $\frac{5}{9} \cdot \frac{9}{5} = 1$
29. $16(3t + 4v) = 48t + 64v$
30. $\sqrt{2} \cdot 3 = 3 \cdot \sqrt{2}$
31. $0.01 \cdot 1 = 0.01$
32. $\frac{3}{2} \cdot \frac{2}{3} = 1$
33. $7 + (-7) = 0$
34. $2(xy) = (2x)y$

Graph the number on the following number line. Estimate if necessary.

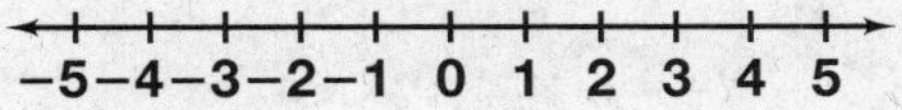

35. $-\sqrt{2}$
36. $\frac{3}{2}$
37. 0.5
38. -1

Find the opposite and the reciprocal of each number.

39. $-2\frac{1}{2}$
40. 3
41. $\frac{5}{9}$
42. -4

Which set of numbers best describes the values of each variable?

43. the number of stops N a commuter train makes on a certain day

44. the high H and low L for a certain stock during a period of n weeks

45. the average time per lap t it takes a race car to complete n laps

Name ______________________ Class ______________ Date ______________

1-1 • Guided Problem Solving

GPS Exercises 79–83

Reasoning Show that each statement is false by finding a counterexample (an example that makes the statement false).

a. The reciprocal of each whole number is a whole number.

b. The opposite of each natural number is a natural number.

c. There is no whole number that has an opposite that is a whole number.

d. There is no integer that has a reciprocal that is an integer.

e. The product of two irrational numbers is an irrational number.

Read and Understand

1. What is a counterexample? ______________________

2. The answers to (a) – (e) may vary. Why? ______________________

Plan and Solve

3. Choose a whole number between 2 and 9. Find its reciprocal. Then write a counterexample for part (a). ______________________

4. Choose a whole number between 2 and 9. Find its opposite. Then write a counterexample for part (b). ______________________

5. For part (c), write the counterexample using the number 0. ______________________

6. Choose the number 1 or -1. Then write a counterexample for part (d). ______________________

7. Choose an irrational number that is the square root of a rational number. Find the product of this number and its opposite. Then write a counterexample for part (e). ______________________

Look Back and Check

8. To check your answers, find another counterexample for each part, if possible. ______________________

Solve Another Problem

9. Show that each statement is false by finding a counterexample.

a. The difference of two whole numbers is a whole number. ______________________

b. The opposite of each integer is a whole number. ______________________

c. The square of a whole number is an even number. ______________________

d. All integers are whole numbers. ______________________

e. The square root of each whole number is an irrational number. ______________________

Name ____________________ Class ____________ Date ____________

Practice 1-2

Algebraic Expressions

Simplify by combining like terms.

1. $6x + x$
2. $11t + 3t - 5$
3. $-6a - 5a + b - 1$
4. $5i + 7j - 3i$
5. $16xy - 4xy$
6. $5x - 3x^2 + 16x^2$
7. $3(m - 2) + m$
8. $\frac{3(a - b)}{9} + \frac{4}{9}b$
9. $t + \frac{t^2}{2} + t^2 + t$
10. $4a - 5(a + 1)$
11. $2(m - n^2) - 6(n^2 + 3m)$
12. $x(x - y) + y(y - x)$
13. The expression $6s^2$ represents the surface area of a cube with edges of length s. Find the surface area of a cube with each edge length.
    a. 3 inches
    b. 1.5 meters
14. The expression $4.95 + 0.07x$ models a household's monthly long-distance charges, where x represents the number of minutes of long-distance calls during the month. Find the monthly charges for 73 minutes.

Evaluate each expression for the given value of the variable.

15. $5y^2 + y + 1;\ y = 4$
16. $a + 6 + 3a;\ a = 5$
17. $-t^2 - (3t + 2);\ t = 5$
18. $i^2 - 5(i^3 - i^2);\ i = 7$
19. $k + 2 - 4k - 1;\ k = -3$
20. $6a - 3a^2 - 2a^3;\ a = 1$
21. $-m(2m + m^2);\ m = -4$
22. $3 - 2n - 5 + n^2;\ n = -3$
23. $12b - 3 + b^2;\ b = 9$
24. $a^2 + b^2;\ a = 3, b = 4$
25. $c(3 - a) - c^2;\ a = 4, c = -1$
26. $-a^2 + 3(d - 2a);\ a = 2, d = -3$
27. Write an expression for the perimeter of the figure as the sum of the lengths of its sides. Then simplify your answer.

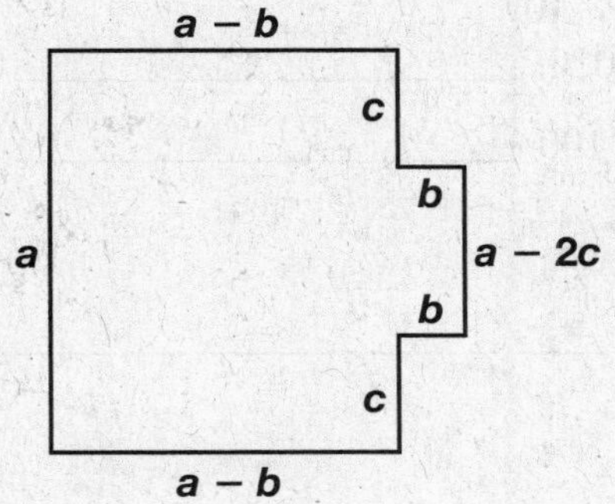

Name ______________________ Class ______________ Date ______________

1-2 • Guided Problem Solving

GPS Exercise 46

Elections The expression $2.6y + 107$ models the number of eligible voters in millions in the United States from 1960 to 2000. In the expression, y represents the number of years since 1960.

a. Find the approximate number of eligible voters in 1988.

b. Assume that the model continues to hold for future years. How many eligible voters will there be in 2012? In 2020?

c. The expression $-0.3y + 61$ models the *percent* of eligible voters who voted in presidential elections from 1960 to 2000. (See Example 3.) Write an expression that models the *number* of voters in presidential elections from 1960 to 2000.

d. Use your model from (c) to find the approximate number of voters who voted for president in 1980.

Read and Understand

1. What does the expression $2.6y + 107$ model? ______________________

2. What does y represent? ______________________

Plan and Solve

3. How many years are there from 1960 to 1988? Substitute your answer into the expression $2.6y + 107$ to approximate the number of eligible voters in 1988. ______________________

4. How many years are there from 1960 to 2012? From 1960 to 2020? ______________________

5. Substitute your answers from Step 4 into the expression $2.6y + 107$ to approximate the number of eligible voters in 2012 and in 2020. ______________________

6. Since $-0.3y + 61$ represents the percent, divide each term by 100. ______________________

7. To find the expression for the *number* of voters, multiply the expression $2.6y + 107$ modeling the eligible voters by the expression you found in Step 6 and simplify. ______________________

8. How many years are there from 1960 to 1980? Substitute your answer into the expression found in Step 7 to approximate the number of voters who voted in 1980. ______________________

Look Back and Check

9. Make a table of years and voters and verify the reasonableness of your answers. ______________________

Solve Another Problem

10. a. Find the approximate number of eligible voters in 1995. ______________________

b. Find the approximate number of voters who voted for president in 1995. ______________________

Name ______________________ Class ______________ Date ______________

Practice 1-3

Solving Equations

Solve each formula for the indicated variable.

1. $V = \frac{\pi}{3} r^2 h$, for h
2. $S = L(1 - r)$, for r
3. $S = \ell w + wh + \ell h$, for w

Solve for x. State any restrictions on the variables.

4. $\frac{4}{9}(x + 3) = g$
5. $a(x + c) = b(x - c)$
6. $\frac{x + 3}{t} = t^2$

7. Two brothers are saving money to buy tickets to a concert. Their combined savings is $55. One brother has $15 more than the other. How much has each saved?

8. The sides of a triangle are in the ratio 5 : 12 : 13. What is the length of each side of the triangle if the perimeter of the triangle is 15 in.?

9. Find three consecutive numbers whose sum is 126.

Solve each equation.

10. $\frac{1}{2}(x - 3) + \left(\frac{3}{2} - x\right) = 5x$
11. $5w + 8 - 12w = 16 - 15w$
12. $7y + 5 = 6y + 11$
13. $1.2(x + 5) = 1.6(2x + 5)$
14. $t - 3\left(t + \frac{4}{3}\right) = 2t + 3$
15. $0.5(c + 2.8) - c = 0.6c + 0.3$
16. $3(x + 1) = 2(x + 11)$
17. $\frac{u}{5} + \frac{u}{10} - \frac{u}{6} = 1$

18. Mike and Adam left a bus terminal at the same time and traveled in opposite directions. Mike's bus was in heavy traffic and had to travel 20 mi/h slower than Adam's bus. After 3 hours, their buses were 270 miles apart. How fast was each bus going?

19. Two trains left a station at the same time. One traveled north at a certain speed and the other traveled south at twice the speed. After 4 hours, the trains were 600 miles apart. How fast was each train traveling?

20. Find four consecutive odd integers whose sum is 336.

21. The length of a rectangle is 5 cm greater than its width. The perimeter is 58 cm. Find the dimensions of the rectangle.

Name _______________ Class _______________ Date _______________

1-3 • Guided Problem Solving

GPS Exercise 52

Investments Suppose you have \$5000 to invest. A certificate of deposit (CD) earns 6% annual interest, while bonds, which are more risky, earn 8% annual interest. You decide to invest \$2000 in a CD and the rest in bonds. How much interest will you have earned at the end of one year? Of two years?

Read and Understand

1. What is the total amount of your investment? _______________

2. How much are you investing in a CD? In bonds? _______________

3. How much interest will the CD earn? Bonds earn? _______________

Plan and Solve

Use the formula $A = P(1 + r)^t$ for finding the total amount (A) after investing a principal of P dollars at an interest rate of r (as a decimal) for t years, compounded annually.

4. What are P, r, and t for the investment in a CD for 1 year? _______________

5. Find A for the 1-year CD investment. _______________

6. What are P, r, and t for the investment in bonds for 1 year? _______________

7. Find A for the 1-year bond investment. _______________

8. Now find just the interest earned after one year for both investments combined. _______________

9. Use the method outlined above to find the interest earned at the end of two years. _______________

Look Back and Check

10. Compare your answers from Steps 8 and 9. Are the answers reasonable? Explain. _______________

Solve Another Problem

11. Suppose you borrow \$800. Your brother charges 3% annual interest, while your sister charges 4% annual interest. Your brother has \$600 to lend, and your sister can lend the rest. How much interest will you owe at the end of one year? Of two years? _______________

Name ______________________ Class ______________ Date ______________

Practice 1-4

Solving Inequalities

Solve each inequality. Graph the solutions.

1. $16 - 4t \leq 36$

2. $2(m + 3) + 1 > 23$

3. $7 + 13(x + 1) \leq 3x$

4. $-6a < 21$

5. $\frac{2}{3}(4x + 5) > \frac{9}{4}x$

6. $2[5x - (3x - 4)] < 3(2x + 3)$

7. $8(x - 5) \geq 56$

8. $6 - x \leq 7x + 3$

9. $10 - x \geq -2(3 + x)$

Solve each compound inequality. Graph the solutions.

10. $-9 \leq 4x + 3 \leq 11$

11. $16x \leq 32$ or $-5x < -40$

12. $9x < 54$ and $-4x < 12$

13. $6(x + 2) \geq 24$ or $5x + 10 \leq 15$

14. $14 > 3x - 1 \geq -10$

15. $4 < 1 - 3x < 7$

16. $2(x - 1) < -4$ or $2(x - 1) > 4$

17. $3x - 5 \geq -8$ and $3x - 5 \leq 1$

Solve each problem by writing an inequality.

18. A salesperson earns \$350 per week plus 10% of her weekly sales. Find the sales necessary for the salesperson to earn at least \$800 in one week.

19. The length of a rectangular yard is 50 ft, and its perimeter is less than 170 ft. Describe the width of the yard.

20. Xul is two years older than his sister Maria. The sum of their ages is greater than 32. Describe Maria's age.

21. A research team estimates that 30% of their questionnaires will not be returned. How many questionnaires should they mail out in order to be reasonably certain that at least 750 will be returned?

Solve each problem by writing a compound inequality.

22. Watermelons cost \$.39 per pound at a local market. Kent's watermelon cost between \$4.00 and \$5.00. What are the possible weights of his watermelon?

23. How much must a carpenter cut off a 48-inch board if the length must be 40 ± 0.25 inches?

24. A concrete slab requires between 10 and 12 yd^3 of concrete. If 2.5 yd^3 of concrete can be poured each hour, how long will it take to pour the slab?

Name ______________________ Class ______________ Date ______________

1-4 • Guided Problem Solving

GPS Exercise 38

Construction A contractor estimated that her expenses for a construction project would be between \$700,000 and \$750,000. She has already spent \$496,000. How much more can she spend and remain within her estimate?

Read and Understand

1. How much are the estimated expenses? ______________________

2. How much has she already spent? ______________________

Plan and Solve

3. Let x be the remaining amount she can spend. Write a compound inequality modeling the problem. ______________________

4. Solve the inequality. ______________________

5. How much more can she spend and remain within her estimate? ______________________

Look Back and Check

6. To check your answers, add the amount she has already spent to the amounts you calculated in Step 5. You should arrive back at the original estimates for the project. ______________________

Solve Another Problem

7. A landscaping company has estimated that a job would take between 45 and 52 hours to complete. If they have already spent 27 hours on the job, how much more time could the job take and remain within the estimate? ______________________

Name_______________________________ Class___________________ Date___________________

Practice 1-5

Absolute Value Equations and Inequalities

Write each specification as an absolute value inequality.

1. $6.3 \leq h \leq 10.3$
2. $-2.5 \leq a \leq 2.5$
3. $22 \leq x \leq 33$

Solve each inequality. Graph the solutions.

4. $|x + 5| > 12$
5. $|k - 3| \leq 19$
6. $|x + 2| \geq 0$
7. $2|t - 5| < 14$
8. $|3x - 2| + 7 \geq 11$
9. $5|2b + 1| - 3 \leq 7$
10. $|2 - 3w| \geq 4$
11. $-3|7m - 8| < 5$
12. $|2u| > 6$

Solve each equation. Check for extraneous solutions.

13. $|4x| = 28$
14. $|3x + 6| = -12$
15. $|z - 1| = 7z - 13$
16. $|s + 12| = 15$
17. $|-3x| = 63$
18. $2|5x + 3| = 16$
19. $|6x + 7| = 5x + 2$
20. $|7r - 4| = 24$
21. $|3c| + 2 = 11$
22. $5|x + 1| + 6 = 21$
23. $|3x + 5| - 2x = 3x + 4$
24. $-|d + 2| = 7$

Write an absolute value inequality and a compound inequality for each length x with the given tolerance.

25. a length of 4.2 cm with a tolerance of 0.01 cm
26. a length of 3.5 m with a tolerance of 0.2 cm
27. a length of 10 ft with a tolerance of 1 in.
28. Write an absolute value inequality and a compound inequality for the temperature T that was recorded to be as low as 65°F and as high as 87°F on a certain day.
29. The weight of a 40-lb bag of fertilizer varies as much as 4 oz from the stated weight. Write an absolute value inequality and a compound inequality for the weight w of a bag of fertilizer.
30. The duration of a telephone call to a software company's help desk is at least 2.5 minutes and at most 25 minutes. Write an absolute value inequality and a compound inequality for the duration d of a telephone call.

Name ______________________ Class ______________ Date ______________

1-5 • Guided Problem Solving

GPS Exercise 34

Solve the equation.

$-|4 - 8b| = 12$

Read and Understand

1. What does it mean to solve an equation? ______________________

2. The absolute value of a number is its ______________ from zero on the number line.

Plan and Solve

3. To solve a multi-step absolute value equation, first isolate the absolute value expression on one side of the equation. ______________

4. Can $|4 - 8b|$ be negative? ______________

5. What is the solution? ______________

Look Back and Check

6. To check your answer, substitute several different values for b in the original equation and notice the pattern of your results. ______________

Solve Another Problem

7. Solve the equation $-|5a + 9| = 24$.

____

Name ______________________ Class ______________ Date ______________

Practice 1-6

Probability

1. You select a number at random from the sample space {1, 2, 3, 4, 5}. Find each theoretical probability.
   a. P(the number is 2)
   b. P(the number is even)
   c. P(the number is prime)
   d. P(the number is less than 5)

2. In a class of 19 students, 10 study Spanish, 7 study French, and 2 study both French and Spanish. One student is picked at random. Find each probability.
   a. P(studying Spanish but not French)
   b. P(studying neither Spanish nor French)
   c. P(studying both Spanish and French)
   d. P(studying French)

3. In a telephone survey of 150 households, 75 respondents answered "Yes" to a particular question, 50 answered "No," and 25 were "Not sure." Find each experimental probability.
   a. P(answer was "Yes")
   b. P(answer was "No")
   c. P(answer was "Not sure")
   d. P(answer was not "Not sure")

4. A wallet contains four bills with denominations of \$1, \$5, \$10, and \$20. You choose two of the four bills from the wallet at random and add the dollar amounts.
   a. What is the sample space? How many outcomes are there?
   b. What is the probability of getting \$15?
   c. What is the probability of getting \$50?
   d. What is the probability of getting at least \$25?

5. A basketball player has attempted 24 shots and made 13. Find the experimental probability that the player will make the next shot that she attempts.

6. A baseball player attempted to steal a base 70 times and was successful 47 times. Find the experimental probability that the player will be successful on his next attempt to steal a base.

For Exercises 7–8, define a simulation by telling how you represent correct answers, incorrect answers, and the quiz. Use your simulation to find each experimental probability.

7. If you guess the answers at random, what is the probability of getting at least three correct answers on a four-question true-false quiz?

8. A five-question multiple-choice quiz has four choices for each answer. If you guess the answers at random, what is the probability of getting at least four correct answers?

9. A circular pool of radius 12 ft is enclosed within a rectangular yard measuring 50 ft by 100 ft. If a ball from an adjacent golf course lands at a random point within the yard, what is the probability that the ball lands in the pool?

10. Five people each flip a coin. What is the theoretical probability that all five will get heads?

Name ______________________ Class ______________ Date ______________

1-6 • Guided Problem Solving

GPS Exercise 38

Suppose you roll two number cubes.

a. What is the sample space?

b. How many outcomes are there?

c. What is the theoretical probability of getting a sum of 12?

d. What is the theoretical probability of getting a sum of 7?

Read and Understand

1. What are the possible outcomes for one of the cubes? ______________

2. What is one possible outcome when you roll two number cubes? ______________

Plan and Solve

3. What is the sample space, or the set of all possible outcomes? ______________

____

4. Count the number of outcomes you listed to find the number of outcomes possible. ______________

5. How many outcomes result in a sum of 12? ______________

6. What is the theoretical probability of getting a sum of 12? ______________

7. How many outcomes result in a sum of 7? ______________

8. What is the theoretical probability of getting a sum of 7? ______________

Look Back and Check

9. Conduct your own experiment by rolling two number cubes. Find the experimental probability of getting a sum of 12 after rolling the cubes 20 times. Your answer should be close to the theoretical probability. ______________

Solve Another Problem

10. Suppose you toss three coins and note whether each lands heads (H) or tails (T).

a. What is the sample space? ______________

b. How many outcomes are there? ______________

c. What is the theoretical probability of getting three heads? ______________

d. What is the theoretical probability of getting one tail and two heads? ______________

Name ______________________ Class ______________ Date ______________

1A: Graphic Organizer

For use after Lesson 1-1

Study Skill Keep notes as you work through each chapter to help you organize your thinking and to make it easier to review the material when you complete the chapter.

Write your answers.

1. What is the chapter title? ______________________________

2. Find the Table of Contents page for this chapter at the front of the book. Name four topics you will study in this chapter.

______________________________ ______________________________

______________________________ ______________________________

3. Complete the graphic organizer as you work through the chapter.

1. Write the title of the chapter in the center oval.
2. When you begin a lesson, write the name of the lesson in a rectangle.
3. When you complete that lesson, write a skill or key concept from that lesson in the outer oval linked to that rectangle.

Continue with steps 2 and 3 clockwise around the graphic organizer.

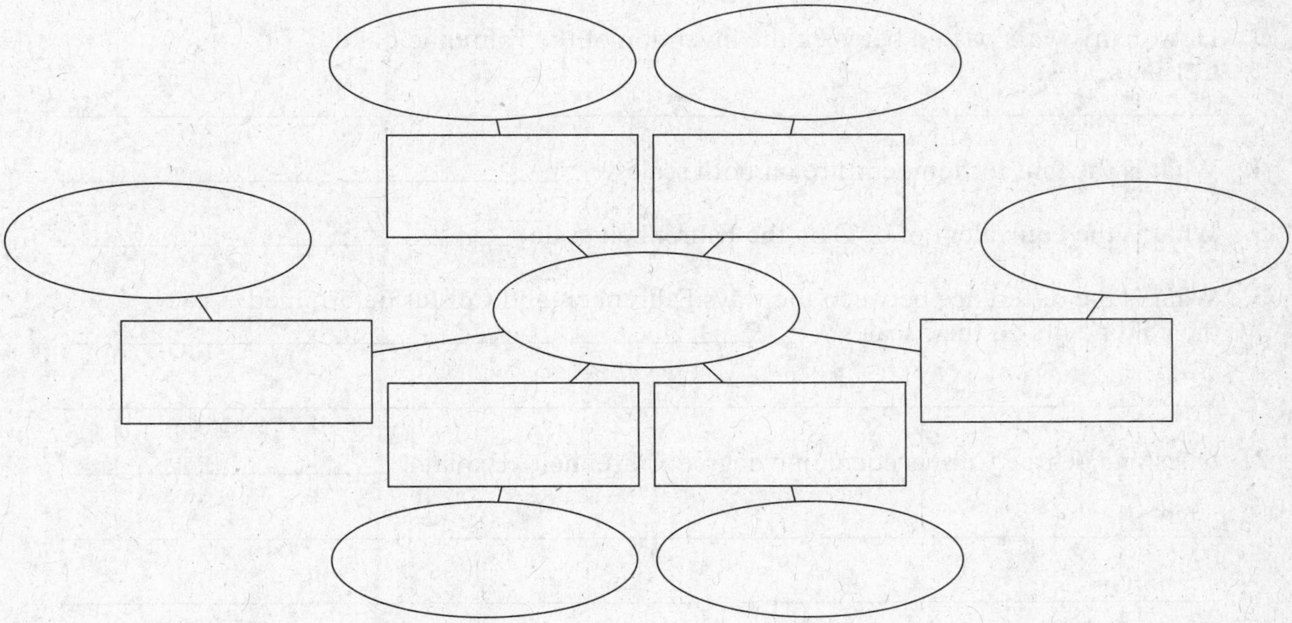

Name ______________________ Class ______________ Date ______________

1B: Reading Comprehension

For use after Lesson 1-3

Study Skill When you read a paragraph, it is a good idea to read it twice, once to get an overview and the second time to find the essential information. If you can mark the page, circle the words that name the topic of the paragraph. Often you may bring knowledge you already have to the subject of the paragraph as you read.

Read the passage below and answer the questions about what you read.

The first temperature scale was devised in 1724 by a German physicist, Gabriel Daniel Fahrenheit. He used as a fixed cold point (which he called 0°, or zero degrees) a mixture of ice and salt, and as a fixed hot point (which he called 96°) normal body temperature. He divided the distance between these two points into 96 equal degrees. (Later it was determined that normal body temperature is actually 98.6° on Fahrenheit's scale.) In 1742 a Swedish astronomer, Anders Celsius, invented an easier temperature scale. He used as a cold point (0°) the freezing point of pure water, and as a hot point (100°) the boiling temperature of water, with 100 evenly spaced degrees between.

1. What is the subject of this paragraph? ______________________

2. What unit of measure is represented by all of the numbers except 1724 and 1742? ______________________

3. How many years passed between the invention of the Fahrenheit and Celsius scales?

____

4. What is the unit for temperature on both scales? ______________________

5. What is the equivalent of 0° C on the Fahrenheit scale? ______________________

6. What is the difference between the ways Fahrenheit and Celsius determined the cold points on their scales? ______________________

____

7. Does one degree Celsius equal one degree Fahrenheit? Explain. ______________________

____

____

8. **High-Use Academic Words** In part 5, what does *equivalent* mean?

a. opposite **b.** equal value

Name ________________ Class ________________ Date ________________

1C: Reading/Writing Math Symbols

For use after Lesson 1-5

Study Skill When you take notes in any subject, you may be able to write more rapidly if you learn to use abbreviations and symbols, such as @ (at); # (number, numbers); w/ (with); w/o (without); s/b (should be).

Vocabulary and Study Skills

Explain the meaning of each mathematical expression using words.

1. $5 \cdot 9$ ________________
2. 1, 2, 3,… ________________
3. $12 \div 0.4$ ________________
4. $\sqrt{7}$ ________________

Write each phrase or statement using math symbols.

5. the absolute value of -3 ________________
6. x divided by 8 ________________
7. w is 29. ________________
8. x raised to the fifth power ________________
9. the square root of 5 ________________
10. 2, 4, 6, and the pattern continues the same way ________________

Name ______________________ Class ______________ Date ______________

1D: Visual Vocabulary Practice

For use after Lesson 1-6

Study Skill The Glossary contains the key vocabulary for this course.

Concept List

absolute value	algebraic expression	coefficient
compound inequality	experimental probability	multiplicative inverse
opposite	term	variable

Write the concept that best describes each exercise. Choose from the concept list above.

1. x ______________	**2.** $7y$ in the expression $7y - 3z$ ______________	**3.** -2 in the expression $-2a + 15$ ______________
4. a and $-a$ ______________	**5.** $\lvert -4x + 12 \rvert$ ______________	**6.** $x \leq -2$ or $x < 3$ ______________
7. a and $\frac{1}{a}$ (for $a \neq 0$) ______________	**8.** $r + 7s$ ______________	**9.** $P(\text{event}) = \frac{\text{number of times the event occurs}}{\text{number of trials}}$ ______________

Name ______________________ Class ______________ Date ______________

1E: Vocabulary Check

For use after Lesson 1-4

Study Skill Strengthen your vocabulary. Use these pages and add cues and summaries by applying the Cornell Notetaking style.

Write the definition for each word at the right. To check your work, fold the paper back along the dotted line to see the correct answers.

______________________ ______________________ ______________________	Opposite
______________________ ______________________ ______________________	Reciprocal
______________________ ______________________ ______________________	Absolute value of a real number
______________________ ______________________ ______________________	Variable expression
______________________ ______________________ ______________________	Solution of an equation

1E: Vocabulary Check (continued)

For use after Lesson 1-4

Write the vocabulary word for each definition. To check your work, fold the paper forward along the dotted line to see the correct answers.

The additive inverse of any number, a, is $-a$. ______________________

The multiplicative inverse of any nonzero number, a, is $\frac{1}{a}$. ______________________

The distance from a real number to zero on the number line. ______________________

An expression that contains one or more variables. ______________________

A number that makes the equation true. ______________________

Name ______________________ Class ______________ Date ______________

1F: Vocabulary Review

For use with Chapter Review

Study Skill Many words in English have more than one meaning. Often a word has one meaning in ordinary conversation and a different meaning when used in math or science. You can often figure out which meaning to use by looking at the sentence that contains the word. To help you decide what a word means, consider the surroundings, or context, in which you see the word.

Fill in the blanks with the following words.

additive inverse

algebraic expression — solution

multiplicative inverse — theoretical probability

1. The ______________ of 3 is $\frac{1}{3}$.
2. The ______________ to the equation $7x = 28$ is $x = 4$.
3. $3 + 7(p + 8)$ is an ______________.
4. The ______________ of –128 is 128.
5. The ______________ of getting heads on a coin toss is 50%.

Create three of your own fill-in-the-blank examples, like the ones above, using the following words.

6. absolute value ______________
7. opposite ______________
8. reciprocal ______________

Name ____________________ Class ____________ Date ____________

Practice 2-1

Relations and Functions

For each function, find $f(-2)$, $f\left(-\frac{1}{2}\right)$, $f(3)$, and $f(7)$.

1. $f(x) = 5x + 2$

2. $f(x) = -\frac{1}{3}x + 1$

3. $f(x) = -3x + 1.8$

Use the vertical line test to determine whether each graph represents a function.

4.

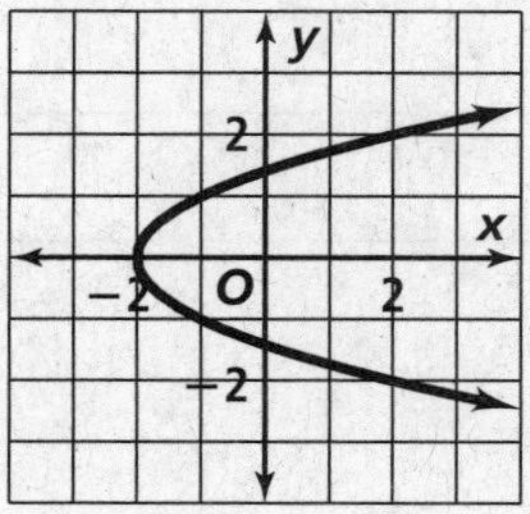

5.

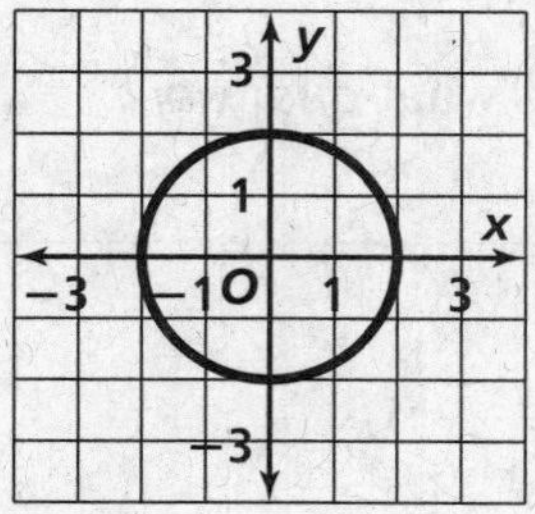

6.

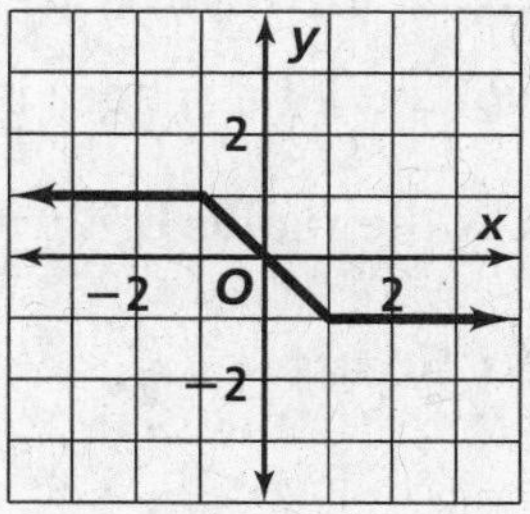

Graph each relation. Find the domain and range.

7. $\left\{(1, -2), \left(2, \frac{3}{4}\right), \left(3, 3\frac{1}{2}\right), (5, 9)\right\}$

8. $\{(-3, 5), (0, -2), (0, 4), (1, -2)\}$

9. $\{(-1, 2), (2, 2), (3, 2)\}$

10. $\{(0.5, -1), (0.5, 0). (0.5, 1), (0.5, 3)\}$

Determine whether each graph represents *y* as a function of *x*.

11.

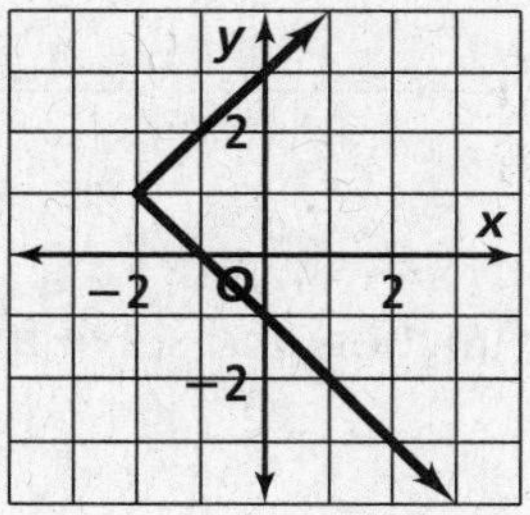

12.

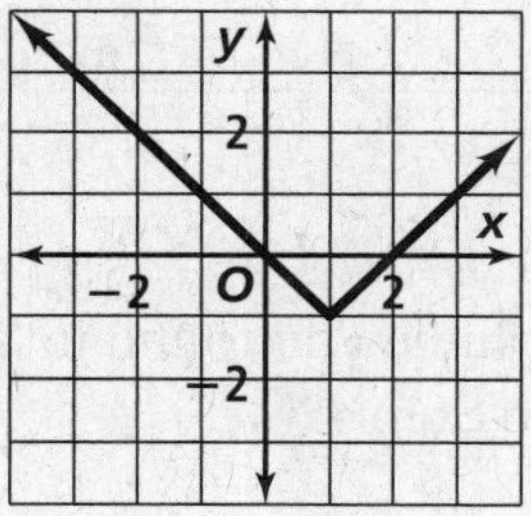

13.

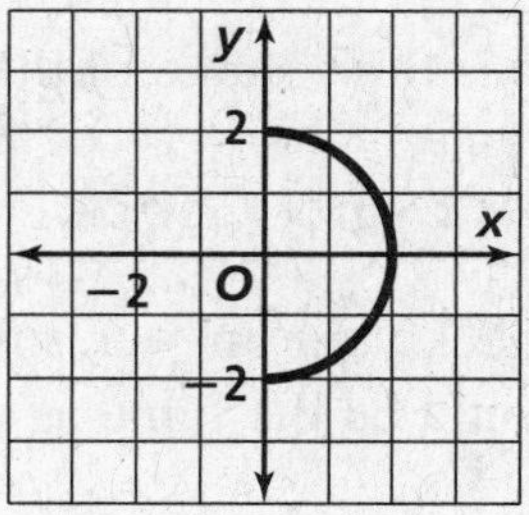

Make a mapping diagram for each relation, and determine whether it is a function.

14. $\{(1, 2), (2, 3), (2, 4), (3, 5)\}$

15. $\{(-1, 1), (0, 0), (1, 1), (2, 4), (3, 9)\}$

Suppose $f(x) = -3x + 2$ and $g(x) = \frac{1}{2}x - 1$. Find each value.

16. $f\left(\frac{1}{3}\right)$

17. $3g(4)$

18. $\dfrac{g(-2)}{f(3)}$

19. $\dfrac{f(-1)}{g(5)}$

Name ______________________ Class ______________ Date ______________

2-1 • Guided Problem Solving

GPS Exercise 47

Sports The volume of a sphere is a function of the radius of the sphere. Write a function for the volume of a ball. Evaluate the function for a volleyball of radius 10.5 cm.

Read and Understand

1. The volume of a sphere is a function of what quantity? ______________

2. What is the radius of the volleyball? ______________

Plan and Solve

3. The volume of a sphere is $\frac{4}{3}\pi$ times the cube of the radius. Let r represent the radius. Write a function for the volume of a ball. ______________

4. To find the volume of the volleyball, what value should you substitute for r? ______________

5. To evaluate the function, the radius is cubed. What will be the units for the volume of the volleyball? ______________

6. What is the volume of the volleyball? ______________

Look Back and Check

7. To check your answer, substitute the volume you found in Step 6 in the function and solve for r. It should be the same as your answer to Step 4.

____

Solve Another Problem

8. The volume of a cube is a function of the length of an edge of the cube. Write a function for the volume of a cube. Evaluate the function for a jewelry box with an edge length of 11.5 cm.

____

Name ____________________ Class ____________ Date ____________

Practice 2-2

Linear Equations

Find the slope of each line.

1. $2x - 5y = 0$

2. $5x - y = -7$

3. $x - \frac{2}{3}y = \frac{1}{4}$

4.

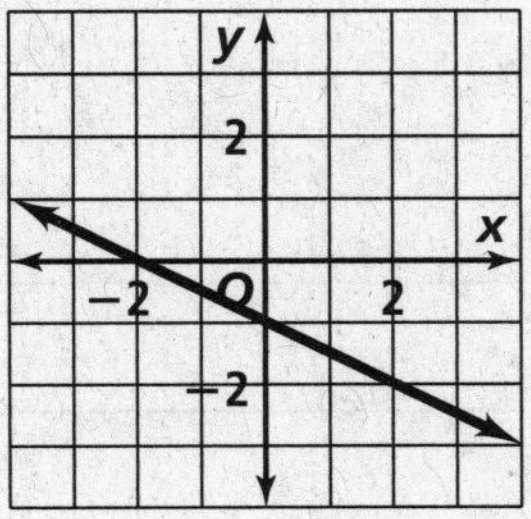

5.

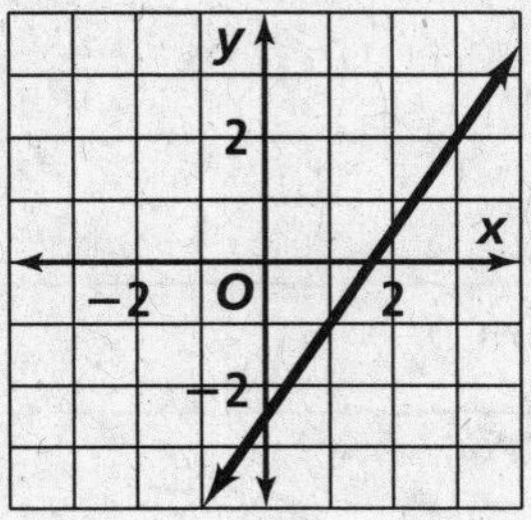

6.

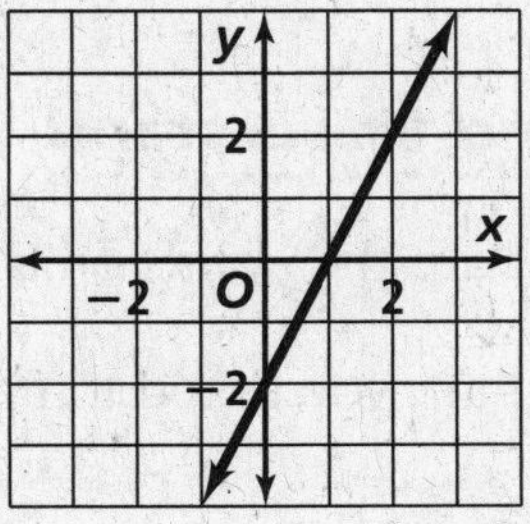

7. through $(4, -1)$ and $(-2, -3)$

8. through $(3, -5)$ and $(1, 2)$

Write in point-slope form the equation of the line through each pair of points.

9. $(0, 1)$ and $(3, 0)$

10. $\left(\frac{1}{2}, \frac{2}{3}\right)$ and $\left(-\frac{3}{2}, \frac{5}{3}\right)$

11. $(-3, -2)$ and $(1, 6)$

Graph each equation.

12. $4x + 3y = 12$

13. $\frac{x}{3} - \frac{y}{6} = 1$

14. $y = -\frac{3}{2}x + \frac{1}{2}$

Write in standard form an equation of the line with the given slope through the given point.

15. slope $= -4$; $(2, 2)$

16. slope $= \frac{2}{5}$; $(-1, 3)$

17. slope $= 0$; $(3, -4)$

Find the slope and the intercepts of each line.

18. $3x - 4y = 12$

19. $y = -2$

20. $f(x) = \frac{4}{5}x + 7$

21. $x = 5$

Write an equation for each line. Then graph the line.

22. through $(-1, 3)$ and parallel to $y = 2x + 1$

23. through $(2, 2)$ and perpendicular to $y = -\frac{3}{5}x + 2$

24. through $(-3, 4)$ and vertical

25. through $(4, 1)$ and horizontal

Name ______________________ Class ______________ Date ______________

2-2 • Guided Problem Solving

GPS Exercise 63

Find the slope of the line through the points $\left(\frac{3}{2}, -\frac{1}{2}\right)$ and $\left(-\frac{2}{3}, \frac{1}{3}\right)$.

Read and Understand

1. What are the points on the line? ______________________

2. What are you asked to find? ______________________

Plan and Solve

3. Write the formula for the slope, where slope $= \dfrac{\text{vertical change (rise)}}{\text{horizontal change (run)}}$.

____

4. Let $(x_1, y_1) = \left(\frac{3}{2}, -\frac{1}{2}\right)$. Then what is (x_2, y_2)? ______________________

5. Substitute the values into the slope formula. ______________________

6. Simplify the equation. What is the slope of the line through the points? ______________________

Look Back and Check

7. To check your answer, let $(x_1, y_1) = \left(-\frac{2}{3}, \frac{1}{3}\right)$ and $(x_2, y_2) = \left(\frac{3}{2}, -\frac{1}{2}\right)$ and find the slope. The slope should be the same as you found above.

____

Solve Another Problem

8. Find the slope of the line through the points $\left(-2, -\frac{1}{2}\right)$ and $\left(-\frac{1}{2}, 4\right)$.

____

Name ____________________ Class ____________ Date ____________

Practice 2-3

Direct Variation

For each direct variation, find the constant of variation. Then find the value of y when $x = 3$.

1. $y = 3$ when $x = -2$

2. $y = \frac{3}{4}$ when $x = \frac{1}{8}$

3. $y = -\frac{3}{8}$ when $x = -\frac{2}{3}$

Determine whether y varies directly as x. If so, find the constant of variation.

4. $y = \frac{4}{9}x$

5. $y = -1.2x$

6. $y + 4x = 0$

7. $y - 3x = 1$

8. $y = 3x$

9. $y + 2 = x$

10. $y - \frac{3}{5}x = 0$

11. $y = -3.5x + 7$

For each function, determine whether y varies directly as x. If so, find the constant of variation and write the equation.

12.

x	y
1	1
2	4
3	9

13.

x	y
−1	−3
1	3
3	9

14.

x	y
−2	−1
2	1
5	$\frac{5}{2}$

15.

x	y
−2	−3
0	1
1	3

Write an equation for a direct variation with a graph that passes through each point.

16. $(6, 2)$

17. $(-1.5, 9)$

18. $(-5, 90)$

19. $(7, 3)$

20. $\left(-1, -\frac{2}{3}\right)$

21. $\left(\frac{3}{5}, -\frac{7}{2}\right)$

22. $(10, 25)$

23. $(3, 165)$

In Exercises 24–27, y varies directly as x.

24. If $y = 3$ when $x = 2$, find x when $y = 5$.

25. If $y = -4$ when $x = \frac{1}{2}$, find y when $x = \frac{2}{3}$.

26. If $y = -14$ when $x = -7$, find x when $y = 22$.

27. If $y = \frac{5}{17}$ when $x = 10$, find y when $x = 5$.

28. A 15-minute long-distance telephone call costs $.90. The cost varies directly as the length of the call. Write an equation that relates the cost to the length of the call. How long is a call that costs $1.32?

29. The distance a spring stretches varies directly as the amount of weight that is hanging on it. A weight of 2.5 pounds stretches a spring 18 inches. Find the stretch of the spring when a weight of 6.4 pounds is hanging on it.

Name ____________ Class ____________ Date ____________

2-3 • Guided Problem Solving

GPS Exercise 52

Gas Mileage Suppose you drive a car 392 mi on one tank of gas. The tank holds 14 gallons. The number of miles traveled varies directly with the number of gallons of gas you use.

a. Write an equation that relates miles traveled to gallons of gas used.

b. You only have enough money to buy 3.7 gallons of gas. How far can you drive before refueling?

c. Last year you drove 11,700 mi. About how many gallons of gas did you use?

Read and Understand

1. How many miles can you travel on one tank of gas? ____________

2. How many gallons does your tank hold? ____________

Plan and Solve

3. To write an equation that relates miles traveled y to gallons of gas used x, substitute the given values into the equation $y = kx$ and solve for k, the constant of variation. ____________

4. Write the equation that relates miles traveled to gallons of gas used. ____________

5. Let $x = 3.7$ gallons and solve for y to find how far you can drive before refueling. ____________

6. Let $y = 11{,}700$ miles and solve for x to find how many gallons you used. ____________

7. Given you can travel 28 mi on 1 gallon of gas and the price of gas is $1.57 per gallon, find the cost per mile. ____________

Look Back and Check

8. To check, substitute your answers for parts (a)–(c) into the direct variation equation $y = kx$ and verify that you obtain the given values in the problem.

____

Solve Another Problem

9. Suppose you drive a motorcycle 406 mi on one tank of gas. The tank holds 7 gallons. The number of miles traveled varies directly with the number of gallons of gas you use.

a. Write an equation that relates miles traveled y to gallons of gas used x. ____________

b. Your tank has 2.5 gallons remaining. How far can you drive before refueling? ____________

c. Last summer on a trip, you drove 4350 mi. About how many gallons of gas did you use? ____________

Name ______________________ Class ______________ Date ______________

Practice 2-4

Using Linear Models

Write an equation for each line.

1. y-intercept of -2.1, x-intercept of 3.5
2. through (1.2, 5.1), x-intercept of 3.7

For each situation, find a linear model and use it to make a prediction.

3. The cost of producing 4 units is $204.80. The cost of producing 8 units is $209.60. How much does it cost to produce 12 units?
4. There were 174 words typed in 3 minutes. There were 348 words typed in 6 minutes. How many words will be typed in 8 minutes?
5. After 5 months the number of subscribers to a newspaper was 5730. After 7 months the number of subscribers to the newspaper was 6022. How many subscribers to the newspaper will there be after 10 months?

Graph each set of data. Decide whether a linear model is reasonable. If so, draw a trend line and write its equation.

6. $\{(1, 2.1), (3, 3.1), (5, 4.0), (7, 5.2), (9, 5.9)\}$
7. $\{(2, 3.5), (4, 4.9), (6, 6.3), (8, 4.6), (10, 2.9)\}$
8. $\{(-2, -3.9), (-1, -1.8), (0, 0.1), (1, 1.9), (2, 3.8)\}$
9. $\{(0.3, 0), (0.8, 3), (1.1, 5), (2.0, 6), (2.5, 6)\}$
10. The table shows the percentage of the population not covered by health insurance in selected states for the years 1990 and 1999.

State	Idaho	Illinois	Michigan	Montana	New York
1990	15.1	10.9	9.4	14.0	12.1
1999	19.1	14.1	11.2	18.6	16.4

Source: *The World Almanac and Book of Facts, 2001*

a. Draw a scatter plot showing the relationship between the percentage not covered by health insurance in 1990 and the percentage not covered in 1999. Use the 1990 percentage as the independent variable.

b. Use your scatter plot to develop a model relating the 1990 percentage to the 1999 percentage.

c. In Wyoming, 12.5% of the population were not covered by health insurance in 1990. Use your model to estimate the percentage who were not covered in 1999.

d. The actual percentage for Wyoming in 1999 was 16.1. Is your model reasonable?

Name ____________________ Class ____________ Date ____________

2-4 • Guided Problem Solving

GPS **Exercise 20**

Nutrition The table below shows the relationship between Calories and fat in various fast-food hamburgers.

Hamburger	A	B	C	D	E	F	G	H	I
Calories	720	530	510	500	305	410	440	320	598
Fat	46	30	27	26	13	20	25	13	26

Source: *The Fat Counter*

a. Develop a model for the relationship between Calories and fat.
b. How much fat would you expect a 330-Calorie hamburger to have?

Read and Understand

1. In what form will your answer to part (a) be? ____________

Plan and Solve

2. The data are plotted on the scatter plot. Is a linear model reasonable? ____________

3. Draw a trend line on the graph.

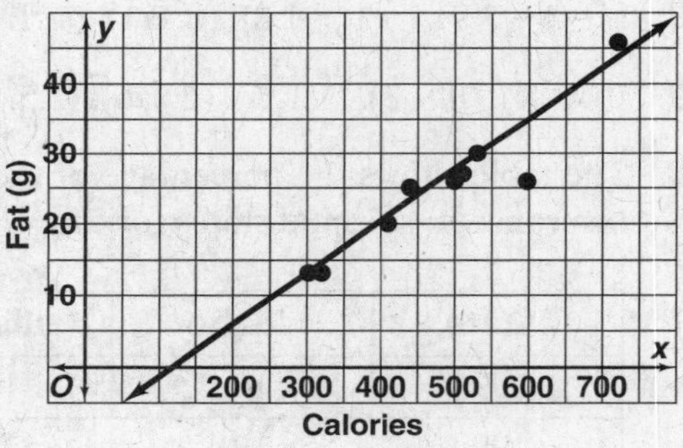

4. Use the points (305, 13) and (530, 30) and the slope formula $m = \frac{y_2 - y_1}{x_2 - x_1}$ to find the slope of the trend line.

____

5. Use the point (530, 30) and the point-slope form $y - y_1 = m(x - x_1)$ to write an equation that models the relationship. ____________

6. Let $x = 330$ in your model to find the expected grams of fat in a 330-Calorie hamburger. ____________

Look Back and Check

7. To check the reasonableness of your answer, graph your equation on the scatter plot above to see if it is a good fit.

Solve Another Problem

8. Use your equation from Step 5 to determine how many calories a hamburger with 36 g of fat might have. ____________

Name ____________________ Class ____________ Date ____________

Practice 2-5

Absolute Value Functions and Graphs

Match each equation with its graph.

1. $y = |x - 1|$
2. $y = 2|x - 1|$
3. $y = |2x| - 1$
4. $y = |x| - 1$
5. $y = |2x - 1|$
6. $y = |2x| - 2$

A.
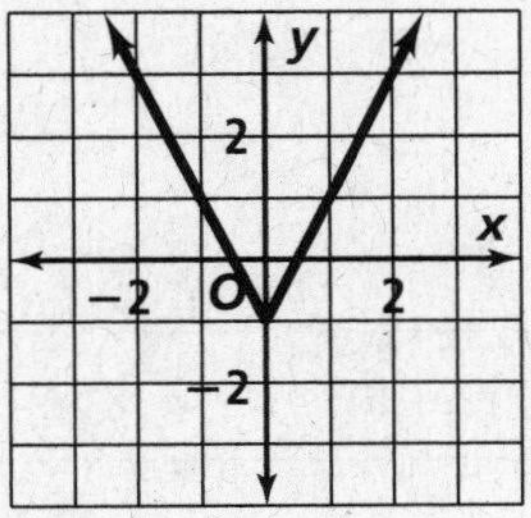

B.
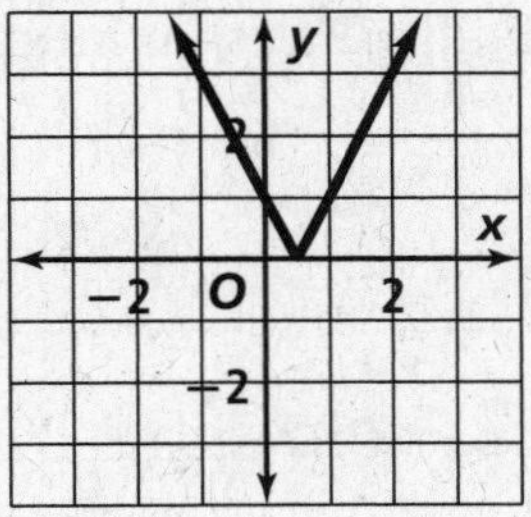

C.
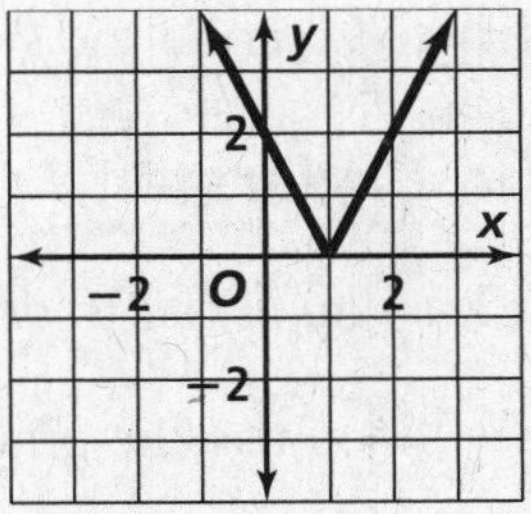

D.
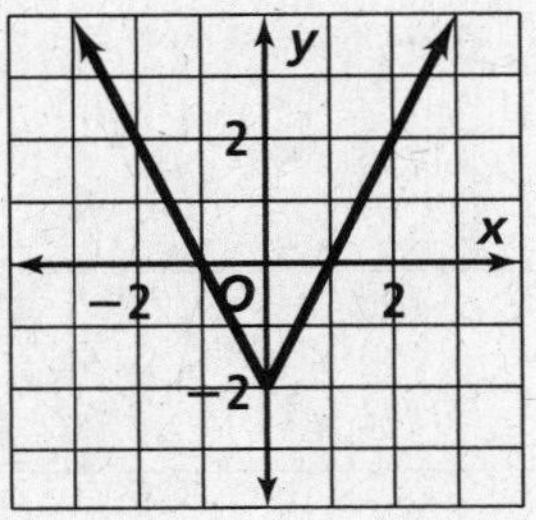

E.
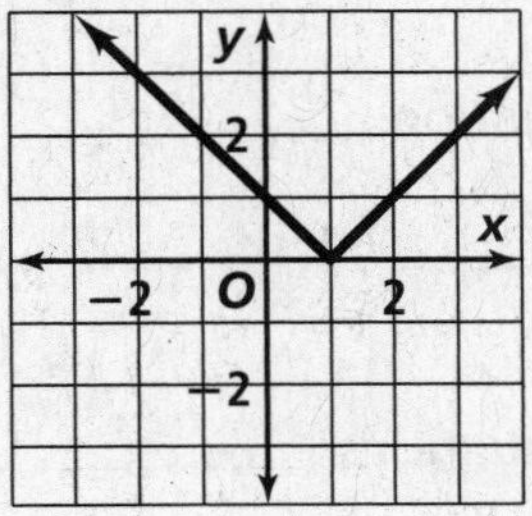

F.
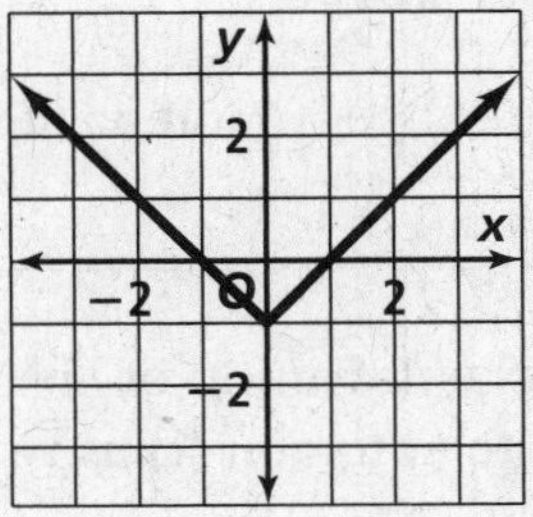

Graph each equation by writing two linear equations.

7. $y = |x - 3|$
8. $y = |2x - 5|$
9. $y = 2|x + 2|$
10. $y = |x + 3| - 1$
11. $y = -|3x + 4|$
12. $y = \left|\frac{1}{2}x - 2\right| + 1$

Graph each absolute value equation.

13. $y = |3 - x|$
14. $y = -\frac{2}{3}\left|\frac{1}{3}x\right|$
15. $y = 3 - |x + 1|$
16. $y = -|-x - 2|$
17. $3y = |2x - 9|$
18. $y = -|x| + 2$
19. $\frac{1}{2}y = |3x - 1| - 2$
20. $y + 3 = |x + 1|$
21. $-2y = |2x - 4|$

Name ______________________ Class ______________ Date ______________

2-5 • Guided Problem Solving

GPS Exercise 52

a. Graph the equations $y = \left|\frac{1}{2}x - 6\right| + 3$ and $y = -\left|\frac{1}{2}x + 6\right| - 3$ on the same set of axes.

b. Writing Describe the similarities and differences in the graphs.

Read and Understand

1. What are you asked to do for part (a)? ______________________

2. How will you use the graphs to answer part (b)? ______________________

Plan and Solve

3. Isolate the absolute value for each equation.

i. ______________________ **ii.** ______________________

4. Use the definition of absolute value to rewrite equation (i) as two separate equations. ______________________

5. Graph each equation for the appropriate domain.

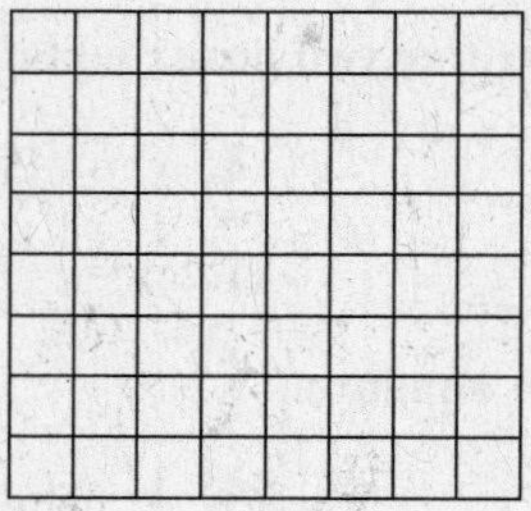

6. Repeat Steps 4–5 for equation (ii). ______________________

____

7. Describe the similarities and differences in the graphs. ______________________

Look Back and Check

8. Check the reasonableness of your answer by choosing a test point on each graph. Substitute into the original equation and verify that a true statement results.

____

Solve Another Problem

9. a. Graph the equations $y = |2x + 3| + 1$ and $y = -|2x - 3| - 1$.

b. Describe the similarities and differences in the graphs. ______________________

Name ______________________ Class ______________ Date ______________

Practice 2-6

Families of Functions

Describe each translation of $f(x) = |x|$ as vertical, horizontal, or combined. Then graph each translation.

1. $f(x) = |x + 2|$

2. $f(x) = |x + 4|$

3. $f(x) = |x| - 5$

4. $f(x) = |x + 1| - 1$

5. $f(x) = |x - 2| + 1$

6. $f(x) = \left|x - \frac{3}{2}\right|$

Write an equation for each translation.

7. $y = |x|$, 1 unit up, 2 units left

8. $y = |x|$, 4 units right

9. $y = -|x|$, 3 units up, 1 unit right

10. $y = -|x|$, $\frac{3}{2}$ units down, $\frac{1}{2}$ unit right

11. $y = |x|$, 2 units down, 3 units left

12. $y = -|x|$, $\frac{3}{5}$ unit up

Write the equation of each translation of $y = |x|$.

13.

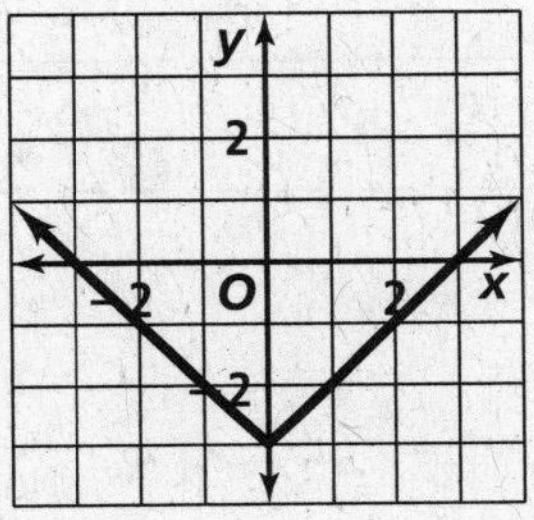

14.

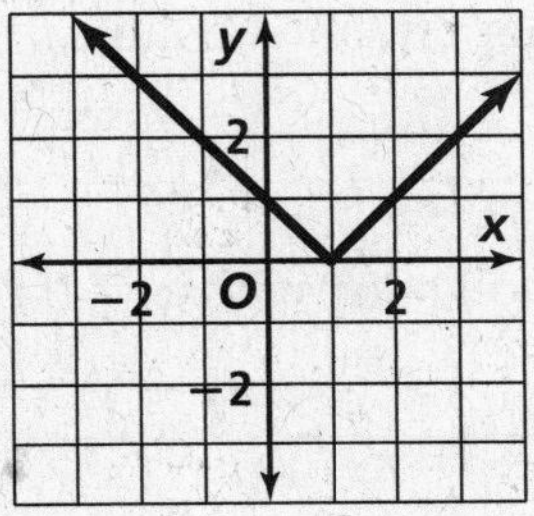

15.

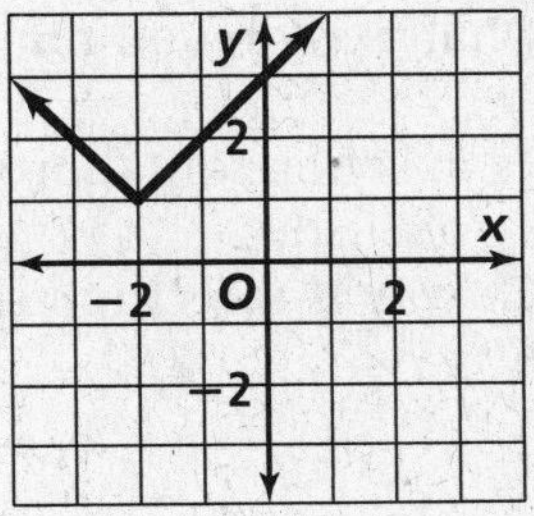

Write the equation of each translation of $y = -|x|$.

16.

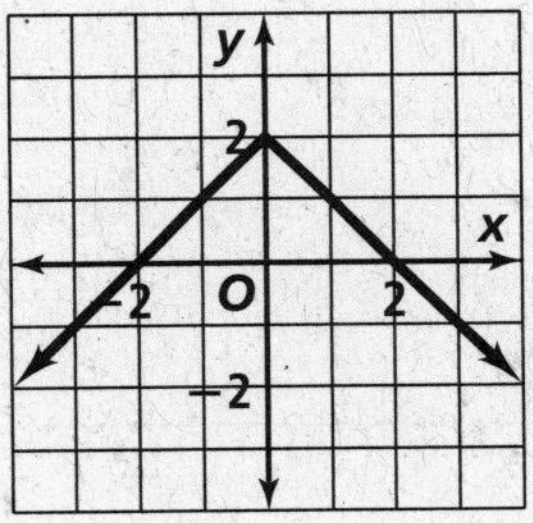

17.

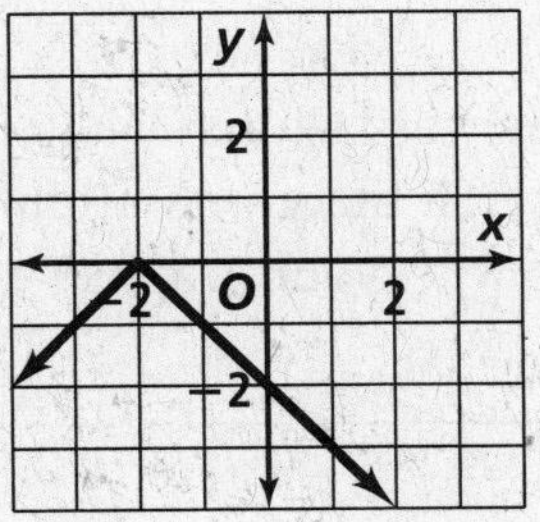

18.

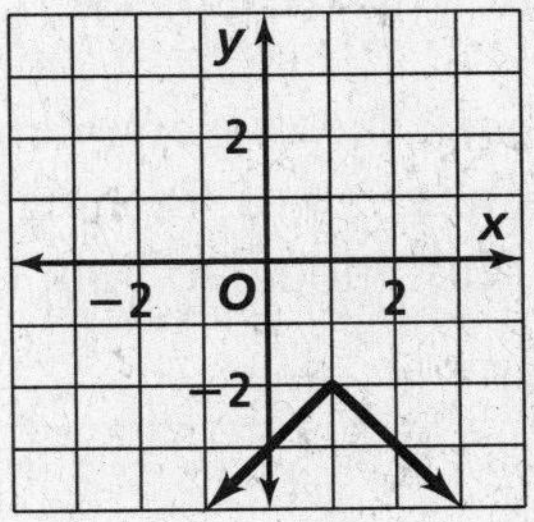

Write the equation for each graph.

19.

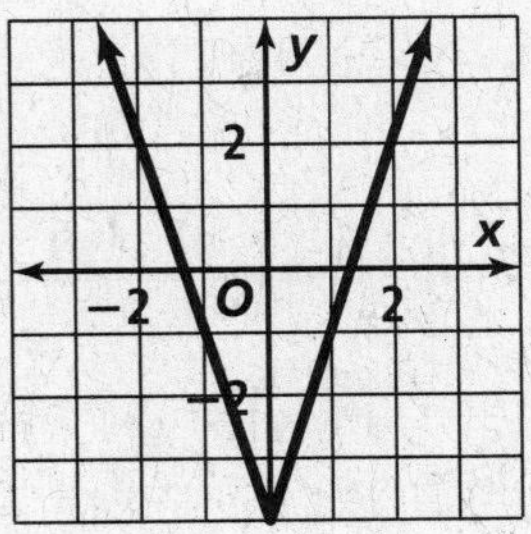

20.

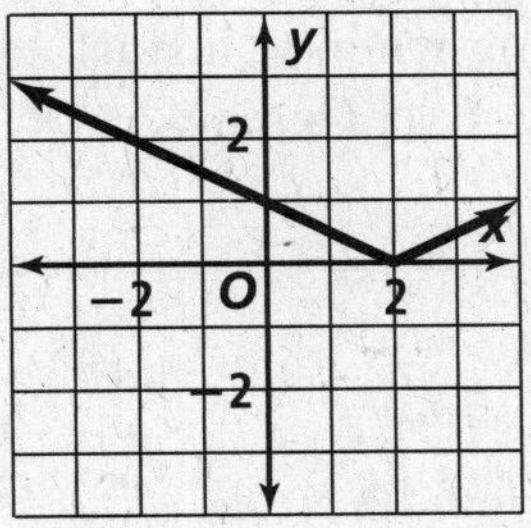

21.

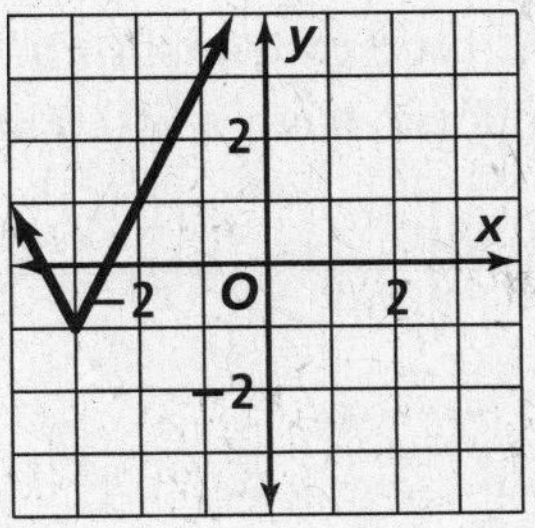

Graph each equation.

22. $y = 3|x|$

23. $y = 2|x| - 3$

24. $y = \frac{1}{2}|x - 1|$

Name ________________ Class ________ Date ________

2-6 • Guided Problem Solving

GPS **Exercise 38**

Data Analysis Suppose you plot data with years as the independent variable. What type of translation are you making when you start with $x = 0$ rather than a year such as 1998? Explain.

Read and Understand

1. Describe possible translations of a graph. ________________

2. What is the independent variable? ________________

Plan and Solve

3. On what axis do you represent the independent variable? ________________

4. Is this axis horizontal or vertical? ________________

5. Which way is the graph shifted when you start with $x = 0$ rather than $x = 1998$?

____

6. What type of translation are you making? ________________

Look Back and Check

7. To check the reasonableness of your answers, sketch what you think a graph of $f(x)$ might be. Then sketch the graph after the translation. Do your answers agree with your graphs?

____

Solve Another Problem

8. Suppose you plot data with income as the dependent variable. What type of translation are you making when you start with an income such as 10,000 rather than $y = 0$? Explain.

____

Name ____________________ Class ____________ Date ____________

Practice 2-7

Two-Variable Inequalities

Write an inequality for each graph. In each case, the equation for the boundary line is given.

1. $y = x - 2$

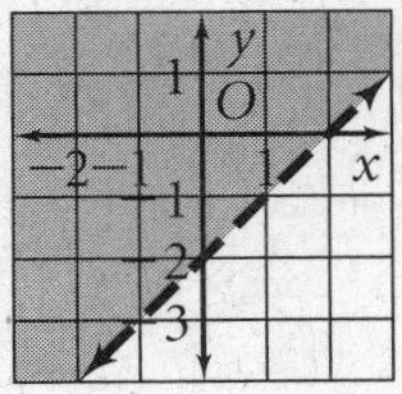

2. $x - 2y = 4$

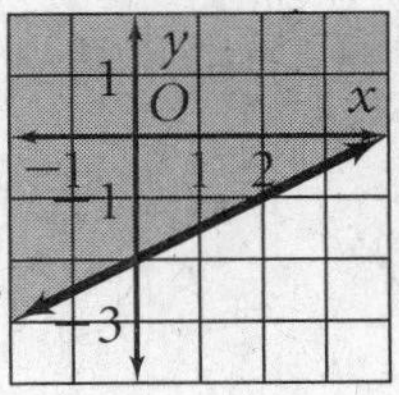

3. $y - 2x = 4$

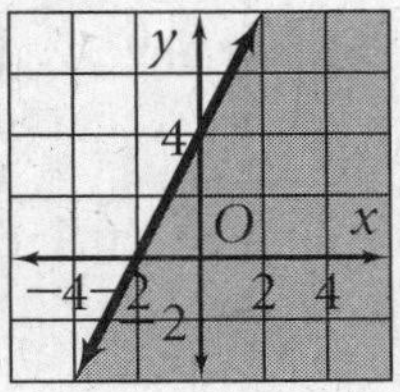

4. $y = -2$

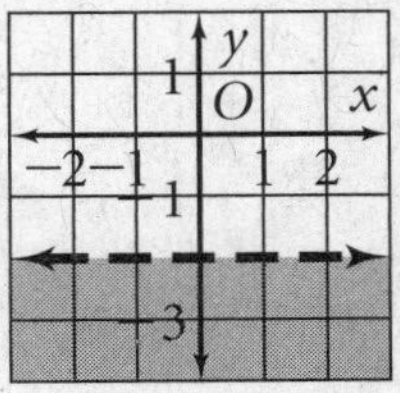

5. $x = 2$

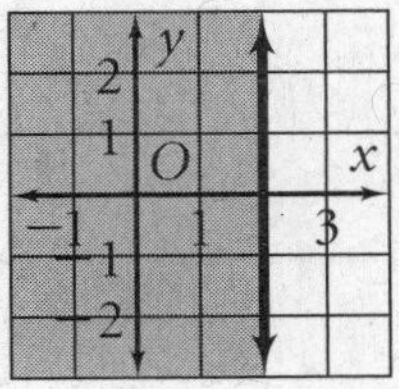

6. $-2x - 3y = 6$

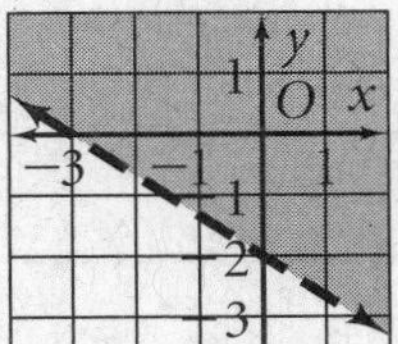

7. $3x - y = 3$

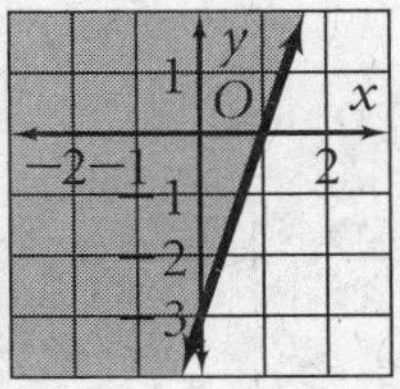

8. $y - 3x = 3$

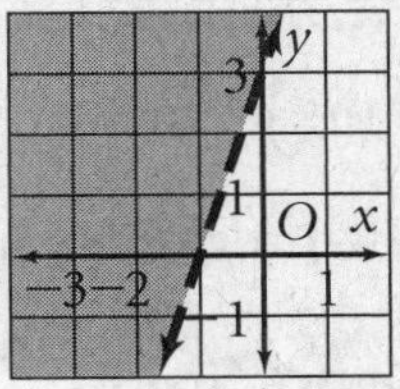

Graph each inequality on a coordinate plane.

9. $y < x$
10. $y \geq x$
11. $y > 2$
12. $y < 2$
13. $x \leq 2$
14. $x > 2$
15. $y \geq |x|$
16. $y > -2x + 1$
17. $y \geq 3x - 4$
18. $4x + 2y \leq 8$
19. $4x - 2y \leq 4$
20. $4y - 2x \geq 4$
21. $y > |x + 2|$
22. $y \leq |x - 2|$
23. $y > |x| + 2$
24. $y < |x| - 2$
25. $y \leq |4x| + 1$
26. $y \geq \left|\frac{1}{6}x\right| - 3$
27. $y > -\frac{1}{6}x - 1$
28. $3x \leq 5y$

29. You need to make at least 150 sandwiches for a picnic. You are making tuna sandwiches and ham sandwiches.
    a. Write an inequality for the number of sandwiches you can make.
    b. Graph the inequality.
    c. Does the point (90, 80) satisfy the inequality? Explain.

30. A salesperson sells two models of vacuum cleaners. One brand sells for \$150 each, and the other sells for \$200 each. The salesperson has a weekly sales goal of at least \$1800.
    a. Write an inequality relating the revenue from the vacuum cleaners to the sales goal.
    b. Graph the inequality.
    c. If the salesperson sold exactly six \$200 models last week, how many \$150 models did she have to sell to make her sales goal?

Name ______________________ Class ______________ Date ______________

2-7 • Guided Problem Solving

GPS Exercise 36

Write an inequality for the graph.

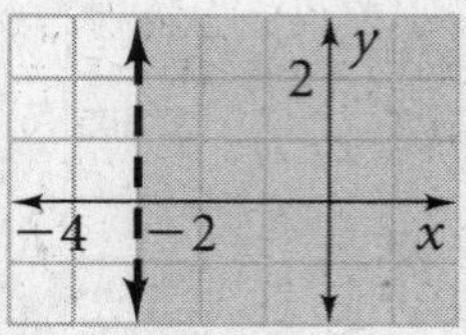

Read and Understand

1. Is the boundary line dashed or solid? ______________________

2. What region is shaded? ______________________

Plan and Solve

3. What is the equation for the boundary line? ______________________

4. Is the boundary line part of the solution? ______________________

5. What inequality symbol should be used? ______________________

6. Write the inequality for the graph. ______________________

Look Back and Check

7. Check if your answer is reasonable by choosing a test point not on the boundary line, such as (0, 0). Does the test point make the inequality true?

____

Solve Another Problem

8. Write an inequality for the graph.

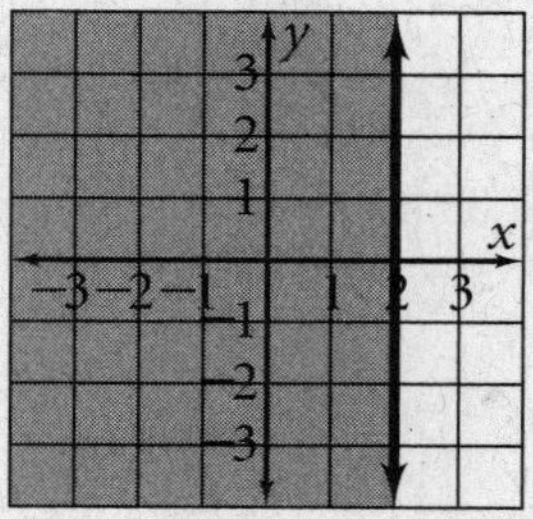

Name ______________________ Class ______________ Date ______________

2A: Graphic Organizer

For use before Lesson 2-1

Study Skill As you begin each new chapter, first survey the material. Next ask yourself questions such as this: *What is the main idea of this chapter?* and *How is the material divided?* Keep notes as you work through each chapter to help you organize your thinking and to make it easier to review the material when you complete the chapter.

Write your answers.

1. What is the chapter title? ______________________

2. Find the Table of Contents page for this chapter at the front of the book. Name four topics you will study in this chapter.

______________________ ______________________

______________________ ______________________

3. Complete the graphic organizer as you work through the chapter.
1. Write the title of the chapter in the center oval.
2. When you begin a lesson, write the name of the lesson in a rectangle.
3. When you complete that lesson, write a skill or key concept from that lesson in the outer oval linked to that rectangle.

Continue with steps 2 and 3 clockwise around the graphic organizer.

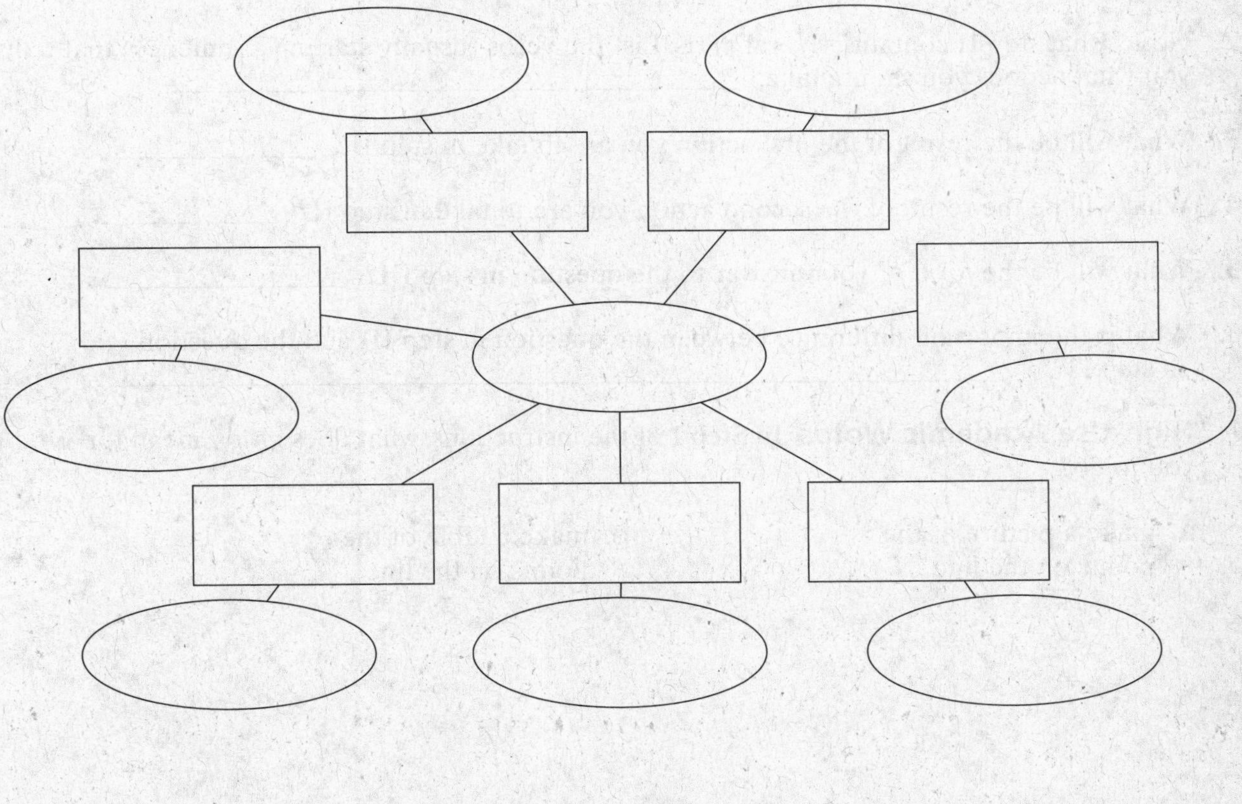

Name ______________________ Class ______________ Date ______________

2B: Reading Comprehension

For use after Lesson 2-7

Study Skill When you are taking notes, whether from your reading, a class discussion or a lecture, you can write more rapidly if you use abbreviations for those words and phrases that occur frequently. You may want to write a brief key for the abbreviations you use, so that you will be able to remember them later as you read over your notes.

Read the instructions in the box, and then answer the questions about the instructions. You do not have to follow the instructions.

I. Graph the line $y = 2x + 3$ on graph paper.

II. (a) Plot each point listed below.
$(3, 2), (1, 5), (1, 7), (-1, 1), (4, 6), (-3, 2)$

(b) Classify each of the points you plotted as *on the line*, *above the line*, or *below the line*.

III. Are all the points that satisfy the inequality $y > 2x + 3$ *above*, *below*, or *on* the line?

IV. Are all the points that satisfy the equation $y = 2x + 3$ *above*, *below*, or *on* the line?

V. Without drawing it, describe the graph of $y \geq 5x + 3$.

1. Read quickly through ALL the steps in the instructions. What supplies will you need to complete this task? ______________________

2. Notice that step II contains several parts. List the verbs (usually starting a sentence) that tell you what actions you should take. ______________________

3. What will be the result of the first action you are to take in step II? ______________

4. What will be the result of the second action you are to take in step II? ______________

5. What will be the *form* of your answer to the question in step III? ______________

6. What is the important difference between the question in step III and the question in step IV? ______________________

7. **High-Use Academic Words** In Step I of the instructions, what does *graph* mean for you to do?

   a. make a picture of the points on the line

   b. make a table of the points on the line

Name ______________________ Class ______________ Date ______________

2C: Reading/Writing Math Symbols

For use after Lesson 2-3

Study Skill When you use abbreviations while taking notes, make sure you can read those abbreviations and symbols later when you review the notes. For example, on the first page of your notebook, you might write a list of the abbreviations and symbols you usually use, and their meanings.

Some of the following mathematical expressions contain letters that are not variables. Write an explanation in words of the meaning for each mathematical expression or equation.

1. $P(3) = \frac{1}{6}$ ______________________

2. P(not taking Spanish) ______________________

3. $f(x)$ ______________________

4. $f(5)$ ______________________

5. $A(s) = s^2$ ______________________

Write each phrase or statement using math symbols.

6. The x-value for the second point is not equal to zero. ______________________

7. the ratio of z to 7 ______________________

8. the theoretical probability of choosing a red marble ______________________

9. 4 is to 10 as x is to 18. ______________________

10. The value of the function g when 7 is the value of the variable. ______________________

Name ____________________ Class ____________ Date ____________

2D: Visual Vocabulary Practice

For use after Lesson 2-6

Study Skill Mathematics builds on itself, so build a strong foundation.

Concept List

absolute value function	constant of variation	point-slope form
scatter plot	slope	slope-intercept form
standard form of a linear equation	translation	trend line

Write the concept that best describes each exercise. Choose from the concept list above.

1. $k = \frac{y}{x}$

____

2. $m = \frac{y_2 - y_1}{x_2 - x_1}$

____

3.

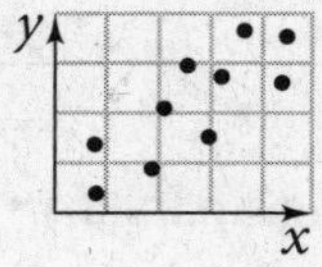

____

4.

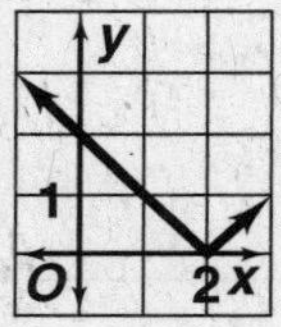

____

5. $Ax + By = C$

____

6. $f(x) = |x|$

____

7.

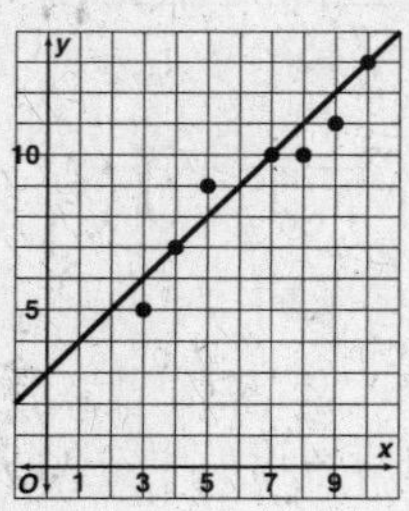

____

8. $y = mx + b$

____

9. $y - y_1 = m(x - x_1)$

____

Name ______________________ Class ______________ Date ______________

2E: Vocabulary Check

For use after Lesson 2-2

Study Skill Strengthen your vocabulary. Use these pages and add cues and summaries by applying the Cornell Notetaking style.

Write the definition for each word at the right. To check your work, fold the paper back along the dotted line to see the correct answers.

______________________	Relation
______________________	Domain
______________________	Range
______________________	Function
______________________	*x*-intercept

Name ______________________ Class ______________ Date ______________

2E: Vocabulary Check (continued)

For use after Lesson 2-2

Write the vocabulary word for each definition. To check your work, fold the paper forward along the dotted line to see the correct answers.

A set of pairs of input and output values. ______________________

The set of all inputs, or x-coordinates, of the ordered pairs of a relation. ______________________

The set of all outputs, or y-coordinates, of the ordered pairs of a relation. ______________________

A relation in which each element of the domain is paired with exactly one element of the range. ______________________

The point at which a line crosses the x-axis (or the x-coordinateof that point). ______________________

Name ______________________ Class ______________ Date ______________

2F: Vocabulary Review Puzzle

For use with Chapter Review

Study Skill Mathematics is a series of concepts you need to learn and remember. It is important to learn the definitions of new terms as soon as they are introduced. Read aloud or recite the new terms as you read them.

Use the words below to complete the crossword puzzle. For help, use the Glossary in your textbook.

translation	linear	range
relation	slope	
domain	function	

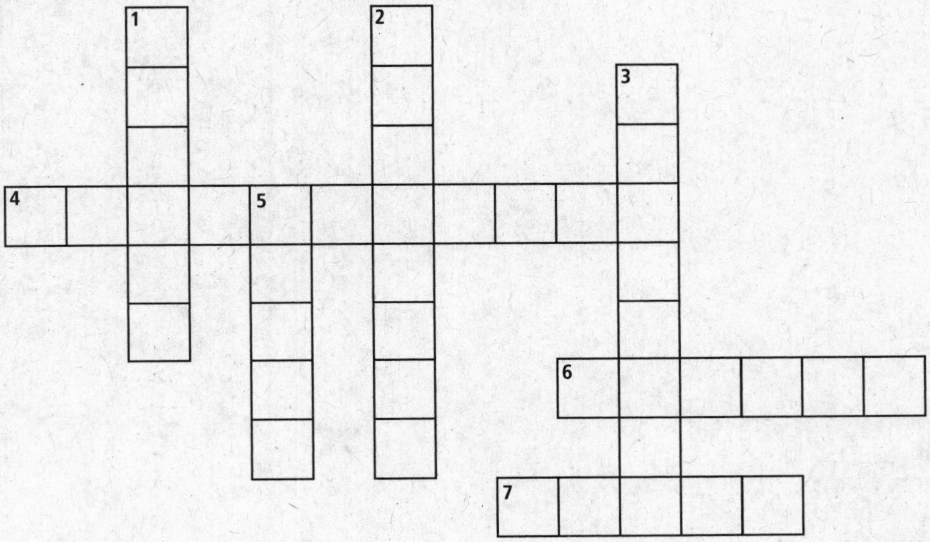

ACROSS

4. a transformation that slides a graph without changing the size or shape

6. graph of this type of equation is a line

7. set of all outputs for a relation

DOWN

1. set of all inputs for a relation

2. a set of ordered pairs

3. a relation in which each element of the domain is paired with exactly one element of the range

5. ratio of the vertical change to the horizontal change

Name ______________________ Class ______________ Date ______________

Practice 3-1

Graphing Systems of Equation

Classify each system without graphing.

1. $\begin{cases} x + y = 3 \\ y = 2x - 3 \end{cases}$

2. $\begin{cases} 2x + y = 3 \\ y = -2x - 1 \end{cases}$

3. $\begin{cases} x + 3y = 9 \\ -2x - 6y = -18 \end{cases}$

4. $\begin{cases} x + y = 4 \\ y = 2x + 1 \end{cases}$

5. $\begin{cases} x + 3y = 9 \\ 9y + 3x = 27 \end{cases}$

6. $\begin{cases} x + 2y = 5 \\ 2x + 3y = 9 \end{cases}$

7. $\begin{cases} 3x + 2y = 7 \\ 3x - 15 = -6y \end{cases}$

8. $\begin{cases} x + y = 6 \\ 3x + 3y = 3 \end{cases}$

9. $\begin{cases} x + y = 11 \\ y = x - 5 \end{cases}$

10. $\begin{cases} x + 2y = 13 \\ 2y = 7 - x \end{cases}$

11. $\begin{cases} y = 12 - 5x \\ x - 4y = -6 \end{cases}$

12. $\begin{cases} 25x - 10y = 0 \\ 2y = 5x \end{cases}$

13. The spreadsheet below shows the monthly income and expenses for a new business.
    a. Find a linear model for monthly income and a linear model for monthly expenses.
    b. Use the models to estimate the month in which income will equal expenses.

	A	B	C
	Month	**Income**	**Expenses**
1	May	$1500	$21,400
2	June	$3500	$18,800
3	July	$5500	$16,200
4	August	$7500	$13,600

Solve each system by graphing. Check your answers.

14. $\begin{cases} y = x - 2 \\ x + y = 10 \end{cases}$

15. $\begin{cases} y = 7 - x \\ x + 3y = 11 \end{cases}$

16. $\begin{cases} x - 2y = 10 \\ y = x - 11 \end{cases}$

17. $\begin{cases} 5x + y = 11 \\ x - y = 1 \end{cases}$

18. $\begin{cases} x + y = -1 \\ x - y = 3 \end{cases}$

19. $\begin{cases} x - y = -1 \\ 2x + 2y = 10 \end{cases}$

20. $\begin{cases} 4x + 3y = -16 \\ -x + y = 4 \end{cases}$

21. $\begin{cases} y = -3x \\ x + y = 2 \end{cases}$

22. $\begin{cases} y = \frac{2}{3}x - 5 \\ y = -\frac{2}{3}x - 3 \end{cases}$

23. $\begin{cases} y = \frac{1}{2}x + 3 \\ y = -\frac{1}{4}x - 3 \end{cases}$

24. $\begin{cases} 2x - 4y = -4 \\ 3x - y = 4 \end{cases}$

25. $\begin{cases} x + y = 6 \\ x - y = 4 \end{cases}$

Name ______________________ Class ______________ Date ______________

3-1 • Guided Problem Solving

GPS Exercise 45

Advertising You and your business partner are mailing advertising flyers to your customers. You address 6 flyers each minute and have already done 80. Your partner addresses 4 flyers each minute and has already done 100. Graph and solve a system of equations to find when the two of you will have addressed equal numbers of flyers.

Read and Understand

1. How many flyers can you do each minute, and how many have you already done?

____

2. How many flyers can your partner do each minute, and how many has he/she already done?

____

Plan and Solve

3. Let x be the number of minutes. What should y represent? ______________

4. Write an equation representing you. ______________

5. Write an equation representing your partner. ______________

6. Graph the system of equations.

7. At what point do the lines meet? ______________

8. After how many minutes will the numbers of flyers be equal? ______________

Look Back and Check

9. To check your answer, substitute the x- and y-values of the intersection point into each equation and verify that correct equations result.

____

Solve Another Problem

10. Miles can deliver 3 newspapers per minute and has already delivered 5 papers. Josh can deliver 2 newspapers per minute and has already delivered 20 papers. Graph and solve a system of equations to find when the two of them will have delivered the same numbers of newspapers.

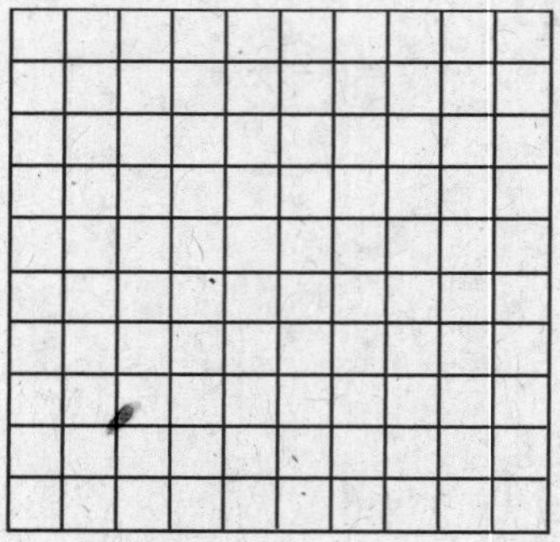

Name ______________________ Class ______________ Date ______________

Practice 3-2

Solving Systems Algebraically

Solve each system by elimination.

1. $\begin{cases} x + y = 10 \\ x - y = 2 \end{cases}$

2. $\begin{cases} -x + 3y = -1 \\ x - 2y = 2 \end{cases}$

3. $\begin{cases} x + y = 7 \\ x + 3y = 11 \end{cases}$

4. $\begin{cases} 4x - 3y = -2 \\ 4x + 5y = 14 \end{cases}$

5. $\begin{cases} x + 2y = 10 \\ 3x - y = 9 \end{cases}$

6. $\begin{cases} 2x - 5y = 11 \\ 4x + 10y = 18 \end{cases}$

7. $\begin{cases} x - y = 0 \\ x + y = 2 \end{cases}$

8. $\begin{cases} x + 3y = -4 \\ y + x = 0 \end{cases}$

9. $\begin{cases} 3x - y = 17 \\ y + 2x = 8 \end{cases}$

10. Suppose your drama club is planning a production that will cost \$525 for the set and \$150 per performance. A sold-out performance will bring in \$325. Write an equation for the cost C and an equation for the income I for p sold-out performances. Find how many sold-out performances will make the cost equal to the income.

Solve each system by substitution. Check your answers.

11. $\begin{cases} y = x + 1 \\ 2x + y = 7 \end{cases}$

12. $\begin{cases} x = y - 2 \\ 3x - y = 6 \end{cases}$

13. $\begin{cases} y = 2x + 3 \\ 5x - y = -3 \end{cases}$

14. $\begin{cases} 6x - 3y = -33 \\ 2x + y = -1 \end{cases}$

15. $\begin{cases} 2x - y = 7 \\ 3x - 2y = 10 \end{cases}$

16. $\begin{cases} 4x = 8y \\ 2x + 5y = 27 \end{cases}$

17. $\begin{cases} x + 3y = -4 \\ y + x = 0 \end{cases}$

18. $\begin{cases} 3x + 2y = 9 \\ x + y = 3 \end{cases}$

19. $\begin{cases} 2y - 3x = 4 \\ x = -4 \end{cases}$

20. Suppose you bought eight oranges and one grapefruit for a total of \$4.60. Later that day, you bought six oranges and three grapefruits for a total of \$4.80. Now you want to find the price of each orange and of each grapefruit. Write an equation for each purchase. Solve the system of equations.

Solve each system.

21. $\begin{cases} y = x + 3 \\ 5x + y = 9 \end{cases}$

22. $\begin{cases} 5x + 4y = 2 \\ -5x - 2y = 4 \end{cases}$

23. $\begin{cases} y = 2x + 3 \\ 5x - y = -3 \end{cases}$

24. $\begin{cases} 14x + 2y = 10 \\ x - 5y = 11 \end{cases}$

25. $\begin{cases} x + 5y = 1 \\ 2x = 2 - 10y \end{cases}$

26. $\begin{cases} 0.3x + 0.4y = 0.8 \\ 0.7x - 0.8y = -6.8 \end{cases}$

27. $\begin{cases} 4x + 3y = -6 \\ 5x - 6y = -27 \end{cases}$

28. $\begin{cases} 2y = -4x \\ 4x + 2y = -11 \end{cases}$

29. $\begin{cases} 1.2x + 1.4y = 2.7 \\ 0.4x - 0.3y = 0.9 \end{cases}$

Name ______________________ Class ______________ Date ______________

3-2 • Guided Problem Solving

GPS **Exercise 62**

Break-Even Point A theater production costs \$40,000 plus \$2800 per performance. A sold-out performance brings in \$3675. How many sold-out performances will the production need to break even?

Read and Understand

1. What are the production costs? ______________________

2. How much money does a sold-out performance bring in? ______________________

Plan and Solve

3. Let x be the number of performances and y be the dollar amount. Write an equation representing the theater costs from x performances. ______________

4. Write an equation representing the income from x performances. ______________

5. Using the two equations and substitution, write an equation with just x. ______________

6. Solve the equation. ______________________

7. How many sold-out performances will the production need to break even?

____

Look Back and Check

8. To check your answer, substitute the value of x into the equations and see if the two dollar amounts are reasonable. ______________

Solve Another Problem

9. It costs \$5,500,000 to build a ferry boat plus \$15,000 in operating costs per trip. A sold-out trip brings in \$24,000. How many sold-out trips will the ferry company need to break even?

____

Name ______________________ Class ______________ Date ______________

Practice 3-3

Systems of Inequalities

Solve each system of inequalities by graphing.

1. $\begin{cases} y > x + 2 \\ y \le -x + 1 \end{cases}$

2. $\begin{cases} y \le x + 3 \\ y \ge x + 2 \end{cases}$

3. $\begin{cases} x + y < 5 \\ y < 3x - 2 \end{cases}$

4. $\begin{cases} x - 2y < 3 \\ 2x + y > 8 \end{cases}$

5. $\begin{cases} -3x + y < 3 \\ x + y > -1 \end{cases}$

6. $\begin{cases} x + 2y > 4 \\ 2x - y > 6 \end{cases}$

7. $\begin{cases} 2x \ge y + 3 \\ x < 3 - 2y \end{cases}$

8. $\begin{cases} 3 < 2x - y \\ x - 3y \le 4 \end{cases}$

9. $\begin{cases} y \ge 2 \\ y \ge |x| \end{cases}$

10. $\begin{cases} y < x - 3 \\ y \ge |x - 4| \end{cases}$

11. $\begin{cases} -2x + y > 1 \\ y > |x| \end{cases}$

12. $\begin{cases} y < -3 \\ y < -|x| \end{cases}$

13. Suppose you are buying two kinds of notebooks for school. A spiral notebook costs $2, and a three-ring notebook costs $5. You must have at least six notebooks. The cost of the notebooks can be no more than $20.
   a. Write a system of inequalities to model the situation.
   b. Graph and solve the system.

14. A camp counselor needs no more than 30 campers to sign up for two mountain hikes. The counselor needs at least 10 campers on the low trail and at least 5 campers on the high trail.
   a. Write a system of inequalities to model the situation.
   b. Graph and solve the system.

Solve each system of inequalities by graphing.

15. $\begin{cases} 2x + y > 2 \\ x - y \ge 3 \end{cases}$

16. $\begin{cases} y \le 3x \\ y \ge -2x + 2 \end{cases}$

17. $\begin{cases} y < 5x - 1 \\ y \ge 7 - 3x \end{cases}$

18. $\begin{cases} y \ge -2x + 2 \\ y \le 3x \end{cases}$

19. $\begin{cases} x + y > 2 \\ 2x - y < 1 \end{cases}$

20. $\begin{cases} y > 3x + 2 \\ y \le -2x + 1 \end{cases}$

21. $\begin{cases} y \ge -2 \\ y \le -|x + 3| \end{cases}$

22. $\begin{cases} y < x + 3 \\ y > |x - 1| \end{cases}$

23. $\begin{cases} y > x \\ y < |x + 2| \end{cases}$

Name ______________________ Class ______________ Date ______________

3-3 • Guided Problem Solving

GPS Exercise 40

Fund-Raising Suppose the Student Council has asked you to form a committee to run a bake sale. The committee needs from 7 to 10 members. The number of seniors should be greater than the number of juniors.

a. Write a system of inequalities to model the problem.

b. Graph the system and list the combinations of juniors and seniors that may participate in the committee.

Read and Understand

1. How many members does the committee need? ______________

2. Is the number of seniors more or less than the number of juniors? ______________

Plan and Solve

3. Let j be the number of juniors and s be the number of seniors. Write an inequality modeling each of the following:

the number of juniors must be positive: ______________

the number of seniors must be positive: ______________

the number of seniors is greater than the number of juniors: ______________

the total number of juniors and seniors is at least 7: ______________

the total number of juniors and seniors is at most 10: ______________

4. Graph the system of equations.

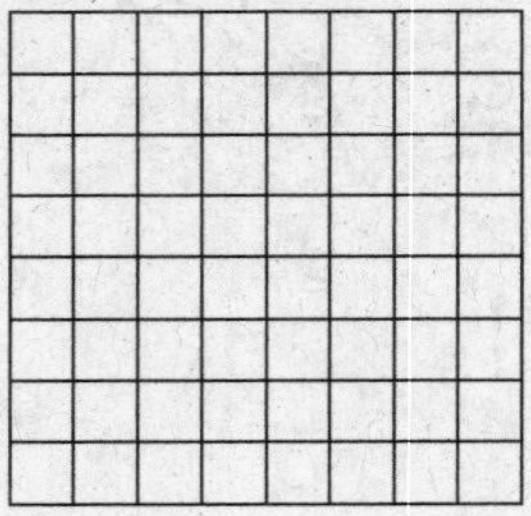

5. Using your graph, list the combinations of juniors and seniors that may participate.

____

____

Look Back and Check

6. To check the reasonableness of your answers, substitute the combinations in each inequality and verify that true statements result. ______________

Solve Another Problem

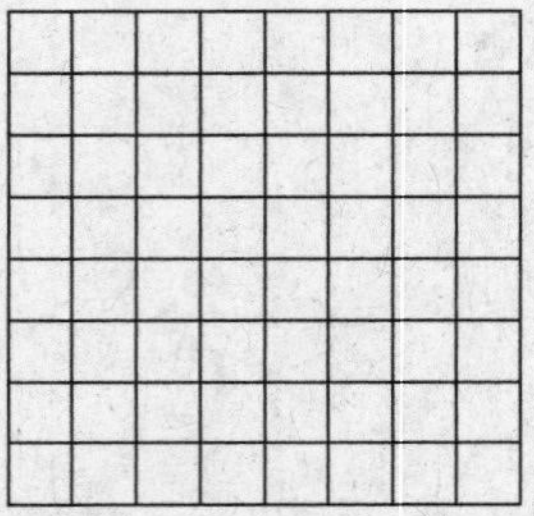

7. A book salesperson is bringing samples of books to a show. He has been asked to bring from 5 to 8 books. The number of paperbacks y should be less than the number of hardcover books x.

a. Write a system of inequalities to model the problem.

b. Graph the system and list the combinations of hardcover books and paperbacks that he can bring.

Name ____________________ Class ____________ Date ____________

Practice 3-4

Linear Programming

Graph each system of constraints. Name all vertices. Then find the values of x and y that maximize or minimize the objective function.

1. $\begin{cases} x + 2y \le 6 \\ x \ge 2 \\ y \ge 1 \end{cases}$

   Minimum for $C = 3x + 4y$

2. $\begin{cases} x + y \le 5 \\ x + 2y \le 8 \\ x \ge 0,\ y \ge 0 \end{cases}$

   Maximum for $P = x + 3y$

3. $\begin{cases} x + y \le 6 \\ 2x + y \le 10 \\ x \ge 0,\ y \ge 0 \end{cases}$

   Maximum for $P = 4x + y$

4. $\begin{cases} 3x + 2y \le 6 \\ 2x + 3y \le 6 \\ x \ge 0,\ y \ge 0 \end{cases}$

   Maximum for $P = 4x + y$

5. $\begin{cases} 4x + 2y \le 4 \\ 2x + 4y \le 4 \\ x \ge 0,\ y \ge 0 \end{cases}$

   Maximum for $P = 3x + y$

6. $\begin{cases} x + y \le 5 \\ 4x + y \le 8 \\ x \ge 0,\ y \ge 0 \end{cases}$

   Minimum for $C = x + 3y$

Find the values of x and y that maximize or minimize the objective function for each graph. Then find the maximum or minimum value.

7.

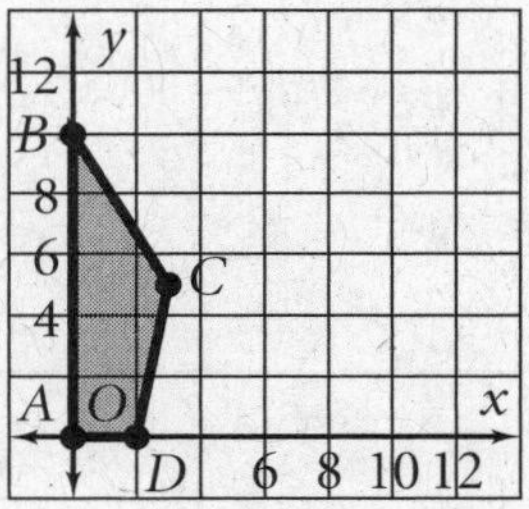

Maximize for $P = 2x + 3y$

8.

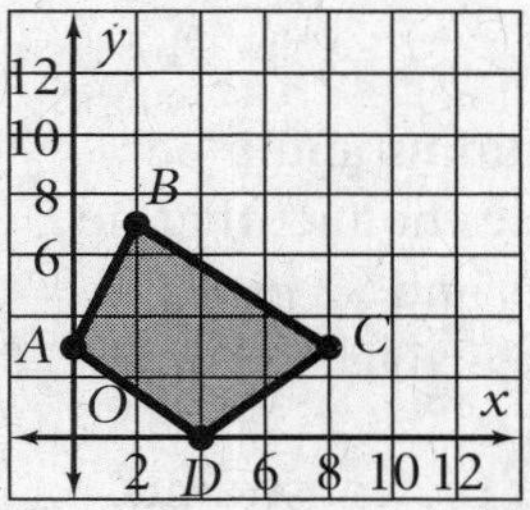

Minimize for $C = x + 2y$

9.

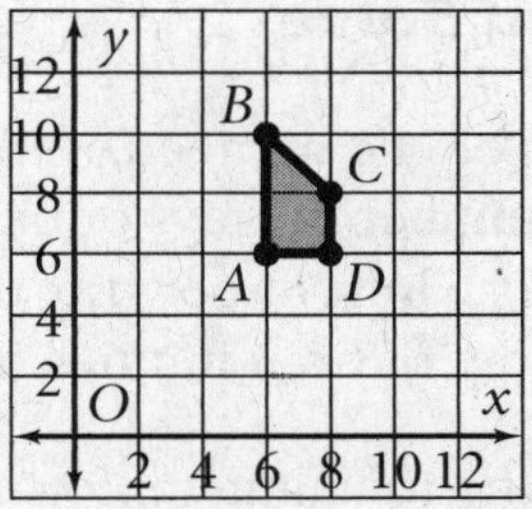

Maximize for $P = 3x + y$

10. You are going to make and sell bread. A loaf of Irish soda bread is made with 2 c flour and $\frac{1}{4}$ c sugar. Kugelhopf cake is made with 4 c flour and 1 c sugar. You will make a profit of \$1.50 on each loaf of Irish soda bread and a profit of \$4 on each Kugelhopf cake. You have 16 c flour and 3 c sugar.

    a. How many of each kind of bread should you make to maximize the profit?

    b. What is the maximum profit?

11. Suppose you make and sell skin lotion. A quart of regular skin lotion contains 2 c oil and 1 c cocoa butter. A quart of extra-rich skin lotion contains 1 c oil and 2 c cocoa butter. You will make a profit of \$10/qt on regular lotion and a profit of \$8/qt on extra-rich lotion. You have 24 c oil and 18 c cocoa butter.

    a. How many quarts of each type of lotion should you make to maximize your profit?

    b. What is the maximum profit?

Name ______________________ Class ______________ Date ______________

3-4 • Guided Problem Solving

GPS Exercise 20

Cooking Baking a tray of corn muffins takes 4 c milk and 3 c wheat flour. A tray of bran muffins takes 2 c milk and 3 c wheat flour. A baker has 16 c milk and 15 c wheat flour. He makes $3 profit per tray of corn muffins and $2 profit per tray of bran muffins. How many trays of each type of muffin should the baker make to maximize his profit?

Read and Understand

1. How much milk does each tray take, and how much milk does the baker have?

____

2. How much flour does each tray take, and how much flour does the baker have?

____

Plan and Solve

3. Let c be the number of trays of corn muffins and b be the number of trays of bran muffins. Use the fact that he makes $3 profit per tray of corn muffins and $2 profit per tray of bran muffins to write the objective function P. ______________

4. Use the remaining information to write the constraints. ______________

5. Graph the constraints. Then find the coordinates of each vertex.

6. Evaluate P at each vertex. ______ At which vertex is the objective function maximized? ______

7. How many trays of each type of muffin should the baker make? ______________

Look Back and Check

8. To verify your answer, select other points in the feasible region and evaluate P. Are the values of P less than that of the vertex chosen? ______________

Solve Another Problem

9. A manufacturer is producing 100 total units. Each unit Q costs $9 for parts and $15 for labor, and each unit R costs $6 for parts and $20 for labor. The manufacturer's budget is $810 for parts and $1800 for labor. If the income per unit is $150 for Q and $175 for R, how many units of each should be manufactured to maximize income?

____

Name ______________________ Class ______________ Date ______________

Practice 3-5

Graphs in Three Dimensions

Describe the location of each point in coordinate space.

1. (3, 0, 0) **2.** (0, 2, 0) **3.** (3, −2, −4) **4.** (−6, −4, −1)

5. (0, 0, 4) **6.** (1, 2, 3) **7.** (3, −1, 6) **8.** (0, 4, −1)

Graph each point in coordinate space.

9. (0, 3, 0) **10.** (2, 0, 0) **11.** (0, 0, 5) **12.** (−1, −4, −2)

13. (2, 3, 1) **14.** (−1, −2, −3) **15.** (6, −1, 0) **16.** (4, −2, 3)

Write the coordinates of each point in the diagram.

17. *A* **18.** *B*

19. *C* **20.** *D*

21. *R* **22.** *T*

23. *U* **24.** *S*

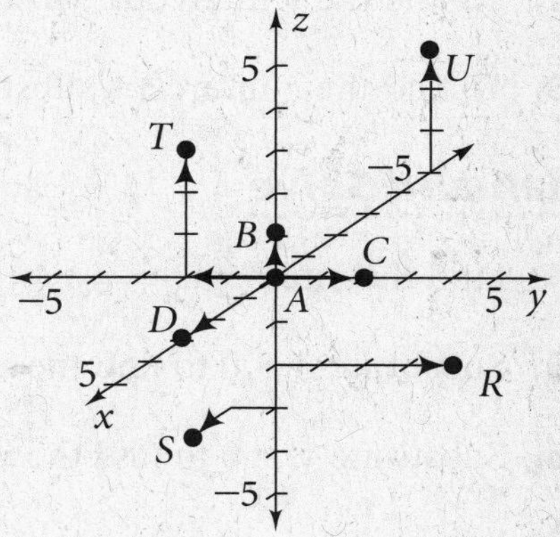

Graph each equation.

25. $x + 2y + 3z = 3$ **26.** $3x - 2y + z = 6$

27. $-6x - 3y + 2z = 6$ **28.** $2x - 3y + 3z = 6$

29. $8x - 2y - 2z = 8$ **30.** $-6x - 12y - 12z = 12$

31. $9x - 3y + z = 9$ **32.** $7x - 1y + 7z = 7$

33. $4x + 3y + 6z = 12$ **34.** $x - y + 2z = 6$

Graph each equation and find the equation of each trace.

35. $x + y + z = 3$ **36.** $x + 2y + 3z = 6$ **37.** $x + 3y + 2z = 6$

38. $2x + 3y + z = 6$ **39.** $-4x + 2y - 4z = 8$ **40.** $4x - 2y + 6z = 12$

41. $6x - 3y + z = 6$ **42.** $7x - 3y + 7z = 21$ **43.** $4x - 3y + 6z = -12$

Name ____________________ Class ____________ Date ____________

3-5 • Guided Problem Solving

GPS Exercise 33

Sketch the graph of the equation and find the equation of each trace.

$6x + 6y - 12z = 36$

Read and Understand

1. To find the x-intercept, substitute 0 for what? ____________

2. To find the y-intercept, substitute 0 for what? ____________

3. To find the z-intercept, substitute 0 for what? ____________

Plan and Solve

4. Find the intercepts. ____________

5. Substitute $z = 0$ to find the xy-trace. ____________

6. Substitute $y = 0$ to find the xz-trace. ____________

7. Substitute $x = 0$ to find the yz-trace. ____________

8. Graph the intercepts. Draw the traces. Shade the plane.

Look Back and Check

9. To check the reasonableness of your answers, simplify $6x + 6y - 12z = 36$ to $x + y - 2z = 6$ and repeat the steps. The results should be the same.

____

Solve Another Problem

10. Sketch the graph of the equation $4x + 9y - 9z = -36$ and find the equation of each trace.

____

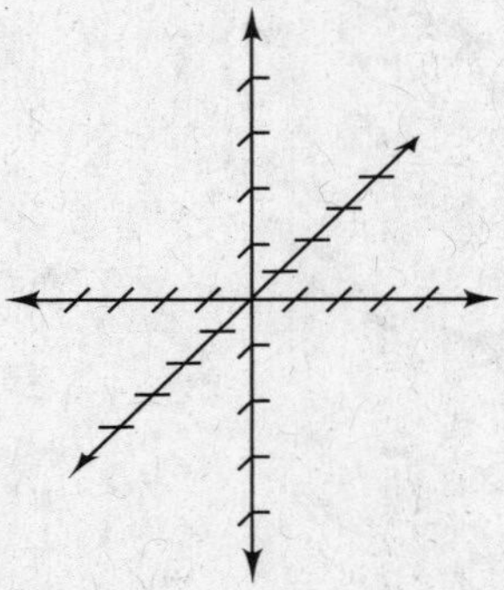

Name ______________________ Class ______________ Date ______________

Practice 3-6

Systems with Three Variables

Solve each system.

1. $\begin{cases} x + y + z = -1 \\ 2x - y + 2z = -5 \\ -x + 2y - z = 4 \end{cases}$

2. $\begin{cases} x + y + z = 3 \\ 2x - y + 2z = 6 \\ 3x + 2y - z = 13 \end{cases}$

3. $\begin{cases} 2x + y = 9 \\ x - 2z = -3 \\ 2y + 3z = 15 \end{cases}$

4. $\begin{cases} x - y + 2z = 10 \\ -x + y - 2z = 5 \\ 3x - 3y + 6z = -2 \end{cases}$

5. $\begin{cases} 2x - y + z = -4 \\ 3x + y - 2z = 0 \\ 3x - y = -4 \end{cases}$

6. $\begin{cases} 2x - y - z = 4 \\ -x + 2y + z = 1 \\ 3x + y + z = 16 \end{cases}$

7. $\begin{cases} x + 5y + 5z = -10 \\ x + y + z = 2 \\ x + 2y + 3z = -3 \end{cases}$

8. $\begin{cases} x - y - z = 0 \\ x - 2y - 2z = 3 \\ -2x + 2y - z = 3 \end{cases}$

9. $\begin{cases} 3x + y + z = 6 \\ 3x - 2y + 2z = 14 \\ 3x + 3y - 3z = -6 \end{cases}$

10. $\begin{cases} x + y + z = -2 \\ 2x + 2y - 3z = 11 \\ 3x - y + z = 4 \end{cases}$

11. $\begin{cases} x - 5y + z = 3 \\ x + 2y - 2z = -12 \\ 2x + 2z = 6 \end{cases}$

12. $\begin{cases} 2x + 3z = 2 \\ 3x + 6y = 6 \\ x - 2z = 8 \end{cases}$

13. $\begin{cases} x + y - z = 0 \\ 3x - y + z = 4 \\ 5x + z = 7 \end{cases}$

14. $\begin{cases} x - 2y = 1 \\ x + 3y + z = 0 \\ 2x - 2z = 18 \end{cases}$

15. $\begin{cases} x + y + 4z = 5 \\ -2x + 2z = 3 \\ 3x + y - 2z = 0 \end{cases}$

16. $\begin{cases} 3x + 2y + 2z = 4 \\ -6x + 4y - 2z = -9 \\ 9x - 2y + 2z = 10 \end{cases}$

17. $\begin{cases} 2x - 3y + z = -3 \\ x - 5y + 7z = -11 \\ -10x + 4y - 6z = 28 \end{cases}$

18. $\begin{cases} x + y + z = -8 \\ x - y - z = 6 \\ 2x - 3y + 2z = -1 \end{cases}$

19. $\begin{cases} 14x - 3y + 5z = -15 \\ 3x + 2y - 6z = 10 \\ 7x - y + 4z = -5 \end{cases}$

20. $\begin{cases} 5x - 3y + 2z = 39 \\ 4x + 4y - 3z = 34 \\ 3x - 2y + 6z = 14 \end{cases}$

21. $\begin{cases} x + y + z = 6 \\ 2x - y + 2z = 6 \\ -x + y + 3z = 10 \end{cases}$

22. $\begin{cases} 2x + y - z = 3 \\ 3x - y + 3z = 3 \\ -x - 3y + 2z = 3 \end{cases}$

23. $\begin{cases} 2x - 3y + z = 4 \\ -2x + 3y - z = -4 \\ 6x - 9y + 3z = 12 \end{cases}$

24. $\begin{cases} x + y - z = 1 \\ x + 2z = 3 \\ 2x + 2y = 4 \end{cases}$

Write and solve a system of equations for each problem.

25. The sum of three numbers is −2. The sum of three times the first number, twice the second number, and the third number is 9. The difference between the second number and half the third number is 10. Find the numbers.

26. Monica has \$1, \$5, and \$10 bills in her wallet that are worth \$96. If she had one more \$1 bill, she would have just as many \$1 bills as \$5 and \$10 bills combined. She has 23 bills total. How many of each denomination does she have?

Name ______________________ Class ______________ Date ______________

3-6 • Guided Problem Solving

GPS Exercise 40

A fish was caught whose tail weighed 9 lb. Its head weighed as much as its tail plus half its body. Its body weighed as much as its head and tail. What did the fish weigh?

Read and Understand

1. What are the three parts of the fish being compared? ______________________
2. How much did the tail weigh? ______________________

Plan and Solve

Let t be the weight of the tail, h be the weight of the head, and b be the weight of the body.

3. Write an equation representing the tail's weight. ______________________
4. Write an equation representing that the head weighed as much as the tail plus half the body.

   ____

5. Write an equation representing that the body weighed as much as the head and tail.

   ____

6. Use substitution to solve the system of equations. ______________________
7. How much does the fish weigh? ______________________

Look Back and Check

8. To check your answer, check that the weight for each part of the fish satisfies each statement in the original problem.

   ____

Solve Another Problem

9. Over the weekend, a student spent 4 hours writing a history report. Also, she spent as much time preparing a speech as she did writing the history report plus twice the time spent on mathematics homework. The time spent on the history report is the same as half the time spent on the speech plus the time spent on mathematics. What is the total amount of time the student spent on homework?

   ____

Name ______________________ Class ______________ Date ______________

3A: Graphic Organizer

For use before Lesson 3-1

Study Skill Previewing a chapter gives you an idea about what you will learn in the chapter. Look at the titles of the lessons in Chapter 3. What do you think you will learn in each lesson, just from the titles? Write down your thoughts, and then as you complete each lesson, compare your recorded thoughts to what you actually learned.

Write your answers.

1. What is the chapter title? ______________________

2. Find the Table of Contents page for this chapter at the front of the book. Name four topics you will study in this chapter.

______________________ ______________________

______________________ ______________________

3. Complete the graphic organizer as you work through the chapter.
   1. Write the title of the chapter in the center oval.
   2. When you begin a lesson, write the name of the lesson in a rectangle.
   3. When you complete that lesson, write a skill or key concept from that lesson in the outer oval linked to that rectangle.

   Continue with steps 2 and 3 clockwise around the graphic organizer.

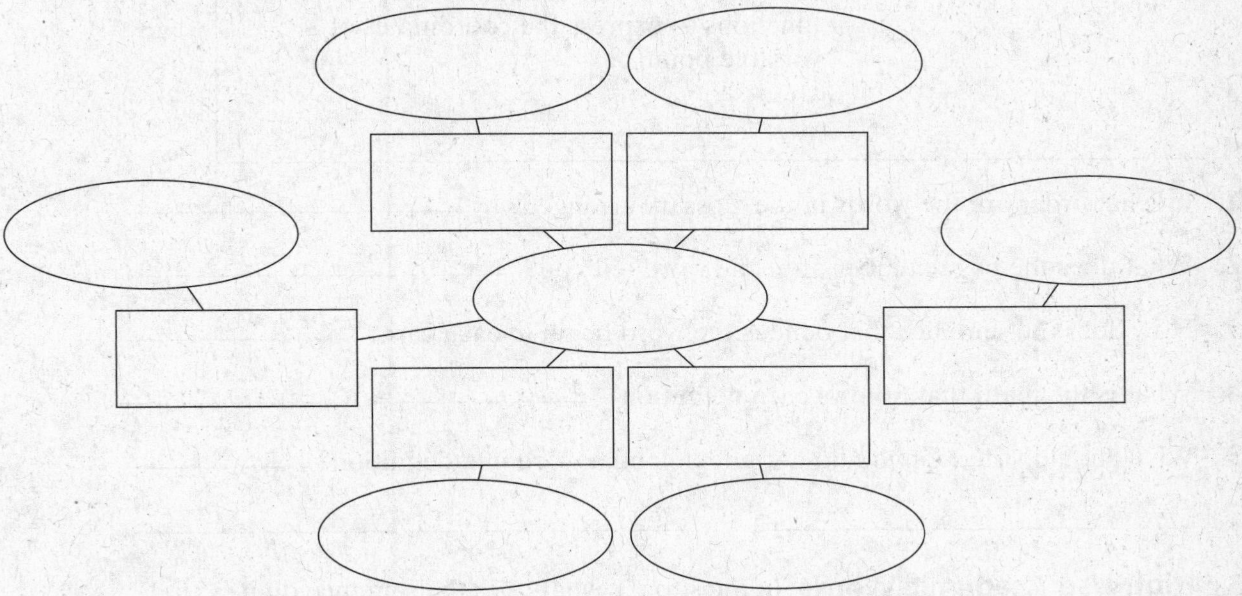

Name ______________________ Class ______________ Date ______________

3B: Reading Comprehension

For use after Lesson 3-5

Study Skill When you are reading, make sure that you understand the meaning of each word that you read. To avoid interrupting your reading, you may sometimes want to make a list of words, and the page on which you encountered them, for which you need to look up the meaning. After you complete writing the definitions in your list, go back to the pages you noted and reread them to make sure you understand each word in context.

Read the example entries from this sample glossary. Then answer the questions about how to read glossary entries.

Dependent system (p. 116)	A dependent system is a system of equations that is true for an infinite number of values of the variables. $\begin{cases} 2x + y = 3 \\ 4x + 2y = 6 \end{cases}$
Inconsistent system (p. 116)	An inconsistent system is a system of equations that is false for all possible values of the variables. It has no solution. $\begin{cases} x + 2y = 3 \\ x + 2y = 5 \end{cases}$
Parameter (p. 126)	A parameter is an independent variable used in a system of equations or functions to express the coordinates of a variable point. $x(t) = 2t$ $y(t) = -t + 4$

1. In what order are the words in the glossary arranged? ______________

2. What does the page number after the word tell you? ______________

3. How does the sentence that defines the word begin in each case? ______________

4. What is the math that follows each definition? ______________

5. What should you do if you do not understand a word in a definition? ______________

____

6. High-Use Academic Words In question 3, what does the sentence do if it *defines* a word?

a. gives the meaning of the word **b.** uses the word incorrectly

Name ____________________ Class ____________ Date ____________

3C: Reading/Writing Math Symbols

For use after Lesson 3-3

Study Skill Taking notes helps you remember the content as you write, but your notes can also be useful when you are reviewing. In order for notes to be helpful later, they must be written clearly enough so that you can read them after you may have forgotten some of the words. If they are scrawled carelessly, you may have trouble making out exactly what you wrote.

Certain letters in mathematics are usually used for specific meanings, for example, A often (though not always) means area, and similarly, V often means volume, P is used for perimeter, C for circumference, and s for side. Clearly these letters are used because they are the first letters of the words they represent. Other letters, by mathematical custom, are also usually used for certain specific purposes.

Write the letter described in each of the following questions.

1. What is the letter that you most often see used to denote a function? ____________
2. What are the two letters that you have seen most often used as the variables in ordered pairs on graphs? ____________
3. What is the letter that is always used for the slope of a line? ____________
4. What is the letter that is usually used to mean width? ____________
5. What is the letter that is usually used to mean length? ____________

Here are two other examples of the customary use of letters in mathematics.

6. What does the m in the expression $m\angle A$ stand for? ____________
7. Write in symbols "the theoretical probability of getting a 7." ____________

Name ____________________ Class ____________________ Date ____________________

3D: Visual Vocabulary Practice
High-Use Academic Words

For use after Lesson 3-6

Study Skills If a word is not in the Glossary, use a dictionary to find its meaning.

Concept List

approximate	compare	define
evaluate	interpret	model
property	set	test

Write the concept that best describes each exercise. Choose from the concept list above.

1. Let w = the width. ____________	**2.** $a = 3$ and $b = -1$, $a - 2b = 3 - 2(-1)$ $= 3 - (-2)$ $= 3 + 2$ $= 5$ ____________	**3.** $\pi \approx \frac{22}{7}$ ____________
4. The equation $y = -\frac{1}{4}x + 6$ models the height of a burning candle. Its slope, $-\frac{1}{4}$, means that the candle burns $\frac{1}{4}$ an inch per hour. ____________	**5.** The equation $y = 0.87x + 2.55$ for the data points shown. 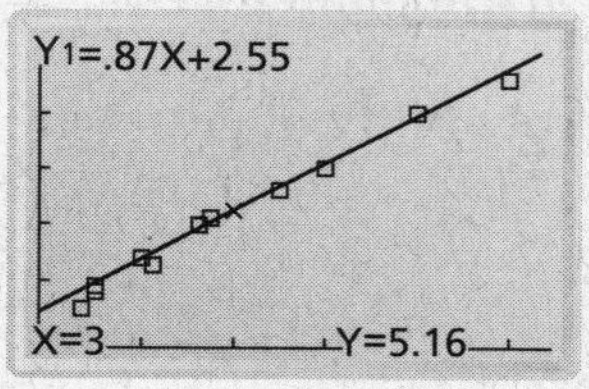 ____________	**6.** All of the numbers that can be written as $\frac{a}{b}$ where a is any integer and b is any nonzero integer. ____________
7. $-0.5 < -0.1$ ____________	**8.** If $a \leq b$ and $c > 0$, then $ac \leq bc$. If $a \leq b$ and $c < 0$, then $ac \geq bc$. ____________	**9.** 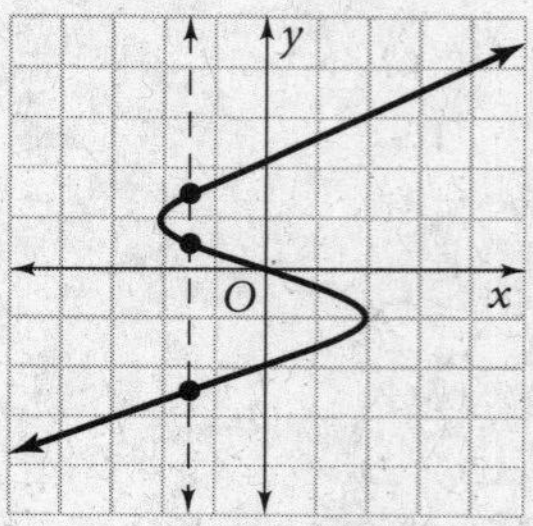 Not a function ____________

Name ______________________ Class ______________ Date ______________

3E: Vocabulary Check

For use after Lesson 3-5

Study Skill Strengthen your vocabulary. Use these pages and add cues and summaries by applying the Cornell Notetaking style.

Write the definition for each word at the right. To check your work, fold the paper back along the dotted line to see the correct answers.

Definition	Word
______________________	Linear system
______________________	Dependent system
______________________	Linear programming
______________________	Objective function
______________________	Trace

Name ______________________ Class ______________ Date ______________

3E: Vocabulary Check (continued)

For use after Lesson 3-5

Write the vocabulary word for each definition. To check your work, fold the paper forward along the dotted line to see the correct answers.

This is a set of two or more linear equations that use the same variables. ______________________

This is a system that does not have a unique solution. ______________________

A technique that identifies the minimum or maximum value of some quantity. This quantity is modeled with an objective function. Limits on the variables in the objective function are constraints, written as linear inequalities. ______________________

In linear programming, this is a model of the quantity that you want to make as large or as small as possible. ______________________

This is a set of ordered pairs that results from substituting 0 for one of the variables in the equation of a plane. ______________________

Name ______________________ Class ______________ Date ______________

3F: Vocabulary Review Puzzle

For use with Chapter Review

Vocabulary and Study Skills

Study Skill Make sure that you are alert when you are learning a new concept, or new vocabulary words. If your mind is wandering as you read or as you listen to a lecture, the concepts you read or hear may not become entrenched in your memory.

Complete the word search puzzle by finding the words that match the descriptions below. For help, use the Glossary in your textbook. Remember a word may go right to left, left to right, up, down, or along a diagonal. Circle the letters that form each word.

1. system of equations that has at least one solution
2. system of equations that has a solution of all points on one line
3. system of equations that has the same solution set as another system
4. system of equations that has no solution
5. system of equations that has a unique solution
6. number of dimensions in coordinate space

E	E	O	E	I	H	I	P	A	D	I	I
T	D	R	E	R	S	Q	E	N	N	N	E
D	N	D	R	D	E	D	I	D	C	E	Q
E	E	E	H	N	P	N	E	O	N	L	U
P	P	R	T	F	I	P	N	P	O	B	I
E	E	E	C	S	E	S	A	A	Q	I	V
N	P	D	E	N	I	O	D	L	E	S	A
D	P	T	D	S	H	S	O	N	D	A	L
E	E	E	T	R	A	E	N	I	L	E	E
N	N	E	H	T	R	E	D	O	R	F	N
T	N	C	Q	E	S	N	H	E	C	P	T
T	S	T	N	I	A	R	T	S	N	O	C

Name ______________________ Class ______________ Date ______________

Practice 4-1

Organizing Data Into Matrices

Write the dimensions of each matrix. Identify the indicated element.

1. $\begin{bmatrix} 2 \\ -3 \\ -6 \end{bmatrix}$; a_{21}

2. $\begin{bmatrix} 5 & -7 & 23 & 10 \\ -9 & 3 & 5 & -2 \\ 1 & 9 & 0 & 2 \end{bmatrix}$; a_{23}

3. $\begin{bmatrix} 2 & 3 & -9 \\ 12 & -8 & 0 \end{bmatrix}$; a_{21}

4. $\begin{bmatrix} x & y & z \\ a & b & c \\ p & q & r \end{bmatrix}$; a_{32}

5. $\begin{bmatrix} 2 & -2 \\ 3 & -3 \\ 4 & -4 \end{bmatrix}$; a_{31}

6. $[5 \quad 8 \quad -7 \quad -4]$; a_{14}

Use the table for Exercises 7–10.

7. Display the data in a matrix with the types of unemployment in the columns.
8. State the dimensions of the matrix.
9. Identify a_{21}, and tell what it represents.
10. Identify a_{16}, and tell what it represents.

Unemployment by Category

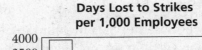

	June, 1992	June, 1996
Construction	17.6%	9.5%
Manufacturing	8.3%	5.1%
Transportation	5.4%	4.5%
Sales	8.7%	6.4%
Finance	4.0%	2.6%
Services	6.6%	5.1%
Government	3.5%	2.7%

Source: *U.S. News & World Report*

Use the table at the right for Exercises 11–14.

11. Write a matrix M to represent the data in the graph, with columns representing years.
12. What are the dimensions of this matrix?
13. What does the first row represent?
14. What does m_{32} represent?

Days Lost to Strikes per 1,000 Employees

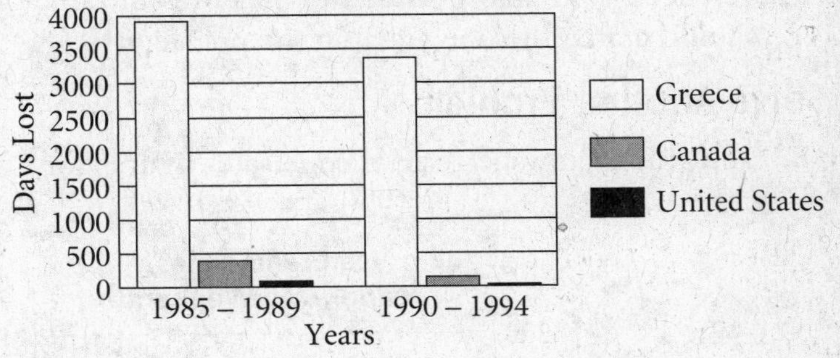

Source: *U.S. News & World Report*

Name ______________________ Class ______________ Date ______________

4-1 • Guided Problem Solving

GPS Exercise 26

Retail Sales The graph shows August sales figures at a music store.

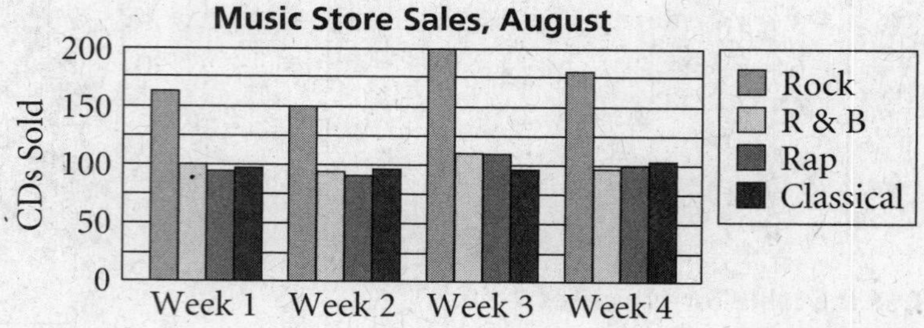

a. Record the data in a table.
b. Show the data in a matrix.
What do the columns represent?
What do the rows represent?

Read and Understand

1. In what form will your answer to (a) be? ______________________

2. In what form will your answer to the first part of (b) be? ______________________

Plan and Solve

3. For the table, let each row represent types of CDs. What will each column represent?

____

4. Estimate the figures in the graph and record the data in a table.

5. Show the data in a matrix.

6. What do the columns represent? What do the rows represent? ______________________

Look Back and Check

7. To check your answers, use the data in your table or matrix to create a bar graph. The result should match the one given in the problem.

Solve Another Problem

8. The graph shows ice cream cone sales figures for Labor Day weekend.

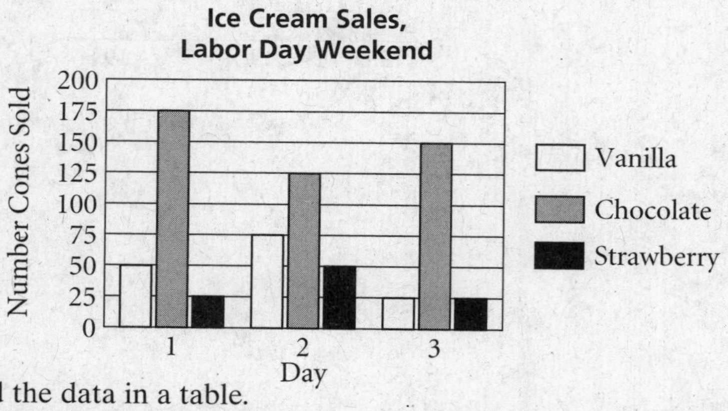

a. Record the data in a table.
b. Show the data in a matrix. What do the columns represent? What do the rows represent?

____

Name ______________________ Class ______________ Date ______________

Practice 4-2

Adding and Subtracting Matrices

Find the value of each variable.

1. $\begin{bmatrix} a & 2b \\ c-2 & d+3 \end{bmatrix} = \begin{bmatrix} 5 & -7 \\ 10 & 10 \end{bmatrix}$

2. $\begin{bmatrix} 3 & 5 & -y & x \\ z & 0 & 3a & b \end{bmatrix} = \begin{bmatrix} 3 & 3c & 7 & 4 \\ \frac{7}{2} & 0 & -9 & 3b \end{bmatrix}$

3. $\begin{bmatrix} 5 & 1 \\ 0 & 2 \end{bmatrix} + \begin{bmatrix} 2 & -13 \\ -10 & -10 \end{bmatrix} = \begin{bmatrix} 2x+1 & -4x \\ 5z & 2.5z - x \end{bmatrix}$

Use the information in the table.

4. Put the data in two matrices: one for males and one for females.

5. Use matrix subtraction to find the difference between the number of males and the number of females in each club each year.

Club Membership at TC High School

	1961–1962		2001–2002	
	Males	**Females**	**Males**	**Females**
Beta	37	23	56	58
Spanish	0	93	76	82
Chess	87	0	102	34
Library	6	18	27	29

Find each sum or difference.

6. $\begin{bmatrix} -1 & 2 \\ 3 & -1 \end{bmatrix} + \begin{bmatrix} -1 & 2 \\ -3 & 1 \end{bmatrix} + \begin{bmatrix} 0 & -1 \\ 2 & 0 \end{bmatrix}$

7. $\begin{bmatrix} 8 & -5 & -5 \\ 4 & -10 & 10 \\ 2 & -15 & -15 \end{bmatrix} - \begin{bmatrix} 0 & 0 & 1 \\ 1 & -2 & -2 \\ -2 & -3 & 3 \end{bmatrix}$

8. $\begin{bmatrix} -2 & -1 \\ -3 & 1 \\ -1 & -1 \end{bmatrix} - \begin{bmatrix} -2 & -2 \\ 3 & -1 \\ 0 & -2 \end{bmatrix} + \begin{bmatrix} -2 & 1 \\ 0 & 3 \\ -3 & -3 \end{bmatrix}$

9. $\begin{bmatrix} 1 \\ 1 \\ 1 \end{bmatrix} + \begin{bmatrix} -1 \\ -3 \\ 5 \end{bmatrix} + \begin{bmatrix} -10 \\ -7 \\ 11 \end{bmatrix} - \begin{bmatrix} -3 \\ -5 \\ -6 \end{bmatrix}$

Solve each matrix equation.

10. $X - \begin{bmatrix} 3 & 4 \\ 4 & 2 \\ 1 & 9 \end{bmatrix} = \begin{bmatrix} 5 & 7 \\ 9 & 12 \\ 3 & 2 \end{bmatrix}$

11. $X + \begin{bmatrix} 20 & -9 & -3 \\ 19 & -2 & -5 \\ -1 & 0 & -8 \end{bmatrix} = \begin{bmatrix} -7 & 92 & -5 \\ 0 & 91 & -6 \\ -9 & -1 & 12 \end{bmatrix}$

12. $\begin{bmatrix} -2 & -3 \\ 2 & 2 \end{bmatrix} = X - \begin{bmatrix} 1 & -1 \\ -2 & 2 \end{bmatrix}$

13. $\begin{bmatrix} 2 & 2 & 0 \\ 1 & -1 & -1 \end{bmatrix} = \begin{bmatrix} 2 & -2 & 3 \\ -3 & -3 & 4 \end{bmatrix} - X$

Determine whether the two matrices in each pair are equal. Justify your reasoning.

14. $\begin{bmatrix} 2 \\ \sqrt{9} \\ 16 \end{bmatrix}; \begin{bmatrix} \frac{4}{2} & 3 & 4^2 \end{bmatrix}$

15. $\begin{bmatrix} 2(3) & 3(1.5) \\ 7 & \frac{10}{2} \end{bmatrix}; \begin{bmatrix} 6 & 4.5 \\ 7 & 5 \end{bmatrix}$

Name ______________________ Class ______________ Date ______________

4-2 • Guided Problem Solving

GPS **Exercise 27**

Manufacturing The table at the right shows the number of beach balls produced during one shift at two manufacturing plants. Plant 1 has two shifts per day, and Plant 2 has three shifts per day.

Beach Ball Production Per Shift

	1-color Plastic	1-color Rubber	3-color Plastic	3-color Rubber
Plant 1	500	700	1300	1900
Plant 2	400	1200	600	1600

a. Write matrices to represent one day's total output at the two plants.

b. Use your results from part (a). Find the difference between production totals at the plants. Which plant produces more three-color plastic balls? Which plant produces more one-color rubber balls?

Read and Understand

1. How many shifts per day does Plant 1 have? Plant 2 have? ______________
2. How many matrices will you write for part (a)? ______________

Plan and Solve

3. Write matrices to represent one *shift's* total output at the two plants. ______________
4. Now write matrices to represent one *day's* total output at the two plants. ______________
5. Find Plant 1 – Plant 2 using matrix subtraction. Write this matrix representing the difference between daily production totals at the plants. ______________
6. Which plant produces more three-color plastic balls? How many more? ______________
7. Which plant produces more one-color rubber balls? How many more? ______________

Look Back and Check

8. Use the table values without matrices to check your answers. ______________

Solve Another Problem

9. The graph below shows the number of packages delivered each hour by two different carriers. Carrier A works 6 hours per day and Carrier B works 5 hours per day.

Package Deliveries Per Hour

	Envelopes Big	Envelopes Small	Boxes Big	Boxes Small
Carrier A	20	45	10	18
Carrier B	32	60	5	20

a. Write matrices to represent one day's total deliveries by the two carriers.

____

b. Use your results from part (a). Find the difference between total deliveries, A – B. Which carrier delivers more big envelopes? Which carrier delivers more small boxes?

____

Name ______________________ Class ______________ Date ______________

Practice 4-3

Matrix Multiplication

Use matrices *A, B, C, D,* and *E* to find each product, sum, or difference, if possible. If not possible, write *product undefined, sum undefined,* or *difference undefined.*

$A = \begin{bmatrix} 1 & -1 \\ 3 & -2 \end{bmatrix}$ $B = \begin{bmatrix} 0 & 2 \\ -2 & 1 \\ -1 & 0 \end{bmatrix}$ $C = \begin{bmatrix} 3 & -3 & -1 \\ 2 & -2 & 4 \end{bmatrix}$ $D = \begin{bmatrix} 1 & 0 \\ 0 & 1 \end{bmatrix}$ $E = \begin{bmatrix} 3 \\ -3 \\ 2 \end{bmatrix}$

1. $3AB$ **2.** $2A + 4D$ **3.** $5D - A$ **4.** $2C - E$ **5.** $3D + A$

6. DA **7.** AE **8.** BD **9.** DB **10.** CE

11. DC **12.** EB **13.** CB **14.** $2D$ **15.** BE

16. $0.2B$ **17.** $\frac{1}{4}C$ **18.** $0.5AC$ **19.** DE **20.** $-3DE$

Find the dimensions of the product matrix. Then find each product.

21. $\begin{bmatrix} 1 \\ 2 \\ 3 \end{bmatrix}\begin{bmatrix} 1 & 2 & 3 & 4 \end{bmatrix}$

22. $\begin{bmatrix} 1 & 2 & 12 \\ 12 & 2 & 1 \end{bmatrix}\begin{bmatrix} 3 & 4 \\ 4 & 3 \\ 5 & 2 \end{bmatrix}$

23. $\begin{bmatrix} 1 & 2 \\ 2 & 1 \end{bmatrix}\begin{bmatrix} 2 & 1 \\ 1 & 2 \end{bmatrix}$

Find each product if possible. If not possible, write *product undefined.*

24. $-12\begin{bmatrix} -6 & -2 \\ -5 & -6 \\ 0 & 1 \end{bmatrix}$

25. $\begin{bmatrix} 3 & 2 \\ 4 & 6 \\ 1 & 1 \end{bmatrix}\begin{bmatrix} -3 & 3 & -2 \\ -2 & 5 & -1 \end{bmatrix}$

26. $\begin{bmatrix} 0 & 1 & 0 \\ 2 & 2 & 1 \end{bmatrix}\begin{bmatrix} -2 & 2 & 2 \\ -1 & 1 & 1 \\ 0 & -1 & -1 \end{bmatrix}$

27. $\begin{bmatrix} 1 & 1 & 1 \\ 1 & 1 & 1 \\ 1 & 1 & 1 \end{bmatrix}\begin{bmatrix} 2 & 3 \\ 4 & 1 \\ 5 & 6 \end{bmatrix}$

28. $\begin{bmatrix} 1 & 0 & 1 \\ 1 & 1 & 0 \\ 1 & 1 & 1 \end{bmatrix}\begin{bmatrix} 6 & 4 & 2 & 8 \\ 10 & 4 & 6 & 2 \\ 2 & 10 & 12 & 4 \end{bmatrix}$

29. $\begin{bmatrix} 4 & 3 \\ 9 & 7 \end{bmatrix}\begin{bmatrix} 6 & 3 \\ 9 & 4 \end{bmatrix}$

Solve each equation. Check your answers.

30. $2\begin{bmatrix} 0 & 1 \\ 3 & -4 \end{bmatrix} - 3X = \begin{bmatrix} 9 & -6 \\ 1 & -2 \end{bmatrix}$

31. $\frac{1}{2}X + \begin{bmatrix} 5 & -1 \\ 0 & \frac{2}{3} \end{bmatrix} = 2\begin{bmatrix} 3 & 0 \\ 1 & 2 \end{bmatrix}$

Name ____________ Class ____________ Date ____________

4-3 • Guided Problem Solving

GPS Exercise 50

Revenue Write a matrix that represents the daily revenue from the play.

Ticket Prices

Orchestra	Mezzanine	Balcony
\$7.00	\$6.00	\$5.00

Number of Tickets Sold

Location	Thursday	Friday	Saturday
Orchestra	150	130	160
Mezzanine	125	130	175
Balcony	60	52	80

Read and Understand

1. Can you determine the answer by using the values on the ticket stub without doing any calculations? ____________
2. Will you use matrix multiplication to answer the question? ____________

Plan and Solve

3. Write a matrix representing the ticket prices. ____________
4. What are the dimensions of this matrix? ____________
5. Write a matrix representing the number of tickets sold. ____________
6. What are the dimensions of this matrix? ____________
7. What will be the dimensions of your answer matrix? ____________
8. Find the matrix that represents the daily revenue from the play. ____________

Look Back and Check

9. To check the reasonableness of your answer, use the values on the ticket to calculate the revenue from one day. Check it against the value in your answer matrix.

____

Solve Another Problem

10. Write a matrix that represents the total cost for each season from the sale of truck models.

Number of Trucks Sold

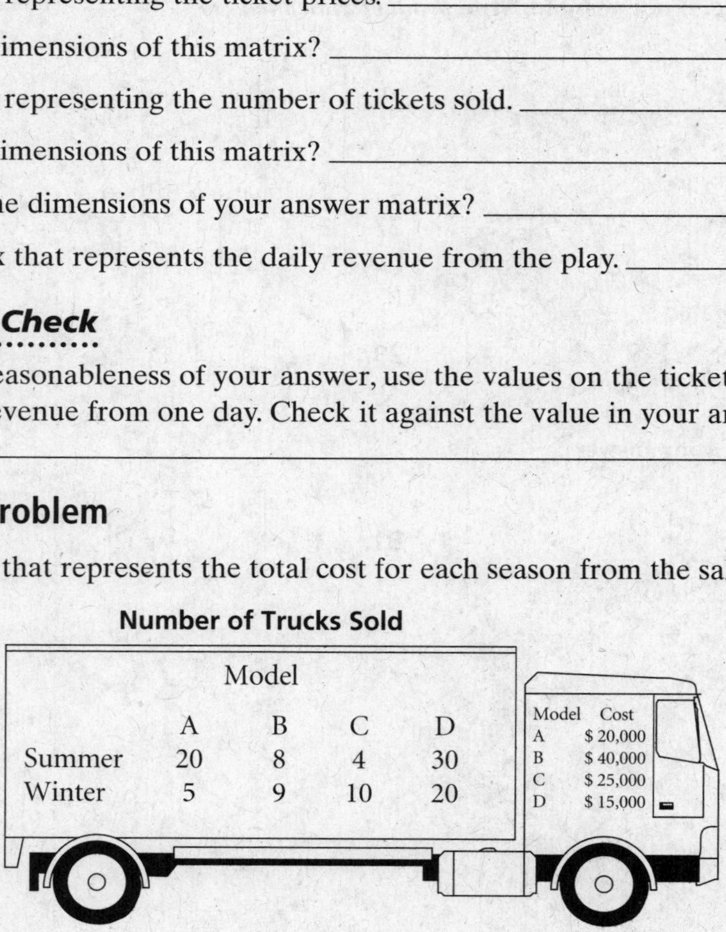

	Model A	B	C	D
Summer	20	8	4	30
Winter	5	9	10	20

Model	Cost
A	\$ 20,000
B	\$ 40,000
C	\$ 25,000
D	\$ 15,000

____

Name ____________________ Class ____________ Date ____________

Practice 4-4

Geometric Transformations With Matrices

For Exercises 1–11, use ΔABC at the right. Find the coordinates of the image under each transformation. Express your answer as a matrix.

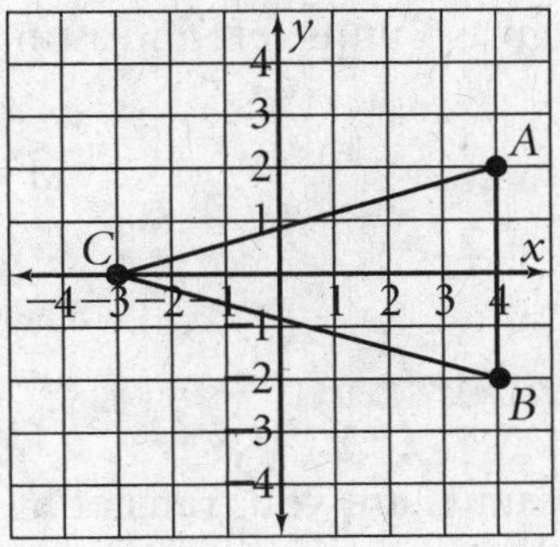

1. a dilation of 11
2. a translation 1 unit right and 4 units up
3. a dilation of 1.5
4. a translation 2 units right and 6 units down
5. a reflection in $y = x$
6. a rotation of 270°
7. a rotation of 90°
8. a translation 1 unit left and 2 units down
9. a translation 3 units left and 1 unit up
10. a dilation of $\frac{1}{2}$
11. a reflection in the x-axis

Graph each figure and its image after the given transformation.

12. $\begin{bmatrix} 2 & -3 & 6 & 4 \\ 0 & 1 & 1 & -4 \end{bmatrix}$; a dilation of 2

13. $\begin{bmatrix} 8 & 3 & -2 & -5 & 2 \\ 7 & 6 & 1 & 0 & -4 \end{bmatrix}$; a translation 2 units left and 1 unit up

14. $\begin{bmatrix} 2 & 4 & 5 & 3 \\ 1 & 1 & 3 & 5 \end{bmatrix}$; a translation 5 units left and 4 units down

15. $\begin{bmatrix} 2 & 1 & 6 & -4 \\ 0 & -3 & 5 & -2 \end{bmatrix}$; a rotation of 180°

16. $\begin{bmatrix} 6 & 5 & 1 & -3 & 6 \\ -1 & 6 & 2 & 0 & -4 \end{bmatrix}$; a reflection in the y-axis

The coordinates of the vertices of a polygon are given. Represent each transformation with matrices. Then express the coordinates of the vertices of the image as a matrix.

17. $I(21, -14), J(0, -7), K(-14, 0), L(0, 7)$; a dilation of $\frac{1}{7}$
18. $M(2, 0), N(0, -2), P(-2, 0)$; a translation 2 units down
19. $Q(2, 0), R(0, -2), S(-2, 0)$; a reflection in $y = -x$

Name ______________________ Class ______________ Date ______________

4-4 • Guided Problem Solving

GPS Exercise 24

Geometry The following matrix represents the vertices of a polygon. Translate the figure 5 units left and 1 unit up. Express your answer as a matrix.

$$\begin{bmatrix} -3 & -3 & 2 & 2 \\ -2 & -4 & -2 & -4 \end{bmatrix}$$

Read and Understand

1. How many units are you translating left? ______________

2. How many units are you translating up? ______________

Plan and Solve

3. To translate the figure left, will you add or subtract to each x-coordinate or y-coordinate? What will you add or subtract? ______________

4. To translate the figure up, will you add or subtract to each x-coordinate or y-coordinate? What will you add or subtract? ______________

5. What matrix will you use to translate the vertices of the polygon? ______________

6. Express the vertices of the image as a matrix. ______________

Look Back and Check

7. To check your answer, graph the polygon and its image using the matrices. Verify that the image is 5 units left and 1 unit up.

____

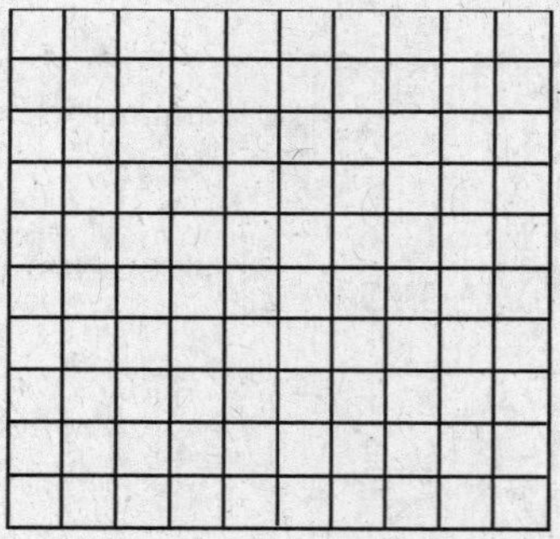

Solve Another Problem

8. The following matrix represents the vertices of a polygon. Translate the figure 3 units right and 2 units down. Express your answer as a matrix.

$$\begin{bmatrix} 4 & -1 & 5 \\ -4 & -6 & 2 \end{bmatrix}$$ ______________

Name ______________________ Class ______________ Date ______________

Practice 4-5

2 × 2 Matrices, Determinants, and Inverses

Find the matrix E^{-1} for each.

1. $E = \begin{bmatrix} 2 & -2 \\ -1 & 2 \end{bmatrix}$
2. $E = \begin{bmatrix} 1 & -1 \\ 1 & 1 \end{bmatrix}$
3. $E = \begin{bmatrix} 2 & -1 \\ 1 & 0 \end{bmatrix}$
4. $E = \begin{bmatrix} 2 & 3 \\ 1 & 1 \end{bmatrix}$
5. $E = \begin{bmatrix} 1 & 4 \\ 1 & 3 \end{bmatrix}$
6. $E = \begin{bmatrix} 4 & 7 \\ 3 & 5 \end{bmatrix}$

Find the inverse of each matrix, if it exists. If it does not exist, write *no inverse* and explain why not.

7. $\begin{bmatrix} 3 & 4 \\ -3 & 4 \end{bmatrix}$
8. $\begin{bmatrix} 3 & 4 \\ 3 & 4 \end{bmatrix}$
9. $\begin{bmatrix} 1 & 2 \\ 3 & 4 \end{bmatrix}$
10. $\begin{bmatrix} 30 & -4 \\ -25 & 3 \end{bmatrix}$

Solve each matrix equation.

11. $\begin{bmatrix} 1 & 2 \\ -1 & -2 \end{bmatrix} X = \begin{bmatrix} 2 \\ -2 \end{bmatrix}$
12. $\begin{bmatrix} 1 & 1 \\ 1 & -1 \end{bmatrix} X = \begin{bmatrix} 3 \\ -1 \end{bmatrix}$
13. $\begin{bmatrix} -2 & 3 \\ -4 & 5 \end{bmatrix} X = \begin{bmatrix} 6 \\ 8 \end{bmatrix}$

Evaluate the determinant of each matrix.

14. $\begin{bmatrix} -3 & 4 \\ 1 & -1 \end{bmatrix}$
15. $\begin{bmatrix} 3 & 9 \\ 3 & 2 \end{bmatrix}$
16. $\begin{bmatrix} 1 & -4 \\ 2 & 6 \end{bmatrix}$
17. $\begin{bmatrix} 4 & -3 \\ 1 & -8 \end{bmatrix}$
18. $\begin{bmatrix} 5 & 4 \\ 4 & 5 \end{bmatrix}$
19. $\begin{bmatrix} 1 & -12 \\ 3 & 0 \end{bmatrix}$

Determine whether the matrices are multiplicative inverses.

20. $\begin{bmatrix} 2 & 1 \\ 5 & 3 \end{bmatrix}, \begin{bmatrix} 3 & -1 \\ -5 & 2 \end{bmatrix}$
21. $\begin{bmatrix} 4 & 9 \\ 2 & 6 \end{bmatrix}, \begin{bmatrix} 1 & -\frac{3}{2} \\ -\frac{1}{3} & \frac{2}{3} \end{bmatrix}$
22. $\begin{bmatrix} 1 & 2 \\ 3 & 4 \end{bmatrix}, \begin{bmatrix} -2 & 1 \\ \frac{3}{2} & -\frac{1}{2} \end{bmatrix}$

Name ______________________ Class ______________ Date ______________

4-5 • Guided Problem Solving

GPS Exercise 42

Solve the matrix equation: $\begin{bmatrix} 4 & 7 \\ 1 & 2 \end{bmatrix} X + \begin{bmatrix} 2 & 7 \\ -3 & 4 \end{bmatrix} = \begin{bmatrix} 6 & 2 \\ -2 & 3 \end{bmatrix}$

Read and Understand

1. To get the equation in the form $AX = B$, what will you do first? ______________

2. To solve for X, by what should you multiply each side of the equation $AX = B$?

____

Plan and Solve

3. Write the equation in the form $AX = B$. ______________

4. To find A^{-1}, you must calculate the determinant of A. Find det A. ______________

5. Now find A^{-1}. ______________

6. Use the equation $X = A^{-1}B$ to solve for X. ______________

Look Back and Check

7. To check your answer, substitute X into the original equation and simplify. The result should be a true statement. ______________

Solve Another Problem

8. Solve the matrix equation: $\begin{bmatrix} 3 & -2 \\ 0 & 1 \end{bmatrix} X - \begin{bmatrix} 8 & 5 \\ -4 & 7 \end{bmatrix} = \begin{bmatrix} 3 & 2 \\ 6 & -9 \end{bmatrix}$ ______________

Name ______________________ Class ______________ Date ______________

Practice 4-6

3×3 Matrices, Determinants, and Inverses

Where necessary, use a graphing calculator. Find the inverse (A^{-1}) of each matrix, if it exists. If it does not exist, write *no inverse*.

1. $\begin{bmatrix} 1 & 2 & 0 \\ -2 & 0 & -3 \\ 3 & -1 & 5 \end{bmatrix}$ **2.** $\begin{bmatrix} 1 & 1 & 1 \\ 2 & 1 & 0 \\ 0 & 2 & 3 \end{bmatrix}$ **3.** $\begin{bmatrix} 2 & 4 & 3 \\ 0 & 5 & -1 \\ 1 & -1 & 2 \end{bmatrix}$ **4.** $\begin{bmatrix} 0 & 2 & 0 \\ 2 & 0 & 2 \\ 0 & 2 & 0 \end{bmatrix}$

5. $\begin{bmatrix} 4 & 5 & 6 \\ 0 & 1 & 2 \\ 8 & 9 & 5 \end{bmatrix}$ **6.** $\begin{bmatrix} 1 & -1 & 1 \\ 0 & 0 & 0 \\ 0 & 0 & 1 \end{bmatrix}$ **7.** $\begin{bmatrix} -1 & 0 & -1 \\ 0 & -2 & 0 \\ -2 & 0 & 3 \end{bmatrix}$ **8.** $\begin{bmatrix} -3 & -2 & -1 \\ 0 & 1 & 2 \\ 3 & 4 & -4 \end{bmatrix}$

Solve each equation for *X*.

9. $\begin{bmatrix} 1 & 0 & 0 \\ 0 & 1 & 0 \\ 0 & 0 & 1 \end{bmatrix} X = \begin{bmatrix} 4 \\ -5 \\ 3 \end{bmatrix}$ **10.** $\begin{bmatrix} 1 & 2 & 0 \\ -2 & 0 & -3 \\ 3 & -1 & 5 \end{bmatrix} X = \begin{bmatrix} -1 \\ 12 \\ -20 \end{bmatrix}$ **11.** $\begin{bmatrix} 0 & 0 & 1 \\ 0 & 0 & 1 \\ 1 & 1 & 1 \end{bmatrix} X = \begin{bmatrix} 3 \\ 4 \\ 3 \end{bmatrix}$

Evaluate the determinant of each matrix.

12. $\begin{bmatrix} -1 & 2 & -2 \\ 0 & 1 & 3 \\ 4 & 2 & -1 \end{bmatrix}$ **13.** $\begin{bmatrix} 2 & 1 & 2 \\ -1 & 0 & 5 \\ 0 & 4 & 1 \end{bmatrix}$ **14.** $\begin{bmatrix} 2 & 4 & 3 \\ -3 & 0 & -2 \\ -1 & 3 & 0 \end{bmatrix}$

15. $\begin{bmatrix} 2 & 6 & -1 \\ 1 & 0 & 0 \\ 1 & 3 & -2 \end{bmatrix}$ **16.** $\begin{bmatrix} -4 & 0 & 3 \\ 0 & -2 & 3 \\ -1 & 4 & -2 \end{bmatrix}$ **17.** $\begin{bmatrix} 7 & -1 & 3 \\ 1 & 2 & 6 \\ 4 & 1 & 3 \end{bmatrix}$

Determine whether the matrices are multiplicative inverses.

18. $A = \begin{bmatrix} -2 & 2 & 3 \\ 1 & -1 & 0 \\ 0 & 1 & 4 \end{bmatrix}, B = \begin{bmatrix} -\frac{4}{3} & -\frac{5}{3} & 1 \\ -\frac{4}{3} & -\frac{8}{3} & 1 \\ 1 & \frac{2}{3} & 0 \end{bmatrix}$ **19.** $A = \begin{bmatrix} 2 & -17 & 11 \\ -1 & 11 & -7 \\ 0 & 3 & -2 \end{bmatrix}, B = \begin{bmatrix} 1 & 1 & 2 \\ 2 & 4 & -3 \\ 3 & 6 & -5 \end{bmatrix}$

Name ____________________ Class ____________ Date ____________

4-6 • Guided Problem Solving

GPS Exercise 16

Evaluate the determinant of the matrix: $\begin{bmatrix} 0 & 2 & -3 \\ 1 & 2 & 4 \\ -2 & 0 & 1 \end{bmatrix}$

Read and Understand

1. Is the determinant of a matrix another matrix? ____________________

2. What type of matrix has a determinant? ____________________

Plan and Solve

3. The determinant of a 3×3 matrix $\begin{bmatrix} a_1 & b_1 & c_1 \\ a_2 & b_2 & c_2 \\ a_3 & b_3 & c_3 \end{bmatrix}$ is $\begin{vmatrix} a_1 & b_1 & c_1 \\ a_2 & b_2 & c_2 \\ a_3 & b_3 & c_3 \end{vmatrix}$. Using the definition of determinants, what is the formula to find the determinant? ____________________

4. Evaluate the determinant of the given matrix. ____________________

Look Back and Check

5. To check the reasonableness of your answer, use a graphing calculator to evaluate the determinant.

____

Solve Another Problem

6. Evaluate the determinant of the matrix: $\begin{bmatrix} 4 & -2 & 5 \\ 5 & 2 & 0 \\ 2 & 0 & 4 \end{bmatrix}$ ____________________

Name ______________________ Class ______________ Date ______________

Practice 4-7

Inverse Matrices and Systems

Solve each system.

1. $\begin{cases} x + y + z = 0.621 \\ 3x - 3y + 2z = -0.007 \\ 4x + 5y - 10z = 1.804 \end{cases}$

2. $\begin{cases} 3x + 4y + 2z = 0.5 \\ 8x - 5y - 5z = 8.1 \\ 5x + 5y + 5z = 1 \end{cases}$

3. $\begin{cases} 5x - 4y + 3z = -30 \\ 18x - 2y - 19z = 103 \\ 2.9x + 0.06y + 17z = -81.8 \end{cases}$

4. $\begin{cases} x + 3y = 5 \\ x + 4y = 6 \end{cases}$

5. $\begin{cases} 4x + y + z = 0 \\ 5x + 2y + 3z = -15 \\ 6x - 5y - 5z = 52 \end{cases}$

6. $\begin{cases} 2x + 3y = 12 \\ x + 2y = 7 \end{cases}$

7. $\begin{cases} x + y + z = 31 \\ x - y + z = 1 \\ x - 2y + 2z = 7 \end{cases}$

8. $\begin{cases} x - 3y = -1 \\ -6x + 19y = 6 \end{cases}$

9. $\begin{cases} x + y + z = 8.8 \\ 2x - 5y + 9z = -4.8 \\ 3x + 2y - 7z = -7.6 \end{cases}$

10. $\begin{cases} -3x + 4y = 2 \\ x - y = -1 \end{cases}$

11. $\begin{cases} 0.5x + 1.5y + z = 7 \\ 3x + 3y + 5z = 3 \\ 2x + y + 2z = -1 \end{cases}$

12. $\begin{cases} x + y + z = -2 \\ 1.5x + 3y + 0.5z = 8 \\ 9x + 4y + 5z = 4 \end{cases}$

Write each system as a matrix equation. Identify the coefficient matrix, the variable matrix, and the constant matrix.

13. $\begin{cases} 6x + 9y = 36 \\ 4x + 13y = 2 \end{cases}$

14. $\begin{cases} 3x - 4y = -9 \\ 7y = 24 \end{cases}$

15. $\begin{cases} 4x - z = 9 \\ 12x + 2y = 17 \\ x - y + 12z = 3 \end{cases}$

Write a system of equations. Solve the system using an inverse matrix.

16. In 1992, there were 548,303 doctors under the age of 65 in the United States. Of those under age 45, 25.53415% were women. Of those between the ages of 45 and 64, 11.67209% were women. There were 110,017 women doctors under the age of 65. How many doctors were under age 45?

17. An apartment building has 50 units. All are one- or two-bedroom units. One-bedroom units rent for $425/mo, and two-bedroom units rent for $550/mo. When all units are occupied, the total monthly income is $25,000. How many apartments of each type are there?

Solve each matrix equation. If the coefficient matrix has no inverse, write *no unique solution.*

18. $\begin{bmatrix} 0.25 & -0.75 \\ 3.5 & 2.25 \end{bmatrix}\begin{bmatrix} x \\ y \end{bmatrix} = \begin{bmatrix} 1.5 \\ -3.75 \end{bmatrix}$

19. $\begin{bmatrix} 3 & -9 \\ 1 & -6 \end{bmatrix}\begin{bmatrix} a \\ b \end{bmatrix} = \begin{bmatrix} 12 \\ 0 \end{bmatrix}$

20. $\begin{bmatrix} 3 & -6 \\ -1 & 2 \end{bmatrix}\begin{bmatrix} u \\ v \end{bmatrix} = \begin{bmatrix} 4 \\ 9 \end{bmatrix}$

21. $\begin{bmatrix} 12 & -3 \\ 16 & 4 \end{bmatrix}\begin{bmatrix} x \\ y \end{bmatrix} = \begin{bmatrix} 144 \\ -64 \end{bmatrix}$

Determine whether each system has a unique solution.

22. $\begin{cases} 4d + 2e = 4 \\ d + 3e = 6 \end{cases}$

23. $\begin{cases} 3x - 2y = 43 \\ 9x - 6y = 40 \end{cases}$

24. $\begin{cases} -y - z = 3 \\ x + 2y + 3z = 1 \\ 4x - 5y - 6z = -50 \end{cases}$

Name ____________________ Class ____________ Date ____________

4-7 • Guided Problem Solving

GPS Exercise 37

Geometry A rectangle is twice as long as it is wide. The perimeter is 840 ft. Find the dimensions of the rectangle.

Read and Understand

1. Let w be the width. What is the length l in terms of w? ____________

2. What is the perimeter? ____________

Plan and Solve

3. Use the equations $2w - l = 0$ and $2w + 2l = 840$ to write the system as a matrix equation of the form $AX = B$.

____

4. To find A^{-1}, you must calculate the determinant of A. Find det A. ____________

5. Now find A^{-1}. ____________

6. Use the equation $X = A^{-1}B$ to solve for X. ____________

7. What are the width and length of the rectangle? ____________

Look Back and Check

8. To check your answer, verify that the length is twice the width and the perimeter is 840.

____

Solve Another Problem

9. A piece of fabric 20 yards long is to be cut into two pieces. One piece will be 2 yards longer than twice the other piece. Find the lengths of the two pieces.

____

Name ______________________ Class ______________ Date ______________

Practice 4-8

Augmented Matrices and Systems

Write a system of equations for each augmented matrix.

1. $\left[\begin{array}{cc|c} 4 & -2 & 3 \\ 6 & 11 & 9 \end{array}\right]$

2. $\left[\begin{array}{cc|c} 12 & 6 & -4 \\ -1 & 0 & 2 \end{array}\right]$

3. $\left[\begin{array}{ccc|c} -2 & 9 & -2 & 20 \\ 3 & -1 & 2 & 29 \\ 6 & 5 & 5 & -4 \end{array}\right]$

Use Cramer's Rule to solve each system.

4. $\begin{cases} 2x + y = 1 \\ 3x - y = 9 \end{cases}$

5. $\begin{cases} 2x - y = 10 \\ x - 3y = 0 \end{cases}$

6. $\begin{cases} 3x + 5y = 1 \\ x + 6y = 9 \end{cases}$

7. $\begin{cases} x + y + z = 1.28 \\ x - 3y + 2z = 1.26 \\ 3x + 2y + 4z = 4.06 \end{cases}$

8. $\begin{cases} 2x + y - z = 0.75 \\ 3x + 3y + 2z = 4 \\ x - 5y + 3z = -2 \end{cases}$

9. $\begin{cases} x + y - z = 6 \\ 3x - 9y + z = -2 \\ 0.2x - 0.3y + 0.71z = -1.12 \end{cases}$

Write an augmented matrix for each system.

10. $\begin{cases} -3x + 4y = -8 \\ 2x - 8y = 16 \end{cases}$

11. $\begin{cases} u + 3v = -30 \\ 4u + v = 1 \end{cases}$

12. $\begin{cases} x - 4y + z = -9 \\ 3x + 2y - 3z = 9 \\ 4x + 2z = -4 \end{cases}$

Use an augmented matrix to solve each system.

13. $\begin{cases} x + y + z = 0 \\ 2x - 2y + 3z = 46 \\ 3x + 7y + 11z = 80 \end{cases}$

14. $\begin{cases} 3x + y + z = 18 \\ 4x + 2y + 3z = 12 \\ 7x + 8y + 5z = 9 \end{cases}$

15. $\begin{cases} 3x + 7y + 10z = 28 \\ 0.7x - 0.6y + 0.8z = 4.3 \\ 12x - 7y - 9z = 77 \end{cases}$

16. $\begin{cases} x - 2y - 3z = 2 \\ 2x + y - 5z = 30 \\ 7x - 11y - z = -48 \end{cases}$

17. $\begin{cases} x + y + z = 6.5 \\ 3x - 5y + 6z = -35 \\ 5x + 2y + 2z = 10 \end{cases}$

18. $\begin{cases} -x + y - z = -2 \\ 3x + 2y + 0.5z = -1.5 \\ 21x + 19y - 2z = -45 \end{cases}$

Use a graphing calculator to solve each system.

19. $\begin{cases} 4x - 2y + 3z = -2 \\ 2x + 2y + 5z = 16 \\ 8x - 5y - 2z = 4 \end{cases}$

20. $\begin{cases} x + y + z = -1 \\ 3x + 5y + 4z = 2 \\ 3x + 6y + 5z = 0 \end{cases}$

21. $\begin{cases} x + 3y - 2z = -3 \\ 2x + y - z = -6 \\ 3x - 2y + 4z = 8 \end{cases}$

Name ______________________ Class ______________ Date ______________

4-8 • Guided Problem Solving

GPS Exercise 32

Business A manufacturer sells pencils and erasers in packages. The price of a package of five erasers and two pencils is \$0.23. The price of a package of seven erasers and five pencils is \$0.41. Find the price of one eraser and one pencil.

Read and Understand

1. What can you buy for \$0.23? ______________________

2. What can you buy for \$0.41? ______________________

Plan and Solve

3. Let e be the price per eraser and p be the price per pencil. Write two equations representing the information in the problem. ______________________

4. Using Cramer's Rule, write and evaluate D. ______________________

5. Write and evaluate D_e. ______________________

6. Write and evaluate D_p. ______________________

7. Find e and p. What are the prices of one eraser and one pencil? ______________________

Look Back and Check

8. To check your answers, use the prices you found to calculate the cost of a package of five erasers and two pencils and the cost of a package of seven erasers and five pencils. Do they match the package prices given in the problem?

____

Solve Another Problem

9. A movie theater has adult tickets and child tickets. One family purchased 2 adult tickets and 3 child tickets for \$32.50, and another family purchased 3 adult tickets and 4 child tickets for \$46. Find the price of one adult ticket and one child ticket.

____

Name ______________________ Class ______________ Date ______________

4A: Graphic Organizer

For use before Lesson 4-1

Study Skill Be sure to read with pencil and paper in hand. Take notes and draw sketches as you look at the new chapter. Formulate questions you might have as you look at each section of the chapter.

Write your answers.

1. What is the chapter title? ______________________

2. Find the Table of Contents page for this chapter at the front of the book. Name four topics you will study in this chapter.

______________________ ______________________

______________________ ______________________

3. Complete the graphic organizer as you work through the chapter.
1. Write the title of the chapter in the center oval.
2. When you begin a lesson, write the name of the lesson in a rectangle.
3. When you complete that lesson, write a skill or key concept from that lesson in the outer oval linked to that rectangle.

Continue with steps 2 and 3 clockwise around the graphic organizer.

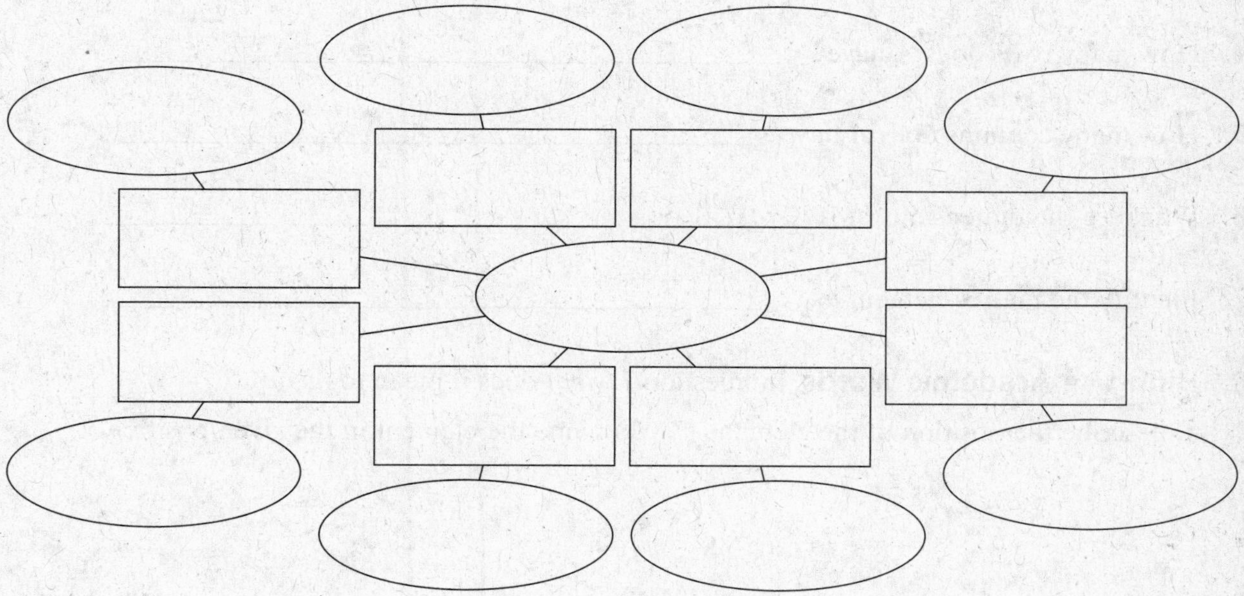

Vocabulary and Study Skills

Name ____________________ Class ____________ Date ____________

4B: Reading Comprehension

For use after Lesson 4-3

Study Skill When you have many assignments to complete, try beginning with the one you find most challenging, while you are fresh, and leaving the ones that require less effort to do later when you may be tired.

Use the given information to answer the questions about reading notation.

$$\begin{cases} x + y \leq 6 \\ 2x + y \leq 10 \\ x \geq 0,\ y \geq 0 \end{cases} \qquad \begin{bmatrix} 3 & -1 & 2 \\ 7 & 5 & -2 \end{bmatrix} = A$$

1. What does the single brace at the left of the inequalities mean?

____

____

2. How many inequalities are grouped together by the brace? ____________

3. How many elements are there in A? ____________

4. How many rows does A have? ____________

5. How many columns does A have? ____________

6. What are the dimensions of A? ____________

7. Identify the matrix element a_{12}. ____________

8. **High-Use Academic Words** In question 7, what does it mean to *identify*?

a. describe the position of the element **b.** name the element in the given position

Name ____________________ Class ____________ Date ____________

4C: Reading/Writing Math Symbols

For use after Lesson 4-6

Study Skill After you take notes on an assignment, go back and use a highlighter to mark key words or phrases that can serve as headings to separate topics. Then, when you review your notes later, you can quickly find the particular information you are seeking.

Vocabulary and Study Skills

All the symbols and numbers in mathematics are not written on the same line, nor are they all the same size. Some symbols are written above the baseline as superscripts, for example, s^2. Others are written below the line as subscripts, for example, (x_1, y_1). Occasionally there may be still another position for a number, a position that has a special meaning mathematically.

Fill in the blanks.

1. A number that is written smaller, to the right, and raised is called an ____________.

2. An exponent tells how many times the ____________ is used as a factor.

3. Write the symbol that means the element in the *m*th row and *n*th column of matrix *A*. ____________

For Exercises 4–7, write an expression for each phrase.

4. the cube of *a* ____________

5. the fourth root of *b* ____________

6. the cube root of $(a + b)$ ____________

7. the square of *a*, plus the square of *b* ____________

Name ______________________ Class ______________ Date ______________

4D: Visual Vocabulary Practice

For use after Lesson 4-6

Study Skill Use the Index to locate the page where a word was first introduced.

Concept List

dilation	matrix	matrix addition
matrix element	matrix equation	matrix multiplication
rotation	scalar multiplication	zero matrix

Write the concept that best describes each exercise. Choose from the concept list above.

1. $\begin{bmatrix} 4 & -1 \\ 0 & -8 \end{bmatrix}$

____

2. $\begin{bmatrix} 0 & 0 \\ 0 & 0 \end{bmatrix}$

____

3. $\begin{bmatrix} -4 & 0 \\ -6 & 5 \end{bmatrix} + \begin{bmatrix} 2 & 1 \\ 8 & 8 \end{bmatrix}$

____

4.

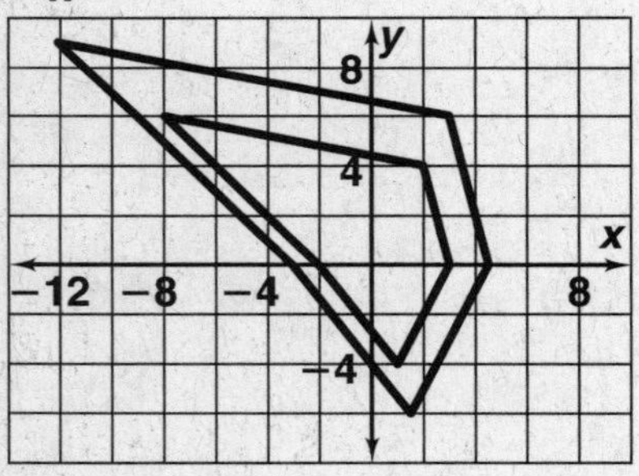

____

5. $\begin{bmatrix} 9 & 0 \\ 3 & 5 \end{bmatrix}\begin{bmatrix} 2 & 1 \\ 5 & 7 \end{bmatrix}$

____

6. $7\begin{bmatrix} -2 & 0 \\ -3 & 9 \end{bmatrix}$

____

7. a_{13} in matrix A

____

8. $X - \begin{bmatrix} 4 & 0 \\ 6 & 5 \end{bmatrix} = \begin{bmatrix} 2 & -1 \\ 5 & -2 \end{bmatrix}$

____

9.

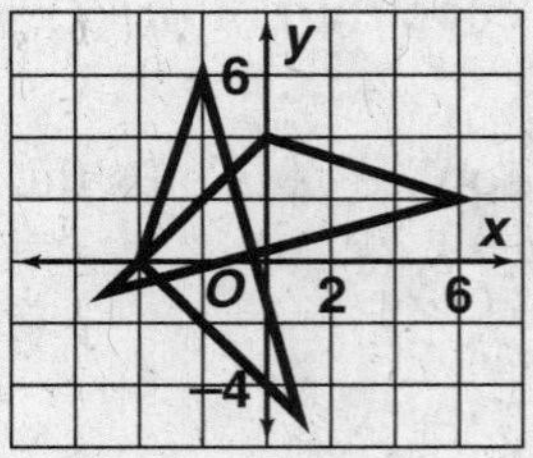

____

4E: Vocabulary Check

For use after Lesson 4-7

Study Skill Strengthen your vocabulary. Use these pages and add cues and summaries by applying the Cornell Notetaking style.

Write the definition for each word at the right. To check your work, fold the paper back along the dotted line to see the correct answers.

______________________________ Square matrix

____

____

______________________________ Determinant

____

____

______________________________ Coefficient matrix

____

____

______________________________ Variable matrix

____

____

______________________________ Constant matrix

____

____

Name ____________________ Class ____________ Date ____________

4E: Vocabulary Check (continued)

For use after Lesson 4-7

Write the vocabulary word for each definition. To check your work, fold the paper forward along the dotted line to see the correct answers.

A matrix with equal numbers of columns and rows. ____________________

A real number $ad - bc$ of a 2×2 matrix $\begin{bmatrix} a & b \\ c & d \end{bmatrix}$. ____________________

When representing a system of equations with a matrix equation, this is the matrix containing the coefficients of the system. ____________________

When representing a system of equations with a matrix equation, this is the matrix containing the variables of the system. ____________________

When representing a system of equations with a matrix equation, this is the matrix containing the constants of the system. ____________________

Name ______________________ Class ______________ Date ______________

4F: Vocabulary Review

For use with Chapter Review

Study Skill Whenever possible, try to draw a sketch or example of what the vocabulary word describes. It is often easier to remember the meaning of a word when you can associate the word with something visual.

Write an example of your own for each term or phrase below.

1. a matrix

2. a 3×2 matrix

3. element a_{23} for this matrix: $\begin{bmatrix} 3 & 4 & -1 & 2 \\ 10 & 7 & 9 & -5 \end{bmatrix}$

4. matrix addition

5. two equal matrices

6. a zero matrix

Name ____________________ Class ____________ Date ____________

Practice 5-1

Modeling Data with Quadratic Functions

Find a quadratic model for each set of values.

1. $(-1, 1), (1, 1), (3, 9)$

2. $(-4, 8), (-1, 5), (1, 13)$

3. $(-1, 10), (2, 4), (3, -6)$

4.

x	-1	0	2
$f(x)$	1	-1	7

5.

x	-4	0	1
$f(x)$	1	9	16

6.

x	-1	2	3
$f(x)$	12	3	4

Identify the vertex and the axis of symmetry of each parabola.

7.

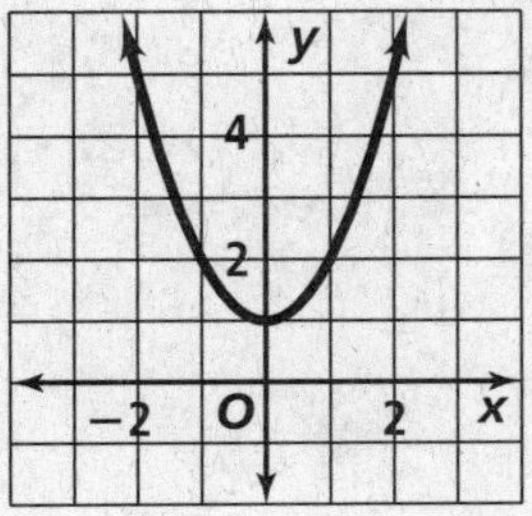

8.

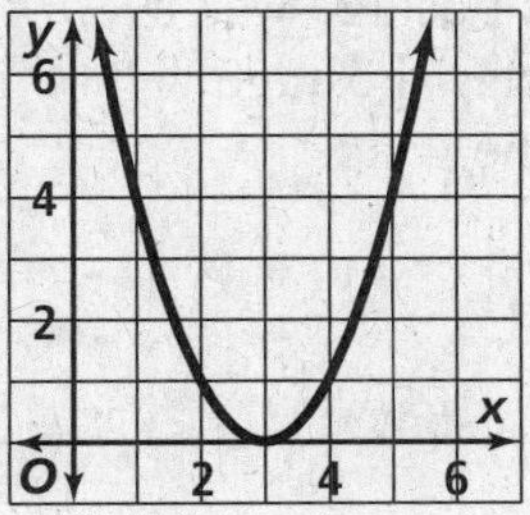

9.

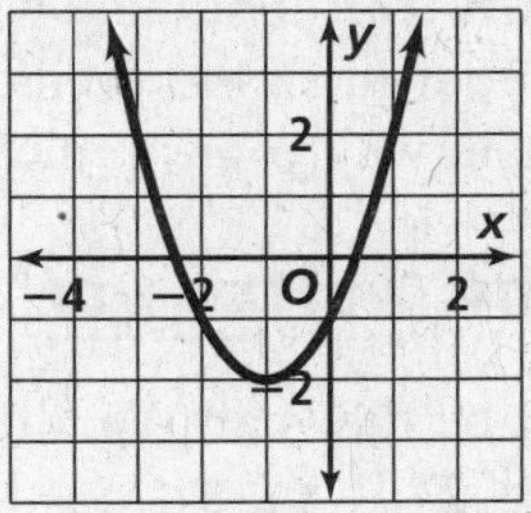

Determine whether each function is linear or quadratic. Identify the quadratic, linear, and constant terms.

10. $y = (x - 2)(x + 4)$

11. $y = 3x(x + 5)$

12. $y = 5x(x - 5) - 5x^2$

13. $f(x) = 7(x - 2) + 5(3x)$

14. $f(x) = 3x^2 - (4x - 8)$

15. $y = 3x(x - 1) - (3x + 7)$

16. $y = 3x^2 - 12$

17. $f(x) = (2x - 3)(x + 2)$

18. $y = 3x - 5$

For each parabola, identify points corresponding to *P* and *Q*.

19.

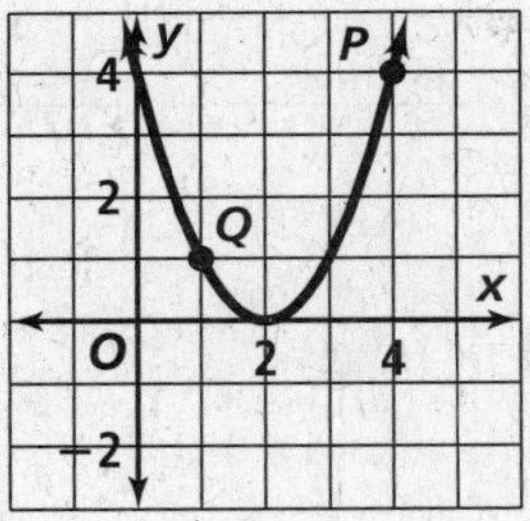

20.

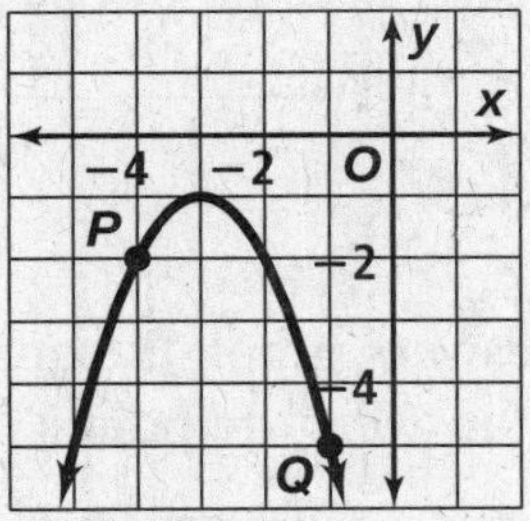

21.

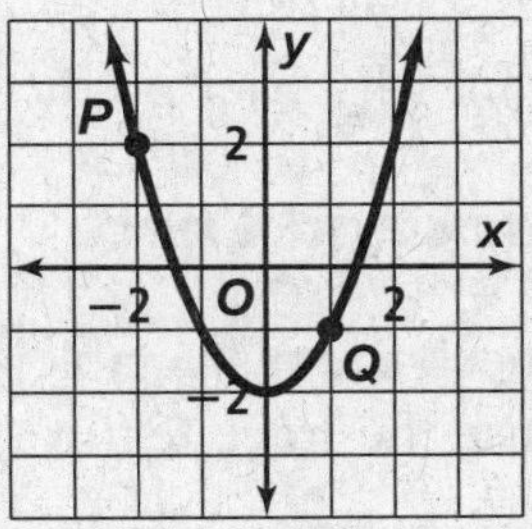

22. A toy rocket is shot upward from ground level. The table shows the height of the rocket at different times.

Time (seconds)	0	1	2	3	4
Height (feet)	0	256	480	672	832

a. Find a quadratic model for this data.

b. Use the model to estimate the height of the rocket after 1.5 seconds.

Name ____________________ Class ____________ Date ____________

5-1 • Guided Problem Solving

GPS Exercise 31

a. **Postal Rates** Find a quadratic model for the data. Use 1974 as year 0.

Year	1974	1978	1981	1983	1988	1995	2001	2002
Price (cents)	10	15	18	20	25	32	34	37

b. Describe a reasonable domain and range for your model. (Hint: This is a discrete, real situation.)
c. **Estimation** Estimate when first-class postage was 29¢.
d. Use your model to predict when first-class postage will be 50¢. Explain why your prediction may not be valid.

Read and Understand

1. Let x be the year. What does $x = 0$ represent? ____________
2. What data points will you use? ____________

Plan and Solve

3. Enter the data. Use the quadratic regression feature of a graphing calculator to model data with a quadratic function. ____________
4. Describe a reasonable domain and range for your model.

____

5. Use the function to estimate when first-class postage was 29¢. ____________
6. Use the function to predict when first-class postage will be 50¢. ____________
7. Explain why your prediction may not be valid. ____________

Look Back and Check

8. To check the reasonableness of your answers, graph the quadratic function and use the trace feature to see if your answers are points on the graph.

____

Solve Another Problem

9. a. **Ice Cream Sales** Find a quadratic model for the data. ____________

Temperature (°F)	10	39	57	60	71	80	88	96
Sales (number of cones)	1	75	124	157	170	172	185	190

b. Describe a reasonable domain and range for your model. ____________
c. **Estimation** Estimate when sales were 120 cones. ____________
d. Use your model to predict when sales will be 206 cones. Explain why your prediction may not be valid. ____________

Name ____________________ Class ____________________ Date ____________________

Practice 5-2

Properties of Parabolas

Graph each function. If $a > 0$, find the minimum value. If $a < 0$, find the maximum value.

1. $y = -x^2 + 2x + 3$

2. $y = 2x^2 + 4x - 3$

3. $y = -3x^2 + 4x$

4. $y = x^2 - 4x + 1$

5. $y = -x^2 - x + 1$

6. $y = 5x^2 - 3$

7. $y = \frac{1}{2}x^2 - x - 4$

8. $y = 5x^2 - 10x - 4$

9. $y = 3x^2 - 12x - 4$

Graph each function.

10. $y = x^2 + 3$

11. $y = x^2 - 4$

12. $y = x^2 + 2x + 1$

13. $y = 2x^2 - 1$

14. $y = -3x^2 + 12x - 8$

15. $y = \frac{1}{3}x^2 + 2x - 1$

16. Suppose you are tossing an apple up to a friend on a third-story balcony. After t seconds, the height of the apple in feet is given by $h = -16t^2 + 38.4t + 0.96$. Your friend catches the apple just as it reaches its highest point. How long does the apple take to reach your friend, and at what height above the ground does your friend catch it?

17. The barber's profit p each week depends on his charge c per haircut. It is modeled by the equation $p = -200c^2 + 2400c - 4700$. Sketch the graph of the equation. What price should he charge for the largest profit?

18. A skating rink manager finds that revenue R based on an hourly fee F for skating is represented by the function $R = -480F^2 + 3120F$. What hourly fee will produce maximum revenues?

19. The path of a baseball after it has been hit is modeled by the function $h = -0.0032d^2 + d + 3$, where h is the height in feet of the baseball and d is the distance in feet the baseball is from home plate. What is the maximum height reached by the baseball? How far is the baseball from home plate when it reaches it's maximum height?

20. A lighting fixture manufacturer has daily production costs of $C = 0.25n^2 - 10n + 800$, where C is the total daily cost in dollars and n is the number of light fixtures produced. How many fixtures should be produced to yield a minimum cost?

Graph each function. Label the vertex and the axis of symmetry.

21. $y = x^2 - 2x - 3$

22. $y = 2x - \frac{1}{4}x^2$

23. $y = x^2 + 6x + 7$

24. $y = x^2 + 2x - 6$

25. $y = x^2 - 8x$

26. $y = 2x^2 + 12x + 5$

27. $y = -3x^2 - 6x + 5$

28. $y = -2x^2 + 3$

29. $y = x^2 - 6$

Name ______________________ Class ______________ Date ______________

5-2 • Guided Problem Solving

GPS **Exercise 42**

Physics Suppose you throw a ball over a 10-ft fence. Barely clearing the fence, the ball reaches its highest point directly above the fence and lands 10 ft from the fence. Using the fence as the axis of symmetry, write a quadratic function that models the ball's height.

Read and Understand

1. How high is the fence? ______________________

2. How far from the fence does the ball land? ______________

Plan and Solve

3. Considering that the fence is the axis of symmetry, what are two points representing the ball's location? Let x = feet from fence and y = height. __________ __________

4. Given the model is of the form $y = ax^2 + c$, substitute the coordinates of your two points into the equation and solve for a and c.
a = __________ c = __________

5. What is the quadratic function that models the ball's height? ______________

Look Back and Check

6. To check the reasonableness of your model, use a graphing calculator to graph the equation. Verify that the two points you found in (3) are on the graph.

____

Solve Another Problem

7. **Physics** Suppose a homemade rocket is projected over a 40-ft tree. Barely clearing the tree, the rocket reaches its highest point directly above the tree and lands 100 ft from the tree. Using the tree as the axis of symmetry, write a quadratic function that models the rocket's height.

____

Name ______________________ Class ______________ Date ______________

Practice 5-3

Transforming Parabolas

Write the equation of the parabola in vertex form.

1.
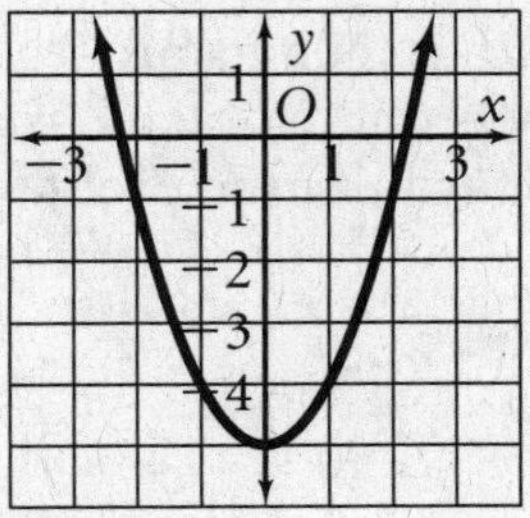

2.
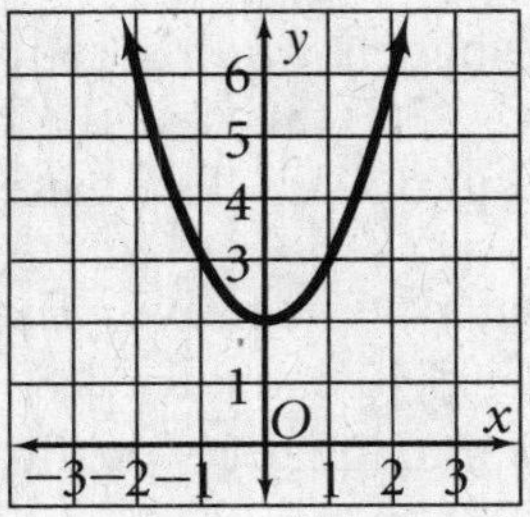

3.
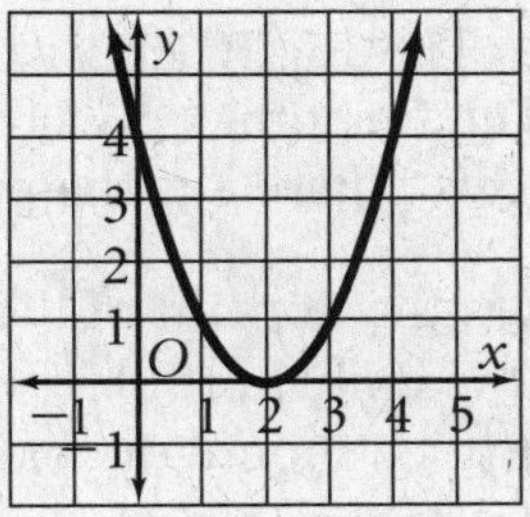

4.
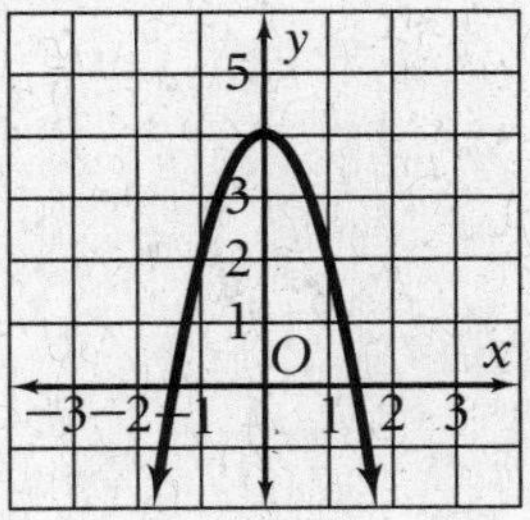

5.
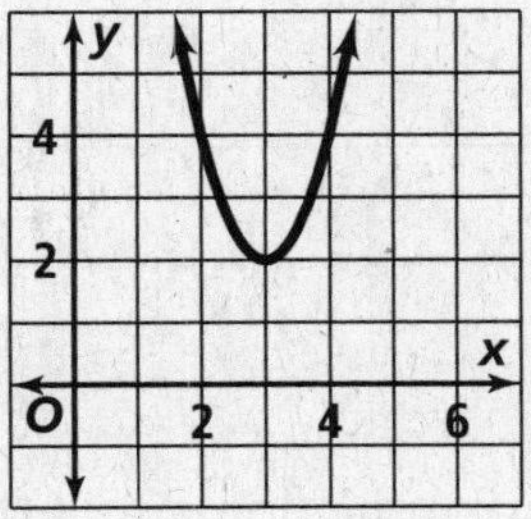

6.
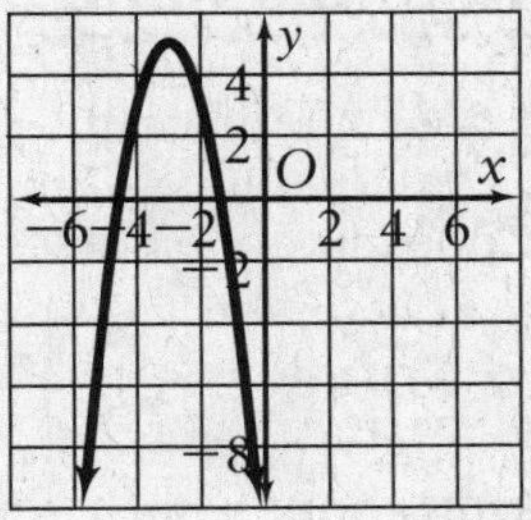

Graph each function.

7. $y = (x - 2)^2 - 3$
8. $y = (x - 6)^2 + 6$
9. $y = \frac{1}{2}(x - 1)^2 - 1$
10. $y = 8(x + 1)^2 - 2$
11. $y = -3(x - 1)^2 + 3$
12. $y = 3(x + 2)^2 + 4$
13. $y = \frac{1}{8}(x + 1)^2 - 1$
14. $y = \frac{1}{2}(x + 6)^2 - 2$
15. $y = 2(x + 3)^2 - 3$
16. $y = 4(x - 2)^2$
17. $y = -2(x + 1)^2 - 5$
18. $y = 4(x - 1)^2 - 2$

Write each function in vertex form.

19. $y = x^2 + 4x$
20. $y = 2x^2 + 8x + 3$
21. $y = -2x^2 - 8x$
22. $y = -x^2 + 4x + 4$
23. $y = x^2 - 4x - 4$
24. $y = x^2 + 5x$
25. $y = 2x^2 - 6$
26. $y = -3x^2 - x - 8$
27. $y = x^2 + 7x + 1$
28. $y = x^2 + 8x + 3$
29. $y = 2x^2 + 6x + 10$
30. $y = x^2 + 4x - 3$

Identify the vertex and the y-intercept of the graph of each function.

31. $y = 3(x - 2)^2 - 4$
32. $y = -\frac{1}{3}(x + 6)^2 + 5$
33. $y = 2(x - 1)^2 - 1$
34. $y = \frac{2}{3}(x + 4)^2 - 3$
35. $y = (x - 1)^2 + 2$
36. $y = -3(x - 2)^2 + 4$
37. $y = 4(x - 5)^2 + 1$
38. $y = -2(x + 5)^2 - 3$
39. $y = -5(x + 2)^2 + 5$

Name ____________________ Class ____________ Date ____________

5-3 • Guided Problem Solving

GPS Exercise 42

Business The Big Brick Bakery sells more bagels when it reduces its prices, but then its profit changes. The function $y = -1000(x - 0.55)^2 + 300$ models the bakery's daily profit in dollars from selling bagels, where x is the price of a bagel in dollars. The bakery wants to maximize the profit.

a. What is the domain of the function? Can x be negative? Explain.
b. Find the daily profit for selling bagels for \$.40 each; for \$.85 each.
c. What price should the bakery charge to maximize its profit from bagels?
d. What is the maximum profit?

Read and Understand

1. What does x represent? ____________________

2. What does y represent? ____________________

Plan and Solve

3. Thinking about what x represents, describe the domain of the function. ____________

4. Given your domain, explain why x can or cannot be negative. ____________

5. Let $x = 0.4$ in the function and solve for y to find the daily profit for selling bagels for \$.40 each. Repeat for \$.85 each. ____________

6. Find the vertex of the function. ____________________

7. Using the x-coordinate of the vertex, what price should the bakery charge to maximize its profit?

____

8. Using the y-coordinate of the vertex, what is the maximum profit? ____________

Look Back and Check

9. To check your answers, graph the function on a graphing calculator and verify your results.

____

Solve Another Problem

10. Movies The Cinemagic Theater keeps track of the price of tickets and the number of people in attendance. The function $y = -10(x - 6.5)^2 + 150$ models the theater attendance y where x is the price of a ticket in dollars. The theater wants to maximize attendance.

a. What is the domain of the function? Can x be negative? Explain. ____________

b. Find the attendance for a ticket price of \$5.50; of \$9.25. ____________

c. What price should the theater charge to maximize its attendance? ____________

d. What is the maximum attendance? ____________

Name ____________________ Class ____________ Date ____________

Practice 5-4

Factoring Quadratic Expression

Factor each expression completely.

1. $x^2 + 4x + 4$
2. $x^2 - 7x + 10$
3. $x^2 + 7x - 8$
4. $x^2 - 6x$
5. $2x^2 - 9x + 4$
6. $x^2 + 2x - 35$
7. $x^2 + 6x + 5$
8. $x^2 - 9$
9. $x^2 - 13x - 48$
10. $x^2 - 4$
11. $4x^2 + x$
12. $x^2 - 29x + 100$
13. $x^2 - x - 6$
14. $9x^2 - 1$
15. $3x^2 - 2x$
16. $x^2 - 64$
17. $x^2 - 25$
18. $x^2 - 81$
19. $x^2 - 36$
20. $x^2 - 100$
21. $x^2 - 1$
22. $4x^2 - 1$
23. $4x^2 - 36$
24. $9x^2 - 4$
25. $x^2 - 7x - 8$
26. $x^2 + 13x + 36$
27. $x^2 - 5x + 6$
28. $x^2 + 5x + 4$
29. $x^2 - 21x - 22$
30. $x^2 + 13x + 40$
31. $2x^2 - 5x - 3$
32. $x^2 + 10x - 11$
33. $x^2 - 14x + 24$
34. $5x^2 + 4x - 12$
35. $2x^2 - 5x - 7$
36. $2x^2 + 13x + 15$
37. $3x^2 - 7x - 6$
38. $3x^2 + 16x + 21$
39. $x^2 + 5x - 24$
40. $x^2 + 34x - 72$
41. $x^2 - 11x$
42. $3x^2 + 21x$
43. $x^2 + 8x + 12$
44. $x^2 - 10x + 24$
45. $x^2 + 7x - 30$
46. $x^2 - 2x - 168$
47. $x^2 - x - 72$
48. $4x^2 - 25$
49. $x^2 - 121$
50. $x^2 + 17x + 16$
51. $10x^2 - 17x + 3$
52. $4x^2 + 12x + 9$
53. $4x^2 - 4x - 15$
54. $9x^2 - 4$
55. $x^2 + 6x - 40$
56. $2x^2 - 8$
57. $x^2 + 18x + 77$
58. $2x^2 - 98$
59. $x^2 + 21x + 98$
60. $x^2 + 20x + 84$
61. $9x^2 + 30x + 16$
62. $8x^2 - 6x - 27$
63. $x^2 - 3x - 54$
64. $x^2 - 169$
65. $25x^2 - 9$
66. $7x^2 + 49$
67. $2x^2 - 10x - 28$
68. $x^2 + 8x + 12$
69. $x^2 - 2x - 35$
70. $x^2 + 2x - 63$
71. $20x^2 - 11x - 3$
72. $12x^2 + 4x - 5$
73. $4x^2 - 5x - 6$
74. $8x^2 + 22x - 21$
75. $3x^2 - 3x - 168$

Name ______________________ Class ______________ Date ______________

5-4 • Guided Problem Solving

GPS **Exercise 49**

Refer to the diagram. Suppose you cut a small square from a square sheet of cardboard. Write an expression for the remaining area. Factor the expression.

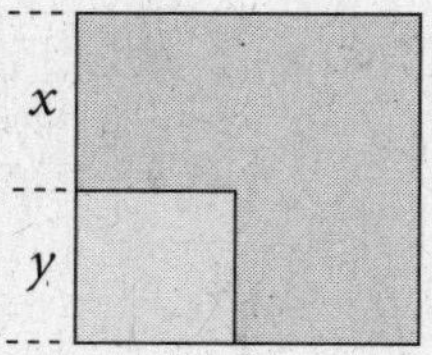

Read and Understand

1. What is the length of one side of the big square, in terms of x and y? ______________

2. What is the length of one side of the small square? ______________

Plan and Solve

3. Write an expression representing the area of the big square. ______________

4. Write an expression representing the area of the small square. ______________

5. Write an expression representing the area remaining after removing the small square from the big square. ______________

6. Factor the expression. ______________

Look Back and Check

7. To check your answer, substitute actual values into the expressions, for example $x = 4$ and $y = 2$, and verify that the calculated areas agree with the diagram.

____

Solve Another Problem

8. Suppose you cut four small squares, each with sides of y, from the square sheet of cardboard. Assume $x > y$. Write an expression for the remaining area. Factor the expression.

____

Name ____________________ Class ____________ Date ____________

Practice 5-5

Quadratic Equations

Solve each equation by factoring, by taking square roots, or by graphing. When necessary, round your answer to the nearest hundredth.

1. $x^2 - 18x - 40 = 0$

2. $16x^2 = 56x$

3. $5x^2 = 15x$

4. $x^2 - 6x - 7 = 0$

5. $x^2 - 49 = 0$

6. $x^2 + 2x + 1 = 0$

7. $x^2 - 1 = 0$

8. $x^2 - 3x - 4 = 0$

9. $x^2 + 9x^2 + 20 = 0$

10. $6x^2 + 9 = -55x$

11. $(x + 5)^2 = 36$

12. $2x^2 - 3x = 0$

13. $2x^2 + x - 10 = 0$

14. $-4x^2 + 3x = -1$

15. $5x^2 - 6x + 1 = 0$

16. $3x^2 + 1 = -4x$

17. $-2x^2 + 2 = -3x$

18. $6x^2 + 1 = 5x$

19. $-2x^2 - x + 1 = 0$

20. $3x^2 + 5x = 2$

21. $x^2 - 6x = -8$

22. $x^2 + 6 = -7x$

23. $6x^2 + 18x = 0$

24. $2x^2 + 5 = 11x$

25. $3x^2 - 7x + 2 = 0$

26. $2x^2 - 3x = -1$

27. $2x^2 - x = 6$

28. $x^2 - 144 = 0$

29. $4x^2 + 2 = 6x$

30. $5x^2 + 2 = -7x$

31. $7x^2 + 6x - 1 = 0$

32. $2x^2 - 6x = -4$

33. $11x^2 - 12x + 1 = 0$

34. $7x^2 + 1 = -8x$

35. $x^2 + 9 = -10x$

36. $(x - 2)^2 = 18$

37. $x^2 - 8x + 7 = 0$

38. $x^2 - 16 = 0$

39. $x^2 + 6x = -8$

40. $x^2 + 3 = 4x$

41. $2x^2 + 6 = -7x$

42. $6x^2 + 2 = 7x$

43. $(x + 7)^2 = \frac{49}{16}$

44. $9x^2 - 8x = 1$

45. $10x^2 + 7x + 1 = 0$

46. $4x^2 + 2 = -9x$

47. $3x^2 + 4 = 8x$

48. $4x^2 + 5 + 9x = 0$

49. $9x^2 + 10x = -1$

50. $2x^2 + 9x + 4 = 0$

51. $2x^2 + 6x = -4$

52. $11x^2 - 1 = -10x$

53. $4x^2 = 1$

54. $6x^2 = 12x$

55. $25x^2 - 9 = 0$

56. $2x^2 + 11x = 6$

57. $8x^2 - 6x + 1 = 0$

58. $x^2 + 11 = -12x$

59. $6x^2 + 2 = 13x$

60. $x^2 = 121$

61. $4x^2 - 11x = 3$

62. $8x^2 + 6x + 1 = 0$

63. $x^2 + 9x + 8 = 0$

64. $x^2 + 8x = -12$

65. $x^2 + 6x = 40$

66. $2x^2 = 8$

67. $x^2 = x + 6$

68. $x^2 + 2x - 6 = 0$

69. $x^2 - 12 = 0$

70. $3x^2 + 4x = 6$

71. $7x^2 - 105 = 0$

72. $16x^2 = 81$

73. $x^2 + 5x + 4 = 0$

74. $x^2 + 36 = -13x$

75. $x^2 + 6 = 5x$

Name ______________________ Class ______________ Date ______________

5-5 • Guided Problem Solving

GPS Exercise 35

Gardening Suppose you want to expand the garden shown here by planting a border of flowers. The border will be of the same width around the entire garden. The flowers you bought will fill an area of 276 ft^2. How wide should the border be?

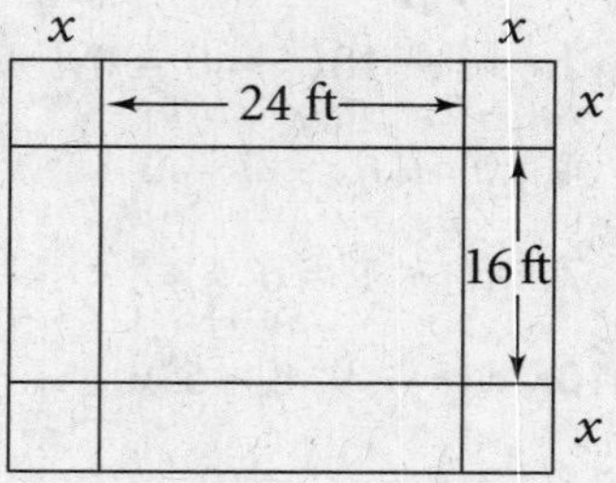

Read and Understand

1. What are the dimensions of the original garden? ______________________

2. What is the area of the original garden? ______________________

3. What is the area of the border that will be filled with flowers? ______________________

Plan and Solve

4. Write two expressions, one representing the length of the new garden and one representing the width of the new garden.
   length ______________ width ______________

5. Write an equation where the area of the border equals the area of the original garden subtracted from the area of the total garden. ______________

6. Solve the quadratic equation by writing in standard form and then using the Zero-Product Property. ______________

7. What is the width of the border? ______________

Look Back and Check

8. Check the reasonableness of your answer by substituting your width value for x. Using the picture of the garden as a reference, calculate the area of the border and verify that it is 276 ft^2.

____

Solve Another Problem

9. Suppose instead of the flower border, you decide to expand the garden shown above by laying a brick path. The path will be of the same width around the entire garden. The bricks you bought will fill an area of 500 ft^2. How wide should the path be?

____

Name ____________________ Class ____________ Date ____________

Practice 5-6

Complex Numbers

Find the first three output values for each function. Use $z = 0$ for the first input value.

1. $f(z) = z^2 + 2i$
2. $f(z) = z^2 + 1 + i$

Find the additive inverse of each of the following.

3. $2 + 3i$
4. $-4 + i$
5. $2i$
6. $-1 - i$
7. $-6i$
8. $5 - 2i$
9. $-2 + 3i$
10. 4

Find each absolute value.

11. $|-2i|$
12. $|5 + 12i|$
13. $|-1 - i|$
14. $|2 + i|$
15. $|4 + 3i|$
16. $|5 - 2i|$
17. $|3 - 2i|$
18. $|-2 + i|$
19. $|3 - 3i|$
20. $|3i|$
21. $|2i|$
22. $|4 + i|$
23. $|6 - 3i|$
24. $|-3 + i|$
25. $|4|$

Simplify each expression.

26. $\sqrt{40}$
27. $\sqrt{-88}$
28. $-\sqrt{-36}$
29. $(1 + 5i) + (1 - 5i)$
30. $(3 + 2i) - (3 + 2i)$
31. $4 - \sqrt{-25}$
32. $(2 + 6i) - (7 + 9i)$
33. $(1 + 5i)(1 - 5i)$
34. $(1 + 5i)(6 - 3i)$
35. $(5 - 6i)(6 - 2i)$
36. $(3 + 4i)(3 + 4i)$
37. $(2 + 3i)(2 - 3i)$
38. $(2 + 2i)(2 - 2i)$
39. $(-3 - 2i)(1 - 3i)$
40. $(3 + 3i) - (4 - 3i)$
41. $\sqrt{-48}$
42. $\sqrt{-300}$
43. $\sqrt{-75}$
44. $\sqrt{-16} + 2$
45. $(4 - i)(4 - i)$
46. $(4 + 2i)(1 - 7i)$
47. $(1 + 3i)(1 - 7i)$
48. $(2 + 4i)(-3 - 2i)$
49. $(11 - 12i)(11 + 12i)$
50. $(2 + 3i) + (-4 + 5i)$
51. $(5 + 14i) - (10 - 2i)$
52. $(5 + 12i)(5 - 12i)$
53. $(3 + 4i)(1 - 2i)$
54. $(6 + 2i)(1 - 2i)$
55. $(5 - 13i)(5 - 13i)$
56. $\sqrt{-44}$
57. $-\sqrt{-63}$
58. $\sqrt{-8}$
59. $(2 + 3i)(4 + 5i)$
60. $(5 + 4i) - (-1 - 2i)$
61. $(1 + 2i)(-1 - 2i)$
62. $(-1 + 4i)(1 - 2i)$
63. $(6 + 2i) + (1 - 2i)$
64. $(3 + 2i)(3 + 2i)$
65. $(-2 + 3i) + (4 + 5i)$
66. $(5 + 4i)(1 + 2i)$
67. $(-1 - 5i)(-1 + 5i)$

Solve each equation.

68. $x^2 + 80 = 0$
69. $5x^2 + 500 = 0$
70. $2x^2 + 40 = 0$
71. $3x^2 + 36 = 0$
72. $3x^2 + 75 = 0$
73. $2x^2 + 144 = 0$
74. $4x^2 + 1600 = 0$
75. $4x^2 + 1 = 0$
76. $2x^2 + 10 = 0$
77. $4x^2 + 100 = 0$
78. $x^2 + 9 = 0$
79. $9x^2 + 90 = 0$

Name ______________________ Class ______________ Date ______________

5-6 • Guided Problem Solving

GPS Exercise 56

Solve $(x + 3i)(x - 3i) = 34$.

Read and Understand

1. Can you multiply two complex numbers of the form $a + bi$ using the procedure for multiplying binomials? ______________
   If not, explain why not. ______________

2. What is the result of this multiplication? $(a + bi)(a - bi) =$ ______________

Plan and Solve

$$(x + 3i)(x - 3i) = 34$$

3. Multiply the binomials on the left side of the equation. ______________ $= 34$

4. Simplify the left side of the equation. ______________ $= 34$

5. Isolate x^2 on the left side of the equation. $x^2 =$ ________

6. Take the square root of both sides to solve for x. $x =$ ________

Look Back and Check

7. To check your answer, substitute your value of x into the original equation and simplify. A true statement should result. ______________

Solve Another Problem

8. Solve $(x - 5i)(x + 5i) = 74$.

____

Name ______________________ Class ______________ Date ______________

Practice 5-7

Completing the Square

1. $x^2 + 6x + \blacksquare$
2. $x^2 - 7x + \blacksquare$
3. $x^2 + 12x + \blacksquare$
4. $x^2 + 3x + \blacksquare$
5. $x^2 - 8x + \blacksquare$
6. $x^2 + 16x + \blacksquare$
7. $x^2 + 21x + \blacksquare$
8. $x^2 - 2x + \blacksquare$

Rewrite each equation in vertex form. Then find the vertex.

9. $y = x^2 + 4x - 6$
10. $y = x^2 - 6x + 6$
11. $y = 4x^2 + 8x - 4$
12. $y = 4x^2 + 4x + 1$
13. $y = 2x^2 + 4x - 5$
14. $y = -3x^2 - 4x - 1$
15. $y = -3x^2 + 3x - 1$
16. $y = x^2 + 2x + 1$
17. $y = -5x^2 + 10x + 1$
18. $y = -2x^2 + 4x + 3$
19. $y = x^2 + 5x + \frac{5}{4}$
20. $y = -2x^2 + 10x - 11$
21. $y = 6x^2 - 12x + 1$
22. $y = -2x^2 + 8x - 9$
23. $y = 3x^2 + 9x + 6$

Solve each quadratic equation by completing the square.

24. $x^2 + 12x + 4 = 0$
25. $x^2 - x - 5 = 0$
26. $3x^2 = -12x - 3$
27. $x^2 - x - 1 = 0$
28. $4x^2 - 8x + 1 = 0$
29. $5x^2 = 8x - 6$
30. $2x^2 - 4x - 3 = 0$
31. $x^2 + 11x = 0$
32. $x^2 = 5x + 14$
33. $2x^2 + x - 1 = 0$
34. $2x^2 + 6x - 7 = 0$
35. $2x^2 = -8x + 45$
36. $x^2 = -3x - 3$
37. $4x^2 = -2x + 1$
38. $3x^2 = -6x + 9$
39. $x^2 = 7x + 12$
40. $x^2 = 3x + 7$
41. $3x^2 = 6x - 9$
42. $x^2 = -3x + 2$
43. $x^2 = -7x - 1$
44. $4x^2 = -3x + 2$
45. $2x^2 = 4x - 5$
46. $2x^2 = 5x + 5$
47. $2x^2 = 6x + 5$
48. $x^2 = 3x$
49. $x^2 = 8x$
50. $4x^2 = -2x - 3$
51. $2x^2 = -2x + 5$
52. $2x^2 = -5x - 5$
53. $3x^2 = -5x + 1$
54. $2x^2 = 2x + 4$
55. $3x^2 = 7x + 8$
56. $2x^2 = -6x + 4$
57. $x^2 = -7x - 9$
58. $2x^2 = 5x$
59. $3x^2 = -42x$
60. $2x^2 = -4x + 5$
61. $4x^2 = -x + 5$
62. $3x^2 = -3x + 1$
63. $x^2 = 3x + 4$
64. $2x^2 = 2x + 8$
65. $3x^2 = x + 4$

Solve each equation.

66. $x^2 + 2x + 1 = 9$
67. $3x^2 - 18x + 27 = 125$
68. $x^2 - 4x + 4 = 5$
69. $x^2 + 3x + \frac{9}{4} = \frac{13}{4}$
70. $x^2 + 3x + \frac{9}{4} = -\frac{15}{4}$
71. $x^2 + 3x + \frac{9}{4} = \frac{41}{4}$
72. $x^2 + 7x + \frac{49}{4} = \frac{53}{4}$
73. $x^2 + 3x + \frac{9}{4} = \frac{29}{4}$
74. $x^2 - 6x + 9 = 7$

Name ______ Class ______ Date ______

5-7 • Guided Problem Solving

GPS Exercise 50

Architecture The shape of the Gateway Arch in St. Louis, Missouri, is a catenary curve, which closely resembles a parabola. The function $y = -\frac{2}{315}x^2 + 4x$ models the shape of the arch, where y is the height in feet and x is the horizontal distance from the base of the left side of the arch in feet.

a. Graph the function and find its vertex.
b. Describe a reasonable domain and range for the function. Explain.
c. According to the model, what is the maximum height of the arch?
d. What is the width of the arch at the base?

Read and Understand

1. What does y represent? ______

2. What does x represent? ______

Plan and Solve

3. Graph the function.

4. What is the vertex? ______

5. Thinking about what x and y represent, describe the domain and range for the function. Explain.

______

6. By using the graph and the coordinates of the vertex, what is the maximum height of the arch?

______

7. What is the width of the arch at the base, considering that it is double the distance from the left side of the arch to the x-coordinate of the vertex?

______

Look Back and Check

8. Check the reasonableness of your answers by rewriting the function in vertex form and verify your answers. ______

Solve Another Problem

9. The function $y = -\frac{1}{200}x^2 + x$ models the shape of another arch.

a. Graph the function and find its vertex. ______

b. According to the model, what is the maximum height of the arch? ______

c. What is the width of the arch at the base? ______

Name ____________________ Class ____________________ Date ____________________

Practice 5-8

The Quadratic Formula

Evaluate the discriminant of each equation. Tell how many solutions each equation has and whether the solutions are real or imaginary.

1. $y = x^2 + 10x - 25$

2. $y = x^2 + 10x + 10$

3. $y = 9x^2 - 24x$

4. $y = 4x^2 - 4x + 1$

5. $y = 4x^2 - 5x + 1$

6. $y = 4x^2 - 3x + 1$

7. $y = x^2 + 3x + 4$

8. $y = x^2 + 7x - 3$

9. $y = -2x^2 + 3x - 5$

10. $y = x^2 - 5x + 4$

11. $y = x^2 + 12x + 36$

12. $y = x^2 + 2x + 3$

13. $y = 2x^2 - 13x - 7$

14. $y = -5x^2 + 6x - 4$

15. $y = -4x^2 - 4x - 1$

Solve each equation using the Quadratic Formula.

16. $x^2 + 6x + 9 = 0$

17. $x^2 - 15x + 56 = 0$

18. $3x^2 - 5x + 2 = 0$

19. $2x^2 + 3x + 5 = 0$

20. $10x^2 - 23x + 12 = 0$

21. $4x^2 + x - 5 = 0$

22. $x^2 + 8x + 15 = 0$

23. $3x^2 + 2x + 1 = 0$

24. $4x^2 + x + 5 = 0$

25. $x^2 - 4x - 12 = 0$

26. $x^2 = 3x + 2$

27. $2x^2 - 5x + 2 = 0$

28. $x^2 + 6x - 4 = 0$

29. $x^2 = 2x - 5$

30. $3x^2 + 7 = -6x$

31. $2x^2 + 6x + 3 = 0$

32. $x^2 = -18x - 80$

33. $x^2 + 9x - 13 = 0$

34. $x^2 - 8x + 25 = 0$

35. $4x^2 + 13x = 12$

36. $3x^2 - 5x = -12$

37. $3x^2 + 4x + 5 = 0$

38. $2x^2 = 3x - 7$

39. $5x^2 + 2x + 1 = 0$

40. $5x^2 + x + 3 = 0$

41. $5x^2 + x = 3$

42. $5x^2 - 2x + 7 = 0$

43. $x^2 - 2x + 3 = 0$

44. $-2x^2 + 3x = 24$

45. $4x^2 = 5x - 6$

46. $x^2 + 6x + 5 = 0$

47. $x^2 - 6x = -8$

48. $x^2 - 6x = -6$

Solve.

49. A model of the daily profits p of a gas station based on the price per gallon g is $p = -15{,}000g^2 + 34{,}500g - 16{,}800$. Use the discriminant to find whether the station can profit \$4000 per day. Explain.

Solve each equation using the Quadratic Formula. Find the exact solutions. Then approximate any radical solutions. Round to the nearest hundredth.

50. $x^2 - 2x - 3 = 0$

51. $x^2 + 5x + 4 = 0$

52. $x^2 - 2x - 8 = 0$

53. $7x^2 - 12x + 3 = 0$

54. $5x^2 + 5x - 1 = 0$

55. $4x^2 + 5x + 1 = 0$

56. $6x^2 + 5x - 4 = 0$

57. $x^2 + x = 6$

58. $x^2 - 13x = 48$

59. $2x^2 + 5x = 0$

60. $x^2 + 3x - 3 = 0$

61. $x^2 - 4x + 1 = 0$

62. $9x^2 - 6x - 7 = 0$

63. $x^2 - 35 = 2x$

64. $x^2 + 7x + 10 = 0$

Name ______________________ Class ______________ Date ______________

5-8 • Guided Problem Solving

GPS Exercise 56

Air Pollution The function $y = 0.0721x^2 - 2.8867x + 117.061$ models the emissions of carbon monoxide in the United States since 1985. In the function, y represents the amount of carbon monoxide released in a year in millions of tons, and $x = 0$ represents the year 1985.

a. How can you use a graph to estimate the year in which less than 100 million tons of carbon monoxide were released into the air?

b. How can you use the Quadratic Formula to estimate the year in which less than 100 million tons of carbon monoxide were released into the air?

c. Which method do you prefer? Explain why.

Read and Understand

1. What does $x = 0$ represent? ______________________

2. What does y represent? ______________________

Plan and Solve

3. Graph $y = 100$ and $y = 0.0721x^2 - 2.8867x + 117.061$ on the same set of axes.

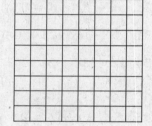

4. What part of the graph represents when less than 100 million tons of carbon monoxide were released? ______________

5. Write an inequality that estimates the year in which less than 100 million tons of carbon monoxide were released into the air. ______________

6. How can you use the Quadratic Formula to solve the inequality? ______________

7. Which method do you prefer? Explain why. ______________

Look Back and Check

8. Check that your methods result in the same answers by solving each and comparing. ______________

Solve Another Problem

9. A manufacturing company uses the function $y = -2x^2 + 100x + 4000$ to model the profit y for x units sold.

a. How can you use a graph to estimate the number of units for which the profit is greater than \$4500? ______________

b. How can you use the Quadratic Formula to estimate the number of units for which the profit is greater than \$4500? ______________

Name ______________________ Class ______________ Date ______________

5A: Graphic Organizer

For use before Lesson 5-1

Study Skill What do the pages before the first page of Chapter 5 tell you? Briefly look over the titles, introductions, objectives and the first few sentences of the chapter. When you read the material, read it as if it were very important. Reading takes a great deal of effort, so pay attention to what you are reading. Take a few notes on what you expect to learn in the chapter based on what you just read.

Write your answers.

1. What is the chapter title? ______________________

2. Find the Table of Contents page for this chapter at the front of the book. Name four topics you will study in this chapter.

______________________ ______________________

______________________ ______________________

3. Complete the graphic organizer as you work through the chapter.
1. Write the title of the chapter in the center oval.
2. When you begin a lesson, write the name of the lesson in a rectangle.
3. When you complete that lesson, write a skill or key concept from that lesson in the outer oval linked to that rectangle.
Continue with steps 2 and 3 clockwise around the graphic organizer.

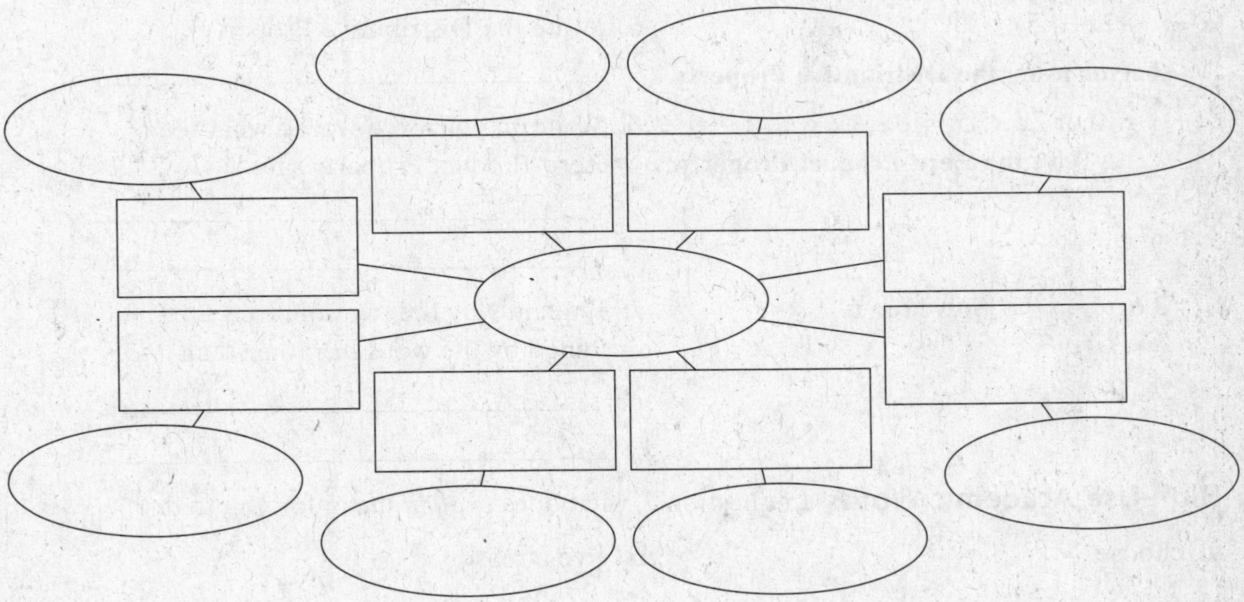

5B: Reading Comprehension

For use after Lesson 5-6

Study Skill Don't rely on your memory when you can take notes and write down instructions. Keep a notebook where you write daily assignments, including special directions, and check work off as you complete it.

Read the steps and notes in the example at the left, and answer the questions at the right.

Solving by Factoring

- Solve $2x^2 - 11x = -15$.

1. Read the title of the example. What process are you going to use to solve this equation?

____

- $2x^2 - 11x + 15 = 0$ **Write in standard form.**

2. What is the standard form for a quadratic equation?

____

- $2x^2 - 5x - 6x + 15 = 0$ **Rewrite the *bx* term.**

3. Why were -5 and -6 chosen in rewriting -11 as a sum?

____

- $x(2x - 5) - 3(2x - 5) = 0$ **Find common factors.**

4. What factor is common to both terms of $x(2x - 5) - 3(2x - 5)$?

____

- $(x - 3)(2x - 5) = 0$ **Factor using the Distributive Property.**

5. Write the Distributive Property:

____

- $x - 3 = 0$ or $2x - 5 = 0$ **Use the Zero-Product Property.**

6. Write, in your own words, what the Zero-Product Property says.

____

____

- $x = 3$ or $x = \frac{5}{2}$ **Solve for *x*.**

7. Explain why the two solutions are joined by the word *or* rather than *and*.

____

____

8. **High-Use Academic Words** In question 7, what does *explain* mean for you to do?

   a. choose

   b. give a reason

5C: Reading/Writing Math Symbols

For use after Lesson 5-3

Study Skill As you take notes, think about how the topic for today relates to a previous topic, or how this content may lead into a future topic. Most material is easier to understand and remember if you connect it to something you already know or want to know.

The position and order of numbers and symbols in mathematics has meaning, as well as the symbols themselves. Answer each of the following questions about the position of numbers.

1. Explain why the graph of the ordered pair (2, 3) is not the same as the graph of the ordered pair (3, 2). Graph both points as part of your explanation.

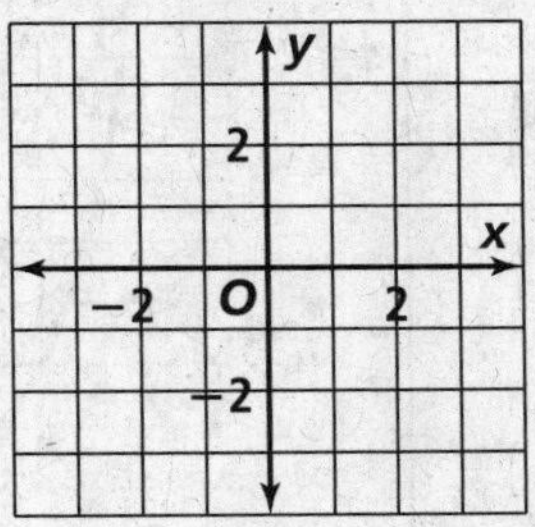

2. Write a 2 × 3 matrix and compare it to a 3 × 2 matrix to explain the order in which matrix dimensions are written.

3. Compare the value and meaning of 12 ÷ 3 with that of 3 ÷ 12.

4. Compare the value and meaning of 15 − 5 with that of 5 − 15.

5. Does the order of two expressions make any difference when you write them with an equal sign between them, as in 4 = 3 + 1 and 3 + 1 = 4?

Name ______________________ Class ______________ Date ______________

5D: Visual Vocabulary Practice

For use after Lesson 5-8

Study Skills When you come across something you don't understand, view it as an opportunity to increase your brain power.

Concept List

absolute value of a complex number	complex number plane	difference of two squares
standard form of a quadratic equation	parabola	perfect square trinomial
vertex form of a quadratic function	imaginary number	Quadratic Formula

Write the concept that best describes each exercise. Choose from the concept list above.

1. $\lvert a + bi \rvert$ ______________	**2.** 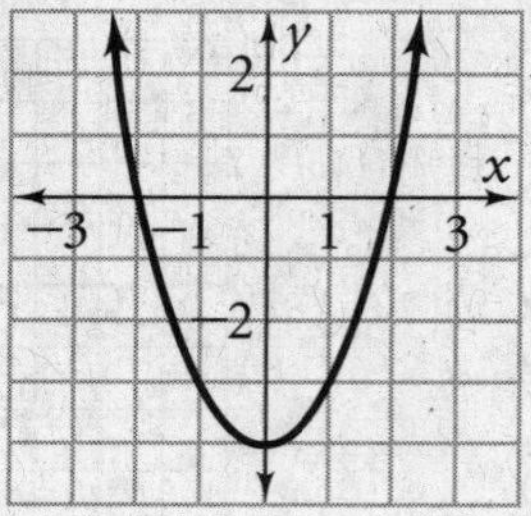 ______________	**3.** $a^2 - b^2$ ______________
4. $a + bi$ ______________	**5.** $x = \dfrac{-b \pm \sqrt{b^2 - 4ac}}{2a}$ ______________	**6.** $y = a(x - h)^2 + k$ ______________
7. $ax^2 + bx + c = 0$ ______________	**8.** 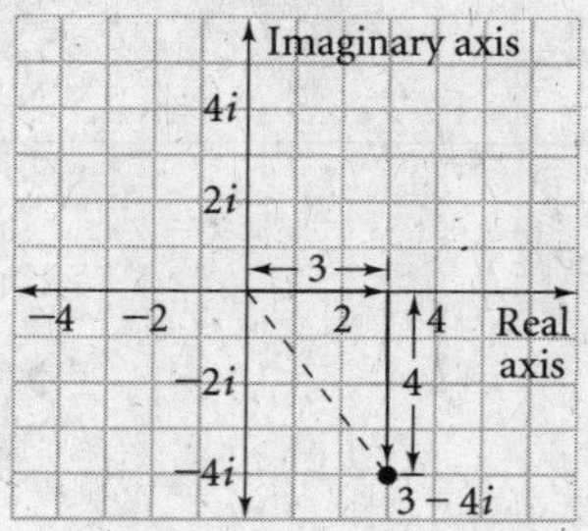 ______________	**9.** $a^2 + 2ab + b^2$ ______________

Name ______________________ Class ______________ Date ______________

5E: Vocabulary Check

For use after Lesson 5-4

Study Skill Strengthen your vocabulary. Use these pages and add cues and summaries by applying the Cornell Notetaking style.

Write the definition for each word at the right. To check your work, fold the paper back along the dotted line to see the correct answers.

______________________ ______________________ ______________________	Quadratic function
______________________ ______________________ ______________________	Axis of symmetry
______________________ ______________________ ______________________	Vertex of a parabola
______________________ ______________________ ______________________	Factoring
______________________ ______________________ ______________________	Greatest common factor (GCF) of an expression

Vocabulary and Study Skills

Name ______________________ Class ______________ Date ______________

5E: Vocabulary Check (continued)

For use after Lesson 5-4

Write the vocabulary word for each definition. To check your work, fold the paper forward along the dotted line to see the correct answers.

A function that can be written in the form $f(x) = ax^2 + bx + c$, where $a \neq 0$. Its graph is a parabola. ______________________

The line that divides a parabola into two parts that are mirror images. ______________________

The point at which the parabola intersects the axis of symmetry. ______________________

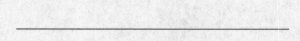

Rewriting an expression as the product of its factors. ______________________

The common factor of each term of the expression that has the greatest coefficient and the greatest exponent. ______________________

Name ______________________ Class ______________ Date ______________

5F: Vocabulary Review Puzzle

For use with Chapter Review

Study Skill Mathematics has its own vocabulary. Many new terms are contained within a chapter. Words that have been familiar may appear with unexpected new meanings. Learn the new terms at the time they are introduced.

Use the words below to complete the crossword puzzle.

parabola	standard	trinomial
vertex	binomial	factor

ACROSS

1. maximum or minimum point of a parabola

4. what you square to get a perfect square trinomial

6. one of the multipliers of a product

DOWN

2. polynomial with three terms

3. a quadratic equation in this form $ax^2 + bx + c = 0$

5. graph of a quadratic function

Name____________________ Class____________ Date____________

Practice 6-1

Polynomial Functions

Find a cubic model for each function. Then use your model to estimate the value of y when $x = 7$.

1.

x	0	2	4	6	8	10
y	25	21	20	23	19	17

2.

x	0	2	4	6	8	10
y	3.1	4.2	4.3	4.4	5.1	6.7

Write each polynomial in standard form. Then classify it by degree and by number of terms.

3. $4x + x + 2$

4. $-3 + 3x - 3x$

5. $6x^4 - 1$

6. $1 - 2s + 5s^4$

7. $5m^2 - 3m^2$

8. $x^2 + 3x - 4x^3$

9. $-1 + 2x^2$

10. $5m^2 - 3m^3$

11. $5x - 7x^2$

12. $2 + 3x^3 - 2$

13. $6 - 2x^3 - 4 + x^3$

14. $6x - 7x$

15. $a^3(a^2 + a + 1)$

16. $x(x + 5) - 5(x + 5)$

17. $p(p - 5) + 6$

18. $(3c^2)^2$

19. $-(3 - b)$

20. $6(2x - 1)$

21. $\frac{2}{3} + s^2$

22. $\frac{2x^4 + 4x - 5}{4}$

23. $\frac{3 - z^5}{3}$

24. The lengths of the sides of a triangle are $x + 4$ units, x units, and $x + 1$ units. Express the perimeter of the triangle as a polynomial in standard form.

25. Find a cubic function to model the data below. (Hint: Use the number of years past 1940 for x.) Then use the function to estimate the average monthly Social Security Benefit for a retired worker in 2010.

Average Monthly Social Security Benefits, 1940–2003

Year	1940	1950	1960	1970	1980	1990	2000	2003
Amount (in dollars)	22.71	29.03	81.73	123.82	321.10	550.50	844.60	922.10

Source: *www.infoplease.com*

26. Find a cubic function to model the data below. (Hint: Use x to represent the gestation period.) Then use the function to estimate the longevity of an animal with a gestation period of 151 days.

Gestation and Longevity of Certain Animals

Animal	Rat	Squirrel	Pig	Cow	Elephant
Gestation (in days)	21	44	115	280	624
Longevity (in years)	3	9	10	12	40

Source: *www.infoplease.com*

Name ______________________ Class ______________ Date ______________

6-1 • Guided Problem Solving

GPS Exercise 31

The diagram at the right shows a cologne bottle that consists of a cylindrical base and a hemispherical top.

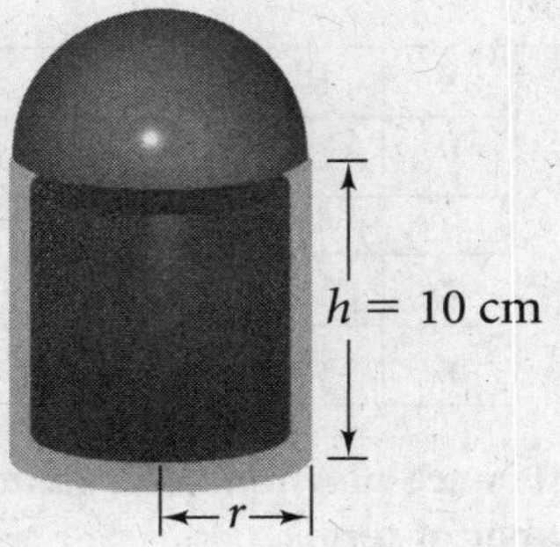

a. Write an expression for the cylinder's volume.
b. Write an expression for the volume of the hemispherical top.
c. Write a polynomial to represent the total volume.

Read and Understand

1. What is the height of the cylindrical base? ______________

2. How is the radius of the cylindrical base related to the radius of the hemispherical top?

____

Plan and Solve

3. What is the formula for the volume of a cylinder with height h and radius r? ______________

4. What is an expression for the volume of the cylindrical base of the bottle? ______________

5. What is the formula for the volume of a sphere with radius r? ______________

6. What is an expression for the volume of the hemispherical top of the bottle? ______________

7. Write a polynomial to represent the total volume. ______________

Look Back and Check

8. Check that your answer is reasonable. Choose a few values for the radius r. Use these specific values to find the volume of cylindrical base and of hemispherical top. Then evaluate the polynomial at these same values of r. The results should be the same. ______________

Solve Another Problem

9. A Norman window is shaped like a rectangle, except the top is a semicircle. To apply a scratch-resistant coating, designers need to know the area of the window. The rectangular portion of the window has a height of 24 inches. The circular portion has a radius of r inches. Write a polynomial to represent the total area of the window.

____

Name ____________________ Class ____________ Date ____________

Practice 6-2

Polynomials and Linear Factors

For each function, determine the zeros. State the multiplicity of any multiple zeros.

1. $y = (x - 5)^3$
2. $y = x(x - 8)^2$
3. $y = (x - 2)(x + 7)^3$
4. $f(x) = x^4 - 8x^3 + 16x^2$
5. $f(x) = 9x^3 - 81x$
6. $y = (2x + 5)(x - 3)^2$

Write each function in standard form.

7. $y = (x - 5)(x + 5)(2x - 1)$
8. $y = (2x + 1)(x - 3)(5 - x)$
9. A rectangular box is 24 in. long, 12 in. wide, and 18 in. high. If each dimension is increased by x in., write a polynomial function in standard form modeling the volume V of the box.

Write a polynomial function in standard form with the given zeros.

10. $-1, 3, 4$
11. $1, 1, 2$
12. $-3, 0, 0, 5$
13. -2 multiplicity 3

Write each expression as a polynomial in standard form.

14. $x(x - 1)^2$
15. $(x + 3)^2(x + 1)$
16. $(x + 4)(2x - 5)(x + 5)^2$

Write each function in factored form. Check by multiplication.

17. $y = 2x^3 + 10x^2 + 12x$
18. $y = x^4 - x^3 - 6x^2$
19. $y = -3x^3 + 18x^2 - 27x$

Find the zeros of each function. Then graph the function.

20. $y = (x + 1)(x - 1)(x - 3)$
21. $y = (x + 2)(x - 3)$
22. $y = x(x - 2)(x + 5)$

Find the relative maximum, relative minimum, and zeros of each function.

23. $f(x) = x^3 - 7x^2 + 10x$
24. $f(x) = x^3 - x^2 - 9x + 9$

Write each polynomial in factored form. Check by multiplication.

25. $x^3 - 6x^2 - 16x$
26. $x^3 + 7x^2 + 12x$
27. $x^3 - 8x^2 + 15x$
28. A rectangular box has a square base. The combined length of a side of the square base, and the height is 20 in. Let x be the length of a side of the base of the box.

    a. Write a polynomial function in factored form modeling the volume V of the box.

    b. What is the maximum possible volume of the box?

Name ____________________ Class ____________ Date ____________

6-2 • Guided Problem Solving

GPS Exercise 58

A storage company needs to design a new storage box that has twice the volume of its largest box. Its largest box is 5 ft long, 4 ft wide, and 3 ft high. The new box must be formed by increasing each dimension by the same amount. Find the increase in each dimension.

Read and Understand

1. What is the width of the company's largest box? ____________

2. How will the volume of the new box compare to that of the largest box? ____________

____

3. If the length is increased by x feet, then the width and the height must be increased by what amount? ____________

Plan and Solve

4. What is the volume of the company's largest box? ____________

5. How many cubic feet will the new box hold? ____________

6. Let x represent the amount of the increase to each dimension. Write a polynomial function $V(x)$ that gives the volume of the new box. ____________

7. Graph $V(x)$. Using the graph and the Table feature of a graphing calculator, what is the value of x where $V(x)$ is the desired volume? ____________

8. To form the new box, what is the increase to each dimension? ____________

Look Back and Check

9. Increase each dimension of the large box by your calculated value of x. Multiply the resulting three numbers together. Verify the resulting volume is twice that of the largest box. ____________

Solve Another Problem

10. A family is redesigning their kitchen. They want the new kitchen drawers to have twice the volume of the old ones. The smallest drawers are 20 in. long, 10 in. wide, and 3 in. high. The new drawers will be formed by increasing the width and the height by the same amount, with the length remaining the same. Find the amount of increase in the width and the height for the smallest drawers.

____

Name ____________________ Class ____________ Date ____________

Practice 6-3

Dividing Polynomials

Determine whether each binomial is a factor of $x^3 + 3x^2 - 10x - 24$.

1. $x + 4$ **2.** $x - 3$ **3.** $x + 6$ **4.** $x + 2$

Divide using synthetic division.

5. $(x^3 - 8x^2 + 17x - 10) \div (x - 5)$

6. $(x^3 + 5x^2 - x - 9) \div (x + 2)$

7. $(-2x^3 + 15x^2 - 22x - 15) \div (x - 3)$

8. $(x^3 + 7x^2 + 15x + 9) \div (x + 1)$

9. $(x^3 + 2x^2 + 5x + 12) \div (x + 3)$

10. $(x^3 - 5x^2 - 7x + 25) \div (x - 5)$

11. $(x^4 - x^3 + x^2 - x + 1) \div (x - 1)$

12. $\left(x^4 + \frac{5}{3}x^3 - \frac{2}{3}x^2 + 6x - 2\right) \div \left(x - \frac{1}{3}\right)$

13. $(x^4 - 5x^3 + 5x^2 + 7x - 12) \div (x - 4)$

14. $(2x^4 + 23x^3 + 60x^2 - 125x - 500) \div (x + 4)$

Use synthetic division and the Remainder Theorem to find $P(a)$.

15. $P(x) = 3x^3 - 4x^2 - 5x + 1;\ a = 2$

16. $P(x) = x^3 + 7x^2 + 12x - 3;\ a = -5$

17. $P(x) = x^3 + 6x^2 + 10x + 3;\ a = -3$

18. $P(x) = 2x^4 - 9x^3 + 7x^2 - 5x + 11;\ a = 4$

Divide using long division. Check your answers.

19. $(x^2 - 13x - 48) \div (x + 3)$

20. $(2x^2 + x - 7) \div (x - 5)$

21. $(x^3 + 5x^2 - 3x - 1) \div (x - 1)$

22. $(3x^3 - x^2 - 7x + 6) \div (x + 2)$

Use synthetic division and the given factor to completely factor each polynomial function.

23. $y = x^3 + 3x^2 - 13x - 15;\ (x + 5)$

24. $y = x^3 - 3x^2 - 10x + 24;\ (x - 2)$

Divide.

25. $(6x^3 + 2x^2 - 11x + 12) \div (3x + 4)$

26. $(x^4 + 2x^3 + x - 3) \div (x - 1)$

27. $(2x^4 + 3x^3 - 4x^2 + x + 1) \div (2x - 1)$

28. $(x^5 - 1) \div (x - 1)$

29. $(x^4 - 3x^2 - 10) \div (x - 2)$

30. $(3x^3 - 2x^2 + 2x + 1) \div \left(x + \frac{1}{3}\right)$

31. A box is to be mailed. The volume in cubic inches of the box can be expressed as the product of its three dimensions: $V(x) = x^3 - 16x^2 + 79x - 120$. The length is $x - 8$. Find linear expressions for the other dimensions. Assume that the width is greater than the height.

Name ____________________ Class ____________ Date ____________

6-3 • Guided Problem Solving

GPS Exercise 48

Use synthetic division to determine whether $x + 3$ is a factor of $3x^3 + 10x^2 - x - 12$.

Read and Understand

1. What is the divisor? ____________________

2. What is the dividend? ____________________

Plan and Solve

3. If $x + 3$ is a factor of $3x^3 + 10x^2 - x - 12$, what will be the remainder?

   ____

4. To use synthetic division, reverse the sign in the divisor. What is the constant term of the divisor with its sign reversed? ____________

5. Perform the synthetic division.

6. From the final column of the synthetic division, what is the remainder? ____________

7. Is $x + 3$ a factor of $3x^3 + 10x^2 - x - 12$? ____________

Look Back and Check

8. Check by multiplying. Multiply the quotient you found by $x + 3$ and add the remainder. Verify the result is $3x^3 + 10x^2 - x - 12$. ____________

9. Check by evaluating. Use the Remainder Theorem and evaluate $3x^3 + 10x^2 - x - 12$ at $x = -3$. Verify the result is the same as your remainder. ____________

Solve Another Problem

10. Use synthetic division to determine whether $x + 2$ is a factor of $2x^3 + 4x^2 - 2x - 8$.

    ____

Name ______________________ Class ______________ Date ______________

Practice 6-4

Solving Polynomial Equations

Factor the expression on the left side of each equation. Then solve the equation.

1. $8x^3 - 27 = 0$

2. $x^3 + 64 = 0$

3. $2x^3 + 54 = 0$

4. $2x^3 - 250 = 0$

5. $4x^3 - 32 = 0$

6. $27x^3 + 1 = 0$

7. $64x^3 - 1 = 0$

8. $x^3 - 27 = 0$

9. $x^4 - 5x^2 + 4 = 0$

10. $x^4 - 12x^2 + 11 = 0$

11. $x^4 - 10x^2 + 16 = 0$

12. $x^4 - 8x^2 + 16 = 0$

13. $x^4 - 9x^2 + 14 = 0$

14. $x^4 + 13x^2 + 36 = 0$

15. $x^4 - 10x^2 + 9 = 0$

16. $x^4 + 3x^2 - 4 = 0$

17. Over 3 yr, Lucia saved \$550, \$600, and \$650 from baby-sitting jobs. The polynomial $550x^3 + 600x^2 + 650x$ represents her savings, with interest, after 3 yr. The annual interest rate equals $x - 1$. Find the interest needed so that she will have \$2000 after 3 yr.

Solve each equation by graphing. Where necessary, round to the nearest hundredth.

18. $2x^4 = 9x^2 - 4$

19. $x^2 - 16x = -1$

20. $6x^3 + 10x^2 + 5x = 0$

21. $36x^3 + 6x^2 = 9x$

22. $15x^4 = 11x^3 + 14x^2$

23. $x^4 = 81x^2$

24. The product of three consecutives integers $n - 1, n$, and $n + 1$ is -336. Write and solve an equation to find the numbers.

Factor each expression.

25. $x^3 - 125$

26. $x^4 - 8x^2 + 15$

27. $x^4 + x^2 - 2$

28. $x^3 + 1$

29. $x^4 - 2x^2 - 24$

30. $x^4 + 10x^2 + 9$

31. $x^3 + 27$

32. $x^4 + 7x^2 - 18$

Solve each equation.

33. $x^4 - x = 0$

34. $3x^4 + 18 = 21x^2$

35. $2x^4 - 26x^2 - 28 = 0$

36. $5x^4 + 50x^2 + 80 = 0$

37. $x^4 - 81 = 0$

38. $x^4 = 25$

39. $x^5 = x^3 + 12x$

40. $x^4 + 12x^2 = 8x^3$

Name ______________________ Class ______________ Date ______________

6-4 • Guided Problem Solving

GPS Exercise 62

Write a polynomial function to describe the volume. Then graph your function to solve the problem.

Geometry The width of a box is 2 m less than the length. The height is 1 m less than the length. The volume is 60 m^3. Find the length of the box.

Read and Understand

1. What is the volume of the box in cubic meters? ______________

2. What quantity does the problem ask you to find? ______________

Plan and Solve

3. Let x represent the length. What is an expression for the width? ______________

4. What is an expression for the height? ______________

5. Write a polynomial function for the volume $V(x)$ of the box. ______________

6. Write an equation that shows the volume of the box is 60 m^3. ______________

7. Use the Intersect feature on a graphing calculator to solve the above equation. Enter $V(x)$ for Y_1 and 60 for Y_2.
   What are the coordinates of the point of intersection? ______________
   What do these coordinates represent? ______________

8. What is the length x of the box? ______________

Look Back and Check

9. Use your proposed length x to determine the corresponding width and height of the box. Multiply the resulting three numbers together. Verify the resulting volume is 60 m^3. ______________

Solve Another Problem

10. Tony is five years older than his sister Sara. Their dog Bark is two years older than Sara. The product of all three of their ages is 1800. How old is Sara?

____

Name ______________________ Class ______________ Date ______________

Practice 6-5

Theorems About Roots of Polynomial Equations

A polynomial equation with rational coefficients has the given roots. Find two additional roots.

1. $2 + 3i$ and $\sqrt{7}$

2. $3 - \sqrt{2}$ and $1 + \sqrt{3}$

3. $-4i$ and $6 - i$

4. $5 - \sqrt{6}$ and $-2 + \sqrt{10}$

Find a fourth-degree polynomial equation with integer coefficients that has the given numbers as roots.

5. $2i$ and $4 - i$

6. $\sqrt{2}$ and $2 - \sqrt{3}$

7. $3i$ and $\sqrt{6}$

8. $2 + i$ and $1 - \sqrt{5}$

Find the roots of each polynomial equation.

9. $x^3 - 5x^2 + 2x + 8 = 0$

10. $x^3 + x^2 - 17x + 15 = 0$

11. $2x^3 + 13x^2 + 17x - 12 = 0$

12. $x^3 - x^2 - 34x - 56 = 0$

13. $x^3 - 18x + 27 = 0$

14. $x^4 - 5x^2 + 4 = 0$

15. $x^3 - 6x^2 + 13x - 10 = 0$

16. $x^3 - 5x^2 + 4x + 10 = 0$

17. $x^3 - 5x^2 + 17x - 13 = 0$

18. $x^3 + x + 10 = 0$

19. $x^3 - 5x^2 - x + 5 = 0$

20. $x^3 - 12x + 16 = 0$

21. $x^3 - 2x^2 - 5x + 6 = 0$

22. $x^3 - 8x^2 - 200 = 0$

23. $x^3 + x^2 - 5x + 3 = 0$

24. $4x^3 - 12x^2 - x + 3 = 0$

25. $x^3 + x^2 - 7x + 2 = 0$

26. $12x^3 + 31x^2 - 17x - 6 = 0$

Use the Rational Root Theorem to list all possible rational roots for each polynomial equation. Then find any actual rational roots.

27. $x^3 + 5x^2 - 2x - 15 = 0$

28. $36x^3 + 144x^2 - x - 4 = 0$

29. $2x^3 + 5x^2 + 4x + 1 = 0$

30. $12x^4 + 14x^3 - 5x^2 - 14x - 4 = 0$

31. $5x^3 - 11x^2 + 7x - 1 = 0$

32. $x^3 + 81x^2 - 49x - 49 = 0$

Find a third-degree polynomial equation with rational coefficients that has the given numbers as roots.

33. $3, 2 - i$

34. $5, 2i$

35. $-1, 3 + i$

36. $-7, i$

37. $-4, 4i$

38. $6, 3 - 2i$

Name ______________________ Class ______________ Date ______________

6-5 • Guided Problem Solving

GPS Exercise 29

Find a fourth-degree polynomial equation with integer coefficients that has $3 + i$ and $-2i$ as roots.

Read and Understand

1. How many roots are given? ______________

2. What will the degree of the polynomial equation be? ______________

Plan and Solve

3. From the Imaginary Root Theorem, complex roots come in conjugate pairs. If $3 + i$ is one root, what must another root be? ______________

4. If $-2i$ is one root, what must another root be? ______________

5. Write the factored form of the polynomial using the Factor Theorem.

____

6. Multiply and write the polynomial in standard form. ______________

7. Write a fourth-degree polynomial equation that has $3 + i$ and $-2i$ as roots.

____

Look Back and Check

8. Use synthetic division to verify that $x - (3 + i)$ and $x + 2i$ are factors of the polynomial. ______________

9. Use a graphing calculator in complex a + b*i* Mode. Evaluate your polynomial at $3 + i$ and $-2i$. Verify that two of the roots are $3 + i$ and $-2i$. ______________

Solve Another Problem

10. Find a fourth-degree polynomial equation with integer coefficients that has $-i$ and $3i$ as roots.

____

Name ____________________ Class ____________ Date ____________

Practice 6-6

The Fundamental Theorem of Algebra

Find all the zeros of each function.

1. $y = 5x^3 - 5x$
2. $f(x) = x^3 - 16x$
3. $g(x) = 12x^3 - 2x^2 - 2x$
4. $y = 6x^3 + x^2 - x$
5. $f(x) = 5x^3 + 6x^2 + x$
6. $y = -4x^3 + 100x$

For each equation, state the number of complex roots, the possible number of real roots, and the possible rational roots.

7. $2x^2 + 5x + 3 = 0$
8. $3x^2 + 11x - 10 = 0$
9. $2x^4 - 18x^2 + 5 = 0$
10. $4x^3 - 12x + 9 = 0$
11. $6x^5 - 28x + 15 = 0$
12. $x^3 - x^2 - 2x + 7 = 0$
13. $x^3 - 6x^2 - 7x - 12 = 0$
14. $2x^4 + x^2 - x + 6 = 0$
15. $4x^5 - 5x^4 + x^3 - 2x^2 + 2x - 6 = 0$
16. $7x^6 + 3x^4 - 9x^2 + 18 = 0$
17. $5 + x + x^2 + x^3 + x^4 + x^5 = 0$
18. $6 - x + 2x^3 - x^3 + x^4 - 8x^5 = 0$

Find all the zeros of each function.

19. $f(x) = x^3 - 9x^2 + 27x - 27$
20. $y = 2x^3 - 8x^2 + 18x - 72$
21. $y = x^3 - 10x - 12$
22. $y = x^3 - 4x^2 + 8$
23. $f(x) = 2x^3 + x - 3$
24. $y = x^3 - 2x^2 - 11x + 12$
25. $g(x) = x^3 + 4x^2 + 7x + 28$
26. $f(x) = x^3 + 3x^2 + 6x + 4$
27. $g(x) = x^4 - 5x^2 - 36$
28. $y = x^4 - 7x^2 + 12$
29. $y = 9x^4 + 5x^2 - 4$
30. $y = 4x^4 - 11x^2 - 3$

Name ______________________ Class ______________ Date ______________

6-6 • Guided Problem Solving

GPS Exercise 21

Find all the zeros of the function $y = x^3 - 4x^2 + 9x - 36$.

Read and Understand

1. What is the degree of the given polynomial function? ______________

2. How many zeros do you expect to find? ______________

Plan and Solve

3. List the possible rational roots. ______________

4. Use synthetic division to test each possible rational root. Which possible root gives a remainder of zero? ______________

5. Write the quadratic quotient from the synthetic division. ______________

6. Find the two zeros of the quadratic function. ______________

7. What are all the zeros of the given function? ______________

Look Back and Check

8. Check by graphing the equation. Verify any real zeros by noting the x-intercepts of the graph. ______________

9. Check by evaluating. Substitute your proposed complex zeros into the function. Verify the result is zero. ______________

Solve Another Problem

10. Find all the zeros of the function $y = x^3 + x^2 + 4x + 4$. ______________

Name ______________________ Class ______________ Date ______________

Practice 6-7

Permutations and Combinations

Indicate whether each situation involves a combination or a permutation.

1. Five apples chosen at random from a case of apples.
2. Ten applicants line up for a job interview.
3. Three students elected president, secretary, and treasurer of the student body.
4. Four students chosen at random from the student body.

Evaluate each expression.

5. ${}_{12}C_{11}$
6. ${}_{12}C_{10}$
7. ${}_{12}C_5$
8. ${}_{12}C_1$
9. ${}_{12}C_{12}$
10. ${}_5C_4 + {}_5C_3$
11. $\frac{{}_5C_3}{{}_5C_2}$
12. $4({}_7C_2)$

How many combinations of five can you make from each set?

13. Xul, Ben, Sue, Tom, and Ria
14. {0, 1, 2, 3, 4, 5, 6, 7, 8, 9}
15. 14 novels on a reading list
16. 50 states

Evaluate each expression.

17. 8!
18. $\frac{11!}{9!}$
19. 6!4!
20. 3(5!)
21. ${}_{12}P_{11}$
22. ${}_{12}P_{10}$
23. ${}_{12}P_5$
24. ${}_{12}P_1$
25. In how many ways can four distinct positions for a relay race be assigned from a team of nine runners?
26. A committee must choose 3 finalists from 15 scholarship candidates. How many ways can the committee choose the three finalists?
27. A traveler can choose from three airlines, five hotels, and four rental car companies. How many arrangements of these services are possible?
28. In how many ways can four students be seated at a table with six chairs?

Assume a and b are positive integers. Decide whether each statement is true or false. If it is true, explain why. If it is false, give a counterexample.

29. $a!b! = b!a!$
30. $(a^2)! = (a!)^2$
31. $a \cdot b! = (ab)!$
32. $(a + 0)! = a!$
33. $(a + b)! = a! + b!$
34. $(a!)! = (a!)^2$

Name ______________________ Class ______________ Date ______________

6-7 • Guided Problem Solving

GPS Exercise 40

Consumer Issues A consumer magazine rates televisions by identifying two levels of price, five levels of repair frequency, three levels of features, and two levels of picture quality. How many different ratings are possible?

Read and Understand

1. When rating one television, how many possible levels are there for each category?

   price ______________ repair frequency ______________

   features ______________ picture quality ______________

2. What does the problem ask you to count? ______________

Plan and Solve

3. There are two levels of price. If you are rating one television set, can you assign more than one price level for that television? Explain. ______________

4. Of the five levels of repair frequency, how many are chosen when rating one television?

   ____

5. Which formula or technique will you use to solve this problem: the permutation formula, the combination formula, or the Multiplication Counting Principle?

   ____

6. Apply your chosen formula or technique. Write an expression for the number of different ways to rate a television. ______________

7. Simplify your expression. How many different ratings are possible? ______________

Look Back and Check

8. Imagine rating your own television using the given rating scheme. What would the rating be? Now list some other possible ratings. Does your answer seem reasonable? ______________

Solve Another Problem

9. A computer program generates characters using five different hairstyles, four different noses, two different face styles, and six different types of eyes. How many different characters are possible? ______________

Name ______________________ Class ______________ Date ______________

Practice 6-8

The Binomial Theorem

Use the Binomial Theorem to expand each binomial.

1. $(x + 2)^4$
2. $(a + 2)^7$
3. $(x + y)^7$
4. $(d - 2)^9$
5. $(2x - 3)^8$
6. $(x - 1)^9$
7. $(2x^2 - 2y^2)^6$
8. $(x^5 + 2y)^7$
9. What is the probability that you will roll exactly five sixes in ten tosses of a number cube?
10. One airline recently had a rate of 52 complaints per 100,000 departures, or a 0.00052 probability of a complaint on each flight.
    a. What is the probability that the airline will not have a complaint in 20 flights?
    b. What is the probability that the airline will not have a complaint in 100 flights?
    c. What is the probability that the airline will have a complaint in 100 flights?
11. 6% of the circuit boards assembled at a certain production plant are defective. If five circuit boards are chosen at random, what is the probability that exactly two are defective?
12. The probability that a baby will be a boy is $\frac{1}{2}$. What is the probability that a family with five children has all boys?
13. Your friend's batting average is 0.225. What is the probability of her getting three or more hits in the next five times at bat?
14. If a classmate randomly guesses on ten multiple choice questions, what is the probability that six or more answers will be right? The probability of each answer being correct is 0.2.

Use Pascal's Triangle to expand each binomial.

15. $(n - 3)^3$
16. $(2n + 2)^4$
17. $(n - 6)^5$
18. $(n - 1)^6$
19. $(2a + 2)^3$
20. $(x^2 - y^2)^4$
21. $(2x + 3y)^5$
22. $(2x^2 + y^2)^6$
23. $(x^2 - y^2)^3$
24. $(2b + c)^4$
25. $(3m - 2n)^5$
26. $(x^3 - y^4)^6$

Expand each binomial.

27. $(x + 1)^7$
28. $(x + 4)^8$
29. $(x - 3y)^6$
30. $(x + 2)^5$
31. $(x^2 - y^2)^5$
32. $(3 + y)^5$
33. $(x^2 + 3)^6$
34. $(x - 5)^7$
35. $(x - 4y)^4$

Name ______________________ Class ______________ Date ______________

6-8 • Guided Problem Solving

GPS Exercise 43

Genetics A family has five children. Assume that the probability of having a boy is 0.5. Write the term in the expansion of $(b + g)^5$ for each outcome described. Then evaluate each probability.

a. exactly 3 boys **b.** exactly 4 boys **c.** exactly 4 girls

Read and Understand

1. For the birth of a single child, what is the probability b of having a boy? ______

2. What is the total number of births? ______

Plan and Solve

3. What is the probability g of having a girl? ______

4. For the desired outcome of exactly 3 boys, how many girls are there? ______

5. Use the number of boys as the exponent on b and the number of girls as the exponent on g. Write the variable part of the corresponding term in the expansion of $(b + g)^5$. ______

6. If 3 out of 5 are boys, write the coefficient of the term in the expansion of $(b + g)^5$. ______

7. Combining the results, what is the term in the expansion of $(b + g)^5$? ______

8. Substitute the values for b and g. Evaluate the probability of having exactly 3 boys. ______

9. For the desired outcome of exactly 4 boys, how many girls are there? ______

10. What is the term in the expansion of $(b + g)^5$ for this outcome? ______

11. Substitute the values for b and g. Evaluate the probability of having exactly 4 boys. ______

12. What is the term in the expansion of $(b + g)^5$ for the outcome of exactly 4 girls? ______

13. Substitute the values for b and g. Evaluate the probability of having exactly 4 girls. ______

Look Back and Check

14. Check that your answers are reasonable. Which seems more likely: 3 boys or 4 boys in the family? Verify that this agrees with your results. How do the outcomes in (b) and (c) compare? Is this what you expected? ______

Solve Another Problem

15. Four students are chosen at random to win an all-expense paid trip to Europe. Assume that the probability of choosing a girl is 0.5. Write the term in the expansion of $(b + g)^4$ for each outcome described. Then evaluate each probability.

a. exactly 2 girls **b.** exactly 3 girls **c.** exactly 3 boys

______ ______ ______

Name ______________________ Class ______________ Date ______________

6A: Graphic Organizer

For use before Lesson 6-1

Study Skill Take a minute to look at the title of Chapter 6. Do you already know what a polynomial is? Look at the titles of the lessons in this chapter. Do they give you any clues about the definition of a polynomial or polynomial function? Record your thoughts. As you complete each lesson, review your notes and update them to reflect what you've learned about polynomials and polynomial functions.

Write your answers.

1. What is the chapter title? ______________________

2. Find the Table of Contents page for this chapter at the front of the book. Name four topics you will study in this chapter.

______________________ ______________________

______________________ ______________________

3. Complete the graphic organizer as you work through the chapter.
1. Write the title of the chapter in the center oval.
2. When you begin a lesson, write the name of the lesson in a rectangle.
3. When you complete that lesson, write a skill or key concept from that lesson in the outer oval linked to that rectangle.

Continue with steps 2 and 3 clockwise around the graphic organizer.

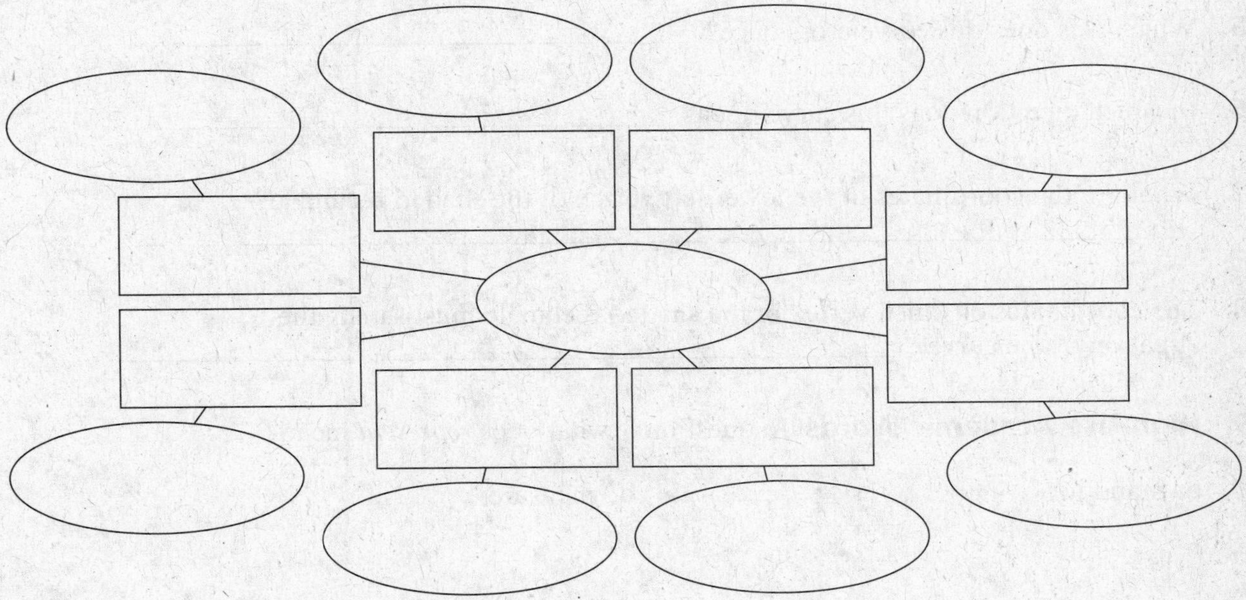

Name ______________________ Class ______________ Date ______________

6B: Reading Comprehension

For use after Lesson 6-7

Study Skill As you read or study a subject, take summary notes of the key points and information. Use your notes when you review for a test.

Answer the questions below about how to read this graph.

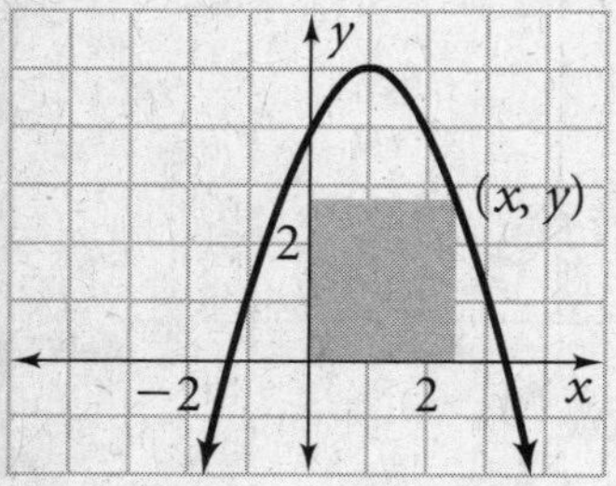

1. What is the label on the horizontal axis? ______________________

2. What is the label on the vertical axis? ______________________

3. How many units does one square on this coordinate grid represent?
____

4. What is the name of the curve in this graph? ______________________

5. Which axis does this curve cross once? ______________________

6. In which direction does this curve open? ______________________

7. What are the coordinates of the lower left vertex of the shaded rectangle?
____

8. The coordinates of which vertex of the shaded rectangle must satisfy the equation of the curve? ______________________

9. **High-Use Academic Words** In question 3, what does *represent* mean?

   a. stand for   **b.** measure

Name ______________________ Class ______________ Date ______________

6C: Reading/Writing Math Symbols

For use after Lesson 6-3

Study Skill When you write symbols in your notes that may be easily confused, make sure you write them clearly so you will not confuse yourself when you review your notes.

A single mathematical expression, such as -1, may have several meanings that are slightly different in various contexts. Answer the following questions about the various meanings of the expression -1.

1. The basic meaning of -1 in the expression $7 - 1$ is to ____________ the number one from seven.

2. In another meaning, -1 is the additive ____________ of 1.

3. A number and its additive inverse add to a value of ____________.

4. When -1 is used as an exponent on an integer, such as 8^{-1}, it denotes the multiplicative ____________ of 8, or the fraction ____________.

5. The product of a number and its multiplicative inverse is __________.

6. When -1 is used as an exponent on a matrix, such as A^{-1}, then the exponent means the multiplicative ____________ of the matrix A.

7. The product of the two matrices, A and A^{-1}, is I, which is the ____________ matrix.

Later on you will see how -1 is also used as an exponent to mean the inverse of a function and also to mean the inverse of a trigonometric function. Watch for these uses, and compare their meanings to the ones you have explored here.

Name ____________________ Class ____________ Date ____________

6D: Visual Vocabulary Practice High-Use Academic Words

For use after Lesson 6-8

Study Skills Use Venn diagrams to understand the relationship between words whose meanings overlap, such as *squares*, *rectangles*, and *quadrilaterals* or *real numbers*, *integers*, and *counting numbers*.

Concept List

always	common	explain
formula	graph	never
simplify	symbol	table

Write the concept that best describes each exercise. Choose from the concept list above.

1. det A and $\begin{vmatrix} a & b \\ c & d \end{vmatrix}$

____

2. $0 = 0$

(millions)

____

3. U.S. Passenger Vehicles and Light Trucks

	Imports	Exports
1996	4.678	1.295
1998	5.185	1.331
2000	6.964	1.402

____

4. The inverse for matrix $M = \begin{bmatrix} 3 & 9 \\ 2 & 6 \end{bmatrix}$ does not exist because det $M = 0$

____

5. **A Day's Commute**

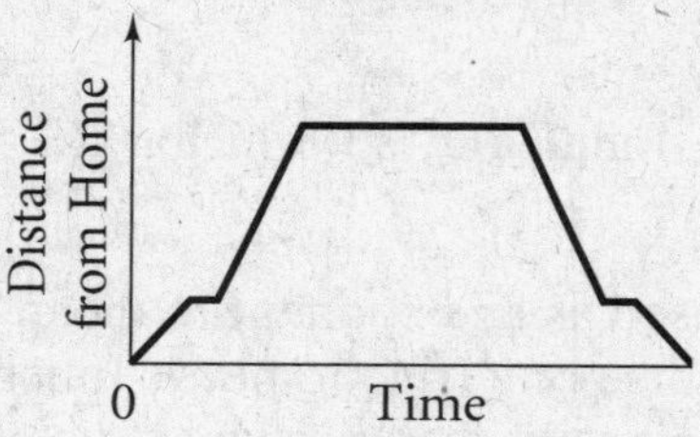

____

6. $x = \dfrac{-b \pm \sqrt{b^2 - 4ac}}{2a}$

____

7. The factor $x + 1$ for $x(x + 1)$ and $7(x + 1)$

____

8. $0 = 12$

____

9. $(2 + 4i) + (4 - i)$
$= (2 + 4) + (4i - i)$
$= 6 + 3i$

____

Name ____________________ Class ____________ Date ____________

6E: Vocabulary Check

For use after Lesson 6-4

Study Skill Strengthen your vocabulary. Use these pages and add cues and summaries by applying the Cornell Notetaking style.

Write the definition for each word at the right. To check your work, fold the paper back along the dotted line to see the correct answers.

____________________	Polynomial
____________________	Degree of a polynomial
____________________	Remainder Theorem
____________________	Multiplicity
____________________	Relative maximum

Name ______________________ Class ______________ Date ______________

6E: Vocabulary Check (continued)

For use after Lesson 6-4

Write the vocabulary word for each definition. To check your work, fold the paper forward along the dotted line to see the correct answers.

A monomial or the sum of monomials. ______________________

The largest degree of any term. ______________________

If a polynomial $P(x)$ of degree $n \geq 1$ is divided by $(x - a)$ where a is a constant, then the remainder is $P(a)$. ______________________

The number of times the related linear factor is repeated in the factored form of the polynomial. ______________________

The y-value of a point on the graph of a function that is higher than other nearby points. ______________________

Name ____________________ Class ____________ Date ____________

6F: Vocabulary Review Puzzle

For use with Chapter Review

Study Skill One of the hardest things about reading a mathematics textbook is the new vocabulary you will encounter. Sometimes you will encounter numerous new terms in just one section. Reciting a rule, definition, or formula can help you to remember and recall it.

In the first column on the left, read the mathematical phrase. The word that fits the mathematical phrase must also fit in the blank in the sentence on the right. In the middle column, write the one word from the list below that matches both columns.

absolute	complex	evaluate	opposite
term	variable		

Mathematical Phrase		Sentence
1. value that tells the distance from zero without direction		It is an ________ certainty that the game will be postponed.
2. when you add this to a number you get zero		Her house is ________ the library on 12th Street.
3. a part of an algebraic expression separated from another part by plus or minus		The ________ of this president will be up next January.
4. a letter in an algebraic expression		The weather is apt to be highly ________ in the early spring.
5. substitute the number and do the calculations		You'll have to ________ the features of this car to see if you want it.
6. a number in the form $a + bi$		It is a ________ situation with many issues to be considered.

Name ______________________ Class ______________ Date ______________

Practice 7-1

Roots and Radical Expressions

Find each real-number root.

1. $\sqrt{144}$
2. $-\sqrt{25}$
3. $\sqrt{-0.01}$
4. $\sqrt[3]{0.001}$
5. $\sqrt[4]{0.0081}$
6. $\sqrt[3]{27}$
7. $\sqrt[3]{-27}$
8. $\sqrt{0.09}$

Find all the real cube roots of each number.

9. 216
10. -343
11. -0.064
12. $\frac{1000}{27}$

Find all the real square roots of each number.

13. 400
14. -196
15. 10,000
16. 0.0625

Find all the real fourth roots of each number.

17. -81
18. 256
19. 0.0001
20. 625

Simplify each radical expression. Use absolute value symbols when needed.

21. $\sqrt{81x^4}$
22. $\sqrt{121y^{10}}$
23. $\sqrt[3]{8g^6}$
24. $\sqrt[3]{125x^9}$
25. $\sqrt[5]{243x^5y^{15}}$
26. $\sqrt[3]{(x-9)^3}$
27. $\sqrt{25(x+2)^4}$
28. $\sqrt[3]{\frac{64x^9}{343}}$

Find the two real-number solutions of each equation.

29. $x^2 = 4$
30. $x^4 = 81$
31. $x^2 = 0.16$
32. $x^2 = \frac{16}{49}$

33. A cube has volume $V = s^3$, where s is the length of a side. Find the side length for a cube with volume 8000 cm^3.

34. The velocity of a falling object can be found using the formula $v^2 = 64h$, where v is the velocity (in feet per second) and h is the distance the object has already fallen.
    a. What is the velocity of the object after a 10-foot fall?
    b. How much does the velocity increase if the object falls 20 feet rather than 10 feet?

Name ______________________ Class ______________ Date ______________

7-1 • Guided Problem Solving

GPS Exercise 38

Boat Building Boat builders share an old rule of thumb for sailboats. The maximum speed K in knots is 1.35 times the square root of the length L in feet of the boat's waterline.

a. A customer is planning to order a sailboat with a maximum speed of 8 knots. How long should the waterline be?

b. How much longer would the waterline have to be to achieve a maximum speed of 10 knots?

Read and Understand

1. What variables represent the maximum speed and the length of the boat's waterline? __________

2. What will you be solving for in (a) and (b), maximum speed or length? __________

Plan and Solve

3. Write a formula for how the maximum speed K is related to the length of the waterline L.

____

4. For (a), substitute $K = 8$ into your formula and solve for L. How long should the waterline be for a maximum speed of 8 knots? __________

5. Now substitute $K = 10$ into your formula and solve for L. How long should the waterline be for a maximum speed of 10 knots? __________

6. For (b), how much longer is the waterline for 10 knots compared to that for 8 knots? __________

Look Back and Check

7. To check the reasonableness of your answers, substitute your answers for length L into the formula and solve for maximum speed K. The values of K should match those given in the problem. __________

Solve Another Problem

8. Pollution Data collected in a particular city show that the amount of pollution P emitted into the air is 0.42 times the square of the number of cars C in thousands.

a. If there are 2175 tons of pollutants in the air, how many cars would you expect in the city?

____

b. How many fewer cars should there be to reduce the pollution to 1800 tons? __________

Name ______________________ Class ______________ Date ______________

Practice 7-2

Multiplying and Dividing Radical Expressions

Multiply and simplify. Assume that all variables are positive.

1. $\sqrt{4} \cdot \sqrt{6}$
2. $\sqrt{9x^2} \cdot \sqrt{9y^5}$
3. $\sqrt[3]{50x^2z^5} \cdot \sqrt[3]{15y^3z}$
4. $4\sqrt{2x} \cdot 3\sqrt{8x}$
5. $\sqrt{xy} \cdot \sqrt{4xy}$
6. $9\sqrt{2} \cdot 3\sqrt{y}$

Rationalize the denominator of each expression. Assume that all variables are positive.

7. $\sqrt{\dfrac{9x}{2}}$
8. $\dfrac{\sqrt{xy}}{\sqrt{3x}}$
9. $\sqrt[3]{\dfrac{x^2}{3y}}$
10. $\dfrac{\sqrt[4]{2x}}{\sqrt[4]{3x^2}}$
11. $\sqrt{\dfrac{x}{8y}}$
12. $\sqrt[3]{\dfrac{3a}{4b^2c}}$

Multiply. Simplify if possible. Assume that all variables are positive.

13. $\sqrt{4} \cdot \sqrt{25}$
14. $\sqrt{81} \cdot \sqrt{36}$
15. $\sqrt{3} \cdot \sqrt{27}$
16. $\sqrt[3]{-3} \cdot \sqrt[3]{9}$
17. $\sqrt{3x} \cdot \sqrt{6x^3}$
18. $\sqrt[3]{2xy^2} \cdot \sqrt[3]{4x^2y^7}$

Simplify. Assume that all variables are positive.

19. $\sqrt{36x^3}$
20. $\sqrt[3]{125y^2z^4}$
21. $\sqrt{18k^6}$
22. $\sqrt[3]{-16a^{12}}$
23. $\sqrt{x^2y^{10}z}$
24. $\sqrt[4]{256s^7t^{12}}$
25. $\sqrt[3]{216x^4y^3}$
26. $\sqrt{75r^3}$
27. $\sqrt[4]{625u^5v^8}$

Divide and simplify. Assume that all variables are positive.

28. $\dfrac{\sqrt{6x}}{\sqrt{3x}}$
29. $\dfrac{\sqrt[3]{4x^2}}{\sqrt[3]{x}}$
30. $\sqrt[4]{\dfrac{243k^3}{3k^7}}$
31. $\dfrac{\sqrt{(2x)^2}}{\sqrt{(5y)^4}}$
32. $\dfrac{\sqrt[3]{18y^2}}{\sqrt[3]{12y}}$
33. $\sqrt{\dfrac{162a}{6a^3}}$

34. The volume of a sphere of radius r is $V = \frac{4}{3}\pi r^3$.

    a. Use the formula to find r in terms of V. Rationalize the denominator.

    b. Use your answer to part (a) to find the radius of a sphere with volume 100 cubic inches. Round to the nearest hundredth.

Name ______________________ Class ______________ Date ______________

7-2 • Guided Problem Solving

GPS **Exercise 55**

Satellites The circular velocity v, in miles per hour, of a satellite orbiting Earth is given by the formula $v = \sqrt{\frac{1.24 \times 10^{12}}{r}}$, where r is the distance in miles from the satellite to the center of Earth. How much greater is the velocity of a satellite orbiting at an altitude of 100 mi than one orbiting at an altitude of 200 mi? (The radius of Earth is 3950 mi.)

Read and Understand

1. What does r represent? ______________

2. What is the radius of Earth? ______________

Plan and Solve

3. What is the value of r for a satellite orbiting at an altitude of 100 mi? ______________

4. Substitute your value from Step 3 into the formula to find the velocity of a satellite orbiting at an altitude of 100 mi. ______________

5. What is the value of r for a satellite orbiting at an altitude of 200 mi? ______________

6. Substitute your value from Step 5 into the formula to find the velocity of a satellite orbiting at an altitude of 200 mi. ______________

7. How much greater is the velocity of a satellite orbiting at an altitude of 100 mi than one orbiting at an altitude of 200 mi? ______________

Look Back and Check

8. To check your answers, substitute your values for v into the equation $v = \sqrt{\frac{1.24 \times 10^{12}}{r}}$. Solve for r and check that they match those used to answer the original question.

____

Solve Another Problem

9. **Music** A string of a certain length and tension on a musical instrument has frequency f, in hertz or vibrations per second, and is given by the formula $f = \frac{1}{94}\sqrt{\frac{6.6 \times 10^{8}}{m}}$, where m is the mass of the string in grams. How much greater is the mass of a string with a frequency of 300 hertz than one with a frequency of 350 hertz?

____

Name ______________________ Class ______________ Date ______________

Practice 7-3

Binomial Radical Expressions

Multiply each pair of conjugates.

1. $(3\sqrt{2} - 9)(3\sqrt{2} + 9)$ **2.** $(1 - \sqrt{7})(1 + \sqrt{7})$ **3.** $(5\sqrt{3} + \sqrt{2})(5\sqrt{3} - \sqrt{2})$

Add or subtract if possible.

4. $9\sqrt{3} + 2\sqrt{3}$ **5.** $5\sqrt{2} + 2\sqrt{3}$ **6.** $3\sqrt{7} - 7\sqrt[3]{x}$ **7.** $14\sqrt[3]{xy} - 3\sqrt[3]{xy}$

Rationalize each denominator. Simplify the answer.

8. $\frac{2}{2\sqrt{3} - 4}$ **9.** $\frac{5}{2 + \sqrt{3}}$ **10.** $\frac{1 + \sqrt{5}}{1 - \sqrt{5}}$ **11.** $\frac{2 + \sqrt{12}}{5 - \sqrt{12}}$

Simplify.

12. $3\sqrt{32} + 2\sqrt{50}$ **13.** $\sqrt{200} - \sqrt{72}$ **14.** $\sqrt[3]{81} - 3\sqrt[3]{3}$ **15.** $2\sqrt[4]{48} + 3\sqrt[4]{243}$

Multiply.

16. $(1 - \sqrt{5})(2 + \sqrt{5})$ **17.** $(1 + 4\sqrt{10})(2 - \sqrt{10})$ **18.** $(1 - 3\sqrt{7})(4 - 3\sqrt{7})$

19. $(4 - 2\sqrt{3})^2$ **20.** $(\sqrt{2} + \sqrt{7})^2$ **21.** $(2\sqrt{3} + 3\sqrt{2})^2$

Simplify. Rationalize all denominators. Assume that all variables are positive.

22. $\sqrt{28} + 4\sqrt{63} - 2\sqrt{7}$ **23.** $6\sqrt{40} - 2\sqrt{90} + 3\sqrt{160}$

24. $3\sqrt{12} + 7\sqrt{75} - \sqrt{54}$ **25.** $4\sqrt[3]{81} + 2\sqrt[3]{72} - 3\sqrt[3]{24}$

26. $3\sqrt{225x} + 5\sqrt{144x}$ **27.** $6\sqrt{45y^2} + 4\sqrt{20y^2}$

28. $(3\sqrt{y} - \sqrt{5})(2\sqrt{y} + 5\sqrt{5})$ **29.** $(\sqrt{x} - \sqrt{3})(\sqrt{x} + \sqrt{3})$

30. $\frac{3 - \sqrt{10}}{\sqrt{5} - \sqrt{2}}$ **31.** $\frac{2 + \sqrt{14}}{\sqrt{7} + \sqrt{2}}$ **32.** $\frac{2 + \sqrt[3]{x}}{\sqrt[3]{x}}$

33. A park in the shape of a triangle has a sidewalk dividing it into two parts.

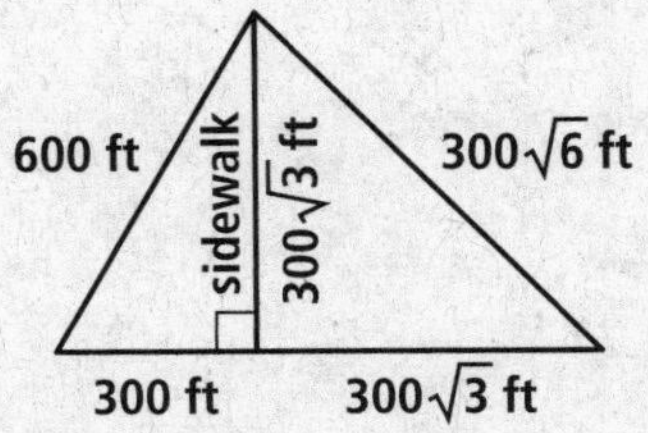

a. If a man walks around the perimeter of the park, how far will he walk?

b. What is the area of the park?

Name ______________________ Class ______________ Date ______________

7-3 • Guided Problem Solving

GPS Exercise 45

The golden ratio is $\frac{1 + \sqrt{5}}{2}$. Find the difference between the golden ratio and its reciprocal.

Read and Understand

1. What is the golden ratio? ______________________

2. What does it mean to find the difference? ______________________

Plan and Solve

3. What is the reciprocal of the golden ratio? ______________________

4. To rationalize the denominator of the reciprocal of the golden ratio, find the conjugate of the denominator. ______________________

5. Rationalize the denominator of the reciprocal of the golden ratio. ______________________

6. Find the difference between the golden ratio and its reciprocal. ______________________

Look Back and Check

7. To check your answer, subtract the result from Step 6 from the golden ratio and verify that it equals the reciprocal of the golden ratio. ______________________

Solve Another Problem

8. Add. $\frac{\sqrt{3} + 2}{5} + \frac{5}{\sqrt{3} + 2}$ ______________________

Name ____________________ Class ____________ Date ____________

Practice 7-4

Rational Exponents

Simplify each expression. Assume that all variables are positive.

1. $27^{\frac{1}{3}}$

2. $\left(81^{\frac{1}{4}}\right)^4$

3. $\left(32^{\frac{1}{5}}\right)^5$

4. $(256^4)^{\frac{1}{4}}$

5. 7^0

6. $8^{\frac{2}{3}}$

7. $(-1)^{\frac{1}{5}}$

8. $(-27)^{\frac{2}{3}}$

9. $16^{\frac{1}{4}}$

10. $x^{\frac{1}{2}} \cdot x^{\frac{1}{3}}$

11. $2y^{\frac{1}{2}} \cdot y$

12. $(8^2)^{\frac{1}{3}}$

13. 3.6^0

14. $\left(\frac{1}{16}\right)^{\frac{1}{4}}$

15. $\left(\frac{27}{8}\right)^{\frac{2}{3}}$

16. $\sqrt[8]{0}$

17. $\left(3x^{\frac{1}{2}}\right)\left(4x^{\frac{2}{3}}\right)$

18. $\dfrac{12y^{\frac{1}{3}}}{4y^{\frac{1}{2}}}$

19. $\left(3a^{\frac{1}{2}}b^{\frac{1}{3}}\right)^2$

20. $\left(y^{\frac{2}{3}}\right)^{-9}$

21. $\left(a^{\frac{2}{3}}b^{-\frac{1}{2}}\right)^{-6}$

22. $y^{\frac{2}{5}} \cdot y^{\frac{3}{8}}$

23. $\left(\dfrac{x^{\frac{4}{7}}}{x^{\frac{2}{3}}}\right)$

24. $\left(2a^{\frac{1}{4}}\right)^3$

25. $81^{-\frac{1}{2}}$

26. $\left(2x^{\frac{2}{5}}\right)\left(6x^{\frac{1}{4}}\right)$

27. $\left(9x^4y^{-2}\right)^{\frac{1}{2}}$

28. The interest rate r required to increase your investment p to the amount a in t years is found by $r = \left(\frac{a}{p}\right)^{\frac{1}{t}} - 1$. What interest rate would be required to increase your investment of \$2700 to \$3600 over three years? Round your answer to the nearest tenth of a percent.

Write each expression in radical form.

29. $x^{\frac{4}{3}}$

30. $(2y)^{\frac{1}{3}}$

31. $a^{1.5}$

32. $b^{\frac{1}{5}}$

33. $z^{\frac{2}{3}}$

34. $(ab)^{\frac{1}{4}}$

35. $m^{2.4}$

36. $t^{-\frac{2}{7}}$

37. $a^{-1.6}$

Write each expression in exponential form.

38. $\sqrt{x^3}$

39. $\sqrt[3]{m}$

40. $\sqrt{5y}$

41. $\sqrt[3]{2y^2}$

42. $\left(\sqrt[4]{b}\right)^3$

43. $\sqrt{-6}$

44. $\sqrt{(6a)^4}$

45. $\sqrt[5]{n^4}$

46. $\sqrt[4]{(5ab)^3}$

Name ________________ Class ________________ Date ________________

7-4 • Guided Problem Solving

GPS Exercise 62

The ratio R of radioactive carbon to nonradioactive carbon left in a sample of an organism that died T years ago can be approximated by the formula $R = A(2.7)^{-\frac{T}{8033}}$. Here A is the ratio of radioactive carbon to nonradioactive carbon in the living organism. What percent of A is left after 2000 years? After 4000 years? After 8000 years?

Read and Understand

1. Express 0.39 as a percent. ________________

2. What does T represent? ________________

Plan and Solve

3. Since R is the ratio of radioactive carbon to nonradioactive carbon left in a sample of an organism that died T years ago and A is the ratio of radioactive carbon to nonradioactive carbon in the living organism, what is $\frac{R}{A}$?

____

4. Solve $R = A(2.7)^{-\frac{T}{8033}}$ for $\frac{R}{A}$.

____

5. Let $T = 2000$. What percent of A is left after 2000 years? ________________

6. Let $T = 4000$. What percent of A is left after 4000 years? ________________

7. Let $T = 8000$. What percent of A is left after 8000 years? ________________

Look Back and Check

8. To check the reasonableness of your answers, substitute your percents into the original equation and solve for T. The values of T should be about 2000, 4000, and 8000. ________________

Solve Another Problem

9. The quantity Q of radium 226 after T years can be approximated by the formula $Q = Q_0 \times 2^{-\frac{T}{1620}}$, where Q_0 represents the initial quantity. What percent of the initial quantity is left after 500 years? After 1000 years? After 5000 years? ________________

Name ______________________ Class ______________ Date ______________

Practice 7-5

Solving Square Root and Other Radical Equations

Solve. Check for extraneous solutions.

1. $(x - 2)^{\frac{1}{3}} = 5$
2. $3x^{\frac{4}{3}} + 5 = 53$
3. $4x^{\frac{3}{2}} - 5 = 103$
4. $\sqrt{x + 1} = x - 1$
5. $\sqrt{2x + 1} = -3$
6. $x^{\frac{1}{2}} - 5 = 0$
7. $\sqrt{x + 7} = x - 5$
8. $(2x + 1)^{\frac{1}{3}} = -3$
9. $2x^{\frac{1}{3}} - 2 = 0$
10. $\sqrt{2x - 5} = 7$
11. $\sqrt{2x - 4} = x - 2$
12. $\sqrt{x} + 6 = x$
13. $\sqrt{x + 2} = 10 - x$
14. $\sqrt{4x + 2} = \sqrt{3x + 4}$
15. $(7x - 3)^{\frac{1}{2}} = 5$
16. $(x - 2)^{\frac{2}{3}} - 4 = 5$
17. $2\sqrt{x - 1} = \sqrt{26 + x}$
18. $2x^{\frac{3}{4}} = 16$
19. $\sqrt{7x - 6} - \sqrt{5x + 2} = 0$
20. $\sqrt{3x - 3} - 6 = 0$
21. $5\sqrt{x + 2} = 12$
22. $2x^{\frac{4}{3}} - 2 = 160$
23. $4x^{\frac{1}{2}} - 5 = 27$
24. $\sqrt{x + 1} = x + 1$
25. $\sqrt{2x + 1} = -5$
26. $x^{\frac{1}{6}} - 2 = 0$
27. $\sqrt{x + 2} = x - 18$
28. $(2x + 1)^{\frac{1}{3}} = 1$
29. $x^{\frac{1}{4}} + 3 = 0$
30. $\sqrt[3]{2x - 4} = -2$

For each equation, let Y1 = left side and Y2 = right side. Find where Y1 = Y2. Use the Technology Activity Steps on page 394 of the text to check that you've found all solutions.

31. $x^{\frac{1}{4}} - 1 = 0$
32. $(x - 2)^{\frac{1}{3}} = -5$
33. $x^{\frac{1}{3}} - 2 = 0$
34. $\sqrt{3x} = 6$
35. $(2x + 7)^{\frac{1}{2}} - x = 2$
36. $\sqrt{4x} - 8 = 0$
37. $\sqrt{3x + 1} - 5 = 0$
38. $3(2x + 4)^{\frac{4}{3}} = 48$
39. $2\sqrt{x} = \sqrt{x + 6}$
40. $(2x + 1)^{\frac{1}{2}} = (5 - 2x)^{\frac{1}{2}}$
41. $(x + 14)^{\frac{1}{4}} = (2x)^{\frac{1}{2}}$
42. $\sqrt[3]{x - 2} = 4$

Name ______________________ Class ______________ Date ______________

7-5 • Guided Problem Solving

GPS Exercise 32

a. Package Design The formula for the area A of a hexagon with a side s units long is $A = \frac{3s^2\sqrt{3}}{2}$. See the figure. Solve the formula for s and rationalize the denominator.

b. A package designer wants the hexagonal base of a hat box to have an area of about 200 in.^{2}. About how long is each side?

c. What is the distance between opposite sides of the hat box?

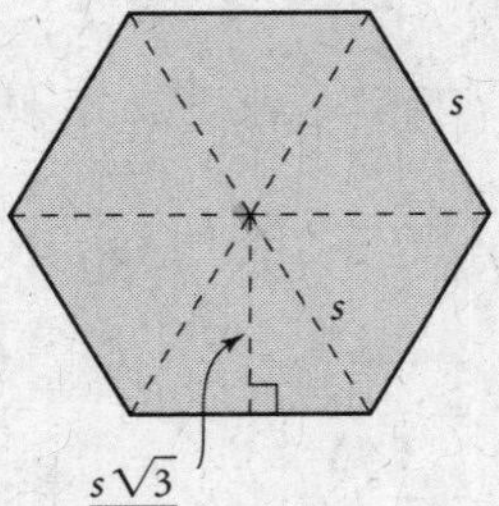

$\frac{s\sqrt{3}}{2}$

Read and Understand

1. From the first figure, how long is half the distance across the hat box, in terms of s?

____

Plan and Solve

2. For part (a), solve the formula for s and rationalize the denominator. $A = \frac{3s^2\sqrt{3}}{2}$

Multiply both sides of the equation by $\frac{2}{3\sqrt{3}}$. ______________ $= s^2$

Rationalize the denominator. ______________ $= s^2$

Solve for s. ______________ $= s$

3. For part (b), let $A = 200$ and solve for s. About how long is each side for an area of about 200 in.^{2}? ______________

4. Use your answer from Step 3 to find the distance between opposite sides of the hat box. ______________

Look Back and Check

5. To check your answer, substitute your value of s into the original equation and simplify. The value of A should be about 200. ______________

Solve Another Problem

6. a. A package designer wants the hexagonal base of a hat box to have an area of about 300 in.^{2}. About how long is each side?

____

b. Another designer wants the distance between opposites sides of the hat box to be 20 in. About how long is each side of the box?

____

Name ________________ Class ________________ Date ________________

Practice 7-6

Function Operations

1. A boutique prices merchandise by adding 80% to its cost. It later decreases by 25% the price of items that don't sell quickly.
   a. Write a function $f(x)$ to represent the price after the 80% markup.
   b. Write a function $g(x)$ to represent the price after the 25% markdown.
   c. Use a composition function to find the price of an item after both price adjustments that originally costs the boutique $150.
   d. Does the order in which the adjustments are applied make a difference? Explain.

Let $f(x) = 4x - 1$ and $g(x) = 2x^2 + 3$. Perform each function operation and then find the domain.

2. $f(x) + g(x)$
3. $f(x) - g(x)$
4. $f(x) \cdot g(x)$
5. $\frac{f(x)}{g(x)}$
6. $g(x) - f(x)$
7. $\frac{g(x)}{f(x)}$

Let $f(x) = -3x + 2$, $g(x) = \frac{x}{5}$, $h(x) = -2x^2 + 9$, and $j(x) = 5 - x$. Find each value or expression.

8. $(f \circ j)(3)$
9. $(j \circ h)(-1)$
10. $(h \circ g)(-5)$
11. $(g \circ f)(a)$
12. $f(x) + j(x)$
13. $f(x) - h(x)$
14. $(g \circ f)(-5)$
15. $(f \circ g)(-2)$
16. $3f(x) + 5g(x)$
17. $g(f(2))$
18. $g(f(x))$
19. $f(g(1))$

Let $g(x) = x^2 - 5$ and $h(x) = 3x + 2$. Perform each function operation.

20. $(h \circ g)(x)$
21. $g(x) \cdot h(x)$
22. $-2g(x) + h(x)$
23. A department store has marked down its merchandise by 25%. It later decreases by $5 the price of items that have not sold.
   a. Write a function $f(x)$ to represent the price after the 25% markdown.
   b. Write a function $g(x)$ to represent the price after the $5 markdown.
   c. Use a composition function to find the price of a $50 item after both price adjustments.
   d. Does the order in which the adjustments are applied make a difference? Explain.

Name ______________________ Class ______________ Date ______________

7-6 • Guided Problem Solving

GPS Exercise 71

Profit A craftsman makes and sells violins. The function $C(x) = 1000 + 700x$ represents his cost in dollars to produce x violins. The function $I(x) = 5995x$ represents the income in dollars from selling x violins.

a. Write and simplify a function $P(x) = I(x) - C(x)$.
b. Find $P(30)$, the profit earned when he makes and sells 30 violins.

Read and Understand

1. What do the functions $C(x)$ and $I(x)$ represent? ______________

2. Describe what $P(x)$ represents. ______________

Plan and Solve

3. What is $I(x)$? ______________

4. What is $C(x)$? ______________

5. Write and simplify a function $P(x) = I(x) - C(x)$. ______________

6. Find $P(30)$. ______________

7. What does $P(30)$ represent? ______________

Look Back and Check

8. To check the reasonableness of your answer, substitute $x = 30$ into each function $I(x)$ and $C(x)$, separately. Then calculate $P(x)$ by finding the difference of your values. The result should be the same as your answer for Step 6.

____

Solve Another Problem

9. **Profit** An artist makes and sells clay pots. The function $C(x) = 30 + 19x$ represents her cost in dollars to produce x pots. The function $I(x) = 75x$ represents the income in dollars from selling x pots.

   a. Write and simplify a function $P(x) = I(x) - C(x)$. ______________

   b. Find $P(250)$, the profit earned when she makes and sells 250 pots. ______________

Name ______________________ Class ______________ Date ______________

Practice 7-7

Inverse Relations and Functions

Graph each relation and its inverse.

1. $y = \frac{x+3}{3}$
2. $y = \frac{1}{2}x + 5$
3. $y = 2x + 5$
4. $y = 4x^2$
5. $y = \frac{1}{2}x^2$
6. $y = \frac{2}{3}x^2$

Find the inverse of each function. Is the inverse a function?

7. $y = x^2 + 2$
8. $y = x + 2$
9. $y = 3(x + 1)$
10. $y = -x^2 - 3$
11. $y = 2x - 1$
12. $y = 1 - 3x^2$
13. $y = 5x^2$
14. $y = (x + 3)^2$
15. $y = 6x^2 - 4$
16. $y = 3x^2 - 2$
17. $y = (x + 4)^2 - 4$
18. $y = -x^2 + 4$

For each function f, find f^{-1} and the domain and range of f and f^{-1}. Determine whether f^{-1} is a function.

19. $f(x) = \frac{1}{6}x$
20. $f(x) = -\frac{1}{5}x + 2$
21. $f(x) = x^2 - 2$
22. $f(x) = x^2 + 4$
23. $f(x) = \sqrt{x - 1}$
24. $f(x) = \sqrt{3x}$

Find the inverse of each relation. Graph the given relation and its inverse.

25.

x	−2	−1	0	1
y	−3	−2	−1	0

26.

x	0	1	2	3
y	−3	−1	0	−2

Let $f(x) = 2x + 5$. Find each value.

27. $(f^{-1} \circ f)(-1)$
28. $(f \circ f^{-1})(3)$
29. $(f \circ f^{-1})\left(-\frac{1}{2}\right)$

30. The equation $f(x) = 198{,}900x + 635{,}600$ can be used to model the number of utility trucks under 6000 pounds that are sold each year in the U.S. with $x = 0$ representing the year 1992. Find the inverse of the function. Use the inverse to estimate in which year the number of utility trucks under 6000 pounds sold in the U.S. will be 4,000,000.
Source: *www.infoplease.com*

Name ______________________ Class ______________ Date ______________

7-7 • Guided Problem Solving

GPS Exercise 44

Water Supply The velocity of the water that flows from an opening at the base of a tank depends on the height of water above the opening. The function $v(x) = \sqrt{2gx}$ models the velocity v in feet per second where g, the acceleration due to gravity, is about 32 ft/s^2 and x is the height in feet of the water. Find the inverse function and use it to find the depth of water when the flow is 40 ft/s, and when the flow is 20 ft/s.

Read and Understand

1. What do each of the following variables represent?

   v ______________________

   g ______________________

   x ______________________

Plan and Solve

2. To find the inverse, solve for x. Do not interchange the variables. $v = \sqrt{2gx}$

   Square both sides. ______________ $= 2gx$

   Divide both sides by $2g$. ______________ $= x$

   Let $g = 32$ and simplify. ______________ $= x$

3. Let $v = 40$ and simplify. ______________________

4. What is the depth of the water when the flow is 40 ft/s? ______________________

5. Let $v = 20$ and simplify. ______________________

6. What is the depth of the water when the flow is 20 ft/s? ______________________

Look Back and Check

7. To check the reasonableness of your answers, substitute your values for x back into the original function $v(x) = \sqrt{2gx}$. The values for v should be 40 and 20.

   ____

Solve Another Problem

8. **Investments** The principal amount P invested at a rate of r per year for 2 years will yield an amount of S dollars according to the function $S(r) = P(1 + r)^2$. Find the inverse function and use it to find the rate for \$2000 to grow to \$2350 in two years. Round your answer to the nearest tenth of a percent. ______________________

Name ______________________ Class ______________ Date ______________

Practice 7-8

Graphing Square Root and Other Radical Functions

Graph each function.

1. $y = -\sqrt{x + 2}$
2. $y = \sqrt{x - 3}$
3. $y = \sqrt{x} + 1$
4. $y = -\sqrt{x} - 1$
5. $y = \sqrt{x - 4} + 2$
6. $y = \sqrt{x + 1} - 3$
7. $y = \sqrt{x + 2} - 6$
8. $y = -\sqrt{x - 2} + 3$
9. $y = -\sqrt{x - 3} + 3$
10. $y = \sqrt{x + 3} - 2$
11. $y = \sqrt{x - 1} - 5$
12. $y = -\sqrt{x - 2} + 5$
13. $y = -\sqrt{x + 1} - 4$
14. $y = -\sqrt{x - 1} + 2$
15. $y = \sqrt{x - 1} + 3$
16. $y = \sqrt{x - 2} + 1$
17. $y = \sqrt{x + 2} - 2$
18. $y = \sqrt{x - 1} + 2$
19. $y = \sqrt{x + 1} + 4$
20. $y = \sqrt{x - 3} + 3$
21. $y = \sqrt{x + 1} - 2$
22. $y = \sqrt{x - 1} - 1$
23. $y = \sqrt{x + 3} - 3$
24. $y = \sqrt{x + 4} - 1$
25. $y = \sqrt{x - 2} - 4$
26. $y = \sqrt{x + 2} + 1$
27. $y = \sqrt{x - 2} + 3$
28. If you know the area A of a circle, you can use the equation $r = \sqrt{\frac{A}{\pi}}$ to find the radius r.
    - **a.** Graph the equation.
    - **b.** What is the radius of a circle with an area of 350 ft^2?

Solve each square root equation by graphing. Round the answer to the nearest hundredth if necessary. If there is no solution, explain why.

29. $\sqrt{x + 6} = 9$
30. $\sqrt{4x - 3} = 5$
31. $\sqrt{3x - 5} = \sqrt{1 - x}$
32. $3\sqrt{2x - 1} = 2\sqrt{x + 6}$

Rewrite each function to make it easy to graph using a translation. Describe the graph.

33. $y = \sqrt{81x + 162}$
34. $y = -\sqrt{4x + 20}$
35. $y = \sqrt[3]{125x - 250}$
36. $y = -\sqrt{64x + 192}$
37. $y = -\sqrt[3]{8x - 56} + 4$
38. $y = \sqrt{25x + 75} - 1$

Graph each function.

39. $y = \sqrt[3]{x - 1}$
40. $y = \sqrt[3]{x + 2} - 3$
41. $y = \sqrt[3]{x + 1} - 2$
42. $y = -\sqrt[3]{x} + 2$
43. $y = 2\sqrt[3]{x - 3}$
44. $y = \sqrt[3]{x + 3} - 1$

Name ____________________ Class ____________ Date ____________

7-8 • Guided Problem Solving

GPS Exercise 52

Circus The time t in seconds for a trapeze to complete one full cycle is given by the function $t = 1.11\sqrt{l}$, where l is the length of the trapeze in feet.

a. Graph the equation on your calculator. Make a sketch of the graph.
b. How long is a full cycle if the trapeze is 15 ft long? 30 ft long?

Read and Understand

1. What does l represent? ____________________

2. What does t represent? ____________________

Plan and Solve

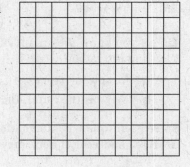

3. Graph $t = 1.11\sqrt{l}$ $\left(\text{or } y = 1.11\sqrt{x}\right)$ on your calculator. Make a sketch of the graph.

4. Let $l = 15$ and simplify. How long is a full cycle if the trapeze is 15 ft long? ____________

5. Let $l = 30$ and simplify. How long is a full cycle if the trapeze is 30 ft long? ____________

Look Back and Check

6. To check the reasonableness of your answers, substitute your values for t back into the original function $t = 1.11\sqrt{l}$ and solve for l. The values for l should be 15 and 30. ____________________

Solve Another Problem

7. **Navigation** To a ship navigator, the distance to the horizon d in nautical miles is given by the function $d = 1.17\sqrt{h}$, where h is the height of the navigator's eyes in feet above sea level. (Note: a nautical mile is about 6080 ft)

   a. Graph the equation on your calculator. Make a sketch of the graph. ____________________

   b. How far is it to the horizon line from a navigator whose eye level is 60 ft above sea level? 100 ft above sea level? ____________________

Name ______________________ Class ______________ Date ______________

7A: Graphic Organizer

For use before Lesson 7-1

Study Skill To best utilize your mathematics textbook, you need to be able to quickly locate information. Pre-reading a chapter enables you to see the new concepts and terms that you will encounter. A graphic organizer like the one below is an excellent way to record the information you find when you pre-read.

Write your answers.

1. What is the chapter title? ______________________

2. Find the Table of Contents page for this chapter at the front of the book. Name four topics you will study in this chapter.

______________________ ______________________

______________________ ______________________

3. Look through the pages of the chapter. List four real-world connections that you see discussed in this chapter.

______________________ ______________________

______________________ ______________________

4. Complete the graphic organizer as you work through the chapter.
1. Write the title of the chapter in the center oval.
2. When you begin a lesson, write the name of the lesson in a rectangle.
3. When you complete that lesson, write a skill or key concept from that lesson in the outer oval linked to that rectangle.

Continue with steps 2 and 3 clockwise around the graphic organizer.

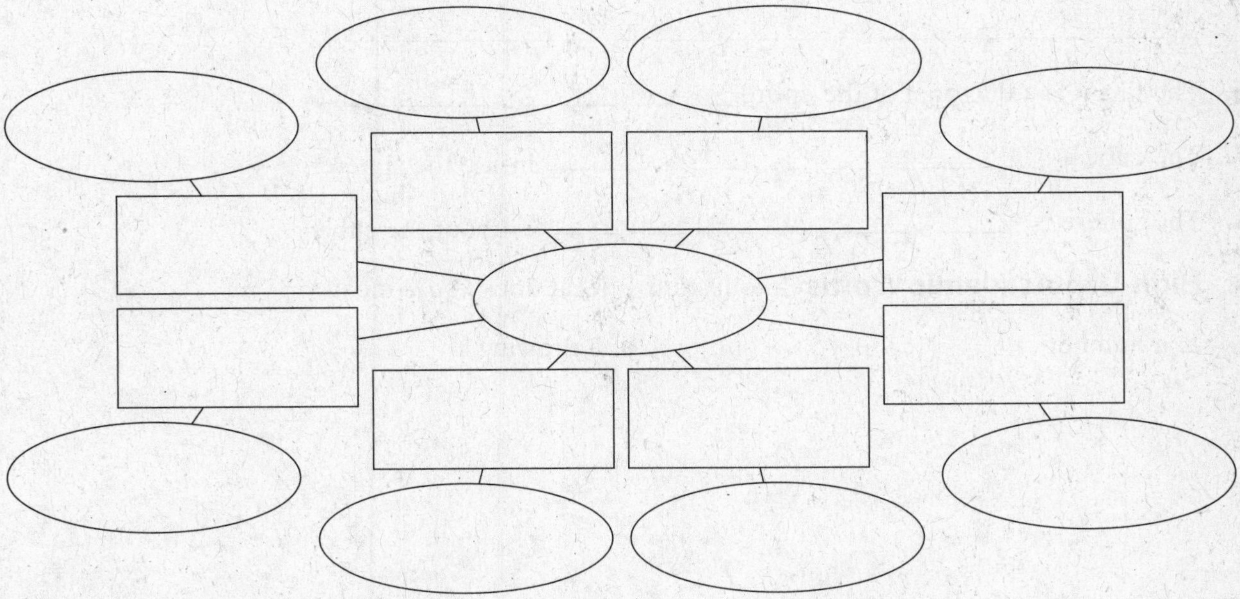

Vocabulary and Study Skills

7B: Reading Comprehension

For use after Lesson 7-6

Study Skill When you have many assignments to complete, try beginning with the one you find most challenging, while you are fresh, and leaving the ones that require less effort to do later when you may be tired.

Look at the figure, then answer the questions about reading this geometric figure.

A Cube Inscribed in a Sphere

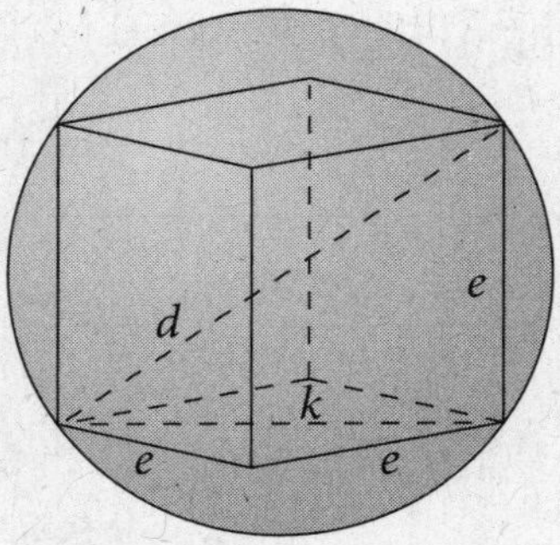

1. What is the name of the three-dimensional figure (polyhedron) shown that has an edge marked *e*? ______________________

2. How many edges, each of length *e*, does this polyhedron have? ______

3. How many vertices does this polyhedron have? ______________

4. What three-dimensional figure is represented in this two-dimensional figure by a circle? ______________________

5. Explain why some lines in the figure are not solid. ______________
____

6. The line *d* is a diagonal of the entire ______________________.

7. The cube is ______________________ inside the sphere.

8. The sphere is ______________________ about the cube.

9. **High-Use Academic Words** In question 1, what does *figure* mean?

   a. a number **b.** a drawing

7C: Reading/Writing Math Symbols

For use after Lesson 7-3

Study Skill When you are doing an assignment, begin by reviewing the instructions or direction line. Make sure you understand exactly what you are asked to do, and what the completed result will look like, before you start to work.

Draw a line from each expression in the left column to the phrase that matches it in the right column. Some items may have more than one match.

Mathematical Expression	Words to Say
1. x^3	**a.** the square root of 32
2. $\sqrt{32}$	**b.** the ordered pair 2, 3
3. $(-2)^3$	**c.** 8 factorial
4. $8!$	**d.** the permutation of 11 items taken 9 at a time
5. ${}_{11}P_9$	**e.** x cubed
6. $(2, 3)$	**f.** the combination of 5 items taken 3 at a time
7. ${}_5C_3$	**g.** negative 2, cubed
8. $\sqrt[3]{a + b}$	**h.** x to the third power
9. $a : b$	**i.** the ratio of a to b
	j. the cube root of the quantity a plus b
	k. $\frac{a}{b}$

Name ______________________ Class ____________ Date ____________

7D: Visual Vocabulary Practice

For use after Lesson 7-8

Study Skill Making sense of mathematical symbols is like reading a foreign language that uses different letters.

Concept List

composite function	inverse functions	inverse relation
like radicals	*n*th root	radical equation
radical function	square root equation	square root function

Write the concept that best describes each exercise. Choose from the concept list above.

1. $\sqrt[n]{a^n} = \lvert a \rvert$ when n is even ________________	**2.** $2\sqrt[3]{x}, -5\sqrt[3]{x}$ ________________	**3.** $f \circ g$ ________________
4. 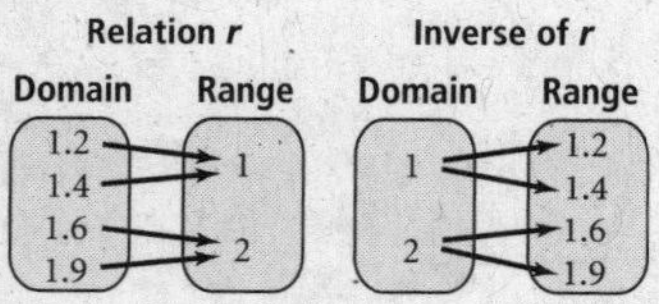 ________________	**5.** $5 + \sqrt{y} = 9$ ________________	**6.** $2(x - 2)^{\frac{2}{3}} = 50$ ________________
7. $f(x) = \sqrt{x} - 5$ ________________	**8.** $f(x) = -4\sqrt[3]{x + 2}$ ________________	**9.** $f(x) = 3x - 1$ and $f^{-1}(x) = \frac{x + 1}{3}$ ________________

Name ________________ Class ________________ Date ________________

7E: Vocabulary Check

For use after Lesson 7-4

Study Skill Strengthen your vocabulary. Use these pages and add cues and summaries by applying the Cornell Notetaking style.

Write the definition for each word at the right. To check your work, fold the paper back along the dotted line to see the correct answers.

Definition	Word
________________	Radicand
________________	Index
________________	Principal root
________________	Rationalize the denominator
________________	Rational exponent

Vocabulary and Study Skills

7E: Vocabulary Check (continued)

For use after Lesson 7-4

Write the vocabulary word for each definition. To check your work, fold the paper forward along the dotted line to see the correct answers.

The number under a radical sign. ______________________

With a radical sign, this indicates the degree of the root. ______________________

When a number has two real roots, this is the positive root. ______________________

Rewrite the denominator of an expression so there are no radicals in any denominator and no denominators in any radical. ______________________

If the nth root of a is a real number and m is an integer, then $a^{\frac{1}{n}} = \sqrt[n]{a}$ and $a^{\frac{m}{n}} = \sqrt[n]{a^m} = \left(\sqrt[n]{a}\right)^m$. If m is negative, $a \neq 0$. ______________________

7F: Vocabulary Review Puzzle

For use with Chapter Review

Study Skill When you complete a puzzle such as a word search, remember to read the list of words carefully and completely. As you identify each word in the word search, circle it and then cross off the word from the list. Pay special attention to the spelling of each word.

Complete the word search puzzle by finding the words that match each description below. For help, use the Glossary in your textbook. Remember a word may go right to left, left to right, up, down, or along a diagonal. Circle the letters that form each word.

1. the number that shows which root to take in a radical expression
2. a relation that "undoes" the original relation
3. the direction the graph is translated if h is negative in $y = (x - h)^2 + k$
4. root that is always indicated by the exponent form
5. type of equation with a variable in a radicand or a variable with a rational exponent
6. an exponent that can be expressed as the ratio of two integers

P	L	I	N	D	E	X	T	E	N	E
R	O	A	R	E	E	D	S	N	G	E
I	N	C	N	I	O	R	D	N	R	X
N	O	T	R	O	E	I	A	I	O	E
C	E	E	V	V	I	H	E	E	H	G
I	G	V	N	A	C	T	L	E	F	T
P	R	I	N	R	O	G	A	I	N	I
A	V	E	E	N	R	R	T	R	R	I
L	E	T	L	A	C	I	D	A	R	R

Name ______________________ Class ______________ Date ______________

Practice 8-1

Exploring Exponential Models

Without graphing, determine whether each equation represents exponential growth or exponential decay.

1. $y = 72(1.6)^x$
2. $y = 24(0.8)^x$
3. $y = 3\left(\frac{6}{5}\right)^x$
4. $y = 7\left(\frac{2}{3}\right)^x$

Sketch the graph of each function. Identify the horizontal asymptote.

5. $y = (0.3)^x$
6. $y = 3^x$
7. $y = 2\left(\frac{1}{5}\right)^x$
8. $y = \frac{1}{2}(3)^x$

9. A new car that sells for $18,000 depreciates 25% each year. Write a function that models the value of the car. Find the value of the car after 4 yr.

10. A new truck that sells for $29,000 depreciates 12% each year. Write a function that models the value of the truck. Find the value of the truck after 7 yr.

11. The bear population increases at a rate of 2% per year. There are 1573 bear this year. Write a function that models the bear population. How many bears will there be in 10 yr?

12. An investment of $75,000 increases at a rate of 12.5% per year. Find the value of the investment after 30 yr.

13. The population of an endangered bird is decreasing at a rate of 0.75% per year. There are currently about 200,000 of these birds. Write a function that models the bird population. How many birds will there be in 100 yr?

Write an exponential function $y = ab^x$ for a graph that includes the given points.

14. (0, 2), (1, 1.3)
15. (−1, 12.5), (4, 4.096)
16. (1, 0.84), (2, 1.008)

For each annual rate of change, find the corresponding growth or decay factor.

17. +45%
18. −10%
19. −40%
20. +200%

For each function, find the annual percent increase or decrease that the function models.

21. $y = 1700(0.75)^x$
22. $y = 30.698\left(\frac{5}{8}\right)^x$
23. $y = 984.5(1.73)^x$

24. The value of a piece of equipment has a decay factor of 0.80 per year. After 5 yr, the equipment is worth $98,304. What was the original value of the equipment?

Name ______________________ Class ______________ Date ______________

8-1 • Guided Problem Solving

GPS Exercise 43

Oceanography The function $y = 20 \cdot 0.975^x$ models the intensity of sunlight beneath the surface of the ocean. The output y represents the percent of surface sunlight intensity that reaches a depth of x feet. The model is accurate from about 20 feet to about 600 feet beneath the surface.

a. Find the percent of sunlight 50 feet beneath the surface of the ocean.
b. Find the percent of sunlight at a depth of 370 ft.

Read and Understand

1. What does the given function model? ______________
2. What does the input x represent? ______________
3. What does the input y represent? ______________

Plan and Solve

4. Consider finding the percent of sunlight 50 feet beneath the surface of the ocean. What is the depth x? ______________
5. Use a calculator to evaluate the function at this value. What is the function output? ______________
6. Interpret the output as percent sunlight. What is the percent of sunlight 50 feet beneath the surface of the ocean? ______________
7. Now consider finding the percent of sunlight at a depth of 370 ft. What is the depth x in this case? ______________
8. Use a calculator to evaluate the function at this value. What is the function output? ______________
9. Interpret the result. What is the percent of sunlight at a depth of 370 ft? ______________

Look Back and Check

10. Which depth has more sunlight? Does this agree with your common sense? Check the reasonableness of your answer by using a graphing calculator to graph the function and verify the percent sunlight at each depth. ______________

Solve Another Problem

11. The function $y = 62 \cdot 1.04^x$ models the quiz score of an average student in an algebra class. The output y represents the percent scored correct on the weekly quiz after spending x hours on homework that week. The model is accurate from about 2 hours to about 12 hours. Find the score of an average student that spends 10 hours per week studying algebra. ______________

Name ______________________ Class ______________ Date ______________

Practice 8-2

Properties of Exponential Functions

Evaluate each expression to four decimal places.

1. e^2
2. $e^{-2.5}$
3. $e^{\frac{1}{3}}$
4. $e^{\sqrt{2}}$

Find the amount in a continuously compounded account for the given conditions.

5. principal: \$5000
annual interest rate: 6.9%
time: 30 yr

6. principal: \$20,000
annual interest rate: 3.75%
time: 2 yr

7. Hg-197 is used in kidney scans. It has a half-life of 64.128 h. Write the exponential decay function for a 12-mg sample. Find the amount remaining after 72 h.

8. Sr-85 is used in bone scans. It has a half-life of 64.9 days. Write the exponential decay function for an 8-mg sample. Find the amount remaining after 100 days.

9. I-123 is used in thyroid scans. It has a half-life of 13.2 h. Write the exponential decay function for a 45-mg sample. Find the amount remaining after 5 h.

Without graphing, determine whether each equation represents exponential growth or exponential decay.

10. $y = \frac{5}{4}(0.11)^x$
11. $A(t) = 1000(1.075)^t$
12. $s(t) = 2.4(0.5)^t$

13. Suppose you invest \$5000 at an annual interest of 6.9%, compounded monthly.
    a. How much will you have in the account after 10 years?
    b. Determine how much more you would have if the interest were compounded continuously.

14. How long would it take to double your principal at an annual interest rate of 7% compounded continuously?

Graph each exponential function.

15. $y = 2^x$
16. $y = 2^{x+1}$
17. $y = -(2)^{x+1}$
18. $y = 5(0.12)^x$
19. $y = 5^x$
20. $y = -0.1(5)^x$
21. $y = 5^{-x}$
22. $y = -0.1(5)^{-x}$
23. $y = \left(\frac{1}{3}\right)^x$
24. $y = 5\left(\frac{1}{3}\right)^x$
25. $y = -5\left(\frac{1}{3}\right)^x$
26. $y = 2(2)^{x+2}$

Name ____________________ Class ____________ Date ____________

8-2 • Guided Problem Solving

GPS Exercise 30

Savings A student wants to save $8000 for college in five years. How much should be put into an account that earns 5.2% annual interest compounded continuously?

Read and Understand

1. What is the student's final goal? ____________________
2. How long will the amount in the account be allowed to grow to reach this goal? ____________
3. How often will the student be putting money into the account? That is, will the student be making monthly deposits into the account or a single one-time deposit? ____________
4. How is the interest compounded? ____________________

Plan and Solve

5. Change the interest rate from a percent to a decimal. ____________
6. Let P represent the initial principal that should be put into the account. Substitute the appropriate values into the continuous compound interest formula. ____________
7. Solve the equation for P. How much should be put into the account? ____________

Look Back and Check

8. Use your answer as the initial principal with the continuous compound interest formula. Make a table to show the account value after one, two, three, four, and five years. Verify the amount after five years matches the student's goal. ____________________
9. Check your answer another way. Determine the effective annual interest rate: how much interest is earned in one year on one dollar? Note that it should be more than 5.2%. Use this effective annual interest rate with the simple interest formula, $I = Prt$. Verify the result is the same. ____________

Solve Another Problem

10. A student wants to save $3000 for a trip to Egypt in four years. How much should be put into an account that earns 4% annual interest compounded continuously? ____________

Name ____________________ Class ____________ Date ____________

Practice 8-3

Logarithmic Functions as Inverses

Write each equation in exponential form.

1. $\log_4 256 = 4$
2. $\log_7 1 = 0$
3. $\log_2 32 = 5$
4. $\log 10 = 1$
5. $\log_5 5 = 1$
6. $\log_8 \frac{1}{64} = -2$
7. $\log_9 59{,}049 = 5$
8. $\log_{17} 289 = 2$
9. $\log_{56} 1 = 0$
10. $\log_{12} \frac{1}{144} = -2$
11. $\log_2 \frac{1}{1024} = -10$
12. $\log_3 6561 = 8$

Write each equation in logarithmic form.

13. $9^2 = 81$
14. $25^2 = 625$
15. $8^3 = 512$
16. $13^2 = 169$
17. $2^9 = 512$
18. $4^5 = 1024$
19. $5^4 = 625$
20. $10^{-3} = 0.001$
21. $4^{-3} = \frac{1}{64}$
22. $5^{-2} = \frac{1}{25}$
23. $8^{-1} = \frac{1}{8}$
24. $11^0 = 1$
25. $6^1 = 6$
26. $6^{-3} = \frac{1}{216}$
27. $17^0 = 1$
28. $17^1 = 17$
29. A single-celled bacterium divides every hour. The number N of bacteria after t hours is given by the formula $\log_2 N = t$. After how many hours will there be 32 bacteria?

Evaluate each logarithm.

30. $\log_2 16$
31. $\log_2 8$
32. $\log_2 4$
33. $\log_2 2$
34. $\log_2 1$
35. $\log_2 \frac{1}{2}$
36. $\log_2 \frac{1}{4}$
37. $\log_2 \frac{1}{8}$
38. $\log_{16} 16$
39. $\log_5 125$
40. $\log_{11} 121$
41. $\log 0.1$
42. $\log 1$
43. $\log_3 1$
44. $\log_6 216$
45. $\log_{12} 12$
46. $\log_{30} 30$
47. $\log 100{,}000$
48. $\log_3 \frac{1}{9}$
49. $\log_3 \frac{1}{27}$
50. $\log \frac{1}{100}$
51. $\log_4 32$
52. $\log_7 \frac{1}{49}$
53. $\log_{81} 9$

For each pH given, find the concentration of hydrogen ions $[H^+]$. Use the formula $pH = -\log[H^+]$.

54. 7.2
55. 7.3
56. 8.2
57. 6.2
58. 5.6
59. 4.6
60. 7.0
61. 2.9

Graph each logarithmic function.

62. $y = \log x$
63. $y = \log_3 x$
64. $y = \log_6 x$
65. $y = \log_{\frac{1}{2}} x$
66. $y = \log_3(x + 1)$
67. $y = \log_2 x - 3$
68. $y = \log_6(x + 2)$
69. $y = \log_5(x - 4) + 1$
70. $y = \log_2(x - 3) + 1$

Name ______________________ Class ______________ Date ______________

8-3 • Guided Problem Solving

GPS Exercise 50

Error Analysis Find the error in the following evaluation of $\log_{27}3$. Then evaluate the logarithm correctly.

$$\begin{aligned}\log_{27}3 &= x\\ 27 &= x^3\\ 3 &= x\\ \log_{27}3 &= 3\end{aligned}$$

Read and Understand

1. What is being evaluated? ______________________

Plan and Solve

2. To evaluate $\log_{27}3$, write an equation in logarithmic form. Does this agree with the first line shown in the evaluation? ______________________

3. Convert the logarithmic form $\log_b y = x$ to exponential form $y = b^x$. ______________________

4. Compare this to the given evaluation. Where is the error? ______________________

5. Write each side of the exponential form using base 3. ______________________

6. Use the Power Property of Exponents to simplify the equation. ______________________

7. Since the bases are the same on each side, the exponents must be equal. Equate exponents by setting the exponents equal to each other. ______________________

8. Solve the equation for x. What is $\log_{27}3$? ______________________

Look Back and Check

9. Check your result using the definition of a logarithm. Evaluating $\log_{27}3$ is the same as asking, "What power do I raise 27 to so that I get 3?" Verify this exponent is the same as your result. ______________________

Solve Another Problem

10. Find the error in the following evaluation of $\log_4 8$. Then evaluate the logarithm correctly.

$$\begin{aligned}\log_4 8 &= x\\ 8 &= 4^x\\ 2^3 &= 4^x\\ 3 &= x\\ \log_4 8 &= 3\end{aligned}$$
____

Name ______________________ Class ______________ Date ______________

Practice 8-4

Properties of Logarithms

For Exercises 1–2, use the formula $L = 10 \log \frac{I}{I_0}$.

1. A sound has an intensity of $5.92 \times 10^{25}\text{W/m}^2$. What is the loudness of the sound in decibels? Use $I_0 = 10^{-12}\text{W/m}^2$.

2. Suppose you decrease the intensity of a sound by 45%. By how many decibels would the loudness be decreased?

Assume that $\log 3 \approx 0.4771$, $\log 4 \approx 0.6021$, and $\log 5 \approx 0.6990$. Use the properties of logarithms to evaluate each expression. Do not use a calculator.

3. $\log 12$ **4.** $\log 16$ **5.** $\log \frac{3}{5}$ **6.** $\log 0.8$

7. $\log 75$ **8.** $\log \frac{16}{5}$ **9.** $\log_6 1 - \log 1$ **10.** $\log 60$

Write each logarithmic expression as a single logarithm.

11. $\log_5 4 + \log_5 3$ **12.** $\log_6 25 - \log_6 5$ **13.** $\log_2 4 + \log_2 2 - \log_2 8$

14. $5 \log_7 x - 2 \log_7 x$ **15.** $\log_4 60 - \log_4 4 + \log_4 x$ **16.** $\log 7 - \log 3 + \log 6$

17. $2 \log x - 3 \log y$ **18.** $\frac{1}{2} \log r + \frac{1}{3} \log s - \frac{1}{4} \log t$ **19.** $\log_3 4x + 2 \log_3 5y$

20. $5 \log 2 - 2 \log 2$ **21.** $\frac{1}{3} \log 3x + \frac{2}{3} \log 3x$ **22.** $2 \log 4 + \log 2 + \log 2$

23. $(\log 3 - \log 4) - \log 2$ **24.** $5 \log x + 3 \log x^2$ **25.** $\log_6 3 - \log_6 6$

26. $\log 2 + \log 4 - \log 7$ **27.** $\log_3 2x - 5 \log_3 y$ **28.** $\frac{1}{3}(\log_2 x - \log_2 y)$

29. $\frac{1}{2} \log x + \frac{1}{3} \log y - 2 \log z$ **30.** $3(4 \log t^2)$ **31.** $\log_5 y - 4(\log_5 r + 2 \log_5 t)$

Expand each logarithm.

32. $\log xyz$ **33.** $\log_2 \frac{x}{yz}$ **34.** $\log 6x^3y$

35. $\log 7(3x - 2)^2$ **36.** $\log \sqrt{\frac{2rst}{5w}}$ **37.** $\log \frac{5x}{4y}$

38. $\log_5 5x^{-5}$ **39.** $\log \frac{2x^2y}{3k^3}$ **40.** $\log_4 (3xyz)^2$

State the property or properties used to rewrite each expression.

41. $\log 6 - \log 3 = \log 2$ **42.** $6 \log 2 = \log 64$ **43.** $\log 3x = \log 3 + \log x$

44. $\frac{1}{3} \log_2 x = \log_2 \sqrt[3]{x}$ **45.** $\frac{2}{3} \log 7 = \log \sqrt[3]{49}$ **46.** $\log_4 20 - 3 \log_4 x = \log_4 \frac{20}{x^3}$

Name ____________________ Class ____________ Date ____________

8-4 • Guided Problem Solving

GPS Exercise 56

Noise Control New components reduce the sound intensity of a certain model of vacuum cleaner from 10^{-4} W/m^2 to 6.31×10^{-6} W/m^2. By how many decibels do these new components reduce the vacuum cleaner's loudness?

Read and Understand

1. What is the sound intensity I_1 of a vacuum without the new components? ____________

2. What is the sound intensity I_2 of a vacuum with the new components? ____________

3. What units measure the apparent loudness of a vacuum? ____________

4. What quantity does the problem ask you to find? ____________

Plan and Solve

5. Let L_1 = loudness without the new components. The relation between apparent loudness L and intensity I is $L = 10 \log \frac{I}{I_0}$. Use the value of I_1 to write an expression for L_1. ____________

6. Let L_2 = loudness with the new components. Use the relation between apparent loudness and intensity with the value of I_2. What is an expression for L_2? ____________

7. The reduction of loudness is the difference of L_1 and L_2. Use the prior results to write an expression for this difference. ____________

8. Apply the quotient property of logarithms. ____________

9. Distribute and combine any like terms. ____________

10. Finish simplifying the expression. By how many decibels is the loudness decreased? ____________

Look Back and Check

11. Use a value of $I_0 = 10^{-12}$W/m^2 for the threshold of hearing. Calculate the values of L_1 and L_2. Find the difference in these values and compare it to your result. ____________

Solve Another Problem

12. A noise-enhancing muffler increases the sound intensity of a certain model of motorcycle from 10^{-3}W/m^2 to 3.1×10^{-2} W/m^2. By how many decibels does the modified muffler increase the motorcycle's loudness?

____

Name ______________________ Class ______________ Date ______________

Practice 8-5

Exponential and Logarithmic Equations

Use the Change of Base Formula to evaluate each expression. Round answers to the nearest hundredth.

1. $\log_2 12$ **2.** $\log_3 40$ **3.** $\log_4 8$ **4.** $\log_5 3$ **5.** $\log_2 1$

6. $\log_5 10$ **7.** $\log_2 8$ **8.** $\log_3 6$ **9.** $\log_9 3$ **10.** $\log_8 3$

Solve each equation. Check your answer. Round answers to the nearest hundredth.

11. $2^x = 243$ **12.** $7^n = 12$ **13.** $5^{2x} = 20$ **14.** $8^{n+1} = 3$

15. $4^{n-2} = 3$ **16.** $4^{3n} = 5$ **17.** $15^{2n-3} = 245$ **18.** $4^x - 5 = 12$

Solve each equation. Check your answer. Round answers to the nearest hundredth.

19. $\log 3x = 2$ **20.** $4 \log x = 4$ **21.** $\log (3x - 2) = 3$

22. $2 \log x - \log 5 = -2$ **23.** $\log 8 - \log 2x = -1$ **24.** $\log (x + 21) + \log x = 2$

25. $8 \log x = 16$ **26.** $\log x = 2$ **27.** $\log 4x = 2$

28. $\log (x - 25) = 2$ **29.** $2 \log x = 2$ **30.** $\log 3x - \log 5 = 1$

Use a table to solve each equation. Round answers to the nearest hundredth.

31. $10^x = 182$ **32.** $8^n = 12$ **33.** $10^{2x} = 9$ **34.** $5^{n+1} = 3$

35. $10^{n-2} = 0.3$ **36.** $3^{3n} = 50$ **37.** $10^{2n-5} = 500$ **38.** $11^x - 50 = 12$

The function $y = 1000(1.005)^x$ models the value of \$1000 deposit at 6% per year (0.005 per month) x months after the money is deposited.

39. Use a graph (on your graphing calculator) to predict how many months it will be until the account is worth \$1100.

40. Predict how many years it will be until the account is worth \$5000.

Solve each equation. Round answers to the nearest hundredth.

41. $2 \log 3x - \log 9 = 1$ **42.** $\log x - \log 4 = -1$ **43.** $\log x - \log 4 = -2$

44. $\log x - \log 4 = 3$ **45.** $2 \log x - \log 4 = 2$ **46.** $\log (2x + 5) = 3$

47. $2 \log (2x + 5) = 4$ **48.** $\log 4x = -1$ **49.** $2 \log x - \log 3 = 1$

Solve by graphing. Round answers to the nearest hundredth.

50. $10^n = 3$ **51.** $10^{3y} = 5$ **52.** $10^{k-2} = 20$

53. $5^x = 4$ **54.** $2^{4x} = 8$ **55.** $3^{x+5} = 15$

Name ____________________ Class ____________ Date ____________

8-5 • Guided Problem Solving

GPS Exercise 49

Seismology An earthquake of magnitude 7.9 occurred in 2001 in Gujarat, India. It was 11,600 times as strong as the greatest earthquake ever to hit Pennsylvania. Find the magnitude of the Pennsylvania earthquake.

Read and Understand

1. What was the magnitude of the 2001 earthquake in India? ____________

2. What are you to find? ____________

Plan and Solve

3. Recall from Lesson 8-3 that the energy released in an earthquake of magnitude M is $E \cdot 30^M$. Write an expression for the energy released in India's earthquake. ____________

4. Let M be the magnitude of the Pennsylvania earthquake. Write an expression for the energy released in the Pennsylvania earthquake. ____________

5. Write an equation that compares the ratio of the two quakes. Use the fact that 11,600 times more energy was released in India's quake. ____________

6. Simplify the equation by canceling any common factors. Then rewrite the ratio as a single exponential with base 30. ____________

7. Take the common logarithm of each side of the equation. ____________

8. Use the power property of logarithms. ____________

9. Solve the equation for M. What was the magnitude of the Pennsylvania earthquake? ____________

Look Back and Check

10. Use a table to solve the exponential equation. Verify the result is the same.

____

11. Using your answer, M, evaluate 30^M. Multiply the result by 11,600. Compare this to $30^{7.9}$.

____

Solve Another Problem

12. After x hours, the number of bacteria in a certain culture is $P \cdot 2^x$. After 5 hours, the population is 8 times larger than when the biologist checked it the first time. When did the biologist first check the culture?

____

Name ______________________ Class ______________ Date ______________

Practice 8-6

Natural Logarithms

The formula $P = 50e^{-\frac{t}{25}}$ gives the power output P, in watts, available to run a certain satellite for t days. Find how long a satellite with the given power output will operate. Round answers to the nearest hundredth.

1. 10 W **2.** 12 W **3.** 14 W

The formula for the maximum velocity v of a rocket is $v = c \ln R$, where c is the velocity of the exhaust in km/s and R is the mass ratio of the rocket. A rocket must reach 7.8 km/s to attain a stable orbit. Round answers to the nearest hundredth.

4. Find the maximum velocity of a rocket with a mass ratio of about 18 and an exhaust velocity of 2.2 km/s. Can this rocket achieve a stable orbit?

5. What mass ratio would be needed to achieve a stable orbit for a rocket with an exhaust velocity of 2.5 km/s?

6. A rocket with an exhaust velocity of 2.4 km/s can reach a maximum velocity of 7.8 km/s. What is the mass ratio of the rocket?

Use natural logarithms to solve each equation. Round answers to the nearest hundredth.

7. $e^x = 15$ **8.** $4e^x = 10$ **9.** $e^{x+2} = 50$ **10.** $4e^{3x-1} = 5$

11. $e^{x-4} = 2$ **12.** $5e^{6x+3} = 0.1$ **13.** $e^x = 1$ **14.** $e^{\frac{x}{5}} = 32$

15. $3e^{3x-5} = 49$ **16.** $7e^{5x+8} = 0.23$ **17.** $6 - e^{12x} = 5.2$ **18.** $e^{\frac{x}{2}} = 25$

19. $e^{2x} = 25$ **20.** $e^{\ln 5x} = 20$ **21.** $e^{\ln x} = 21$ **22.** $e^{x+6} + 5 = 1$

Solve each equation. Check your answer. Round answers to the nearest hundredth.

23. $4 \ln x = -2$ **24.** $2 \ln (3x - 4) = 7$ **25.** $5 \ln (4x - 6) = -6$

26. $-7 + \ln 2x = 4$ **27.** $3 - 4 \ln (8x + 1) = 12$ **28.** $\ln x + \ln 3x = 14$

29. $2 \ln x + \ln x^2 = 3$ **30.** $\ln x + \ln 4 = 2$ **31.** $\ln x - \ln 5 = -1$

32. $\ln e^x = 3$ **33.** $3 \ln e^{2x} = 12$ **34.** $\ln e^{x+5} = 17$

35. $\ln 3x + \ln 2x = 3$ **36.** $5 \ln (3x - 2) = 15$ **37.** $7 \ln (2x + 5) = 8$

38. $\ln (3x + 4) = 5$ **39.** $\ln \frac{2x}{41} = 2$ **40.** $\ln (2x - 1)^2 = 4$

Write each expression as a single natural logarithm.

41. $\ln 16 - \ln 8$ **42.** $3 \ln 3 + \ln 9$ **43.** $a \ln 4 - \ln b$

44. $\ln z - 3 \ln x$ **45.** $\frac{1}{2} \ln 9 + \ln 3x$ **46.** $4 \ln x + 3 \ln y$

Name ______________________ Class ______________ Date ______________

8-6 • Guided Problem Solving

GPS Exercise 40

Space Use the formula for maximum velocity $v = -0.0098t + c \ln R$. Find the mass ratio of a rocket with an exhaust velocity of 3.1 km/s, a firing time of 50 s, and a maximum shuttle velocity of 6.9 km/s.

Read and Understand

1. Connect the formula to the given rocket specifications. Refer to Example 2 in your textbook, if needed. What do the variables v, t, c, and R represent in the velocity formula?

   v is ______________ t is ______________

   c is ______________ R is ______________

2. What are the given values for these variables, if known?

   $v =$ ________ $t =$ ________ $c =$ ________ $R =$ ________

Plan and Solve

3. Use the velocity formula. Substitute the values for the variables as determined above.

   ____

4. Isolate the logarithm on one side of the equation. ______________
5. Rewrite the equation in exponential form, using e as the base. ______________
6. Evaluate the exponential expression. What is mass ratio of the rocket? ______________

Look Back and Check

7. Make sure you have properly applied the formula. Use the units given with each quantity to double-check your interpretation of the variables. Then verify your substitutions.
8. Does the answer make sense? Recall from Example 2 in your textbook, the mass ratio of the rocket is the ratio that compares the mass of the rocket filled with fuel to its mass without fuel. Should this ratio be less than one or greater than one? Explain. Then verify your answer meets this requirement. ______________
9. Solve the equation using a table. Verify the result is the same. ______________

Solve Another Problem

10. Find the mass ratio of a rocket with an exhaust velocity of 2.8 km/s, a firing time of 60 s, and a maximum shuttle velocity of 7.8 km/s. ______________

Name ____________________ Class ____________ Date ____________

8A: Graphic Organizer

For use before Lesson 8-1

Study Skill Be sure to read with pencil and paper in hand. Take notes and draw sketches as you look at the new chapter. Formulate questions you might have as you look at each section of the chapter.

Write your answers.

1. What is the chapter title? ____________________

2. Find the Table of Contents page for this chapter at the front of the book. Name four topics you will study in this chapter.

____________________ ____________________

____________________ ____________________

3. Complete the graphic organizer as you work through the chapter.
1. Write the title of the chapter in the center oval.
2. When you begin a lesson, write the name of the lesson in a rectangle.
3. When you complete that lesson, write a skill or key concept from that lesson in the outer oval linked to that rectangle.

Continue with steps 2 and 3 clockwise around the graphic organizer.

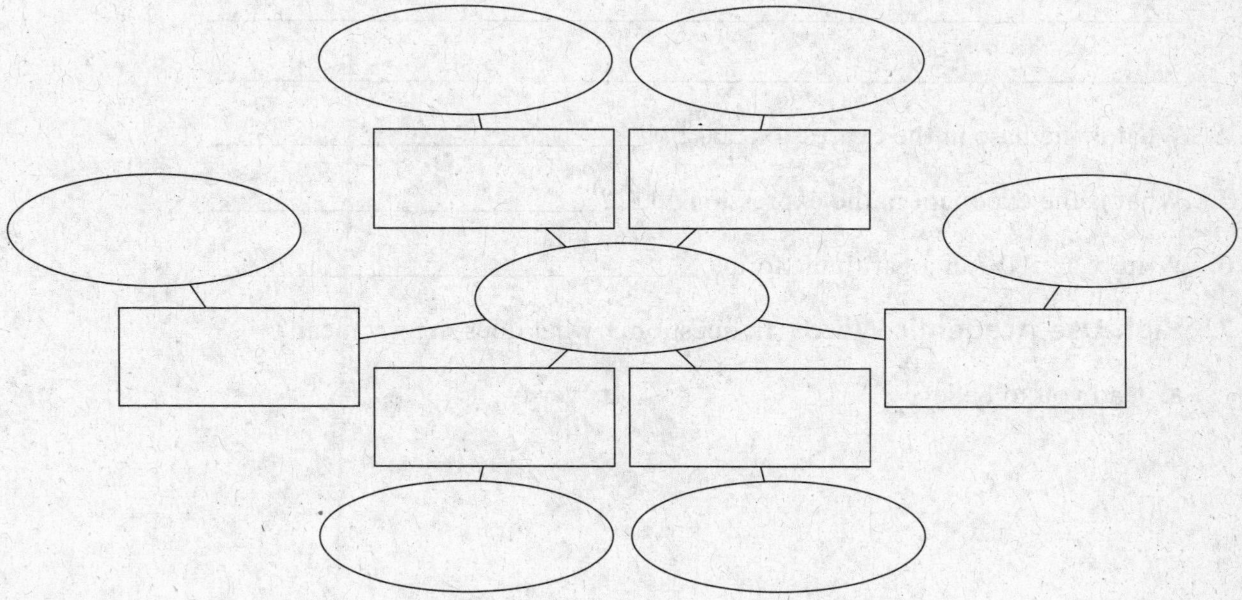

Name ______________________ Class ______________ Date ______________

8B: Reading Comprehension

For use after Lesson 8-5

Study Skill When you read a paragraph, it may help you to visualize by forming a clear picture in your mind of what you want to remember. Make mental pictures of the content you are reading, like a "mind movie," to help you recall the content later.

Read the passage below and answer the questions that follow.

> In the twentieth century, both common and natural logarithms have been used in the design of electronic computers and calculators. Since pocket calculators are now widely available, you might wonder how useful or necessary logarithms are today. In working with very large or very small numbers, you will find that the pocket calculator has its limitations. For example, a number such as 500^{39} is too large for most pocket calculators, yet the answer can be quickly and easily approximated using logarithms.

1. What is the subject of this paragraph? ______________________

2. What are the two types of logarithms? ______________________

3. The source for this passage is a book published in 1982. What content in the passage might suggest that it was written some time ago?

   ____

   ____

4. What is the base in the expression 500^{39}? ______________________

5. What is the exponent in the expression 500^{39}? ______________________

6. Write $x = 500^{39}$ in logarithmic form. ______________________

7. **High-Use Academic Words** In question 3, what does *suggest* mean?

   a. lead you to believe **b.** verify

Name ______________________ Class ______________ Date ______________

8C: Reading/Writing Math Symbols

For use after Lesson 8-3

Study Skill Have a dictionary and the Glossary for your text (if available) close by as you study. Look up any symbols or words whose meaning you are not sure of, and add the symbol or word and its definition to your written vocabulary list.

Grouping symbols, such as parentheses, carry much of the meaning in mathematics. Compare the meaning of the following expressions by evaluating each one for $a = 2$ and $b = -3$. The first one is done for you.

1. $(a + b)^2 =$ ___1___ $a^2 + b^2 =$ ___13___

Is $(a + b)^2$ the same as $a^2 + b^2$? ___no___

2. $|a + b| =$ ________ $|a| + |b| =$ ________

Is $|a + b|$ the same as $|a| + |b|$? ________________

3. $(a, b) =$ ________ $(b, a) =$ ________

Is the point (a, b) the same as the point (b, a)? ________________

4. $|a - b| =$ ________ $|a| - |b| =$ ________

Is $|a - b|$ the same as $|a| - |b|$? ________________

5. $(a^2)^3 =$ ________ $(a^3)^2 =$ ________

Is $(a^2)^3$ the same as $(a^3)^2$? ________________

6. $-(b^2) =$ ________ $(-b^2) =$ ________ $(-b)^2 =$ ________

Is $-(b^2)$ the same as either $(-b^2)$ or $(-b)^2$? ________________

Name ____________________ Class ____________ Date ____________

8D: Visual Vocabulary Practice

For use after Lesson 8-6

Study Skill When learning a new concept, try to draw a picture to illustrate it.

Concept List

change of base formula	common logarithm	continuously compounded interest
decay factor	exponential equation	growth factor
logarithmic equation	logarithmic function	natural logarithmic function

Write the concept that best describes each exercise. Choose from the concept list above.

1. $\log 100$ ________________	**2.** $\log_8 3 = \dfrac{\log 3}{\log 8}$ ________________	**3.** $4^{2x} = 135$ ________________
4. $y = 100(2)^x$ ________________	**5.** $\log(2x + 1) = 5$ ________________	**6.** $A = Pe^{rt}$ ________________
7. $y = \log_2 x$ ________________	**8.** $y = 50\left(\frac{1}{2}\right)^{12.5}$ ________________	**9.** $y = \ln x$ ________________

Name ________________ Class ________________ Date ________________

8E: Vocabulary Check

For use after Lesson 8-4

Study Skill Strengthen your vocabulary. Use these pages and add cues and summaries by applying the Cornell Notetaking style.

Write the definition for each word at the right. To check your work, fold the paper back along the dotted line to see the correct answers.

________________ ________________ ________________	Asymptote
________________ ________________ ________________	Logarithmic function
________________ ________________ ________________	Exponential function
________________ ________________ ________________	Common Logarithm
________________ ________________ ________________	Growth factor

8E: Vocabulary Check (continued)

For use after Lesson 8-4

Write the vocabulary word for each definition. To check your work, fold the paper forward along the dotted line to see the correct answers.

A line that a graph approaches but never reaches. ____________________

The inverse of an exponential function. ____________________

The general form is $y = ab^x$, where x is a real number, $b > 0$, and $b \neq 1$. ____________________

A logarithm that uses base 10. ____________________

The value b in $y = ab^x$, where $b > 1$. ____________________

Name ____________________ Class ____________ Date ____________

8F: Vocabulary Review

For use with Chapter Review

Study Skill Math vocabulary may seem less important than being able to solve problems, but without knowing the vocabulary words from previous lessons or chapters, you may have trouble understanding new concepts as they are introduced.

Draw a line from each word or phrase in the left column to the example that matches it in the right column. For help, use the Glossary in your textbook.

Word(s)	Example
1. asymptote	**a.** $y = \log 5$
2. continuously compounded interest formula	**b.** $y = ab^x$
3. decay factor	**c.** 3 in $y = 7(3)^x$
4. exponential function	**d.** $A = Pe^{rt}$
5. growth factor	**e.** the x-axis for $y = \left(\frac{1}{2}\right)^x$
6. logarithmic function	**f.** 0.4 in $y = 2(0.4)^x$
7. inverse functions	**g.** $y = e^x$ and $\ln y = x$
8. Use of Change of Base Formula	**h.** $\log_3 15 = \frac{\log 15}{\log 3}$

Name ______________________ Class ______________ Date ______________

Practice 9-1

Inverse Variation

Each ordered pair is from an inverse variation. Find the constant of variation.

1. $\left(3, \frac{1}{3}\right)$
2. $(0.2, 6)$
3. $(10, 5)$
4. $\left(\frac{5}{7}, \frac{2}{5}\right)$
5. $(3.5, 1.2)$

Suppose that x and y vary inversely. Write a function that models each inverse variation.

6. $x = 7$ when $y = 2$
7. $x = 4$ when $y = 9$
8. $x = -3$ when $y = 8$
9. $x = 5$ when $y = -6$
10. $x = 1$ when $y = 0.8$
11. $x = -4$ when $y = -2$
12. $x = \frac{3}{5}$ when $y = 5$
13. $x = 3$ when $y = 2.1$
14. $x = -\frac{1}{3}$ when $y = \frac{9}{10}$

Describe the combined variation that is modeled by each formula.

15. $I = \frac{120}{R}$
16. $A = \frac{1}{2}bh$
17. $h = \frac{3V}{B}$
18. $V = \frac{4}{3}\pi r^3$

Each pair of values is from an inverse variation. Find the missing value.

19. $(2, 4)$ and $(6, y)$
20. $\left(\frac{1}{3}, 6\right)$ and $\left(x, -\frac{1}{2}\right)$
21. $(1.2, 4.5)$ and $(2.7, y)$

Suppose that x and y vary inversely. Write a function that models each inverse variation, and find y when $x = 8$.

22. $x = 4$ when $y = 2$
23. $x = -3$ when $y = \frac{1}{3}$
24. $x = 6$ when $y = 1.2$

Write the function that models each relationship. Find z when $x = 6$ and $y = 4$.

25. z varies jointly with x and y. When $x = 7$ and $y = 2$, $z = 28$.
26. z varies directly with x and inversely with the cube of y. When $x = 8$ and $y = 2$, $z = 3$.

Is the relationship between the values in each table a direct variation, an inverse variation, or neither? Write equations to model the direct and inverse variations.

27.

x	2	4	5	20
y	10	5	4	1

28.

x	1	3	7	10
y	2	8	20	29

29.

x	1	2	5	7
y	6	12	30	42

30.

x	0.2	0.5	2	3
y	25	62.5	250	375

31.

x	0.1	0.5	1.5	2
y	31	7	3	2.5

32.

x	3	1.5	0.5	0.3
y	5	10	30	50

Name ______________________ Class ______________ Date ______________

9-1 • Guided Problem Solving

GPS Exercise 53

Suppose that y varies directly with x and inversely with z^2, and $x = 48$ when $y = 8$ and $z = 3$. Find x when $y = 12$ and $z = 2$.

Read and Understand

1. How do x and y vary? ______________________

2. How do y and z^2 vary? ______________________

3. When x is 48 and z is 3, what is the value of y? ______________________

4. What quantity are you to find? ______________________

Plan and Solve

5. Use the fact that y varies directly with x and inversely with z^2. Write y as a function of x and z, using k for the constant of variation. ______________________

6. Substitute the given values for the three variables into your equation. ______________________

7. Solve the equation for k. ______________________

8. Substitute this value of k into your function from Step 5. ______________________

9. Substitute $y = 12$ and $z = 2$. Solve for x. ______________________

Look Back and Check

10. Look at your initial function from Step 5. Check that it agrees with the described combined variation. Specifically, is y varying directly or inversely with x in your function? Ignoring x, does y vary with z or with the square of z in your function? Is this a direct variation or an inverse variation? ______________________

    ____

11. Determine the value of k differently. Substitute your value for x together with $y = 12$ and $z = 2$ into your function from Step 5. Solve for k and verify it is the same value you found in Step 7.

    ____

Solve Another Problem

12. Suppose that c varies directly with b and inversely with a, and $a = 3$ when $c = 4$ and $b = 6$. Find a when $c = 5$ and $b = 10$. ______________________

Name ______________________ Class ______________ Date ______________

Practice 9-2

Graphing Inverse Variations

Write an equation for a translation of $y = -\frac{3}{x}$ that has the given asymptotes.

1. $x = 2; y = 1$
2. $x = -1; y = 3$
3. $x = 4; y = -2$
4. $x = 0; y = 6$
5. $x = 3; y = 0$
6. $x = 1; y = 2$
7. $x = -3; y = -1$
8. $x = -2; y = 1$

Sketch the asymptotes and the graph of each equation.

9. $y = \frac{3}{x - 1} + 2$
10. $y = \frac{2}{x + 1}$
11. $y = \frac{11}{x + 3} - 3$
12. $y = -\frac{4}{x - 2} - 2$
13. $y = \frac{1}{x} + 3$
14. $y = \frac{1}{x + 1} - 2$
15. $y = \frac{1}{x - 2} + 1$
16. $y = \frac{1}{x - 1} - 1$
17. $y = \frac{2}{x}$
18. $y = -\frac{3}{x - 3} + 1$
19. $y = \frac{1}{x + 1} + 2$
20. $y = \frac{3}{4x} + \frac{1}{2}$
21. $y = \frac{3}{x + 3} - 1$
22. $y = \frac{2}{x - 5}$
23. $y = -\frac{6}{x - 3} - 2$
24. $y = \frac{5}{x}$
25. $y = \frac{1}{x - 1} + 1$
26. $y = \frac{1}{x}$
27. $y = -\frac{3}{x - 4} - 2$
28. $y = -\frac{1}{x - 2} - \frac{1}{2}$

The length of a panpipe p (in feet) is inversely proportional to its pitch ℓ (in hertz). The inverse variation is modeled by the equation $p = \frac{495}{\ell}$.

29. Find the length required to produce a pitch of 220 Hz.
30. What pitch would be produced by a pipe with a length of 1.2 ft?
31. Find the pitch of a 0.6-ft pipe.
32. Find the pitch of a 3-ft pipe.

The junior class is buying keepsakes for the junior-senior prom. The price of each keepsake p is inversely proportional to the number of keepsakes s bought. The equation $p = \frac{1800}{s}$ models this inverse variation.

33. If they buy 240 keepsakes, how much can the class spend for each?
34. If they spend $5.55 for each keepsake, how many can the class buy?
35. If 400 keepsakes are bought, how much can be spent for each?
36. If the class buys 50 keepsakes, how much can be spent for each?

Name ______________________ Class ______________ Date ______________

9-2 • Guided Problem Solving

GPS Exercise 47

a. Gasoline Mileage Suppose you drive an average of 10,000 miles each year. Your gasoline mileage (mi/gal) varies inversely with the number of gallons of gasoline you use each year. Write and graph a model for your average mileage m in terms of the gallons g of gasoline used.

b. After you begin driving on the highway more often, you use 50 gal less per year. Write and graph a new model to include this information.

c. Calculate your old and new mileage assuming that you originally used 400 gal of gasoline per year.

Read and Understand

1. What is the average number of miles driven in one year? ______________________

2. What units measure the gasoline mileage m? ______________

3. When you make the graphs, what will the x-axis represent? ______________________

Plan and Solve

4. Use the fact that gas mileage m varies inversely with the number of gallons g of gas used. Write a function that models this inverse variation. ______________________

5. Make a table of values for some positive values of g. Then graph the function.

g						
m						

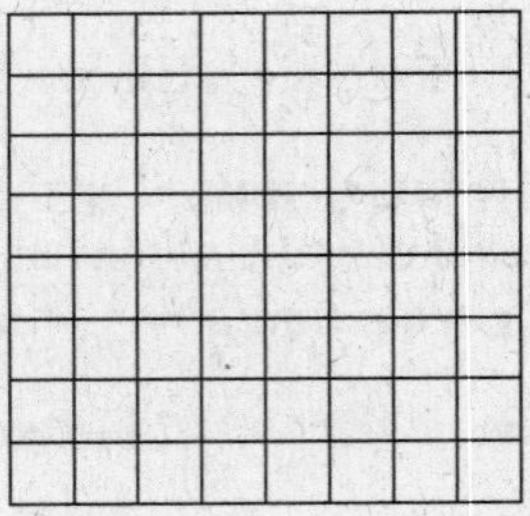

6. Now assume you use 50 gal less gas. How will this effect your graph?

____

7. Write a new model to show you use 50 gal less gas during the year. Then graph the new model. Show your graph above, on the coordinate grid from Step 5.

____

8. Use your two models to calculate your mileage m for the two cases indicated.
mileage using 400 gal per year ______________ mileage using (400–50) gal per year ______________

Look Back and Check

9. Less gas is used in the new model. Should the new mileage be less than the old mileage? Do your answers seem reasonable? ______________________

Solve Another Problem

10. Suppose you get a new car that is twice as fuel efficient. That is, you still drive 10,000 miles each year, but you now use half as much gas. Write two models to describe the old and new mileage. Then describe how the graphs are related. ______________________

Name ______________________ Class ______________ Date ______________

Practice 9-3

Rational Functions and Their Graphs

Find any points of discontinuity for each rational function.

1. $y = \frac{x+3}{(x-4)(x+3)}$
2. $y = \frac{x-2}{x^2-4}$
3. $y = \frac{(x-3)(x+1)}{(x-2)}$
4. $y = \frac{3x(x+2)}{x(x+2)}$
5. $y = \frac{2}{(x+1)}$
6. $y = \frac{4x}{x^3-9x}$

Find the horizontal asymptote of the graph of each rational function.

7. $y = \frac{2}{x-6}$
8. $y = \frac{x+2}{x-4}$
9. $y = \frac{(x+3)}{2(x+4)}$
10. $y = \frac{2x^2+3}{x^2-6}$
11. $y = \frac{3x-12}{x^2-2}$
12. $y = \frac{3x^3-4x+2}{2x^3+3}$

Sketch the graph of each rational function.

13. $y = \frac{3}{x-2}$
14. $y = \frac{3}{(x-2)(x+2)}$
15. $y = \frac{x}{x(x-6)}$
16. $y = \frac{2x}{x-6}$
17. $y = \frac{x^2-1}{x^2-4}$
18. $y = \frac{2x^2+10x+12}{x^2-9}$
19. $y = \frac{x}{x^2+4}$
20. $y = \frac{x+2}{x-1}$
21. $y = \frac{x+3}{x+1}$

Describe the vertical asymptotes and holes for the graph of each rational function.

22. $y = \frac{x-2}{(x+2)(x-2)}$
23. $y = -\frac{x}{x(x-1)}$
24. $y = \frac{5-x}{x^2-1}$
25. $y = \frac{x^2-2}{x+2}$
26. $y = \frac{x^2-4}{x^2+4}$
27. $y = \frac{x+3}{x^2-9}$
28. $y = \frac{x^2-25}{x-4}$
29. $y = \frac{(x-2)(2x+3)}{(5x+4)(x-3)}$
30. $y = \frac{15x^2-7x-2}{x^2-4}$

31. Suppose you start a home business typing technical research papers for college students. You must spend \$3500 to replace your computer system. Then you estimate the cost of typing each page will be \$.02.

 a. Write a rational function modeling your average cost per page. Graph the function.

 b. How many pages must you type to bring your average cost per page to less than \$1.50 per page, the amount you plan to charge?

 c. How many pages must you type to have the average cost per page equal \$1.00?

 d. How many pages must you type to have the average cost per page equal \$.50?

 e. What are the vertical and horizontal asymptotes of the graph of the function?

Name ______________________ Class ______________ Date ______________

9-3 • Guided Problem Solving

GPS Exercise 42

Basketball A basketball player has made 21 of her last 30 free throws—an average of 70%. To model the player's rate of success if she makes x more consecutive free throws, use the function $y = \frac{21 + x}{30 + x}$.

a. Graph the function.

b. Use the graph to find the number of consecutive free throws the player needs to raise her success rate to 75%.

Read and Understand

1. What does y represent? ______________________

2. Does the problem ask for an x- or y-value? What does this value represent? ______________

Plan and Solve

3. What is a good viewing window for the function?

Xmin = __________ Xmax = __________

Ymin = __________ Ymax = __________

4. Graph the function using a graphing calculator. Adjust the viewing window accordingly.

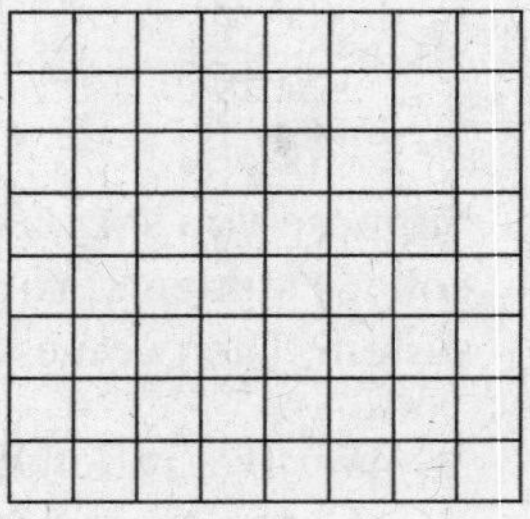

5. Explain how you will use your graph to find the number of consecutive free throws the player needs. Which feature of your calculator might you use? ______________________

____

6. How many consecutive free throws does the player need to raise her success rate to 75%? __________

Look Back and Check

7. If she makes no more free throws, what will her average be? Does this agree with the y-intercept of your graph? If she kept on making free throws, what should her average approach? Does this agree with horizontal asymptote of your graph? ______________________

8. Substitute your final answer into the given function. Verify that the result is 0.75. __________

Solve Another Problem

9. A student has turned in 12 of his last 20 homework assignments—an average of 60%. To model the student's homework score if he turns in the next x assignments, use the function $y = \frac{12 + x}{20 + x}$. Use the graph of the function to find the number of assignments the student should turn in to raise his score to 80%. ______________________

Name ______________________ Class ______________ Date ______________

Practice 9-4

Rational Expressions

Simplify each rational expression. State any restrictions on the variable.

1. $\frac{20 + 40x}{20x}$
2. $\frac{4x + 6}{2x + 3}$
3. $\frac{3y^2 - 3}{y^2 - 1}$
4. $\frac{4x + 20}{3x + 15}$
5. $\frac{x^2 + x}{x^2 + 2x}$
6. $\frac{3x + 6}{5x + 10}$
7. $\frac{2y}{y^2 + 6y}$
8. $\frac{x^2 - 5x}{x^2 - 25}$
9. $\frac{x^2 + 3x - 18}{x^2 - 36}$
10. $\frac{x^2 + 13x + 40}{x^2 - 2x - 35}$
11. $\frac{3x^2 - 12}{x^2 - x - 6}$
12. $\frac{4x^2 - 36}{x^2 + 10x + 21}$
13. $\frac{2x^2 + 11x + 5}{3x^2 + 17x + 10}$
14. $\frac{6x^2 + 5x - 6}{3x^2 - 5x + 2}$
15. $\frac{7x - 28}{x^2 - 16}$
16. $\frac{x^2 - 9}{2x + 6}$

Multiply or divide. Write the answer in simplest form. State any restrictions on the variables.

17. $\frac{5a}{5a + 5} \cdot \frac{10a + 10}{a}$
18. $\frac{9 - x^2}{5x^3 + 17x^2 + 6x} \cdot \frac{5x^2 + 2x}{x - 3}$
19. $\frac{(x - 1)(2x - 4)}{x + 4} \cdot \frac{(x + 1)(x + 4)}{2x - 4}$
20. $\frac{(x + 3)(x + 4)}{(x + 1)(x + 3)} \cdot \frac{(x + 3)(x + 1)}{x + 4}$
21. $\frac{5y - 20}{3y + 15} \cdot \frac{7y + 35}{10y + 40}$
22. $\frac{3x^3}{x^2 - 25} \cdot \frac{x^2 + 6x + 5}{x^2}$
23. $\frac{3y + 3}{6y + 12} \div \frac{18}{5y + 5}$
24. $\frac{6x + 6}{7} \div \frac{4x + 4}{x - 2}$
25. $\frac{y^2 - 2y}{y^2 + 7y - 18} \cdot \frac{y^2 - 81}{y^2 - 11y + 18}$
26. $\frac{(y + 6)^2}{y^2 - 36} \cdot \frac{3y - 18}{2y + 12}$
27. $\frac{y^2 - 49}{(y - 7)^2} \div \frac{5y + 35}{y^2 - 7y}$
28. $\frac{x^2 - 3x - 10}{2x^2 - 11x + 5} \div \frac{x^2 - 5x + 6}{2x^2 - 7x + 3}$
29. $\frac{x^2 - 5x + 4}{x^2 - 1} \cdot \frac{x^2 + 5x + 4}{x^2 - 9}$
30. $\frac{x^2 - 5x}{x^2 + 3x} \cdot \frac{x + 3}{x - 5}$
31. $\frac{x^2 - 4}{x^2 + 6x + 9} \cdot \frac{x^2 - 9}{x^2 + 4x + 4}$
32. $\frac{x^2 - 6x}{x^2 - 36} \cdot \frac{x + 6}{x^2}$
33. $\frac{x^2 + 10x + 16}{x^2 - 6x - 16} \div \frac{x + 8}{x^2 - 64}$
34. $\frac{5y}{2x^2} \div \frac{5y^2}{8x^2}$
35. $\frac{6x^2 - 32x + 10}{3x^2 - 15x} \div \frac{3x^2 + 11x - 4}{2x^2 - 32}$
36. $\frac{7x^4}{24y^5} \div \frac{21x}{12y^4}$
37. $\frac{2x + 4}{10x} \cdot \frac{15x^2}{x + 2}$
38. $\frac{x^2 + 6x}{3x^2 + 6x - 24} \cdot \frac{x^2 + 2x - 8}{x + 6}$
39. $\frac{x^2 - 5x + 4}{x^2 + 3x - 28} \cdot \frac{x^2 + 2x - 3}{x^2 + 10x + 21}$
40. $\frac{x^2 + 2x + 1}{x^2 - 1} \cdot \frac{x^2 + 3x + 2}{x^2 + 4x + 4}$

Name ______________________ Class ______________ Date ______________

9-4 • Guided Problem Solving

GPS Exercise 26

Industrial Design A storage tank will have a circular base of radius r and a height of r. The tank can be either cylindrical or hemispherical (half a sphere).

a. Write and simplify an expression for the ratio of the volume of the hemispherical tank to its surface area (including the base). For a sphere, $V = \frac{4}{3}\pi r^3$ and S.A. $= 4\pi r^2$.

b. Write and simplify an expression for the ratio of the volume of the cylindrical tank to its surface area (including the bases).

c. Compare the ratios of volume to surface area for the two tanks.

d. Compare the volumes of the two tanks.

Read and Understand

1. What is the radius and height of the storage tank? ______________

2. What are the two possible shapes of the storage tank? ______________

Plan and Solve

3. What is the volume of the hemispherical tank? ______________

4. What is the surface area of the hemispherical tank (including the base)? ______________

5. Write and simplify the ratio of the volume to surface area for this tank. ______________

6. What is the volume of the cylindrical tank? ______________

7. What is the surface area of the cylindrical tank (including the base)? ______________

8. Write and simplify the ratio of the volume to surface area for this tank. ______________

9. Compare the ratios of volume to surface area for the two tanks. ______________

10. Compare the volumes of the two tanks. ______________

Look Back and Check

11. Check that your answers seem reasonable. Can you fit a hemispherical tank inside a cylindrical one? What does this suggest about the volumes of the two tanks? Verify that this agrees with your answer to Step 10. ______________

Solve Another Problem

12. A company makes hemispherical and cylindrical steel tanks. Both tanks have radius r and height r. Compare the volume-to-surface-area ratios to find which tank uses less material per gallon of liquid held. ______________

Name ______________________ Class ______________ Date ______________

Practice 9-5

Adding and Subtracting Rational Expressions

Find the least common multiple of each pair of polynomials.

1. $3x(x + 2)$ and $6x(2x - 3)$

2. $2x^2 - 8x + 8$ and $3x^2 + 27x - 30$

3. $4x^2 + 12x + 9$ and $4x^2 - 9$

4. $2x^2 - 18$ and $5x^3 + 30x^2 + 45x$

Simplify.

5. $\frac{x^2}{5} + \frac{x^2}{5}$

6. $\frac{x^2 - 2}{12} + \frac{x}{6}$

7. $\frac{12}{xy^3} - \frac{9}{xy^3}$

8. $-\frac{2}{n + 4} - \frac{n^2}{n^2 - 16}$

9. $\frac{x}{9} - \frac{2x}{9}$

10. $\frac{2y + 1}{3y} + \frac{5y + 4}{3y}$

11. $\frac{6y - 4}{y^2 - 5} + \frac{3y + 1}{y^2 - 5}$

12. $\frac{6}{5x^2y} + \frac{5}{10xy^2}$

13. $\frac{3}{8x^3y^3} - \frac{1}{4xy}$

14. $\frac{4}{x^2 - 25} + \frac{6}{x^2 + 6x + 5}$

15. $\frac{3}{7x^2y} + \frac{4}{21xy^2}$

16. $\frac{xy - y}{x - 2} - \frac{y}{x + 2}$

17. $\frac{x + 2}{x^2 + 4x + 4} + \frac{2}{x + 2}$

18. $\frac{3}{x^2 - x - 6} + \frac{2}{x^2 + 6x + 5}$

19. $\frac{1}{6x^2 - 11x + 3} + \frac{1}{8x^2 - 18}$

20. $\frac{4}{x^2 - 3x} + \frac{6}{3x - 9}$

21. $\frac{3}{x^2 + 3x - 10} + \frac{1}{x^2 + 6x + 5}$

22. $\frac{3}{x - 9} + 4x$

23. $3 - \frac{1}{x^2 + 5}$

24. $5 + \frac{1}{x^2 - 5x + 6}$

25. $1 + \frac{2x + 7}{3x - 1}$

26. $\frac{2a}{a + 2} + \frac{3a}{a - 2}$

27. $\frac{4c}{c - 3} + \frac{4c}{c + 3}$

28. $\frac{f + 1}{fgh} + \frac{f - 1}{fgh}$

29. $\frac{2 - t}{t - 5} + \frac{2 + t}{t + 5}$

30. $\frac{4r}{r - 2} + \frac{4r}{r + 2}$

31. $\frac{x - y}{x + y} + \frac{y}{x}$

32. $\frac{\frac{2}{x}}{\frac{3}{y}}$

33. $\frac{1 + \frac{2}{x}}{4 - \frac{6}{x}}$

34. $\frac{\frac{1}{x - 2}}{2 + \frac{1}{x}}$

35. $\frac{y}{4y + 8} - \frac{1}{y^2 + 2y}$

36. $\frac{1 + \frac{2}{3}}{\frac{4}{9}}$

37. $\frac{6x^2}{3x - 2} + \frac{5x - 6}{3x - 2}$

38. $\frac{\frac{3}{x + 1}}{\frac{5}{x - 1}}$

39. $\frac{\frac{2}{x} + 6}{\frac{1}{y}}$

40. $\frac{2y}{y^2 - 4y - 12} + \frac{y}{y^2 - 10y + 24}$

41. The total resistance for a parallel circuit is given by $\frac{1}{R} = \frac{1}{R_1} + \frac{1}{R_2} + \frac{1}{R_3}$.

a. If $R = 1$ ohm, $R_2 = 6$ ohms, and $R_3 = 8$ ohms, find R_1.

b. If $R_1 = 3$ ohms, $R_2 = 4$ ohms, and $R_3 = 6$ ohms, find R.

Name ____________________ Class ____________ Date ____________

9-5 • Guided Problem Solving

GPS Exercise 52

Music The harmonic mean of two numbers a and b equals $\frac{2}{\frac{1}{a} + \frac{1}{b}}$. As you vary the length of a violin or guitar string, its pitch changes. If a full-length string is 1 unit long, then many lengths that are simple fractions produce pitches that harmonize, or sound pleasing together. The harmonic mean relates three lengths that produce harmonious sounds. For example, $\frac{1}{3}$ is the harmonic mean of $\frac{1}{2}$ and $\frac{1}{4}$, and strings of these lengths produce harmonious sounds. Find the harmonic mean for strings of lengths 1 and $\frac{1}{2}$, $\frac{3}{4}$ and $\frac{1}{2}$, and $\frac{3}{4}$ and $\frac{3}{5}$.

Read and Understand

1. How long is a full-length string? ____________

2. Suppose a musician makes three harmonious pitches. For the first, she presses down on a string so that its length is $\frac{1}{2}$ unit. For the second, the length is $\frac{1}{4}$ unit. Using the given example in the problem, what is the length for the third pitch that sounds pleasing? ____________

Plan and Solve

3. Let $a = 1$ and $b = \frac{1}{2}$. Find $\frac{1}{a}$ and $\frac{1}{b}$. ____________

4. Substitute these values into the expression for the harmonic mean. ____________

5. Write the resulting fraction in simplest form. What is the harmonic mean of 1 and $\frac{1}{2}$? ____________

6. Now let $a = \frac{3}{4}$ and $b = \frac{1}{2}$. Find $\frac{1}{a}$ and $\frac{1}{b}$. ____________

7. Substitute these values into the expression for the harmonic mean. Then multiply both the numerator and denominator by the LCD. What is the harmonic mean of $\frac{3}{4}$ and $\frac{1}{2}$? ____________

8. Use a similar technique to find the harmonic mean of $\frac{3}{4}$ and $\frac{3}{5}$. ____________

Look Back and Check

9. Rewrite the formula as $\frac{2ab}{a + b}$. Then use this alternative formula to find the harmonic means. ____________

10. Use a guitar, violin, or a homemade instrument with a board and rubber bands. Test that the pitches do in fact sound harmonious together. ____________

Solve Another Problem

11. Find the harmonic mean of 2 and 4. ____________

Name________________________ Class______________ Date______________

Practice 9-6

Solving Rational Equations

Solve each equation. Check each solution.

1. $\frac{1}{x} = \frac{x}{9}$
2. $\frac{4}{x} = \frac{x}{4}$
3. $\frac{3x}{4} = \frac{5x+1}{3}$
4. $-\frac{4}{x+1} = \frac{5}{3x+1}$
5. $\frac{3}{2x-3} = \frac{1}{5-2x}$
6. $\frac{x-4}{3} = \frac{x-2}{2}$
7. $\frac{3}{1-x} = \frac{2}{1+x}$
8. $\frac{2x-3}{4} = \frac{2x-5}{6}$
9. $\frac{1}{x} = \frac{2}{x+3}$
10. $\frac{x-1}{6} = \frac{x}{4}$
11. $\frac{3-x}{6} = \frac{6-x}{12}$
12. $\frac{4}{x+3} = \frac{10}{2x-1}$
13. $\frac{x-2}{10} = \frac{x-7}{5}$
14. $\frac{3}{3-x} = \frac{4}{2-x}$
15. $\frac{1}{4-5x} = \frac{3}{x+9}$
16. $x + \frac{10}{x-2} = \frac{x^2+3x}{x-2}$
17. $\frac{2}{x+3} + \frac{5}{3-x} = \frac{6}{x^2-9}$
18. $\frac{1}{2x+2} + \frac{5}{x^2-1} = \frac{1}{x-1}$
19. $\frac{2}{6x+2} = \frac{x}{3x^2+11}$
20. $\frac{3}{2x-4} = \frac{5}{3x+7}$
21. $\frac{2y}{5} + \frac{2}{6} = \frac{y}{2} - \frac{1}{6}$
22. $\frac{1}{2x+2} = \frac{1}{x-1}$
23. $\frac{2}{x+2} + \frac{5}{x-2} = \frac{6}{x^2-4}$
24. $5 + \frac{5}{x} = \frac{6}{5x}$
25. $\frac{4}{x-1} = \frac{5}{x-2}$
26. $\frac{2x-1}{x+3} = \frac{5}{3}$
27. $\frac{7}{2} = \frac{7x}{8} - 4$
28. $5 - \frac{4}{x+1} = 6$
29. $\frac{x}{x+3} - \frac{x}{x-3} = \frac{x^2+9}{x^2-9}$
30. $\frac{x}{3} + \frac{x}{2} = 10$
31. $\frac{2}{3} + \frac{3x-1}{6} = \frac{5}{2}$
32. $4 + \frac{2y}{y-5} = \frac{8}{y-5}$
33. $\frac{4}{x-3} = \frac{2}{x+1} + \frac{16}{x^2-2x-3}$
34. $\frac{7}{x^2-5x} + \frac{2}{x} = \frac{3}{2x-10}$
35. $\frac{x+3}{x^2+3x-4} = \frac{x+2}{x^2-16}$
36. $\frac{3y}{5} + \frac{1}{2} = \frac{y}{10}$

37. A round trip flight took 3.9 h flying time. The plane traveled the 510 mi to the city at 255 mi/h with no wind. How strong was the wind on the return flight? Was the wind a head wind or a tail wind?

38. A round trip flight took 5 h flying time. The plane traveled the 720 mi to the city at 295 mi/h with no wind. How strong was the wind on the return flight? Was the wind a head wind or a tail wind?

39. If one student can complete the decorations for the prom in 5 days working alone, another student could do it in 3 days, and a third could do it in 4 days, how long would it take them working together?

40. Tom and Huck start a business painting fences. They paint Aunt Polly's fence and find that they can paint a 200-ft^2 fence in 40 min if they work together. If Huck works four times faster than Tom, how long would it take each of them to paint a 500-ft^2 fence working alone?

Name ______________________ Class ______________ Date ______________

9-6 • Guided Problem Solving

GPS Exercise 55

Transportation A plane flies from New York to Chicago (about 700 miles) at a speed of 360 mi/h.

a. The speed s of the plane is given by $s = \frac{d}{t}$. d represents the distance and t is the time. Solve the equation for t.

b. Find the time for the trip.

c. On the return trip from Chicago to New York, a tail wind helps the plane move faster. Write an expression for the speed of the plane on the return trip. Let x represent the speed of the tail wind.

d. The total flying time for the round trip is 3.5 h. Write a rational equation for the sum of the flying times. Find the speed x of the tail wind.

Read and Understand

1. What is the approximate distance d from New York to Chicago? ______________

2. What is the speed s of the plane? ______________

Plan and Solve

3. Solve the equation $s = \frac{d}{t}$ for t by multiplying both sides by t and then dividing by s. ______________

4. Substitute the known values for d and s. What is the time for the trip? ______________

5. On the return trip, will the tail wind make the plane fly faster or slower? ______________

6. Write an expression for the speed of the plane on the return trip. ______________

7. Use your answer from Step 3 that gives the time it takes for a plane to fly d miles at a speed s. Substitute the known value of d and the expression for the speed on the return trip. What is an expression for the time on the return trip? ______________

8. Add the results from Step 4 (time for first trip) and step 7 (time for return trip) to get the total flight flying time. Write an equation showing the total flying time is 3.5 h. ______________

9. Solve your equation for x. What is the speed of the tail wind? ______________

Look Back and Check

10. Add the speed of the tail wind to the speed of the plane. How long does it take to fly from Chicago to New York at this rate? Verify that this return flight takes less time than the initial flight from New York to Chicago. Add the two flight times and verify that the sum is 3.5 hours.

Solve Another Problem

11. A small plane flies 300 miles at a speed of 150 mi/h. On the trip back, the plane maintains this same air speed, but the return trip takes one hour more due to a head wind. Find the speed of the head wind. ______________

Name ____________________ Class ____________ Date ____________

Practice 9-7

Probability of Multiple Events

Integers from 1 to 100 are randomly selected. State whether the events are mutually exclusive.

1. Even integers and multiples of 3
2. Integers less than 40 and integers greater than 50
3. Odd integers and multiples of 4
4. Integers less than 50 and integers greater than 40

Classify each pair of events as *dependent* or *independent*.

5. A member of the junior class and a second member of the same class are randomly selected.
6. A member of the junior class and a member of another class are randomly chosen.
7. An odd-numbered problem is assigned for homework, and an even-numbered problem is picked for a test.
8. The sum and the product of two rolls of a number cube

Find each probability.

9. A flavored-water company wants to know how many people prefer its new lemon-flavored water over two competitors' brands. The company hires you to survey 1000 people and ask them to rank the three drinks in order of preference. After conducting the survey, you find that 35% prefer the lemon-flavored water over Competitor A, 38% prefer the lemon-flavored water over Competitor B, and 47% did not prefer the lemon-flavored water over either competitor's brand. What is the probability that someone prefers the lemon-flavored water over both competitors' brands?
10. A natural number from 1 to 10 is randomly chosen.
    a. $P(\text{even or } 7)$
    b. $P(\text{even or odd})$
    c. $P(\text{multiple of 2 or multiple of 3})$
    d. $P(\text{odd or less than } 3)$
11. A standard number cube is tossed.
    a. $P(\text{even or } 3)$
    b. $P(\text{less than 2 or even})$
    c. $P(\text{prime or } 4)$
    d. $P(2 \text{ or greater than } 6)$
12. Only 93% of the airplane parts Salome is examining pass inspection. What is the probability that all of the next five parts pass inspection?
13. There is a 50% chance of thunderstorms the next three days. What is the probability that there will be thunderstorms each of the next three days?

Q and R are independent events. Find $P(Q \text{ and } R)$.

14. $P(Q) = \frac{1}{8}, P(R) = \frac{2}{5}$
15. $P(Q) = 0.8, P(R) = 0.2$
16. $P(Q) = \frac{1}{4}, P(R) = \frac{1}{5}$

M and N are mutually exclusive events. Find $P(M \text{ or } N)$.

17. $P(M) = \frac{3}{4}, P(N) = \frac{1}{6}$
18. $P(M) = 10\%, P(N) = 45\%$
19. $P(M) = \frac{1}{5}, P(N) = 18\%$

Name ____________________ Class ____________ Date ____________

9-7 • Guided Problem Solving

GPS Exercise 45

Tests A multiple-choice test has four choices for each answer.

a. What is the probability that a random guess on a question will yield the correct answer?

b. Suppose you need to make a random guess on three of the ten test questions. What is the probability that you will answer all three correctly?

Read and Understand

1. What sort of test is given? ____________

2. For part (b), how many questions are you guessing at random? ____________

Plan and Solve

3. When answering a single question on the test, how many choices do you have? ____________

4. How many of these choices match the correct answer for that test question? ____________

5. For a single question, what is the probability you will guess correctly? ____________

6. Now consider answering three questions. Suppose you've guessed the first question correctly. Does this affect the outcome for the second question? ____________

7. Define events A, B, and C as follows.
A: 1st is correct B: 2nd is correct C: 3rd is correct
Are the events independent or dependent? ____________

8. Use the result from part (a) to assign the probability of each event.
$P(A) =$ ________ $P(B) =$ ________ $P(C) =$ ________

9. Use the appropriate principle of probability. Write an expression for $P(A \text{ and } B \text{ and } C)$.

____

10. Simplify your expression. What is the probability that all three guesses are correct? ____________

Look Back and Check

11. Check your logic by imagining a similar situation. For example, suppose you have three jars, each with 4 different colored balls. Let the red ball play the role of the correct answer. If you randomly pick the red ball from the first jar, does this change the probability of picking a red ball from the second jar? Verify that this agrees with your answers in Steps 4 and 5. ____________

Solve Another Problem

12. The last part of a test has three true/false questions. What is the probability that a student will get this portion of the test 100% correct if she guesses at random? ____________

Name ____________________ Class ____________ Date ____________

9A: Graphic Organizer

For use before Lesson 9-1

Study Skill As you approach the latter part of the book, take a minute to flip back through the chapters that you have already covered. Think about some of the things that you have already learned. What was your favorite chapter? What was your least favorite? How do you think you will use what you've already learned in this chapter? Record your responses in your notebook.

Write your answers.

1. What is the chapter title? ____________________

2. Find the Table of Contents page for this chapter at the front of the book. Name four topics you will study in this chapter.

____________________ ____________________

____________________ ____________________

3. Complete the graphic organizer as you work through the chapter.
1. Write the title of the chapter in the center oval.
2. When you begin a lesson, write the name of the lesson in a rectangle.
3. When you complete that lesson, write a skill or key concept from that lesson in the outer oval linked to that rectangle.

Continue with steps 2 and 3 clockwise around the graphic organizer.

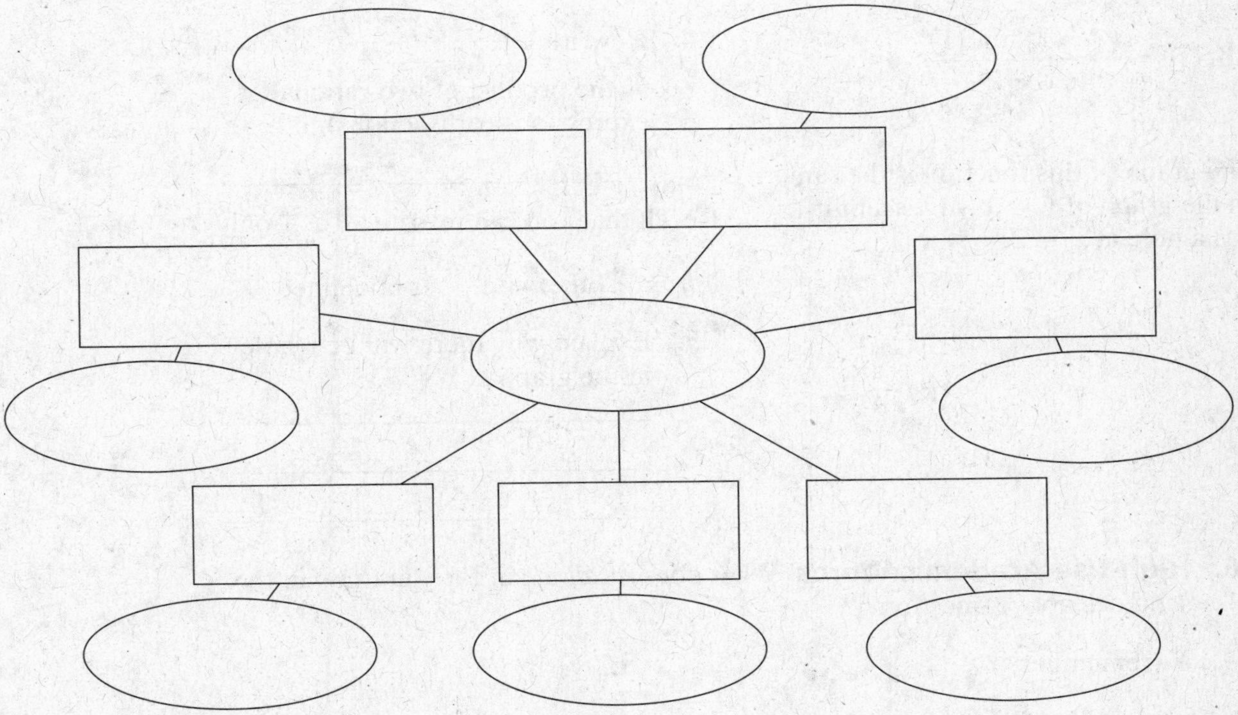

Name ______________________ Class ______________ Date ______________

9B: Reading Comprehension

For use after Lesson 9-3

Study Skill When you take notes in class, make sure that you write down the most important information. In general, most things that your teacher writes on the chalkboard or overhead projector should go into your notes.

Read the steps and comments in the example at the left, and answer the questions at the right.

Describe the vertical asymptotes and holes for the graph of each rational function.

As you read the instructions, review in your mind the meaning of the words, and draw mental pictures.

1. A vertical asymptote is parallel to which axis? ______________

a. $y = \dfrac{x + 1}{(x - 2)(x - 3)}$

2. When is a function a rational function? ______________

____

Since 2 and 3 are the zeros of the denominator and neither is a zero of the numerator, $x = 2$ and $x = 3$ are vertical asymptotes.

3. Explain what it means to say that 2 is a *zero* of the denominator.

____

____

---

b. $y = \dfrac{(x - 2)(x - 1)}{x - 2}$

4. Rewrite $\dfrac{(x - 2)(x - 1)}{x - 2}$ as the product of two rational expressions (or fractions).

____

The graph of this function is the same as the graph of $y = x - 1$, except it has a hole at $x = 2$.

Recall that you can rewrite $\dfrac{n}{n}$ as 1 only if $n \neq 0$; otherwise, $\dfrac{n}{n}$ is undefined.

5. Explain why there will be a hole in the graph at $x = 2$.

____

____

____

6. High-Use Academic Words What does *recall* mean for you to do in the sentence above question 5?

a. remember

b. verify

Name ______________________ Class ______________ Date ______________

9C: Reading/Writing Math Symbols

For use after Lesson 9-5

Study Skill Clearly written and easily understandable notes make doing your homework or studying for a test easier.

Fill in the blanks.

Sometimes letters in mathematics represent constants rather than variables.

1. In the general form of a complex number, $a + bi$, what is the value represented by the letter i? ______________________

2. In the expression for a natural logarithm, $\log_e y = x$, what is the approximate value represented by the letter e rounded to the nearest thousandth? ______________

3. In the formula for a circle, $C = 2\pi r$, what is the approximate value represented by the Greek letter π? ______________________

Sometimes ordinary English punctuation marks have a special meaning in mathematics.

4. Explain the meaning of the exclamation point (!) in the expression 7!.

   ____

5. Explain the meaning of the colon (:) in the expression 3 : 5.

   ____

6. Explain the meaning of the period in the expression 12.8.

   ____

7. Explain the meaning of the dot in the expression $7 \cdot 9$.

   ____

Name ____________________ Class ____________ Date ____________

9D: Visual Vocabulary Practice
High-Use Academic Words

For use after Lesson 9-7

Study Skills Mathematics is like learning a foreign language. You have to know the vocabulary before you can speak the language correctly.

Concept List

apply	approach	arrange
composition	equivalent	exclude
notation	pattern	solve

Write the concept that best describes each exercise. Choose from the concept list above.

1. $n!$

____

2. If $f(x) = x - 2$ and $g(x) = x^2$, $(g\ f)(x) = (x - 2)^2$

____

3.
abc
acb
bac
bca
cab
cba

____

4.
1
1 1
1 2 1
1 3 3 1
1 4 6 4 1
⋮

____

5. Value of y as x increases

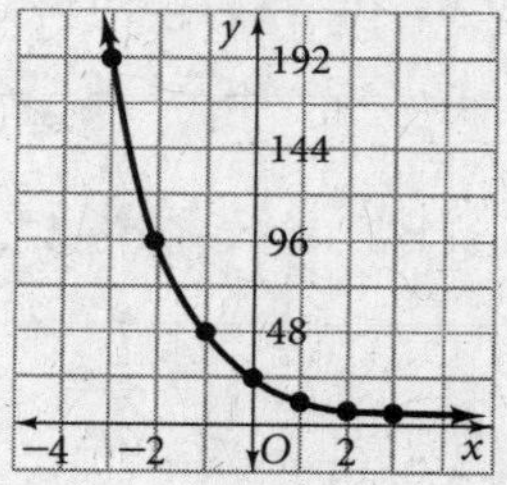

____

6. $25 = 5^2$ and $\log_5 25 = 2$

____

7. The function $h = -16t^2 + 34t$ models the height of the ball in feet at t seconds. When will the ball hit the ground?

____

8. $x = 3$ for the domain of the function $y = \frac{1}{x - 3}$

____

9.
$$2 + \sqrt{3x - 2} = 6$$
$$\sqrt{3x - 2} = 4$$
$$3x - 2 = 16$$
$$3x = 18$$
$$x = 6$$

____

Name ____________________ Class ____________ Date ____________

9E: Vocabulary Check

For use after Lesson 9-4

Study Skill Strengthen your vocabulary. Use these pages and add cues and summaries by applying the Cornell Notetaking style.

Write the definition for each word at the right. To check your work, fold the paper back along the dotted line to see the correct answers.

____________________ ____________________ ____________________	Branch
____________________ ____________________ ____________________	Inverse variation
____________________ ____________________ ____________________	Rational function
____________________ ____________________ ____________________	Joint variation
____________________ ____________________ ____________________	Point of discontinuity

Vocabulary and Study Skills

Name ______________________ Class ______________ Date ______________

9E: Vocabulary Check (continued)

For use after Lesson 9-4

Write the vocabulary word for each definition. To check your work, fold the paper forward along the dotted line to see the correct answers.

A piece of a discontinuous graph. ______________________

An equation of the form $y = \frac{k}{x}$ or $xy = k$, where $k \neq 0$. ______________________

$f(x) = \frac{P(x)}{Q(x)}$, where $P(x)$ and $Q(x)$ are polynomial functions and $Q(x) \neq 0$. ______________________

An equation of the form $z = kxy$, where $k \neq 0$. ______________________

Occurs at $x = a$, if a is a real number for which the denominator of a rational function f is zero. ______________________

9F: Vocabulary Review Puzzle

For use with Chapter Review

Study Skill Try writing vocabulary words on note cards, with the definitions on the back of the cards. You can then flip through the cards and say the definitions to yourself as you read each word. If you need help remembering the definition, flip the card over.

Unscramble the UPPERCASE letters to form a math word or phrase that completes each sentence.

1. A rational expression is in TESSPILM MORF when its numerator and denominator are polynomials that have no common divisors.
   ____
2. A fraction that has a fraction in either its numerator or denominator is XLEMPOC. ______________________
3. A value that satisfies the derived equation but not the original equation is a(n) TEXNAESOUR TOOSNUIL. ______________________
4. A point on the graph where the denominator of a rational function is zero is a(n) TININICOUDTYS. ______________________
5. Events for which the outcome of one event does not affect the outcome of a second are called TENPENNIDED. ______________________
6. Each of the two parts of a graph is called a(n) NARBCH.
   ____
7. A function of x that can be written as the quotient of two other polynomial functions of x (with the divisor not equal to zero) is called LATNOIRA. ______________________
8. When events are PTENDNEED, the outcome of one affects the outcome of the second. ______________________
9. A variation that puts together direct and inverse variation is called BODENMIC. ______________________
10. When two events cannot happen at the same time, the events are LYTMUULA CLEESIVUX. ______________________

Name ______________________ Class ______________ Date ______________

Practice 10-1

Identify the center and intercepts of each conic section. Give the domain and range of each graph.

1.

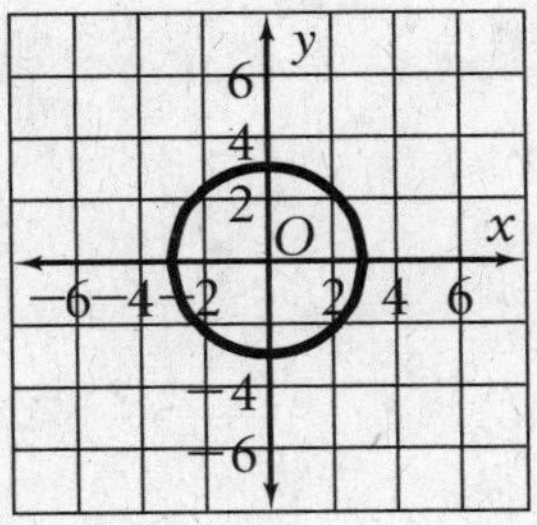

2.

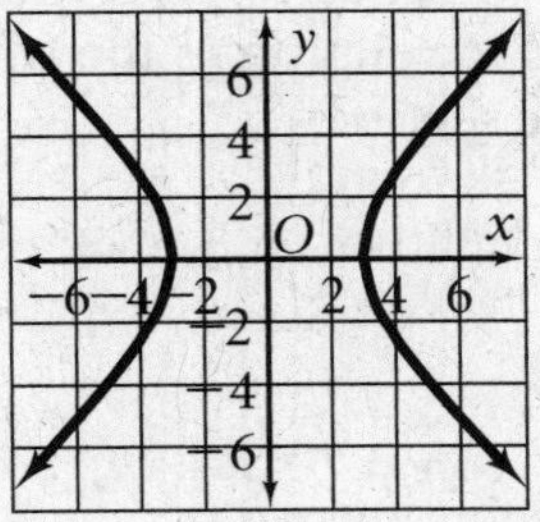

3.

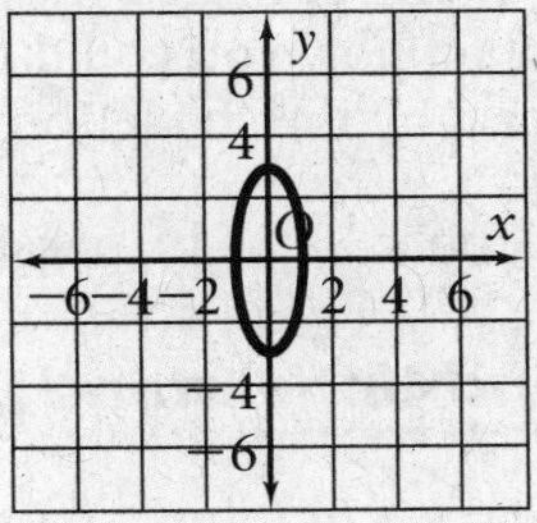

4.

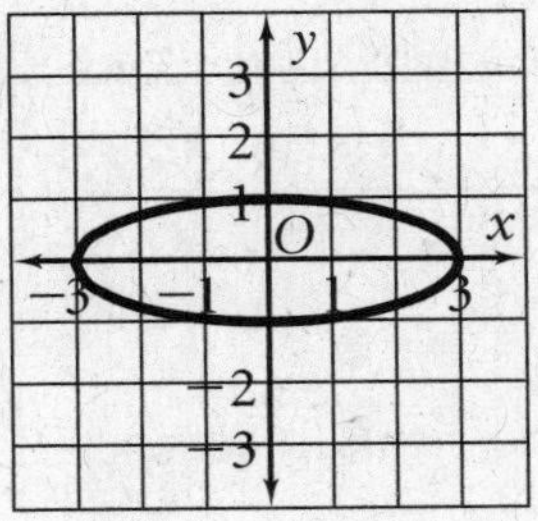

5.

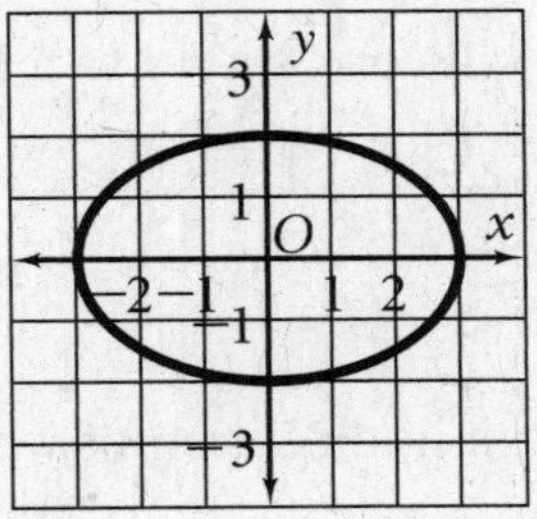

6.

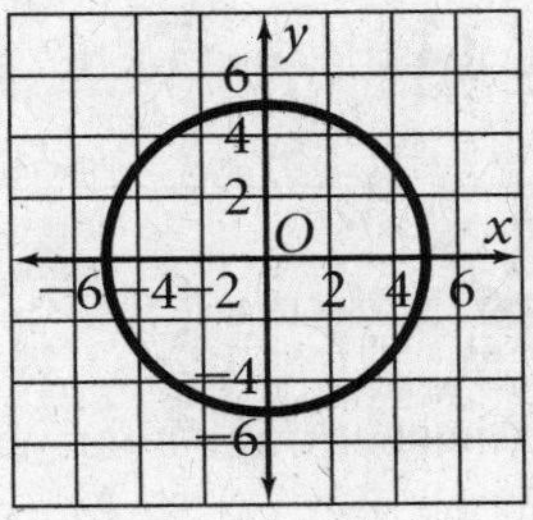

Graph each equation. Identify the conic section and its lines of symmetry. Then find the domain and range.

7. $x^2 + 4y^2 = 4$

8. $4x^2 + y^2 - 4 = 0$

9. $9x^2 + 4y^2 = 36$

10. $x^2 - y^2 = 4$

11. $x^2 - y^2 - 9 = 0$

12. $4x^2 - 9y^2 - 36 = 0$

13. $5x^2 + 5y^2 = 45$

14. $2x^2 + 2y^2 - 4 = 0$

15. $8x^2 + 8y^2 = 40$

16. $3x^2 + 6y^2 - 6 = 0$

17. $3x^2 - 6y^2 = 6$

18. $6y^2 - 3x^2 - 6 = 0$

19. $5x^2 - 5y^2 = 25$

20. $5x^2 + 5y^2 = 125$

21. $9x^2 + 16y^2 = 144$

22. $16y^2 - 9x^2 = 144$

23. $9x^2 - 16y^2 = 144$

24. $9x^2 + 9y^2 = 1$

25. $x^2 - y^2 = 49$

26. $2x^2 + 2y^2 - 32 = 0$

27. $2x^2 + 8y^2 = 32$

28. $y^2 - x^2 + 4 = 0$

29. $49x^2 - y^2 - 48 = 1$

30. $x^2 + y^2 - 40 = 9$

31. $5x^2 - 5y^2 - 45 = 0$

32. $25x^2 + y^2 = 25$

33. $9x^2 + 36y^2 = 36$

34. $25x^2 - y^2 - 25 = 0$

35. $y^2 - x^2 = 9$

36. $4y^2 - 9x^2 = 36$

37. $x^2 + y^2 = 4$

38. $x^2 + y^2 = 36$

39. $3x^2 + 3y^2 - 9 = 0$

40. $4x^2 + 9y^2 - 36 = 0$

41. $6x^2 + y^2 - 12 = 0$

42. $9x^2 + y^2 = 9$

Name ____________________ Class ____________ Date ____________

10-1 • Guided Problem Solving

GPS Exercise 33

Light The light emitted from a lamp with a shade forms a shadow on the wall. Explain how you could turn the lamp in relation to the wall so that the shadow cast by the shade forms each conic section.

a. hyperbola **b.** parabola **c.** ellipse **d.** circle

Read and Understand

1. To make a different shadow, what is being turned? ____________

2. Describe the part of the shadow that will correspond to a conic section. ____________

Plan and Solve

3. A conic section is a curve formed by the intersection of what two geometrical objects? ____________

4. Describe how these two objects are related to the wall and the shade of the lamp. ____________

5. Suppose the lamp is sitting in a normal, upright position. If its shade is nearly touching the wall, which conic section is cast? ____________

6. Now suppose the lamp is turned at some angle so that the shade contacts the wall along a vertical line. Which conic section is cast? ____________

7. Suppose the lamp is turned exactly 90° from its normal, upright position so that the light comes through the hole in the top of the lampshade. Which conic section is cast? ____________

8. From the position in Step 7, describe how to turn the lamp slightly so the remaining conic section is cast. ____________

Look Back and Check

9. Test your conjectures using a real lamp. Verify that you can form the desired conic sections.

____

Solve Another Problem

10. Cut a circular hole in a flat piece of cardboard. Using the sun or a strong light, turn your cardboard to cast different shadows. Use chalk to trace the outline of the shadows cast. Describe the outcome of your experiments.

____

Name ____________________ Class ____________ Date ____________

Practice 10-2

Parabolas

Determine whether each parabola opens upward, downward, to the left, or to the right.

1. $x = -2y^2$
2. $y = -6x^2$
3. $-8x = y^2$
4. $-2y = -3x^2$
5. $-2y + x^2 = 0$
6. $2x + 6y^2 = 0$
7. $-3x + 4y^2 = 0$
8. $y + 12x^2 = 0$

Identify the focus and the directrix of the graph of each equation.

9. $y = -\frac{1}{32}x^2$
10. $y = -8x^2$
11. $x = \frac{1}{3}y^2$
12. $x = 12y^2$
13. $y + 3x^2 = 0$
14. $x - 5y^2 = 0$
15. $-y + x^2 = 3$
16. $-x - 3y^2 = 0$
17. $8x = y^2 + 6y + 9$
18. $\frac{1}{8}x = y^2$
19. $-8y = -x^2$
20. $-\frac{1}{8}y = -x^2$

Write an equation of a parabola with vertex at the origin.

21. focus at $(-2, 0)$
22. focus at $(0, 4)$
23. directrix at $x = 3$
24. directrix at $y = 4$
25. focus at $(0, -3)$
26. directrix at $x = -2$
27. directrix at $y = -3$
28. focus at $(3, 0)$
29. directrix at $x = 6$
30. focus at $(-5, 0)$
31. focus at $(0, 5)$
32. directrix at $y = -7$

Write the equation whose graph is the set of all points in the plane equidistant from the given point and the given line.

33. $F(0, 8)$ and $y = -8$
34. $F(1, 0)$ and $x = -1$
35. $F(6, 0)$ and $x = -6$
36. $F(0, -4)$ and $y = 4$
37. $F(0, 1)$ and $y = -1$
38. $F(-3, 0)$ and $x = 3$
39. $F(-1, 0)$ and $x = 1$
40. $F(-10, 0)$ and $x = 10$
41. $F(0, -3)$ and $y = 3$
42. $F(5, 0)$ and $x = -5$
43. $F(0, 5)$ and $y = -5$
44. $F(3, 0)$ and $x = -3$
45. A pipe with a diameter of 0.5 in. is located 10 in. from a mirror used as a parabolic solar collector. The pipe is at the focus of the parabola.
    a. Write an equation to model the cross section of the mirror.
    b. The pipe receives 25 times more sunlight than it would without the mirror. The amount of light collected by the mirror is directly proportional to its diameter. Find the width of the mirror.

Write an equation of a parabola opening upward with a vertex at the origin.

46. focus 2 units from vertex
47. focus $\frac{1}{4}$ unit from vertex

Identify the vertex, focus, and directrix of the graph of each equation. Then sketch the graph.

48. $y + 1 = -\frac{1}{4}(x - 3)^2$
49. $x = 2y^2$
50. $y^2 - 4x - 2y = 3$

Name ______________________ Class ______________ Date ______________

10-2 • Guided Problem Solving

GPS **Exercise 42**

Earth Science Tsunamis are ocean waves that result from an undersea earthquake. As the waves approach shallow water, the depth decreases and their speed decreases. The equation $d = \frac{1}{10}s^2$ relates the depth d (in meters) of the ocean to the speed s (in meters per second) at which tsunamis travel. Graph the equation.

Read and Understand

1. What units measure the depth d of the ocean? ______________________

2. What does s represent? ______________________

Plan and Solve

3. Identify the vertex of the parabola. ______________________

4. Compare the given equation to the general form $y = ax^2$. Identify the value of a and determine the direction in which the parabola opens. ______________________

5. Use the fact that $|a| = \frac{1}{4c}$ to determine the value of c. ______________________

6. Identify the focus $F(0, c)$ and the directrix $y = -c$ of the parabola. ______________________

7. Select some values for s, such as $s = 10$. Then use the given equation to determine the corresponding d-value(s). List at least two points (s, d) on the parabola.

____

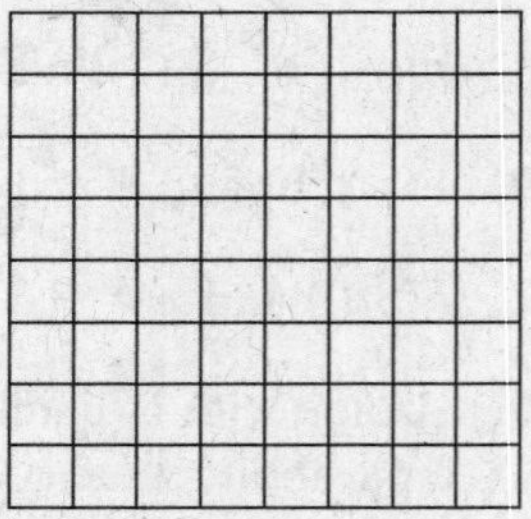

8. Graph the parabola.

Look Back and Check

9. Verify that your graph agrees with the described behavior of a tsunami. Choose two points on the parabola in the first quadrant. Is the speed s of the wave less at the point with the shallower depth d?

____

Solve Another Problem

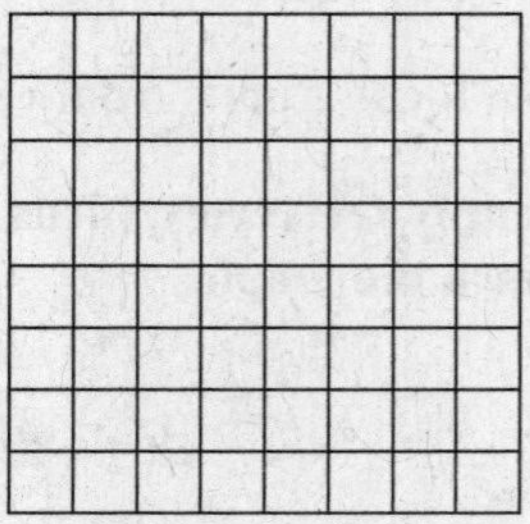

10. The equation $d = \frac{1}{32}t^2$ gives the distance d (in feet) that a ball rolls down a ramp at time t (in seconds). Graph the equation.

Name ______________________ Class ______________ Date ______________

Practice 10-3

Circles

Write an equation in standard form for each circle.

1.
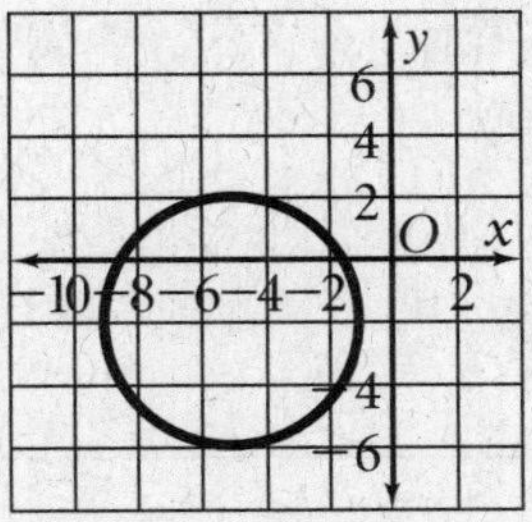

2.
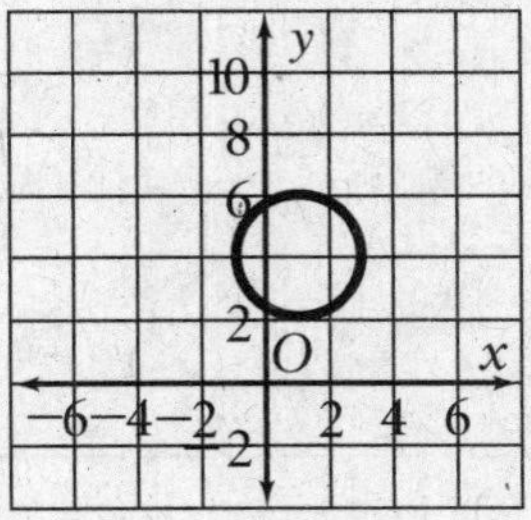

3.
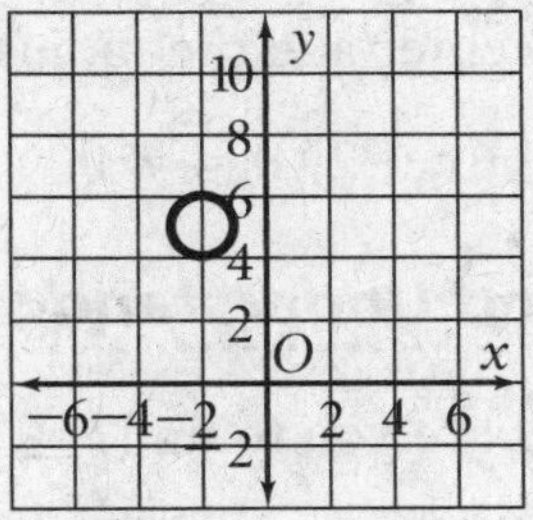

4.
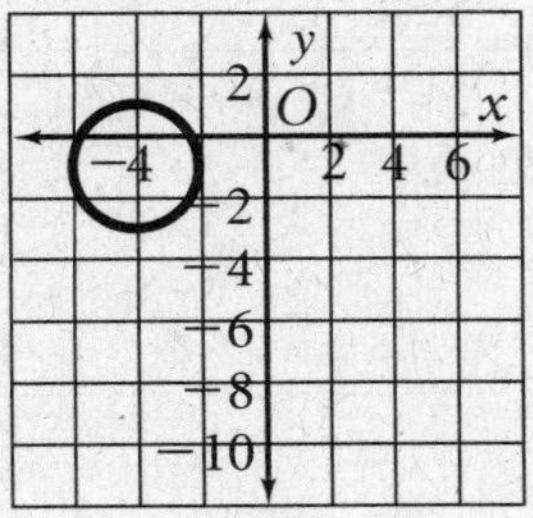

5.
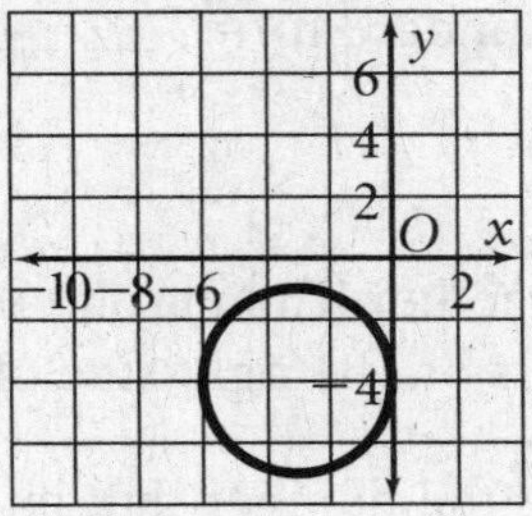

6.
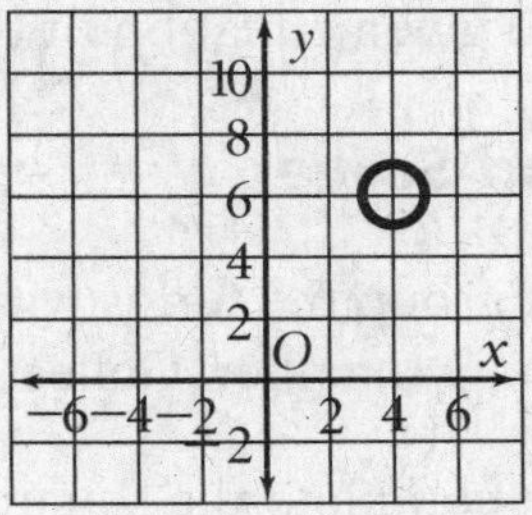

Write an equation of a circle with the given center and radius. Check your answers.

7. center $(0, 0)$, radius 3
8. center $(0, 1)$, radius 2
9. center $(-1, 0)$, radius 6
10. center $(2, 0)$, radius 1
11. center $(0, -3)$, radius 5
12. center $(4, -4)$, radius 1.5
13. center $(-2, 6)$, radius 4
14. center $(5, -1)$, radius 1.1
15. center $(1, -5)$, radius 2.5
16. center $(2, 3)$, diameter 1

Write an equation for each translation.

17. $x^2 + y^2 = 9$; right 4 and down 2
18. $x^2 + y^2 = 12$; left 2 and up 5
19. $x^2 + y^2 = 49$; right 1 and up 7
20. $x^2 + y^2 = 1$; right 5 and up 5
21. $x^2 + y^2 = 25$; up 10
22. $x^2 + y^2 = 36$; left 8 and down 6

Find the center and radius of each circle.

23. $(x + 1)^2 + (y - 8)^2 = 1$
24. $x^2 + (y + 3)^2 = 9$
25. $(x + 3)^2 + (y + 1)^2 = 2$
26. $(x - 6)^2 + y^2 = 5$
27. $(x - 6)^2 + (y - 9)^2 = 4$
28. $x^2 + y^2 = 144$

Use the center and radius to graph each circle.

29. $(x + 9)^2 + (y - 2)^2 = 81$
30. $x^2 + (y + 3)^2 = 121$
31. $(x - 8)^2 + (y + 9)^2 = 64$
32. $(x + 8)^2 + y^2 = 49$
33. $(x - 6)^2 + (y - 3)^2 = 75$
34. $(x + 9)^2 + (y + 9)^2 = 36$
35. $(x + 7)^2 + (y + 2)^2 = 80$
36. $(x - 5)^2 + (y + 7)^2 = 25$

Name ______________________ Class ______________ Date ______________

10-3 • Guided Problem Solving

GPS Exercise 63

Find the center and the radius of the circle.

$x^2 + y^2 - 6x - 2y + 4 = 0$

Read and Understand

1. What are you to find? ______________________

2. Is the given equation of the circle in standard form? ______________________

Plan and Solve

3. First, group the terms with x^2 and x together. Then group the terms with y^2 and y together. Collect any constants on the right side of the equation. ______________________

4. Next, complete the square in x. To find the number that must be added to both sides, take one half of -6 (the coefficient of the x-term) and square it. Add the resulting number to each side of the equation. ______________________

5. Complete the square in y. To find the number that must be added to both sides, take one half of -2 (the coefficient of the y-term) and square it. Add the resulting number to each side of the equation. ______________________

6. Write the standard form of the equation for the circle. ______________________

7. Write the standard form of the equation of a circle with center (h, k) and radius r.

8. Compare the two equations in Steps 6 and 7. Find h, k, and r for the given circle.

   $h =$ ______________ $k =$ ______________ $r =$ ______________

9. What is the center of the circle? ______________________

10. What is the radius of the circle? ______________________

Look Back and Check

11. Check that you have correctly completed the squares. Work backwards from your result in Step 6, the equation written in standard form. Square each binomial on the left side of the equation. Combine like terms. Verify that the result is equivalent to the original equation.

Solve Another Problem

12. Find the center and the radius of the circle $x^2 - 4x + y^2 - 6y = 3$ ______________________

Name ______________________ Class ______________ Date ______________

Practice 10-4

Ellipses

Find the foci for each equation of an ellipse. Then graph the ellipse.

1. $\frac{x^2}{36} + \frac{y^2}{81} = 1$
2. $x^2 + \frac{y^2}{36} = 1$
3. $\frac{x^2}{9} + \frac{y^2}{100} = 1$
4. $16x^2 + 25y^2 = 1600$
5. $4x^2 + y^2 = 49$
6. $\frac{x^2}{64} + \frac{y^2}{144} = 1$
7. $9x^2 + 25y^2 = 225$
8. $25x^2 + 4y^2 = 100$
9. $\frac{x^2}{81} + \frac{y^2}{9} = 1$
10. $\frac{x^2}{121} + \frac{y^2}{4} = 1$
11. $49x^2 + y^2 = 49$
12. $4x^2 + 9y^2 = 36$
13. $\frac{x^2}{4} + \frac{y^2}{9} = 1$
14. $\frac{x^2}{9} + \frac{y^2}{4} = 1$
15. $\frac{x^2}{16} + y^2 = 1$
16. $\frac{x^2}{25} + \frac{y^2}{36} = 1$
17. $\frac{x^2}{81} + \frac{y^2}{16} = 1$
18. $x^2 + \frac{y^2}{25} = 1$
19. $3x^2 + 9y^2 = 9$
20. $4x^2 + 8y^2 = 16$
21. $12x^2 + 4y^2 = 48$

Write an equation of each ellipse in standard form with center at the origin and with the given characteristics.

22. height 8; width 18
23. vertices $(\pm 4, 0)$; co-vertices $(0, \pm 2)$
24. foci $(\pm 5, 0)$; co-vertices $(0, \pm 2)$
25. foci $(0, \pm 2)$; co-vertices $(\pm 1, 0)$
26. foci $(\pm 3, 0)$; co-vertices $(0, \pm 1)$
27. height 10; width 8
28. height 3; width 1
29. vertices $(\pm 2, 0)$; co-vertices $(0, \pm 1)$
30. foci $(\pm 1, 0)$; co-vertices $(0, \pm 2)$
31. foci $(0, \pm 3)$; co-vertices $(\pm 3, 0)$
32. vertex $(6, 0)$; co-vertex $(0, -5)$
33. vertex $(0, 10)$; co-vertex $(-7, 0)$
34. height 28 ft; width 20 ft
35. height 20 ft; width 28 ft
36. height 50 ft; width 40 ft
37. height 9 cm; width 12 cm
38. vertex $(0, 2)$; co-vertex $(-1, 0)$
39. vertex $(4, 0)$; co-vertex $(0, 2)$
40. foci $(0, \pm 4)$; co-vertices $(\pm 4, 0)$
41. foci $(\pm 4, 0)$; co-vertices (0 ± 2)
42. vertex $(9, 0)$; co-vertex $(0, -6)$
43. vertex $(11, 0)$; co-vertex $(0, -10)$
44. foci $(\pm 2, 0)$; co-vertices $(0, \pm 4)$
45. foci $(\pm 1, 0)$; co-vertices $(0, \pm 5)$
46. foci $(\pm 3, 0)$; co-vertices $(0, \pm 3)$
47. foci $(0, \pm 2)$; co-vertices $(\pm 1, 0)$
48. vertex $(-7, 0)$; co-vertex $(0, -5)$
49. vertex $(-2, 0)$; co-vertex $(0, -1)$
50. Blinn College is building a new track for cycling teams. The track is to be elliptical. The available land is 200 yd long and 100 yd wide. Find the equation of the ellipse.

Name ____________________ Class ____________ Date ____________

10-4 • Guided Problem Solving

GPS Exercise 41

The eccentricity of an ellipse is a measure of how nearly circular it is. Eccentricity is defined as $\frac{c}{a}$, where c is the distance from the center to a focus and a is the distance from the center to a vertex.

a. Find the eccentricity of an ellipse with foci $(\pm 9, 0)$ and vertices $(\pm 10, 0)$. Sketch the graph.
b. Find the eccentricity of an ellipse with foci $(\pm 1, 0)$ and vertices $(\pm 10, 0)$. Sketch the graph.
c. Describe the shape of an ellipse that has an eccentricity close to 0.
d. Describe the shape of an ellipse that has an eccentricity close to 1.

Read and Understand

1. How is the eccentricity for an ellipse related to a and c? ____________________

Plan and Solve

2. For an ellipse with foci $(\pm 9, 0)$ and vertices $(\pm 10, 0)$, determine the values of a and c.

$a =$ ____________ $c =$ ____________

3. Use the given formula to compute the eccentricity. ____________________

4. Recall $c^2 = a^2 - b^2$. Find the co-vertices $(0, \pm b)$; then sketch the graph of this ellipse.

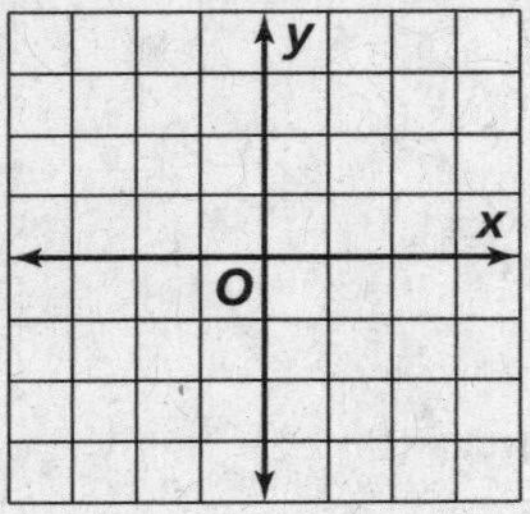

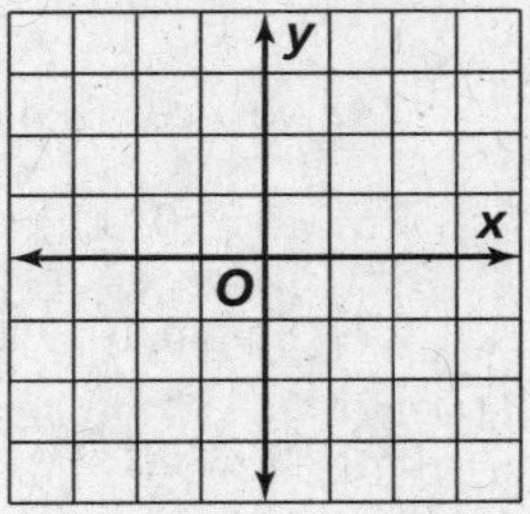

5. Now for an ellipse with foci $(\pm 1, 0)$ and vertices $(\pm 10, 0)$, find the indicated values.

$a =$ ____________ $b =$ ____________ $c =$ ____________ $\frac{c}{a} =$ ____________

6. Sketch the graph of this ellipse above in the second coordinate grid of Step 4.

7. Using your graphs as a guide, describe the shape of an ellipse with an eccentricity close to 0. Then describe the shape of an ellipse with an eccentricity close to 1. ____________________

____

Look Back and Check

8. Is it possible for the eccentricity of an ellipse to be greater than 1? Explain. ____________________

____

Solve Another Problem

9. Write an equation of an ellipse that is very eccentric, with a vertical major axis. ____________________

____

Name ______________________ Class ______________ Date ______________

Practice 10-5

Hyperbolas

Find the foci of each hyperbola. Then draw the graph.

1. $\frac{x^2}{4} - \frac{y^2}{4} = 1$
2. $\frac{y^2}{9} - \frac{x^2}{25} = 1$
3. $\frac{x^2}{49} - \frac{y^2}{36} = 1$
4. $4y^2 - 36x^2 = 144$
5. $x^2 - 9y^2 = 9$
6. $16x^2 - y^2 = 64$
7. $9y^2 - 16x^2 = 144$
8. $4x^2 - 9y^2 = 36$
9. $121y^2 - 4x^2 = 121$
10. $\frac{y^2}{16} - \frac{x^2}{9} = 1$
11. $\frac{x^2}{64} - \frac{y^2}{9} = 1$
12. $\frac{y^2}{100} - \frac{x^2}{4} = 1$
13. $25y^2 - 4x^2 = 100$
14. $49y^2 - x^2 = 49$
15. $4x^2 - 100y^2 = 100$
16. $\frac{x^2}{25} - \frac{y^2}{4} = 1$
17. $y^2 - \frac{x^2}{9} = 1$
18. $\frac{y^2}{25} - \frac{x^2}{16} = 1$
19. $\frac{y^2}{4} - \frac{x^2}{9} = 1$
20. $x^2 - \frac{y^2}{16} = 1$
21. $\frac{x^2}{4} - \frac{y^2}{16} = 1$
22. $\frac{x^2}{36} - y^2 = 1$
23. $\frac{x^2}{64} - \frac{y^2}{16} = 1$
24. $y^2 - x^2 = 16$
25. $y^2 - 4x^2 = 16$
26. $4x^2 - 4y^2 = 100$
27. $25x^2 - 4y^2 = 100$
28. $16y^2 - 4x^2 = 80$
29. $9y^2 - 4x^2 = 36$
30. $4x^2 - 36y^2 = 36$
31. $x^2 - 25y^2 = 25$
32. $4x^2 - y^2 = 16$
33. $9y^2 - 16x^2 = 225$
34. $16y^2 - 9x^2 = 225$
35. $4x^2 - 9y^2 = 36$
36. $9x^2 - 4y^2 = 36$
37. $\frac{y^2}{9} - x^2 = 1$
38. $\frac{x^2}{9} - \frac{y^2}{16} = 1$
39. $\frac{y^2}{4} - \frac{x^2}{16} = 1$
40. $\frac{x^2}{25} - \frac{y^2}{16} = 1$
41. $y^2 - \frac{x^2}{16} = 1$
42. $\frac{x^2}{9} - \frac{y^2}{36} = 1$
43. $4y^2 - 25x^2 = 100$
44. $y^2 - 4x^2 = 16$
45. $16x^2 - y^2 = 64$

Find the equation of a hyperbola with the given *a* and *c* values. Assume that the transverse axis is horizontal.

46. $a = 432{,}356,\ c = 1{,}984{,}576$
47. $a = 176{,}398,\ c = 1{,}984{,}576$
48. $a = 7,\ c = 9$
49. $a = 292{,}954,\ c = 365{,}987$
50. $a = 5,\ c = 15$
51. $a = 7654,\ c = 8675$
52. $a = 67,\ c = 92$
53. $a = 75,\ c = 180$
54. $a = 8,\ c = 20$
55. $a = 6,\ c = 9$
56. $a = 6, c = 10$
57. $a = 6, c = 8$
58. $a = 1, c = 9$
59. $a = 3, c = 7$
60. $a = 8, c = 10$
61. $a = 9, c = 12$

Name ______________________ Class ______________ Date ______________

10-5 • Guided Problem Solving

GPS Exercise 36

Rewrite the equation $x^2 - 4y^2 = 4$ in standard form. Then write the equation for a translation right 1 unit and down 1 unit. Draw the graph of each.

Read and Understand

1. In the translated graph, what is the vertical translation desired? ______________

Plan and Solve

2. Divide both sides by 4. What is $x^2 - 4y^2 = 4$ in standard form? ______________

3. Graph the hyperbola defined in Step 2.

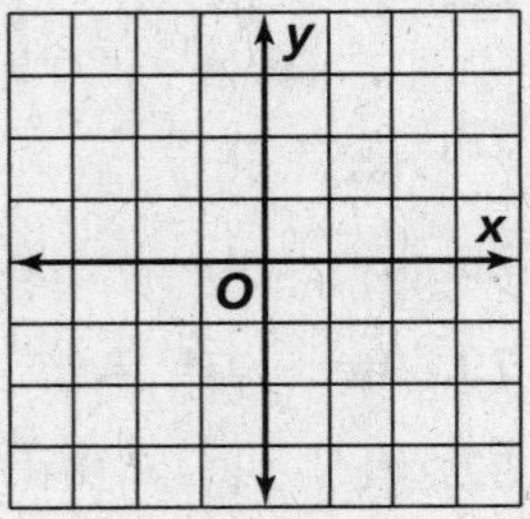

4. For a translation to the right of 1 unit, will you add or subtract 1 from x? ______________

5. For a translation down 1 unit, will you add or subtract 1 from y? ______________

6. Write the equation for a translation right 1 unit and down 1 unit. ______________

7. Use the graph from Step 3. Translate the vertices, the central rectangle, and the asymptotes right 1 unit and down 1 unit.

Look Back and Check

8. Choose some values for x. Use your equation from Step 6 to find the associated y-value. Verify these points are on your graph.

Solve Another Problem

9. Rewrite the equation $9x^2 - 4y^2 = 36$ in standard form. Then write the equation for a translation left 1 unit and up 2 units. Draw the graph.

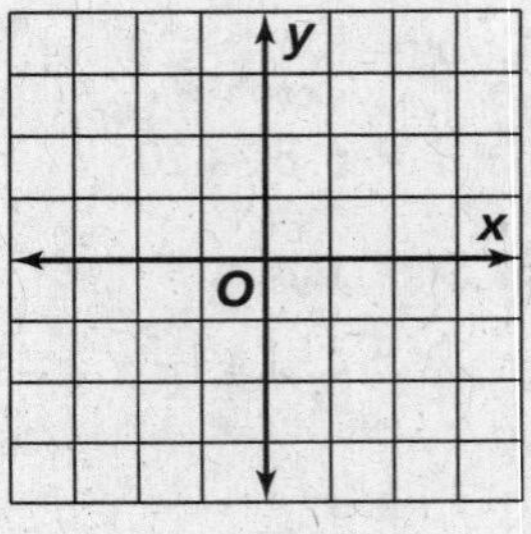

Name ______________________ Class ______________ Date ______________

Practice 10-6

Translating Conic Sections

Identify the conic section represented by each equation by writing the equation in standard form. For a parabola, give the vertex. For a circle, give its center and radius. For an ellipse or hyperbola, give its center and foci. Sketch the graph.

1. $3x^2 + 6x + 5y^2 - 20y - 13 = 0$

2. $x^2 - 9y^2 + 36y - 45 = 0$

3. $x^2 + 4y^2 + 8x - 48 = 0$

4. $x^2 + y^2 - 8x - 4y + 19 = 0$

5. $x^2 + y^2 + 6y - 27 = 0$

6. $x^2 - 10x - 4y^2 + 24y - 15 = 0$

7. $16x^2 - 96x - 9y^2 + 36y - 36 = 0$

8. $10x^2 + 10y^2 - 70 = 0$

9. $x^2 + 2x + y^2 + 14y - 31 = 0$

10. $25x^2 + 50x - 9y^2 - 18y - 209 = 0$

11. $4x^2 - 16x + 4y^2 - 16y - 4 = 0$

12. $x^2 + 4y^2 - 4x + 8y = 0$

13. $x^2 - 10x + y^2 + 4y - 7 = 0$

14. $x^2 + 2x + y^2 - 10y - 38 = 0$

15. $x^2 - 2x - y + 3 = 0$

16. $x^2 + 6x - y + 7 = 0$

17. $x^2 + 8x + y^2 + 2y + 1 = 0$

18. $x^2 - y^2 - 4 = 0$

19. $y^2 + 2y - x + 3 = 0$

20. $x^2 - 4x + 3 - y = 0$

Write an equation of a conic section with the given characteristics.

21. circle with center $(-4, 5)$, radius 6

22. hyperbola with center $(-4, 5)$, one vertex $(-4, 7)$, one focus $(-4, 8)$

23. Points on the hyperbola are 96 units closer to one focus than to the other. The foci are located at $(0, 0)$ and $(100, 0)$.

24. parabola with vertex $(1, -2)$, x-intercept 3, and opens to the right

25. ellipse with center $(0, 2)$, horizontal major axis of length 6, minor axis of length 4

26. ellipse with center $(-4, -5)$, endpoints of major and minor axes $(-4, -7), (-4, -3), (-1, -5), (-7, -5)$

27. circle with center $(-1, 2)$, diameter 12

28. parabola with vertex $(-1, 5)$, y-intercept 4, and opens downward

29. hyperbola with vertices $(0, 2)$ and $(4, 2)$, foci $(-1, 2)$ and $(5, 2)$

30. ellipse with center $(2, -5)$, one end of each axis $(2, -9)$ and $(-3, -5)$

31. Points on the hyperbola are 12 units closer to one focus than to the other. The foci are located at $(0, 0)$ and $(250, 0)$.

32. ellipse with center $(0, -2)$, vertical major axis of length 5, minor axis of length 3

Name ______________________ Class ______________ Date ______________

10-6 • Guided Problem Solving

GPS Exercise 34

Write the equation of the graph.

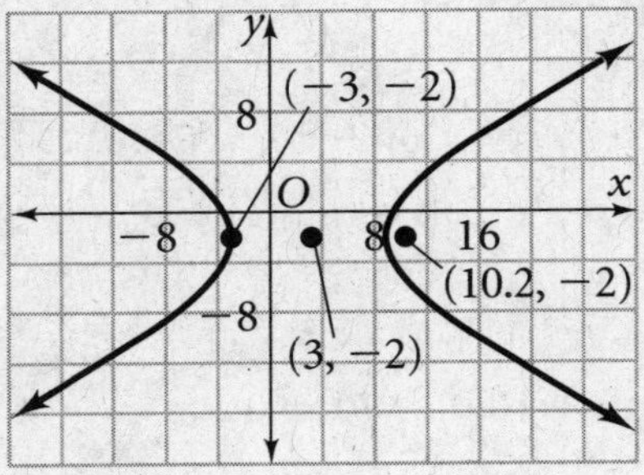

Read and Understand

1. What kind of conic section is represented in the graph? ______________________

2. Where is the center (h, k) of the conic section? ______________________

Plan and Solve

3. What are the coordinates of the labeled vertex? ______________________

4. Find the distance between the center and this vertex. What is the value of a? ______________

5. What are the coordinates of the labeled focus? ______________________

6. Find the distance between the center and this focus. What is the value of c? ______________

7. Find b^2 using the Pythagorean theorem. ______________________

8. Is the transverse axis passing through the vertices horizontal or vertical? ______________

9. Will the equation be in the form $\frac{(x-h)^2}{a^2} - \frac{(y-k)^2}{b^2} = 1$ or in the form $\frac{(y-k)^2}{a^2} - \frac{(x-h)^2}{b^2} = 1$?

10. What is the equation of the graph? ______________________

Look Back and Check

11. Choose some values for x. Use your equation from Step 6 to find the associated y-value. Verify these points are on the graph shown above.

Solve Another Problem

12. Write the equation of the graph shown at right.

____

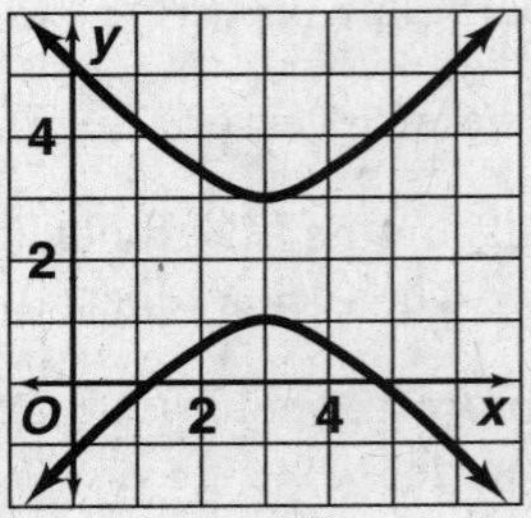

Name ______________________ Class ______________ Date ______________

10A: Graphic Organizer

For use before Lesson 10-1

Study Skill Sometimes the chapter title can reveal quite a bit about what you will learn in the chapter. Chapter 10 is entitled *Quadratic Relations*. Think about what you already know about quadratic equations. Write down what this term means. If you are not sure, look it up. Then skim the chapter to compare what you already know to what you will learn about this concept in this chapter.

Write your answers.

1. What is the chapter title? ______________________

2. Find the Table of Contents page for this chapter at the front of the book. Name four topics you will study in this chapter.

   ______________________ ______________________

   ______________________ ______________________

3. What is the topic of the Test-Taking Strategies page? ______________________

4. Look through the pages of the chapter. List four real-world connections that you see discussed in this chapter.

   ______________________ ______________________

   ______________________ ______________________

5. Complete the graphic organizer as you work through the chapter.
   1. Write the title of the chapter in the center oval.
   2. When you begin a lesson, write the name of the lesson in a rectangle.
   3. When you complete that lesson, write a skill or key concept from that lesson in the outer oval linked to that rectangle.

   Continue with steps 2 and 3 clockwise around the graphic organizer.

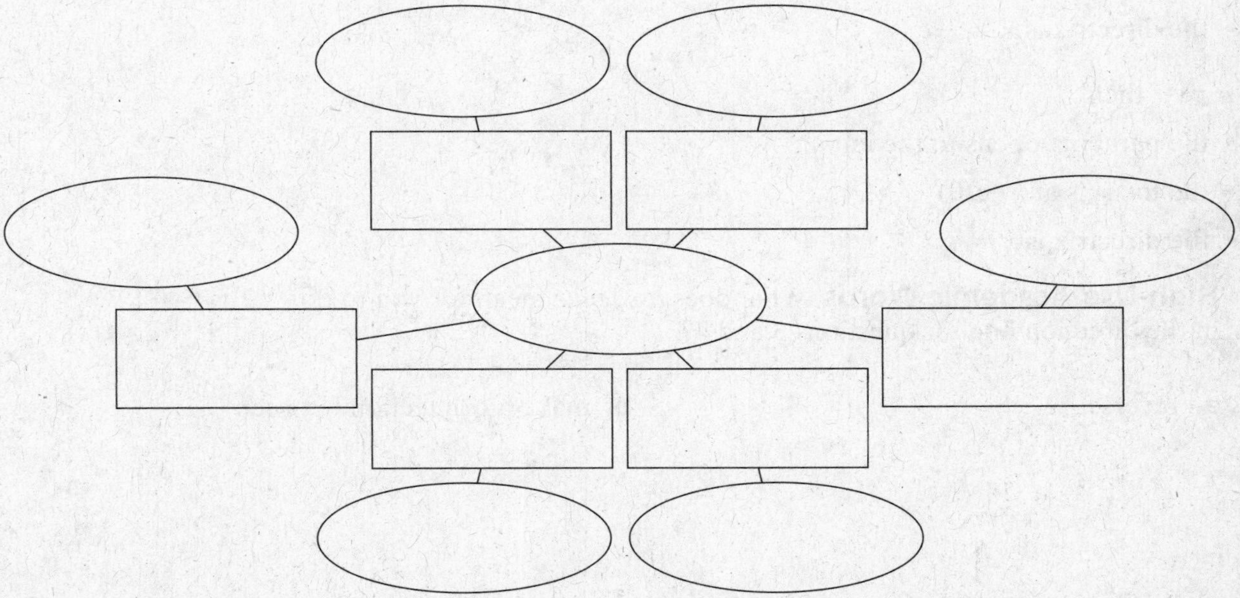

Name ______________________ Class ______________ Date ______________

10B: Reading Comprehension

For use after Lesson 10-3

Study Skill When you are trying to memorize, it can be helpful to read the material aloud. Reciting a rule, formula, or definition can help you to remember it. When you involve more than one of your senses, such as both sight and hearing, in learning the material, you will be better able to recall the content.

Read the review at the left, and then answer the questions and fill in the blanks at the right.

Summary of the graph of any parabola with the equation $y = ax^2$.

If $a > 0$, then

- the parabola opens upward
- the focus is at $(0, c)$
- the directrix is $y = -c$

If $a < 0$, then

- the parabola opens downward
- the focus is at $(0, -c)$
- the directrix is $y = c$

Summary of the graph of any parabola with the equation $x = ay^2$.

If $a > 0$, then

- the parabola opens to the right
- the focus is at $(c, 0)$
- the directrix is $x = -c$

If $a < 0$, then

- the parabola opens to the left
- the focus is at $(-c, 0)$
- the directrix is $x = c$

As you look at the description of the four graphs, make associations to help you remember each of the four.

1. The graphs of parabolas of the type $y = ax^2$ are symmetric about which axis?

____

2. The graphs of parabolas of the type $x = ay^2$ are symmetric about which axis?

____

Associate the direction of the opening with the sign of a.

3. If $a > 0$, the graph opens either ______________ or ______________.

4. If $a < 0$, the graph opens either ______________ or ______________.

5. High-Use Academic Words What does *associate* mean for you to do in the direction line for questions 3 and 4?

a. reverse

b. make a connection between

Name ____________________ Class ____________ Date ____________

10C: Reading/Writing Math Symbols

For use after Lesson 10-5

Vocabulary and Study Skills

Study Skill Set builder notation may look very abstract and complicated at first. Read it part by part, saying the words aloud as you go.

Write the words that tell how to read each of the following.

1. $\{x \mid x \in \text{real numbers}\}$ ____________________

2. $\{x \mid x > 0\}$ ____________________

3. $\{y \mid y < -1\}$ ____________________

4. $\{x \mid 5 < x < 9\}$ ____________________

5. $\{(x, y) \mid x = y\}$ ____________________

6. $\{(x, y) \mid y = 3x\}$ ____________________

Name ______________________ Class ______________ Date ______________

10D: Visual Vocabulary Practice

For use after Lesson 10-6

Study Skill Math symbols give us a way to express complex ideas in a small space.

Concept List

circle	ellipse	foci of an ellipse
foci of a hyperbola	hyperbola	parabola
radius	vertices of an ellipse	vertices of a hyperbola

Write the concept that best describes each exercise. Choose from the concept list above.

1.

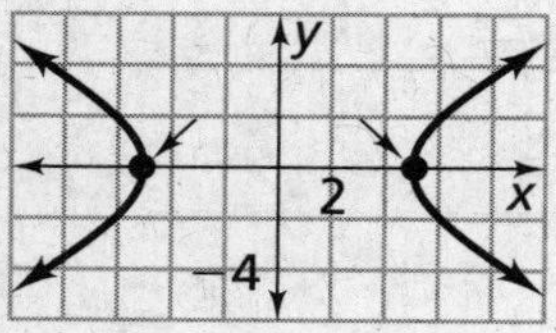

____

2. $\frac{x^2}{4} + \frac{y^2}{9} = 1$

____

3.

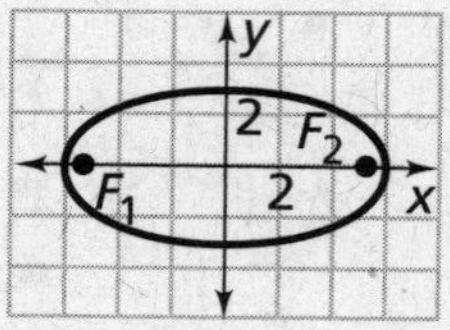

____

4. $x = 4(y + 1)^2$

____

5.

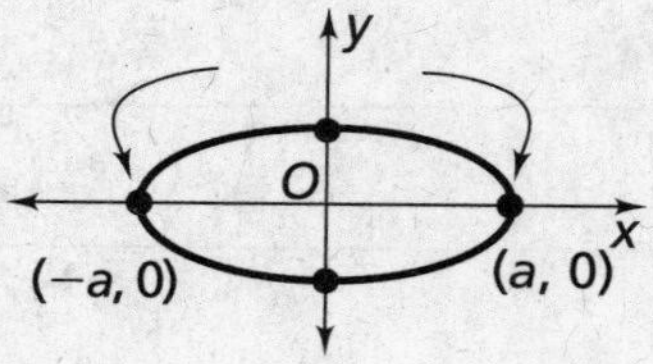

____

6. $\frac{x^2}{9} - \frac{y^2}{16} = 1$

____

7.

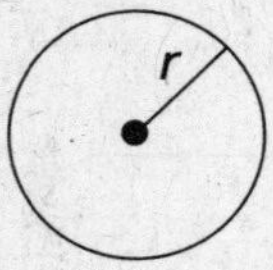

____

8. $(x - 1)^2 + (y + 2)^2 = 5^2$

____

9.

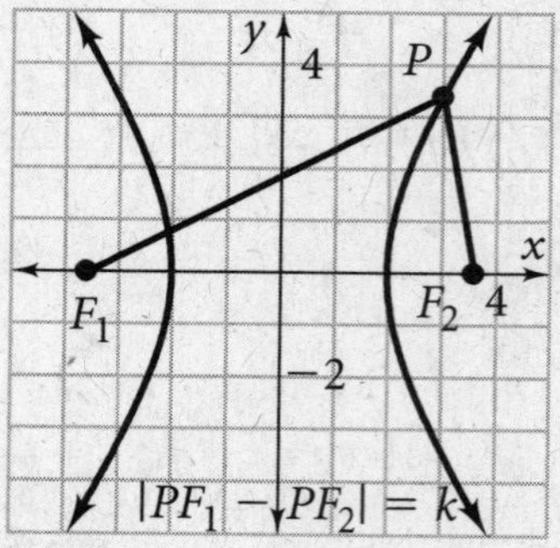

____

Name ______________________ Class ______________ Date ______________

10E: Vocabulary Check

For use after Lesson 10-4

Vocabulary and Study Skills

Study Skill Strengthen your vocabulary. Use these pages and add cues and summaries by applying the Cornell Notetaking style.

Write the definition for each word at the right. To check your work, fold the paper back along the dotted line to see the correct answers.

______________________ ______________________ ______________________	Radius
______________________ ______________________ ______________________	Conic section
______________________ ______________________ ______________________	Directrix
______________________ ______________________ ______________________	Circle
______________________ ______________________ ______________________	Center

Name ____________________ Class ____________ Date ____________

10E: Vocabulary Check (continued)

For use after Lesson 10-4

Write the vocabulary word for each definition. To check your work, fold the paper forward along the dotted line to see the correct answers.

The distance between the center of a circle and any point on the circumference. ____________________

A curve formed by the intersection of a plane and a double cone. ____________________

The fixed line used to define a parabola. Each point of the parabola is the same distance from the focus and this line. ____________________

The set of all points in a plane at a distance *r* from a given point. ____________________

The point that is the same distance from every point on the circle. ____________________

Name ______________________ Class ______________ Date ______________

10F: Vocabulary Review Puzzle

For use with Chapter Review

Study Skill Mathematics has its own vocabulary, often with many new terms in each chapter. Some mathematics vocabulary terms may have different meanings in everyday language. Make sure you understand the two different meanings of such words.

Use the given words to complete the crossword puzzle. For help, use the Glossary in your textbook.

ellipse	circle	parabola
hyperbola	focus	directrix
radius	axis	

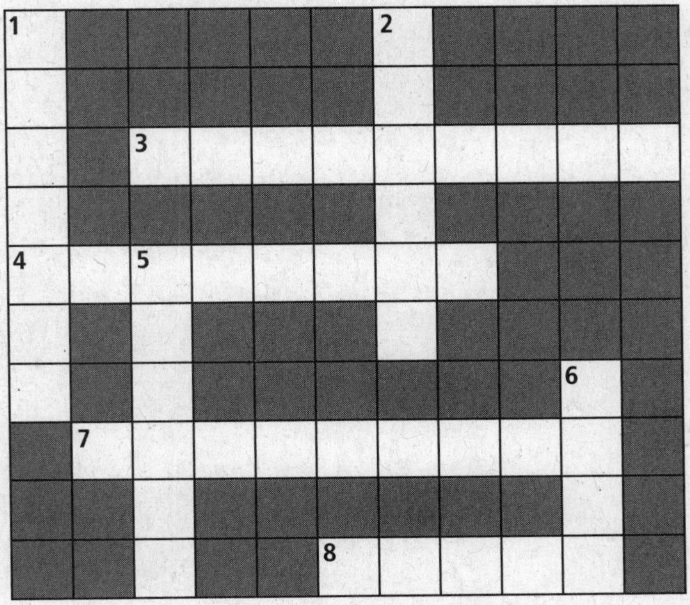

ACROSS

3. the set of points P in a plane such that the difference between the distances from P to two fixed points F_1 and F_2 is a constant

4. the set of points P in a plane that are the same distance from a fixed point F and a line d

7. the fixed line used to define a parabola

8. a point used to define a conic section

DOWN

1. the set of points P in a plane such that the sum of the distances from P to two fixed points F_1 and F_2 is a constant

2. the set of points in a plane that is a constant distance from a given point

5. the distance between the center of a circle and any point on the circle

6. a line segment that connects the vertices or co-vertices of an ellipse

Name ______________________ Class ______________ Date ______________

Practice 11-1

Mathematical Patterns

Write a recursive formula for each sequence. Then find the next term.

1. $-14, -8, -2, 4, 10, \ldots$
2. $6, 5.7, 5.4, 5.1, 4.8, \ldots$
3. $1, -2, 4, -8, 16, \ldots$
4. $1, 3, 9, 27, \ldots$
5. $1, \frac{1}{2}, \frac{1}{4}, \frac{1}{8}, \frac{1}{16}, \ldots$
6. $\frac{2}{3}, 1, 1\frac{1}{3}, 1\frac{2}{3}, 2, \ldots$
7. $36, 39, 42, 45, 48, \ldots$
8. $36, 30, 24, 18, 12, \ldots$
9. $9.6, 4.8, 2.4, 1.2, 0.6, \ldots$

Write an explicit formula for each sequence. Then find a_{20}.

10. $7, 14, 21, 28, 35, \ldots$
11. $2, 8, 14, 20, 26, \ldots$
12. $5, 6, 7, 8, 9, \ldots$
13. $-1, 0, 1, 2, 3, \ldots$
14. $3, 5, 7, 9, 11, \ldots$
15. $0.8, 1.6, 2.4, 3.2, 4, \ldots$
16. $\frac{1}{4}, \frac{1}{2}, \frac{3}{4}, 1, \frac{5}{4}, \ldots$
17. $\frac{1}{2}, \frac{1}{4}, \frac{1}{6}, \frac{1}{8}, \frac{1}{10}, \ldots$
18. $\frac{2}{3}, 1\frac{2}{3}, 2\frac{2}{3}, 3\frac{2}{3}, 4\frac{2}{3}, \ldots$

Describe each pattern formed. Find the next three terms.

19. $1, 2, 4, 8, 16, \ldots$
20. $44, 39, 34, 29, 24, \ldots$
21. $0.7, 0.8, 0.9, 1.0, 1.1, \ldots$
22. $4, 11, 18, 25, 32, \ldots$
23. $1\frac{1}{4}, 2\frac{1}{2}, 5, 10, 20, \ldots$
24. $-6, -9, -12, -15, -18, \ldots$

Decide whether each formula is *explicit* or *recursive*. Then find the first five terms of each sequence.

25. $a_n = \frac{1}{3}n$
26. $a_n = n^2 - 6$
27. $a_1 = 5, a_n = 3a_{n-1} - 7$
28. $a_n = \frac{1}{2}(n - 1)$
29. $a_1 = 5, a_n = 3 - a_{n-1}$
30. $a_1 = -4, a_n = 2a_{n-1}$

31. The first figure of a fractal contains one segment. For each successive figure, six segments replace each segment.
    a. How many segments are in each of the first four figures of the sequence?
    b. Write a recursive formula for the sequence.

32. The sum of the measures of the exterior angles of any polygon is 360. All the angles have the same measure in a regular polygon.
    a. Find the measure of one exterior angle in a regular hexagon (six angles).
    b. Write an explicit formula for the measure of one exterior angle in a regular polygon with n angles.
    c. Why would this formula not be meaningful for $n = 1$ or $n = 2$?

Name ______________________ Class ______________ Date ______________

11-1 • Guided Problem Solving

GPS Exercise 32

Entertainment Suppose you are building a tower of cards with levels as displayed here. Complete the table, assuming the pattern continues.

Levels	1	2	3	4	5
Cards Needed	2	7			

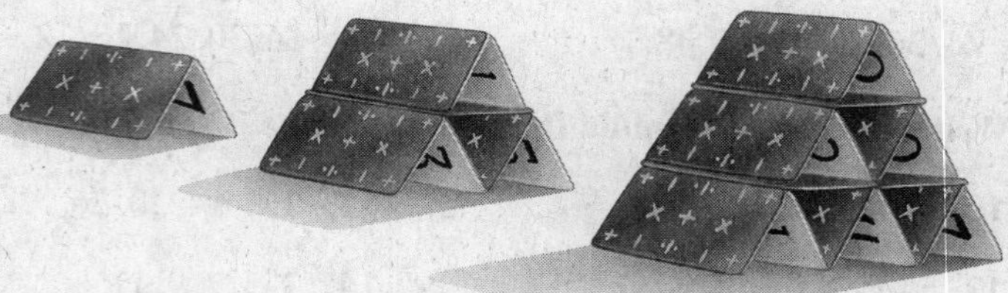

Read and Understand

1. How many cards are needed for level 1? ______

2. How many cards are needed for level 2? ______

Plan and Solve

3. Using the given picture, count the number of cards in the third tower to find the cards needed for level 3. ______

4. For each next level n, keep the previous cards and add a bottom row of cards and their lids. Write the recursive formula for a_n. ______

5. Use the recursive formula to find the cards needed for level 4. ______

6. Use the recursive formula to find the cards needed for level 5. ______

7. Complete the table. ______

Look Back and Check

8. To check your answers, build towers of cards with 4 and 5 levels. Then count the number of cards in each level. ______

Solve Another Problem

9. **Entertainment** Suppose you are building a tower of blocks with levels as displayed here. Complete the table, assuming the pattern continues.

Levels	1	2	3	4	5
Blocks Needed	1	3			

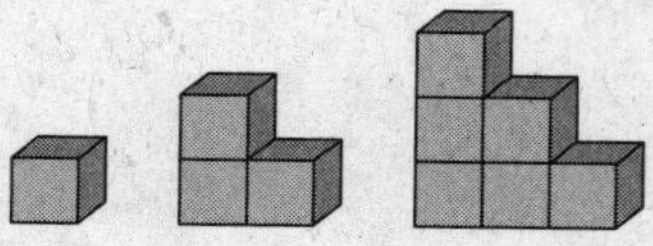

Name ______________________ Class ______________ Date ______________

Practice 11-2

Arithmetic Sequences

Find the 43rd term of each sequence.

1. 12, 14, 16, 18, ...

2. 13.1, 3.1, −6.9, −16.9, ...

3. 19.5, 19.9, 20.3, 20.7, ...

4. 27, 24, 21, 18, ...

5. 2, 13, 24, 35, ...

6. 21, 15, 9, 3, ...

7. 1.3, 1.4, 1.5, 1.6, ...

8. −2.1, −2.3, −2.5, −2.7, ...

9. 45, 48, 51, 54, ...

Is the given sequence arithmetic? If so, identify the common difference.

10. 2, 3, 5, 8, ...

11. 0, −3, −6, −9, ...

12. 0.9, 0.5, 0.1, −0.3, ...

13. 3, 8, 13, 18, ...

14. 14, −15, −44, −73, ...

15. 3.2, 3.5, 3.8, 4.1, ...

16. −34, −28, −22, −16, ...

17. 2.3, 2.5, 2.7, 2.9, ...

18. 127, 140, 153, 166, ...

Find the missing term of each arithmetic sequence.

19. ... 23, ■, 49, ...

20. 14, ■, 28, ...

21. ... 29, ■, 33, ...

22. ... 14, ■, 15, ...

23. ... −45, ■, −39, ...

24. ... −5, ■, −2, ...

25. −2, ■, 2, ...

26. ... −6, ■, 2, ...

27. −34, ■, 77, ...

28. ... −45, ■, −12, ...

29. −2, ■, 456, ...

30. ... 34, ■, 345, ...

Find the arithmetic mean a_n of the given terms.

31. $a_{n-1} = 2, a_{n+1} = 7$

32. $a_{n-1} = 13.2, a_{n+1} = 15.8$

33. $a_{n-1} = 29, a_{n+1} = -11$

34. $a_{n-1} = \frac{2}{5}, a_{n+1} = \frac{4}{5}$

35. $a_{n-1} = 15, a_{n+1} = -17$

36. $a_{n-1} = -6, a_{n+1} = -7$

37. Each year, a volunteer organization expects to add 5 more people to the number of shut-ins for whom the group provides home maintenance services. This year, the organization provides the service for 32 people.

a. Write a recursive formula for the number of people the organization expects to serve each year.

b. Write the first five terms of the sequence.

c. Write an explicit formula for the number of people the organization expects to serve each year.

d. How many people would the organization expect to serve in the 20th year?

Name ______________________ Class ______________ Date ______________

11-2 • Guided Problem Solving

GPS Exercise 62

Transportation Suppose a trolley stops at a certain intersection every 14 min. The first trolley of the day gets to the stop at 6:43 A.M. How long do you have to wait for a trolley if you get to the stop at 8:15 A.M.? At 3:20 P.M.?

Read and Understand

1. Let 6:43 A.M. be given in minutes as $6(60) + 43 = 403$. Write the arithmetic sequence representing the trolley stop times, including the first three terms. ______________

2. What is the first term of the sequence a_1 and the common difference d? ______________

Plan and Solve

3. Write the explicit formula for finding the nth term of the arithmetic sequence of trolley stop times. ______________

4. Give 8:15 A.M. in minutes. Let this value be a_n. ______________

5. Substitute a_n in the explicit formula and solve for n, rounding up. ______________

6. Use this value of n to find the nth term of the sequence. This is the time the trolley stops closest to the time after you arrive. ______________

7. Subtract the time, in minutes, you arrived (Step 4) from the trolley's time (Step 6) to calculate the number of minutes you have to wait. ______________

8. Give 3:20 P.M. in minutes (remember to add 12 hours since it is P.M.) and repeat the steps above to find how long you have to wait for a trolley if you get to the stop at 3:20 P.M. ______________

Look Back and Check

9. To check the reasonableness of your answer to Step 7, write out the first several terms of the sequence. Using the value of the sequence that is greater than your arrival time, find the difference and compare the wait times. ______________

Solve Another Problem

10. Find the 40th term of the arithmetic sequence whose 1st and 15th terms are -9 and 19, respectively. ______________

Name ____________________ Class ____________ Date ____________

Practice 11-3

Geometric Sequences

Find the missing term of each geometric sequence.

1. 4, ■ , 16, . . .

2. 9, ■ , 16, . . .

3. 2, ■ , 8, . . .

4. 3, ■ , 12, . . .

5. 2, ■ , 50, . . .

6. 4, ■ , 5.76, . . .

Is the given sequence geometric? If so, identify the common ratio and find the next two terms.

7. 3, 9, 27, 81, . . .

8. 4, 8, 16, 32, . . .

9. 4, 8, 12, 16, . . .

10. 4, −8, 16, −32, . . .

11. 1, 0.5, 0.25, 0.125, . . .

12. 100, 30, 9, 2.7, . . .

13. −5, 0, 5, 10, . . .

14. 64, −32, 16, −8, . . .

15. 1, 4, 9, 16, . . .

Identify each sequence as *arithmetic, geometric,* or *neither.* Then find the next two terms.

16. $9, 3, 1, \frac{1}{3}, \ldots$

17. 1, 0, −2, −5, . . .

18. 2, −2, 2, −2, . . .

19. −3, 2, 7, 12, . . .

20. 1, −2, −5, −8, . . .

21. 1, −2, 3, −4, . . .

Write the explicit formula for each sequence. Then generate the first five terms.

22. $a_1 = 3, r = -2$

23. $a_1 = 5, r = 3$

24. $a_1 = -1, r = 4$

25. $a_1 = -2, r = -3$

26. $a_1 = 32, r = -0.5$

27. $a_1 = 2187, r = \frac{1}{3}$

28. $a_1 = 9, r = 2$

29. $a_1 = -4, r = 4$

30. $a_1 = 0.1, r = -2$

31. When a pendulum swings freely, the length of its arc decreases geometrically. Find each missing arc length.

a. 20th arc is 20 in.; 22nd arc is 18.5 in.

b. 8th arc is 27 mm; 10th arc is 3 mm

32. The deer population in an area is increasing. This year, the population was 1.025 times last year's population of 2537.

a. Assuming that the population increases at the same rate for the next few years, write an explicit formula for the sequence.

b. Find the expected deer population for the fourth year of the sequence.

33. You enlarge a picture to 150% of its size several times. After the first increase, the picture is 1 in. wide.

a. Write an explicit formula to model the size after each increase.

b. How wide is the photo after the 2nd increase?

c. How wide is the photo after the 3rd increase?

d. How wide is the photo after the 12th increase?

Name ______________________ Class ______________ Date ______________

11-3 • Guided Problem Solving

GPS Exercise 41

a. Open-Ended Choose two positive numbers. Find their geometric mean.

b. Find the common ratio for a geometric sequence that includes the terms from part (a) in order from least to greatest or from greatest to least.

c. Find the 9th term of the geometric sequence from part (b).

d. Find the geometric mean of the term from part (c) and the first term of your sequence. What term of the sequence have you just found?

Read and Understand

1. What is the formula for finding the geometric mean? ______________________

2. What is the explicit formula for a geometric sequence? ______________________

Plan and Solve

3. Choose two positive numbers and find their geometric mean. ______________________

4. Find the common ratio r for a geometric sequence that includes the terms from Step 3 in order from least to greatest or from greatest to least. ______________

5. Using the explicit formula for a geometric sequence and $n = 9$, find the 9th term of the geometric sequence from Step 4. ______________

6. Find the geometric mean of the 9th term a_9 and the first term a_1 of your sequence. ______________________

7. What term of the sequence have you just found? ______________________

Look Back and Check

8. To check the reasonableness of your answers, write out the first 9 terms of the sequence and check your answers. ______________

Solve Another Problem

9. Open-Ended Choose two other positive numbers and repeat the steps above. Is your answer to Step 7 the same or different? Explain. ______________

Name ______________________ Class ______________ Date ______________

Practice 11-4

Arithmetic Series

For each sum, find the number of terms, the first term, and the last term. Then evaluate the series.

1. $\sum_{n=1}^{4}(n - 1)$

2. $\sum_{n=2}^{6}(2n - 1)$

3. $\sum_{n=3}^{8}(n + 25)$

4. $\sum_{n=2}^{5}(5n + 3)$

5. $\sum_{n=1}^{4}(2n + 0.5)$

6. $\sum_{n=1}^{6}(3 - n)$

7. $\sum_{n=5}^{10}n$

8. $\sum_{n=1}^{4}(-n - 3)$

9. $\sum_{n=3}^{6}(3n + 2)$

Write the related series for each finite sequence. Then evaluate each series.

10. 1, 3, 5, . . . , 15

11. 5, 8, 11, . . . , 26

12. 4, 9, 14, 19, . . . , 44

13. 10, 25, 40, 55, 70, 85

14. 17, 25, 33, 41, 49, 57, 65

15. 125, 126, 127, . . . , 131

Use summation notation to write each arithmetic series for the specified number of terms.

16. $1 + 3 + 5 + \ldots; n = 7$

17. $2.3 + 2.6 + 2.9 + \ldots; n = 5$

18. $4 + 8 + 12 + \ldots; n = 4$

19. $10 + 7 + 4 + \ldots; n = 6$

20. $3 + 7 + 11 + \ldots; n = 8$

21. $15 + 25 + 35 + \ldots; n = 7$

Tell whether each list is a *series* or a *sequence*. Then tell whether it is *finite* or *infinite*.

22. 7, 12, 17, 22, 27

23. $3 + 5 + 7 + 9 + \ldots$

24. 8, 8.2, 8.4, 8.6, 8.8, 9.0, . . .

25. $1 + 5 + 9 + 13 + 17$

26. 40, 20, 10, 5, 2.5, 1.25, . . .

27. $10 + 20 + 30 + 40 + 50$

Each sequence has six terms. Evaluate each related series.

28. 1, 0, −1, . . . , −4

29. 4, 5, 6, . . . , 9

30. −7, −9, −11, . . . , −17

31. −6, −7, −8, . . . , −11

32. 0, 0.3, 0.6, . . . , 1.5

33. 5, 7, 9, . . . , 15

34. An embroidery pattern calls for 5 stitches in the first row and for three more stitches in each successive row. The 25th row, which is the last row, has 77 stitches. Find the total number of stitches in the pattern.

35. A marching band formation consists of 6 rows. The first row has 9 musicians, the second has 11, the third has 13 and so on. How many musicians are in the last row and how many musicians are there in all?

Name ____________________ Class ____________ Date ____________

11-4 • Guided Problem Solving

GPS Exercise 31

Architecture A 20-row theater has three sections of seating. In each section, the number of seats in a row increases by one with each successive row. The first row of the middle section has 10 seats. The first row of each of the two side sections has 4 seats.

a. Find the total number of chairs in each section. Then find the total seating capacity of the theater.
b. Write an arithmetic series to represent each section.
c. After every five rows, the ticket price goes down by $5. Front-row tickets cost $60. What is the total amount of money generated by a full house?

Read and Understand

1. How many rows are in the theater? ____________

2. How many seats are in the first row of each section? ____________

3. How many seats are in the last row of each section? ____________

Plan and Solve

4. Use the formula for the sum of a finite arithmetic series, $S_n = \frac{n}{2}(a_1 + a_n)$, to find the total number of chairs in each section. ____________

5. What is the total seating capacity of the theater? ____________

6. Use summation notation to write an arithmetic series to represent each section. ____________

7. Find the total amount of money generated by a full house, starting with the money from the front row and moving to the back, i.e., $60(4 + 4 + 10) + 60(5 + 5 + 11) + \dots$. ____________

Look Back and Check

8. To check the reasonableness of your answers, draw a picture. Use the picture to calculate the answers and compare. ____________

Solve Another Problem

9. The first term of an arithmetic series is 9, the last term is 147, and the sum is 1872. Find the number of terms and the common difference. ____________

Name ______________________ Class ______________ Date ______________

Practice 11-5

Geometric Series

Decide whether each infinite geometric series *diverges* or *converges*. State whether each series has a sum.

1. $3 + \frac{3}{2} + \frac{3}{4} + \dots$

2. $4 + 2 + 1 + \dots$

3. $17 + 15.3 + 13.77 + \dots$

4. $6 + 11.4 + 21.66 + \dots$

5. $-20 - 8 - 3.2 - \dots$

6. $50 + 70 + 98 + \dots$

Evaluate each infinite series that has a sum.

7. $\sum_{n=1}^{\infty} 5\left(\frac{2}{3}\right)^{n-1}$

8. $\sum_{n=1}^{\infty} (-2.1)^{n-1}$

9. $\sum_{n=1}^{\infty} \left(-\frac{1}{2}\right)^{n-1}$

10. $\sum_{n=1}^{\infty} 2\left(\frac{5}{3}\right)^{n-1}$

Evaluate each infinite geometric series.

11. $8 + 4 + 2 + 1 + \dots$

12. $1 + \frac{1}{3} + \frac{1}{9} + \frac{1}{27} + \dots$

13. $120 + 96 + 76.8 + 61.44 + \dots$

14. $1000 + 750 + 562.5 + 421.875 + \dots$

Determine whether each series is *arithmetic* or *geometric*. Then evaluate the series to the given term.

15. $2 + 5 + 8 + 11 + \dots; S_9$

16. $\frac{1}{8} + \frac{1}{16} + \frac{1}{32} + \frac{1}{64} + \dots; S_8$

17. $-3 + 6 - 12 + 24 - \dots; S_{10}$

18. $-2 + 2 + 6 + 10 + \dots; S_{12}$

Evaluate the finite series for the specified number of terms.

19. $40 + 20 + 10 + \dots; n = 10$

20. $4 + 12 + 36 + \dots; n = 15$

21. $15 + 12 + 9.6 + \dots; n = 40$

22. $27 + 9 + 3 + \dots; n = 100$

23. $0.2 + 0.02 + 0.002 + \dots; n = 8$

24. $100 + 200 + 400 + \dots; n = 6$

25. This month, Julia deposits \$400 to save for a vacation. She plans to deposit 10% more each successive month for the next 11 months. How much will she have saved after the 12 deposits?

26. Suppose your business made a profit of \$5500 the first year. If the profit increases 20% per year, find the total profit over the first 5 yr.

27. The end of a pendulum travels 50 cm on its first swing. Each swing after the first travels 99% as far as the preceding one. How far will the pendulum travel before it stops?

28. A seashell has chambers that are each 0.82 times the length of the next chamber. The outer chamber is 32 mm around. Find the total length of the shell's spiraled chambers.

29. The first year a toy manufacturer introduces a new toy, its sales total \$495,000. The company expects its sales to drop 10% each succeeding year. Find the total expected sales in the first 6 yr. Find the total expected sales if the company offers the toy for sale for as long as anyone buys it.

Name ______________________ Class ______________ Date ______________

11-5 • Guided Problem Solving

GPS Exercise 30

Communications Many companies use a telephone chain to notify employees of a closing due to bad weather. Suppose the first person in the chain calls four people. Then each of these people calls four others, and so on.

a. Make a tree diagram to show the first three stages in the telephone chain. How many calls are made at each stage?
b. Write the series that represents the total number of calls made through the first six stages.
c. How many employees have been notified after stage six?

Read and Understand

1. How many people does the first person call? ______________

2. How many people does each of those people call? ______________

Plan and Solve

3. Make a tree diagram to show the first three stages in the telephone chain. ______________

4. How many calls are made at each stage? ______________

5. What is the common ratio *r* of the geometric series? ______________

6. Using the common ratio, write the series that represents the total number of calls made through the first six stages. ______________

7. Find the sum of the finite geometric series in Step 6. How many employees have been notified after stage six? ______________

Look Back and Check

8. To check your answer to Step 7, write the formula for the sum of a finite geometric series. Then use this formula to find the sum of the first six terms. ______________

Solve Another Problem

9. **Savings** A student has decided to start a savings plan. She saves $10 after the first month and saves twice as much in each successive month as in the previous month.

   a. How much money is saved each month for the first three months? ______________

   b. Write the series that represents the amount saved through the first five months. ______________

   c. How much money has been saved after five months? ______________

Name ______________________ Class ______________ Date ______________

Practice 11-6

Area Under a Curve

Write and evaluate a sum to approximate the area under each curve for the domain $0 \leq x \leq 2$.

a. Use inscribed rectangles 0.5 unit wide.
b. Use circumscribed rectangles 0.5 unit wide.

1. $y = -x^2 + 4$

2. $f(x) = -2x^2 + 16$

3. $g(x) = -0.5x^2 + 2$

4. $f(x) = x^2 + 4$

5. $y = 2x^2 + 6$

6. $h(g) = 0.5x^2 + 2$

7. $y = -3x^2 + 15$

8. $f(x) = 3x^2 + 2$

9. $f(x) = 10 - x^2$

10. **a.** Graph the curve $y = 2x^2 + 1$.

b. Use inscribed rectangles to approximate the area under the curve for the interval $0 \leq x \leq 2$ and rectangle width of 0.5 unit.

c. Repeat part b using circumscribed rectangles.

d. Find the mean of the areas you found in parts b and c. Of the three estimates, which best approximates the area for the interval?

Use your graphing calculator to find the area under each curve for the domain $-2 \leq x \leq 1$.

11. $y = -x^3 + 1$

12. $f(x) = -2x^3 + 3$

13. $f(x) = 2x^2 + 1$

14. $g(x) = 3x^2 + 1$

15. $y = -\frac{1}{4}x^2 + 1$

16. $f(x) = 4x^2 + 2$

17. $y = -x^2 + 4$

18. $f(x) = x^2 + 1$

19. $y = \sqrt{x + 3}$

Given each set of axes, what does the area under the curve represent?

20. *y*-axis: feet per second, *x*-axis: seconds

21. *y*-axis: computers produced per day, *x*-axis: days

22. *y*-axis: miles per hour, *x*-axis: hours

23. *y*-axis: gallons per minute, *x*-axis: minutes

24. *y*-axis: molecules per second, *x*-axis: seconds

25. *y*-axis: price per pound of apples, *x*-axis: pounds of apples

Graph each curve. Use inscribed rectangles to approximate the area under the curve for the interval and rectangle width given.

26. $y = \frac{1}{4}x^2, 2 \leq x \leq 4, 1$

27. $y = x^3 + 1, 0 \leq x \leq 2, 0.5$

Name ______________________ Class ______________ Date ______________

11-6 • Guided Problem Solving

GPS **Exercise 30**

a. Graph the curve $y = \frac{1}{3}x^3$.

b. Use inscribed rectangles to approximate the area under the curve for the interval $0 \le x \le 3$ and rectangle width of 1 unit.

c. Repeat part (b) using circumscribed rectangles.

d. Find the mean of the areas you found in parts (b) and (c). Of the three estimates, which best approximates the area for the interval? Explain.

Read and Understand

1. Using inscribed rectangles, the area approximation is ____________ than the actual area.

2. Using circumscribed rectangles, the area approximation is ____________ than the actual area.

Plan and Solve

3. Graph the curve $y = \frac{1}{3}x^3$.

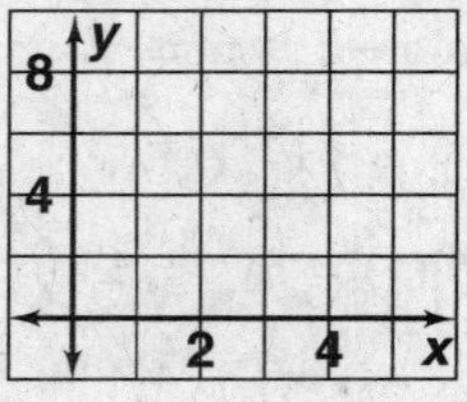

4. Add inscribed rectangles to your graph under the curve for the interval $0 \le x \le 3$.

5. Use the formula $A = \sum_{n=1}^{b} (w)f(a_n)$ and your inscribed rectangles to approximate the area. ____________

6. Repeat Steps 3–5 using circumscribed rectangles.

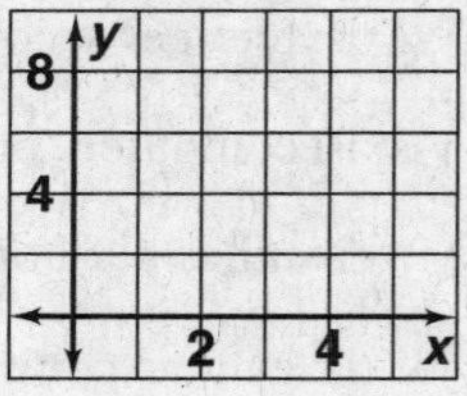

7. Find the mean of the areas you found in parts (b) and (c). ____________

8. Of the three estimates, which best approximates the area for the interval? Explain. ____________

____

Look Back and Check

9. To check your answers, repeat the process using rectangles of width 0.5 unit. ____________

Solve Another Problem

10. Repeat the given problem for the curve $y = \frac{1}{2}x^2$ with the interval $0 \le x \le 4$ and rectangle width of 1 unit. ____________

Name ______________________ Class ______________ Date ______________

11A: Graphic Organizer

For use before Lesson 11-1

Study Skill Skimming and selective reading are quick and efficient ways for getting what you need from a mathematics textbook or magazine article. It is always important to preview the chapter to see what new concepts are being developed and to link them to previous knowledge.

Write your answers.

1. What is the chapter title? ______________________

2. Find the Table of Contents page for this chapter at the front of the book. Name four topics you will study in this chapter.

______________________ ______________________

______________________ ______________________

3. Look through the pages of the chapter. List four real-world connections that you see discussed in this chapter.

______________________ ______________________

______________________ ______________________

4. Complete the graphic organizer as you work through the chapter.
1. Write the title of the chapter in the center oval.
2. When you begin a lesson, write the name of the lesson in a rectangle.
3. When you complete that lesson, write a skill or key concept from that lesson in the outer oval linked to that rectangle.

Continue with steps 2 and 3 clockwise around the graphic organizer.

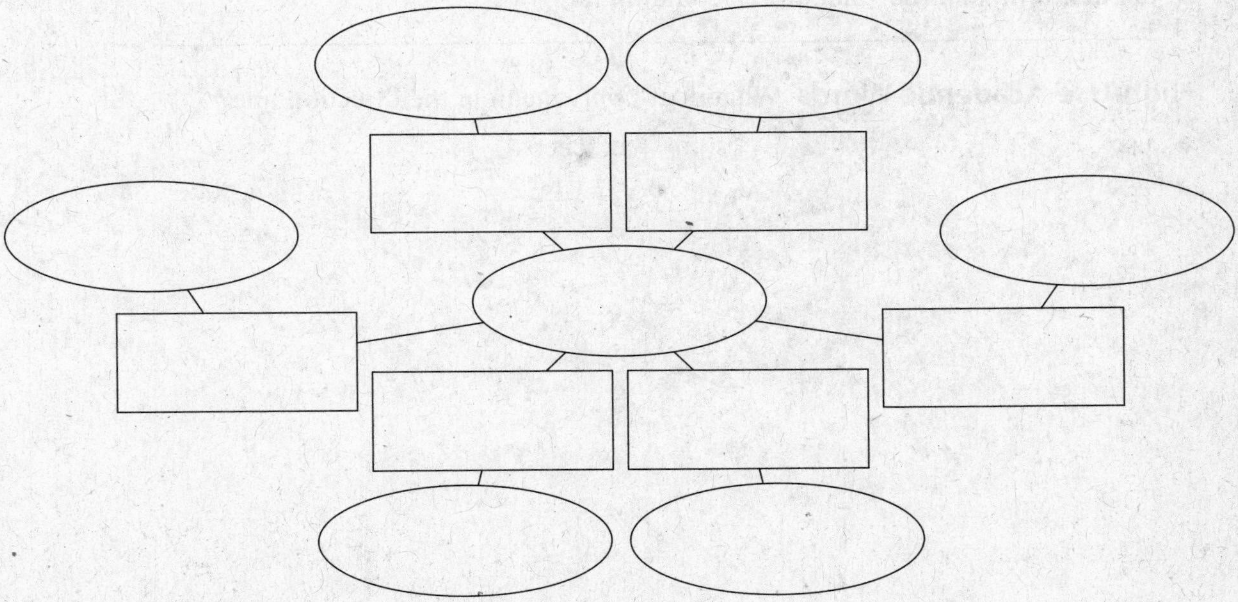

Name ______________________ Class ______________ Date ______________

11B: Reading Comprehension

For use after Lesson 11-3

Study Skill Before you dive into the main content of a paragraph, a graph, or a diagram, read all the captions and titles. These labels tell you the topic, and often contain other important information.

Look at the formulas. Then answer the questions that follow about how to read and apply a formula.

Geometric Sequence Formulas

Recursive Formula	Explicit Formula
a_1 = a given value, $a_n = a_{n-1} \cdot r$	$a_n = a_1 \cdot r^{n-1}$

In these formulas, a_n is the nth term, a_1 is the first term, n is the number of the term, and r is the common ratio.

1. What will both of these formulas help you to find?

   ____

2. What is the difference between the left sides of the two formulas?

   ____

3. Explain the difference in meaning of $n - 1$ in a_{n-1} and in r^{n-1}.

   ____

4. Which formula would you use to find the nth term if you knew the value of the term just before the nth term and the value of the common ratio?

   ____

5. Which formula would you use to find the nth term if you knew the value of the first term and the value of the common ratio?

   ____

6. **High-Use Academic Words** What does *apply* mean in the direction line?

   a. use **b.** check

Name ________________ Class ________________ Date ________________

11C: Reading/Writing Math Symbols

For use after Lesson 11-5

Study Skill When you are reading, use the context to help you decide which of several meanings a word has. Clues from the context can sometimes also help you decide the meanings of terms with which you are not familiar.

The notation used for geometry has several special math symbols. Write the words that tell how to read each of these.

1. $\overleftrightarrow{AB}$ ________________
2. $\overline{CD}$ ________________
3. $\angle A$ ________________
4. $\triangle XYZ$ ________________

In some of the previous examples, line segments used in symbols above the letters had various meanings. The length of a line segment can also have meaning.

5. Explain the difference in meaning, and how you read them, between the − symbol in −5 and in 7 − 5.

____

____

6. The letter *m* can also have more than one meaning in geometry. Explain the difference between *m* and $m\angle A$.

____

____

Vocabulary and Study Skills

11D: Visual Vocabulary Practice

For use after Lesson 11-6

Study Skill When interpreting an illustration, look for the most specific concept represented.

Concept List

arithmetic mean	arithmetic sequence	arithmetic series
circumscribed rectangles	explicit formula	geometric mean
geometric sequence	geometric series	inscribed rectangles

Write the concept that best describes each exercise. Choose from the concept list above.

1. 5, 10, 15, 20, . . .

____

2.

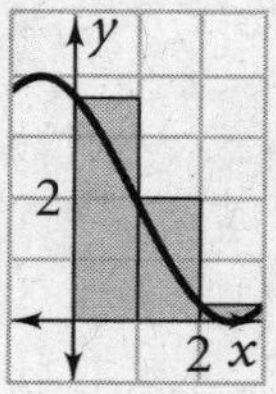

____

3. $\frac{\text{sum of two numbers}}{2}$

____

4. $\sqrt{\text{product of two numbers}}$

____

5. $80 + 40 + 20 + 10$

____

6. 5, 10, 20, 40, . . .

____

7. $1 + 4 + 7 + 10 + 13$

____

8.

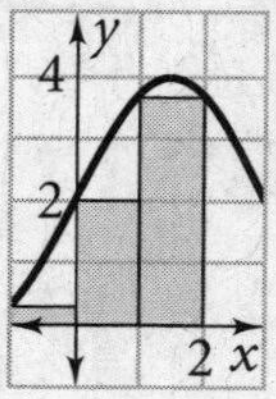

____

9. $a_n = a_1 + (n - 1)d$

____

Name ______________________ Class ______________ Date ______________

11E: Vocabulary Check

For use after Lesson 11-4

Study Skill Strengthen your vocabulary. Use these pages and add cues and summaries by applying the Cornell Notetaking style.

Write the definition for each word at the right. To check your work, fold the paper back along the dotted line to see the correct answers.

Definition	Word
______________________	Sequence
______________________	Term
______________________	Common ratio
______________________	Series
______________________	Limit

11E: Vocabulary Check (continued)

For use after Lesson 11-4

Write the vocabulary word for each definition. To check your work, fold the paper forward along the dotted line to see the correct answers.

An ordered list of numbers. ______________________

Each number in a sequence. ______________________

The ratio of consecutive terms of a geometric sequence. ______________________

The sum of the terms of a sequence. ______________________

The least and greatest integer values of *n* in summation notation. ______________________

Name ______________________ Class ______________ Date ______________

11F: Vocabulary Review

For use with Chapter Review

Vocabulary and Study Skills

Study Skill Many mathematical ideas are opposites, inverses, or contrasts. In any course when you learn new vocabulary, it is good to take the time to go back and review some of the vocabulary terms from previous chapters.

For each pair of vocabulary words, write a brief statement that describes how to distinguish between the two mathematical ideas in the pair. For help, use the Glossary in your textbook.

1. sequence
series

____

____

____

2. circumscribed rectangles
inscribed rectangles

____

____

____

3. common difference
common ratio

____

____

____

4. arithmetic sequence
geometric sequence

____

____

____

Name ____________________ Class ____________ Date ____________

Practice 12-1

Probability Distributions

1. Use the frequency table to find each probability.

a. What is the probability that a person living alone is 45 or older?

b. In a sample of 100 persons living alone, predict how many are age 35 and older.

c. Find *P*(15 to 24 years of age)

d. Find *P*(35 to 44 years of age)

e. Find *P*(65 years and older)

Persons Living Alone in 1999 (in thousands)

15 to 24 years of age	1,313
25 to 34 years of age	3,714
35 to 44 years of age	4,074
45 to 64 years of age	7,757
65 years and older	9,747

Source: *www.infoplease.com*

2. You roll two number cubes. Make a table to show the probability distribution for each sample space.

a. {the sum of the cubes is 5 or less, the sum is greater than 5}

b. {the sum of the cubes is prime, the sum is composite}

c. {only one cube shows 2, both cubes show the same number, the cubes show different numbers and neither is a 2}

3. A survey of student pizza preferences showed that 43 students preferred cheese, 56 preferred sausage, 39 preferred pepperoni, 28 preferred supreme, 31 preferred another kind, and 19 did not like any type of pizza.

a. Organize this data in a frequency table.

b. Find the experimental probability for each outcome in the table. Round to the nearest tenth of a percent. What is the sum of the experimental probabilities? Explain.

c. Graph the probability distribution for {pizza, no pizza}.

d. Graph the probability distribution for {cheese, sausage or pepperoni, supreme or other, no pizza}.

e. How are the probability distributions related?

4. Visitors to the game preserve see up to eight species of large mammals as they drive through. A survey shows that the number of species seen varies according to the distribution below.

Probability Distribution for Number of Species Seen

s	0	1	2	3	4	5	6	7	8
P(*s*)	0.08	0.12	0.21	0.18	0.12	0.11	0.09	0.08	0.01

a. Use random numbers to simulate the number of species seen in each of 20 visits to the preserve. What is the average per visit?

b. You donate \$5 to the preserve for upkeep of each species you see. On the basis of your simulation, how much would you donate in 20 visits?

Name ______________________ Class ______________ Date ______________

12-1 • Guided Problem Solving

GPS Exercise 18

Odds The odds in favor of an event equal the ratio of the number of times the event occurs to the number of times the event does not occur. The odds in favor of event A are 1 : 4. The odds in favor of event B are 2 : 3. The odds in favor of event C are 1 : 3. The odds in favor of event D are 1 : 7. Graph the probability distribution of events A, B, C, and D.

Read and Understand

1. What are the odds in favor of an event? ______________________

2. What are the odds of each event: A, B, C, and D? ______________________

Plan and Solve

3. To graph the probability distribution, the odds of each event need to be changed into what?

   ____

4. How do you use the odds to calculate the total times an event occurred and did not occur?

   ____

5. Find the probability of each event.

   $$P(A) = \frac{\text{number of times event occurs}}{\text{total number of times event occurs and does not occur}} = \frac{1}{1+4} = \frac{1}{5} = \_\_\_\_\_\_$$

   $P(B) =$ ______________________

   $P(C) =$ ______________________

   $P(D) =$ ______________________

6. Graph the probability distribution of events A, B, C, and D. ______________________

Look Back and Check

7. To check your answer, use the graph of the probabilities to convert to odds and compare to the information given in the problem.

Solve Another Problem

8. The odds in favor of event W are 3 : 7. The odds in favor of event X are 2 : 3. The odds in favor of event Y are 9 : 1. The odds in favor of event Z are 4 : 1. Graph the probability distribution of events W, X, Y, and Z. ______________________

Name _______________ Class _______________ Date _______________

Practice 12-2

Conditional Probability

1. The table contains information about the 1205 employees at one business. Find each probability. Round to the nearest tenth of a percent.

Education and Salary of Employees

	Under $20,000	$20,000 to $30,000	Over $30,000
Less than high school	69	36	2
High school	112	98	14
Some college	102	193	143
College degree	13	178	245

   a. *P*(employee has less than a high school education)
   b. *P*(employee earns under $20,000)
   c. *P*(employee earns over $30,000 and has less than a high school education)
   d. *P*(employee earns under $20,000 and has a college degree)
   e. given that the employee has only a high school education, the probability that the employee earns over $30,000
   f. given that the employee earns over $30,000, the probability that the employee has only a high school education or less

2. High school students in one school chose their favorite leisure activity. Find each probability. Round to the nearest tenth of a percent.

Favorite Leisure Activities

	Sports	Hiking	Reading	Phoning	Shopping	Other
Female	39	48	85	62	71	29
Male	67	58	76	54	68	39

   a. *P*(sports | female) b. *P*(female | sports) c. *P*(reading | male) d. *P*(male | reading)
   e. *P*(hiking | female) f. *P*(hiking | male) g. *P*(male | shopping) h. *P*(female | shopping)

3. The senior class is 55% female, and 32% are females who play a competitive sport. Find the probability that a student plays a competitive sport, given that the student is female.

Draw a tree diagram. Find each probability.

4. A softball game has an 80% chance of being canceled for a light drizzle and a 30% chance of being canceled for a heavy fog when there is no drizzle. There is a 70% chance of heavy fog and a 30% chance of light drizzle.
   a. Find the probability that the game will be canceled.
   b. Find the probability there will be a light drizzle and the game will not be canceled.

5. The students of a high school are 51% males; 45% of the males and 49% of the females attend concerts.
   a. Find the probability that a student attends concerts.
   b. Find the probability that a student is a female and does not attend concerts.

Name ____________________ Class ____________________ Date ____________________

12-2 • Guided Problem Solving

GPS Exercise 13

Suppose A and B are independent events, with $P(A) = 0.60$ and $P(B) = 0.25$. Find each probability.

a. $P(A \text{ and } B)$.
b. $P(A \mid B)$
c. What do you notice about $P(A)$ and $P(A \mid B)$?
d. Critical Thinking One way to describe A and B as independent events is *The occurrence of B has no effect on the probability of A.* Explain how the answer to part (c) illustrates this relationship.

Read and Understand

1. What does it mean to say that A and B are independent events? ____________________

2. What is the probability of event A? event B? ____________________

Plan and Solve

3. Since A and B are independent events, $P(A \text{ and } B) = P(A) \cdot P(B)$. Find $P(A \text{ and } B)$. ____________________

4. What is the formula for finding the conditional probability $P(A \mid B)$? ____________________

5. Find $P(A \mid B)$. ____________________

6. What do you notice about $P(A)$ and $P(A \mid B)$? ____________________

7. Explain how your answer to Step 6 illustrates that A and B are independent events. ____________________

____

Look Back and Check

8. To check the reasonableness of your answers, repeat the steps using other independent events and see if you come up with the same conclusions. ____________________

Solve Another Problem

9. Suppose Q and R are dependent events, with $P(Q) = P(\text{Queen}) = \frac{1}{13}$ and $P(R) = P(\text{Red card}) = \frac{1}{2}$ and $P(Q \text{ and } R) = P(\text{Red Queen}) = \frac{1}{26}$.
Find each probability.

   a. $P(Q \text{ and } R)$ ____________________

   b. $P(Q \mid R)$ ____________________

   c. What do you notice about $P(Q)$ and $P(Q \mid R)$? ____________________

Name ______________________ Class ______________ Date ______________

Practice 12-3

Analyzing Data

Identify the outliers of each set of values.

1. 23 76 79 76 77 74 75

2. 43 46 49 50 52 54 78 47

3. 32 35 3 36 37 35 38 40 42 34

4. 153 156 176 156 165 110 159 169 172

Find the mean, median, and mode of each set of values.

5. 98 87 79 82 101 99 97 97 102 91 93

6. 41 41 45 46 54 52 53 50 49 47 49 48 44

7. 2.3 2.4 2.5 2.8 2.4 2.4 2.9 2.6 2.4 2.9

8. 15.2 15.3 15.9 16.1 16.3 15.4 15.5 15.6 15.8

9. 245 345 365 566 442 476 423 495 412

10. 1002 1005 1023 1034 1012 1054 1023

11. 0.019 0.021 0.018 0.019 0.018 0.020

12. 23 29 31 32 29 27 21 19 25 26 28 29 24

13. 45 49 41 45 51 39 42 46 49 48 42 40

14. 3 5 31 35 41 49 50 51 52 53 54 69 81 99

15. 14 15 19 15 15 16 19 20 21 29 16 17

16. 1.8 1.3 1.9 1.5 1.6 1.5 1.8 1.5 1.3 1.4 1.3

17. 8.7 8.8 8.9 9.4 10.2 9.8 9.0 8.1 9.5

18. 101 114 128 106 125 122 120 114 116

19. 4.25 4.46 4.19 4.23 4.25 4.28 4.27 4.35

20. 11 15 18 22 25 29 32 36 39 41 42 45 48 51

Make a box-and-whisker plot for each set of values.

21. 2 8 3 7 3 6 4 9 10 15 21 29 32 30 5 7 32 4 11 13 11 14 10 12 13 15

22. 1054 1165 1287 1385 1456 1398 1298 1109 1067 1384 1499 1032 1222 1045

23. 43.4 46.5 47.9 51.0 50.2 49.5 42.5 41.6 46.8 50.0

24. 19 20 21 22 23 25 27 12 19 31 53 52 48 41 29 33 48 46 44 42

Find the values at the 20th and 80th percentiles for each set of values.

25. 188 168 174 198 186 178 184 190 176 172 170 180 182 186 176

26. 376 324 346 348 350 352 356 368 345 360

27. 98 99 96 94 95 96 97 99 95 94 93 96 97 98 99 97 96 94 92 97

28. 2 12 17 20 22 28 32 37 38 41 44 51 53 59 62 78 86 92 102 112

29. The data shows the average temperatures in January for several cities in the mid-South.
49.1 50.8 42.9 44.0 44.2 51.4 45.7 39.9 50.8 46.7 52.4 50.4

a. Find the mean of the temperatures.
b. Find the median of the temperatures.
c. Find the mode of the temperatures.
d. Find the quartiles of the data. Sketch a box-and-whisker plot, and label the quartiles.

Name ______________________ Class ______________ Date ______________

12-3 • Guided Problem Solving

GPS Exercise 13

Meteorology On May 3, 1999, 59 tornadoes hit Oklahoma in the largest tornado outbreak ever recorded in the state. Sixteen of these were classified as strong (F2 or F3) or violent (F4 or F5).

a. Make a box-and-whisker plot of the data for length of path.
b. Identify the outliers. Remove them from the data set and make a revised box-and-whisker plot.
c. Writing How does the removal of the outliers affect the box-and-whisker plot? How does it affect the median of the data set?

Major Tornadoes in Oklahoma, May 3, 1999

Length of Path (miles)	Intensity
6	F3
9	F3
4	F2
38	F5
7	F2
12	F3
8	F2
7	F2
15	F4
20	F4
1	F5
22	F3
16	F3
8	F2
13	F3
2	F2

SOURCE: National Oceanic & Atmospheric Administration

Read and Understand

1. How many values are in the data set? ______________
2. List the values in order from smallest to largest.

____

Plan and Solve

3. Find the quartile values, the minimum value, and the maximum value.

____

4. Make a box-and-whisker plot of the data.
5. Identify the outlier(s).
6. Remove the outlier(s) and find the quartile values, the minimum value, and the maximum value. ______________
7. Make a revised box-and-whisker plot.
8. How does the removal of the outlier(s) affect the box-and-whisker plot? ______________
9. How does the removal of the outlier(s) affect the median of the data set? ______________

Look Back and Check

10. To check your answers, use the plot to identify the quartile values and the minimum and maximum values. Confirm that these values match those calculated from the data set. ______________

Solve Another Problem

11. The following data are the heights of a basketball team's players, in inches: 73, 72, 74, 74, 77, 76, 69, 70, 70, 74, 73. Make a box-and-whisker plot of the data. ______________

Name ______________________ Class ______________ Date ______________

Practice 12-4

Standard Deviation

Find the mean and the standard deviation for each set of values. Round to the nearest tenth.

1. 232 254 264 274 287 298 312 342 398
2. 26 27 28 28 28 29 30 30 32 35 35 36
3. 2.2 2.2 2.3 2.4 2.4 2.4 2.5 2.5 2.5 2.6
4. 75 73 77 79 79 74 81 74 70 68 70 72
5. 87 21 90 43 54 23 123 110 90 44 50

Find the range, mean, and interquartile range of each set of values.

6. 10 12 13 10 9 5 6 11
7. 23 56 59 60 123 164 180 212
8. 524 526 532 531 534 539 530 535
9. 1.4 1.6 1.9 2.2 2.6 2.7 2.9 3.1
10. 45 48 46 47 45 48 46 49 46 47
11. 97 102 99 105 100 101 99 101

Determine the number of standard deviations that includes all data values.

12. The mean test score on a standardized test is 216; the standard deviation is 52.
    127 98 236 192 267 335 217 365 472 177
13. The mean age of students in a school is 16.4 years; the standard deviation is 1.5.
    13 17 18 15 16 14 15 18 17 16 15 16 13
14. The average rainfall for the month of April for several Eastern cities is as follows:
    3.0 3.4 4.3 3.6 3.6 2.9 2.8 3.9 2.8 2.9 4.5 3.8 4.2 3.6 4.0 2.9 3.1
    a. Find the mean of the data.
    b. Find the standard deviation of the data.
    c. Find the range of the data.
    d. Within how many standard deviations is a rainfall of 2.8 in.? 4.0 in.?
15. The test scores on a college algebra test are as follows:
    67 69 71 75 78 78 83 85 85 85 85 86 87 89 92 95 98 98 98 100 100 100 100 100 100
    a. Find the range of the data.
    b. Find the interquartile range.
    c. Find the mean of the data.
    d. Find the standard deviation.
    e. Within how many standard deviations of the mean is a score of 65?
    f. Within how many standard deviations of the mean is a score of 100?
16. A set of values has a mean of 67 and a standard deviation of 8. Find the z-score of the value 70.
17. A set of values has a mean of 102 and a standard deviation of 12. Find the z-score of the value 135.

Name ______________________ Class ______________ Date ______________

12-4 • Guided Problem Solving

GPS Exercise 22

Another measure of variation is variance, which equals s^2. Find the variance and the standard deviation of the data set: 12 h 3 h 2 h 4 h 5 h 7 h

Read and Understand

1. What is the formula for the variance of a data set? ______________________

2. What is the formula for the standard deviation of a data set? ______________________

Plan and Solve

3. Find the mean of the data set: $\overline{x}$. ______________________

4. Find the difference between each value and the mean: $x - \overline{x}$. ______________________

5. Square each difference: $(x - \overline{x})^2$. ______________________

6. How many data values are there? Find n. ______________________

7. What is the variance? ______________________

8. What is the standard deviation? ______________________

Look Back and Check

9. To check the reasonableness of your answers, enter the data on a calculator and use the CALC menu of the STAT feature to find the standard deviation. ______________________

Solve Another Problem

10. Find the variance and the standard deviation of the data set: \$800, \$500, \$1000, \$450, \$750.

____

Name ______________________ Class ______________ Date ______________

Practice 12-5

Working with Samples

1. In a survey, participants were asked their opinion of a new government program. The response scale ranged from 1 to 4, with 4 being a favorable response to the program. Which sample was largest? Explain.

Sample	Score	Standard Deviation
A	3.0	1.1
B	2.8	1.3
C	2.9	0.8

Identify any bias in each sampling method. When appropriate, suggest a sampling method that is more likely to produce a random sample.

2. A committee wants to find how much time students spend reading each week. They ask the students as they enter the library.

3. The students planning the junior class party want to know what kinds of pizza to buy. They ask the pizza restaurant what kinds sell the most.

4. The county road department wants to know which roads cause the most concern among the residents of the county. They ask the local restaurant to hand out survey forms.

5. A politician wants to know what issues are most important to the voters in his district. He spends all day Tuesday talking to people as they enter the grocery store.

6 A politician wants to know the voters' views on an important issue. She has her campaign workers call people randomly from the phone book.

Find the sample size that produces each margin of error.

7. $\pm 15\%$

8. $\pm 2\%$

9. $\pm 0.9\%$

10. $\pm 0.6\%$

For each sample find the sample proportion, the margin of error, and an interval likely to contain the true population proportion. Round to the nearest percent.

11. In a survey of 38 parents of preschool children, 20 would like to have their local school district provide play group sessions at least one evening a month.

12. In a random sample of 526 visitors to the craft center, 378 want the craft center to be open later in the evenings.

13. In a survey of 165 visitors to the library, 102 want the library to have more novels available.

14. In one lake, 98 of the last 323 fish caught have a certain chemical present in their body.

15. In a traffic survey, 537 of the 1287 drivers passing through the checkpoint were traveling more than 100 miles from home.

Name ____________________ Class ____________ Date ____________

12-5 • Guided Problem Solving

GPS Exercise 17

Surveys In a random sample of 408 grocery shoppers, 258 prefer one large trip per week to several smaller ones. Find (a) the sample proportion, (b) the margin of error, and (c) the interval likely to contain the true population proportion.

Read and Understand

1. How many shoppers are in the random sample n? ____________

2. How many shoppers prefer one large trip x? ____________

Plan and Solve

3. What is the formula for finding the sample proportion? ____________

4. Find the sample proportion. Round to the nearest whole percent. ____________

5. What is the formula for finding the margin of error? ____________

6. Find the margin of error. Round to the nearest whole percent. ____________

7. Use the margin of error along with the sample proportion to determine the interval likely to contain the true population proportion. ____________

Look Back and Check

8. To check your answers, find the midpoint of your interval. What should the value be? Is it? ____________

Solve Another Problem

9. **Sales** In a random sample of 64 calls, a salesperson was able to make 11 sales. Find (a) the sample proportion, (b) the margin of error, and (c) the interval likely to contain the true population proportion. ____________

Name ____________________ Class ____________ Date ____________

Practice 12-6

Binomial Distributions

1. The probability that a baby is a male is 50%. Use a tree diagram to find each probability.
   - a. P(at least 1 baby in a family with 3 children is a male)
   - b. P(at least 2 babies in a family of 3 children are male)
   - c. P(exactly 2 of 3 babies born in the hospital on any day are male)

For each situation, describe a trial and a success. Then design and run a simulation to find the probability.

2. The probability that the weather will be acceptable for a launch of the space shuttle over the next 3 days is 70% each day. Find the probability that the weather will be acceptable at least one of the next three days.

3. A poll shows that 30% of the voters favor an earlier curfew. Find the probability that all of five people chosen at random favor an earlier curfew.

4. The probability that a machine part is defective is 10%. Find the probability that exactly one part is defective in a sample of five parts.

Find the probability of x successes in n trials for the given probability of success p on each trial.

5. $x = 5, n = 5, p = 0.4$

6. $x = 2, n = 8, p = 0.9$

7. $x = 3, n = 10, p = 0.25$

8. $x = 1, n = 3, p = 0.2$

Use the binomial expansion of $(p + q)^n$ to calculate and graph each binomial distribution.

9. $n = 5, p = 0.6$

10. $n = 3, p = 0.7$

11. $n = 3, p = 0.1$

12. $n = 4, p = 0.8$

13. There is a 60% probability of rain each of the next 5 days. Find each probability. Round to the nearest percent.
   - a. P(rain at least 3 of the next 5 days)
   - b. P(rain at least 1 of the next 5 days)
   - c. P(rain at least 1 of the next 4 days)
   - d. P(rain at least 1 of the next 2 days)

14. In one area the probability of a power outage during a rainstorm is 4%. Find each probability. Round to the nearest percent.
   - a. P(at least 1 outage in the next 5 rainstorms)
   - b. P(at least 2 outages in the next 10 rainstorms)
   - c. P(at least 1 outage in the next 20 rainstorms)

Name ______________________ Class ______________ Date ______________

12-6 • Guided Problem Solving

GPS **Exercise 22**

Quality Control A company claims that 99% of its cereal boxes have at least as much cereal by weight as the amount stated on the box.

a. At a quality control checkpoint, 1 box out of a random sample of 10 boxes falls short of its stated weight. What is the probability of this happening due to chance variation in box weights?

b. Suppose 3 of 10 boxes fail to have the claimed weight. What would you conclude? Explain why.

Read and Understand

1. Let a success be the number of cereal boxes that have at least as much cereal by weight as the amount stated on the box. What is the probability of a success p? ______________

2. Let a failure be the number of cereal boxes that fall short of the stated weight. What is the probability of a failure q? ______________

Plan and Solve

3. What is the formula for the probability of x successes in n trials for repeated independent trials, each with a probability of success p and a probability of failure q? ______________

4. If 1 box out of a random sample of 10 boxes falls short, what are n and x? ______________

5. What is the probability of this happening due to chance variation in box weights? ______________

6. If 3 boxes out of a random sample of 10 boxes fall short, what are n and x? ______________

7. What is the probability of this happening due to chance variation in box weights? ______________

8. Considering this probability of 3 of 10 boxes falling short, what would you conclude about the machinery? Explain. ______________

Look Back and Check

9. To check that your answers are reasonable, find the probability of 2 boxes out of a random sample of 10 falling short. This value should be between the two you calculated. ______________

Solve Another Problem

10. Pet Health A study shows that 39% of all dogs in a city are overweight. A veterinarian selected a random sample of dogs and found that 4 out of 9 were overweight. What is the probability of this happening due to chance variation?

____

Name ______________________ Class ______________ Date ______________

Practice 12-7

Normal Distributions

A set of data with a mean of 45 and a standard deviation of 8.3 is normally distributed. Find each value, given its distance from the mean.

1. +1 standard deviation from the mean
2. +3 standard deviations from the mean
3. −1 standard deviation from the mean
4. −2 standard deviations from the mean

Sketch a normal curve for each distribution. Label the *x*-axis at one, two, and three standard deviations from the mean.

5. mean = 95; standard deviation = 12
6. mean = 100; standard deviation = 15
7. mean = 60; standard deviation = 6
8. mean = 23.8; standard deviation = 5.2
9. mean = 676; standard deviation = 60
10. mean = 54.2; standard deviation = 12.3

A set of data has a normal distribution with a mean of 5.1 and a standard deviation of 0.9. Find the percent of data within each interval.

11. between 4.2 and 5.1
12. between 6.0 and 6.9
13. greater than 6.9
14. between 4.2 and 6.0
15. less than 4.2
16. less than 5.1

17. Scores on an exam are normally distributed with a mean of 76 and a standard deviation of 10.
    a. In a group of 230 tests, how many students score above 96?
    b. In a group of 230 tests, how many students score below 66?
    c. In a group of 230 tests, how many students score within one standard deviation of the mean?

18. The number of nails of a given length is normally distributed with a mean length of 5.00 in. and a standard deviation of 0.03 in.
    a. Find the number of nails in a bag of 120 that are less than 4.94 in. long.
    b. Find the number of nails in a bag of 120 that are between 4.97 and 5.03 in. long.
    c. Find the number of nails in a bag of 120 that are over 5.03 in. long.

19. The actual weights of bags of pet food are normally distributed. The mean of the weights is 50.0 lb, with a standard deviation of 0.2 lb. Use the graph for a–c.
    a. About what percent of bags of pet food weigh less than 49.8 lb?
    b. In a group of 250 bags, how many would you expect to weigh more than 50.4 lb?
    c. In a group of 50 bags, how many would you expect to be within 1.5 standard deviations of the mean?

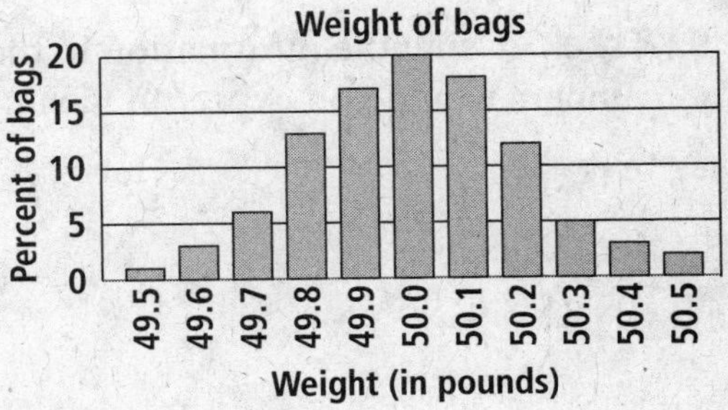

Name _______________ Class _______________ Date _______________

12-7 • Guided Problem Solving

GPS Exercise 18

Track To qualify as a contestant in a race, a runner has to be in the fastest 16% of all applicants. The running times are normally distributed, with a mean of 63 min and a standard deviation of 4 min. To the nearest minute, what is the qualifying time for the race?

Read and Understand

1. What is the mean of the running times? _______________

2. What is the standard deviation of the running times? _______________

Plan and Solve

3. Using the standard normal curve, what percent of the data fall less than two standard deviations below the mean? _______________

4. Using the standard normal curve, what percent of the data fall between one and two standard deviations below the mean? _______________

5. Using the standard normal curve, what percent of the data fall less than one standard deviation below the mean? _______________

6. Did any of your answers equal 16%? _______________

7. Now use the mean and the standard deviation of running times to find the qualifying time. _______________

Look Back and Check

8. To check your answer, choose a time that is less than the qualifying time and find the z-score. Is the z-score what you expect? _______________

Solve Another Problem

9. **Track** Using the information in the problem, how many runners would you expect to have times between 55 min and 67 min? _______________

Name ________________ Class ________________ Date ________________

12A: Graphic Organizer

For use before Lesson 12-1

Study Skill As you start a new chapter, take a minute to look at the title and then compare it to the titles of the chapter before and the chapter after. Ask yourself how the chapters may be related. What did you learn in the previous chapter that you may need in order to learn new concepts in this chapter? What will you learn in this chapter that will apply to the next chapter?

Write your answers.

1. What is the chapter title? ________________

2. Find the Table of Contents page for this chapter at the front of the book. Name four topics you will study in this chapter.

________________ ________________

________________ ________________

3. Look through the pages of the chapter. List four real-world connections that you see discussed in this chapter.

________________ ________________

________________ ________________

4. Complete the graphic organizer as you work through the chapter.
1. Write the title of the chapter in the center oval.
2. When you begin a lesson, write the name of the lesson in a rectangle.
3. When you complete that lesson, write a skill or key concept from that lesson in the outer oval linked to that rectangle.

Continue with steps 2 and 3 clockwise around the graphic organizer.

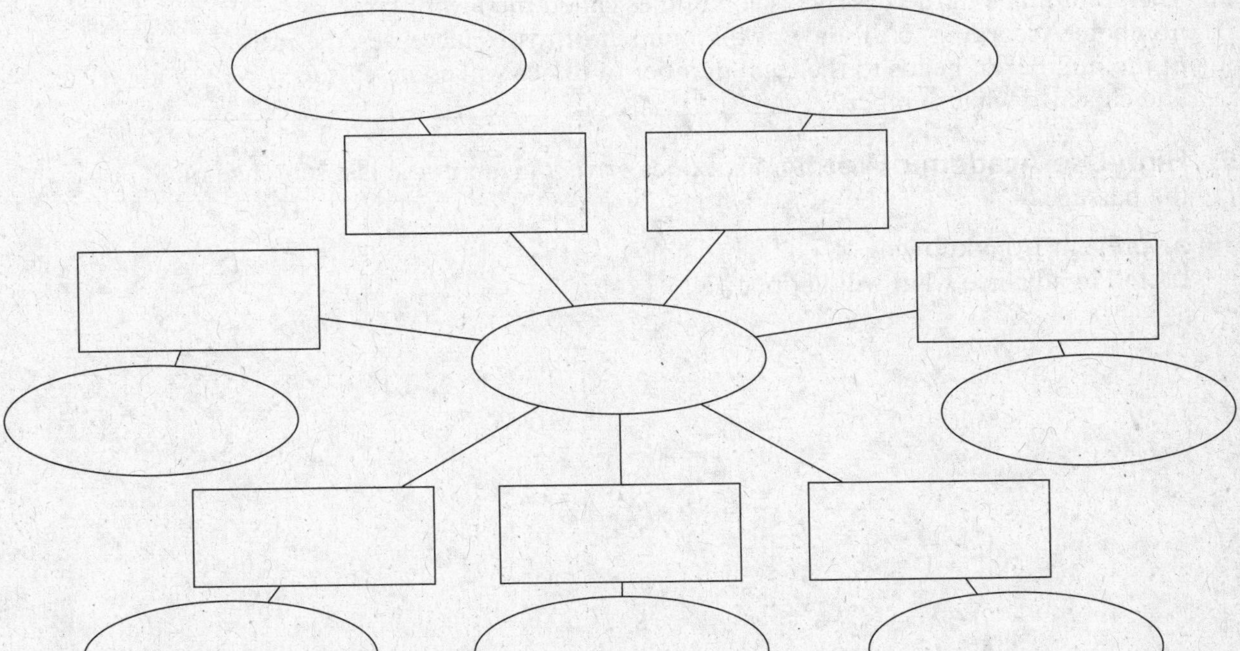

Name ______________________ Class ______________ Date ______________

12B: Reading Comprehension

For use after Lesson 12-3

Study Skill When you have a number of pages to read, look up from your reading every two or three pages, and reflect on what you have just read. It may also help to change from one subject to another as a way to stay alert.

Read the passage below and answer the questions that follow.

> The probability of an event is not much good as a predictor of what will happen in a small number of cases. For example, although the probability of getting heads in one toss of a coin is $\frac{1}{2}$, this does not mean that if you toss a coin twice, you will get one head and one tail. Nor does it mean that if you toss the coin 10 times, it will come up heads $\frac{1}{2}$ of 10, or 5 times. But it does mean that if you toss the coin a great number of times, it is likely to come up heads half the time. The laws of probability predict only what will happen when a very large number of events is surveyed.
>
> *The Prentice-Hall Encyclopedia of Mathematics*

1. What is the subject of this paragraph? ______________________

2. What probability is expressed by the numbers in the paragraph?
____

3. According to the passage, what is the theoretical probability of getting heads in one toss of a coin? ______________________

4. What kind of probability is the passage talking about? ______________________

5. The point made in the passage is sometimes called the law of large numbers. According to this law, as the number of tosses increases, the ratio of the number of heads to the total number of tosses will come closer and closer to what number? ______________________

6. **High-Use Academic Words** What does *predict* mean in the last sentence of the passage?
   a. prevent from knowing
   b. tell in advance what will happen

Name ______________________ Class ______________ Date ______________

12C: Reading/Writing Math Symbols

For use after Lesson 12-2

Study Skill When you are reading a passage, consider the point of view and purpose of the writer to help you evaluate what the passage says.

Sentences in both English and math are joined with conjunctions, but the meaning of these joining symbols and words in math is very specific.

$-9 < x < 9$

1. Name one negative and one positive integer that make this sentence true. ______________________
2. Does 9 make this sentence true? ______________________
3. Does 0 make this sentence true? ______________________

$x < -3$ or $x > 3$

4. Name one negative and one positive integer that are solutions to this system. ______________________
5. Does 3 make this system true? ______________________
6. Does 0 make this system true? ______________________

$P(R|Q)$

7. Write the words for reading this expression aloud.

____

8. What is the meaning of the symbol | in this expression?

____

Vocabulary and Study Skills

Name ____________________ Class ____________ Date ____________

12D: Visual Vocabulary Practice

For use after Lesson 12-4

Study Skill When learning a new symbol, it helps to know if it is an operation or a relationship or other type of notation.

Concept List

box-and-whisker plot	conditional probability	frequency table
interquartile range	mean	probability distribution
quartiles	standard deviation	*z*-score

Write the concept that best describes each exercise. Choose from the concept list above.

1. 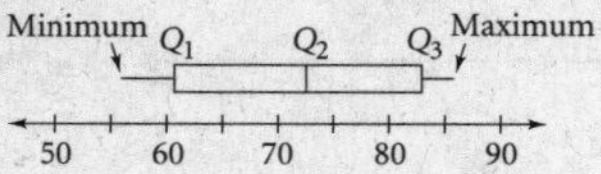

____

2. Q_1, Q_2, Q_3

____

3. $\overline{x}$

____

4. $P(B \mid A)$

____

5.

Type	Number
A	3
B	9
C	7
Total	19

____

6. 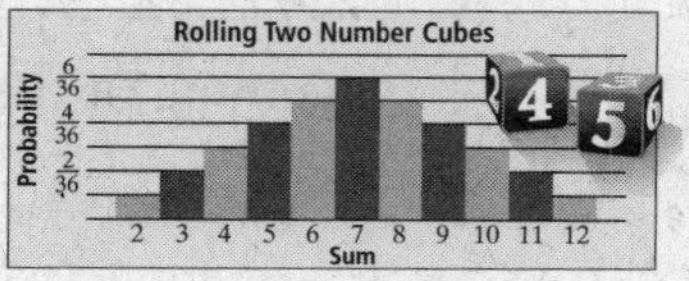

____

7. $\dfrac{\text{value} - \text{mean}}{\text{standard deviation}}$

____

8. $Q_3 - Q_1$

____

9. $\sigma = \sqrt{\dfrac{\Sigma(x - \overline{x})^2}{n}}$

____

Name ______________________ Class ______________ Date ______________

12E: Vocabulary Check

For use after Lesson 12-5

Study Skill Strengthen your vocabulary. Use these pages and add cues and summaries by applying the Cornell Notetaking style.

Write the definition for each word at the right. To check your work, fold the paper back along the dotted line to see the correct answers.

______________________ ______________________ ______________________	Median
______________________ ______________________ ______________________	Outlier
______________________ ______________________ ______________________	Sample
______________________ ______________________ ______________________	Sample proportion
______________________ ______________________ ______________________	Margin of error

Vocabulary and Study Skills

Name ________________ Class ________________ Date ________________

12E: Vocabulary Check (continued)

For use after Lesson 12-5

Write the vocabulary word for each definition. To check your work, fold the paper forward along the dotted line to see the correct answers.

The middle value in a data set. ________________

An item of data with a substantially different value from the rest of the items in the data set. ________________

Information gathered from only part of a population. ________________

$\frac{x}{n}$, where x is the number of times an event occurs in a sample of size n. ________________

An estimate of error of a sample proportion. ________________

Name ______________________ Class ______________ Date ______________

12F: Vocabulary Review Puzzle

For use with Chapter Review

Study Skill Most math exams do not have a vocabulary section, only problems to be solved. However, in order to solve the problems you must understand the vocabulary being used in the questions. The next time you study for a math test, spend some time studying the vocabulary of the chapter.

Unscramble the UPPERCASE letters to form a math word or phrase that completes each sentence.

1. The arithmetic average, or $\overline{x}$ is the NAEM. ______________

2. An item of data with a value substantially different from the rest of the items in the data set is called a(n) RIELTOU. ______________

3. REALQUITS are the values that separate the data set into four equal parts. ______________

4. The DEMANI is the value that separates the data set into two equal parts. ______________

5. All members of the population are equally likely to be chosen in a(n) MORNAD LEPMAS. ______________

6. The value that occurs most frequently in a data set is the DOME. ______________

Name ____________________ Class ____________________ Date ____________________

Practice 13-1

Exploring Periodic Data

Determine whether each function *is* or *is not* periodic. If it is, find the period.

1.

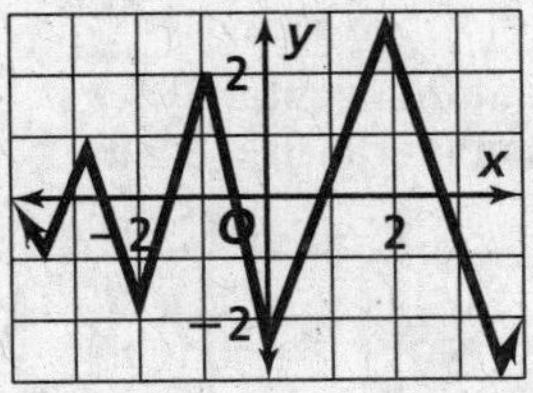

2.

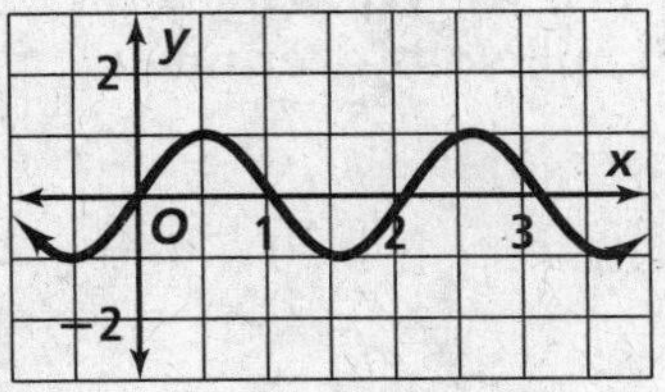

3.

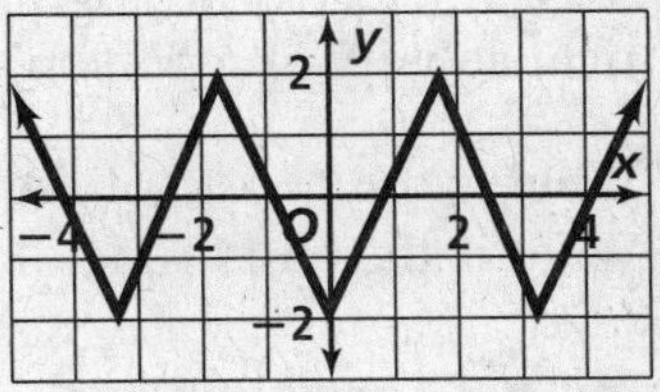

For each function, identify one cycle in two different ways. Then determine the period of the function.

4.

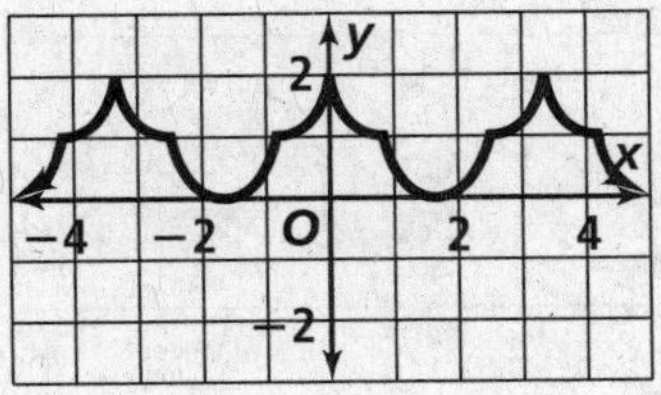

5.

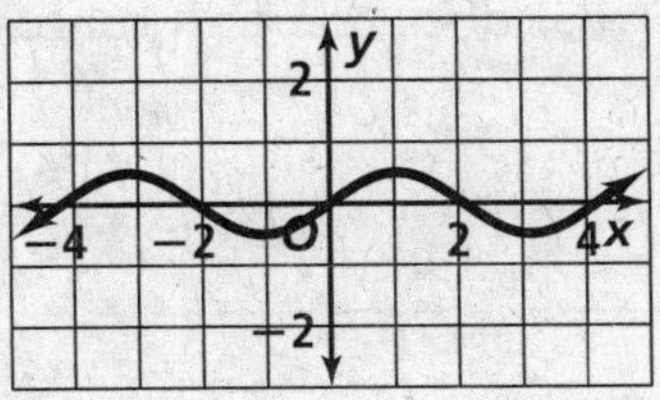

6.

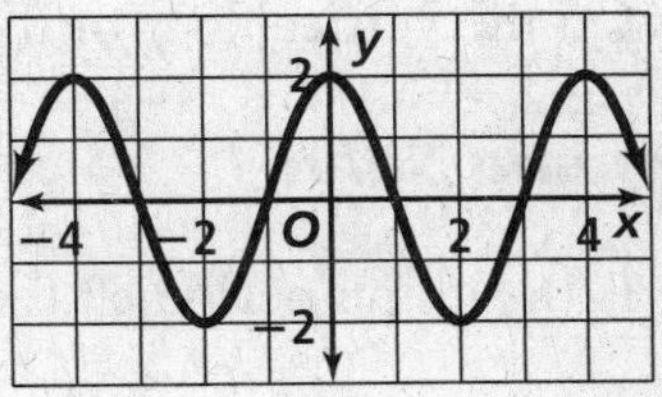

Find the period and amplitude of each periodic function.

7.

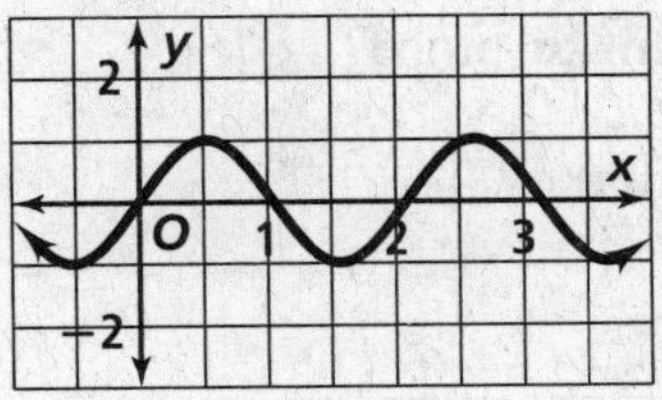

8.

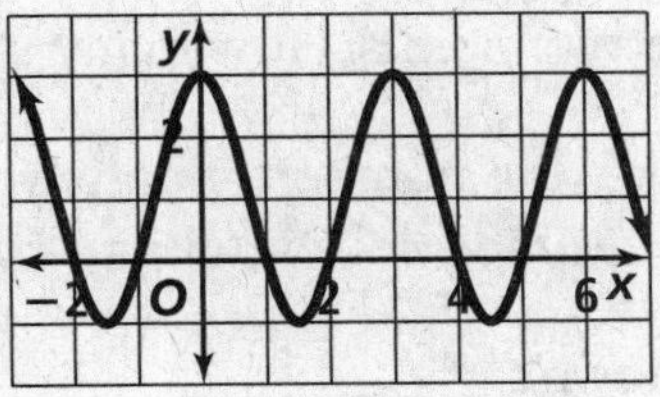

9.

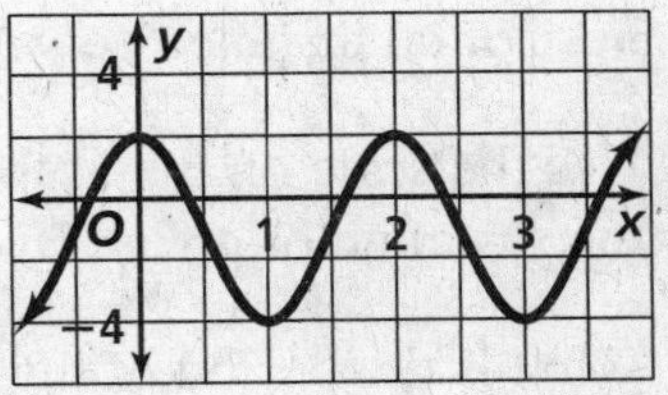

10.

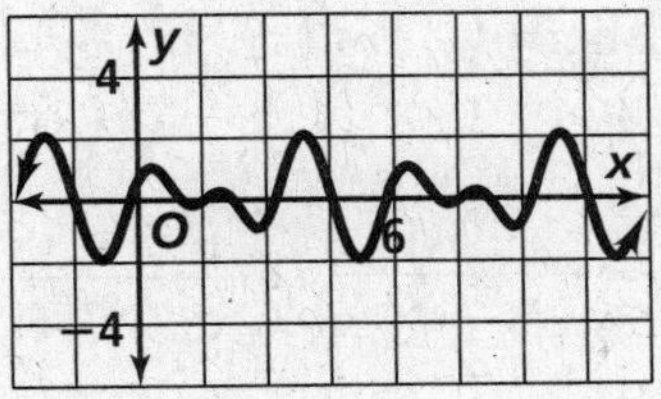

11.

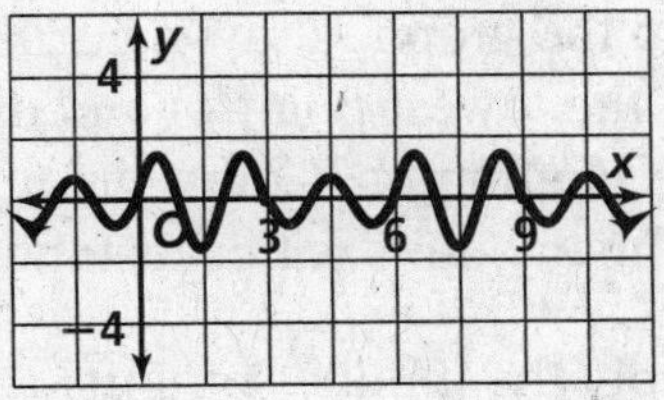

12.

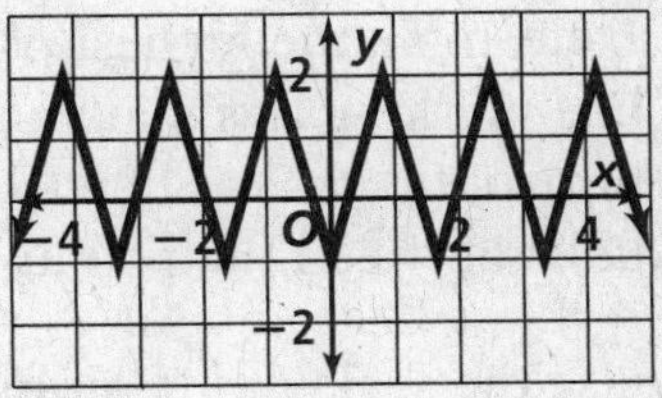

13.

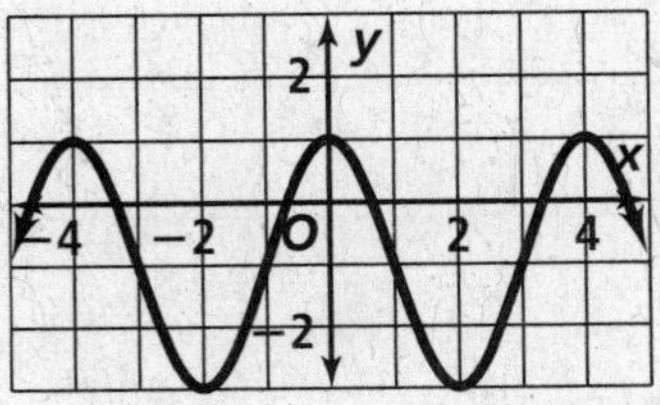

14.

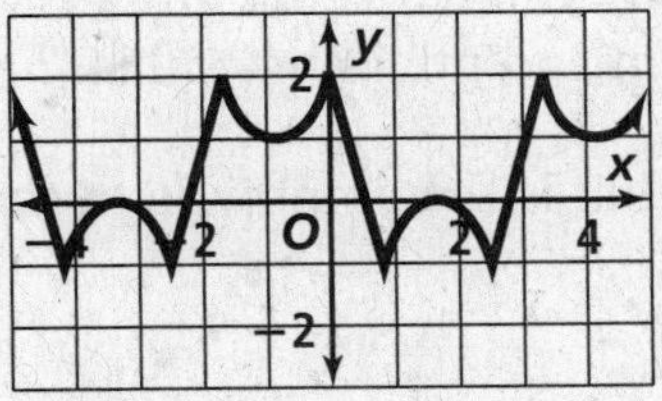

15.

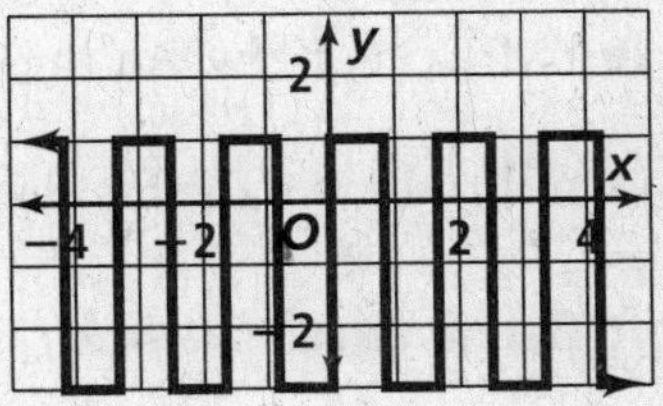

16.

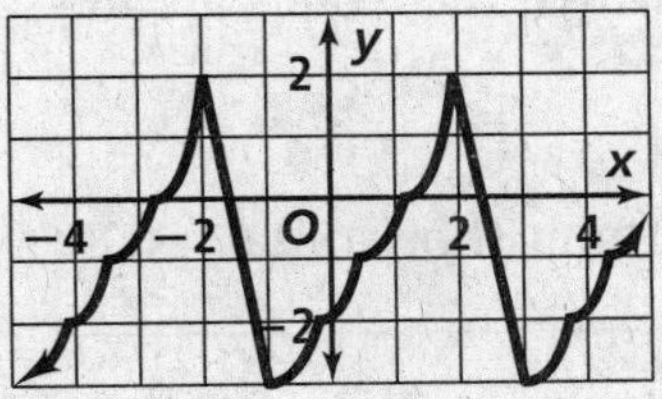

17.

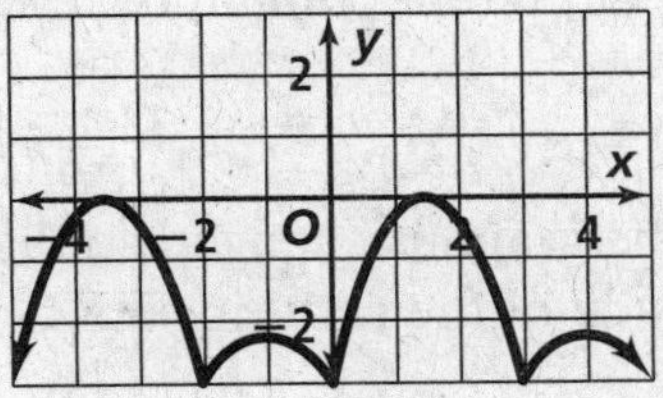

18.

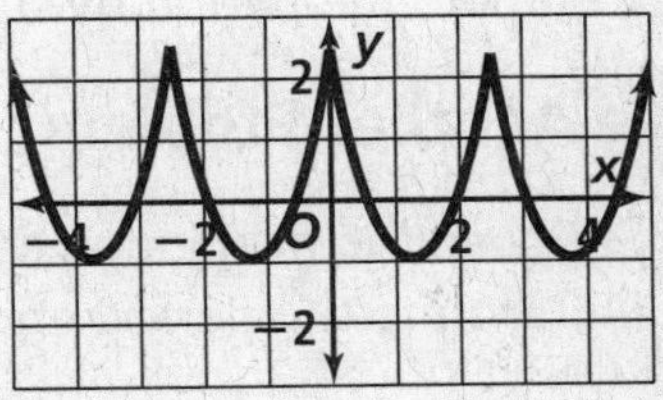

Name ______________________ Class ______________ Date ______________

13-1 • Guided Problem Solving

GPS Exercise 21

Health An electrocardiogram (EKG or ECG) measures the electrical activity of a person's heart in millivolts over time.

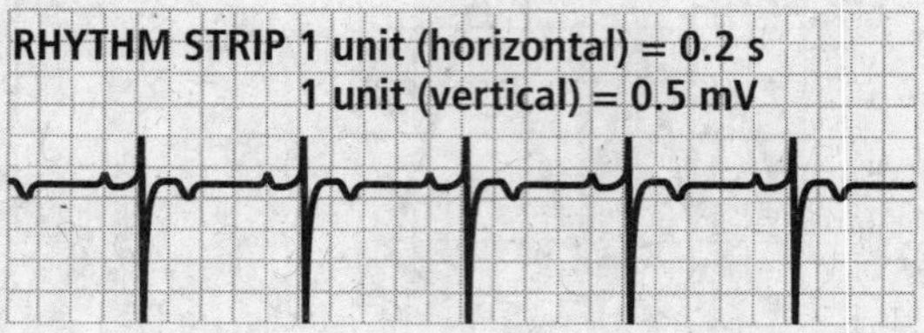

a. What is the period of the EKG shown?
b. What is the amplitude of the EKG?

Read and Understand

1. On the horizontal axis of the graph, what does one unit represent? ______________

2. On the vertical axis of the graph, what does one unit represent? ______________

Plan and Solve

3. Is the graph periodic? Explain. ______________

4. How many complete cycles does the graph show? ______________

5. Trace one complete cycle on the graph. Mark where you start and where you end. Count the horizontal distance between these two points. How many units is this distance? ______________

6. Use the scale on the graph. Multiply the number of units you counted by the scale factor given. How many seconds does it take to complete one cycle? ______________

7. What is the period of the EKG shown? ______________

8. Determine the highest point(s) on the graph. Draw a horizontal dashed line marking this maximum. Find the lowest point(s) and draw another horizontal dashed line to mark this minimum. Count the number of units between the two lines. How many units is this distance? ______________

9. Use the scale on the graph. Multiply the number of units you counted by the scale factor given. What is the difference in millivolts between the maximum and minimum values? ______________

10. Amplitude is half this distance. What is the amplitude of the EKG? ______________

Look Back and Check

11. Compute the period by starting at a different point in the cycle. Verify that the results are the same.

Solve Another Problem

12. Suppose the horizontal scale on the graph is changed so that now 1 unit (horizontal) is 0.1 s. Determine the period and amplitude of the resulting EKG. ______________

Name ______________________ Class ______________ Date ______________

Practice 13-2

Angles and the Unit Circle

Sketch each angle in standard position.

1. 30° **2.** 60° **3.** 100° **4.** 135° **5.** 210°

6. 270° **7.** 330° **8.** −30° **9.** −90° **10.** −190°

11. −150° **12.** −330° **13.** −45° **14.** 315° **15.** −180°

16. 120° **17.** −120° **18.** 145° **19.** −145° **20.** −355°

Find the measure of an angle between 0° and 360° coterminal with each given angle.

21. −100° **22.** −60° **23.** −225° **24.** −145° **25.** 372°

26. −15° **27.** 482° **28.** 484° **29.** −20° **30.** 421°

31. 409° **32.** −38° **33.** 376° **34.** −210° **35.** 387°

36. 390° **37.** 660° **38.** 440° **39.** −170° **40.** 370°

41. −700° **42.** 458° **43.** 480° **44.** 406° **45.** −120°

46. 460° **47.** −222° **48.** −330° **49.** −127° **50.** 377°

Find the exact values of the cosine and sine of each angle. Then find the decimal equivalents. Round your answers to the nearest hundredth.

51. 45° **52.** 225° **53.** −225° **54.** −45° **55.** 330°

56. −330° **57.** 150° **58.** −150° **59.** 300° **60.** −300°

61. 240° **62.** 120° **63.** −90° **64.** 360° **65.** 720°

66.

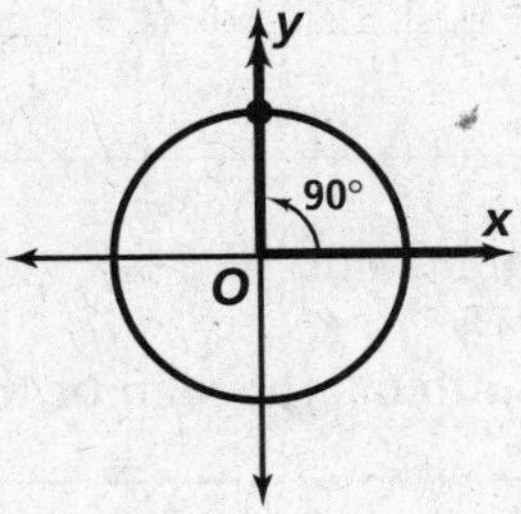

67.

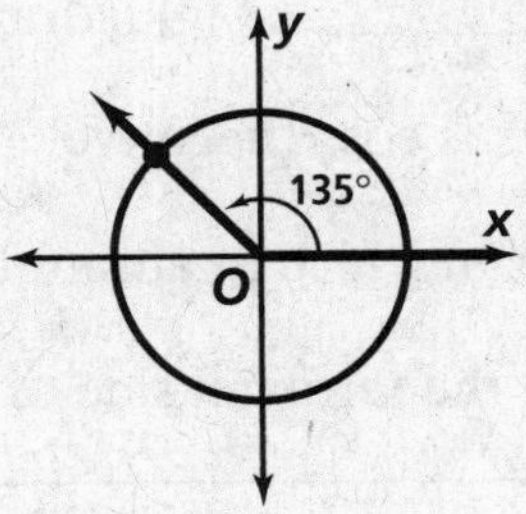

68.

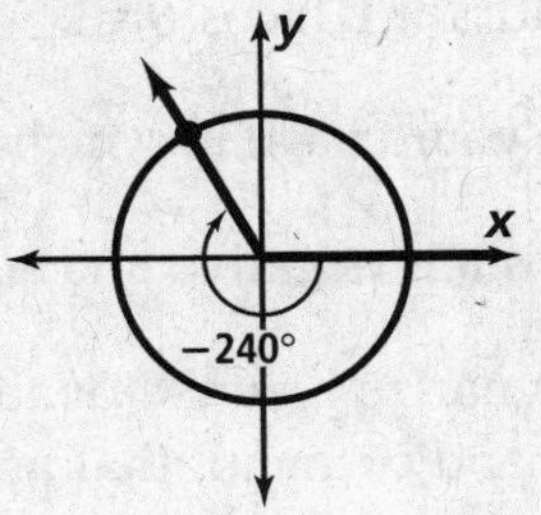

Find the measure of each angle in standard position.

69.

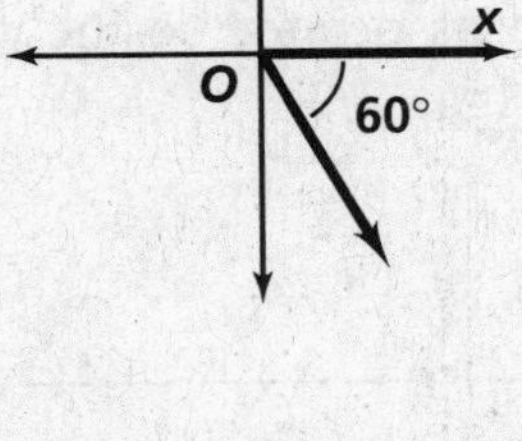

70.

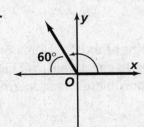

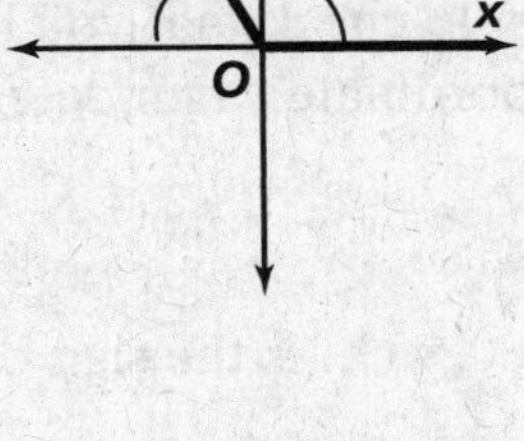

71.

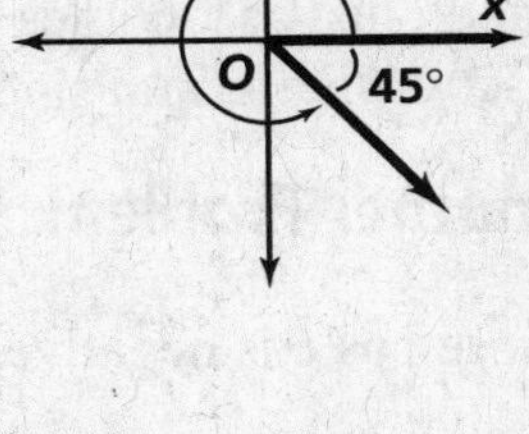

Name ______________________ Class ______________ Date ______________

13-2 • Guided Problem Solving

GPS Exercise 50

a. Copy and complete the chart at the right.

b. Suppose you know that cos θ is negative and sin θ is positive. In which quadrant does the terminal side of the angle lie?

c. **Writing** Summarize how the quadrant in which the terminal side of an angle lies affects the sign of the sine and cosine of that angle.

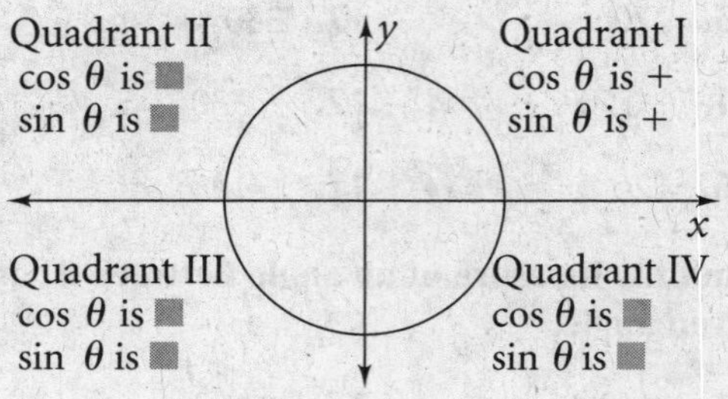

Read and Understand

1. Which quadrant in the chart has no missing information? ______________

Plan and Solve

2. Draw an angle θ that terminates in Quadrant II. Mark the point where it intersects the unit circle. Is the x-coordinate of this point negative (to the left of the origin) or positive (to the right of the origin)? ______________

3. Is the y-coordinate of this point negative or positive? ______________

4. In terms of cosine and sine, what are the coordinates of this point? ______________

5. Combine the prior results. What are the signs of cos θ and sin θ in Quadrant II? ______________

6. Draw an angle θ that terminates in each of the other quadrants. Use similar reasoning to find the sign of cos θ and sin θ in those quadrants.

Quadrant III: cos θ = ______, sin θ = ______   Quadrant IV: cos θ = ______, sin θ = ______

7. Use your chart. In which two quadrants is cos θ negative? ______________

8. If cos θ is negative and sin θ is positive, in which quadrant does the terminal side of θ lie? ______

9. Summarize how the quadrant in which the terminal side of an angle lies affects the sign of the sine and cosine of that angle. ______________

____

Look Back and Check

10. To connect cosine and sine with the point of intersection, notice that c comes before s in the alphabet, just as x comes before y. Double-check that you have correctly associated cosine with the x-coordinate, and sine with the y-coordinate when determining the signs.

Solve Another Problem

11. Suppose cos θ is negative. If $0 < \theta < 180$, what is the sign of sin θ? ______________

Name ____________________ Class ____________ Date ____________

Practice 13-3

Radian Measure

Write each measure in radians. Express your answer in terms of π.

1. 45° **2.** 90° **3.** 30° **4.** 150° **5.** 180°

6. 240° **7.** 270° **8.** 300° **9.** 360° **10.** 40°

11. 80° **12.** 110° **13.** 160° **14.** 200° **15.** 220°

Write each measure in degrees. Round your answer to the nearest degree, if necessary.

16. π **17.** 2π **18.** $\frac{5\pi}{6}$ **19.** $\frac{3\pi}{4}$ **20.** $\frac{3\pi}{2}$

21. $\frac{\pi}{6}$ **22.** $\frac{7\pi}{6}$ **23.** $\frac{11\pi}{6}$ **24.** $\frac{\pi}{3}$ **25.** $\frac{4\pi}{3}$

26. $\frac{5\pi}{4}$ **27.** $\frac{7\pi}{4}$ **28.** $\frac{2\pi}{3}$ **29.** $\frac{\pi}{9}$ **30.** $\frac{2\pi}{9}$

The measure θ of an angle in standard position is given. Find the exact values of $\cos\theta$ and $\sin\theta$ for each angle measure.

31. $\frac{\pi}{6}$ radians **32.** $\frac{\pi}{3}$ radians **33.** $-\frac{3\pi}{4}$ radians **34.** $\frac{7\pi}{4}$ radians

35. $\frac{5\pi}{6}$ radians **36.** $\frac{4\pi}{3}$ radians **37.** $\frac{11\pi}{6}$ radians **38.** $\frac{2\pi}{3}$radians

Use each circle to find the length of the indicated arc. Round your answer to the nearest tenth.

39.

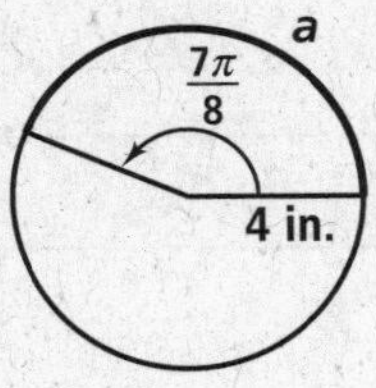

40.

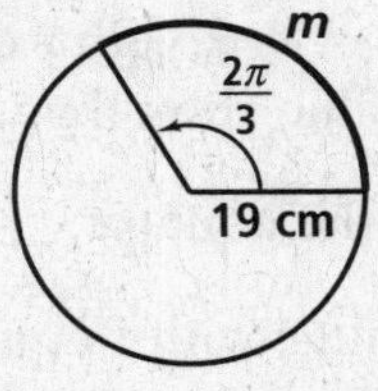

41.

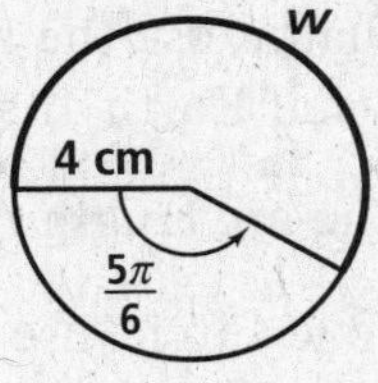

42.

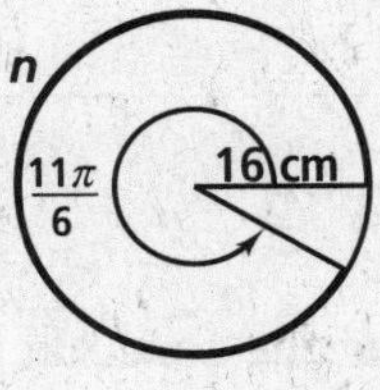

43.

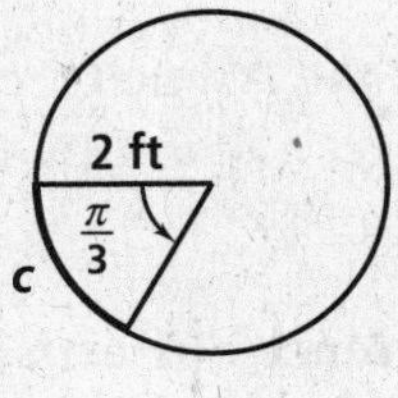

44.

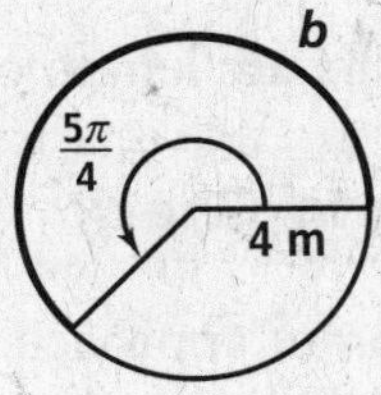

45. A pendulum swings through an angle of 1.8 radians. The distance the tip of the pendulum travels is 32 in. How long is the pendulum?

46. A 0.8 m pendulum swings through an angle of 1.5 radians. What distance does the tip of the pendulum travel?

Name ______________________ Class ______________ Date ______________

13-3 • Guided Problem Solving

GPS Exercise 30

Geography The 24 lines of longitude that approximate the 24 standard time zones are equally spaced around the equator.

a. Suppose that you use 24 central angles to divide a circle into 24 equal arcs. Express the measure of each angle in degrees and in radians.

b. The radius of the equator is about 3960 mi. About how wide is each time zone at the equator?

c. The radius of the Arctic Circle is about 1580 mi. About how wide is each time zone at the Arctic Circle?

Read and Understand

1. How many different time zones are there? ______________

Plan and Solve

2. How many degrees are in a circle? ______________
3. Divide this measure by 24. How many degrees are there for each time zone? ______________
4. How many radians are in a circle? ______________
5. Divide this measure by 24. How many radians are there for each time zone? ______________
6. For the equator, use the arc length formula $s = r\theta$, with r equal to the given radius of Earth at the equator. What value should you use for θ? ______________
7. Compute the arc length of one time zone at the equator. ______________
8. For the Arctic Circle, use the arc length formula, with r equal to the given radius of Earth at the Arctic Circle. What value should you use for θ? ______________
9. Compute the arc length of one time zone at the Arctic Circle. ______________

Look Back and Check

10. Use a different approach. Find the circumference of Earth at the equator using the formula $C = 2\pi r$. Divide the circumference into 24 parts. Verify that the result is the same width you found in Step 7. ______________
11. Repeat Step 10 for the Arctic Circle. ______________
12. Check that your answers are reasonable. Should the width of a time zone at the equator be more or less than the width of a time zone at the Arctic Circle? Explain. ______________

____

Solve Another Problem

13. If the sun rises at 7 o'clock at the eastern edge of a time zone at the equator, what time does it rise at the western edge of this same time zone at the equator? ______________

Name ____________________ Class ____________ Date ____________

Practice 13-4

The Sine Function

Find the amplitude and period of each sine curve. Then write an equation for each curve.

1.

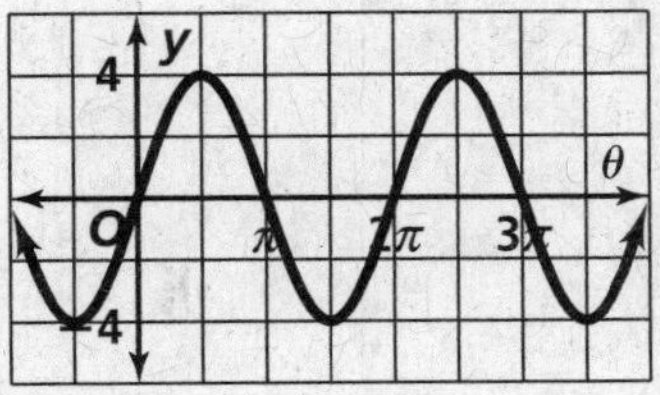

2.

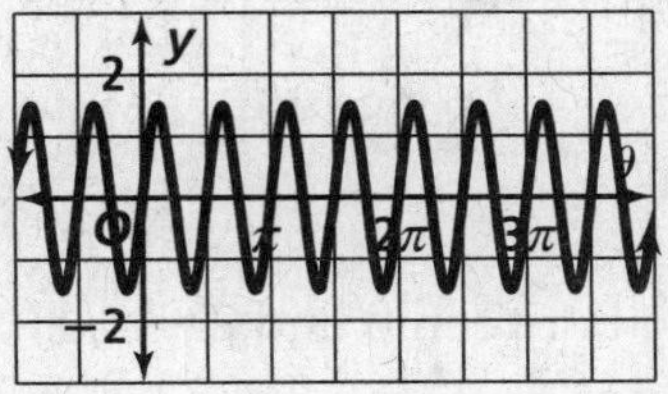

3.

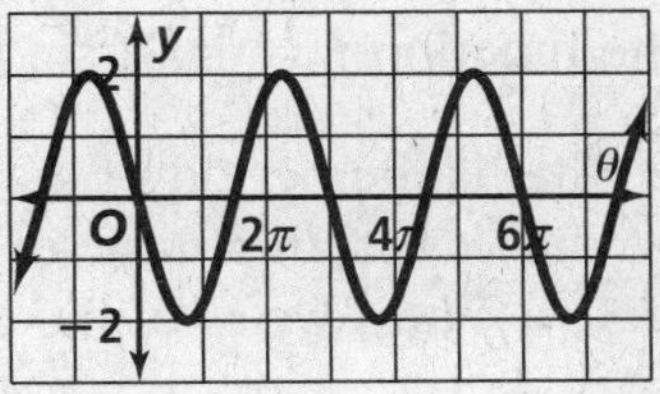

4.

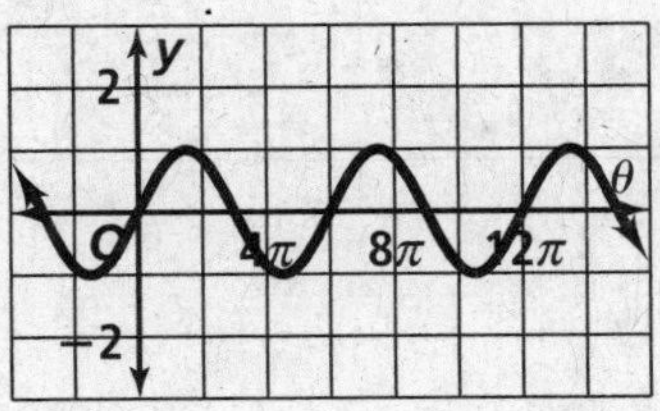

5.

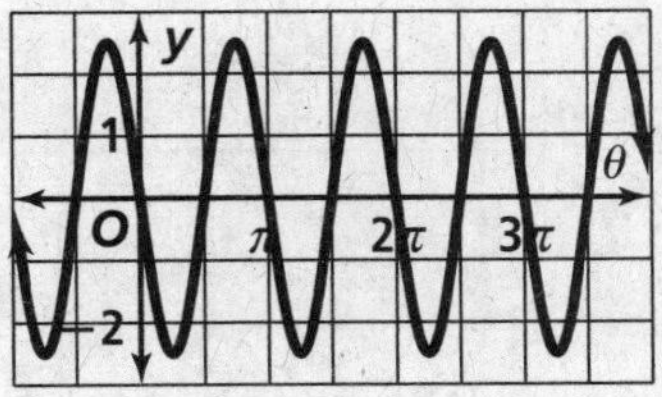

6.

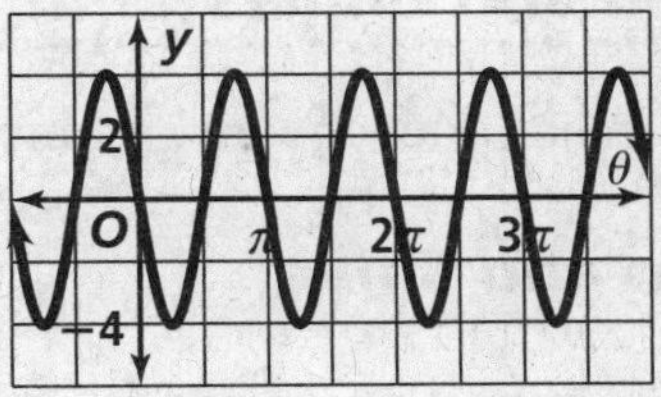

Sketch one cycle of each sine curve. Assume $a > 0$. Write an equation for each graph.

7. amplitude $= 2$; period $= \pi$

8. amplitude $= 3$; period $= 2\pi$

9. amplitude $= 2$; period $= \frac{\pi}{2}$

10. amplitude $= 2$; period $= \frac{\pi}{4}$

11. amplitude $= 1.5$; period $= \frac{\pi}{3}$

12. amplitude $= 2.5$; period $= 2\pi$

Sketch one cycle of the graph of each sine function.

13. $y = 2 \sin \theta$

14. $y = -2 \sin 4\theta$

15. $y = \sin 2\theta$

16. $y = 3 \sin \frac{\theta}{2}$

17. $y = -\sin 2\theta$

18. $y = -5 \sin 3\theta$

19. $y = -3 \sin 2\theta$

20. $y = 4 \sin 5\theta$

21. $y = -4 \sin \frac{\theta}{2}$

Use the graph at the right to find the value of $y = 0.3 \sin \theta$ for each value of θ.

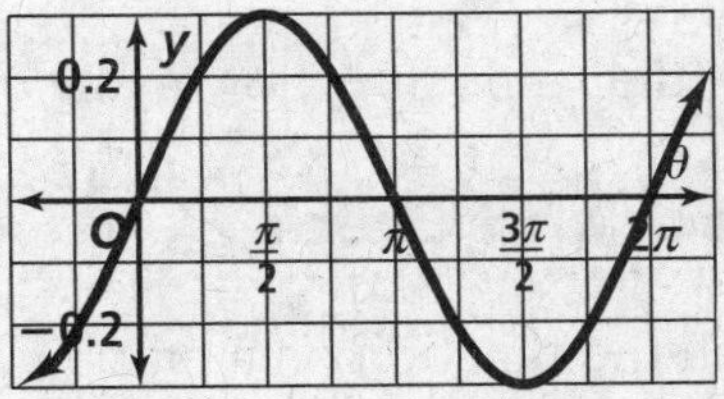

22. 6 radians

23. $\frac{\pi}{4}$ radians

24. $\frac{3\pi}{4}$ radians

25. $\frac{\pi}{2}$ radian

Use the graph at the right to find the value of $y = 0.3 \sin \theta$ for each value of θ.

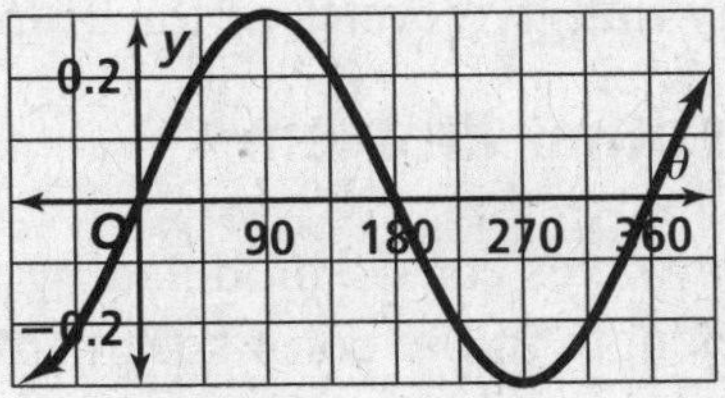

26. 160°

27. 135°

28. 270°

29. 225°

Name ______________________ Class ______________ Date ______________

13-4 • Guided Problem Solving

GPS Exercise 43

Music The sound wave for the note A above middle C can be modeled by the function $y = 0.001 \sin 880\pi\theta$.

a. What is the period of the function?
b. What is the amplitude of the function?
c. How many cycles of the graph are between 0 and 2π?

Read and Understand

1. What does the given function model? ______________________

Plan and Solve

2. Compare the given function to the general form of a sine function, $y = a \sin b\theta$. Identify the values of a and b.

$a =$ ____________ $b =$ ____________

3. What does a represent? ______________________

4. What does b represent? ______________________

5. How is b related to the period of the function? ______________________

6. From the value of a, what is the amplitude of the given function? ______________

7. Using the value of b, what is an expression for the period of the given function? ______________

8. Simplify this expression by writing the fraction in simplest form. What is the period? ______________

9. From the value of b, how many cycles of the graph are between 0 and 2π? ______________

Look Back and Check

10. Graph the function on a graphing calculator. Set the Window as follows.
$x\text{Min} = 0$, $x\text{Max} =$ twice the period (from Step 8)
$y\text{Min} = -a$, $y\text{Max} = a$ (from Step 6)
Verify that two cycles of the graph exactly fit in the window.

Solve Another Problem

11. Light waves can be modeled by $y = \sin b\theta$, where the value of b depends on the particular wavelength in the color spectrum. One shade of blue can be modeled by the function $y = \sin \frac{\pi}{240}\theta$. What are the period and the amplitude of the function? ______________

____

Name____________________ Class____________ Date____________

Practice 13-5

The Cosine Function

Sketch the graph of each function in the interval from 0 to 2π.

1. $y = \cos\theta$
2. $y = 2\cos\pi\theta$
3. $y = 5\cos\theta$
4. $y = -\cos\theta$
5. $y = -5\cos\theta$
6. $y = \cos 2\pi\theta$
7. $y = -2\cos 2\theta$
8. $y = 3\cos 4\theta$
9. $y = \cos\frac{\theta}{2}$
10. $y = 3\cos 8\theta$
11. $y = -4\cos\pi\theta$
12. $y = 0.5\cos\pi\theta$
13. $y = -\cos 2\theta$
14. $y = -3\cos\frac{\pi}{2}\theta$
15. $y = 4\cos\pi\theta$
16. Suppose 12 in. waves occur every 5 s. Write an equation using a cosine function that models the height of a water particle as it moves from crest to crest.

Write an equation of a cosine function for each graph.

17.

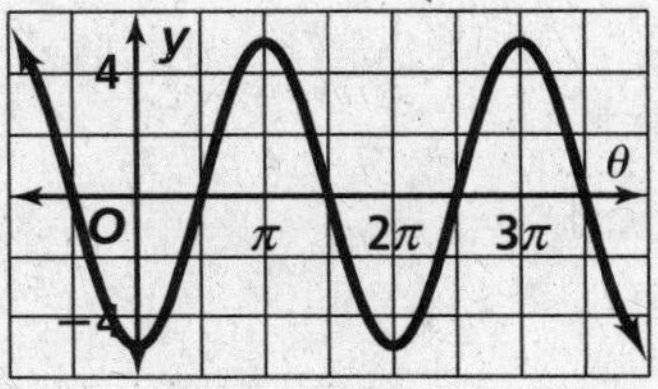

18.

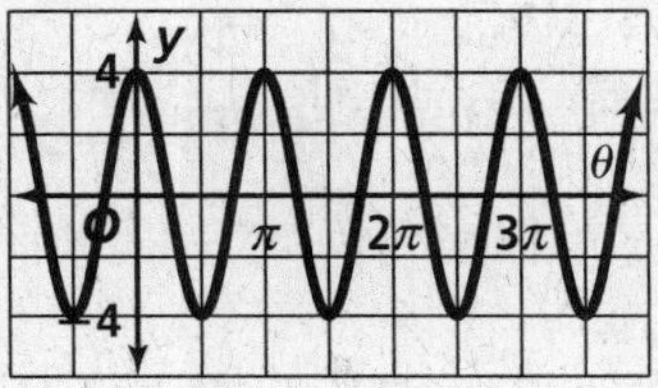

19.

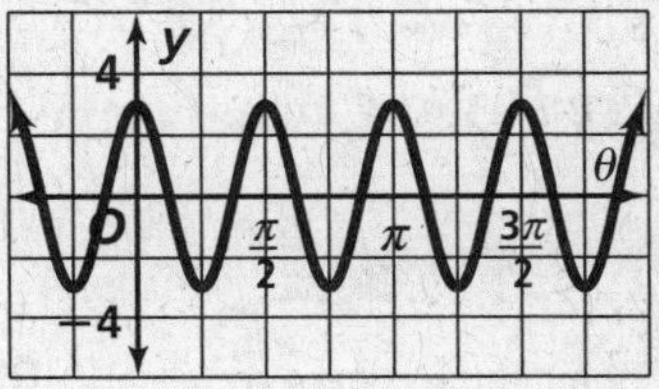

Find the period and amplitude of each cosine function. Identify where the maximum value(s), minimum value(s), and zeros occur in the interval from 0 to 2π.

20.

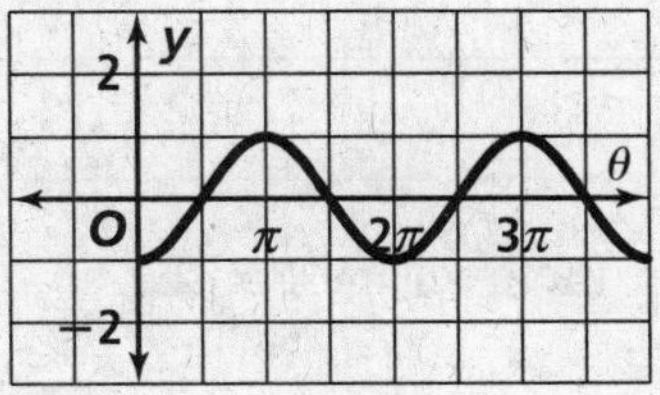

21.

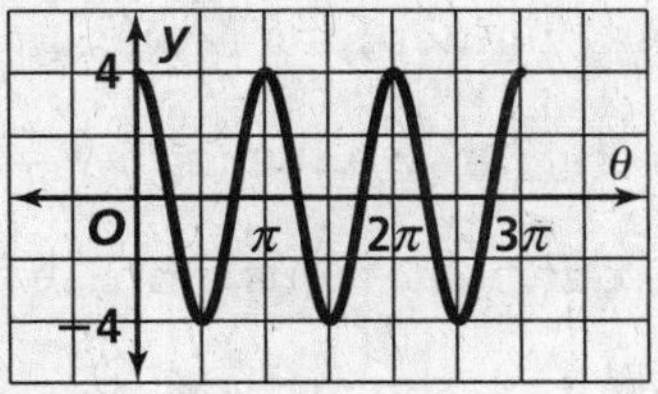

22.

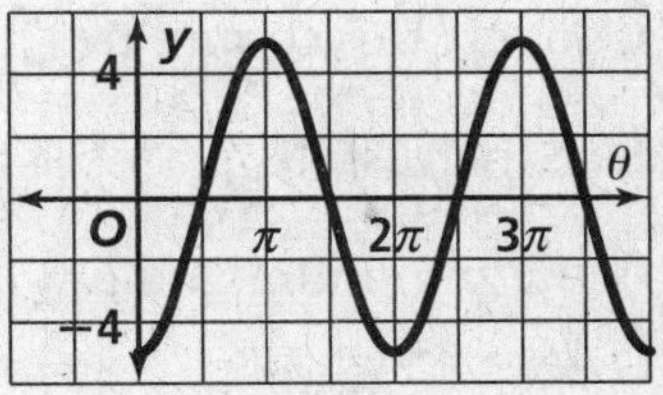

Solve each equation in the interval from 0 to 2π. Round to the nearest hundredth.

23. $2\cos 3\theta = 1.5$
24. $\cot\frac{t}{3} = 1$
25. $1.5\cos\pi\theta = -1.5$
26. $3\cos\frac{\pi}{5}\theta = 2$
27. $3\cos t = 2$
28. $0.5\cos\frac{\theta}{2} = 0.5$
29. $4\cos\frac{\pi}{4}\theta = -2$
30. $3\cos\frac{\theta}{4} = 1.5$
31. $3\cos\theta = -3$

Write a cosine function for each description. Assume that $a > 0$.

32. amplitude $= 2\pi$, period $= 1$
33. amplitude $= \frac{1}{2}$, period $= \pi$

Name ______________________ Class ______________ Date ______________

13-5 • Guided Problem Solving

GPS Exercise 35

Tides The table at the right shows the times for high tide and low tide. The markings on the side of a local pier showed a high tide of 7 ft and a low tide of 4 ft on the previous day.

a. What is the average depth of water at the pier? What is the amplitude of the variation from the average depth?

b. How long is one cycle of the tide?

c. Write a cosine function that models the relationship between the depth of water and the time of day. Use $y = 0$ to represent the average depth of water. Use $t = 0$ to represent the time 4:03 A.M.

d. Critical Thinking Suppose your boat needs at least 5 ft of water to approach or leave the pier. Between what times could you come and go?

Tide Table	
High tide	4:03 A.M.
Low tide	10:14 A.M.
High tide	4:25 P.M.
Low tide	10:36 P.M.

Read and Understand

1. At 4:03 A.M., what is the depth of the water at the pier? ____________

Plan and Solve

2. For the average depth, find the average of 4 ft and 7 ft. ____________
3. Find the amplitude by computing half the difference between 4 ft and 7 ft. ____________
4. From the tide table, how many hours are there between the two high tides? ____________
5. Convert this to minutes. How many minutes long is one cycle? ____________
6. Use the results in Step 3 and Step 5 to write a function $y = a \cos bt$. ____________
7. Is the minimum amount of water your boat needs more or less than the average depth? ____________
8. Write this minimum as the distance from the average depth. ____________
9. Use a graphing calculator to find where your function intersects the horizontal line from Step 8. What are the points of intersection? ____________
10. Use the fact that $t = 0$ is 4:03 A.M. What times can you come or go? ____________

Look Back and Check

11. Verify that your graph reaches a high of 7 ft at 4:03 A.M. ($t = 0$) and 4:25 P.M. ($t = 742$), and a low of 4 ft at 10:14 A.M. ($t = 371$) and 10:36 P.M. ($t = 1113$).

Solve Another Problem

12. The water at a pier reaches a high of 12 ft at 3:00 A.M. and a low of 8 ft at 9 A.M. Write a cosine function that models the relationship between the depth of the water and the time in minutes past 3:00 A.M. Use $y = 0$ to represent the average depth of the water. ____________

Name ______________________ Class ______________ Date ______________

Practice 13-6

The Tangent Function

Identify the period and tell where the asymptotes occur, in the interval from 0 to 2π, for each function.

1. $y = \tan\theta$ **2.** $y = 2\tan\frac{\theta}{2}$ **3.** $y = 3\tan\frac{\theta}{4}$

4. $y = 4\tan 2\theta$ **5.** $y = -\tan\frac{\pi}{2}\theta$ **6.** $y = -2\tan\pi\theta$

7. $y = -3\tan 2\theta$ **8.** $y = -4\tan\theta$ **9.** $y = 0.5\tan\pi\theta$

Sketch two cycles of the graph of each function.

10. $y = \tan\theta$ **11.** $y = 2\tan\theta$ **12.** $y = -\tan\theta$

13. $y = -2\tan\theta$ **14.** $y = -0.5\tan 2\theta$ **15.** $y = 3\tan\theta$

16. $y = -3\tan 2\theta$ **17.** $y = 5\tan\frac{\pi}{2}\theta$ **18.** $y = 2\tan 3\theta$

19. $y = 0.5\tan 2\theta$ **20.** $y = -2.5\tan\frac{\pi}{2}\theta$ **21.** $y = -5\tan 2\pi\theta$

22. $y = -2\tan 4\theta$ **23.** $y = -0.25\tan 3\theta$ **24.** $y = -4\tan 4\pi\theta$

25. $y = -2.25\tan\theta$ **26.** $y = -0.25\tan\frac{\pi}{3}\theta$ **27.** $y = 0.75\tan 4\theta$

Identify the period of each tangent function.

28.

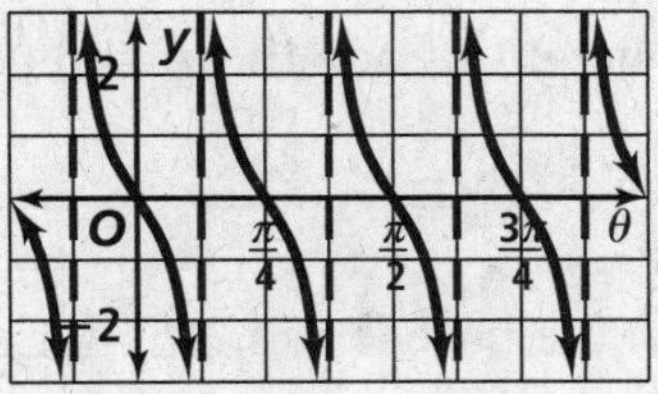

29.

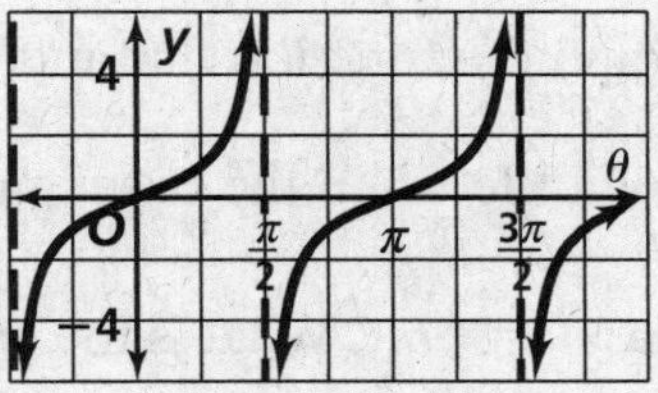

30.

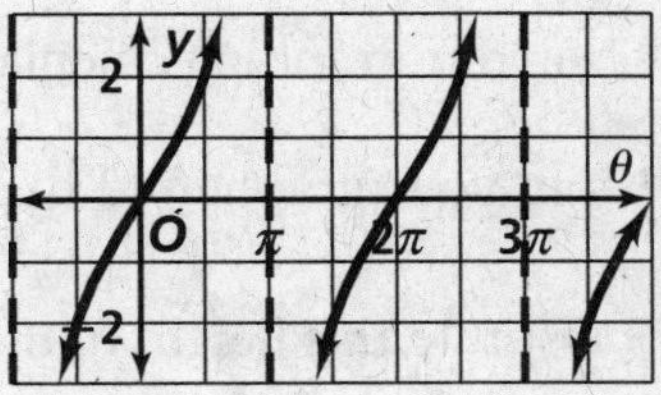

Use the graph of $y = \tan\theta$ to find each value. If the tangent is undefined at that point, write *undefined*.

31. $\tan\frac{\pi}{2}$ **32.** $\tan\left(-\frac{3\pi}{4}\right)$

33. $\tan\left(-\frac{\pi}{4}\right)$ **34.** $\tan\frac{3\pi}{2}$

Using your graphing calculator, graph each function on the interval $0° < x < 470°$ and $-300 < y < 300$. Evaluate the function at $x = 45°, 90°$, and $135°$.

35. $y = 200\tan x$ **36.** $y = -75\tan\left(\frac{1}{4}x\right)$ **37.** $y = -50\tan x$

Name ______________________ Class ______________ Date ______________

13-6 • Guided Problem Solving

GPS Exercise 30

Ceramics An artist is creating triangular ceramic tiles for a triangular patio. The patio will be an equilateral triangle with base 18 ft and height 15.6 ft.

a. Find the area of the patio in square feet.
b. The artist uses tiles that are isosceles triangles with base 6 in. The function $y = 3 \tan \theta$ models the height of the tiles, where θ is the measure of one of the base angles. Graph the function. Find the height of the tile when $\theta = 30°$ and when $\theta = 60°$.
c. Find the area of one tile in square inches when $\theta = 30°$ and $\theta = 60°$.
d. Find the number of tiles the patio will require if $\theta = 30°$ and if $\theta = 60°$.

Read and Understand

1. What does θ represent in this problem? ______________________

Plan and Solve

2. Use the formula $A = \frac{1}{2}bh$ to find the area of the patio in square feet. ______________

3. Use your graphing calculator to graph the function that models the height of one tile, $y = 3 \tan \theta$.

4. From your graph, find the height of a tile when the base angle is $\theta = 30°$. ______________

5. Substitute this height in the formula $A = \frac{1}{2}bh$. What is the area when the base is 6 in.? ______________

6. Use a similar technique to find the area of one tile in square inches when $\theta = 60°$. ______________

7. Convert the total area of the patio to square inches. ______________________

8. Divide the total area of the patio by the area of one tile.
number of tiles when $\theta = 30°$ ______________ number of tiles when $\theta = 60°$ ______________

Look Back and Check

9. Compute the answer a different way. How many of the 30° tiles does it take to make a square foot? How many would it take to cover the patio? Verify that this agrees with your result from Step 8. Should it take more or fewer of the 60° tiles to cover the same area? ______________

____

Solve Another Problem

10. Suppose the dimensions of the equilateral triangle are changed so that the base is 16 ft and the height is 14.1 ft. Find the number of tiles the patio will require for $\theta = 30°$. ______________

Name ______________________ Class ______________ Date ______________

Practice 13-7

Translating Sine and Cosine Functions

Graph each function in the interval from 0 to 2π.

1. $y = -\sin\left(x + \frac{\pi}{2}\right)$
2. $y = 3\sin\left(x - \frac{\pi}{4}\right) + 2$
3. $y = \cos\frac{1}{2}x + 1$
4. $y = 3\cos(x - 2)$
5. $y = \sin 3(x - \pi)$
6. $y = \cos(x + 4)$
7. $y = \cos x + 3$
8. $y = -2\sin x + 1$
9. $y = -\cos 2\left(x + \frac{\pi}{4}\right)$
10. $y = \frac{1}{2}\cos x + 3$
11. $y = \sin\frac{1}{2}(x + \pi)$
12. $y = \cos\left(x + \frac{\pi}{6}\right)$
13. $y = -2\cos x + 3$
14. $y = \sin 2x + 1$
15. $y = \sin 2\left(x - \frac{\pi}{3}\right)$

Write an equation for each translation.

16. $y = \sin x$, 2 units down
17. $y = \cos x$, π units left
18. $y = \cos x$, $\frac{\pi}{4}$ units up
19. $y = \sin x$, 3.2 units to the right

Find the amplitude and period of each function. Describe any phase shift and vertical shift in the graph.

20. $y = 3\cos x + 2$
21. $y = -2\sin\left(x + \frac{\pi}{2}\right)$
22. $y = \cos 2x + 1$
23. $y = -\sin\left(x - \frac{\pi}{3}\right)$
24. $y = \frac{1}{2}\cos x - 3$
25. $y = \cos\frac{1}{2}x - 2$

Use the function $f(x)$ at the right. Graph each translation.

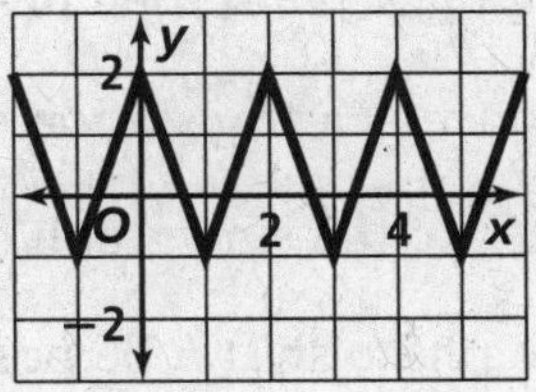

26. $f(x) + 3$
27. $f(x + 1)$
28. $f(x) - 5$
29. $f(x + 3)$
30. $f(x + 2) - 1$
31. $f(x) - 4$

What is the value of h in each translation? Describe each phase shift (use a phrase like *3 units to the left*).

32. $g(x) = f(x + 2)$
33. $g(x) = f(x - 1)$
34. $h(t) = f(t + 1.5)$
35. $f(x) = g(x - 1)$
36. $y = \cos\left(x - \frac{\pi}{2}\right)$
37. $y = \cos(x + \pi)$

Name ______________________ Class ______________ Date ______________

13-7 • Guided Problem Solving

GPS Exercise 43

The graphs of $y = \sin x$ and $y = \cos x$ are shown at the right.

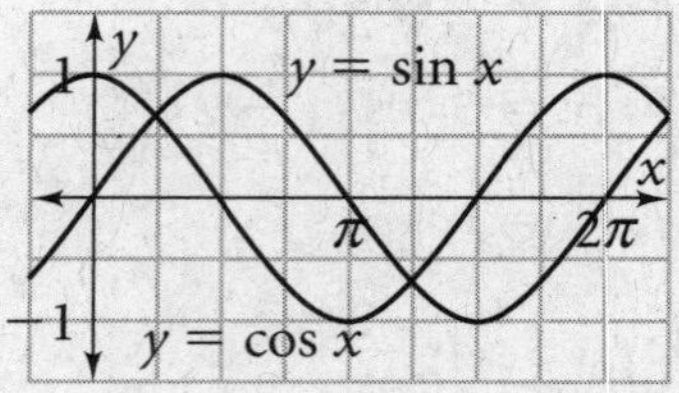

a. What phase shift will translate the cosine graph onto the sine graph? Write your answer as an equation in the form $\sin x = \cos(x - h)$.

b. What phase shift will translate the sine graph onto the cosine graph? Write your answer as an equation in the form $\cos x = \sin(x - h)$.

Read and Understand

1. What two graphs are shown? ______________________

2. Is a phase shift a vertical or a horizontal translation? ______________________

Plan and Solve

3. Read the graphs from left to right. Mark the first point on the graph of $y = \cos x$ where the cosine function reaches its maximum value. Mark the point on the graph of $y = \sin x$ where the sine function reaches its maximum value. Find the horizontal distance between these two points. ______________

4. To translate the cosine graph onto the sine graph, will the shift be to the right or the left? ________

5. Will the phase shift h be positive or negative in this case? What is the value of h? ________

6. Write $\sin x$ as a translation of $\cos x$, in the form $\sin x = \cos(x - h)$. ______________

7. To translate the sine graph onto the cosine graph, will the shift be to the right or the left? ______

8. Will the phase shift h be positive or negative in this case? What is the value of h? ________

9. Write $\cos x$ as a translation of $\sin x$, in the form $\cos x = \sin(x - h)$. ______________

Look Back and Check

10. Use the unit circle. Substitute some standard values for x and evaluate both sides of $\cos x = \sin(x - h)$ with the phase shift h you found. Verify that they are identical. Repeat for $\sin x = \cos(x - h)$. ______________________

11. It is often said "sine leads the cosine." Interpret this remark in terms of translation. By how much does sine "lead" the cosine? ______________________

____

Solve Another Problem

12. Suppose the equation $T = 65\cos\left(\frac{\pi}{12}x\right) + 6$ models the temperature in degrees x hours after 4 P.M. Rewrite the model using a sine function. ______________

Name ______________________ Class ______________ Date ______________

Practice 13-8

Reciprocal Trigonometric Functions

Evaluate each expression. Each angle is given in radians. Round to the nearest hundredth, if necessary.

1. cot 4
2. csc $\frac{\pi}{6}$
3. csc (-2)
4. sec π
5. cot $(-\pi)$
6. sec (-3.5)
7. cot $\frac{\pi}{3}$
8. sec 1.5
9. csc (-1.5)
10. cot π
11. sec 3
12. csc $\frac{\pi}{4}$

Evaluate each expression. Write your answer in exact form. If appropriate, also state it as a decimal rounded to the nearest hundredth. If the expression is undefined, write *undefined*.

13. sec 45°
14. cot 180°
15. sec 30°
16. csc 30°
17. cot (−180°)
18. csc (−45°)
19. csc 180°
20. cot 45°
21. sec 90°
22. sec (−30°)
23. csc (−60°)
24. sec 60°
25. Suppose $\tan\theta = \frac{6}{9}$. Find $\cot\theta$
26. Suppose $\sin\theta = \frac{2}{5}$. Find $\csc\theta$
27. Suppose $\cos\theta = \frac{14}{20}$. Find $\sec\theta$
28. Suppose $\tan\theta = -\frac{2}{3}$. Find $\cot\theta$

Graph each function in the interval from 0 to 2π.

29. $y = \cot 2\theta$
30. $y = -\cot \frac{1}{2}\theta$
31. $y = \sec\left(\theta - \frac{\pi}{2}\right)$
32. $y = \csc 2\theta + 1$
33. $y = -\csc 3\theta$
34. $y = \sec\theta + 2$
35. $y = \cot(\theta + \pi)$
36. $y = \sec \frac{1}{4}\theta$
37. $y = \csc\theta - 1$

Use the graph of the appropriate reciprocal trigonometric function to find each value. Round to the nearest hundredth, if necessary.

38. cot 30°
39. csc 180°
40. cot 70°
41. sec 100°
42. sec 50°
43. csc 100°
44. cot 20°
45. sec 120°
46. A fire truck is parked on the shoulder of a freeway next to a long wall. The red light on the top of the truck rotates through one complete revolution every 2 seconds. The function $y = 10\sec\pi t$ models the length of the beam in feet to a point on the wall in terms of time t.
    a. Graph the function.
    b. Find the length at time 1.75 seconds
    c. Find the length at time 2 seconds.

Name ____________________ Class ____________ Date ____________

13-8 • Guided Problem Solving

GPS Exercise 60

a. Graph $y = \tan x$ and $y = \cot x$ on the same axes.
b. State the domain, the range, and the asymptotes of each function.
c. **Writing** Compare the two graphs. How are they alike? How are they different?
d. **Geometry** The graph of the cotangent function can be reflected about a line to graph the tangent function. Name at least two lines that have this property.

Read and Understand

1. What are the names of the functions you will graph? ____________________

Plan and Solve

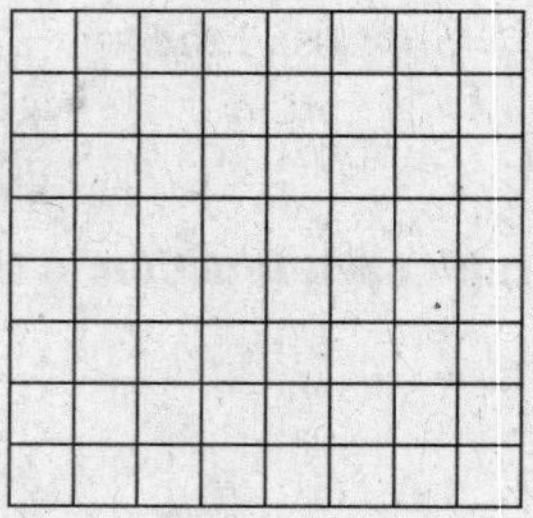

2. Make a table of values for each function. Use a calculator to find additional values if needed. Then plot the points and sketch the graphs.

3. What are the domain, range, and location of the asymptotes of the tangent function? ____________________

____

4. What are the domain, range, and location of the asymptotes of the cotangent function? ____________________

____

5. Compare the two graphs. What is the same about the two graphs? ____________________

____

6. What is different about the two graphs? ____________________

____

7. Mark a point where the two graphs intersect. Draw a vertical line through it. Is the graph of the cotangent function reflected about this line the graph of the tangent function? Name at least two lines that have this property. ____________________

Look Back and Check

8. Graph the two functions on the same screen on a graphing calculator. Use the Intersect feature to verify your result in Step 8.

Solve Another Problem

9. The graph of $y = 4\cot\frac{\theta}{2}$ can be reflected about a line to graph $y = 4\tan\frac{\theta}{2}$. Name at least two lines that have this property. ____________________

Name ______________________ Class ______________ Date ______________

13A: Graphic Organizer

For use before Lesson 13-1

Study Skill As you near the end of the book, take a while to start reviewing the previous chapters, rather than waiting until the end of the course. Studying for a final exam is much easier if you've already begun your review.

Write your answers.

1. What is the chapter title? ______________________________

2. Find the Table of Contents page for this chapter at the front of the book. Name four topics you will study in this chapter.

______________________ ______________________

______________________ ______________________

3. Complete the graphic organizer as you work through the chapter.
1. Write the title of the chapter in the center oval.
2. When you begin a lesson, write the name of the lesson in a rectangle.
3. When you complete that lesson, write a skill or key concept from that lesson in the outer oval linked to that rectangle.

Continue with steps 2 and 3 clockwise around the graphic organizer.

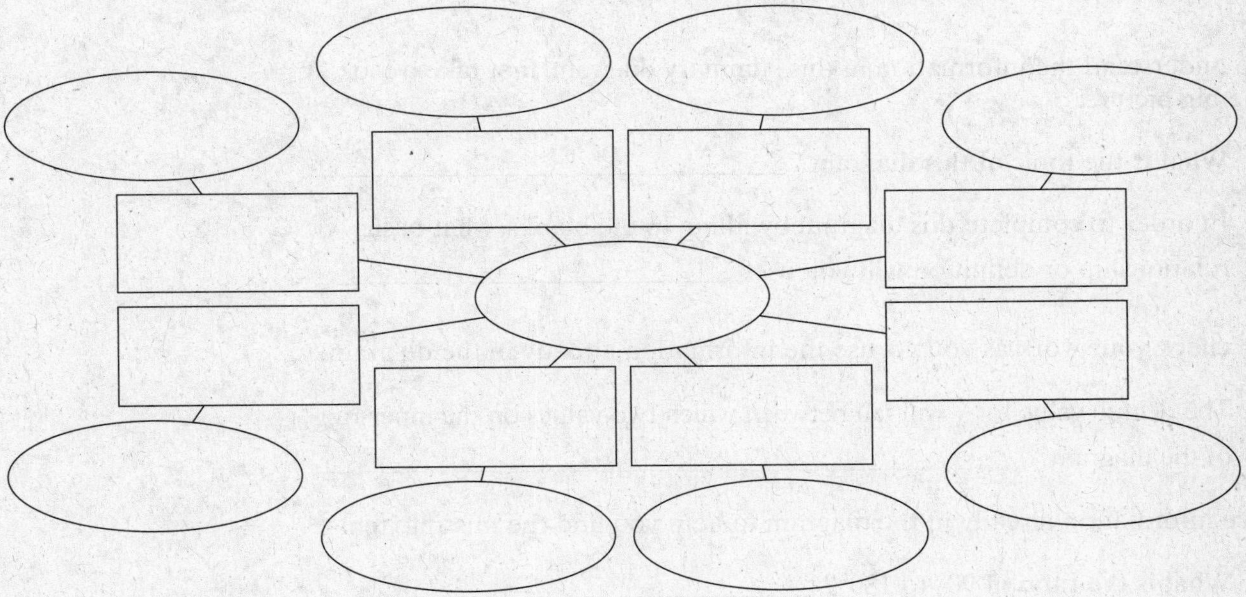

Name ______________________ Class ______________ Date ______________

13B: Reading Comprehension

For use after Lesson 13-3

Study Skill When you read a diagram to answer questions, be sure to look at the entire diagram, including the title and all labels. If you only look at the diagram for specific information, you may miss crucial information.

Look at the summary diagram and then answer the questions.

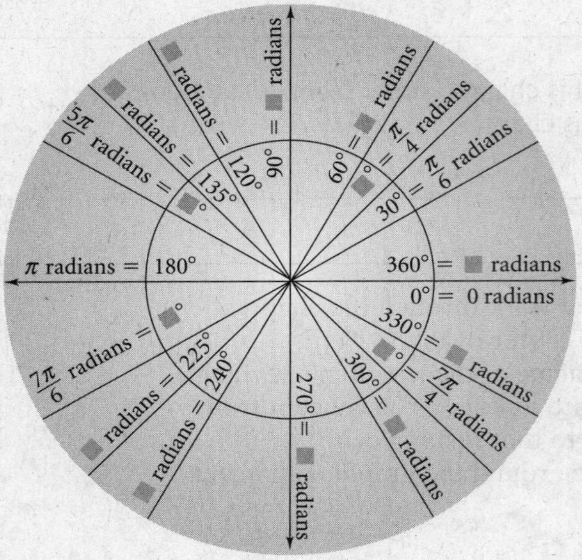

To understand the information in this summary diagram, first take a look at the big picture.

1. What is the topic of this diagram? ______________________

2. In order to complete this diagram by filling in the blanks, what basic relationship or definition will you use? ______________________

To check your work as you go, use the information already in the diagram.

3. The degree value for $\frac{\pi}{4}$ will fall between which two values on the inner ring of the diagram? ______________________

Use information already in the diagram to help you find the missing items.

4. What is the ratio of 90° to 180°? ______________________

5. Multiply this same ratio by the radians equal to 180° to find the radians equal to 90°. ______________________

6. High-Use Academic Words What does *topic* mean in question 1?

a. subject **b.** shape

Name ____________________ Class ____________ Date ____________

13C: Reading/Writing Math Symbols

For use after Lesson 13-7

Study Skill There are many symbols or abbreviations that are standard. It is helpful to learn as many of these as possible. With this knowledge, you may be able to understand what other people write when they use symbols or abbreviations.

The first column shows the lowercase letters of the Greek alphabet. The second column shows the names of the Greek letters. The third column shows the uppercase forms of the same letters. Use the Greek alphabet to answer the questions that follow.

α	alpha	A
β	beta	B
γ	gamma	Γ
δ	delta	Δ
ε	epsilon	E
Θ	theta	Θ
λ	lambda	Λ
μ	mu	M
π	pi	Π
ρ	rho	P
σ	sigma	Σ
ω	omega	Ω

1. Write the Greek letter that is used to represent the irrational number that shows the ratio between the circumference and the diameter of a circle. ____________

2. What is the name of the Greek letter you wrote in question 1? ____________

3. Write the (uppercase) Greek letter that is used to represent the sum of the terms in a series. ____________

4. What is the name of the Greek letter you wrote in question 3? ____________

5. Write the Greek letter that tells the number of radians in 180°. ____________

6. Write the Greek letter often used to name an angle in trigonometry. ____________

7. What is the name of the Greek letter you wrote in question 6? ____________

Name ______________________ Class ____________ Date ____________

13D: Visual Vocabulary Practice

For use after Lesson 13-8

Study Skill When interpreting an illustration, notice the information that is given and also notice what is not given. Do not make assumptions.

Concept List

cosecant	cosine function	cotangent
coterminal angles	periodic function	phase shift
secant	sine function	unit circle

Write the concept that best describes each exercise. Choose from the concept list above.

1.

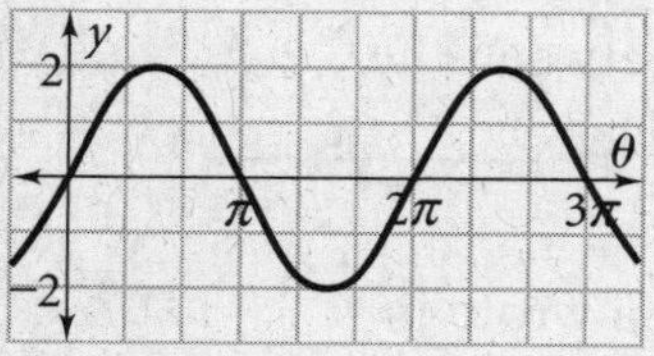

____

2. $\dfrac{1}{\cos 45°}$

____

3.

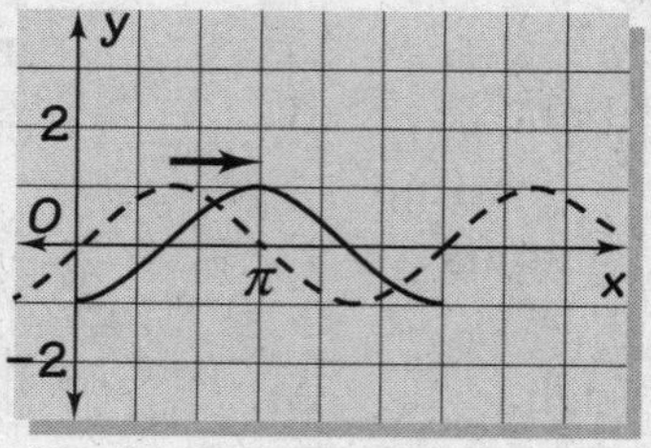

____

4.

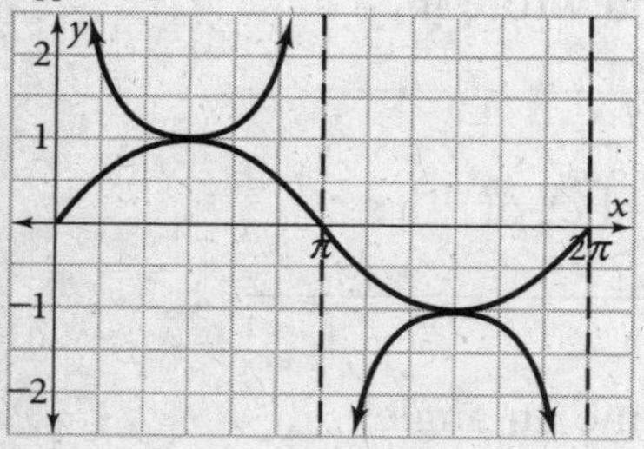

____

5.

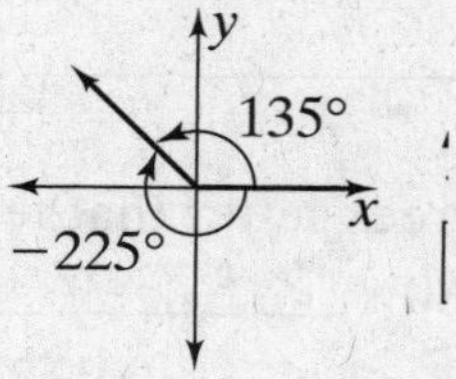

____

6.

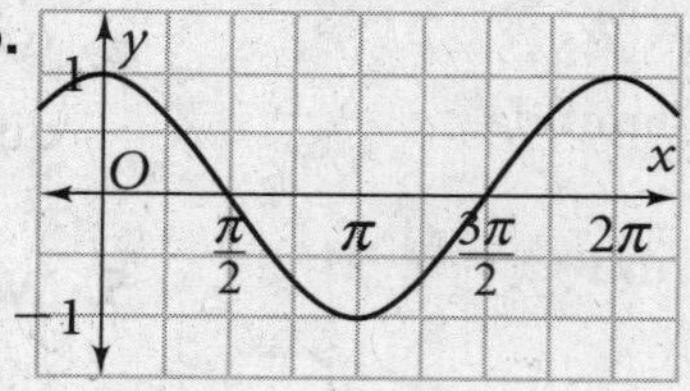

____

7.

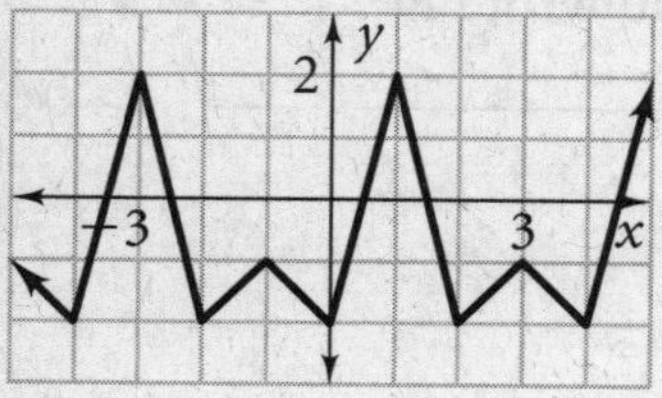

____

8. $\dfrac{1}{\tan x}$

____

9.

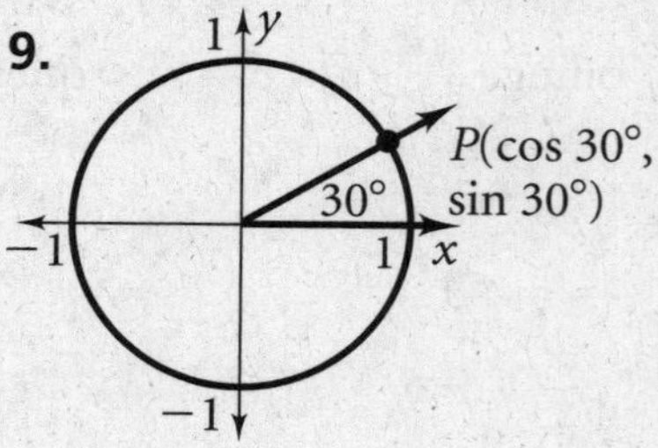

____

Name ____________________ Class ____________ Date ____________

13E: Vocabulary Check

For use after Lesson 13-4

Study Skill Strengthen your vocabulary. Use these pages and add cues and summaries by applying the Cornell Notetaking style.

Write the definition for each word at the right. To check your work, fold the paper back along the dotted line to see the correct answers.

____________________	Periodic function
____________________	Cosine θ
____________________	Central angle
____________________	Intercepted arc
____________________	Radian

Vocabulary and Study Skills

Name ______________________ Class ______________ Date ______________

13E: Vocabulary Check (continued)

For use after Lesson 13-4

Write the vocabulary word for each definition. To check your work, fold the paper forward along the dotted line to see the correct answers.

Repeats a pattern of y-values at regular intervals. ______________________

The x-coordinate of the point at which the terminal side of the angle θ intersects the unit circle. ______________________

An angle whose vertex is at the center of a circle. ______________________

The portion of a circle whose endpoints are on the sides of a central angle of the circle and whose remaining points lie in the interior angle. ______________________

The measure of a central angle of a circle that intercepts an arc of equal length to a radius of the circle. ______________________

Name ______________________ Class ______________ Date ______________

13F: Vocabulary Review Puzzle

For use with Chapter Review

Study Skill Consider working with a partner to learn new vocabulary terms. Drill each other by saying the term and having your partner repeat the definition to you. You may also wish to make flash cards to help you and your partner drill.

Find the words in this puzzle that match the given definitions. Complete the word search puzzle. For help, use the Glossary in your textbook. Remember a word may go right to left, left to right, up, down, or along a diagonal. Circle the letters that form each word.

1. half the difference between the maximum and minimum values of a function
2. direction of rotation of a negative angle
3. ratio of side adjacent over hypotenuse
4. one complete pattern of a periodic graph
5. horizontal length of one cycle
6. ratio of side opposite over hypotenuse
7. ratio of side opposite to side adjacent

C	T	C	N	E	T	W	E	A
L	N	R	Y	I	D	N	M	M
O	E	N	D	C	I	P	T	I
C	G	R	E	S	L	O	R	E
K	N	I	O	I	Z	E	W	P
W	A	C	T	Y	E	I	S	S
I	T	U	W	N	R	E	R	U
S	D	P	E	R	I	O	D	E
E	T	I	N	U	O	O	Y	I

Name ______________________ Class ______________ Date ______________

Practice 14-1

Trigonometric Identities

Verify each identity.

1. $\sin\theta \sec\theta \cot\theta = 1$
2. $\csc\theta = \cot\theta \sec\theta$
3. $\frac{\sin\theta}{\csc\theta} = \sin^2\theta$
4. $\cos\theta \csc\theta \tan\theta = 1$
5. $\sin\theta \tan\theta + \cos\theta = \sec\theta$
6. $\frac{\csc\theta}{\cot\theta} = \sec\theta$
7. $\sec\theta = \tan\theta \csc\theta$
8. $\tan\theta + \cot\theta = \sec\theta \csc\theta$
9. $\tan^2\theta + 1 = \sec^2\theta$
10. $\cos\theta \cot\theta + \sin\theta = \csc\theta$
11. $\frac{\sec\theta}{\csc\theta} = \tan\theta$
12. $\sec\theta \cot\theta = \csc\theta$
13. $\sec^2\theta - \tan^2\theta = 1$
14. $\sec\theta = \csc\theta \tan\theta$
15. $\frac{\sin\theta + \cos\theta}{\sin\theta} = 1 + \cot\theta$
16. $\cos\theta(\sec\theta - \cos\theta) = \sin^2\theta$
17. $\cot\theta \sec\theta = \csc\theta$
18. $(1 - \sin\theta)(1 + \sin\theta) = \cos^2\theta$

Simplify each trigonometric expression.

19. $1 - \sec^2\theta$
20. $\frac{\sec\theta}{\tan\theta}$
21. $\csc\theta \tan\theta$
22. $\sec\theta \cos^2\theta$
23. $\csc^2\theta - \cot^2\theta$
24. $1 - \sin^2\theta$
25. $\tan\theta \cot\theta$
26. $\cos\theta \cot\theta + \sin\theta$
27. $\cos\theta \tan\theta$
28. $\frac{\sin\theta \cot\theta}{\cos\theta}$
29. $\sec\theta \tan\theta \csc\theta$
30. $\sec\theta \cot\theta$
31. $\frac{\sin\theta}{\csc\theta} + \frac{\cos\theta}{\sec\theta}$
32. $\frac{\tan\theta \csc\theta}{\sec\theta}$
33. $\cot^2\theta - \csc^2\theta$
34. $\frac{\cot\theta}{\csc\theta}$

Name _______________ Class _______________ Date _______________

14-1 • Guided Problem Solving

GPS Exercise 45

Verify the identity $\sin^2\theta\tan^2\theta = \tan^2\theta - \sin^2\theta$.

Read and Understand

1. What does it mean to verify an identity? _______________

2. Write the tangent and cotangent identities. _______________

Plan and Solve

3. Use the tangent identity to rewrite $\tan^2\theta$. $\qquad \sin^2\theta\tan^2\theta = \sin^2\theta$ _______________

4. Use the Pythagorean identity $\cos^2\theta + \sin^2\theta = 1$ to rewrite $\sin^2\theta$. $\qquad =$ _______________

5. Use the distributive property to write the numerator. $\qquad = \dfrac{\_\_\_\_\_\_\_\_}{\cos^2\theta}$

6. Rewrite as two separate fractions. $\qquad = \dfrac{\_\_\_\_\_\_}{\cos^2\theta} - \dfrac{\_\_\_\_\_\_}{\cos^2\theta}$

7. Simplify. $\qquad =$ _______________

Look Back and Check

8. To check your answer, verify the identity by starting with the right side and transforming it until it is the same as the left side. _______________

Solve Another Problem

9. Verify the identity $\sin^2\theta\csc^2\theta - \sin^2\theta = \cos^2\theta$. _______________

____

Name ______________________ Class ______________ Date ______________

Practice 14-2

Solving Trigonometric Equations Using Inverses

Solve each equation for $0 \le \theta < 2\pi$.

1. $2 \tan \theta + 2 = 0$
2. $2 \cos \theta = 1$
3. $2 \cos \theta + \sqrt{3} = 0$
4. $\sqrt{3} \cot \theta - 1 = 0$
5. $4 \sin \theta - 3 = 0$
6. $4 \sin \theta + 3 = 0$
7. $\left(2 \cos \theta + \sqrt{3}\right)(2 \cos \theta + 1) = 0$
8. $\sqrt{3} \tan \theta - 2 \sin \theta \tan \theta = 0$
9. $2 \cos^2 \theta + \cos \theta = 0$
10. $5 \cos \theta - 3 = 0$
11. $\tan \theta - 2 \cos \theta \tan \theta = 0$
12. $\tan \theta (\tan \theta + 1) = 0$
13. $(\cos \theta - 1)(2 \cos \theta - 1) = 0$
14. $\tan^2 \theta - \tan \theta = 0$
15. If a projectile is fired into the air with an initial velocity v at an angle of elevation θ, then the height h of the projectile at time t is given by $h = -16t^2 + vt \sin \theta$.
    a. Find the angle of elevation θ of a rifle barrel, to the nearest tenth of a degree, if a bullet fired at 1500 ft/s takes 2 s to reach a height of 750 ft.
    b. Find the angle of elevation of a rifle, to the nearest tenth of a degree, if a bullet fired at 1500 ft/s takes 3 s to reach a height of 750 ft.

Use a calculator and inverse functions to find the radian measures of the angles.

16. angles whose tangent is 2.5
17. angles whose sine is 0.75
18. angles whose cosine is (−0.24)
19. angles whose cosine is 0.45

Use a unit circle and 45°–45°–90° triangles to find the degree measures of the angles.

20. angles whose sine is $\frac{\sqrt{2}}{2}$
21. angles whose tangent is 1
22. angles whose cosine is $\frac{\sqrt{2}}{2}$
23. angle whose sine is 1

Use the graph of the inverse of $y = \cos \theta$ at the right.

24. Find the measures of the angles whose cosine is −1.
25. Find the measures of the angles whose cosine is 0.

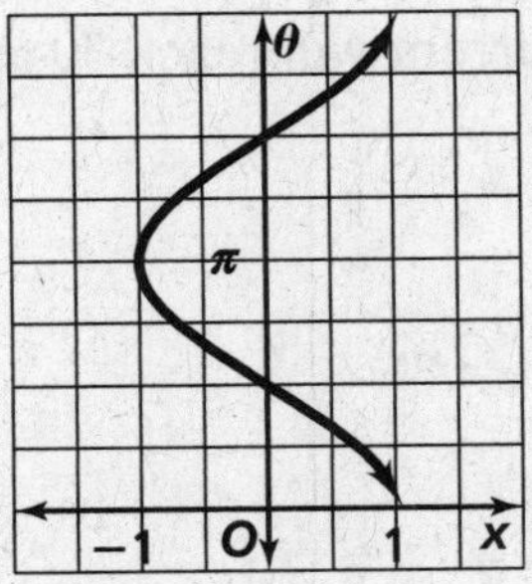

Name ______ Class ______ Date ______

14-2 • Guided Problem Solving

GPS Exercise 44

Electricity The function $I = 40 \sin 60\pi t$ models the current I in amps that an electric generator is producing after t seconds. When is the first time that the current will reach 20 amps? −20 amps?

Read and Understand

1. What does I represent in the function? ______

2. What does t represent in the function? ______

Plan and Solve

3. Solve the function for t.

$$I = 40\sin 60\pi t$$

$$\_\_\_\_\_\_ = \sin 60\pi t$$

$$\_\_\_\_\_\_ = 60\pi t$$

$$\_\_\_\_\_\_ = t$$

4. Let $I = 20$ and solve for t. ______

5. When is the first time that the current will reach 20 amps? ______

6. Let $I = -20$ and solve for t. ______

7. When is the first time that the current will reach −20 amps? ______

Look Back and Check

8. To check the reasonableness of your answers, substitute your values for the number of seconds into the original equation and solve for I. Does I equal 20 and −20, respectively? ______

Solve Another Problem

9. Using the same function, $I = 40\sin 60\pi t$, when is the first time that the current will reach 30 amps? −30 amps? ______

Name ________________ Class ________________ Date ________________

Practice 14-3

Right Triangles and Trigonometric Ratios

Use the triangle at the right to find the exact values of the trigonometric ratios.

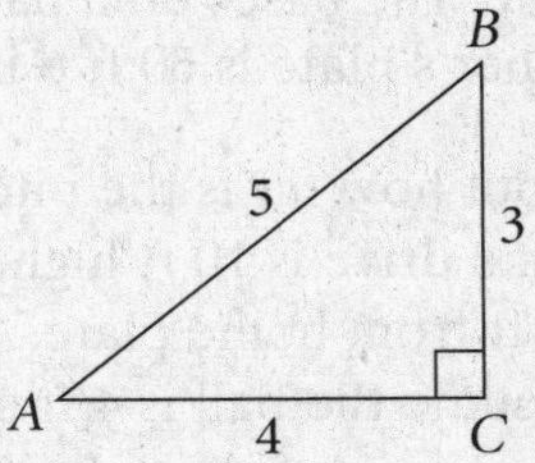

1. $\cos A$ **2.** $\cos B$

3. $\tan A$ **4.** $\tan B$

5. $\cot B$ **6.** $\sec A$

7. $\csc A$ **8.** $\sin B$

In $\triangle DEF$, $\angle D$ is a right angle. Find the remaining sides and angles. Round answers to the nearest tenth.

9. $f = 8, e = 15$ **10.** $f = 1, d = 2$ **11.** $f = 1, e = 2$ **12.** $f = 2, e = 1$

13. $f = 1, d = 500$ **14.** $d = 21, e = 8$ **15.** $e = 6, d = 12$ **16.** $e = 5, f = 1$

17. Suppose you are standing on one bank of a river. A tree on the other side of the river is known to be 150 ft tall. A line from the top of the tree to the ground at your feet makes an angle of 11° with the ground. How far from you is the base of the tree?

18. A kite string makes a 62° angle with the horizontal, and 300 ft of string is let out. The string is held 6 ft off the ground. How high is the kite?

19. You are designing several access ramps. What angle would each ramp make with the ground, to the nearest 0.1°?

a. 20 ft long, rises 16 in. **b.** 8 ft long, rises 8 in. **c.** 12 ft long, rises 6 in.

d. 30 ft long, rises 32 in. **e.** 4 ft long, rises 6 in. **f.** 6 ft long, rises 14 in.

20. In $\triangle ABC$, $\angle C$ is a right angle and $\tan A = \frac{2}{3}$. Draw a diagram and find each value in fraction form and in decimal form.

a. $\cos A$ **b.** $\tan B$ **c.** $\sin A$

d. $\cot B$ **e.** $\sec A$ **f.** $\csc B$

Find the measure of each angle to the nearest tenth of a degree.

21. $\sin^{-1}\left(\frac{\sqrt{2}}{2}\right)$ **22.** $\cos^{-1}(0.5)$ **23.** $\tan^{-1}\left(\sqrt{3}\right)$ **24.** $\sin^{-1}(0.3232)$

25. $\cos^{-1}(0.8)$ **26.** $\tan^{-1}(1)$ **27.** $\cos^{-1}(0.4)$ **28.** $\tan^{-1}(3.2678)$

29. $\sin^{-1}(0.75)$ **30.** $\tan^{-1}(0.5)$ **31.** $\tan^{-1}(12.0001)$ **32.** $\sin^{-1}(0.1044)$

Name ____________________ Class ____________ Date ____________

14-3 • Guided Problem Solving

GPS Exercise 48

Baseball The bases on a baseball diamond form a square 90 ft on a side. The pitcher's plate is 60 ft 6 in. from the back corner of home plate.

a. About how far is the pitcher's plate from second base?

b. A line drive is 10 ft high when it passes over the third baseman, who is 100 ft from home plate. At what angle did the ball leave the bat? (Assume the ball is 4 ft above the ground when it is hit.)

Read and Understand

1. What is the measure of each side of the square formed by the baseball diamond? ____________

2. How far is the pitcher's plate from the back corner of home plate, in feet? ____________

Plan and Solve

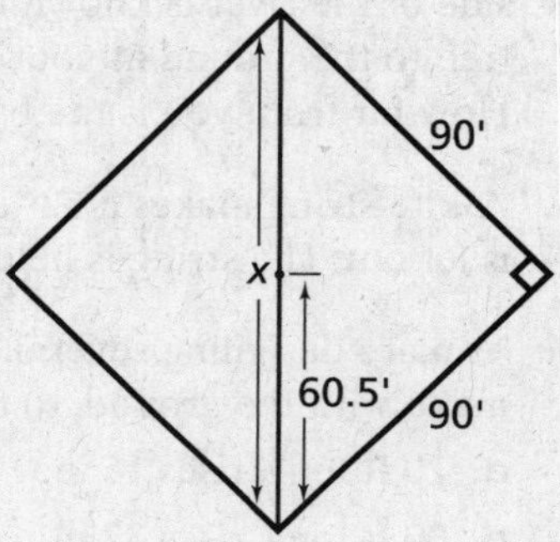

3. Let x = the distance from second base to home plate. See the diagram. Use the Pythagorean Theorem to write an equation to solve for x. ____________

4. Solve the equation for x. ____________

5. What is the distance from the pitcher's plate to second base? ____________

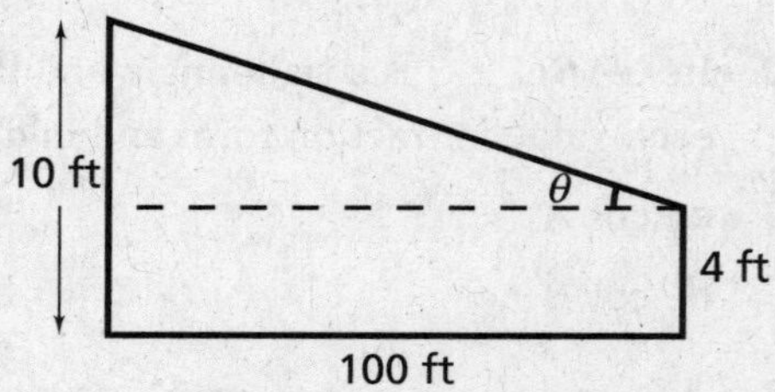

6. Let θ = the angle at which the ball leaves the bat. See the diagram. What is the length of the leg opposite angle θ? ____________

7. Use a trigonometric ratio for a right triangle to write an equation to solve for θ. ____________

8. Solve the equation for θ. ____________

Look Back and Check

9. To check, substitute your answers in trigonometric ratios and verify that true statements result.

____

Solve Another Problem

10. Suppose the shortstop is standing exactly halfway between second base and third base on the base line. How far is the shortstop from home plate, rounded to the nearest tenth? ____________

Name ______________________ Class ______________ Date ______________

Practice 14-4

Area and the Law of Sines

Use the Law of Sines. Find the measure of the indicated part of each triangle. Round answers to the nearest tenth.

1. Find $m\angle X$ if $x = 10$, $y = 12$, and $m\angle Y = 18°$.
2. Find x if $y = 21$, $m\angle X = 31°$, and $m\angle Y = 43°$.
3. Find z if $y = 15$, $m\angle Y = 79°$, and $m\angle Z = 79°$.
4. Find $m\angle Z$ if $y = 23$, $z = 19$, and $m\angle Y = 123°$.
5. Find y if $z = 54$, $m\angle Y = 65°$, and $m\angle Z = 21°$.
6. Find $m\angle Y$ if $y = 36$, $z = 42$, and $m\angle Z = 39°$.
7. Find $m\angle X$ if $x = 54$, $z = 63$, and $m\angle Z = 33°$.
8. Find x if $z = 18$, $m\angle X = 25°$, and $m\angle Z = 31°$.
9. Find x if $y = 20$, $m\angle X = 30°$, and $m\angle Y = 60°$.
10. Find $m\angle X$ if $x = 63$, $y = 72$, and $m\angle Y = 45°$.
11. Find $m\angle Z$ if $y = 7$, $z = 3$, and $m\angle Y = 31°$.
12. Find x if $y = 35$, $m\angle X = 118°$, and $m\angle Y = 20°$.
13. Find $m\angle X$ if $x = 9$, $y = 15$, and $m\angle Y = 62°$.
14. Find y if $z = 70$, $m\angle Y = 25°$, and $m\angle Z = 100°$.

Find the area of each triangle.

15.

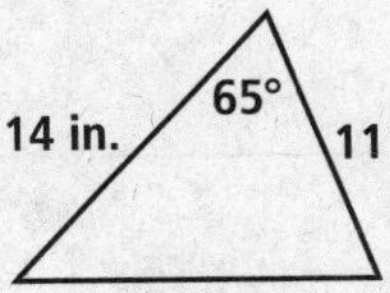

16.

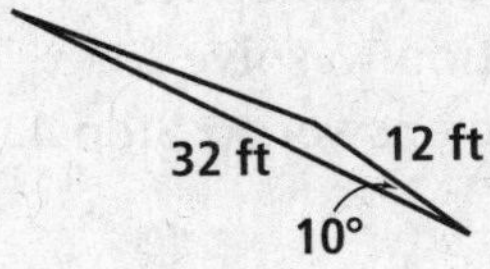

17.

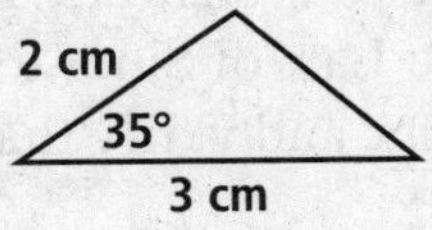

18. A triangle has sides of lengths 15 in. and 22 in., and the measure of the angle between them is 95°. Find the area of the triangle.

19. A hot-air balloon is observed from two points, A and B, on the ground 800 ft apart as shown in the diagram. The angle of elevation of the balloon is 65° from point A and 37° from point B. Find the distance from point A to the balloon.

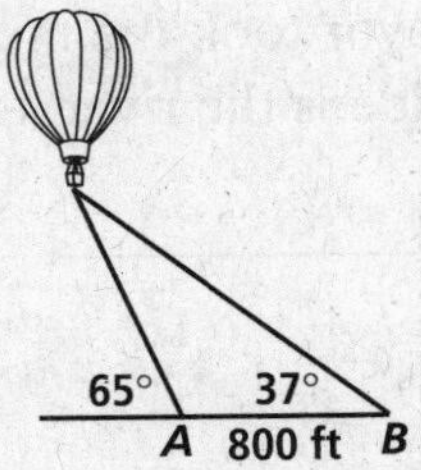

20. Two searchlights on the shore of a lake are located 3020 yd apart as shown in the diagram. A ship in distress is spotted from each searchlight. The beam from the first searchlight makes an angle of 38° with the baseline. The beam from the second light makes an angle of 57° with the baseline. Find the ship's distance from each searchlight.

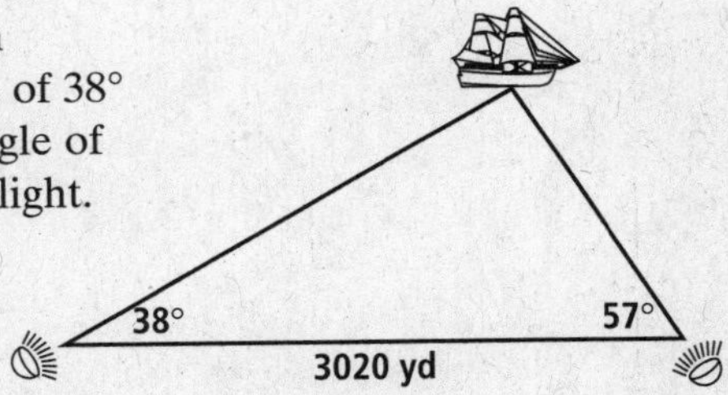

Name ______________________ Class ______________ Date ______________

14-4 • Guided Problem Solving

GPS Exercise 42

Measurement A vacant lot is in the shape of an isosceles triangle. It is between two streets that intersect at an 85.9° angle. Each of the sides of the lot that face these streets is 150 ft long. Find the length of the third side, to the nearest foot.

Read and Understand

1. What is an isosceles triangle? ______________________

2. What is the sum of the interior angles of a triangle? ______________________

Plan and Solve

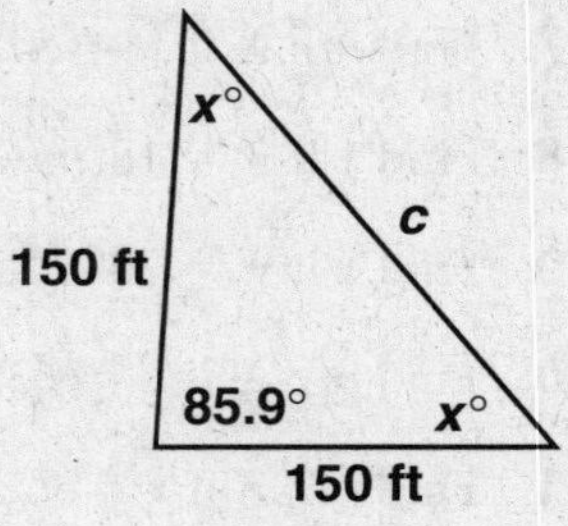

3. Using the figure, write an equation with x that represents the sum of the interior angles. ______________________

4. Solve for x. What is the measure of each unknown angle? ______________________

5. Use the Law of Sines to write an equation with c. ______________________

6. Solve for c. How long is the third side, to the nearest foot? ______________________

Look Back and Check

7. To check your answers, use the value you obtained for c and the Law of Sines to write an equation to solve for x. Solve for x and verify that it matches the answer to Step 4. ______________________

Solve Another Problem

8. A surveyor took the measurements shown in the figure. How wide is the river, to the nearest tenth of a yard?

____

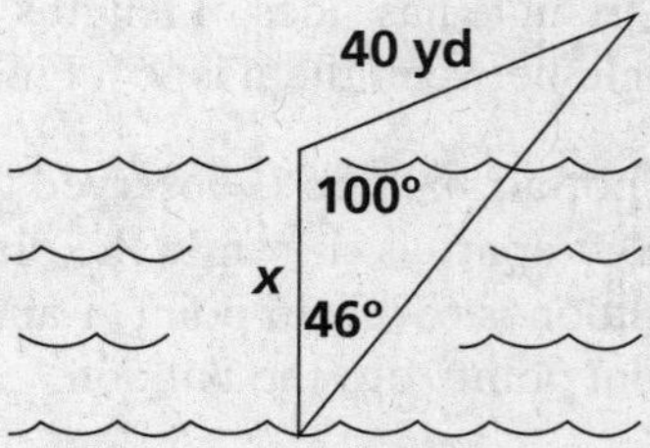

Name ______________________ Class ______________ Date ______________

Practice 14-5

The Law of Cosines

Use the Law of Cosines. Find the measure of the indicated part of each triangle. Round answers to the nearest tenth.

1. Find x if $y = 4$, $z = 9$, and $m\angle X = 16°$.
2. Find y if $x = 8$, $z = 5$, and $m\angle Y = 8°$.
3. Find $m\angle Y$ if $x = 17.2$, $y = 22.1$, and $z = 31.3$.
4. Find z if $x = 32$, $y = 25$, and $m\angle Z = 21°$.
5. Find $m\angle Y$ if $x = 14$, $y = 6$, and $z = 10$.
6. Find $m\angle X$ if $x = 24.9$, $y = 32.0$, and $z = 42.3$.
7. Find x if $y = 16$, $z = 4$, and $m\angle X = 123°$.
8. Find $m\angle Z$ if $x = 6.2$, $y = 5.9$, and $z = 3.4$.
9. Find z if $x = 321$, $y = 543$, and $m\angle Z = 54°$.
10. Find $m\angle Z$ if $x = 235$, $y = 154$, and $z = 239$.
11. Find x if $y = 10$, $z = 12$, and $m\angle X = 29°$.
12. Find y if $x = 3$, $z = 6$, and $m\angle Y = 15°$.
13. Find x if $y = 8$, $z = 7$, and $m\angle X = 149°$.
14. Find z if $x = 7$, $y = 22$, and $m\angle Z = 12°$.
15. Find z if $x = 46$, $y = 67$, and $m\angle Z = 85°$.
16. Find $m\angle X$ if $x = 4$, $y = 7$, and $z = 10$.
17. Find $m\angle Y$ if $x = 32$, $y = 79$, and $z = 86$.
18. Find $m\angle Z$ if $x = 3$, $y = 2.9$, and $z = 4.6$.
19. Find $m\angle Y$ if $x = 34.7$, $y = 18.9$, and $z = 21.5$.
20. Find $m\angle Z$ if $x = 14$, $y = 16$, and $z = 18$.
21. The sides of a triangular lot are 158 ft, 173 ft, and 191 ft. Find the measure of the angle opposite the longest side to the nearest tenth of a degree.
22. A car travels 50 miles due west from point A. At point B, the car turns and travels at an angle of 35° north of due east. The car travels in this direction for 40 miles, to point C. How far is point C from point A?

Name ____________________ Class ____________ Date ____________

14-5 • Guided Problem Solving

GPS Exercise 34

Navigation A pilot is flying from city A to city B, which is 85 mi due north. After flying 20 mi, the pilot must change course and fly 10° east of north to avoid a cloudbank.

a. If the pilot remains on this course for 20 mi, how far will the plane be from city B?

b. How many degrees will the pilot have to turn to the left to fly directly to city B? How many degrees from due north is this course?

Read and Understand

1. How far is it from city A to city B? ____________

2. How far does the pilot fly directly north from A to B? ____________

Plan and Solve

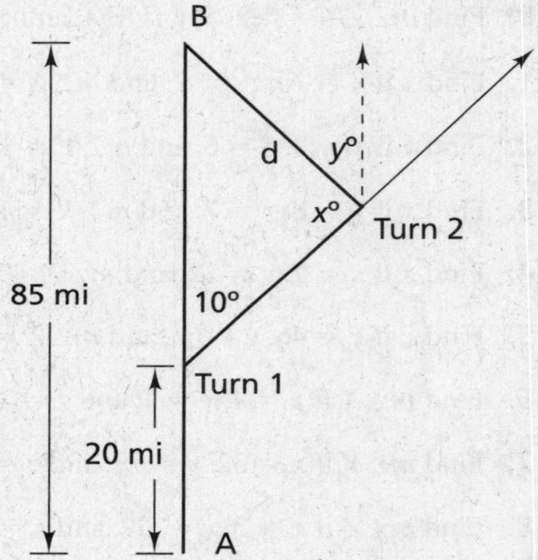

3. See the figure. How far is the place where the pilot first changed course from city B? ____________

4. How far does the pilot travel after the first change of course? ____________

5. Use the Law of Cosines to write an equation with *d*, the distance to city B. ____________

6. Solve for *d*. How far is the plane from city B?

____

7. Use your answer from step 6 along with the Law of Sines to write an equation and solve for *x*. ____________

8. Using your value for *x*, calculate how many degrees the pilot will have to turn to the left to fly directly to city B. ____________

9. Using your answer from step 8, find *y*. In other words, how many degrees from due north is this new course? ____________

Look Back and Check

10. To check your answers, use the Law of Sines or Cosines to find the remaining measures. Verify that they make sense in the problem. ____________

Solve Another Problem

11. In $\triangle QRS$, $m\angle R = 80°$, $q = 5$ mi, $s = 8$ mi. Find r, to the nearest tenth. ____________

Name ______________________ Class ______________ Date ______________

Practice 14-6

Angle Identities

Find each exact value. Use a sum or difference identity.

1. $\sin 240°$
2. $\tan(-300°)$
3. $\sin(-105°)$
4. $\cos 15°$
5. $\sin 15°$
6. $\sin 135°$
7. $\cos 225°$
8. $\tan 225°$
9. $\tan 240°$
10. $\cos 390°$
11. $\sin(-300°)$
12. $\tan(-75°)$

Verify each identity.

13. $\cot\left(\theta - \frac{\pi}{2}\right) = -\tan\theta$
14. $\sin\left(\theta - \frac{\pi}{2}\right) = -\cos\theta$
15. $\cos\left(\theta - \frac{\pi}{2}\right) = \sin\theta$
16. $\sec\left(\theta - \frac{\pi}{2}\right) = \csc\theta$

Use the definitions of the trigonometric ratios for a right triangle to derive each cofunction identity.

17. A cofunction identity for $\tan(90° - A)$
18. A cofunction identity for $\cos(90° - A)$

Solve each trigonometric equation for $0 \leq \theta < 2\pi$.

19. $2\sin\left(\frac{\pi}{2} - \theta\right)\tan\theta = 1$
20. $\cos\left(\frac{\pi}{2} - \theta\right)\tan\theta - \sec(-\theta) = 1$
21. $\sin^2\theta + \cos^2\theta = \tan\theta$
22. $2\sin^2\theta = \sin(-\theta)$
23. $\sqrt{3}\cos\left(\frac{\pi}{2} - \theta\right) = \cos(-\theta)$
24. $\cot\left(\frac{\pi}{2} - \theta\right) = \sin\theta$
25. $\csc\left(\frac{\pi}{2} - \theta\right) = \tan\theta$
26. $2\cos\left(\frac{\pi}{2} - \theta\right) = \tan(-\theta)$
27. $\csc^2\theta - \cot^2\theta = 2\cos\theta$
28. $\sin\left(\theta - \frac{\pi}{2}\right)\cos\theta = 0$

Use mental math to find the value of each trigonometric expression.

29. $\sin 10° \cos 80° + \cos 10° \sin 80°$
30. $\cos 110° \cos 70° - \sin 110° \sin 70°$
31. $\sin 310° \cos 130° - \cos 310° \sin 130°$
32. $\cos 95° \cos 50° + \sin 95° \sin 50°$

Name ______________________ Class ______________ Date ______________

14-6 • Guided Problem Solving

GPS Exercise 51

Gears The diagram shows a gear whose radius is 10 cm. Point A represents a 60° counterclockwise rotation of point $P(10, 0)$. Point B represents a θ-degree rotation of point A. The coordinates of B are $(10\cos(\theta + 60°), 10\sin(\theta + 60°))$. Write these coordinates in terms of $\cos\theta$ and $\sin\theta$.

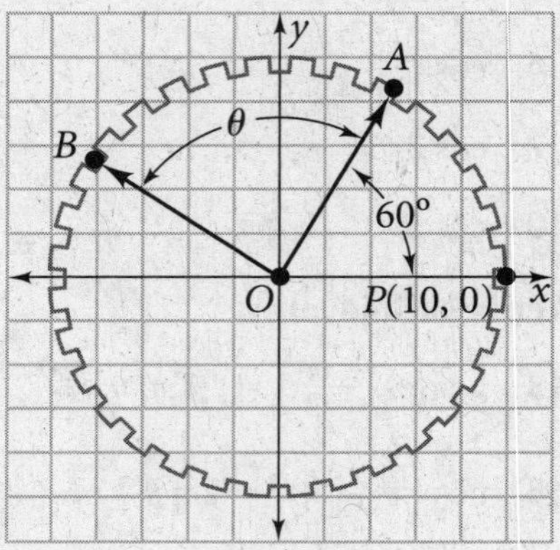

Read and Understand

1. What is the x-coordinate of B? ______________

2. What is the y-coordinate of B? ______________

Plan and Solve

3. What is the angle sum identity for $\cos(A + B)$? ______________

4. Use this angle sum identity to rewrite the x-coordinate of point B. ______________

5. Simplify the equation in Step 4. ______________

6. What is the angle sum identity for $\sin(A + B)$? ______________

7. Use this angle sum identity to rewrite the y-coordinate of point B. ______________

8. Simplify the equation in Step 7. ______________

9. What are the coordinates of B in terms of $\cos\theta$ and $\sin\theta$? ______________

Look Back and Check

10. To check that your answers are reasonable, substitute a value for θ in each set of coordinates. Simplify and verify that your coordinates are the same. ______________

Solve Another Problem

11. Rewrite the expression $\sin 7\theta \cos 4\theta - \cos 7\theta \sin 4\theta$ as a trigonometric function of a single angle measure. ______________

Name ______________________ Class ______________ Date ______________

Practice 14-7

Double-Angle and Half-Angle Identities

Given $\sin\theta = \frac{7}{25}$ and $90° < \theta < 180°$, find the exact value of each expression.

1. $\cos\frac{\theta}{2}$
2. $\sin\frac{\theta}{2}$
3. $\tan\frac{\theta}{2}$
4. $\sec\frac{\theta}{2}$
5. $\csc\frac{\theta}{2}$
6. $\cot\frac{\theta}{2}$

Given $\cos\theta = -\frac{8}{17}$ and $180° < \theta < 270°$, find the exact value of each expression.

7. $\sin\frac{\theta}{2}$
8. $\cos\frac{\theta}{2}$
9. $\cot\frac{\theta}{2}$
10. $\tan\frac{\theta}{2}$
11. $\csc\frac{\theta}{2}$
12. $\sec\frac{\theta}{2}$

Use an angle sum identity to verify each identity.

13. $\cos 2\theta = \cos^2\theta - \sin^2\theta$
14. $\cos 2\theta = 2\cos^2\theta - 1$
15. $\cos 2\theta = 1 - 2\sin^2\theta$
16. $\sin 2\theta = 2\sin\theta\cos\theta$

Verify each identity.

17. $\cos^2\theta = \frac{1 + \cos 2\theta}{2}$
18. $\cot\theta = \frac{\sin 2\theta}{1 - \cos 2\theta}$
19. $\tan\theta + \cot\theta = 2\csc 2\theta$
20. $\frac{\cos 2\theta}{\sin\theta\cos\theta} = \cot\theta - \tan\theta$

Use a double-angle identity to find the exact value of each expression.

21. $\sin 120°$
22. $\tan 600°$
23. $\sin 660°$
24. $\cos 660°$
25. $\tan 90°$
26. $\cos 90°$
27. $\tan 660°$
28. $\sin 240°$
29. $\tan 120°$

Use a half-angle identity to find the exact value of each expression.

30. $\cos 15°$
31. $\cos 7.5°$
32. $\tan 7.5°$
33. $\sin 7.5°$
34. $\cos 45°$
35. $\tan 22.5°$
36. $\cos 22.5°$
37. $\sin 90°$
38. $\cos 90°$

Name ____________________ Class ____________ Date ____________

14-7 • Guided Problem Solving

GPS Exercise 42

Use identities to write the equation $4 \sin 2\theta - 3 \cos \theta = 0$ in terms of the single angle θ. Then solve the equation for $0 \le \theta < 2\pi$.

Read and Understand

1. What is a double-angle identity for $\sin 2\theta$? ____________

2. What is a double-angle identity for $\cos 2\theta$? ____________

Plan and Solve

$4\sin 2\theta - 3\cos \theta = 0$

3. Use the double-angle identity to rewrite $\sin 2\theta$. $4(\_\_\_\_\_\_\_\_) - 3\cos\theta = 0$

4. Multiply the quantity by 4. $\_\_\_\_\_\_\_\_ - 3\cos\theta = 0$

5. Factor out $\cos \theta$. $\cos\theta(\_\_\_\_\_\_\_\_) = 0$

6. Rewrite as two separate equations. $\cos\theta = 0$ or $\_\_\_\_\_\_\_\_ = 0$

7. Solve for θ. $\theta =$ ____________

Look Back and Check

8. To check your answer, substitute the value(s) for θ into the original equation and verify that a true statement results. ____________

Solve Another Problem

9. Use identities to write the equation $\cos 2\theta = \cos \theta$ in terms of the single angle θ. Then solve the equation for $0 \le \theta < 2\pi$. ____________

Name ________________ Class ________ Date ________

14A: Graphic Organizer

For use before Lesson 14-1

Study Skill As you complete the book, consider creating a graphic organizer for the entire book. In the center write the title of the book. Then write the chapter names in rectangles. Look back through the chapters and write important concepts in circles linked to the chapter blocks. Use the graphic organizer as you study for your final exam.

Write your answers.

1. What is the chapter title? ________________

2. Find the Table of Contents page for this chapter at the front of the book. Name four topics you will study in this chapter.

________________ ________________

________________ ________________

3. Look through the pages of the chapter. List four real-world connections that you see discussed in this chapter.

________________ ________________

________________ ________________

4. Complete the graphic organizer as you work through the chapter.
1. Write the title of the chapter in the center oval.
2. When you begin a lesson, write the name of the lesson in a rectangle.
3. When you complete that lesson, write a skill or key concept from that lesson in the outer oval linked to that rectangle.

Continue with steps 2 and 3 clockwise around the graphic organizer.

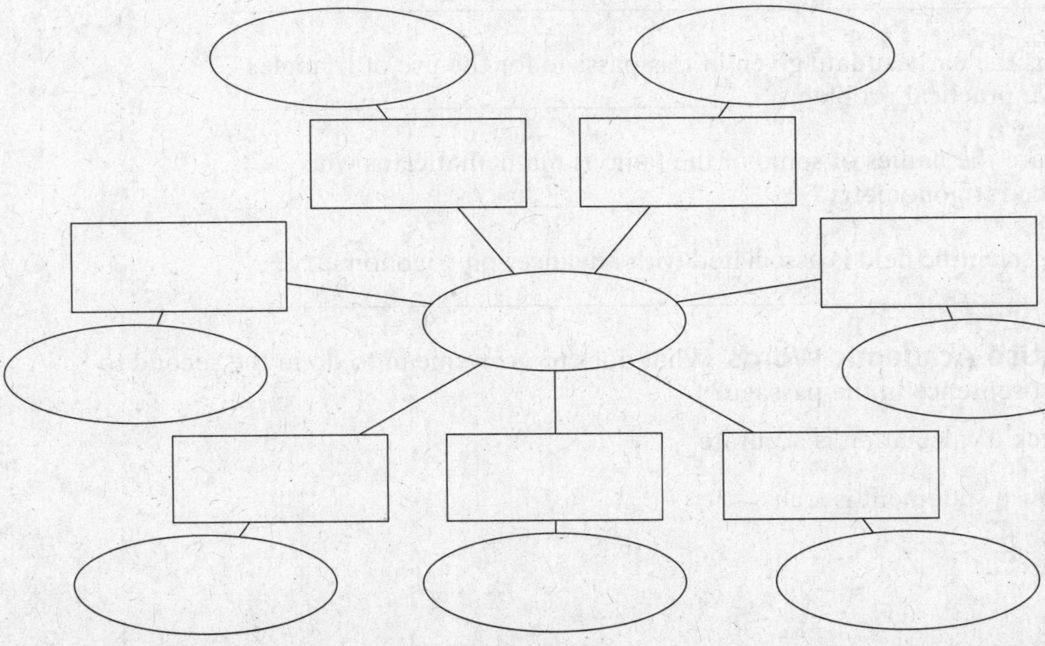

Name ______________________ Class ______________ Date ______________

14B: Reading Comprehension

For use after Lesson 14-6

Study Skill After you read a long paragraph, pause and review the essential information in that paragraph. Remember that the first sentence of a paragraph often introduces the topic and the last sentence may summarize the content.

Read the passage below and answer the questions that follow.

From very early times, surveyors, navigators, and astronomers have employed triangles to measure distances that could not be measured directly. Babylonian clay tablets and ancient Egyptian papyri, dating from at least 1600 B.C., show considerable evidence of practical problems solved by triangle measurement. Trigonometry as the science of trigonometric ratios grew out of early astronomical observations, such as those of Hipparchus of Alexandria, about 140 B.C. By the second century A.D., there existed Claudius Ptolemy's "Table of Chords" and Menelaus of Alexandria's treatise on spherical geometry and trigonometry. And it was astronomy again which led to vast improvements in trigonometry. In the early sixteenth century, the Polish astronomer Nicolas Copernicus challenged the prevailing view of the universe by proposing the theory of a sun-centered solar system rather than the traditional earth-centered universe. To prove or disprove the Copernican theory, more accurate astronomical observations and calculations were needed, leading to the extension of trigonometric tables to ten and fifteen places, for every angle from 0° to 90°, in ten-second increments. By 1700 this enormous task had been accomplished, entirely by hand calculation.

1. What is the subject of this paragraph? ______________

2. Is the year 150 A.D. or the year 250 A.D. in the second century A.D.?
____

3. What is the earliest date given in this passage for the use of triangles to solve practical problems? ______________

4. What are the names of some of the famous mathematicians who advanced trigonometry? ______________

5. Which scientific field is associated with advances on trigonometry?
____

6. **High-Use Academic Words** What does to *prove* mean to do in the second to the last sentence in the passage?

   a. check a calculation is accurate

   b. show a statement is true

Name ______________________ Class ______________ Date ______________

14C: Reading/Writing Math Symbols

For use after Lesson 14-3

Study Skill Plan your time, whether you are studying or taking a test. Look at the entire amount of time you have and divide it into portions that you allocate to each task. Keep track of whether you are on schedule.

The meaning of an expression containing an exponent may be different, depending upon where the exponent is placed. The general rule is that an exponent applies only to the base to which it is directly attached. Use this information to evaluate the expressions and answer the questions below.

1. Evaluate 5^2. ______________________

2. Evaluate -5^2. ______________________

3. Evaluate $\sin 30°$. ______________________

4. Evaluate $(\sin 30°)^2$. ______________________

5. Evaluate $\sin^2 30°$. ______________________

6. If $f(x) = x - 5$, find f^{-1}. ______________________

7. Evaluate $\sin^{-1} \frac{1}{2}$. ______________________

Name ______________________ Class ______________ Date ____________

14D: Visual Vocabulary Practice

For use after Lesson 14-5

Study Skill When making a sketch, make it simple but make it complete.

Concept List

cosecant	cosine	cotangent
Law of Cosines	Law of Sines	secant
sine function	Transitive Property of Equality	trigonometric identity

Write the concept that best describes each exercise. Choose from the concept list above.

1. $y = \cos\theta$

____

2. $\sec\theta = \dfrac{1}{\cos\theta}$

____

3. $\cot\theta = \dfrac{1}{\tan\theta}$

____

4. $\cos^2\theta + \sin^2\theta = 1$

____

5.

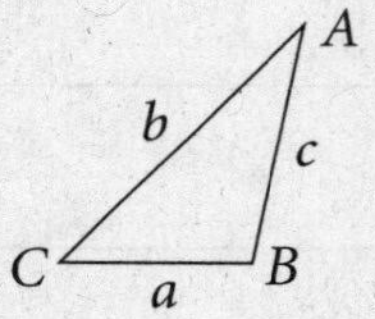

$$\frac{\sin A}{a} = \frac{\sin B}{b} = \frac{\sin C}{c}$$

____

6. If $a = b$ and $b = c$, then $a = c$.

____

7.

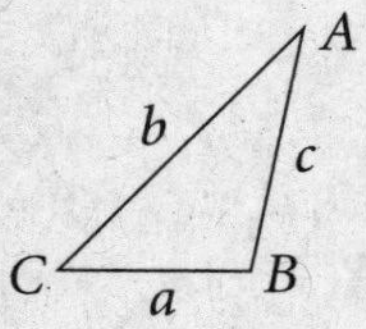

$$a^2 = b^2 + c^2 - 2bc\cos A$$

____

8. $\csc\theta = \dfrac{1}{\sin\theta}$

____

9.

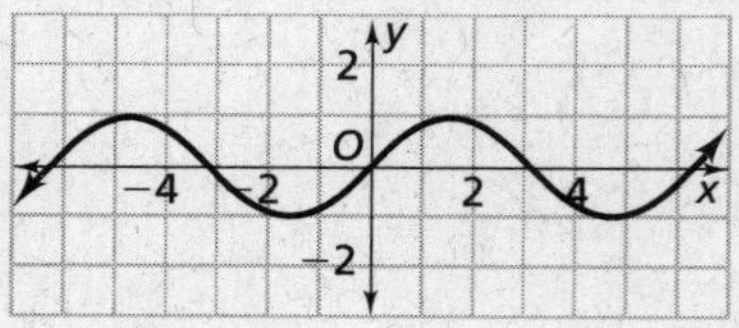

____

Name ______________________ Class ______________ Date ______________

14E: Vocabulary Check

For use after Lesson 14-4

Study Skill Strengthen your vocabulary. Use these pages and add cues and summaries by applying the Cornell Notetaking style.

Write the definition for each word at the right. To check your work, fold the paper back along the dotted line to see the correct answers.

Definition	Word
______________________	Trigonometric identity
______________________	Radian
______________________	Function
______________________	Tangent function
______________________	Trigonometric ratios for a right triangle

Name ________________ Class ________________ Date ________________

14E: Vocabulary Check (continued)

For use after Lesson 14-4

Write the vocabulary word for each definition. To check your work, fold the paper forward along the dotted line to see the correct answers.

A trigonometric equation that is true for all values except those for which an expression on either side of the equal sign is undefined. ________________

The measure of a central angle of a circle that intercepts an arc equal in length to a radius of the circle. ________________

A relation in which each element of the domain is paired with exactly one element of the range. ________________

A function that matches the measure θ of an angle in standard position with the y-coordinate of the point at which the line containing the terminal side of a central angle of the unit circle intersects the tangent line $x = 1$. ________________

The six different ratios of the sides of a right triangle. ________________

14F: Vocabulary Review

For use with Chapter Review

Study Skill To be successful in mathematics, you need to be able to understand meanings of words that you know and ones that you don't. Learn each term one at a time, moving on to the next when you are confident of your knowledge of the first.

Draw a line from each word or phrase in the left column to the statement or phrase that matches it in the right column. Some items may have more than one match. For help, use the Glossary in your textbook.

Word(s)

1. Law of Cosines
2. Law of Sines
3. trigonometric identity
4. trigonometric ratio for a right triangle
5. frequency table
6. measures of central tendency
7. periodic function
8. phase shift
9. unit circle
10. initial side

Phrase

a. mean, median, and mode
b. lists how often each outcome occurs
c. $\cos^2 \theta + \sin^2 \theta = 1$
d. $\tan A = \frac{a}{b}$
e. $\frac{\sin A}{a} = \frac{\sin B}{b} = \frac{\sin C}{c}$
f. $\sin A = \frac{a}{c}$
g. $1 + \tan^2 \theta = \sec^2 \theta$
h. $a^2 = b^2 + c^2 - 2bc \cos A$
i. $b^2 = a^2 + c^2 - 2ac \cos B$
j. has a radius of 1 unit and its center at origin
k. a horizontal translation of a periodic function
l. ray on the x-axis
m. repeats a pattern of y-values at regular intervals